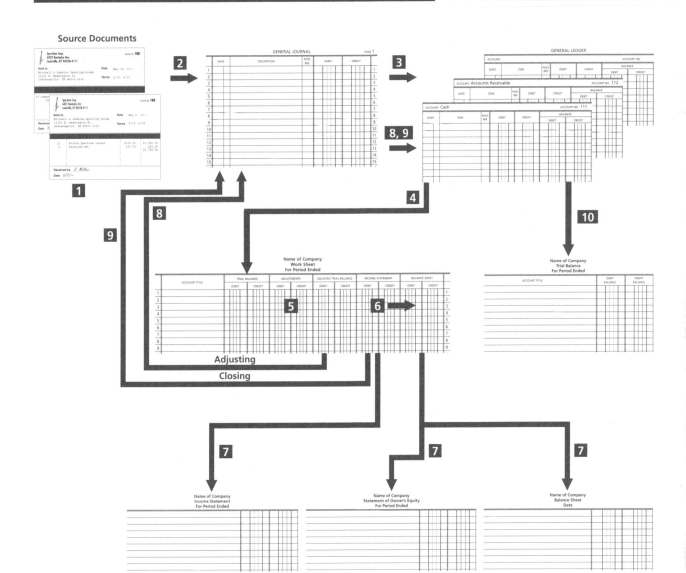

Steps in the Accounting Cycle

During Accounting Period:
1. Analyze source documents.
2. Journalize the transactions.
3. Post to the ledger accounts.

End of Accounting Period:
4. Prepare a trial balance.
5. Determine and prepare the needed adjustments on the work sheet.
6. Complete an end-of-period work sheet.
7. Prepare an income statement, statement of owner's equity, and balance sheet.
8. Journalize and post the adjusting entries.
9. Journalize and post the closing entries.
10. Prepare a post-closing trial balance.

15TH EDITION

CHAPTERS 1-

College
accounting

JAMES A. HEINTZ, DBA, CPA
Professor of Accounting
University of Connecticut
Storrs, Connecticut

ROBERT W. PARRY, JR., PHD
Associate Professor of Accounting
Indiana University
Bloomington, Indiana

SOUTH-WESTERN College Publishing

An International Thomson Publishing Company

Publishing Team Director:	Diane Longworth Myers
Senior Acquisitions Editor:	Gary L. Bauer
Developmental Editors:	Tom Bormann, Minta Berry
Production Editor:	Shelley Brewer
Production House:	Berry Publication Services
Cover Design:	Fusion Design
Cover Photograph:	Guildhaus Photography
Internal Design:	Lesiak/Crampton Design
Opener Illustrations:	Cary Rillo
Manufacturing Coordinator:	Sue Disselkamp
Marketing Manager:	Dreis Van Landuyt

Library of Congress Cataloging-in-Publication Data:
Heintz, James A.
    College accounting / James A. Heintz, Robert W. Parry, Jr. -- 15th
  ed.
      p.   cm.
    Includes index.
    ISBN 0-538-85202-X
    1. Accounting.   I. Parry, Robert W.   . II. Title.
  HF5635.H444 1995
  657'.044--dc20   95-9583
                                                    CIP

Annotated Instructor's Edition, Chapters 1–28 ISBN: 0-538-85245-3
Annotated Instructor's Edition, Chapters 1–15 ISBN: 0-538-85543-6
Student Edition, Chapters 1–28   ISBN: 0-538-85202-X
Student Edition, Chapters 1–20   ISBN: 0-538-85205-4
Student Edition, Chapters 1–15   ISBN: 0-538-85204-6
Student Edition, Chapters 1–10   ISBN: 0-538-85203-8

3 4 5 6 7 8 9 Ki 3 2 1 0 9 8 7
Printed in the United States of America

I ⓉP
International Thomson Publishing
South-Western College Publishing is an ITP Company.
The ITP trademark is used under license.

Dedication

We are grateful to our wives,

Celia Heintz and Jane Parry

and our children,

Andrea Heintz, John Heintz, Jessica Jane Parry, and Mitch Parry

for their love, support, and assistance during the creation of this fifteenth edition. We especially appreciate Jessie Parry's willingness to let us use her name throughout the first six chapters.

PREFACE

Anyone who desires a successful career in business and not-for-profit organizations must understand accounting. This textbook is designed for students of accounting, business administration, office technology, computer science, and other disciplines. As students begin their study of accounting, this book will thoroughly and efficiently introduce fundamental accounting concepts and principles. This new edition maintains the strong tradition of emphasizing student understanding.

IMPORTANT FEATURES OF THE FIFTEENTH EDITION

The basic foundation that has made this text a market leader for many years has been retained in the fifteenth edition. In response to user feedback, focus group interviews, surveys, and independent reviews by accounting educators, numerous improvements have been made. The text presentation has been refined throughout, new materials have been added, and both print and computerized supplements have been revised and added. The text and all accompanying supplements have been crafted to guide students to success.

Learning Objectives

Each chapter begins with learning objectives. The learning objectives are restated at the beginning of the appropriate text section for ease of reference. The learning objectives are also keyed to the Key Points summaries, end of chapter exercises and problems, testbank, and study guide.

    The following illustration shows Learning Objective 5 from Chapter 3 as it appears in the text, in the Key Points summary, and in an exercise.

THE TRIAL BALANCE

LO5 Prepare a trial balance.

5 A trial balance shows that the debit and credit totals are equal. A trial balance can also be used in preparing the financial statements.

5 **EXERCISE 3A9 TRIAL BALANCE**   The following accounts have normal balances. Prepare a trial balance for Juanita's Delivery Service as of September 30, 19--.

Chapter Opening Vignettes

Along with the learning objectives, each chapter begins with a brief narrative that sets the stage for the chapter material. These vignettes include realistic business decisions and pose real-world questions. They are designed to help students understand the purpose of the chapter and why the chapter topics are important.

Learning Keys

Throughout the text, learning keys emphasize important new points. These keys direct student attention to such things as the application of new accounting concepts, how to journalize and post a transaction, relationships among accounts, and how to make an important calculation. A learning key from page 45 is shown below.

 Debits are always on the left and credits are always on the right for all accounts.

Key Steps

Key steps are incorporated frequently to show students how to accomplish specific objectives. The steps are used for many purposes, including how to prepare a bank reconciliation or a work sheet, how to post subsidiary and general ledger accounts, and how to find the cause of errors in a bank reconciliation or trial balance.

Illustrations

Accounting documents and records, diagrams, and flow charts are used throughout the text to help students visualize important concepts. Illustrations are used particularly when any new accounting principles or procedures are introduced. Important examples are as follows:

- **Use of the accounting equation.**   In analyzing business transactions, students must understand the impact of an event on specific accounts in the accounting equation. Throughout Chapters 2 and 3, we repeat the accounting equation as a header for each entry made for specific transactions. This enables the student to see where each account fits in the equation, how the account is increased or decreased, and the effect each entry has on the balance of the equation.
- **Owner's equity umbrella.**   In Chapter 3, the owner's equity umbrella illustrates how revenue, expense, and drawing affect owner's equity.
- **Accounting equation and financial statements.**   In Chapter 2, we illustrate the direct linkages between the balances in the accounting equation and the financial statements.
- **Trial balance and financial statements.**   In Chapter 3, we show how a trial balance is used to develop a set of financial statements.
- **Work sheet and financial statements.**   In Chapter 6, we show the linkages (a) between the Income Statement columns of the work sheet and the income statement, and (b) between the Balance Sheet

columns of the work sheet and the statement of owner's equity and balance sheet.

- **Work sheet and cost of goods sold.** In Chapter 14, we illustrate the linkages between the information extended to the Income Statement columns of the work sheet and the cost of goods sold section of the income statement.

- **Work sheet and closing entries.** In Chapter 15, we illustrate the linkages between the Income Statement and Balance Sheet columns of the work sheet and the closing entries.

Key Points

Each chapter ends with a summary of key points. This provides an efficient way for students to review important chapter material.

Key Terms

At the end of each chapter, a list is provided of all important new terms introduced in the chapter. Each term is followed by the page number on which the term is first used in the chapter and a definition.

Review Questions

Review questions are provided at the end of each chapter. The questions provide students with an opportunity to immediately test their recall of important chapter concepts.

Managing Your Writing

A new and innovative section on Managing Your Writing has been added to Chapter 1. This section presents a twelve-step process that will help students become more efficient and effective writers. As part of this emphasis on writing, we have added a Managing Your Writing assignment at the end of each chapter. Each assignment provides an opportunity to apply critical thinking and writing skills to issues directly related to material in the chapter.

Demonstration Problem and Solution

Complete demonstration problems and solutions are provided for each chapter. The problems are a comprehensive application of key concepts and principles introduced in the chapter. They are useful in a variety of classroom settings. Students may work through the problems and solutions independently to gain confidence before working the Series A and B problems. Demonstration problems also can be used effectively as in-class examples.

Exercises and Problems

Three complete sets of exercises and problems have been prepared to facilitate instructor usage and student learning. At the end of each chapter, there are two sets (Series A and B) of exercises and problems. A third set, with and without solutions, is available when the study guide is adopted. Each exercise reinforces one concept developed in the chapter. Each problem links related concepts. All exercises and problems are keyed to the chapter learning objectives.

Mastery Problems

A comprehensive mastery problem follows the exercises and problems at the end of each chapter. This problem is usually similar to the demonstration problem in content and purpose. Mastery problems help develop critical thinking skills and can be used either to test or to further strengthen the students' overall grasp of the chapter materials.

Comprehensive Problems

A comprehensive problem is provided at the end of Chapter 6 and Chapter 15. Each problem permits the student to review the entire accounting cycle. Comprehensive Problem 1 deals with a service business; a merchandising business is the focus of Comprehensive Problem 2.

EMPHASIS ON SOUND PEDAGOGY

Our concern throughout the text is to facilitate student learning. Several dimensions of this sound pedagogy are worth emphasizing.

- **Work sheet acetates.** This multi-layer presentation (Chapter 5) of the work sheet provides the most effective demonstration of work sheet preparation found anywhere. Students easily see how the work sheet is built.
- **Accounts receivable—Notes receivable.** Notes receivable generally appear before accounts receivable on the balance sheet. In terms of student understanding, however, these two accounts come in the opposite order. Therefore, we cover the simpler, easier to understand subject of accounts receivable first (Chapter 16). Students are then better able to follow the notes receivable presentation (Chapter 17).
- **Payroll.** This sometimes difficult subject is taught in two chapters, taking advantage of the natural break between employee and employer taxes and related issues. All coverage is current as of the date of publication, including the separation of the FICA tax into its Social Security and Medicare components.
- **Voucher system.** This important topic is integrated into the sequence on accounting for a merchandising business (Chapters 11–15). By presenting this subject immediately following purchases and cash payments (Chapter 12), the student is shown the voucher system as a natural expansion of accounting for purchases.
- **Sales and cash receipts—Purchases and cash payments.** For sound learning and efficiency of presentation, each of these pairs of topics belongs together. The natural sequence of sales and cash receipts is reflected in Chapter 11. Similarly, Chapter 12 addresses the related activities of purchases and cash payments.

- **Depreciation methods.**   Complete coverage of various depreciation methods is provided in Chapter 19. In addition, to accommodate students who may not enroll in a course that covers Chapter 19, Chapter 5 and its Appendix introduce the straight-line, sum-of-the-years'-digits, double-declining-balance, and modified accelerated cost recovery system depreciation methods.
- **Statement of cash flows.**   We provide the most thorough coverage of the statement of cash flows of any text in our market. Because of the importance of the statement of cash flows today, we provide an introduction to this financial statement early in the text in an Appendix to Chapter 6. This Appendix explains the purpose of the statement of cash flows; illustrates the statement format using the direct method; and introduces operating, investing, and financing activities that are key sections of the statement. This early presentation allows students to develop a sense of the importance of managing cash flows without introducing the complexities of preparing the formal financial statement.

    Chapter 24 contains a complete discussion and illustration of the direct method of reporting cash flows from operating activities, which is preferred by the FASB. The Appendix to Chapter 24 illustrates the indirect method, which currently is used by most companies.
- **Accounting forms.**   All journals, ledgers, and statements are presented on rulings. This emphasizes structure and helps students learn more quickly how to prepare these documents.
- **Color.**   All journals are on blue rulings to differentiate these chronological records from ledgers and other processing documents, which are shown in yellow. Financial statements are white. Source documents vary in color, in the same manner as real-life documents.
- **Accounting relationships.**   Color is used to show accounting relationships. This helps the student see the important relationships more easily. Pages 28 and 66 are two examples of this frequently used pedagogical aid.
- **Arrow pointers and text pointers.**   Arrow pointers and text pointers emphasize the sources and calculations of numbers. For example, Figure 6-3 shows number pointers that point from the source number to the resulting number, and text pointers contain additional information.

FOR THE INSTRUCTOR

All complete learning packages include strong supplements. The supplements that have been designed for use by instructors are described below.

Annotated Instructor's Edition

New for this edition of the text is a complete Annotated Instructor's Edition. This special volume contains many valuable features. The first 32 pages are designed as a "walk through" the **College Accounting** learning package. In addition to introducing the package, the authors have included material on classroom preparation techniques and cooperative learning ideas. The remainder of the Annotated Instructor's Edition contains teaching tips, active learning ideas, check figures, and references to the teaching transparencies. All these components appear in the margins next to the appropriate material in the student text.

Solutions Manual

Two volumes (Chapters 1–15 and Chapters 16–28) contain complete solutions to Review Questions, Managing Your Writing activities, Series A and Series B Exercises and Problems, Mastery Problems, and Comprehensive Problems. The solutions appear on accounting rulings.

Solutions Transparencies

Series A and Series B Exercises and Problems, Mastery Problems, and Comprehensive Problems are supplied on acetates for use in classroom presentations. All solutions appear on accounting rulings.

Instructor's Resource Guide

This helpful resource supplements the Annotated Instructor's Edition. It provides complete teaching outlines with examples and activities for each chapter. In addition, brief class quizzes are included.

Testbank, Microexam, and Teletests

Over 2,000 true/false, multiple choice, and problem items are included in the testbank. Completely revised to match the changes made in this edition of the text, the testbank is a useful resource for developing testing materials. In addition to the printed supplement, Microexam provides access to the testbank in a computerized format. This easy-to-use software creates customized tests. Teletests are also available with this edition of the text.

Achievement Tests

Two sets of preprinted achievement tests are available. The tests have been completely restructured, with two tests now available for each chapter.

Teaching Transparencies

New, full-color transparencies of many illustrations in the text are available for classroom use. These transparencies are referenced in the Annotated Instructor's Edition for ease of use.

PowerPoint® Presentations

Complete classroom presentations for each chapter have been designed using Microsoft's popular presentation software. The presentations may be used with any computer that has PowerPoint installed.

Videos

Videos are available for Chapters 1–15 of the text. The videos highlight the key points of each chapter and present a problem and solution that correlates with the topics addressed in the chapter.

FOR THE STUDENT

Working Papers

Accounting rulings are available for all Series A and Series B Exercises and Problems, Mastery Problems, and Comprehensive Problems. Separate books are available for Chapters 1–10, Chapters 1–15, Chapters 11–20, and Chapters 16–28.

Study Guide

A solid tool for reinforcement, the study guide contains a discussion of learning objectives, questions, exercises, problems, and practice test questions. The study guide is available both with and without solutions, so that instructors can decide how the study guides will be used. Separate books are available for Chapters 1–10, Chapters 1–15, Chapters 11–20, and Chapters 16–28.

Solutions Software

General ledger software designed by Klooster and Allen is available for use with selected problems and practice sets. Opening balances, charts of accounts, and problem setup are provided for these problems. As students complete the problems, they gain valuable experience with full-functioning general ledger software.

Spreadsheet Software

Selected problems from the text can be completed using commercial spreadsheet software. Templates contain the basic problem setup; students learn to use the spreadsheet to solve the problems.

Tutorial Software

This computerized study guide is ideal to reinforce the concepts introduced in class, to allow students to review material missed, and to help students prepare for tests.

Practice Sets

Numerous practice sets (manual and computerized) are available for use with **_College Accounting_**. Each practice set is self contained; most include realistic source documents.

Check Figures

Check figures for the Series A and Series B Exercises and Problems and Mastery Problems are available on separate printed sheets.

RELATED MATERIALS

As world leader in accounting publishing, South-Western College Publishing has a wealth of resources available to complement its texts. Several have been designed to specifically accompany *College Accounting*. These include *Accounting for a Legal Office* and *Accounting for a Medical Office* and *Integrated Accounting*. The first two can be used in any classroom setting where additional coverage of specialized accounting procedures is desired. They are especially helpful to students preparing for a career in the legal or medical fields.

Integrated Accounting is available for IBM (DOS and Windows™) and Macintosh computers. Accounting applications for proprietorships, partnerships, and corporations; service and merchandising businesses; departmentalized and nondepartmentalized businesses; and voucher systems are included.

ACKNOWLEDGMENTS

We gratefully acknowledge the helpful input received from instructors and students. Your suggestions in reviews, surveys, feedback, and focus groups were instrumental in the preparation of the 15th edition. Several individuals deserve special recognition for their in-depth reviews, verification of solutions, and help with the text and supplements: Doug Cloud, Pepperdine University; Lynne Fowler, Heald Business College; Beth King, Heald Business College; Michael D. Lawrence, Portland Community College; Greg Lowry; Thomas E. Lynch, Hocking College; Leland Mansuetti, Sierra College; Fred McCracken, Indiana Business College; Betsy Ray, Indiana Business College; Marsha Schomburg; and Keith Weidkamp, Sierra College.

Further we would like to thank the Community and Career College Team members at South-Western College Publishing who worked with us on this edition: Diane Longworth Myers, Publishing Team Director; Gary Bauer, Senior Acquisitions Editor; Tom Bormann, Developmental Editor; Shelley Brewer, Production Editor; Sue Disselkamp, Manufacturing Coordinator; Dreis Van Landuyt, Marketing Manager; and Holly Knoechel and Meghan Kenney, Team Assistants. In addition, we thank Berry Publication Services for coordinating the development and production of the text. The following individuals deserve special recognition for their work with Berry Publication Services: Sara Myers, Joe Myers, Scott Ellis, and especially Minta Berry who played a key role in every phase of this revision of *College Accounting*.

Jim Heintz
Rob Parry

CONTENTS IN BRIEF

CONTENTS

Part 1 Accounting for a Service Business   1

CHAPTER 3   THE DOUBLE-ENTRY FRAMEWORK   44

Part 2 Specialized Accounting Procedures for Service Businesses and Proprietorships 203

Part 4 Specialized Accounting Procedures for Merchandising Businesses and Partnerships 555

CHAPTER 18   ACCOUNTING FOR MERCHANDISE INVENTORY   617

CHAPTER 19   ACCOUNTING FOR LONG-TERM ASSETS   649

CHAPTER 20   ACCOUNTING FOR PARTNERSHIPS   683

PART

1

Accounting for a Service Business

1

Introduction to Accounting

So, you have decided to study accounting. Good decision. A solid foundation in accounting concepts and techniques will be helpful. This is true whether you take a professional position in accounting or business, or simply want to better understand your personal finances and dealings with businesses. Knowledge of how accounting works will help you evaluate the financial health of businesses and other organizations. It will also give you a solid approach to dealing with financial and business transactions in your personal life.

Accounting is the language of business. You must learn this language to understand the impact of economic events on a specific company. Common, everyday terms have very precise meanings when used in accounting. For example, you have probably heard terms like asset, liability, revenue, expense, and income. Take a moment to jot down a brief definition for each of these terms. After reading and studying Chapter 2, compare your definitions with those developed in this text. This comparison will show whether you can trust your current understanding of accounting terms. Whether you intend to pursue a career in accounting or simply wish to understand the impact of business transactions, you need a clear understanding of this language.

THE PURPOSE OF ACCOUNTING

LO1 Describe the purpose of accounting.

The purpose of accounting is to provide financial information about the current operations and financial condition of a business to individuals, agencies, and organizations. As shown in Figure 1-1, owners, managers, creditors, and government agencies all need accounting information. Other users of accounting information include customers, clients, labor unions, stock exchanges, and financial analysts.

FIGURE 1-1 Users of Accounting Information

USER	INFORMATION NEEDED
Owners— Present and future	Firm's profitability and current financial condition
Managers— May or may not own business	Detailed measures of business performance
Creditors— Present and future	Whether the firm can pay bills on time so they can decide whether to extend credit
Government Agencies— National, state, and local	To determine taxes which must be paid and for purposes of regulation

THE ACCOUNTING PROCESS

LO2 Describe the accounting process.

Accounting is the art of gathering financial information about a business and reporting this information to users. The six major steps of the accounting process are analyzing, recording, classifying, summarizing, reporting, and interpreting (Figure 1-2). Computers are often used in the recording, classifying, summarizing, and reporting steps.

- **Analyzing** is looking at events that have taken place and thinking about how they affect the business.
- **Recording** is entering financial information about events into the accounting system. Although this can be done with paper and pencil, most businesses use computers to perform routine record keeping operations.
- **Classifying** is sorting and grouping similar items together rather than merely keeping a simple, diary-like record of numerous events.
- **Summarizing** is bringing the various items of information together to determine a result.
- **Reporting** is telling the results. In accounting, it is common to use tables of numbers to report results.
- **Interpreting** is deciding the importance of the information in various reports. This may include percentage analyses and the use of ratios to help explain how pieces of information relate to one another.

FIGURE 1-2 The Accounting Process

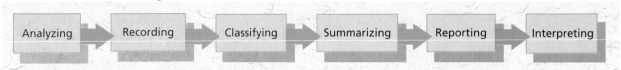

Generally accepted accounting principles (GAAP) are followed during the accounting process. The Financial Accounting Standards Board develops these accounting rules, called GAAP, to provide procedures and guidelines to be followed in the accounting and reporting process.

THREE TYPES OF OWNERSHIP STRUCTURES

LO3 Define three types of business ownership structures.

One or more persons may own a business. Businesses are classified according to who owns them and the specific way they are organized. Three types of ownership structures are (1) sole proprietorship, (2) partnership, and (3) corporation (Figure 1-3). Accountants provide information to owners of all three types of ownership structures.

Sole Proprietorship

A **sole proprietorship** is owned by one person. The owner is often called a proprietor. The proprietor often manages the business. The owner assumes all risks for the business, and personal assets can be taken to pay creditors. The advantage of a sole proprietorship is that the owner can make all decisions.

FIGURE 1-3   Types of Ownership Structures—Advantages and Disadvantages

TYPES OF OWNERSHIP STRUCTURES		
Proprietorship	**Partnership**	**Corporation**
■ One owner	■ Two or more partners	■ Stockholders
■ Owner assumes all risk	■ Partners share risks	■ Stockholders have limited risk
■ Owner makes all decisions	■ Partners may disagree on how to run business	■ Stockholders may have little influence on business decisions

Partnership

A **partnership** is owned by more than one person. One or more partners may manage the business. Like proprietors, partners assume the risks for the business, and their assets may be taken to pay creditors. An advantage of a partnership is that owners share risks and decision making. A disadvantage is that partners may disagree about the best way to run the business.

Corporation

A **corporation** is owned by stockholders (or shareholders). Corporations may have many owners, and they usually employ professional managers. The owners' risk is usually limited to their initial investment, and they usually have very little influence on the business decisions.

TYPES OF BUSINESSES

LO4   Classify different types of businesses by activities.

Businesses are classified according to the type of service or product provided. Some businesses provide a service. Others sell a product. A business that provides a service is called a **service business**. A business that buys a product from another business to sell to customers is called a **merchandising business**. A business that makes a product to sell is called a **manufacturing business**. You will learn about all three types of businesses in this book. Figure 1-4 lists examples of types of businesses organized by activity.

CAREER OPPORTUNITIES IN ACCOUNTING

LO5   Identify career opportunities in accounting.

Accounting offers many career opportunities. The positions described below require varying amounts of education, experience, and technological skill.

FIGURE 1-4   Types and Examples of Businesses Organized by Activities

SERVICES	MERCHANDISING	MANUFACTURING
Travel Agency	Department Store	Automobile Manufacturer
Computer Consultant	Pharmacy	Furniture Maker
Physician	Jewelry Store	Toy Factory

Accounting Clerks

> **ACCOUNTING CLERK**
>
> Travel agency is looking for an accounting clerk to handle book-keeping tasks. 1–3 years experience with an automated accounting system required.

Businesses with large quantities of accounting tasks to perform daily often employ **accounting clerks** to record, sort, and file accounting information. Often accounting clerks will specialize in cash, payroll, accounts receivable, accounts payable, inventory, or purchases. As a result, they are involved with only a small portion of the total accounting responsibilities for the firm. Accounting clerks usually have at least one year of accounting education.

Bookkeepers and Para-Accountants

> **BOOKKEEPING/ACCOUNTING**
>
> Service company has an opening for a full charge bookkeeper/accountant. Previous accounting experience with an associates degree preferred. Salary commensurate with experience. Excellent knowledge of LOTUS 1-2-3 required.

Bookkeepers generally supervise the work of accounting clerks, help with daily accounting work, and summarize accounting information. In small-to-medium-sized businesses, the bookkeeper may also help managers and owners interpret the accounting information. Bookkeepers usually have one to two years of accounting education and experience as an accounting clerk.

Para-accountants provide many accounting, auditing, or tax services under the direct supervision of an accountant. A typical para-accountant has a two-year degree or significant accounting and bookkeeping experience.

Accountants

> **ACCOUNTANT**
>
> Responsibilities include accounts receivable, accounts payable, and general ledger. Familiarity with computerized systems a must. Supervisory experience a plus.

The difference between accountants and bookkeepers is not always clear, particularly in smaller firms where bookkeepers also help analyze the accounting information. In large firms, the distinction is clearer. Bookkeepers focus on the processing of accounting data. **Accountants** design the accounting information system and focus on analyzing and interpreting information. They also look for important trends in the data and study the impact of alternative decisions.

Most accountants enter the field with a college degree in accounting. Accountants are employed in public accounting, private (managerial) accounting, and in governmental and not-for-profit accounting (Figure 1-5).

Public Accounting.   Public accountants offer services in much the same way as doctors and lawyers. The public accountant can achieve professional recognition as a **Certified Public Accountant** (CPA). This is done by meeting certain education and experience requirements as determined by each state, and passing a uniform examination prepared by the American Institute of Certified Public Accountants.

Many CPAs work alone, while others work for major accounting firms that vary in scope and size. Services offered by public accountants are listed on the next page.

FIGURE 1-5 Accounting Careers

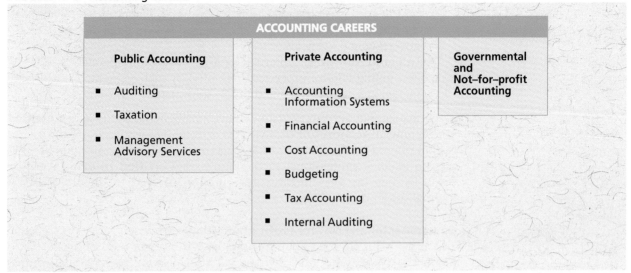

- **Auditing.**   Auditing involves the application of standard review and testing procedures to be certain that proper accounting policies and practices have been followed. The purpose of the audit is to provide an independent opinion that the financial information about a business is fairly presented.
- **Taxation.**   Tax specialists advise on tax planning, prepare tax returns, and represent clients before governmental agencies such as the Internal Revenue Service.
- **Management Advisory Services.**   Given the financial training and business experience of public accountants, many businesses seek their advice on a wide variety of managerial issues. Often accounting firms are involved in designing computerized accounting systems.

CONTROLLER
$40,000–$45,000

Service company seeks financial manager to oversee all general accounting and financial reporting. PC skills important. 4+ years in corporate or public accounting will qualify.

Private Accounting (Managerial Accounting).   Many accountants are employees of private business firms. The **controller** oversees the entire accounting process and is the principal accounting officer of the company. Private or managerial accountants perform a wide variety of services for the business. These services are listed below.

- **Accounting Information Systems.**   Accountants in this area design and implement manual and computerized accounting systems.
- **Financial Accounting.**   Based on the accounting data prepared by the bookkeepers and accounting clerks, the accountant prepares various reports and financial statements.
- **Cost Accounting.**   The cost of producing specific products or providing services must be measured. Further analysis is also done to determine whether the products and services are produced in the most cost-effective manner.
- **Budgeting.**   In the budgeting process, accountants help managers develop a financial plan.

- **Tax Accounting.**   Instead of hiring a public accountant, a firm may have its own accountants. They focus on tax planning, preparation of tax returns, and dealing with the Internal Revenue Service and other governmental agencies.
- **Internal Auditing.**   Internal auditors review the operating and accounting control procedures adopted by management. They also make sure that accurate and timely information is provided.

A managerial accountant can achieve professional status as a **Certified Management Accountant** (CMA). This is done by passing a uniform examination offered by the Institute of Management Accounting. An internal auditor can achieve professional recognition as a **Certified Internal Auditor** (CIA) by passing the uniform examination offered by the Institute of Internal Auditors.

Governmental and Not-for-Profit Accounting.   Thousands of governmental and not-for-profit organizations (states, cities, schools, churches, and hospitals) gather and report financial information. These organizations employ a large number of accountants. While the rules are somewhat different for governmental and not-for-profit organizations, many accounting procedures are similar to those found in profit-seeking enterprises.

ACCOUNTANT

Assist fiscal officer in not-for-profit accounting. Experience in payroll, payroll taxes, and LOTUS 1-2-3 helpful. Qualifications: accounting degree or equivalent. $22–$25K.

Job Opportunities

Job growth in some areas will be much greater than in others. Notice in newspaper advertisements that accountants and accounting clerks are expected to have computer skills. Computer skills definitely increase the opportunities available to you in your career. Almost every business needs accountants, accounting clerks, and bookkeepers. Figure 1-6 shows the expected growth for different types of businesses. Notice that growth will be greatest in the service businesses. Chapters 2 through 10 introduce accounting skills that you will need to work in a service business. Chapter 11 begins the discussion of merchandising businesses. Accounting for manufacturing businesses is addressed in the last chapters of the book. Figure 1-7 shows the expected demand for accounting skills.

Regardless of the type of career you desire, writing skills are important in business and your personal life. Becoming a good writer requires practice and a strategy for the process used to prepare memos, letters, and other documents. On pages 10 and 11, Ken Davis offers an excellent approach to managing your writing. Take a moment to read Ken's tips. Then, practice his approach by completing the writing assignments as you finish each chapter.

KEY POINTS

1   The purpose of accounting is to provide financial information about a business to individuals and organizations.

2   The six major steps of the accounting process are analyzing, recording, classifying, summarizing, reporting, and interpreting.

FIGURE 1-6   Expected Growth

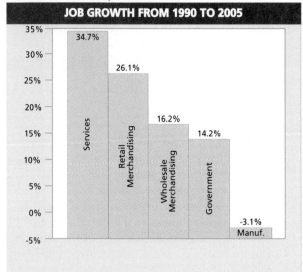

The growth in the number of new jobs from 1990 to 2005 will vary according to industry. The major area of growth is in service businesses. Service businesses that provide services to health care and business will provide the most opportunities. For example, many job opportunities will be available with temporary help agencies and computer and data processing services. Opportunities within manufacturing businesses will decrease. Part of the decrease will result from continued automation. Employment for technical workers within manufacturing will probably even increase.

Source: Bureau of Labor Statistics (1992)

FIGURE 1-7   Expected Demand

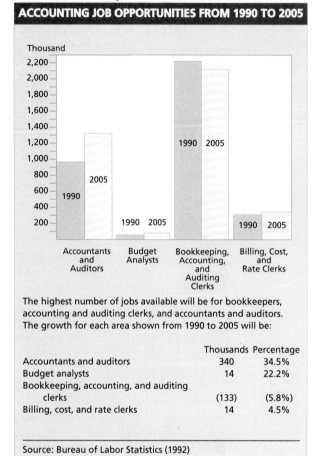

The highest number of jobs available will be for bookkeepers, accounting and auditing clerks, and accountants and auditors. The growth for each area shown from 1990 to 2005 will be:

	Thousands	Percentage
Accountants and auditors	340	34.5%
Budget analysts	14	22.2%
Bookkeeping, accounting, and auditing clerks	(133)	(5.8%)
Billing, cost, and rate clerks	14	4.5%

Source: Bureau of Labor Statistics (1992)

3   Three types of business ownership structures are sole proprietorship, partnership, and corporation.

4   Different types of businesses classified by activities are a service business, a merchandising business, and a manufacturing business.

5   Career opportunities in accounting include work in public accounting, private accounting, and governmental and not-for-profit accounting.

KEY TERMS

accountant 6   Designs the accounting information system and focuses on analyzing and interpreting information.

accounting 3   The art of gathering financial information about a business and reporting this information to users.

accounting clerk 6   Records, sorts, and files accounting information.

Managing Your Writing

KEN DAVIS

Here's a secret: the business writing that you and I do—the writing that gets the world's work done—requires no special gift. It can be *managed,* like any other business process.

Managing writing is largely a matter of managing time. Writing is a process, and like any process it can be done efficiently or inefficiently. Unfortunately, most of us are pretty inefficient writers. That's because we try to get each word, each sentence, right the first time. Given a letter to write, we begin with the first sentence. We think about that sentence, write it, revise it, even check its spelling, before going on to the second sentence. In an hour of writing, we might spend 45 or 50 minutes doing this kind of detailed drafting. We spend only a few minutes on overall planning at the beginning and only a few minutes on overall revising at the end.

That approach to writing is like building a house by starting with the front door: planning, building, finishing—even washing the windows—before doing anything with the rest of the house. No wonder most of us have so much trouble writing.

Efficient, effective writers take better charge of their writing time. They *manage* their writing. Like building contractors, they spend time planning before they start construction. Once construction has started, they don't try to do all of the finishing touches as they go.

As the illustration on the next page shows, many good writers break their writing process into three main stages: planning, drafting, and revising. They spend more time at the first and third stages than at the second. They also build in some "management" time at the beginning and the end, and some break time in the middle. To manage *your* writing time, try the following steps.

At the *MANAGING* stage (perhaps two or three minutes for a one-hour writing job), remind yourself that writing *can* be managed and that it's largely a matter of managing time. Plan your next hour.

At the *PLANNING* stage (perhaps 20 minutes out of the hour):

1. *Find the "we."* Define the community to which you and your reader belong. Then ask, "How are my reader and I alike and different?"—in knowledge, attitudes, and circumstances.

2. *Define your purpose.* Remember the advice a consultant once gave Stanley Tool executives: "You're not in the business of making drills; you're in the business of making holes." Too many of us lose sight of the difference between making drills and making holes when we write letters and memos. We focus on the piece of writing—the tool itself—not its purpose. The result: our writing often misses the chance to be as effective as it could be. When you're still at the planning stage, focus on the outcome you want, not on the means you will use to achieve it.

3. *Get your stuff together.* Learn from those times when you've turned a one-hour home-improvement project into a three- or four-hour job by having to make repeated trips to the hardware store for tools or parts. Before you start the drafting stage of writing, collect the information you need.

4. *Get your ducks in a row.* Decide on the main points you want to make. Then, make a list or rough outline placing your points in the most logical order.

At the *DRAFTING* stage (perhaps 5 minutes out of the hour):

5. *Do it wrong the first time.* Do a "quick and dirty" draft, without editing. Think of your draft as a "prototype," written not for the end user but for your own testing and improvement. Stopping to edit while you draft breaks your train of thought and keeps you from being a good writer. (Hint: if you are writing at a computer, try turning off the monitor during the drafting stage.)

At the *BREAK* stage (perhaps 5 minutes):

6. *Take a break and change hats.* Get away from your draft, even if for only a few minutes. Come back with a fresh perspective—the reader's perspective.

At the *REVISING* stage (perhaps 25 minutes):

7. *Signal your turns.* Just as if you were driving a car, you're leading your reader through new territory. Use "turn signals"—*and, in addition, but, however, or, therefore, because, for example*—to guide your reader from sentence to sentence.

8. *Say what you mean.* Put the point of your sentences in the subjects and verbs. For example, revise "There are drawbacks to using this accounting method" to "This accounting method has some drawbacks." You'll be saying

what you mean, and you'll be a more effective communicator.

9. *Pay by the word.* Reading your memo requires work. If your sentences are wordy and you are slow to get to the point, the reader may decide that it is not worth the effort. Pretend you are paying the reader by the word to read your memo. Then, revise your memo to make it as short and to the point as possible.

10. *Translate into English.* Keep your words simple. (Lee Iacocca put both these tips in one "commandment of good management": "Say it in English and keep it short.") Remember that you write to express, not impress.

11. Finish the job. Check your spelling, punctuation, and mechanics.

Finally, at the *MANAGING* stage again (2 to 3 minutes):

12. Evaluate your writing process. Figure out how to improve it next time.

By following these 12 steps, you can take charge of your writing time. Begin today to *manage your writing*. As a United Technologies Corporation advertisement in *The Wall Street Journal* admonished, "If you want to manage somebody, manage yourself. Do that well and you'll be ready to stop managing and start leading."

Dr. Ken Davis is Professor of English and coordinator of the Applied Writing Group at Indiana University-Purdue University at Indianapolis. He is president of Komei, Inc., a global communication consulting company.

accounting information systems 7   Accountants in this area design and implement manual and computerized accounting systems.

analyzing 4   Looking at events that have taken place and thinking about how they affect the business.

auditing 7   Reviewing and testing to be certain that proper accounting policies and practices have been followed.

bookkeeper 6   Generally supervise the work of accounting clerks, help with daily accounting work, and summarize accounting information.

budgeting 7   The process in which accountants help managers develop a financial plan.

Certified Internal Auditor 8   An internal auditor who has achieved professional recognition by passing the uniform examination offered by the Institute of Internal Auditors.

Certified Management Accountant 8   An accountant who has passed an examination prepared by the Institute of Management Accounting.

Certified Public Accountant 6   A public accountant who has met certain education and experience requirements and has passed an examination prepared by the American Institute of Certified Public Accountants.

classifying 4   Sorting and grouping similar items together rather than merely keeping a simple, diary-like record of numerous events.

controller 7   The accountant who oversees the entire accounting process in a private business firm.

corporation 5   A type of ownership structure in which stockholders own the business. The owners' risk is usually limited to their initial investment, and they usually have very little influence on the business decisions.

cost accounting 7   Determining the cost of producing specific products or providing services and analyzing for cost effectiveness.

financial accounting 7   Preparing various reports and financial statements based on the accounting data prepared by the bookkeepers and accounting clerks.

generally accepted accounting principles 4   Procedures and guidelines developed by the Financial Accounting Standards Board to be followed in the accounting process.

internal auditing 8   Reviewing the operating and accounting control procedures adopted by management and seeing that accurate and timely information is provided.

interpreting 4   Deciding the importance of the information on various reports.

management advisory services 7   Providing advice to businesses on a wide variety of managerial issues.

manufacturing business 5   A business that makes a product to sell.

merchandising business 5   A business that buys products to sell.

para-accountant 6   A paraprofessional that provides many accounting, auditing, or tax services under the direct supervision of an accountant.

partnership 5   A type of ownership structure in which more than one person owns the business.

recording 4   Entering financial information into the accounting system.

reporting 4   Telling the results of the financial information.

service business 5   A business that provides a service.

sole proprietorship 4   A type of ownership structure in which one person owns the business.

summarizing 4   Bringing the various items of information together to explain a result.

tax accounting 8   Accountants in this area focus on planning, preparing tax returns, and dealing with the Internal Revenue Service and other governmental agencies.

REVIEW QUESTIONS

1. What is the purpose of accounting?
2. Identify four user groups normally interested in financial information about a business.
3. Identify the six major steps of the accounting process and explain each step.
4. Identify the three types of ownership structures and discuss the advantages and disadvantages of each.
5. Identify three types of businesses according to activities.
6. What are the main functions of an accounting clerk?
7. Name and describe three areas of specialization for a public accountant.
8. Name and describe six areas of specialization for a managerial accountant.

MANAGING YOUR WRITING

1. Prepare a one-page memo to your instructor that explains what you hope to learn in this course and how this knowledge will be useful to you.
2. If you started a business, what would it be? Prepare a one-page memo that describes the type of business you would enjoy the most. Would it be a service, merchandising, or manufacturing business? Explain what form of ownership you would prefer and why.

SERIES A   EXERCISES

1   **EXERCISE 1A1 PURPOSE OF ACCOUNTING**   Match the following users with the information needed.

1. Owners
2. Managers
3. Creditors
4. Government agencies

a. Whether the firm can pay its bills on time
b. Detailed, up-to-date information to measure business performance (and plan for future operations)
c. To determine taxes to be paid and whether other regulations are met
d. The firm's current financial condition

2 **EXERCISE 1A2 ACCOUNTING PROCESS**   List the six major steps of the accounting process in order (1–6) and define each.

_____   Recording
_____   Summarizing
_____   Reporting
_____   Analyzing
_____   Interpreting
_____   Classifying

SERIES B EXERCISES

1 **EXERCISE 1B1 PURPOSE OF ACCOUNTING** Describe the kind of information needed by the users listed.

Owners (present and future)
Managers
Creditors (present and future)
Government agencies

2 **EXERCISE 1B2 ACCOUNTING PROCESS**   Match the following steps of the accounting process with their definitions.

Analyzing	**a.** Telling the results
Recording	**b.** Looking at events that have taken place and thinking about how they affect the business
Classifying	**c.** Deciding the importance of the various reports
Summarizing	**d.** Bringing together information to explain a result
Reporting	**e.** Sorting and grouping like items together
Interpreting	**f.** Entering financial information into the accounting system

2

Analyzing Transactions: The Accounting Equation

Have you ever heard the expression "garbage in, garbage out"? Computer users commonly use it to mean that if input to the computer system is not correctly entered, the output from the system will be worthless. The same expression applies in accounting. If the economic events and their impact on the accounting equation are not properly understood, the events will not be correctly entered into the accounting system. This will make the outputs from the system (the financial statements) worthless.

The entire accounting process is based on one simple equation, called the accounting equation. In this chapter, you will learn how to use this equation to analyze business transactions. You also will learn how to prepare financial statements that report the effect of these transactions on the financial condition of a business.

THE ACCOUNTING ELEMENTS

LO1 Define the accounting elements.

Before the accounting process can begin, the entity to be accounted for must be defined. A **business entity** is an individual, association, or organization that engages in economic activities and controls specific economic resources. This definition allows the personal and business finances of an owner to be accounted for separately.

Three basic accounting elements exist for every business entity: assets, liabilities, and owner's equity. These elements are defined below.

 Pay close attention to the definitions for the basic accounting elements. A clear understanding of these definitions will help you analyze even the most complex business transactions.

Assets

Assets are items owned by a business that will provide future benefits. Examples include money, merchandise, furniture, fixtures, machinery, buildings, and land.

Liabilities

Liabilities represent something owed to another business entity. The amount owed represents a probable future outflow of assets as a result of a past event or transaction. Liabilities are debts or obligations of the business that can be paid with cash, goods, or services.

The most common liabilities are accounts payable and notes payable. An **account payable** is an unwritten promise to pay a supplier for assets purchased or services received. Formal written promises to pay suppliers or lenders specified sums of money at definite future times are known as **notes payable**.

Owner's Equity

Owner's equity is the amount by which the business assets exceed the business liabilities. Other terms used for owner's equity include **net worth** and **capital**. If there are no business liabilities, the owner's equity is equal to the total assets.

The owner of a business may have business assets and liabilities as well as nonbusiness assets and liabilities. For example, the business owner probably owns a home, clothing, and a car, and perhaps owes the dentist for dental service. These are personal, nonbusiness assets and liabilities. According to the **business entity concept**, nonbusiness assets and liabilities are not included in the business entity's accounting records.

 The business entity's accounting records are separate from the owner's nonbusiness assets and liabilities.

If the owner invests money or other assets in the business, the item invested is reclassified from a nonbusiness asset to a business asset. If the owner withdraws money or other assets from the business for personal use, the item withdrawn is reclassified from a business asset to a nonbusiness asset. These distinctions are important and allow the owner to make decisions based on the financial condition and results of the business apart from nonbusiness affairs.

THE ACCOUNTING EQUATION

LO2 Construct the accounting equation.

The relationship between the three basic accounting elements—assets, liabilities, and owner's equity—can be expressed in the form of a simple equation known as the **accounting equation**.

$$\text{Assets} = \text{Liabilities} + \text{Owner's Equity}$$

 If you know two accounting elements, you can calculate the third element.

Total assets	$60,400
Total liabilities	−5,400
Owner's equity	$55,000

This equation reflects the fact that both outsiders and insiders have an interest in all of the assets of a business. *Liabilities represent the outside interests of creditors. Owner's equity represents the inside interests of owners. When two elements are known, the third can always be calculated.* For example, assume that assets on December 31 total $60,400. On that same day, the business liabilities consist of $5,400 owed for equipment. Owner's equity is calculated by subtracting total liabilities from total assets, $60,400 − $5,400 = $55,000.

$$\text{Assets} = \text{Liabilities} + \text{Owner's Equity}$$

$$\$60,400 = \$5,400 + \$55,000$$
$$\$60,400$$

ANALYZING BUSINESS TRANSACTIONS

LO3 Analyze business transactions.

A **business transaction** is an economic event that has a direct impact on the business. A business transaction almost always requires an exchange between the business and another outside entity. We must be able to measure this exchange in dollars. Examples of business transactions include buying goods and services, selling goods and services, buying and selling assets, making loans, and borrowing money.

All business transactions affect the accounting equation through specific accounts. An **account** is a separate record used to summarize changes in each asset, liability, and owner's equity of a business. **Account titles** provide a description of the particular type of asset, liability, or owner's equity affected by a transaction.

Three basic questions must be answered when analyzing the effects of a business transaction on the accounting equation.

1. **What happened?**
   ▪ Make certain you understand the event that has taken place.
2. **Which accounts are affected?**
   ▪ Identify the accounts that are affected.
   ▪ Classify these accounts as assets, liabilities, or owner's equity.
3. **How is the accounting equation affected?**
   ▪ Determine which accounts have increased or decreased.
   ▪ Make certain that the accounting equation remains in balance after the transaction has been entered.

EFFECT OF TRANSACTIONS ON THE ACCOUNTING EQUATION

LO4 Show the effects of business transactions on the accounting equation.

Each transaction affects one or more of the three basic accounting elements. A transaction increases or decreases a specific asset, liability, or owner's equity account. Assume that the following transactions occurred during June 19--, the first month of operations for Jessie Jane's Campus Delivery.

TRANSACTION (a):   **Investment by owner**

An Increase in an Asset Offset by an Increase in Owner's Equity.   Jessica Jane opened a bank account with a deposit of $2,000 for her business. The new business now has $2,000 of the asset Cash. Since Jane contributed the asset, the owner's equity element, Jessica Jane, Capital, increases by the same amount.

Assets	=	Liabilities	+	Owner's Equity
Items Owned		Amounts Owed		Owner's Investment
				Jessica Jane,
Cash	=			Capital
(a) $2,000				$2,000

TRANSACTION (b):   **Purchase of an asset for cash**

An Increase in an Asset Offset by a Decrease in Another Asset.   Jane decided that the fastest and easiest way to get around campus and find parking is on a motor scooter. Thus, she bought a motor scooter (delivery equipment) for

$1,200, cash. Jane exchanged one asset, cash, for another, delivery equipment. This transaction reduces Cash and creates a new asset, Delivery Equipment.

	Assets		=	Liabilities	+	Owner's Equity
	Items Owned			Amounts Owed		Owner's Investment
	Cash +	Delivery Equipment =				Jessica Jane, Capital
	$2,000					$2,000
(b)	−1,200	+$1,200				
	$ 800	$1,200				$2,000
	└── $2,000 ──┘			└── $2,000 ──┘		

TRANSACTION (c):   Purchase of an asset on account

An Increase in an Asset Offset by an Increase in a Liability.   Jane hired a friend to work for her, which meant that a second scooter would be needed. Given Jane's limited cash, she bought the dealer's demonstration model for $900. The seller agreed to allow Jane to spread the payments over the next three months. This transaction increased an asset, Delivery Equipment, by $900 and increased the liability, Accounts Payable, by an equal amount.

	Assets		=	Liabilities	+	Owner's Equity
	Items Owned			Amounts Owed		Owner's Investment
	Cash +	Delivery Equipment =		Accounts Payable	+	Jessica Jane, Capital
	$ 800	$1,200				$2,000
(c)		+ 900		+900		
	$ 800	$2,100		$900		$2,000
	└── $2,900 ──┘			└── $2,900 ──┘		

TRANSACTION (d):   Payment on a loan

A Decrease in an Asset Offset by a Decrease in a Liability.   Jane paid the first installment on the scooter of $300. (See transaction (c).) This payment decreased the asset, Cash, and the liability, Accounts Payable, by $300.

	Assets		=	Liabilities	+	Owner's Equity
	Items Owned			Amounts Owed		Owner's Investment
	Cash +	Delivery Equipment =		Accounts Payable	+	Jessica Jane, Capital
	$ 800	$2,100		$900		$2,000
(d)	−300			−300		
	$ 500	$2,100		$600		$2,000
	└── $2,600 ──┘			└── $2,600 ──┘		

Expanding the Accounting Equation: Revenues, Expenses, and Withdrawals

In the preceding sections, three key accounting elements of every business entity were defined and explained: assets, liabilities, and owner's equity. To complete the explanation of the accounting process, three additional elements must be added to the discussion: revenues, expenses, and withdrawals.

Revenues.   **Revenues** represent the amount a business charges customers for products sold or services performed. Customers generally pay with cash or a credit card, or they promise to pay at a later date. Most businesses recognize revenues when earned, even if cash has not yet been received. *Revenues increase both assets and owner's equity.*

Expenses.   **Expenses** represent the decrease in assets (or increase in liabilities) as a result of efforts made to produce revenues. Common examples of expenses are rent, salaries, supplies consumed, and taxes. As expenses are incurred, either assets are consumed (supplies), cash is paid (wages), or a promise is made to pay cash at a future date. The promise to pay in the future represents a liability. Most businesses recognize expenses when incurred, even if cash has not yet been paid. *Expenses either decrease assets or increase liabilities. Expenses always reduce owner's equity.*

 LEARNING KEY   It is important to remember that expenses do not always reduce cash.

If total revenues exceed total expenses of the period, the excess is the **net income** or net profit for the period.

Revenues Greater than Expenses = Net Income

On the other hand, if expenses exceed revenues of the period, the excess is a **net loss** for the period.

Expenses Greater than Revenues = Net Loss

The owner can determine the time period used in the measurement of net income or net loss. It may be a month, a quarter (three months), a year, or some other time period. The concept that income determination can be made on a periodic basis is known as the **accounting period concept**. Any accounting period of twelve months is called a **fiscal year**. The fiscal year frequently coincides with the calendar year.

Withdrawals

LEARNING KEY

Owner's Equity	
Decrease	Increase
Expenses	Revenues
Drawing	Investments

Withdrawals, or **drawing**, reduce owner's equity as a result of the owner taking cash or other assets out of the business for personal use. Since earnings are expected to offset withdrawals, this reduction is viewed as temporary.

The accounting equation is expanded to include revenues, expenses, and withdrawals. Note that revenues increase owner's equity, while expenses and drawing reduce owner's equity.

Assets		=	Liabilities	+	Owner's Equity				
Items Owned			Amounts Owed		Owner's Investment + Earnings				
Cash +	Delivery Equipment =		Accounts Payable	+	Jessica Jane, Capital	Jessica Jane, – Drawing	+ Revenues	– Expenses	
Balance $500	$2,100		$600		$2,000				
⌊— $2,600 —⌋			⌊———————— $2,600 ————————⌋						

Effect of Revenue, Expense, and Withdrawal Transactions on the Accounting Equation

To show the effects of revenue, expense, and withdrawal transactions, the example of Jessie Jane's Campus Delivery will be continued. Assume that the following transactions took place in Jane's business during June 19--.

TRANSACTION (e):   Delivery revenues earned in cash

An Increase in an Asset Offset by an Increase in Owner's Equity Resulting from Revenue.   Jane received $500 cash from clients for delivery services. This transaction increased the asset, Cash, and increased owner's equity by $500. The increase in owner's equity is shown by increasing the revenue, Delivery Fees, by $500.

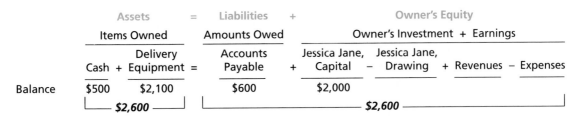

Assets		=	Liabilities	+	Owner's Equity				
Items Owned			Amounts Owed		Owner's Investment + Earnings				
Cash +	Delivery Equipment =		Accounts Payable	+	Jessica Jane, Capital	Jessica Jane, – Drawing	+ Revenues	– Expenses	Description
$ 500	$2,100		$600		$2,000				
(e) +500							+$500		Delivery fees
$1,000	$2,100		$600		$2,000		$500		
⌊— $3,100 —⌋			⌊———————— $3,100 ————————⌋						

TRANSACTION (f):   Paid rent for month

A Decrease in an Asset Offset by a Decrease in Owner's Equity Resulting from an Expense.   Jane rents a small office on campus. She paid $200 for office rent for June. This transaction decreased both Cash and owner's equity by $200. The decrease in owner's equity is shown by increasing an expense called Rent Expense by $200. An increase in an expense decreases owner's equity.

	Assets		=	Liabilities	+		Owner's Equity				
	Items Owned			Amounts Owed			Owner's Investment + Earnings				
	Cash +	Delivery Equipment =		Accounts Payable	+	Jessica Jane, Capital	− Jessica Jane, Drawing	+ Revenues	− Expenses		Description
	$1,000	$2,100		$600		$2,000		$500			
(f)	−200								+$200		Rent Expense
	$ 800	$2,100		$600		$2,000		$500	$200		
		$2,900					$2,900				

TRANSACTION (g):   Paid telephone bill

A Decrease in an Asset Offset by a Decrease in Owner's Equity Resulting from an Expense. Jane paid $50 in cash for telephone service. This transaction, like the previous one, decreased both Cash and owner's equity. This decrease in owner's equity is shown by increasing an expense called Telephone Expense by $50.

	Assets		=	Liabilities	+		Owner's Equity				
	Items Owned			Amounts Owed			Owner's Investment + Earnings				
	Cash +	Delivery Equipment =		Accounts Payable	+	Jessica Jane, Capital	− Jessica Jane, Drawing	+ Revenues	− Expenses		Description
	$800	$2,100		$600		$2,000		$500	$200		
(g)	− 50								+ 50		Telephone Exp.
	$750	$2,100		$600		$2,000		$500	$250		
		$2,850					$2,850				

> 🔑 **LEARNING KEY**   Revenue is recognized even though cash is not received.

TRANSACTION (h):   Delivery revenues earned on account

An Increase in an Asset Offset by an Increase in Owner's Equity Resulting from Revenue. Jane extends credit to regular customers. Often delivery services are performed for which payment will be received later. This is known as offering services "on account." Since revenues are recognized when earned, an increase in owner's equity must be reported by increasing the revenue account. Since no cash is received at this time, Cash cannot be increased. Instead, an increase is reported for another asset, Accounts Receivable. *The total of Accounts Receivable at any point in time reflects the amount owed to Jane by her customers.* Deliveries made on account amounted to $600. Accounts Receivable and Delivery Fees are increased.

	Assets			=	Liabilities	+		Owner's Equity				
	Items Owned				Amounts Owed			Owner's Investment + Earnings				
	Cash +	Accounts Receivable +	Delivery Equipment =		Accounts Payable	+	Jessica Jane, Capital	− Jessica Jane, Drawing	+ Revenues	− Expenses		Description
	$750		$2,100		$600		$2,000		$ 500	$250		
(h)		+$600							+600			Delivery Fees
	$750	$600	$2,100		$600		$2,000		$1,100	$250		
			$3,450					$3,450				

TRANSACTION (i):   Purchase of supplies

An Increase in an Asset Offset by a Decrease in an Asset.   Jane bought pens, paper, delivery envelopes, and other supplies for $80 cash. These supplies should last for several months. Since they will generate future benefits, the supplies should be recorded as an asset. The accounting equation will show an increase in an asset, Supplies, and a decrease in Cash.

	Assets			=	Liabilities	+	Owner's Equity				
	Items Owned				Amounts Owed		Owner's Investment + Earnings				
Cash +	Accounts Receivable +	Supplies +	Delivery Equipment =		Accounts Payable	+	Jessica Jane, Capital −	Jessica Jane, Drawing +	Revenues −	Expenses	Description
$750	$600		$2,100		$600		$2,000		$1,100	$250	
−80		+$80									
$670	$600	$80	$2,100		$600		$2,000		$1,100	$250	

(i) on left margin.

Assets total: **$3,450**   Liabilities + Owner's Equity total: **$3,450**

TRANSACTION (j):   Payment of insurance premium

 LEARNING KEY | Both supplies and insurance are recorded as assets because they will last for several months.

An Increase in an Asset Offset by a Decrease in an Asset.   Since Jane plans to graduate next January, she paid $200 for an eight-month liability insurance policy. Insurance is paid in advance and will provide future benefits. Thus, it is treated as an asset. We must expand the equation to include another asset, Prepaid Insurance, and show that Cash has been reduced.

	Assets				=	Liabilities	+	Owner's Equity				
	Items Owned					Amounts Owed		Owner's Investment + Earnings				
Cash +	Accounts Receivable +	Supplies +	Prepaid Insurance +	Delivery Equipment =		Accounts Payable	+	Jessica Jane, Capital −	Jessica Jane, Drawing +	Revenues −	Expenses	Description
$670	$600	$80		$2,100		$600		$2,000		$1,100	$250	
−200			+$200									
$470	$600	$80	$200	$2,100		$600		$2,000		$1,100	$250	

(j) on left margin.

Assets total: **$3,450**   Liabilities + Owner's Equity total: **$3,450**

TRANSACTION (k):   Cash receipts from prior sales on account

An Increase in an Asset Offset by a Decrease in an Asset.   Jane received $570 in cash for delivery services performed for customers earlier in the month (see transaction (h)). Receipt of this cash increases the cash account and reduces the amount due from customers reported in the accounts receivable account. *Notice that owner's equity is not affected in this transaction. Owner's equity increased in transaction (h) when revenue was recognized as it was earned, rather than now when cash is received.*

	Assets				=	Liabilities	+	Owner's Equity					
	Items Owned					Amounts Owed		Owner's Investment + Earnings					
Cash +	Accounts Receivable +	Supplies +	Prepaid Insurance +	Delivery Equipment =		Accounts Payable	+	Jessica Jane, Capital −	Jessica Jane, Drawing +	Revenues −	Expenses	Description
$ 470	$600	$80	$200	$2,100		$600		$2,000		$1,100	$250	
(k) +570	−570											
$1,040	$ 30	$80	$200	$2,100		$600		$2,000		$1,100	$250	
		$3,450						$3,450				

TRANSACTION (l):   Purchase of an asset on credit making a partial payment

An Increase in an Asset Offset by a Decrease in an Asset and an Increase in a Liability. With business increasing, Jane hired a second employee and bought a third motor scooter. The scooter cost $1,500. Jane paid $300 in cash and will spread the remaining payments over the next four months. The asset Delivery Equipment increases by $1,500, Cash decreases by $300, and the liability, Accounts Payable, increases by $1,200. *Note that this transaction changes three accounts. Even so, the accounting equation remains in balance.*

	Assets				=	Liabilities	+	Owner's Equity					
	Items Owned					Amounts Owed		Owner's Investment + Earnings					
Cash +	Accounts Receivable +	Supplies +	Prepaid Insurance +	Delivery Equipment =		Accounts Payable	+	Jessica Jane, Capital −	Jessica Jane, Drawing +	Revenues −	Expenses	Description
$1,040	$30	$80	$200	$2,100		$ 600		$2,000		$1,100	$250	
(l) −300				+1,500		+1,200						
$ 740	$30	$80	$200	$3,600		$1,800		$2,000		$1,100	$250	
		$4,650						$4,650				

TRANSACTION (m):   Payment of wages

A Decrease in an Asset Offset by a Decrease in Owner's Equity Resulting from an Expense. Jane paid her part-time employees $650 in wages. This represents an additional business expense. As with other expenses, Cash is reduced and owner's equity is reduced by increasing an expense.

	Assets				=	Liabilities	+	Owner's Equity					
	Items Owned					Amounts Owed		Owner's Investment + Earnings					
Cash +	Accounts Receivable +	Supplies +	Prepaid Insurance +	Delivery Equipment =		Accounts Payable	+	Jessica Jane, Capital −	Jessica Jane, Drawing +	Revenues −	Expenses	Description
$740	$30	$80	$200	$3,600		$1,800		$2,000		$1,100	$250	
(m) −650											+650	Wages Expense
$ 90	$30	$80	$200	$3,600		$1,800		$2,000		$1,100	$900	
		$4,000						$4,000				

TRANSACTION (n):   Deliveries made for cash and credit

An Increase in Two Assets Offset by an Increase in Owner's Equity. Total delivery fees for the remainder of the month amounted to $900: $430 in cash and $470 on account. Since all of these delivery fees have been earned, the revenue account increases by $900. Also, Cash increases by $430 and Accounts Receivable increases by $470. Thus, revenues increase assets and owner's equity. Note, once again, that one event impacts three accounts while the equation remains in balance.

		Assets			=	Liabilities	+		Owner's Equity				
		Items Owned				Amounts Owed		Owner's Investment + Earnings					
Cash +	Accounts Receivable +	Supplies +	Prepaid Insurance +	Delivery Equipment =		Accounts Payable	+	Jessica Jane, Capital	– Jessica Jane, Drawing	+ Revenues	– Expenses		Description
$ 90	$ 30	$80	$200	$3,600		$1,800		$2,000		$1,100	$900		
(n) +430	+470									+900			Delivery Fees
$520	$500	$80	$200	$3,600		$1,800		$2,000		$2,000	$900		
└──────── $4,900 ────────┘						└──────── $4,900 ────────┘							

TRANSACTION (o):   **Withdrawal of cash from business**

> Withdrawals by the owner are reported in the drawing account. Withdrawals are the opposite of investments by the owner. Recall the business entity concept. The owner of the business and the business are separate economic entities. Thus, personal transactions must not be included with those of the business. If this is allowed, it will be very difficult to evaluate the performance of the business.

A Decrease in an Asset Offset by a Decrease in Owner's Equity Resulting from a Withdrawal by the Owner.   At the end of the month, Jane took $150 in cash from the business to purchase books for her classes. Since the books are not business related, this is a withdrawal. Withdrawals can be viewed as the opposite of investments by the owner. Both owner's equity and Cash decrease.

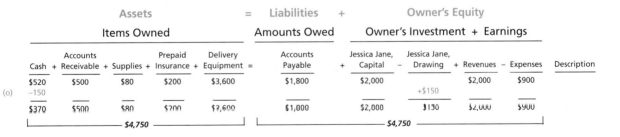

Figure 2-1 shows a summary of the transactions. Use this summary to test your understanding of transaction analysis by describing the economic event represented by each transaction. At the bottom of Figure 2-1, the asset accounts and their totals are compared with the liability and owner's equity accounts and their totals.

FIGURE 2-1   Summary of Transactions Illustrated

	SUMMARY										

	Assets					**=**	**Liabilities**	**+**	**Owner's Equity**		
	Items Owned						Amounts Owed		Owner's Investment + Earnings		

Transaction	Cash	+ Accounts Receivable	+ Supplies	+ Prepaid Insurance	+ Delivery Equipment =	Accounts Payable	+ Jessica Jane, Capital	– Jessica Jane, Drawing	+ Revenues	– Expenses	Description
Balance											
(a)	2,000	____	__	__	____	____	2,000	__	____	__	
Balance	2,000						2,000				
(b)	(1,200)				1,200						
Balance	800	____	__	__	1,200	____	2,000		____	__	
(c)					900	900					
Balance	800	____	__	__	2,100	900	2,000		____	__	
(d)	(300)					(300)					
Balance	500				2,100	600	2,000				
(e)	500								500		Delivery Fees
Balance	1,000	____	__	__	2,100	600	2,000		500		
(f)	(200)									200	Rent Exp.
Balance	800	____	__	__	2,100	600	2,000		500	200	
(g)	(50)									50	Tele. Exp.
Balance	750	____	__	__	2,100	600	2,000		500	250	
(h)		600							600		Delivery Fees
Balance	750	600	____	__	2,100	600	2,000		1,100	250	
(i)	(80)		80								
Balance	670	600	80	____	2,100	600	2,000		1,100	250	
(j)	(200)			200							
Balance	470	600	80	200	2,100	600	2,000		1,100	250	
(k)	570	(570)									
Balance	1,040	30	80	200	2,100	600	2,000		1,100	250	
(l)	(300)				1,500	1,200					
Balance	740	30	80	200	3,600	1,800	2,000		1,100	250	
(m)	(650)									650	Wages Exp.
Balance	90	30	80	200	3,600	1,800	2,000		1,100	900	
(n)	430	470							900		Delivery Fees
Balance	520	500	80	200	3,600	1,800	2,000		2,000	900	
(o)	(150)							150			
Balance	370	500	80	200	3,600	1,800	2,000	150	2,000	900	

Cash	$ 370	Accounts Payable	$1,800
Accounts Receivable	500	Jessica Jane, Capital	2,000
Supplies	80	Jessica Jane, Drawing	(150)
Prepaid Insurance	200	Delivery Fees	2,000
Delivery Equipment	3,600	Rent Expense	(200)
		Telephone Expense	(50)
Total assets	$4,750	Wages Expense	(650)
		Total liabilities and owner's equity	$4,750

> Amounts in ( ) are subtracted

> As with the running totals in the table, the listing immediately following provides proof that the accounting equation is in balance.

FINANCIAL STATEMENTS

LO5 Prepare a simple income statement, statement of owner's equity, and balance sheet.

Three financial statements commonly prepared by a business entity are the income statement, statement of owner's equity, and balance sheet. The transaction information gathered and summarized in the accounting equation may be used to prepare these financial statements. Figure 2-2 shows the following:

1. A summary of the specific revenue and expense transactions and the ending totals for the asset, liability, capital, and drawing accounts from the accounting equation.
2. The financial statements and their linkages with the accounting equation and each other.

Note that each of the financial statements in Figure 2-2 has a heading consisting of:

HEADING FOR FINANCIAL STATEMENTS	1. The name of the firm	Jessie Jane's Campus Delivery
	2. The title of the statement	Income Statement, Statement of Owner's Equity, or Balance Sheet
	3. The time period covered or the date of the statement.	For Month Ended June 30, 19—, or June 30, 19—

The income statement and statement of owner's equity provide information concerning events covering a period of time, in this case, *the month ended* June 30, 19--. The balance sheet, on the other hand, offers a picture of the business *on a specific date*, June 30, 19--.

The Income Statement

Income Statement		Income Statement	
Revenues	$500	Revenues	$500
Expenses	400	Expenses	700
Net income	$100	Net loss	$200

The **income statement**, sometimes called the **profit and loss statement** or **operating statement**, reports the profitability of business operations for a specific period of time. Jane's income statement shows the revenues earned

FIGURE 2-2 Summary and Financial Statements

Transaction	Cash	+	Accounts Receivable	+	Supplies	+	Prepaid Insurance	+	Delivery Equipment	=	Accounts Payable	+	Jessica Jane, Capital	–	Jessica Jane, Drawing	+	Revenues	–	Expenses	Description
(e)																	500			Delivery Fees
(f)																			200	Rent Exp.
(g)																			50	Tele. Exp.
(h)																	600			Delivery Fees
(m)																			650	Wages Exp.
(n)																	900			Delivery Fees
Balance	370		500		80		200		3,600		1,800		2,000		150		2,000		900	

Assets = Liabilities + Owner's Equity
Items Owned | Amounts Owed | Owner's Investment + Earnings

Jessie Jane's Campus Delivery
Income Statement
For Month Ended June 30, 19--

Revenues			
Delivery fees			$2 0 0 0 00
Expenses			
Wages expense	$ 6 5 0 00		
Rent expense	2 0 0 00		
Telephone expense	5 0 00		
Total expenses		9 0 0 00	
Net income			$1 1 0 0 00

$ at top of column

Subtotal underline

Jessie Jane's Campus Delivery
Statement of Owner's Equity
For Month Ended June 30, 19--

Jessica Jane, capital, June 1, 19--		$2 0 0 0 00
Net income for June	$1 1 0 0 00	
Less withdrawals for June	1 5 0 00	
Increase in capital		9 5 0 00
Jessica Jane, capital, June 30, 19--		$2 9 5 0 00

$ on total

Jessie Jane's Campus Delivery
Balance Sheet
June 30, 19--

Assets		Liabilities	
Cash	$ 3 7 0 00	Accounts payable	$1 8 0 0 00
Accounts receivable	5 0 0 00		
Supplies	8 0 00	Owner's Equity	
Prepaid insurance	2 0 0 00	Jessica Jane, capital	2 9 5 0 00
Delivery equipment	3 6 0 0 00		
		Total liabilities and	
Total assets	$4 7 5 0 00	owner's equity	$4 7 5 0 00

Double underline

for the month of June. Next, the expenses incurred as a result of the efforts made to earn these revenues are deducted. If the revenues are greater than the expenses, net income is reported. If not, a net loss is reported.

By carefully studying the income statement, it is clear that Jane earns revenues in only one way: by making deliveries. If other types of services were offered, these revenues would also be identified on the statement. Further, the reader can see the kinds of expenses that were incurred. The reader can make a judgment as to whether these seem reasonable given the amount of revenue earned. Finally, the most important number on the statement is the net income reported. This is known as the "bottom line."

The Statement of Owner's Equity

Owner's equity is affected by two basic types of transactions:

INFORMATION ON STATEMENT OF OWNER'S EQUITY	1. Investments and withdrawals by the owner, and
	2. Profits and losses generated through operating activities.

The **statement of owner's equity** illustrated in Figure 2-2 reports on these activities for the month of June. Jane started her business with an investment of $2,000. During the month of June she earned $1,100 in net income and withdrew $150 for personal expenses. This resulted in a net increase in Jane's capital of $950. Jane's $2,000 original investment, plus the net increase of $950, results in her ending capital of $2,950.

Note that Jane's original investment and later withdrawal are taken from the accounting equation. *The net income figure could have been computed from information in the accounting equation. However, it is easier to simply transfer net income as reported on the income statement to the statement of owner's equity.* This is an important linkage between the income statement and statement of owner's equity.

If Jane had a net loss of $500 for the month, the statement of owner's equity would be prepared as shown in Figure 2-3.

FIGURE 2-3   Statement of Owner's Equity with Net Loss

Jessie Jane's Campus Delivery Statement of Owner's Equity For Month Ended June 30, 19--		
Jessica Jane, capital, June 1, 19--		$2 0 0 0 00
Less: Net loss for June	$ 5 0 0 00	
Withdrawals for June	1 5 0 00	
Decrease in capital		6 5 0 00
Jessica Jane, capital, June 30, 19--		$1 3 5 0 00

The Balance Sheet

The **balance sheet** reports a firm's assets, liabilities, and owner's equity on a specific date. It is called a balance sheet because it confirms that the accounting equation has remained in balance. It is also referred to as a **statement of financial position** or **statement of financial condition**.

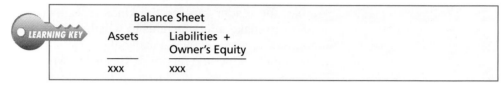

As illustrated in Figure 2-2, the asset and liability accounts are taken from the accounting equation and reported on the balance sheet. *The total of Jane's capital account on June 30 could have been computed from the owner's equity accounts in the accounting equation ($2,000 – $150 + $2,000 – $900). However, it is simpler to take the June 30, 19--, capital as computed on the statement of owner's equity and transfer it to the balance sheet.* This is an important linkage between these two statements.

GUIDELINES FOR PREPARING FINANCIAL STATEMENTS
1. Financial statements are prepared primarily for users not associated with the firm. Therefore, to make a good impression and enhance understanding, they must follow a standard form with careful attention to placement, spacing, and indentations.
2. All statements have a heading with the name of the company, name of the statement, and accounting period or date.
3. Single rules (lines) indicate that the numbers above the line have been added or subtracted. Double rules (double underlines) indicate a total.
4. Dollar signs are used at the top of columns and for the first amount entered in a column beneath a ruling.
5. On the income statement, a common practice is to list expenses from highest to lowest dollar amount, with miscellaneous expense listed last.
6. On the balance sheet, assets are listed from most liquid to least liquid. **Liquidity** measures the ease with which the asset will be converted to cash. Liabilities are listed from most current to least current.

OVERVIEW OF THE ACCOUNTING PROCESS

LO6 Define the three basic phases of the accounting process.

Figure 2-4 shows the three basic phases of the accounting process in terms of input, processing, and output.

- **Input.** Business transactions provide the necessary **input**.
- **Processing.** Recognizing the effect of these transactions on the assets, liabilities, owner's equity, revenues, and expenses of a business is the **processing** function.
- **Output.** The financial statements are the **output**.

FIGURE 2-4 Input, Processing, and Output

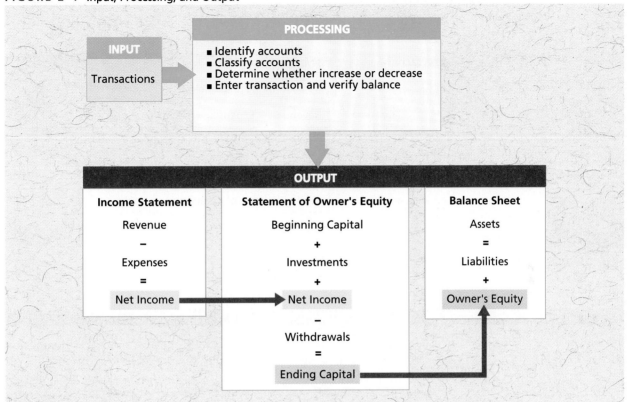

KEY POINTS

1 The three key accounting elements are assets, liabilities, and owner's equity. Owner's equity is expanded to include revenues, expenses, and drawing.

2 The accounting equation is:

Assets = Liabilities + Owner's Equity

3 Three questions must be answered in analyzing business transactions.

1. What happened?
2. Which accounts are affected?
3. How is the accounting equation affected?

4 Each transaction affects one or more of the three basic accounting elements. The transactions described in this chapter can be classified into five groups:

1. Increase in an asset offset by an increase in owner's equity.
2. Increase in an asset offset by a decrease in another asset.
3. Increase in an asset offset by an increase in a liability.
4. Decrease in an asset offset by a decrease in a liability.
5. Decrease in an asset offset by a decrease in owner's equity.

5 The purposes of the income statement, statement of owner's equity, and balance sheet can be summarized as follows.

STATEMENT	PURPOSE
Income statement	Reports net income or loss
	Revenues − Expenses = Net Income or Loss
Statement of owner's equity	Shows changes in the owner's capital account
	Beginning Capital + Investments + Net Income − Withdrawals = Ending Capital
Balance sheet	Verifies balance of accounting equation
	Assets = Liabilities + Owner's Equity

KEY TERMS

account 18   An account is a separate record used to summarize changes in each asset, liability, and owner's equity of a business.

account title 18   An account title provides a description of the particular type of asset, liability, owner's equity, revenue, or expense.

account payable 16   An unwritten promise to pay a supplier for assets purchased or services rendered.

accounting equation 17   The accounting equation consists of the three basic accounting elements: assets = liabilities + owner's equity.

accounting period concept 20   The concept that income determination can be made on a periodic basis.

assets 16   Items a business owns that will provide future benefits.

balance sheet 30   Reports assets, liabilities, and owner's equity on a specific date. It is called a balance sheet because it confirms that the accounting equation is in balance.

business entity 16   An individual, association, or organization that engages in economic activities and controls specific economic resources.

business entity concept 17   The concept that nonbusiness assets and liabilities are not included in the business entity's accounting records.

business transaction 17   An economic event that has a direct impact on the business.

capital 16   Another term for owner's equity, the amount by which the business assets exceed the business liabilities.

drawing 21   Withdrawals that reduce owner's equity as a result of the owner taking cash or other assets out of the business for personal use.

expenses 20   The decrease in assets (or increase in liabilities) as a result of efforts to produce revenues.

fiscal year 20   Any accounting period of twelve months' duration.

income statement 27 Reports the profitability of business operations for a specific period of time. (Also called the profit and loss statement or operating statement.)

input 30 Business transactions provide the necessary input for the accounting information system.

liability 16 Something owed to another business entity.

net income 20 The excess of total revenues over total expenses for the period.

net loss 20 The excess of total expenses over total revenues for the period.

net worth 16 Another term for owner's equity, the amount by which the business assets exceed the business liabilities.

note payable 16 A formal written promise to pay a supplier or lender a specified sum of money at a definite future time.

operating statement 27 Another name for the income statement, which reports the profitability of business operations for a specific period of time.

output 30 The financial statements are the output of the accounting information system.

owner's equity 16 The amount by which the business assets exceed the business liabilities.

processing 30 Recognizing the effect of transactions on the assets, liabilities, owner's equity, revenues, and expenses of a business.

profit and loss statement 27 Another name for the income statement, which reports the profitability of business operations for a specific period of time.

revenues 20 The amount a business charges customers for products sold or services performed.

statement of financial condition 30 Another name for the balance sheet, which reports assets, liabilities, and owner's equity on a specific date.

statement of financial position 30 Another name for the balance sheet, which reports assets, liabilities, and owner's equity on a specific date.

statement of owner's equity 29 Reports beginning capital plus net income less withdrawals to compute ending capital.

withdrawals 21 Reduce owner's equity as a result of the owner taking cash or other assets out of the business for personal use.

REVIEW QUESTIONS

1. Why is it necessary to distinguish between business assets and liabilities and nonbusiness assets and liabilities of a single proprietor?
2. List the three basic questions that must be answered when analyzing the effects of a business transaction on the accounting equation.
3. Name and define the six major elements of the accounting equation.
4. What is the function of an income statement?
5. What is the function of a statement of owner's equity?
6. What is the function of a balance sheet?
7. What are the three basic phases of the accounting process?

MANAGING YOUR WRITING

Write a brief memo that explains the differences and similarities between expenses and withdrawals.

DEMONSTRATION PROBLEM

Damon Young has started his own business, Home and Away Inspections. He inspects property for buyers and sellers of real estate. Young rents office space and has a part-time assistant to answer the phone and help with inspections. The transactions for the month of September are as follows:

(a) On the first day of the month, Young invested cash by making a deposit in a bank account for the business, $15,000.
(b) Paid rent for September, $300.
(c) Bought a used truck for cash, $8,000.
(d) Purchased tools on account from Crafty Tools, $3,000.
(e) Paid electricity bill, $50.
(f) Paid two-year premium for liability insurance on truck, $600.
(g) Received cash from clients for service performed, $2,000.
(h) Paid part-time assistant (wages) for first half of month, $200.
(i) Performed inspection services for clients on account, $1,000.
(j) Paid telephone bill, $35.
(k) Bought office supplies costing $300. Paid $100 cash and will pay the balance next month, $200.
(l) Received cash from clients for inspections performed on account in (i), $300.
(m) Paid part-time assistant (wages) for last half of month, $250.
(n) Made partial payment on tools bought in (d), $1,000.
(o) Earned additional revenues amounting to $2,000: $1,400 in cash and $600 on account.
(p) Young Withdrew cash at the end of the month for personal expenses, $500.

REQUIRED

1. Enter the transactions in an accounting equation similar to the one illustrated below. After each transaction, show the new amount for each account.

Assets						=	Liabilities	+	Owner's Equity				
Items Owned							Amounts Owed		Owner's Investment + Earnings				
Cash +	Accounts Receivable +	Supplies +	Prepaid Insurance +	Tools +	Truck =		Accounts Payable	+	Damon Young, Capital	Damon Young, – Drawing +	Revenues –	Expenses	Description

2. Compute the ending balances for all accounts.
3. Prepare an income statement for Home and Away Inspections for the month of September 19--.

4. Prepare a statement of owner's equity for Home and Away Inspections for the month of September 19--.

5. Prepare a balance sheet for Home and Away Inspections as of September 30, 19--.

SOLUTION

1, 2.

	Assets						=	Liabilities	+	Owner's Equity				
	Items Owned							Amounts Owed		Owner's Investment + Earnings				
	Cash +	Accounts Receivable +	Supplies +	Prepaid Insurance +	Tools +	Truck =		Accounts Payable	+	Damon Young, Capital	Damon Young, − Drawing	+ Revenues	− Expenses	Description
Bal. (a)	15,000									15,000				
Bal.	15,000									15,000				
(b)	(300)												300	Rent Exp.
Bal.	14,700									15,000			300	
(c)	(8,000)					8,000								
Bal.	6,700					8,000				15,000			300	
(d)					3,000			3,000						
Bal.	6,700				3,000	8,000		3,000		15,000			300	
(e)	(50)												50	Utilities Exp.
Bal.	6,650				3,000	8,000		3,000		15,000			350	
(f)	(600)		600											
Bal.	6,050		600		3,000	8,000		3,000		15,000			350	
(g)	2,000											2,000		Inspect. Fees
Bal.	8,050		600		3,000	8,000		3,000		15,000		2,000	350	
(h)	(200)												200	Wages Exp.
Bal.	7,850		600		3,000	8,000		3,000		15,000		2,000	550	
(i)		1,000										1,000		Inspect. Fees
Bal.	7,850	1,000	600		3,000	8,000		3,000		15,000		3,000	550	
(j)	(35)												35	Teleph. Exp.
Bal.	7,815	1,000	600		3,000	8,000		3,000		15,000		3,000	585	
(k)	(100)		300					200						
Bal.	7,715	1,000	300	600	3,000	8,000		3,200		15,000		3,000	585	
(l)	300	(300)												
Bal.	8,015	700	300	600	3,000	8,000		3,200		15,000		3,000	585	
(m)	(250)												250	Wages Exp.
Bal.	7,765	700	300	600	3,000	8,000		3,200		15,000		3,000	835	
(n)	(1,000)							(1,000)						
Bal.	6,765	700	300	600	3,000	8,000		2,200		15,000		3,000	835	
(o)	1,400	600										2,000		Inspect. Fees
Bal.	8,165	1,300	300	600	3,000	8,000		2,200		15,000		5,000	835	
(p)	(500)										500			
Bal.	7,665	1,300	300	600	3,000	8,000		2,200		15,000	500	5,000	835	

Cash	$ 7,665	Accounts Payable	$ 2,200	
Accounts Receivable	1,300	Damon Young, Capital	15,000	
Supplies	300	Damon Young, Drawing	(500)	
Prepaid Insurance	600	Inspection Fees	5,000	
Tools	3,000	Rent Expense	(300)	
Truck	8,000	Utilities Expense	(50)	
		Wages Expense	(450)	
Total assets	$20,865	Telephone Expense	(35)	
		Total liabilities and owner's equity	$20,865	

3.

Home and Away Inspections
Income Statement
For Month Ended September 30, 19--

Revenues		
Inspection fees		$5 0 0 0 00
Expenses		
Wages expense	$ 4 5 0 00	
Rent expense	3 0 0 00	
Utilities expense	5 0 00	
Telephone expense	3 5 00	
Total expenses		8 3 5 00
Net income		$4 1 6 5 00

4.

Home and Away Inspections
Statement of Owner's Equity
For Month Ended September 30, 19--

Damon Young, capital, September 1, 19--		$15 0 0 0 00
Net income for September	$4 1 6 5 00	
Less withdrawals for September	5 0 0 00	
Increase in capital		3 6 6 5 00
Damon Young, capital, September 30, 19--		$18 6 6 5 00

5.

Home and Away Inspections
Balance Sheet
September 30, 19--

Assets		Liabilities	
Cash	$7 6 6 5 00	Accounts payable	$2 2 0 0 00
Accounts receivable	1 3 0 0 00		
Supplies	3 0 0 00	Owner's Equity	
Prepaid insurance	6 0 0 00	Damon Young, capital	18 6 6 5 00
Tools	3 0 0 0 00		
Truck	8 0 0 0 00	Total liabilities and	
Total assets	$20 8 6 5 00	owner's equity	$20 8 6 5 00

SERIES A   EXERCISES

1 **EXERCISE 2A1 ACCOUNTING ELEMENTS**   Label each of the following accounts as an asset (A), a liability (L), or owner's equity (OE), using a format as follows.

Item	Account	Classification
Money in bank	Cash	
Office supplies	Supplies	
Money owed	Accounts Payable	
Office chairs	Office Furniture	
Net worth of owner	John Smith, Capital	
Money taken by owner	John Smith, Drawing	
Money owed by customers	Accounts Receivable	

2 **EXERCISE 2A2 THE ACCOUNTING EQUATION**   Using the accounting equation, compute the missing elements.

Assets	=	Liabilities	+	Owner's Equity
_____	=	$24,000	+	$10,000
$25,000	=	$18,000	+	_____
$40,000	=	_____	+	$15,000

3 **EXERCISE 2A3 EFFECTS OF TRANSACTIONS (BALANCE SHEET ACCOUNTS)**   Alice Stern started a business. During the first month (February 19--), the following transactions occurred. Show the effect of each transaction on the accounting equation: *Assets = Liabilities + Owner's Equity*. After each transaction, show the new account totals.

(a) Invested cash in the business, $20,000.
(b) Bought office equipment on account, $3,500.
(c) Bought office equipment for cash, $1,200.
(d) Paid cash on account to supplier in (b), $1,500.

4 **EXERCISE 2A4 EFFECTS OF TRANSACTIONS (REVENUE, EXPENSE, WITHDRAWALS)**   Assume Alice Stern completed the following additional transactions during February. Show the effect of each transaction on the basic elements of the expanded accounting equation: *Assets = Liabilities + Owner's Equity [Capital – Drawing + Revenues – Expenses]*. After each transaction show the new account totals.

(e) Received cash from a client for professional services, $2,500.
(f) Paid office rent for February, $900.
(g) Paid February telephone bill, $73.
(h) Withdrew cash for personal use, $500.
(i) Performed services for clients on account, $1,000.
(j) Paid wages to part-time employee, $600.
(k) Received cash for services performed on account in (i), $600.

1/5   **EXERCISE 2A5 FINANCIAL STATEMENT ACCOUNTS**   Label each of the following accounts as an asset (A), liability (L), owner's equity (OE), revenue (R), or expense (E). Indicate the financial statement on which the account belongs: income statement (IS), statement of owner's equity (SOE), or balance sheet (B), in a format similar to the following.

Account	Classification	Financial Statement
Cash		
Rent Expense		
Accounts Payable		
Service Fees		
Supplies		
Wages Expense		
Ramon Martinez, Drawing		
Ramon Martinez, Capital		
Prepaid Insurance		
Accounts Receivable		

5   **EXERCISE 2A6 STATEMENT OF OWNER'S EQUITY REPORTING NET INCOME**   Betsy Ray started an accounting service on June 1, 19--, by investing $20,000. Her net income for the month was $10,000 and she withdrew $8,000. Prepare a statement of owner's equity for the month of June.

5   **EXERCISE 2A7 STATEMENT OF OWNER'S EQUITY REPORTING NET LOSS**   Based on the information provided in Exercise 2A6, prepare a statement of owner's equity assuming Ray had a net loss of $3,000.

SERIES A   PROBLEMS

1   **PROBLEM 2A1 THE ACCOUNTING EQUATION**   Dr. John Schleper is a chiropractor. As of December 31, he owned the following property that related to his professional practice:

Cash	$ 4,750
Office Equipment	$ 6,200
X-ray Equipment	$11,680
Laboratory Equipment	$ 7,920

He also owes the following business suppliers:

Chateau Gas Company	$2,420
Aloe Medical Supply Company	$3,740

REQUIRED

1. From the preceding information, compute the accounting elements and enter them in the accounting equation shown as follows.

Assets	=	Liabilities	+	Owner's Equity
_____	+	_____	+	_____

2. During January, the assets increase by $7,290, and the liabilities increase by $4,210. Compute the resulting accounting equation.

3. During February, the assets decrease by $2,920, and the liabilities increase by $2,200. Compute the resulting accounting equation.

2 **PROBLEM 2A2 EFFECT OF TRANSACTIONS ON ACCOUNTING EQUATION**   Jay Pembroke started a business. During the first month (April 19--), the following transactions occurred.

(a) Invested cash in business, $18,000.
(b) Bought office supplies for $4,600: $2,000 in cash and $2,600 on account.
(c) Paid one-year insurance premium, $1,200.
(d) Earned revenues totaling $3,300: $1,300 in cash and $2,000 on account.
(e) Paid cash on account to the company that supplied the office supplies in (b), $2,300.
(f) Paid office rent for the month, $750.
(g) Withdrew cash for personal use, $100.

REQUIRED

Show the effect of each transaction on the basic elements of the accounting equation: *Assets = Liabilities + Owner's Equity [Capital – Drawing + Revenues – Expenses]*. After each transaction, show the new account totals.

5 **PROBLEM 2A3 INCOME STATEMENT**   Based on Problem 2A2, prepare an income statement for Jay Pembroke for the month of April 19--.

5 **PROBLEM 2A4 STATEMENT OF OWNER'S EQUITY**   Based on Problem 2A2, prepare a statement of owner's equity for Jay Pembroke for the month of April 19--.

5 **PROBLEM 2A5 BALANCE SHEET**   Based on Problem 2A2, prepare a balance sheet for Jay Pembroke as of April 30, 19--.

SERIES B EXERCISES

1 **EXERCISE 2B1 ACCOUNTING ELEMENTS**   Label each of the following accounts as an asset (A), liability (L), or owner's equity (OE) using the following format.

Account	Classification
Cash	
Accounts Payable	
Supplies	
Bill Jones, Drawing	
Prepaid Insurance	

continued

Account	Classification
Accounts Receivable	
Bill Jones, Capital	

2 **EXERCISE 2B2 THE ACCOUNTING EQUATION**   Using the accounting equation, compute the missing elements.

Assets	=	Liabilities	+	Owner's Equity
_____	=	$20,000	+	$5,000
$30,000	=	$15,000	+	_____
$20,000	=	_____	+	$10,000

3 **EXERCISE 2B3 EFFECTS OF TRANSACTIONS (BALANCE SHEET ACCOUNTS)**   Jon Wallace started a business. During the first month (March 19--), the following transactions occurred. Show the effect of each transaction on the accounting equation: *Assets = Liabilities + Owner's Equity*. After each transaction, show the new account totals.

(a)   Invested cash in the business $30,000.
(b)   Bought office equipment on account, $4,500.
(c)   Bought office equipment for cash, $1,600.
(d)   Paid cash on account to supplier in (b), $2,000.

4 **EXERCISE 2B4 EFFECTS OF TRANSACTIONS (REVENUE, EXPENSE, WITHDRAWALS)**   Assume Jon Wallace completed the following additional transactions during March. Show the effect of each transaction on the basic elements of the expanded accounting equation: *Assets = Liabilities + Owner's Equity [Capital – Drawing + Revenues – Expenses]*. After each transaction show the new account totals.

(e)   Performed services and received cash, $3,000.
(f)   Paid rent for March, $1,000.
(g)   Paid March telephone bill, $68.
(h)   Jon Wallace withdrew cash for personal use, $800.
(i)   Performed services for clients on account, $900.
(j)   Paid wages to part-time employee, $500.
(k)   Received cash for services performed on account in (i), $500.

1 **EXERCISE 2B5 FINANCIAL STATEMENT ACCOUNTS**   Label each of the following accounts as an asset (A), liability (L), owner's equity (OE), revenue (R), or expense (E). Indicate the financial statement on which the account belongs: income statement (IS), statement of owner's equity (SOE), or balance sheet (B), in a format similar to the following.

Account	Classification	Financial Statement
Cash		
Rent Expense		
Accounts Payable		
Service Fees		

continued

Account	Classification	Financial Statement
Supplies		
Wages Expense		
Amanda Wong, Drawing		
Amanda Wong, Capital		
Prepaid Insurance		
Accounts Receivable		

5 **EXERCISE 2B6 STATEMENT OF OWNER'S EQUITY REPORTING NET INCOME** Efran Lopez started a financial consulting service on June 1, 19--, by investing $15,000. His net income for the month was $6,000 and he withdrew $7,000 for personal use. Prepare a statement of owner's equity for the month of June.

5 **EXERCISE 2B7 STATEMENT OF OWNER'S EQUITY REPORTING NET LOSS** Based on the information provided in Exercise 2B6, prepare a statement of owner's equity assuming Lopez had a net loss of $2,000.

SERIES B PROBLEMS

1 **PROBLEM 2B1 THE ACCOUNTING EQUATION** Dr. Patricia Parsons is a dentist. As of January 31, Parsons owned the following property that related to her professional practice:

Cash	$3,560
Office Equipment	$4,600
X-ray Equipment	$8,760
Laboratory Equipment	$5,940

She also owes the following business suppliers:

Cupples Gas Company	$1,815
Swan Dental Lab	$2,790

REQUIRED

1. From the preceding information, compute the accounting elements and enter them in the accounting equation as show below.

Assets	=	Liabilities	+	Owner's Equity
_____	=	_____	+	_____

2. During February, the assets increase by $4,565, and the liabilities increase by $3,910. Compute the resulting accounting equation.
3. During March, the assets decrease by $2,190, and the liabilities increase by $1,650. Compute the resulting accounting equation.

2 **PROBLEM 2B2 EFFECT OF TRANSACTIONS ON ACCOUNTING EQUATION** David Segal started a business. During the first month (October 19--), the following transactions occurred.

(a) Invested cash in the business, $15,000.
(b) Bought office supplies for $3,800: $1,800 in cash and $2,000 on account.
(c) Paid one-year insurance premium, $1,000.
(d) Earned revenues amounting to $2,700: $1,700 in cash and $1,000 on account.
(e) Paid cash on account to the company that supplied the office supplies in (b), $1,800.
(f) Paid office rent for the month, $650.
(g) Withdrew cash for personal use, $150.

REQUIRED

Show the effect of each transaction on the basic elements of the accounting equation: *Assets = Liabilities + Owner's Equity [Capital – Drawing + Revenues – Expenses]*. After each transaction, show the new account totals.

5 **PROBLEM 2B3 INCOME STATEMENT**   Based on Problem 2B2, prepare an income statement for David Segal for the month of October 19--.

5 **PROBLEM 2B4 STATEMENT OF OWNER'S EQUITY**   Based on Problem 2B2, prepare a statement of owner's equity for David Segal for the month of October 19--.

5 **PROBLEM 2B5 BALANCE SHEET**   Based on Problem 2B2, prepare a balance sheet for David Segal as of October 31, 19--.

MASTERY PROBLEM

Lisa Vozniak started her own business, We Do Windows. She offers interior and exterior window cleaning for local area residents. Lisa rents a garage to store her tools and cleaning supplies and has a part-time assistant to answer the phone and handle third-story work. (Lisa is afraid of heights.) The transactions for the month of July are as follows:

(a) On the first day of the month, Vozniak invested cash by making a deposit in a bank account for the business, $8,000.
(b) Paid rent for July, $150.
(c) Purchased a used van for cash, $5,000.
(d) Purchased tools on account from Clean Tools, $600.
(e) Purchased cleaning supplies that cost $300. Paid $200 cash and will pay the balance next month, $100.
(f) Paid part-time assistant (wages) for first half of month, $100.
(g) Paid for advertising, $75.
(h) Paid two-year premium for liability insurance on van, $480.
(i) Received cash from clients for services performed, $800.
(j) Performed cleaning services for clients on account, $500.
(k) Paid telephone bill, $40.
(l) Received cash from clients for window cleaning performed on account in (j), $200.

(m) Paid part-time assistant (wages) for last half of month, $150.
(n) Made partial payment on tools purchased in (d), $200.
(o) Earned additional revenues amounting to $800: $600 in cash and $200 on account.
(p) Vozniak withdrew cash at the end of the month for personal expenses, $100.

REQUIRED

1. Enter the above transactions in an accounting equation similar to the one illustrated below. After each transaction, show the new amount for each account.

Assets						=	Liabilities	+	Owner's Equity					
Items Owned							Amounts Owed		Owner's Investment + Earnings					
	Accounts		Prepaid				Accounts		Lisa Vozniak,	Lisa Vozniak,				
Cash +	Receivable +	Supplies +	Insurance +	Tools +	Van =		Payable	+	Capital	– Drawing	+ Revenues	– Expenses	Description

2. Compute the ending balances for all accounts.
3. Prepare an income statement for We Do Windows for the month of July 19--.
4. Prepare a statement of owner's equity for We Do Windows for the month of July 19--.
5. Prepare a balance sheet for We Do Windows as of July 31, 19--.

3

The Double-Entry Framework

How do you keep track of your personal finances? Perhaps you make a list of your earnings and other cash inflows. Then you prepare a list of how the money was spent. Businesses need to do this, too. However, since businesses earn and spend money in many different ways, and enter thousands of transactions, a systematic approach must be followed. This is called the double-entry framework.

The terms asset, liability, owner's equity, revenue, and expense were explained in Chapter 2. Examples showed how individual business transactions change one or more of these basic accounting elements. Each transaction had a dual effect. An increase or decrease in any asset, liability, owner's equity, revenue, or expense was *always* accompanied by an offsetting change within the basic accounting elements. The fact that each transaction has a dual effect upon the accounting elements provides the basis for what is called **double-entry accounting**. To understand double-entry accounting, it is important to learn how T accounts work and the role of debits and credits in accounting.

THE T ACCOUNT

LO1   Define the parts of a T account.

The assets of a business may consist of a number of items, such as cash, accounts receivable, equipment, buildings, and land. The liabilities may consist of one or more items, such as accounts payable and notes payable. Similarly, owner's equity may consist of the owner's investments and various revenue and expense items. A separate account is used to record the increases and decreases in each type of asset, liability, owner's equity, revenue, and expense.

The T account gets its name from the fact that it resembles the letter T. As shown below, there are three major parts of an account:

1. the title,
2. the debit, or left side, and
3. the credit, or right side.

Title	
Debit = Left	Credit = Right

 LEARNING KEY   Debits are always on the left and credits are always on the right for all accounts.

The debit side is always on the left and the credit side is always on the right. This is true for all types of asset, liability, owner's equity, revenue, and expense accounts.

BALANCING A T ACCOUNT

LO2   Foot and balance a T account.

To determine the balance of a T account at any time, simply total the dollar amounts on the debit and credit sides. These totals are known as **footings**. The difference between the footings is called the **balance** of the account. This amount is then written on the side with the larger footing.

In Chapter 2, the accounting equation was used to analyze business transactions. This required columns in which to record the increases and decreases in various accounts. Let's compare this approach with the use of a

T account for the transactions affecting cash. When a T account is used, increases in cash are recorded on the debit side and decreases are recorded on the credit side. Transactions for Jessie Jane's Campus Delivery are shown below.

COLUMNAR SUMMARY (From Chapter 2, page 26)		T ACCOUNT FORM	

COLUMNAR SUMMARY
(From Chapter 2, page 26)

Transaction	Cash
(a)	2,000
(b)	(1,200)
(d)	(300)
(e)	500
(f)	(200)
(g)	(50)
(i)	(80)
(j)	(200)
(k)	570
(l)	(300)
(m)	(650)
(n)	430
(o)	(150)
Balance	370

T ACCOUNT FORM

Cash

(a)	2,000	(b)	1,200
(e)	500	(d)	300
(k)	570	(f)	200
(n)	430	(g)	50
		(i)	80
footing → 3,500		(j)	200
		(l)	300
		(m)	650
		(o)	150
			3,130 ← *footing*
Balance	370		

DEBITS AND CREDITS

LO3   Describe the effects of debits and credits on specific types of accounts.

To **debit** an account means to enter an amount on the left or debit side of the account. To **credit** an account means to enter an amount on the right or credit side of the account. *Debits may increase* **or** *decrease the balances of specific accounts. This is also true for credits. To learn how to use debits and credits, it is best to reflect on the accounting equation.*

Assets		=	Liabilities		+	Owner's Equity	
Debit	Credit		Debit	Credit		Debit	Credit
+	−		−	+		−	+

 Debits increase assets and decrease liabilities and owner's equity. Credits decrease assets and increase liabilities and owner's equity.

Assets

Assets are on the left side of the accounting equation. Therefore, increases are entered on the left (debit) side of an asset account and decreases are entered on the right (credit) side.

Liabilities and Owner's Equity

Liabilities and owner's equity are on the right side of the equation. Therefore, increases are entered on the right (credit) side and decreases are entered on the left (debit) side.

Normal Balances

A **normal balance** is the side of an account that is increased. Since assets are debited for increases, these accounts normally have **debit balances**. Since liability and owner's equity accounts are credited for increases, these accounts normally have **credit balances**. Figure 3-1 shows the relationship between normal balances and debits and credits.

FIGURE 3-1   Normal Balances

ACCOUNT	ACCOUNTING EQUATION	INCREASE	DECREASE	NORMAL BALANCE
Assets	Left	Debit	Credit	Debit
Liabilities	Right	Credit	Debit	Credit
Owner's Equity	Right	Credit	Debit	Credit

Expanding the accounting equation helps illustrate the use of debits and credits for revenue, expense, and drawing. Since these accounts affect owner's equity, they are shown under the "umbrella" of owner's equity in the accounting equation in Figure 3-2.

FIGURE 3-2 The Accounting Equation and the Owner's Equity Umbrella

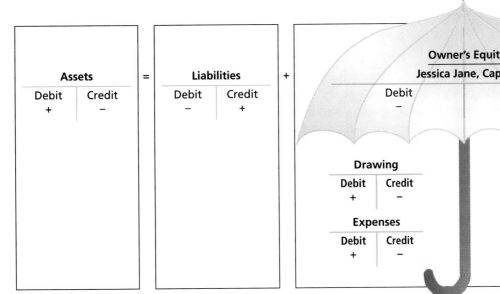

Revenues

Revenues increase owner's equity. Revenues could be recorded directly on the credit side of the owner's capital account. However, readers of financial statements are interested in the specific types of revenues earned.

Therefore, specific revenue accounts, like delivery fees, sales, and service fees, are used. These specific accounts are credited when revenue is earned.

Expenses

As expenses increase, owner's equity decreases. Expenses could be recorded on the debit side of the owner's capital account. However, readers of financial statements want to see the types of expenses incurred during the accounting period. Thus, specific expense accounts are maintained for items like rent, wages, advertising, and utilities. These specific accounts are debited as expenses are incurred.

> You could credit the owner's capital account for revenues and debit the capital account for expenses and withdrawals. However, using specific accounts provides additional information. Remember: an increase in an expense decreases owner's equity.

Drawing

Withdrawals of cash and other assets by the owner for personal reasons decrease owner's equity. Withdrawals could be debited directly to the owner's capital account. However, readers of financial statements want to know the amount of withdrawals for the accounting period. Thus, it is easier to maintain this information in a separate account.

Normal Balances for the Owner's Equity Umbrella

Since expense and drawing accounts are debited for increases, these accounts normally have **debit balances**. Since revenue accounts are credited for increases, these accounts normally have **credit balances**. Figure 3-3 shows the normal balances for the owner's equity accounts.

FIGURE 3-3   Normal Balances for the Owner's Equity Umbrella

ACCOUNT	OWNER'S EQUITY UMBRELLA	INCREASE	DECREASE	NORMAL
Revenues	Right	Credit	Debit	Credit
Expenses	Left	Debit	Credit	Debit
Drawing	Left	Debit	Credit	Debit

TRANSACTION ANALYSIS

LO4   Use T accounts to analyze transactions.

In Chapter 2, you learned how to analyze transactions by using the accounting equation. Here, we continue to use the accounting equation, but add debits and credits by using T accounts. As shown in Figure 3-4, the three basic questions that must be answered when analyzing a transaction are essentially the same, but expanded slightly to address the use of T accounts. You must determine the location of the account within the accounting equation. You must also determine whether the accounts should be debited or credited.

FIGURE 3-4   Steps in Transaction Analysis

1. What happened?
Make certain you understand the event that has taken place.

2. Which accounts are affected?
Once you have determined what happened, you must:
- Identify the accounts that are affected.
- Classify these accounts as assets, liabilities, owner's equity, revenues, or expenses.
- Identify the location of the accounts in the accounting equation and/or the owner's equity umbrella—left or right.

3. How is the accounting equation affected?
- Determine whether the accounts have increased or decreased.
- Determine whether the accounts should be debited or credited.
- Make certain that the accounting equation remains in balance after the transaction has been entered.
  (1) Assets = Liabilities + Owner's Equity.
  (2) Debits = Credits for every transaction.

 LEARNING KEY | Proper use of debits and credits helps to keep the accounting equation in balance.

Debits and Credits: Asset, Liability, and Owner's Equity Accounts

Transactions (a) through (d) from Jessie Jane's Campus Delivery (Chapter 2) demonstrate the double-entry process for transactions affecting asset, liability, and owner's equity accounts.

As you study each transaction, answer the three questions: (1) What happened? (2) Which accounts are affected? and (3) How is the accounting equation affected? The transaction statement tells you what happened. The analysis following the illustration of each transaction tells which accounts are affected. The illustration shows you how the accounting equation is affected.

TRANSACTION (a):   Investment by owner

Jessica Jane opened a bank account with a deposit of $2,000 for her business (Figure 3-5).

Analysis: As a result of this transaction, the business acquired an asset, Cash. In exchange for the asset, the business gave Jessica Jane owner's equity. The owner's equity account is called Jessica Jane, Capital. The transaction is entered as an increase in an asset and an increase in owner's equity. Debit Cash and credit Jessica Jane, Capital for $2,000.

FIGURE 3-5 Transaction (a): Investment by Owner

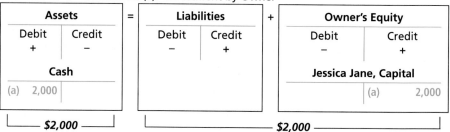

ACCOUNT AFFECTED	CLASSIFICATION	LOCATION IN EQUATION	INCREASE OR DECREASE	DEBIT OR CREDIT
Cash	Asset	Left	Increase	Debit
Capital	Owner's Equity	Right	Increase	Credit

TRANSACTION (b):   **Purchase of an asset for cash**

Jane bought a motor scooter (delivery equipment) for $1,200 cash (Figure 3-6).

FIGURE 3-6 Transaction (b): Purchase of an Asset for Cash

Assets		=	Liabilities		+	Owner's Equity	
Debit +	Credit −		Debit −	Credit +		Debit −	Credit +
Cash						**Jessica Jane, Capital**	
Bal. 2,000	(b) 1,200						Bal. 2,000
Bal. 800							
Delivery Equipment							
(b) 1,200							
—— $2,000 ——			—— $2,000 ——				

Analysis: Jane exchanged one asset, Cash, for another, Delivery Equipment. Debit Delivery Equipment and credit Cash for $1,200. Notice that the total assets are still $2,000 as they were following transaction (a). Transaction (b) shifted assets from cash to delivery equipment, but total assets remained the same.

ACCOUNT AFFECTED	CLASSIFICATION	LOCATION IN EQUATION	INCREASE OR DECREASE	DEBIT OR CREDIT
Delivery Equipment	Asset	Left	Increase	Debit
Cash	Asset	Left	Decrease	Credit

TRANSACTION (c):   **Purchase of an asset on account**

Jane bought a second motor scooter on account for $900 (Figure 3-7).

FIGURE 3-7   Transaction (c): Purchase of an Asset on Account

Assets		=	Liabilities		+	Owner's Equity	
Debit +	Credit −		Debit −	Credit +		Debit −	Credit +
Cash			**Accounts Payable**			**Jessica Jane, Capital**	
Bal. 800				(c) 900			Bal. 2,000
Delivery Equipment							
Bal. 1,200							
(c) 900							
Bal. 2,100							

└──── $2,900 ────┘   └──────── $2,900 ────────┘

Analysis: The asset, Delivery Equipment, increases by $900 and the liability, Accounts Payable, increases by the same amount. Thus, debit Delivery Equipment and credit Accounts Payable for $900.

ACCOUNT AFFECTED	CLASSIFICATION	LOCATION IN EQUATION	INCREASE OR DECREASE	DEBIT OR CREDIT
Delivery Equipment	Asset	Left	Increase	Debit
Accounts Payable	Liability	Right	Increase	Credit

TRANSACTION (d):   **Payment on a loan**

Jane made the first $300 payment on the scooter purchased in transaction (c) (Figure 3-8).

FIGURE 3-8   Transaction (d): Payment on a Loan

Assets		=	Liabilities		+	Owner's Equity	
Debit +	Credit −		Debit −	Credit +		Debit −	Credit +
Cash			**Accounts Payable**			**Jessica Jane, Capital**	
Bal. 800				Bal. 900			Bal. 2,000
	(d) 300		(d) 300				
Bal. 500				Bal. 600			
Delivery Equipment							
Bal. 2,100							

└──── $2,600 ────┘   └──────── $2,600 ────────┘

Analysis: This payment decreases the asset, Cash, and decreases the liability, Accounts Payable. Debit Accounts Payable and credit Cash for $300.

ACCOUNT AFFECTED	CLASSIFICATION	LOCATION IN EQUATION	INCREASE OR DECREASE	DEBIT OR CREDIT
Accounts Payable	Liability	Right	Decrease	Debit
Cash	Asset	Left	Decrease	Credit

Notice that for transactions (a) through (d), the debits equal credits and the accounting equation is in balance. Review transactions (a) through (d). Again, identify the accounts that were affected and how they were classified (assets, liabilities, or owner's equity). Finally, note each account's location within the accounting equation.

Debits and Credits: Including Revenues, Expenses, and Drawing

> Revenues increase owner's equity and are on the credit side of the capital account. Expenses and drawing reduce owner's equity and are on the debit side of the capital account.

Transactions (a) through (d) involved only assets, liabilities, and the owner's capital account. To complete the illustration of Jessie Jane's Campus Delivery, the equation is expanded to include revenues, expenses, and drawing. Remember, revenues increase owner's equity and are shown under the credit side of the capital account. Expenses and drawing decrease owner's equity and are shown under the debit side of the capital account. The expanded equation is shown in Figure 3-9.

FIGURE 3-9 The Expanded Accounting Equation

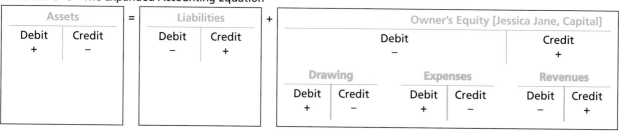

TRANSACTION (e):   Delivery revenues earned in cash

Jane made deliveries and received $500 cash from clients (Figure 3-10).

FIGURE 3-10   Transaction (e): Delivery Revenues Earned in Cash

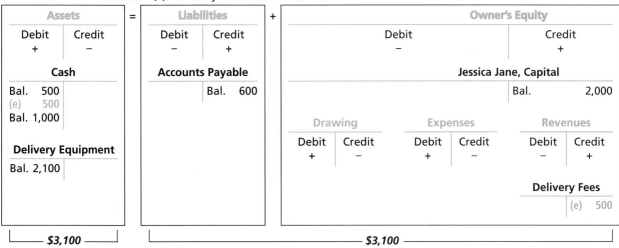

Analysis: The asset, Cash, and the revenue, Delivery Fees, increase. Debit Cash and credit Delivery Fees for $500.

ACCOUNT AFFECTED	CLASSIFICATION	LOCATION IN EQUATION	INCREASE OR DECREASE	DEBIT OR CREDIT
Cash	Asset	Left	Increase	Debit
Delivery Fees	Revenue	Right O.E.—Right Side	Increase	Credit

TRANSACTION (f):   **Paid rent for month**

Jane paid $200 for office rent for June (Figure 3-11).

FIGURE 3-11   Transaction (f): Paid Rent for Month

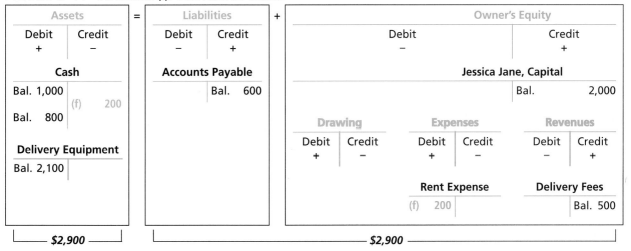

Analysis: Rent Expense increases and Cash decreases. Debit Rent Expense and credit Cash for $200.

A debit to an expense account increases that expense and decreases owner's equity. Notice that the placement of the plus and minus signs for expenses are opposite the placement of the signs for owner's equity. Note also that expenses are located on the left (debit) side of the owner's equity umbrella.

ACCOUNT AFFECTED	CLASSIFICATION	LOCATION IN EQUATION	INCREASE OR DECREASE	DEBIT OR CREDIT
Rent Expense	Expense	Right O.E.—Left Side	Exp.— Increases; O.E.— Decreases	Debit
Cash	Asset	Left	Decrease	Credit

TRANSACTION (g):   **Paid telephone bill**

Jane paid for telephone service, $50 (Figure 3-12).

FIGURE 3-12   Transaction (g): Paid Telephone Bill

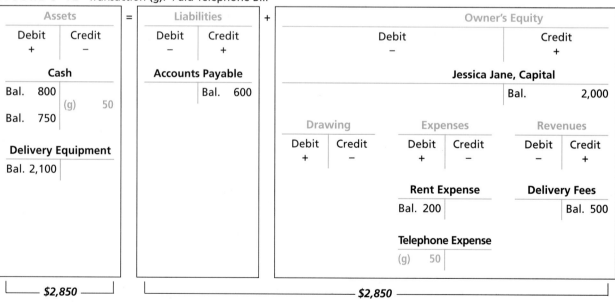

Analysis: This transaction, like the previous one, increases an expense and decreases an asset. Debit Telephone Expense and credit Cash for $50.

ACCOUNT AFFECTED	CLASSIFICATION	LOCATION IN EQUATION	INCREASE OR DECREASE	DEBIT OR CREDIT
Telephone Expense	Expense	Right O.E.—Left Side	Exp.— Increases; O.E.— Decreases	Debit
Cash	Asset	Left	Decrease	Credit

TRANSACTION (h):   Delivery revenues earned on account

Jane made deliveries on account for $600 (Figure 3-13).

FIGURE 3-13   Transaction (h): Delivery Revenues Earned on Account

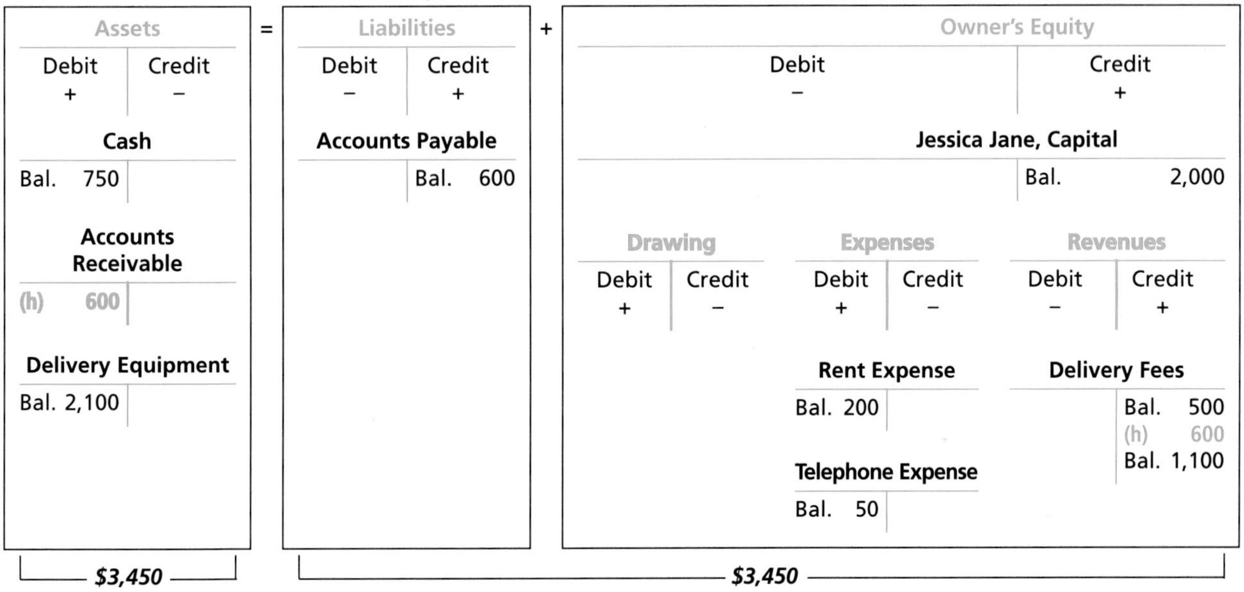

Analysis: As discussed in Chapter 2, delivery services are performed for which payment will be received later. This is called offering services "on account" or "on credit." Instead of receiving cash, Jane receives a promise that her customers will pay cash in the future. Therefore, the asset, Accounts Receivable, increases. Since revenues are recognized when earned, the revenue account, Delivery Fees, also increases. Debit Accounts Receivable and credit Delivery Fees for $600.

ACCOUNT AFFECTED	CLASSIFICATION	LOCATION IN EQUATION	INCREASE OR DECREASE	DEBIT OR CREDIT
Accounts Receivable	Asset	Left	Increase	Debit
Delivery Fees	Revenue	Right O.E.—Left Side	Increase	Credit

Review transactions (e) through (h). Two of these transactions are expenses and two are revenue transactions. Each of these transactions affected the owner's equity umbrella. Three transactions affected Cash and one transaction affected Accounts Receivable. Keep in mind that expense and revenue transactions do not always affect cash.

Notice that the debits equal credits and the accounting equation is in balance after each transaction. As you review transactions (e) through (h), identify the accounts that were affected and classify each account (assets, liabilities, owner's equity, revenue, or expense). Notice each account's location within the accounting equation and the owner's equity umbrella.

TRANSACTION (i):   Purchase of supplies

Jane bought pens, paper, delivery envelopes, and other supplies for $80 cash (Figure 3-14).

FIGURE 3-14 Transaction (i): Purchase of Supplies

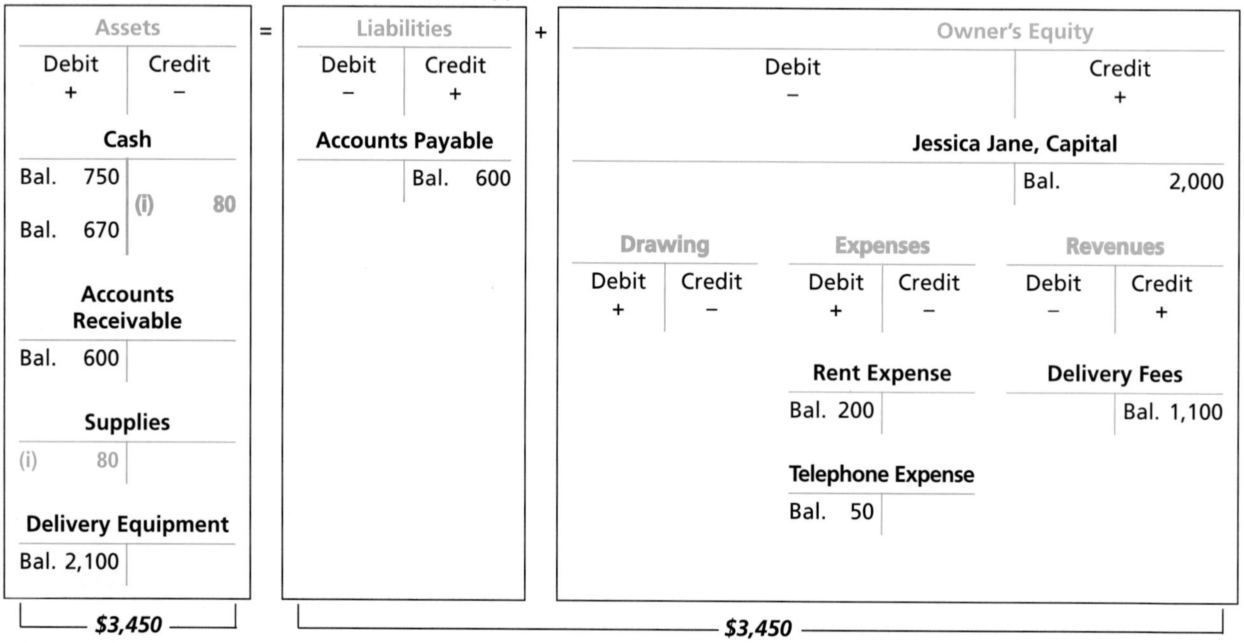

Analysis: These supplies will last for several months. Since they will generate future benefits, the supplies should be recorded as an asset. An asset, Supplies, increases, and an asset, Cash, decreases. Debit Supplies and credit Cash for $80.

ACCOUNT AFFECTED	CLASSIFICATION	LOCATION IN EQUATION	INCREASE OR DECREASE	DEBIT OR CREDIT
Supplies	Asset	Left	Increase	Debit
Cash	Asset	Left	Decrease	Credit

TRANSACTION (j):   **Payment of insurance premium**

Jane paid $200 for an eight-month liability insurance policy (Figure 3-15).

FIGURE 3-15 Transaction (j): Payment of Insurance Premium

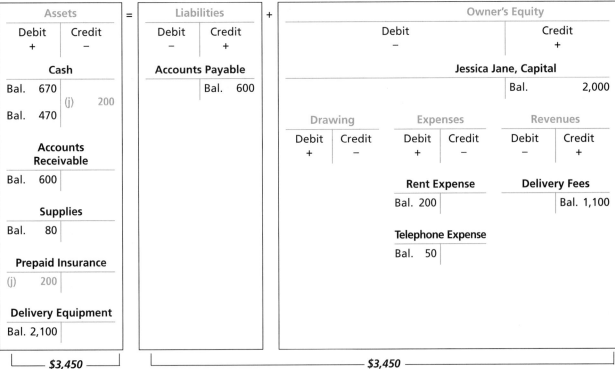

Analysis: Since insurance is paid in advance and will provide future benefits, it is treated as an asset. Therefore, one asset, Prepaid Insurance, increases and another, Cash, decreases. Debit Prepaid Insurance and credit Cash for $200.

ACCOUNT AFFECTED	CLASSIFICATION	LOCATION IN EQUATION	INCREASE OR DECREASE	DEBIT OR CREDIT
Prepaid Insurance	Asset	Left	Increase	Debit
Cash	Asset	Left	Decrease	Credit

Transactions (i) and (j) both involve an exchange of cash for another asset. As you analyze these two transactions and answer the three questions about these transactions, you may wonder why prepaid insurance and supplies are assets while the rent and telephone bill in transactions (f) and (g) are expenses. Prepaid insurance and supplies are assets because they will last for more than one month. Jessica Jane pays her rent and her telephone bill each month so they are classified as expenses. If Jessica Jane paid her rent only once every three months, she would need to set up an asset account called Prepaid Rent. She would debit this account when she paid the rent.

TRANSACTION (k):   Received cash from prior sales on account

Jane received $570 in cash for delivery services performed for customers earlier in the month (see transaction (h)) (Figure 3-16).

FIGURE 3-16 Transaction (k): Received Cash from Prior Sales on Account

Assets		=	Liabilities		+	Owner's Equity	
Debit +	Credit −		Debit −	Credit +		Debit −	Credit +
Cash			**Accounts Payable**			**Jessica Jane, Capital**	
Bal. 470				Bal. 600			Bal. 2,000
(k) 570							
Bal. 1,040							

Drawing

Debit +	Credit −

Expenses

Debit +	Credit −

Rent Expense

Bal. 200	

Telephone Expense

Bal. 50	

Revenues

Debit −	Credit +

Delivery Fees

	Bal. 1,100

Accounts Receivable

Bal. 600	
	(k) 570
Bal. 30	

Supplies

Bal. 80	

Prepaid Insurance

Bal. 200	

Delivery Equipment

Bal. 2,100	

—— $3,450 ——   —— $3,450 ——

Analysis: This transaction increases Cash and reduces the amount due from customers reported in Accounts Receivable. Debit Cash and credit Accounts Receivable $570.

As you analyze transaction (k), notice which accounts are affected and the location of these accounts in the accounting equation. Jessica Jane received cash, but this transaction did not affect revenue. The revenue was recorded in transaction (h). Transaction (k) is an exchange of one asset (Accounts Receivable) for another asset (Cash).

ACCOUNT AFFECTED	CLASSIFICATION	LOCATION IN EQUATION	INCREASE OR DECREASE	DEBIT OR CREDIT
Cash	Asset	Left	Increase	Debit
Accounts Receivable	Asset	Left	Decrease	Credit

TRANSACTION (I):   **Purchase of an asset on credit making a partial payment**

Jane bought a third motor scooter for $1,500. Jane made a down payment of $300 and spread the remaining payments over the next four months (Figure 3-17).

FIGURE 3-17   Transaction (l): Purchase of an Asset on Credit Making a Partial Payment

Assets			Liabilities			Owner's Equity		
Debit **+**	**Credit** **−**	=	**Debit** **−**	**Credit** **+**	+	**Debit** **−**	**Credit** **+**	

Assets:
- **Cash** — Bal. 1,040 | (l) 300 → Bal. 740
- **Accounts Receivable** — Bal. 30
- **Supplies** — Bal. 80
- **Prepaid Insurance** — Bal. 200
- **Delivery Equipment** — Bal. 2,100 | (l) 1,500 | Bal. 3,600

Liabilities:
- **Accounts Payable** — Bal. 600 | (l) 1,200 | Bal. 1,800

Owner's Equity:
- **Jessica Jane, Capital** — Bal. 2,000

Drawing		Expenses		Revenues	
Debit **+**	**Credit** **−**	**Debit** **+**	**Credit** **−**	**Debit** **−**	**Credit** **+**

- **Rent Expense** — Bal. 200
- **Telephone Expense** — Bal. 50
- **Delivery Fees** — Bal. 1,100

Assets total: *$4,650*   Liabilities + Owner's Equity total: *$4,650*

Analysis: The asset, Delivery Equipment, increases by $1,500, Cash decreases by $300, and the liability, Accounts Payable, increases by $1,200. Thus, debit Delivery Equipment for $1,500, credit Cash for $300, and credit Accounts Payable for $1,200. This transaction requires one debit and two credits. Even so, total debits ($1,500) equal the total credits ($1,200 + $300) and the accounting equation remains in balance.

ACCOUNT AFFECTED	CLASSIFICATION	LOCATION IN EQUATION	INCREASE OR DECREASE	DEBIT OR CREDIT
Delivery Equipment	Asset	Left	Increase	Debit
Cash	Asset	Left	Decrease	Credit
Accounts Payable	Liability	Right	Increase	Credit

TRANSACTION (m):   Payment of wages

Jane paid her part-time employees $650 in wages (Figure 3-18).

FIGURE 3-18 Transaction (m): Payment of Wages

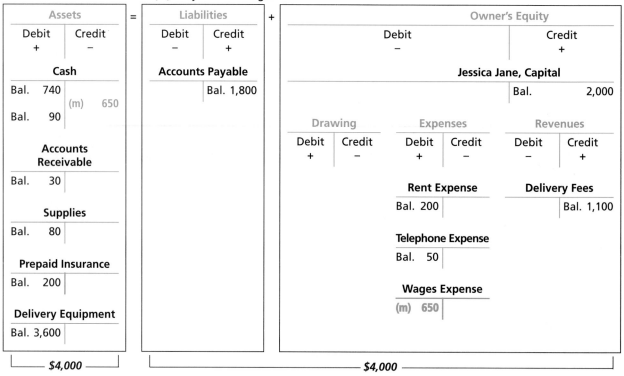

Analysis: This is an additional business expense. Expenses increase and Cash decreases. Debit Wages Expense and credit Cash for $650.

ACCOUNT AFFECTED	CLASSIFICATION	LOCATION IN EQUATION	INCREASE OR DECREASE	DEBIT OR CREDIT
Wage Expense	Expense	Right O.E.—Left Side	Exp.— Increases; O.E.— Decreases	Debit
Cash	Asset	Left	Decrease	Credit

TRANSACTION (n):   Deliveries made for cash and credit

Total delivery fees for the remainder of the month amounted to $900: $430 in Cash and $470 on account (Figure 3-19).

FIGURE 3-19   Transaction (n): Deliveries Made for Cash and Credit

Assets			=	Liabilities			+	Owner's Equity				

Assets

Debit +	Credit −

Cash

Bal.	90	
(n)	430	
Bal.	520	

Accounts Receivable

Bal.	30	
(n)	470	
Bal.	500	

Supplies

Bal.	80	

Prepaid Insurance

Bal.	200	

Delivery Equipment

Bal. 3,600	

$4,900

Liabilities

Debit −	Credit +

Accounts Payable

	Bal. 1,800

Owner's Equity

Debit −	Credit +

Jessica Jane, Capital

	Bal. 2,000

Drawing

Debit +	Credit −

Expenses

Debit +	Credit −

Rent Expense

Bal. 200	

Telephone Expense

Bal. 50	

Wages Expense

Bal. 650	

Revenues

Debit −	Credit +

Delivery Fees

	Bal. 1,100
	(n) 900
	Bal. 2,000

$4,900

Analysis: Since the delivery fees have been earned, the revenue account increases by $900. Also, Cash increases by $430 and Accounts Receivable increases by $470. Note once again that one event impacts three accounts. This time we have debits of $430 to Cash and $470 to Accounts Receivable, and a credit of $900 to Delivery Fees. As before, the total debits ($430 + $470) equal the total credits ($900) and the accounting equation remains in balance.

ACCOUNT AFFECTED	CLASSIFICATION	LOCATION IN EQUATION	INCREASE OR DECREASE	DEBIT OR CREDIT
Cash	Asset	Left	Increase	Debit
Accounts Receivable	Asset	Left	Increase	Debit
Delivery Fees	Revenue	Right O.E. Right Side	Increase	Credit

TRANSACTION (o):   **Withdrawal of cash from business**

At the end of the month, Jane withdrew $150 in cash from the business to purchase books for her classes (Figure 3-20).

FIGURE 3-20 Transaction (o): Withdrawal of Cash from Business

Assets			=	Liabilities			+	Owner's Equity			

Assets
Debit +	Credit −
Cash	
Bal. 520	
	(o) 150
Bal. 370	
Accounts Receivable	
Bal. 500	
Supplies	
Bal. 80	
Prepaid Insurance	
Bal. 200	
Delivery Equipment	
Bal. 3,600	

$4,750

= Liabilities
Debit −	Credit +
Accounts Payable	
	Bal. 1,800

+ Owner's Equity
Debit −	Credit +
Jessica Jane, Capital	
	Bal. 2,000

Drawing		Expenses		Revenues	
Debit +	Credit −	Debit +	Credit −	Debit −	Credit +
Jessica Jane, Drawing		**Rent Expense**		**Delivery Fees**	
(o) 150		Bal. 200			Bal. 2,000
		Telephone Expense			
		Bal. 50			
		Wages Expense			
		Bal. 650			

$4,750

Analysis: Cash withdrawals decrease owner's equity and decrease cash. Debit Jessica Jane, Drawing and credit Cash for $150.

Withdrawals are reported in the drawing account. Withdrawals by an owner are the opposite of an investment. You could debit the owner's capital account for withdrawals. However, using a specific account tells the user of the accounting information how much was withdrawn for the period.

ACCOUNT AFFECTED	CLASSIFICATION	LOCATION IN EQUATION	INCREASE OR DECREASE	DEBIT OR CREDIT
Drawing	Drawing	Right O.E.—Left Side	Drawing Increases; O.E. Decreases	Debit
Cash	Asset	Left	Decrease	Credit

As you analyze transactions (l) through (o), make certain that you understand what has happened in each transaction. Identify the accounts that are affected and the locations of these accounts within the accounting equation. Notice that the accounting equation remains in balance after every transaction and debits equal credits for each transaction.

Summary of Transactions

In illustrating transactions (a) through (o), each T account for Jessie Jane's Campus Delivery shows a balance before and after each transaction. To focus your attention on the transaction being explained, only a single entry was shown. In practice, this is not done. Instead, each account gathers all transactions for a period. Jessica Jane's accounts, with all transactions listed, are shown in Figure 3-21. Note the following:

1. The footings are directly under the debit (left) and credit (right) sides of the T account for those accounts with more than one debit or credit.
2. The balance is shown on the side with the larger footing.
3. The footing serves as the balance for accounts with entries on only one side of the account.
4. If an account has only a single entry, it is not necessary to enter a footing or balance.

FIGURE 3-21   Summary of Transactions (a) Through (o)

	Assets		=		Liabilities		+		Owner's Equity	

Assets =

Debit +		Credit −	

Cash

(a)	2,000	(b)	1,200
(e)	500	(d)	300
(k)	570	(f)	200
(n)	430	(g)	50
	3,500	(i)	80
		(j)	200
		(l)	300
		(m)	650
		(o)	150
			3,130
Bal.	370		

Accounts Receivable

(h)	600	(k)	570
(n)	470		
	1,070		
Bal.	500		

Supplies

(i)	80	

Prepaid Insurance

(j)	200	

Delivery Equipment

(b)	1,200	
(c)	900	
(l)	1,500	
Bal.	3,600	

────── $4,750 ──────

Liabilities +

Debit −		Credit +	

Accounts Payable

(d)	300	(c)	900
		(l)	1,200
			2,100
		Bal.	1,800

Owner's Equity

Debit −		Credit +	

Jessica Jane, Capital

		(a)	2,000

Drawing

Debit +	Credit −

Jessica Jane, Drawing

(o)	150	

Expenses

Debit +	Credit −

Rent Expense

(f)	200	

Telephone Expense

(g)	50	

Wages Expense

(m)	650	

Revenues

Debit −	Credit +

Delivery Fees

		(e)	500
		(h)	600
		(n)	900
		Bal.	2,000

──────────────── $4,750 ────────────────

THE TRIAL BALANCE

LO5   Prepare a trial balance.

 A trial balance provides proof that total debits equal total credits and shows that the accounting equation is in balance.

Recall the two very important rules in double-entry accounting.

1. The sum of the debits must equal the sum of the credits. This means that at least two accounts are affected by each transaction.
2. The accounting equation must remain in balance.

In illustrating the transactions for Jessie Jane's Campus Delivery, the equality of the accounting equation was verified after each transaction. Because of the large number of transactions entered each day, this is not done in practice. Instead, a trial balance is prepared periodically to determine the equality of the debits and credits. A **trial balance** is a list of all accounts showing the title and balance of each account.

A trial balance of Jessica Jane's accounts, taken on June 30, 19--, is shown in Figure 3-22. This date is shown on the third line of the heading. The trial balance shows that the debit and credit totals are equal in amount. This is proof that (1) in entering transactions (a) through (o), the total of the debits was equal to the total of the credits, and (2) the accounting equation has remained in balance.

A trial balance is not a formal statement or report. Normally, it is only seen by the accountant. As shown in the summary illustration on page 66, a trial balance can be used as an aid in preparing the financial statements.

FIGURE 3-22   Trial Balance

Jessie Jane's Campus Delivery
Trial Balance
June 30, 19--

ACCOUNT TITLE	ACCOUNT NO.	DEBIT BALANCE	CREDIT BALANCE
Cash		3 7 0 00	
Accounts Receivable		5 0 0 00	
Supplies		8 0 00	
Prepaid Insurance		2 0 0 00	
Delivery Equipment		3 6 0 0 00	
Accounts Payable			1 8 0 0 00
Jessica Jane, Capital			2 0 0 0 00
Jessica Jane, Drawing		1 5 0 00	
Delivery Fees			2 0 0 0 00
Rent Expense		2 0 0 00	
Telephone Expense		5 0 00	
Wages Expense		6 5 0 00	
		5 8 0 0 00	5 8 0 0 00

KEY POINTS

1 The parts of a T account are:

1. the title,
2. the debit or left side, and
3. the credit or right side.

Title	
Debit = Left	Credit = Right

2 Rules for footing and balancing T accounts are:

1. The footings are directly under the debit (left) and credit (right) sides of the T account for those accounts with more than one debit or credit.
2. The balance is shown on the side with the larger footing.
3. The footing serves as the balance for accounts with entries on only one side of the account.
4. If an account has only a single entry, it is not necessary to enter a footing or balance.

3 Rules for debits and credits. (See illustration on page 67.)

1. Assets are on the left side of the accounting equation. Therefore, increases are entered on the left (debit) side of an asset account and decreases are entered on the right (credit) side.
2. Liabilities and owner's equity are on the right side of the accounting equation. Therefore, increases are entered on the right (credit) side and decreases are entered on the left (debit) side.
3. Revenues are on the right side of the owner's equity umbrella. Therefore, increases are entered on the right (credit) side and decreases are entered on the left (debit) side.
4. Expenses and drawing are on the left side of the owner's equity umbrella. Therefore, increases are entered on the left (debit) side and decreases are entered on the right (credit) side.

4 Picture the accounting equation in your mind as you analyze transactions. When entering transactions in T accounts:

1. The sum of the debits must equal the sum of the credits.
2. At least two accounts are affected by each transaction.
3. When finished, the accounting equation must remain in balance.

5 A trial balance shows that the debit and credit totals are equal. A trial balance can also be used in preparing the financial statements.

SUMMARY

Jessie Jane's Campus Delivery
Trial Balance
June 30, 19--

ACCOUNT TITLE	ACCOUNT NO.	DEBIT BALANCE	CREDIT BALANCE
Cash		3 7 0 00	
Accounts Receivable		5 0 0 00	
Supplies		8 0 00	
Prepaid Insurance		2 0 0 00	
Delivery Equipment		3 6 0 0 00	
Accounts Payable			1 8 0 0 00
Jessica Jane, Capital			2 0 0 0 00
Jessica Jane, Drawing		1 5 0 00	
Delivery Fees			2 0 0 0 00
Rent Expense		2 0 0 00	
Telephone Expense		5 0 00	
Wages Expense		6 5 0 00	
		5 8 0 0 00	5 8 0 0 00

Jessie Jane's Campus Delivery
Income Statement
For Month Ended June 30, 19--

Revenue:		
Delivery fees		$2 0 0 0 00
Expenses:		
Wages expense	$ 6 5 0 00	
Rent expense	2 0 0 00	
Telephone expense	5 0 00	
Total expenses		9 0 0 00
Net income		$1 1 0 0 00

Jessie Jane's Campus Delivery
Statement of Owner's Equity
For Month Ended June 30, 19--

Jessica Jane, capital, June 1, 19--		$2 0 0 0 00
Net income for June	$1 1 0 0 00	
Less withdrawals for June	1 5 0 00	
Increase in capital		9 5 0 00
Jessica Jane, capital, June 30, 19--		$2 9 5 0 00

Jessie Jane's Campus Delivery
Balance Sheet
June 30, 19--

Assets			Liabilities	
Cash	$ 3 7 0 00		Accounts payable	$1 8 0 0 00
Accounts receivable	5 0 0 00			
Supplies	8 0 00		Owner's Equity	
Prepaid insurance	2 0 0 00		Jessica Jane, capital	2 9 5 0 00
Delivery equipment	3 6 0 0 00			
			Total liabilities and	
Total assets	$4 7 5 0 00		owner's equity	$4 7 5 0 00

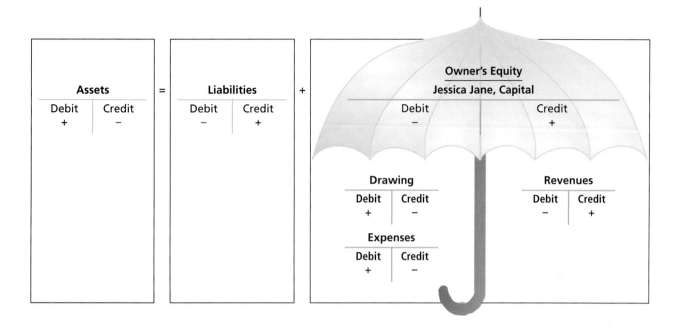

balance 45   The difference between the footings of an account.

credit 46   To enter an amount on the right side of an account.

credit balance 47   The normal balance of liability, owner's equity, and revenue accounts.

debit 46   To enter an amount on the left side of an account.

debit balance 47   The normal balance of asset, expense, and drawing accounts.

double-entry accounting 45   A system in which each transaction has a dual effect on the accounting elements.

footings 45   The total dollar amounts on the debit and credit sides of an account.

normal balance 47   The side of an account that is increased.

trial balance 64   A list of accounts showing the title and balance of each account.

REVIEW QUESTIONS

1. What are the three major parts of a T account?

2. What is the left side of the T account called? the right side?

3. What is a footing?

4. What is the relationship between the revenue and expense accounts and the owner's equity account?

5. What is the function of the trial balance?

MANAGING YOUR WRITING

Write a one-page memo to your instructor explaining how you could use the double-entry system to maintain records of your personal finances. What types of accounts would you use for the accounting elements?

DEMONSTRATION PROBLEM

Celia Pints opened We-Buy, You-Pay Shopping Services. For a fee that is based on the amount of research and shopping time required, Pints and her associates will shop for almost anything from groceries to home furnishings. Business is particularly heavy around Christmas and in early summer. The business operates from a rented store front. The associates receive a commission based on the revenues they produce and a mileage reimbursement for the use of their personal automobiles for shopping trips. Pints decided to use the following accounts to record transactions:

Assets	Owner's Equity
Cash	Celia Pints, Capital
Accounts Receivable	Celia Pints, Drawing
Office Equipment	Revenue
Computer Equipment	Shopping Fees
Liabilities	Expenses
Accounts Payable	Rent Expense
Notes Payable	Telephone Expense
	Commissions Expense
	Utilities Expense
	Travel Expense

The following transactions are for the month of December 19--.

(a) Pints invested cash in the business, $30,000.
(b) Bought office equipment for $10,000. Paid $2,000 in cash and promised to pay the balance over the next four months.
(c) Paid rent for December, $500.
(d) Provided shopping services for customers on account, $5,200.
(e) Paid telephone bill, $90.
(f) Borrowed cash from the bank by signing a note payable, $5,000.
(g) Bought a computer and printer, $4,800.
(h) Collected cash from customers for services performed on account, $4,000.
(i) Paid commissions to associates for revenues generated during the first half of the month, $3,500.
(j) Paid utility bill, $600.
(k) Paid cash on account for the office equipment purchased in transaction (b), $2,000.
(l) Earned shopping fees of $13,200: $6,000 in cash and $7,200 on account.
(m) Paid commissions to associates for last half of month, $7,000.

(n) Paid mileage reimbursements for the month, $1,500.
(o) Paid cash on note payable to bank, $1,000.
(p) Pints withdrew cash for personal use, $2,000.

REQUIRED

1. Enter the transactions for December in T accounts. Use the accounting equation as a guide for setting up the T accounts.
2. Foot the T accounts and determine their balances as necessary.
3. Prepare a trial balance of the accounts as of December 31 of the current year.
4. Prepare an income statement for the month ended December 31 of the current year.
5. Prepare a statement of owner's equity for the month ended December 31 of the current year.
6. Prepare a balance sheet as of December 31 of the current year.

SOLUTION

1, 2.

Assets		=	Liabilities		+	Owner's Equity	

Assets =

	Debit +	Credit −

Cash

(a)	30,000	(b)	2,000
(f)	5,000	(c)	500
(h)	4,000	(e)	90
(l)	6,000	(g)	4,800
	45,000	(i)	3,500
		(j)	600
		(k)	2,000
		(m)	7,000
		(n)	1,500
		(o)	1,000
		(p)	2,000
			24,990
Bal.	20,010		

Accounts Receivable

(d)	5,200	(h)	4,000
(l)	7,200		
	12,400		
Bal.	8,400		

Office Equipment

| (b) | 10,000 | |

Computer Equipment

| (g) | 4,800 | |

—— **$43,210** ——

Liabilities

Debit −	Credit +

Accounts Payable

| (k) | 2,000 | (b) | 8,000 |
| | | Bal. | 6,000 |

Notes Payable

| (o) | 1,000 | (f) | 5,000 |
| | | Bal. | 4,000 |

Owner's Equity

Debit −	Credit +

Celia Pints, Capital

| | | (a) | 30,000 |

Drawing

| Debit + | Credit − |

Celia Pints, Drawing

| (p) | 2,000 | |

Expenses

| Debit + | Credit − |

Rent Expense

| (c) | 500 | |

Telephone Expense

| (e) | 90 | |

Commissions Expense

(i)	3,500	
(m)	7,000	
Bal.	10,500	

Utilities Expense

| (j) | 600 | |

Travel Expense

| (n) | 1,500 | |

Revenues

| Debit − | Credit + |

Shopping Fees

		(d)	5,200
		(l)	13,200
		Bal.	18,400

—— **$43,210** ——

3.

We-Buy, You-Pay Shopping Services
Trial Balance
December 31, 19--

ACCOUNT TITLE	DEBIT BALANCE	CREDIT BALANCE
Cash	20 0 1 0 00	
Accounts Receivable	8 4 0 0 00	
Office Equipment	10 0 0 0 00	
Computer Equipment	4 8 0 0 00	
Accounts Payable		6 0 0 0 00
Notes Payable		4 0 0 0 00
Celia Pints, Capital		30 0 0 0 00
Celia Pints, Drawing	2 0 0 0 00	
Shopping Fees		18 4 0 0 00
Rent Expense	5 0 0 00	
Telephone Expense	9 0 00	
Commissions Expense	10 5 0 0 00	
Utilities Expense	6 0 0 00	
Travel Expense	1 5 0 0 00	
	58 4 0 0 00	58 4 0 0 00

4.

We Buy, You-Pay Shopping Services
Income Statement
For Month Ended December 31, 19--

Revenue:		
Shopping fees		$18 4 0 0 00
Expenses:		
Commissions expense	$10 5 0 0 00	
Travel expense	1 5 0 0 00	
Utilities expense	6 0 0 00	
Rent expense	5 0 0 00	
Telephone expense	9 0 00	
Total expenses		13 1 9 0 00
Net income		$ 5 2 1 0 00

5.

We-Buy, You-Pay Shopping Services
Statement of Owner's Equity
For Month Ended December 31, 19--

Celia Pints, capital, December 1, 19--		$30 0 0 0 00
Net income for December	$5 2 1 0 00	
Less withdrawals for December	2 0 0 0 00	
Increase in capital		3 2 1 0 00
Celia Pints, capital, December 31, 19--		$33 2 1 0 00

6.

We-Buy, You-Pay Shopping Services
Balance Sheet
December 31, 19--

Assets		Liabilities	
Cash	$20 0 1 0 00	Accounts payable	$ 6 0 0 0 00
Accounts receivable	8 4 0 0 00	Notes payable	4 0 0 0 00
Office equipment	10 0 0 0 00	Total liabilities	$10 0 0 0 00
Computer equipment	4 8 0 0 00		
		Owner's Equity	
		Celia Pints, capital	33 2 1 0 00
		Total liabilities and	
Total assets	$43 2 1 0 00	owner's equity	$43 2 1 0 00

SERIES A   EXERCISES

2 **EXERCISE 3A1 FOOT AND BALANCE A T ACCOUNT**   Foot and balance the cash T account shown.

Cash

500	100
400	200
600	

3 **EXERCISE 3A2 DEBIT AND CREDIT ANALYSIS**   Complete the following questions using either "debit" or "credit."

(a) The cash account is increased with a _____.
(b) The owner's capital account is increased with a _____.
(c) The delivery equipment account is increased with a _____.
(d) The cash account is decreased with a _____.
(e) The liability account Accounts Payable is increased with a _____.
(f) The revenue account Delivery Fees is increased with a _____.

continued

(g) The asset account Accounts Receivable is increased with a _____ .

(h) The rent expense account is increased with a _____ .

(i) The owner's drawing account is increased with a _____ .

2/3/4 **EXERCISE 3A3 ANALYSIS OF T ACCOUNTS** Jim Arnold began a business called Arnold's Shoe Repair.

1. Create T accounts for Cash; Supplies; Jim Arnold, Capital; and Utilities Expense. Identify the following transactions by letter and place on the proper side of the T accounts.
   (a) Arnold invested cash in the business, $5,000.
   (b) Purchased supplies for cash, $800.
   (c) Paid utility bill, $1,500.
2. Foot the T account for Cash and enter the ending balance.

3 **EXERCISE 3A4 NORMAL BALANCE OF ACCOUNT** Indicate the normal balance (debit or credit) for each of the following accounts.

1. Cash
2. Wages Expense
3. Accounts Payable
4. Owner's Drawing
5. Supplies
6. Owner's Capital
7. Equipment

4 **EXERCISE 3A5 TRANSACTION ANALYSIS** Sheryl Hansen started a new business on May 1, 19--. Analyze the following transactions for the first month of business using T accounts. Label each T account with the title of the account affected and then place the dollar amount on the debit or credit side.

(a) Hansen invested cash in the business, $4,000.
(b) Bought equipment for cash, $500.
(c) Bought equipment on account, $800.
(d) Paid cash on account for equipment purchased in transaction (c), $300.
(e) Owner withdrew cash for personal use, $700.

2 **EXERCISE 3A6 ANALYSIS OF T ACCOUNT** From the transactions in exercise 3A5, analyze the transactions affecting Cash, foot the T account, and indicate the ending balance.

2/4 **EXERCISE 3A7 ANALYSIS OF TRANSACTIONS** Charles Chadwick began a new business called Charlie's Detective Service in January 19--. Set up T accounts for the following accounts: Cash; Accounts Receivable; Office Supplies; Computer Equipment; Office Furniture; Accounts Payable; Charles Chadwick, Capital; Charles Chadwick, Drawing; Professional Fees; Rent Expense; and Utilities Expense.

The following transactions occurred during the first month of business. Record these transactions in T accounts. After all transactions are recorded, foot and balance the accounts if necessary.

(a) Chadwick invested cash in the business, $30,000.
(b) Bought office supplies for cash, $300.
(c) Bought office furniture for cash, $5,000.
(d) Purchased computer and printer on account, $8,000.
(e) Received cash from clients for services, $3,000.
(f) Paid cash on account for computer and printer purchased in transaction (d), $4,000.
(g) Earned professional fees on account during the month, $9,000.
(h) Paid cash for office rent for January, $1,500.
(i) Paid utility bills for the month, $800.
(j) Received cash from clients billed in transaction (g), $6,000.
(k) Chadwick withdrew cash for personal use, $3,000.

5 **EXERCISE 3A8 TRIAL BALANCE**   Based on the transactions recorded in Exercise 3A7, prepare a trial balance for Charlie's Detective Service as of January 31, 19--.

5 **EXERCISE 3A9 TRIAL BALANCE**   The following accounts have normal balances. Prepare a trial balance for Juanita's Delivery Service as of September 30, 19--.

Cash	$5,000
Accounts Receivable	3,000
Supplies	800
Prepaid Insurance	600
Delivery Equipment	8,000
Accounts Payable	2,000
Juanita Raye, Capital	10,000
Juanita Raye, Drawing	1,000
Delivery Fees	9,400
Wages Expense	2,100
Rent Expense	900

EXERCISE 3A10 INCOME STATEMENT   From the information in Exercise 3A9, prepare an income statement for Juanita's Delivery Service for the month ended September 30, 19--.

EXERCISE 3A11 STATEMENT OF OWNER'S EQUITY   From the information in Exercise 3A9, prepare a statement of owner's equity for Juanita's Delivery Service for the month ended September 30, 19--.

EXERCISE 3A12 BALANCE SHEET   From the information in Exercise 3A9, prepare a balance sheet for Juanita's Delivery Service as of September 30, 19--.

SERIES A PROBLEMS

2/4/5   **PROBLEM 3A1 T ACCOUNTS AND TRIAL BALANCE**   Harold Long started a business in May 19-- called Harold's Home Repair. Long hired a part-time college student as an assistant. Long has decided to use the following accounts for recording transactions:

Assets	Owner's Equity
Cash	Harold Long, Capital
Accounts Receivable	Harold Long, Drawing
Office Supplies	Revenue
Prepaid Insurance	Service Fees
Equipment	Expenses
Van	Rent Expense
Liabilities	Wages Expense
Accounts Payable	Telephone Expense
	Gas and Oil Expense

The following transactions occurred during May.

(a) Long invested cash in the business, $20,000.
(b) Purchased a used van for cash, $7,000.
(c) Purchased equipment on account, $5,000.
(d) Received cash for services rendered, $6,000.
(e) Paid cash on amount owed from transaction (c), $2,000.
(f) Paid rent for the month, $900.
(g) Paid telephone bill, $200.
(h) Earned revenue on account, $4,000.
(i) Purchased office supplies for cash, $120.
(j) Paid wages to student, $600.
(k) Purchased insurance, $1,200.
(l) Received cash from services performed in transaction (h), $3,000.
(m) Paid cash for gas and oil expense on the van, $160.
(n) Purchased additional equipment for $3,000, paying $1,000 cash and spreading the remaining payments over the next 10 months.
(o) Service fees earned for the remainder of the month amounted to $3,200: $1,800 in cash and $1,400 on account.
(p) Long withdrew cash at the end of the month, $2,800.

REQUIRED

1. Enter the transactions in T accounts, identifying each transaction with its corresponding letter.
2. Foot and balance the accounts where necessary.
3. Prepare a trial balance as of May 31, 19--.

PROBLEM 3A2 NET INCOME AND CHANGE IN OWNER'S EQUITY   Refer to the trial balance of Harold's Home Repair in Problem 3A1 to determine the following information. Use the format provided on the next page.

1. a. Total revenue for the month _____
  b. Total expenses for the month _____
  c. Net income for the month _____
2. a. Harold Long's original investment in the business _____
    + the net income for the month _____
    − owner's drawing _____
    = ending owner's equity _____
  b. End of month accounting equation:

ASSETS   =   LIABILITIES   + OWNER'S EQUITY

_____ = _____ + _____

PROBLEM 3A3 FINANCIAL STATEMENTS   Refer to the trial balance in Problem 3A1 and to the analysis of the change in owner's equity in Problem 3A2.

REQUIRED

1. Prepare an income statement for Harold's Home Repair for the month ended May 31, 19--.
2. Prepare a statement of owner's equity for Harold's Home Repair for the month ended May 31, 19--.
3. Prepare a balance sheet for Harold's Home Repair as of May 31, 19--.

SERIES B   EXERCISES

2   **EXERCISE 3B1 FOOT AND BALANCE A T ACCOUNT**   Foot and balance the accounts payable T account shown.

Accounts Payable	
300	450
250	350
	150

3   **EXERCISE 3B2 DEBIT AND CREDIT ANALYSIS**   Complete the following questions using either "debit" or "credit."

(a) The asset account Prepaid Insurance is increased with a _____ .
(b) The owner's drawing account is increased with a _____ .
(c) The asset account Accounts Receivable is decreased with a ,
(d) The liability account Accounts Payable is decreased with a _____ .
(e) The owner's capital account is increased with a _____ .
(f) The revenue account Professional Fees is increased with a _____ .
(g) The expense account Repair Expense is increased with a _____ .
(h) The asset account Cash is decreased with a _____ .
(i) The asset account Accounts Receivable is increased with a _____ .

2/3/4   **EXERCISE 3B3 ANALYSIS OF T ACCOUNTS**   Roberto Alvarez began a business called Roberto's Fix-It Shop.

1. Create T accounts for Cash; Supplies; Roberto Alvarez, Capital; and Utilities Expense. Identify the following transactions by letter and place them on the proper side of the T accounts.
   (a) Alvarez invested cash in the business, $6,000.
   (b) Purchased supplies for cash, $1,200.
   (c) Paid utility bill, $900.
2. Foot the T account for Cash and enter the ending balance.

3   **EXERCISE 3B4 NORMAL BALANCE OF ACCOUNT**   Indicate the normal balance (debit or credit) for each of the following accounts.

1. Cash
2. Rent Expense
3. Notes Payable
4. Owner's Drawing
5. Accounts Receivable
6. Owner's Capital
7. Tools

4   **EXERCISE 3B5 TRANSACTION ANALYSIS**   George Atlas started a new business on June 1, 19--. Analyze the following transactions for the first month of business using T accounts. Label each T account with the title of the account affected and then place the dollar amount on the debit or credit side.

(a) Atlas invested cash in the business, $7,000.
(b) Purchased equipment for cash, $900.
(c) Purchased equipment on account, $1,500.
(d) Paid $800 on account for equipment purchased in transaction (c).
(e) Atlas withdrew cash for personal use, $1,100.

2   **EXERCISE 3B6 ANALYSIS OF T ACCOUNT**   From the transactions in Exercise 3B5, analyze the transactions affecting Cash, foot the T account, and indicate the ending balance.

2/4   **EXERCISE 3B7 ANALYSIS OF TRANSACTIONS**   Nicole Lawrence began a new business called Nickie's Neat Ideas in January 19--. Set up T accounts for the following accounts: Cash; Accounts Receivable; Office Supplies; Computer Equipment; Office Furniture; Accounts Payable; Nicole Lawrence, Capital; Nicole Lawrence, Drawing; Professional Fees; Rent Expense; and Utilities Expense.

The following transactions occurred during the first month of business. Record these transactions in T accounts. After all transactions have been recorded, foot and balance the accounts if necessary.

(a) Lawrence invested cash in the business, $18,000.
(b) Purchased office supplies for cash, $500.

continued

(c) Purchased office furniture for cash, $8,000.

(d) Purchased computer and printer on account, $5,000.

(e) Received cash from clients for services, $4,000.

(f) Paid cash on account for computer and printer purchased in transaction (d), $2,000.

(g) Earned professional fees on account during the month, $7,000.

(h) Paid office rent for January, $900.

(i) Paid utility bills for the month, $600.

(j) Received cash from clients that were billed previously in transaction (g), $3,000.

(k) Lawrence withdrew cash for personal use, $4,000.

5 **EXERCISE 3B8 TRIAL BALANCE** Based on the transactions recorded in Exercise 3B7, prepare a trial balance for Nickie's Neat Ideas as of January 31, 19--.

5 **EXERCISE 3B9 TRIAL BALANCE** The following accounts have normal balances. Prepare a trial balance for Bill's Delivery Service as of September 30, 19--.

Cash	$ 7,000
Accounts Receivable	4,000
Supplies	600
Prepaid Insurance	900
Delivery Equipment	9,000
Accounts Payable	3,000
Bill Swift, Capital	12,000
Bill Swift, Drawing	2,000
Delivery Fees	12,500
Wages Expense	3,000
Rent Expense	1,000

EXERCISE 3B10 INCOME STATEMENT From the information in Exercise 3B9, prepare an income statement for Bill's Delivery Service for the month ended September 30, 19--.

EXERCISE 3B11 STATEMENT OF OWNER'S EQUITY From the information in Exercise 3B9, prepare a statement of owner's equity for Bill's Delivery Service for the month ended September 30, 19--.

EXERCISE 3B12 BALANCE SHEET From the information in Exercise 3B9, prepare a balance sheet for Bill's Delivery Service as of September 30, 19--.

2/4/5   **PROBLEM 3B1 T ACCOUNTS AND TRIAL BALANCE**   Sue Jantz started a business in August 19-- called Jantz Plumbing Service. Jantz hired a part-time college student as an administrative assistant. Jantz has decided to use the following accounts:

Assets
  Cash
  Accounts Receivable
  Office Supplies
  Prepaid Insurance
  Plumbing Equipment
  Van
Liabilities
  Accounts Payable

Owner's Equity
  Sue Jantz, Capital
  Sue Jantz, Drawing
Revenue
  Service Fees
Expenses
  Rent Expense
  Wages Expense
  Telephone Expense
  Advertising Expense

The following transactions occurred during August.

(a) Jantz invested cash in the business, $30,000.
(b) Purchased a used van for cash, $8,000.
(c) Purchased plumbing equipment on account, $4,000.
(d) Received cash for services rendered, $3,000.
(e) Paid cash on amount owed from transaction (c), $1,000.
(f) Paid rent for the month, $700.
(g) Paid telephone bill, $100.
(h) Earned revenue on account, $4,000.
(i) Purchased office supplies for cash, $300.
(j) Paid wages to student, $500.
(k) Purchased insurance, $800.
(l) Received cash from services performed in transaction (h), $3,000.
(m) Paid cash for advertising expense, $2,000.
(n) Purchased additional plumbing equipment for $2,000, paying $500 cash and spreading the remaining payments over the next 6 months.
(o) Revenue earned from services for the remainder of the month amounted to $2,800: $1,100 in cash and $1,700 on account.
(p) Jantz withdrew cash at the end of the month, $3,000.

REQUIRED

1. Enter the transactions in T accounts, identifying each transaction with its corresponding letter.
2. Foot and balance the accounts where necessary.
3. Prepare a trial balance as of August 31, 19--.

PROBLEM 3B2 NET INCOME AND CHANGE IN OWNER'S EQUITY   Refer to the trial balance of Jantz Plumbing Service in Problem 3B1 to determine the following information. Use the format provided below.

1. a. Total revenue for the month _____

   b. Total expenses for the month _____

   c. Net income for the month _____

2. a. Sue Jantz's original investment in the business _____

   + the net income for the month _____

   – owner's drawing _____

   = ending owner's equity _____

   b. End of month accounting equation:

   ASSETS = LIABILITIES + OWNER'S EQUITY

   _____ = _____ + _____

PROBLEM 3B3 FINANCIAL STATEMENTS Refer to the trial balance in Problem 3B1 and to the analysis of the change in owner's equity in Problem 3B2.

REQUIRED

1. Prepare an income statement for Jantz Plumbing Service for the month ended August 31, 19--.
2. Prepare a statement of owner's equity for Jantz Plumbing Service for the month ended August 31, 19--.
3. Prepare a balance sheet for Jantz Plumbing Service as of August 31, 19--.

MASTERY PROBLEM

Craig Fisher started a lawn service called Craig's Quick Cut to earn money over the summer months. Fisher has decided to use the following accounts for recording transactions:

Assets
  Cash
  Accounts Receivable
  Mowing Equipment
  Lawn Tools
Liabilities
  Accounts Payable
  Notes Payable
Owner's Equity
  Craig Fisher, Capital
  Craig Fisher, Drawing

Revenue
  Lawn Fees
Expenses
  Rent Expense
  Wages Expense
  Telephone Expense
  Gas and Oil Expense
  Transportation Expense

Transactions for the month of June are listed below.

(a) Fisher invested cash in the business, $3,000.
(b) Bought mowing equipment for $1,000: paid $200 in cash and promised to pay the balance over the next four months.
(c) Paid garage rent for June, $50.
(d) Provided lawn services for customers on account, $520.
(e) Paid telephone bill, $30.

continued

(f) Borrowed cash from the bank by signing a note payable, $500.

(g) Bought lawn tools, $480.

(h) Collected cash from customers for services performed on account in transaction (d), $400.

(i) Paid associates for lawn work done during the first half of the month, $350.

(j) Paid for gas and oil for the equipment, $60.

(k) Paid cash on account for the mowing equipment purchased in transaction (b), $200.

(l) Earned lawn fees of $1,320: $600 in cash and $720 on account.

(m) Paid associates for last half of month, $700.

(n) Reimbursed associates for expenses associated with using their own vehicles for transportation, $150.

(o) Paid on note payable to bank, $100.

(p) Fisher withdrew cash for personal use, $200.

REQUIRED

1. Enter the transactions for June in T accounts. Use the accounting equation as a guide for setting up the T accounts.
2. Foot and balance the T accounts where necessary.
3. Prepare a trial balance of the accounts as of June 30, 19--.
4. Prepare an income statement for the month ended June 30, 19--.
5. Prepare a statement of owner's equity for the month ended June 30, 19--.
6. Prepare a balance sheet as of June 30, 19--.

4

Journalizing and Posting Transactions

"Jim, come here," called Mary. "Look at how Rob entered this transaction. What was he thinking? Why does he make these entries in ink? Do you have an ink eraser?" Should Mary try to correct Rob's error by erasing his work and reentering the transaction?

The double-entry framework of accounting was explained and illustrated in Chapter 3. To demonstrate the use of debits and credits, business transactions were entered directly into T accounts. Now we will take a more detailed look at the procedures used to account for business transactions.

FLOW OF DATA

LO1 Describe the flow of data from source documents through the trial balance.

This chapter traces the flow of financial data from the source documents through the accounting information system. This process includes the following steps:

1. Analyze what happened by using information from source documents and the firm's chart of accounts.
2. Enter business transactions in the general journal.
3. Post entries to accounts in the general ledger.
4. Prepare a trial balance.

The flow of data from the source documents through the preparation of a trial balance is shown in Figure 4-1.

FIGURE 4-1   Flow of Data from Source Documents Through Trial Balance

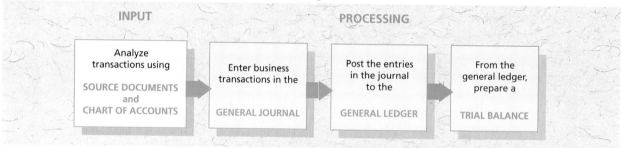

THE CHART OF ACCOUNTS

LO2 Describe the chart of accounts as a means of classifying financial information.

You learned in Chapters 2 and 3 that there are three basic questions that must be answered when analyzing transactions:

1. What happened?
2. Which accounts are affected?
3. How is the accounting equation affected?

To determine which accounts are affected (step 2), the accountant must know the accounts being used by the business. A list of all accounts used by a business is called a **chart of accounts**.

The chart of accounts includes the account titles in numeric order for all assets, liabilities, owner's equity, revenues, and expenses. The numbering should follow a consistent pattern. In Jessie Jane's Campus Delivery, asset accounts begin with "1," liability accounts begin with "2," owner's equity accounts begin with "3," revenue accounts begin with "4," and expense accounts begin with "5." Jane uses three-digit numbers for all accounts.

A chart of accounts for Jessie Jane's Campus Delivery is shown in Figure 4-2. Jane would not need many accounts initially because the business is new. Additional accounts can easily be added as needed. Note that the accounts are arranged according to the accounting equation.

FIGURE 4-2   Chart of Accounts

Jessie Jane's Campus Delivery Chart of Accounts			
Assets	**(100–199)**	**Revenues**	**(400–499)**
111	Cash	411	Delivery Fees
131	Accounts Receivable		
151	Supplies	**Expenses**	**(500–599)**
155	Prepaid Insurance	541	Rent Expense
185	Delivery Equipment	542	Wages Expense
		545	Telephone Expense
Liabilities	**(200–299)**		
216	Accounts Payable		
Owner's Equity	**(300–399)**		
311	Jessica Jane, Capital		
312	Jessica Jane, Drawing		

Assets begin with 1
Liabilities begin with 2
Owner's Equity begin with 3
Revenues begin with 4
Expenses begin with 5

SOURCE DOCUMENTS

LO3 Describe and explain the purpose of source documents.

Almost any document that provides information about a business transaction can be called a **source document**. A source document triggers the analysis of what happened. It begins the process of entering transactions into the accounting system. Examples of source documents are shown in Figure 4-3. These source documents provide information that is useful in determining the effect of business transactions on specific accounts.

In addition to serving as input for transaction analysis, source documents serve as objective evidence of business transactions. If anyone questions the accounting records, these documents may be used as objective, verifiable evidence of the accuracy of the accounting records. For this reason, source documents are filed for possible future reference. *Having objective, verifiable evidence that a transaction occurred is an important accounting concept.*

FIGURE 4-3   Source Documents

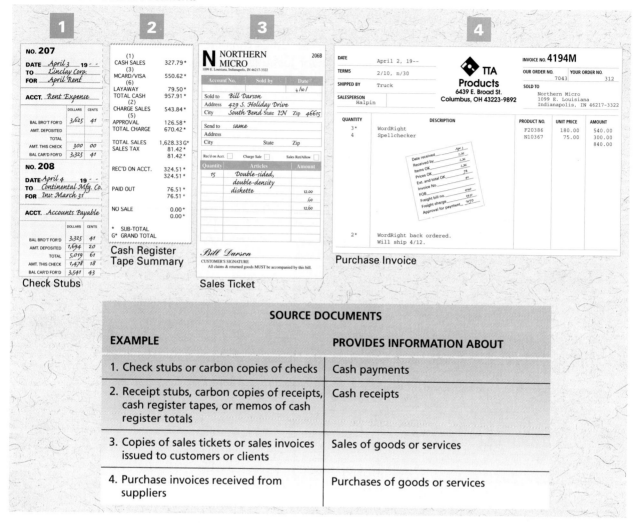

SOURCE DOCUMENTS	
EXAMPLE	**PROVIDES INFORMATION ABOUT**
1. Check stubs or carbon copies of checks	Cash payments
2. Receipt stubs, carbon copies of receipts, cash register tapes, or memos of cash register totals	Cash receipts
3. Copies of sales tickets or sales invoices issued to customers or clients	Sales of goods or services
4. Purchase invoices received from suppliers	Purchases of goods or services

THE GENERAL JOURNAL

LO4 Journalize transactions.

A day-by-day listing of the transactions of a business is called a **journal**. The purpose of a journal is to provide a record of all transactions completed by the business. The journal shows the date of each transaction, titles of the accounts to be debited and credited, and the amounts of the debits and credits.

 LEARNING KEY | A journal provides a day-by-day listing of all transactions completed by the business.

A journal is commonly referred to as a **book of original entry** because it is here that the first formal accounting record of a transaction is made.

Although many types of journals are used in business, the simplest journal form is a two-column general journal (Figure 4-4). Any kind of business transaction may be entered into a general journal.

FIGURE 4-4   Two-Column General Journal

DATE	DESCRIPTION	POST. REF.	DEBIT	CREDIT	
GENERAL JOURNAL					PAGE **1**
19--					
1	2	3	4	5	

A **two-column general journal** is so-named because it has only two amount columns, one for debit amounts and one for credit amounts. Journal pages are numbered in the upper right-hand corner. The five column numbers in Figure 4-4 are explained in Figure 4-5.

FIGURE 4-5   The Columns in a Two-Column General Journal

Column **1** Date	The year is entered in small figures at the top of the column immediately below the column heading. The year is repeated only at the top of each new page. The month is entered for the first entry on the page and for the first transaction of the month. The day of the month is recorded for every transaction, even if it is the same as the prior entry.
Column **2** Description	The **Description** or **Explanation** column is used to enter the titles of the accounts affected by each transaction, and to provide a very brief description of the transaction. Each transaction affects two or more accounts. The account(s) to be debited are entered first at the extreme left of the column. The account(s) to be credited are listed after the debits and indented about one-half inch. The description should be entered immediately following the last credit entry and indented an additional one-half inch.
Column **3** Posting Reference	No entries are made in the **Posting Reference column** during journalizing. Entries are made in this column when the debits and credits are copied to the proper accounts in the ledger. This process will be explained in detail later in this chapter.
Column **4** Debit **Amount**	The **Debit amount column** is used to enter the amount to be debited to an account. The amount should be entered on the same line as the title of that account.
Column **5** Credit **Amount**	The **Credit amount column** is used to enter the amount to be credited to an account. The amount should be entered on the same line as the title of that account.

Journalizing

Entering the transactions in a journal is called **journalizing.** For every transaction, the entry should include the date, the title of each account affected, the amounts, and a brief description.

To illustrate the journalizing process, transactions for the first month of operations of Jessie Jane's Campus Delivery will be journalized. The transactions are listed in Figure 4-6. Since you analyzed these transactions in Chapters 2 and 3, the journalizing process should be easier to understand. Let's start with a close look at the steps followed when journalizing the first transaction, Jane's initial investment of $2,000.

When journalizing, the exact account titles shown in the chart of accounts must be used. Refer to the chart of accounts in Figure 4-2 as you review the entries for Jessie Jane's Campus Delivery.

FIGURE 4-6   Summary of Transactions

		Summary of Transactions Jessie Jane's Campus Delivery
Transaction		
(a)	June 1	Jessica Jane invested cash in her business, $2,000.
(b)	3	Bought delivery equipment for cash, $1,200.
(c)	5	Bought delivery equipment on account from Big Red Scooters, $900.
(d)	6	Paid first installment from transaction (c) to Big Red Scooters, $300.
(e)	6	Received cash for delivery services rendered, $500.
(f)	7	Paid cash for June office rent, $200.
(g)	15	Paid telephone bill, $50.
(h)	15	Made deliveries on account for a total of $600: Accounting Department ($400) and the School of Optometry ($200).
(i)	16	Bought supplies for cash, $80.
(j)	18	Paid cash for an eight-month liability insurance policy, $200. Coverage began on June 1.
(k)	20	Received $570 in cash for services performed in transaction (h): $400 from the Accounting Department and $170 from the School of Optometry.
(l)	25	Bought a third scooter from Big Red Scooters, $1,500. Paid $300 cash, with the remaining payments expected over the next four months.
(m)	27	Paid part-time employees wages, $650.
(n)	30	Earned delivery fees for the remainder of the month amounting to $900: $430 in cash and $470 on account. Deliveries on account: Accounting Department ($100) and Athletic Ticket Office ($370).
(o)	30	Jane withdrew cash for personal use, $150.

TRANSACTION (a)

June 1   Jessica Jane opened a bank account with a deposit of $2,000 for her business.

STEP 1   **Enter the date.**   Since this is the first entry on the journal page, the year is entered on the first line of the Date column (in small print at the top of the line). The month and day are entered on the same line, below the year, in the Date column.

GENERAL JOURNAL   PAGE 1

	DATE		DESCRIPTION	POST. REF.	DEBIT	CREDIT	
	19--						
1	June	1					1
2							2

STEP 2   **Enter the debit.**   Cash is entered on the first line at the extreme left of the Description column. The amount of the debit, $2,000, is entered on the same line in the Debit column.

GENERAL JOURNAL   PAGE 1

	DATE		DESCRIPTION	POST. REF.	DEBIT	CREDIT	
	19--						
1	June	1	Cash		2 0 0 0 00		1
2							2

STEP 3   **Enter the credit.**   The title of the account to be credited, Jessica Jane, Capital, is entered on the second line, indented one-half inch from the left side of the Description column. The amount of the credit, $2,000, is entered on the same line in the Credit column.

GENERAL JOURNAL   PAGE 1

	DATE		DESCRIPTION	POST. REF.	DEBIT	CREDIT	
	19--						
1	June	1	Cash		2 0 0 0 00		1
2			Jessica Jane, Capital			2 0 0 0 00	2

STEP 4   **Enter the explanation.**   The explanation of the entry is entered on the next line, indented an additional one-half inch. The second line of the explanation, if needed, is also indented the same distance as the first.

GENERAL JOURNAL   PAGE 1

	DATE		DESCRIPTION	POST. REF.	DEBIT	CREDIT	
	19--						
1	June	1	Cash		2 0 0 0 00		1
2			Jessica Jane, Capital			2 0 0 0 00	2
3			Owner's original investment in				3
4			delivery business				4

To enter transaction (b), the purchase of a motor scooter for $1,200 cash, we skip a line and follow the same four steps. In practice, you probably would not skip a line to prevent inappropriate changes to entries. Note that the month and year do not need to be repeated. The day of the month must, however, be entered.

GENERAL JOURNAL PAGE **1**

	DATE		DESCRIPTION	POST. REF.	DEBIT	CREDIT	
	19--						
1	June	1	Cash		2 0 0 0 00		1
2			Jessica Jane, Capital			2 0 0 0 00	2
3			Owner's original investment in				3
4			delivery business				4
5							5
6		3	Delivery Equipment		1 2 0 0 00		6
7			Cash			1 2 0 0 00	7
8			Purchased delivery equipment				8
9			for cash				9

Skip a line

The journal entries for the month of June are shown in Figure 4-7. Note that the entries on June 25 and June 30 affect more than two accounts. These are called **compound entries**.

FIGURE 4-7   General Journal Entries

GENERAL JOURNAL PAGE **1**

	DATE		DESCRIPTION	POST. REF.	DEBIT	CREDIT	
	19--						
1	June	1	Cash		2 0 0 0 00		1
2			Jessica Jane, Capital			2 0 0 0 00	2
3			Owner's original investment in				3
4			delivery business				4
5							5
6		3	Delivery Equipment		1 2 0 0 00		6
7			Cash			1 2 0 0 00	7
8			Purchased delivery equipment				8
9			for cash				9
10							10
11		5	Delivery Equipment		9 0 0 00		11
12			Accounts Payable			9 0 0 00	12
13			Purchased delivery equipment				13
14			on account from Big Red				14
15			Scooters				15

List debits first
List credits second and indented 1/2"
Explanation is third and indented another 1/2"
Space to make entries easier to read

In practice, this might not be done to prevent inappropriate changes to entries.

FIGURE 4-7   General Journal Entries (continued)

GENERAL JOURNAL   PAGE **1**

	DATE		DESCRIPTION	POST. REF.	DEBIT	CREDIT	
17		6	Accounts Payable		3 0 0 00		17
18			Cash			3 0 0 00	18
19			Made partial payment to Big				19
20			Red Scooters				20
21							21
22		6	Cash		5 0 0 00		22
23			Delivery Fees			5 0 0 00	23
24			Received cash for delivery				24
25			services				25
26							26
27		7	Rent Expense		2 0 0 00		27
28			Cash			2 0 0 00	28
29			Paid office rent for June				29
30							30
31		15	Telephone Expense		5 0 00		31
32			Cash			5 0 00	32
33			Paid telephone bill for June				33
34							34
35		15	Accounts Receivable		6 0 0 00		35
36			Delivery Fees			6 0 0 00	36
37			Deliveries made on account for				37
38			Accounting Department ($400)				38
39			and School of Optometry ($200)				39
40							40

GENERAL JOURNAL   PAGE **2**

	DATE		DESCRIPTION	POST. REF.	DEBIT	CREDIT	
1	19-- June	16	Supplies		8 0 00		1
2			Cash			8 0 00	2
3			Purchased supplies for cash				3
4							4
5		18	Prepaid Insurance		2 0 0 00		5
6			Cash			2 0 0 00	6
7			Paid premium for eight-month				7
8			insurance policy				8

FIGURE 4-7   General Journal Entries (continued)

GENERAL JOURNAL   PAGE 2

	DATE	DESCRIPTION	POST. REF.	DEBIT	CREDIT	
	19--					
10	20	Cash		5 7 0 00		10
11		Accounts Receivable			5 7 0 00	11
12		Received cash on account from				12
13		Accounting Department ($400)				13
14		and School of Optometry ($170)				14
15						15
16	25	Delivery Equipment		1 5 0 0 00		16
17		Accounts Payable			1 2 0 0 00	17
18		Cash			3 0 0 00	18
19		Purchased scooter with down				19
20		payment; balance on account				20
21		from Big Red Scooters				21
22						22
23	27	Wages Expense		6 5 0 00		23
24		Cash			6 5 0 00	24
25		Paid employees				25
26						26
27	30	Cash		4 3 0 00		27
28		Accounts Receivable		4 7 0 00		28
29		Delivery Fees			9 0 0 00	29
30		Deliveries made for cash and				30
31		on account to Accounting				31
32		Department ($100) and				32
33		Athletic Ticket Office ($370)				33
34						34
35	30	Jessica Jane, Drawing		1 5 0 00		35
36		Cash			1 5 0 00	36
37		Owner's withdrawal				37

Compound entry (pointing to row 16)

Compound entry (pointing to row 27)

THE GENERAL LEDGER

LO5   Post to the general ledger.

The journal provides a day-by-day record of business transactions. To determine the current balance of specific accounts, however, the information in the journal must be copied to accounts similar to the T accounts illustrated in Chapter 3.

While the journal provides a day-by-day record of business transactions, the ledger provides a record of the transactions entered in each account.

A complete set of all the accounts used by a business is known as the **general ledger**. The general ledger provides a complete record of the transactions entered in each account. The accounts are numbered and arranged in the same order as the chart of accounts. That is, accounts are numbered and grouped by classification: assets, liabilities, owner's equity, revenues, and expenses.

Four-Column Account

For purposes of illustration, the T account was introduced in Chapter 3. In practice, businesses are more likely to use a version of the account called the **four-column account**. A four-column account contains columns for the debit or credit transaction and columns for the debit or credit running balance. In addition, there are columns for the date, description of the item, and posting reference. The "Item" column is used to provide descriptions of special entries. For example, "Balance" is written in this column when the balance of an account is transferred to a new page. The "Posting Reference" column is used to indicate the journal page from which an entry was posted, or a check mark (✓) is inserted to indicate that no posting was required. Figure 4-8 compares the cash T account from Chapter 3 for Jessie Jane's Campus Delivery and a four-column cash account summarizing the same cash transactions.

FIGURE 4-8   Comparison of T Account and Four-Column Account

Cash

(a)	2,000	(b)	1,200
(e)	500	(d)	300
(k)	570	(f)	200
(n)	430	(g)	50
	3,500	(i)	80
		(j)	200
		(l)	300
		(m)	650
		(o)	150
			3,130
Bal.	370		

GENERAL LEDGER

ACCOUNT: **CASH**   ACCOUNT NO. **111**

DATE		ITEM	POST. REF.	DEBIT	CREDIT	BALANCE DEBIT	BALANCE CREDIT
19-- June	1			2 0 0 0 00		2 0 0 0 00	
	3				1 2 0 0 00	8 0 0 00	
	6				3 0 0 00	5 0 0 00	
	6			5 0 0 00		1 0 0 0 00	
	7				2 0 0 00	8 0 0 00	
	15				5 0 00	7 5 0 00	
	16				8 0 00	6 7 0 00	
	18				2 0 0 00	4 7 0 00	
	20			5 7 0 00		1 0 4 0 00	
	25				3 0 0 00	7 4 0 00	
	27				6 5 0 00	9 0 00	
	30			4 3 0 00		5 2 0 00	
	30				1 5 0 00	3 7 0 00	

└ Transaction Amount ┘└ Running Balances ┘

The primary advantage of the four-column account over the T account is that the four-column account maintains a running balance.

As shown in Figure 4-8, the primary advantage of the T account is that the debit and credit sides of the account are easier to identify. Thus, for demonstration purposes and analyzing what happened, T accounts are very helpful. However, computing the balance of a T account is cumbersome. The primary advantage of the four-column account is that it maintains a running balance.

Note that the heading for the four-column account has the account title and an account number. The account number is taken from the chart of accounts and is used in the posting process.

Posting to the General Ledger

The process of copying the debits and credits from the journal to the ledger accounts is known as **posting**. All amounts entered in the journal must be posted to the general ledger accounts.

> Posting is simply the copying of the exact dates and dollar amounts from the journal to the ledger.

Posting from the journal to the ledger is done daily or at frequent intervals. There are five steps.

STEPS IN THE POSTING PROCESS

In the ledger account:

STEP 1 Enter the date of the transaction in the Date column. There is no need to repeat the month and year, but the day must be entered even if it is the same date as in the previous transaction.

STEP 2 Enter the amount of the debit or credit in the Debit or Credit column.

STEP 3 Enter the new balance in the Balance columns under Debit or Credit. If the balance of the account is zero, draw a line through the debit and credit columns.

STEP 4 Enter the journal page number from which each transaction is posted in the Posting Reference column.

In the journal:

STEP 5 Enter the ledger account number in the Posting Reference column of the journal for each transaction that is posted.

Step 5 is the last step in the posting process. After this step is completed, the posting references will indicate which journal entries have been posted to the ledger accounts. This is very helpful, particularly if you are interrupted during the posting process. The information in the posting reference columns of the journal and ledger provides a link between the journal and ledger known as a **cross-reference**.

> Posting references indicate that a journal entry has been posted to the general ledger.

To illustrate the posting process, the first journal entry for Jessie Jane's Campus Delivery will be posted step-by-step. First, let's post the debit to Cash (Figure 4-9).

FIGURE 4-9 Posting a Debit

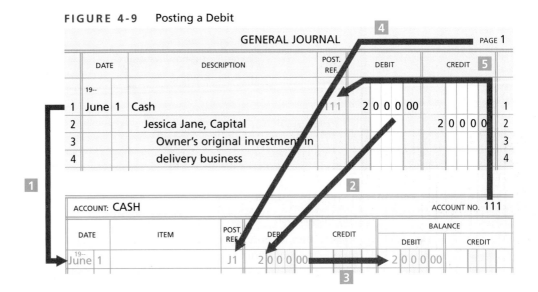

In the ledger account:

STEP 1 Enter the year, "19--," the month, "June," and the day, "1," in the Date column of the cash account.

STEP 2 Enter the amount, "$2,000," in the Debit column.

STEP 3 Enter the $2,000 balance in the Balance columns under Debit.

STEP 4 Enter "J1" in the Posting Reference column since the posting came from page 1 of the Journal.

In the journal:

STEP 5 Enter the account number for cash, 111 (see chart of accounts in Figure 4-2 on page 83), in the Posting Reference column of the journal on the same line as the debit to Cash for $2,000.

Now let's post the credit portion of the first entry (Figure 4-10).

In the ledger account:

STEP 1 Enter the year, "19 ," the month, "June," and the day, "1," in the Date column of the Jessica Jane, capital account.

STEP 2 Enter the amount, "$2,000," in the Credit column.

STEP 3 Enter the $2,000 balance in the Balance columns under Credit.

STEP 4 Enter "J1" in the Posting Reference column since the posting came from Page 1 of the Journal.

FIGURE 4-10   Posting a Credit

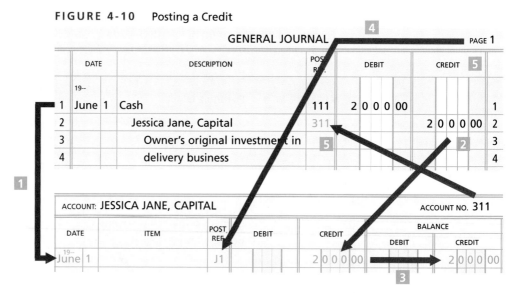

In the journal:

STEP 5   Enter the account number for Jessica Jane, Capital, 311, in the Posting Reference column.

After posting the journal entries for Jessie Jane's Campus Delivery for the month of June, the general journal and general ledger should appear as illustrated in Figures 4-11 and 4-12 on pages 94–98. *Note that the Posting Reference column of the journal has been filled in because the entries have been posted.*

FIGURE 4-11   General Journal After Posting

GENERAL JOURNAL   PAGE 1

	DATE		DESCRIPTION	POST. REF.	DEBIT	CREDIT	
1	19-- June	1	Cash	111	2 0 0 0 00		1
2			Jessica Jane, Capital	311		2 0 0 0 00	2
3			Owner's original investment in				3
4			delivery business				4
5							5
6		3	Delivery Equipment	185	1 2 0 0 00		6
7			Cash	111		1 2 0 0 00	7
8			Purchased delivery equipment				8
9			for cash				9
10							10
11		5	Delivery Equipment	185	9 0 0 00		11
12			Accounts Payable	216		9 0 0 00	12
13			Purchased delivery equipment				13
14			on account from Big Red				14
15			Scooters				15

FIGURE 4-11 General Journal After Posting (continued)

GENERAL JOURNAL PAGE 1

	DATE	DESCRIPTION	POST. REF.	DEBIT	CREDIT	
16						16
17	6	Accounts Payable	216	3 0 0 00		17
18		Cash	111		3 0 0 00	18
19		Made partial payment to Big				19
20		Red Scooters				20
21						21
22	6	Cash	111	5 0 0 00		22
23		Delivery Fees	411		5 0 0 00	23
24		Received cash for delivery				24
25		services				25
26						26
27	7	Rent Expense	541	2 0 0 00		27
28		Cash	111		2 0 0 00	28
29		Paid office rent for June				29
30						30
31	15	Telephone Expense	545	5 0 00		31
32		Cash	111		5 0 00	32
33		Paid telephone bill for June				33
34						34
35	15	Accounts Receivable	131	6 0 0 00		35
36		Delivery Fees	411		6 0 0 00	36
37		Deliveries made on account for				37
38		Accounting Department ($400)				38
39		and School of Optometry ($200)				39

GENERAL JOURNAL PAGE 2

	DATE		DESCRIPTION	POST. REF.	DEBIT	CREDIT	
	19--						
1	June	16	Supplies	151	8 0 00		1
2			Cash	111		8 0 00	2
3			Purchased supplies for cash				3
4							4
5		18	Prepaid Insurance	155	2 0 0 00		5
6			Cash	111		2 0 0 00	6
7			Paid premium for eight-month				7
8			insurance policy				8
9							9

FIGURE 4-11   General Journal After Posting (concluded)

	DATE	DESCRIPTION	POST. REF.	DEBIT	CREDIT	
10	20	Cash	111	5 7 0 00		10
11		Accounts Receivable	131		5 7 0 00	11
12		Received cash on account from				12
13		Accounting Department ($400)				13
14		and School of Optometry ($170)				14
15						15
16	25	Delivery Equipment	185	1 5 0 0 00		16
17		Accounts Payable	216		1 2 0 0 00	17
18		Cash	111		3 0 0 00	18
19		Purchased scooter with down				19
20		payment; balance on account				20
21		from Big Red Scooters				21
22						22
23	27	Wages Expense	542	6 5 0 00		23
24		Cash	111		6 5 0 00	24
25		Paid employees				25
26						26
27	30	Cash	111	4 3 0 00		27
28		Accounts Receivable	131	4 7 0 00		28
29		Delivery Fees	411		9 0 0 00	29
30		Deliveries made for cash and				30
31		on account to Accounting				31
32		Department ($100) and				32
33		Athletic Ticket Office ($370)				33
34						34
35	30	Jessica Jane, Drawing	312	1 5 0 00		35
36		Cash	111		1 5 0 00	36
37		Owner's withdrawal				37
38						38
39						39
40						40
41						41
42						42
43						43
44						44
45						45
46						46
47						47
48						48
49						49

GENERAL JOURNAL   PAGE 2

FIGURE 4-12   General Ledger After Posting

GENERAL LEDGER

ACCOUNT: **Cash**   ACCOUNT NO. **111**

DATE		ITEM	POST. REF.	DEBIT	CREDIT	BALANCE DEBIT	BALANCE CREDIT
19-- June	1		J1	2 0 0 0 00		2 0 0 0 00	
	3		J1		1 2 0 0 00	8 0 0 00	
	6		J1		3 0 0 00	5 0 0 00	
	6		J1	5 0 0 00		1 0 0 0 00	
	7		J1		2 0 0 00	8 0 0 00	
	15		J1		5 0 00	7 5 0 00	
	16		J2		8 0 00	6 7 0 00	
	18		J2		2 0 0 00	4 7 0 00	
	20		J2	5 7 0 00		1 0 4 0 00	
	25		J2		3 0 0 00	7 4 0 00	
	27		J2		6 5 0 00	9 0 00	
	30		J2	4 3 0 00		5 2 0 00	
	30		J2		1 5 0 00	3 7 0 00	

ACCOUNT: **Accounts Receivable**   ACCOUNT NO. **131**

DATE		ITEM	POST. REF.	DEBIT	CREDIT	BALANCE DEBIT	BALANCE CREDIT
19-- June	15		J1	6 0 0 00		6 0 0 00	
	20		J2		5 7 0 00	3 0 00	
	30		J2	4 7 0 00		5 0 0 00	

ACCOUNT: **Supplies**   ACCOUNT NO. **151**

DATE		ITEM	POST. REF.	DEBIT	CREDIT	BALANCE DEBIT	BALANCE CREDIT
19-- June	16		J2	8 0 00		8 0 00	

ACCOUNT: **Prepaid Insurance**   ACCOUNT NO. **155**

DATE		ITEM	POST. REF.	DEBIT	CREDIT	BALANCE DEBIT	BALANCE CREDIT
19-- June	18		J2	2 0 0 00		2 0 0 00	

ACCOUNT: **Delivery Equipment**   ACCOUNT NO. **185**

DATE		ITEM	POST. REF.	DEBIT	CREDIT	BALANCE DEBIT	BALANCE CREDIT
19-- June	3		J1	1 2 0 0 00		1 2 0 0 00	
	5		J1	9 0 0 00		2 1 0 0 00	
	25		J2	1 5 0 0 00		3 6 0 0 00	

FIGURE 4-12   General Ledger After Posting (concluded)

ACCOUNT: **Accounts Payable**   ACCOUNT NO. **216**

DATE		ITEM	POST. REF.	DEBIT	CREDIT	BALANCE	
						DEBIT	CREDIT
19-- June	5		J1		9 0 0 00		9 0 0 00
	6		J1	3 0 0 00			6 0 0 00
	25		J2		1 2 0 0 00		1 8 0 0 00

ACCOUNT: **Jessica Jane, Capital**   ACCOUNT NO. **311**

DATE		ITEM	POST. REF.	DEBIT	CREDIT	BALANCE	
						DEBIT	CREDIT
19-- June	1		J1		2 0 0 0 00		2 0 0 0 00

ACCOUNT: **Jessica Jane, Drawing**   ACCOUNT NO. **312**

DATE		ITEM	POST. REF.	DEBIT	CREDIT	BALANCE	
						DEBIT	CREDIT
19-- June	30		J2	1 5 0 00		1 5 0 00	

ACCOUNT: **Delivery Fees**   ACCOUNT NO. **411**

DATE		ITEM	POST. REF.	DEBIT	CREDIT	BALANCE	
						DEBIT	CREDIT
19-- June	6		J1		5 0 0 00		5 0 0 00
	15		J1		6 0 0 00		1 1 0 0 00
	30		J2		9 0 0 00		2 0 0 0 00

ACCOUNT: **Rent Expense**   ACCOUNT NO. **541**

DATE		ITEM	POST. REF.	DEBIT	CREDIT	BALANCE	
						DEBIT	CREDIT
19-- June	7		J1	2 0 0 00		2 0 0 00	

ACCOUNT: **Wages Expense**   ACCOUNT NO. **542**

DATE		ITEM	POST. REF.	DEBIT	CREDIT	BALANCE	
						DEBIT	CREDIT
19-- June	27		J2	6 5 0 00		6 5 0 00	

ACCOUNT: **Telephone Expense**   ACCOUNT NO. **545**

DATE		ITEM	POST. REF.	DEBIT	CREDIT	BALANCE	
						DEBIT	CREDIT
19-- June	15		J1	5 0 00		5 0 00	

The Trial Balance

In Chapter 3, a **trial balance** was used to prove that the totals of the debit and credit balances in the T accounts were equal. In this chapter, a trial balance is used to prove the equality of the debits and credits in the ledger accounts. A trial balance can be prepared daily, weekly, monthly, or whenever desired. Before preparing a trial balance, all transactions should be journalized and posted so that the effect of all transactions will be reflected in the ledger accounts.

The trial balance for Jessie Jane's Campus Delivery shown in Figure 4-13 was prepared from the balances in the general ledger in Figure 4-12. The accounts are listed in the order used in the chart of accounts. This order is also often used when preparing financial statements. In Chapter 2, we pointed out that many firms list expenses from highest to lowest amounts. Some firms list expenses according to the chart of accounts. We will follow the latter approach in the text and assignment material.

LEARNING KEY | The chart of accounts determines the order for listing accounts in the general ledger and trial balance. This order may also be used when preparing financial statements.

FIGURE 4-13   Trial Balance

Jessie Jane's Campus Delivery
Trial Balance
June 30, 19--

ACCOUNT TITLE	ACCOUNT NO.	DEBIT BALANCE	CREDIT BALANCE
Cash	111	3 7 0 00	
Accounts Receivable	131	5 0 0 00	
Supplies	151	8 0 00	
Prepaid Insurance	155	2 0 0 00	
Delivery Equipment	185	3 6 0 0 00	
Accounts Payable	216		1 8 0 0 00
Jessica Jane, Capital	311		2 0 0 0 00
Jessica Jane, Drawing	312	1 5 0 00	
Delivery Fees	411		2 0 0 0 00
Rent Expense	541	2 0 0 00	
Wages Expense	542	6 5 0 00	
Telephone Expense	545	5 0 00	
		5 8 0 0 00	5 8 0 0 00

Even though the trial balance indicates that the ledger is in balance, the ledger can still contain errors. For example, if a journal entry was made debiting or crediting the wrong accounts, or if an item was posted to the wrong account, the ledger will still be in balance. It is important, therefore, to be very careful in preparing the journal entries and in posting them to the ledger accounts.

FINDING AND CORRECTING ERRORS IN THE TRIAL BALANCE

LO6 Explain how to find and correct errors.

Tips are available to help if your trial balance has an error. Figure 4-14 offers hints for finding the error when your trial balance does not balance.

FIGURE 4-14   Tips for Finding Errors in the Trial Balance

1. Double check your addition.

2. Find the difference between the debits and the credits.
   a. If the difference is equal to the amount of a specific transaction, perhaps you forgot to post the debit or credit portion of this transaction.
   b. Divide the difference by **2**. If the difference is evenly divisible by 2, you may have posted two debits or two credits for a transaction. If a debit was posted as a credit, it would mean that one transaction had two credits and no debits. The difference between the total debits and credits would be twice the amount of the debit that was posted as a credit.
   c. Divide the difference by **9**. If the difference is evenly divisible by 9, you may have committed a **slide error** or a **transposition error**. A slide occurs when debit or credit amounts "slide" a digit or two to the left or right when entered. For example, if **$250** was entered as **$25**:

$$\$250 - 25 = \$225$$
$$\$225 \div 9 = \$25$$

The difference is evenly divisible by 9.

A transposition occurs when two digits are reversed. For example, if **$250** was entered as **$520**:

$$\$520 - 250 = \$270$$
$$\$270 \div 9 = \$30$$

Again, the difference is evenly divisible by 9.

Profiles in Accounting

JEFF CLIFTON, Account Supervisor

Jeff Clifton maintained a 4.0 GPA with nearly perfect attendance while earning an Associate Degree in Accounting Automation. He performed an externship with Brooke County Taxing Authority and then began working as an accounts receivable clerk with the DeBartolo Properties Management, Inc., in Youngstown, OH.

He was promoted and is now an account supervisor where duties include management of accounts receivable for 20 development properties across the United States, supervising five employees and interviewing prospective employees.

According to Jeff, being self motivated is the main key to success. You need to work hard and success will come. Accounting interested Jeff because he enjoys working with numbers and considers himself to be very analytical.

If the tips in Figure 4-14 don't work, you must retrace your steps through the accounting process. Double check your addition for the ledger accounts. Also trace all postings. Be patient as you search for your error. Use this process as an opportunity to reinforce your understanding of the flow of information through the accounting system. Much can be learned while looking for an error.

Once you have found an error, there are two methods of making the correction. Although you may want to erase when correcting your homework, this is not acceptable in practice. An erasure may suggest that you are trying to hide something. Instead you should use the ruling method or make a correcting entry.

Ruling Method

The **ruling method** should be used to correct two types of errors:

1. When an incorrect journal entry has been made, but not yet posted.
2. When a proper entry has been made but posted incorrectly.

When using the ruling method, draw a line through the incorrect account title or amount and write the correct information directly above the line. Corrections should be initialed so the source and reason for the correction can be traced. This type of correction may be made in the journal or ledger accounts, as shown in Figure 4-15.

FIGURE 4-15 Ruling Method of Making a Correction

GENERAL JOURNAL

PAGE 2

	DATE	DESCRIPTION	POST. REF.	DEBIT	CREDIT	
1	19-- Sept. 17	~~Wages Expense~~ *RP* ~~Entertainment Expense~~		6 5 0 00		1
2		Cash			6 5 0 00	2
3		Paid employees				3
4				*RP* 2 0 0 00 ~~2 0 00~~		4
5	18	Prepaid Insurance			*RP* 2 0 0 00	5
6		Cash			~~2 0 00~~	6
7		Paid premium for eight-month				7
8		insurance policy				8
9						9

Slide

GENERAL LEDGER

ACCOUNT: Accounts Payable ACCOUNT NO. 216

DATE	ITEM	POST. REF.	DEBIT	CREDIT	BALANCE DEBIT	BALANCE CREDIT
19-- Sept. 8		J1		7 0 0 00		9 0 0 00
15		J1	2 0 0 00			5 0 0 00
25		J2		*1 2 0 0 00* *RP* ~~2 1 0 0 00~~		*RP* *1 2 0 0 00* ~~2 6 0 0 00~~

Transposition

Correcting Entry Method

If an incorrect entry has been journalized and posted to the wrong account, a **correcting entry** should be made. For example, assume that a $400 payment for Rent Expense was incorrectly debited to Repair Expense and correctly credited to Cash. This requires a correcting entry and explanation as shown in Figure 4-16. Figure 4-17 shows the effects of the correcting entry on the ledger accounts.

FIGURE 4-16 Correcting Entry Method

GENERAL JOURNAL   PAGE 6

	DATE	DESCRIPTION	POST. REF.	DEBIT	CREDIT	
1	19-- Sept. 25	Rent Expense	541	4 0 0 00		1
2		Repair Expense	565		4 0 0 00	2
3		To correct error in which				3
4		payment for rent was debited				4
5		to Repair Expense				5

FIGURE 4-17 Effects of Correcting Entry on Ledger Accounts

GENERAL LEDGER

ACCOUNT: Rent Expense   ACCOUNT NO. 541

DATE	ITEM	POST. REF.	DEBIT	CREDIT	BALANCE DEBIT	BALANCE CREDIT
19-- Sept. 25		J6	4 0 0 00		4 0 0 00	

ACCOUNT: Repair Expense   ACCOUNT NO. 565

DATE	ITEM	POST. REF.	DEBIT	CREDIT	BALANCE DEBIT	BALANCE CREDIT
19-- Sept. 10		J5	5 0 00		5 0 00	
15		J5	4 0 0 00		4 5 0 00	
25		J6		4 0 0 00	5 0 00	

KEY POINTS

1 The flow of data from the source documents through the trial balance is:

1. Analyze business transactions.
2. Journalize transactions in the general journal.
3. Post journal entries to the general ledger.
4. Prepare a trial balance.

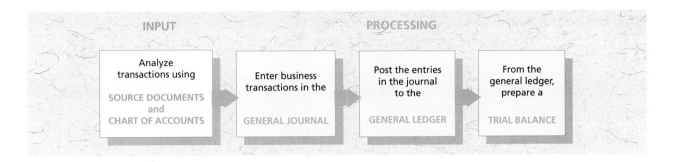

2   The chart of accounts includes the account titles in numeric order for all assets, liabilities, owner's equity, revenues, and expenses. The chart of accounts is used in classifying information about transactions.

3   Source documents trigger the analysis of business transactions and the entries into the accounting system.

4   A journal provides a day-by-day listing of transactions. The journal shows the date, titles of the accounts to be debited or credited, and the amounts of the debits and credits. The steps in the journalizing process are:

1. Enter the date.
2. Enter the debit. Accounts to be debited are entered first.
3. Enter the credit. Accounts to be credited are entered after the debits and are indented one-half inch.
4. Enter the explanation. A brief explanation of the transaction should be entered in the description column on the line following the last credit. The explanation should be indented an additional one-half inch.

5   The general ledger is a complete set of all accounts used by the business. The steps in posting from the general journal to the general ledger are:

In the general ledger:
1. Enter the date of each transaction.
2. Enter the amount of each debit or credit in the Debit or Credit column.
3. Enter the new balance.
4. Enter the journal page number from which each transaction is posted in the Posting Reference column.

In the journal:
5. Enter the account number in the Posting Reference column for each transaction that is posted.

6   When an error is discovered, use the ruling method or the correcting entry method to correct the error.

KEY TERMS

book of original entry 84 The journal or the first formal accounting record of a transaction.

chart of accounts 82 A list of all accounts used by a business.

compound entry 88 A general journal entry that affects more than two accounts.

correcting entry 102 An entry to correct an incorrect entry that has been journalized and posted to the wrong account.

cross-reference 92 The information in the Posting Reference columns of the journal and ledger that provides a link between the journal and ledger.

four-column account 91 An account with columns for the debit or credit transaction and columns for the debit or credit running balance.

general ledger 91 A complete set of all the accounts used by a business.

journal 84 A day-by-day listing of the transactions of a business.

journalizing 85 Entering the transactions in a journal.

posting 92 Copying the debits and credits from the journal to the ledger accounts.

ruling method 101 A method of correcting an entry in which a line is drawn through the error and the correct information is placed above it.

slide error 100 An error that occurs when debit or credit amounts "slide" a digit or two to the left or right.

source document 83 Any document that provides information about a business transaction.

transposition error 100 Occurs when two digits are reversed.

trial balance 99 A list used to prove that the totals of the debit and credit balances in the ledger accounts are equal.

two-column general journal 85 A journal with only two amount columns, one for debit amounts and one for credit amounts.

REVIEW QUESTIONS

1. Trace the flow of accounting information through the accounting system.
2. Explain the purpose of a chart of accounts.
3. Name the five types of financial statement classifications for which it is ordinarily desirable to keep separate accounts.
4. Name a source document that provides information about each of the following types of business transactions:
   a. Cash payment
   b. Cash receipt
   c. Sale of goods or services
   d. Purchase of goods or services
5. Where is the first formal accounting record of a business transaction usually made?
6. Describe the four steps required to journalize a business transaction in a general journal.
7. In what order are the accounts customarily placed in the ledger?
8. Explain the primary advantage of a four-column ledger account.

9. Explain the five steps required when posting the journal to the ledger.
10. What information is entered in the Posting Reference column of the journal as an amount is posted to the proper account in the ledger?
11. Explain why the ledger can still contain errors even though the trial balance is in balance. Give examples of two such types of errors.
12. What is a slide error?
13. What is a transposition error?
14. What is the ruling method of correcting an error?
15. What is the correcting entry method?

MANAGING YOUR WRITING

You are a public accountant with many small business clients. During a recent visit to a client's business, the bookkeeper approached you with a problem. The columns of the trial balance were not equal. You helped the bookkeeper find and correct the error, but believe you should go one step further. Write a memo to all of your clients that explains the purpose of the double-entry framework, the importance of maintaining the equality of the accounting equation, the errors that might cause an inequality, and suggestions for finding the errors.

DEMONSTRATION PROBLEM

George Fielding is a financial planning consultant. He provides budgeting, estate planning, tax planning, and investing advice for professional golfers. He developed the following chart of accounts for his business.

Assets
111   Cash
152   Office Supplies

Revenues
411   Professional Fees

Liabilities
216   Accounts Payable

Owner's Equity
311   George Fielding, Capital
312   George Fielding, Drawing

Expenses
541   Rent Expense
542   Wages Expense
545   Telephone Expense
546   Automobile Expense
555   Utilities Expense
557   Charitable Contributions Expense

The following transactions took place during the month of December of the current year.

Dec.   1   Fielding invested cash to start the business, $20,000.
       3   Paid Bollhorst Real Estate for December office rent, $1,000.
       4   Received cash from Aaron Patton, a client, for services, $2,500.

Dec. 6 Paid T. Z. Anderson Electric for December heating and light, $75.
7 Received cash from Andrew Conder, a client, for services, $2,000.
12 Paid Fichter's Super Service for gasoline and oil purchases, $60.
14 Paid Hillenburg Staffing for temporary secretarial services during the past two weeks, $600.
17 Bought office supplies from Bowers Office Supply on account, $280.
20 Paid Mitchell Telephone Co. for business calls during the past month, $100.
21 Fielding withdrew cash for personal use, $1,100.
24 Made donation to the National Multiple Sclerosis Society, $100.
27 Received cash from Billy Walters, a client, for services, $2,000.
28 Paid Hillenburg Staffing for temporary secretarial services during the past two weeks, $600.
29 Made payment on account to Bowers Office Supply, $100.

REQUIRED

1. Record the preceding transactions in a general journal.
2. Post the entries to the general ledger.
3. Prepare a trial balance.

SOLUTION

1.

GENERAL JOURNAL PAGE 1

DATE		DESCRIPTION	POST. REF.	DEBIT	CREDIT
19-- Dec.	1	Cash	111	20 000 00	
		George Fielding, Capital	311		20 000 00
		Owner's original investment in			
		consulting business			
	3	Rent Expense	541	1 000 00	
		Cash	111		1 000 00
		Paid rent for December			
	4	Cash	111	2 500 00	
		Professional Fees	411		2 500 00
		Received cash for services			
		rendered			

1. continued

	GENERAL JOURNAL					PAGE 1

	DATE	DESCRIPTION	POST. REF.	DEBIT	CREDIT	
15	6	Utilities Expense	555	7 5 00		15
16		Cash	111		7 5 00	16
17		Paid utilities				17
18						18
19	7	Cash	111	2 0 0 0 00		19
20		Professional Fees	411		2 0 0 0 00	20
21		Received cash for services				21
22		rendered				22
23						23
24	12	Automobile Expense	546	6 0 00		24
25		Cash	111		6 0 00	25
26		Paid for gas and oil				26
27						27
28	14	Wages Expense	542	6 0 0 00		28
29		Cash	111		6 0 0 00	29
30		Paid temporary secretaries				30
31						31
32	17	Office Supplies	152	2 8 0 00		32
33		Accounts Payable	216		2 8 0 00	33
34		Purchased office supplies on				34
35		account from Bowers Office				35
36		Supply				36

	GENERAL JOURNAL					PAGE 2

	DATE	DESCRIPTION	POST. REF.	DEBIT	CREDIT	
1	Dec. 20	Telephone Expense	545	1 0 0 00		1
2		Cash	111		1 0 0 00	2
3		Paid telephone bill				3
4						4
5	21	George Fielding, Drawing	312	1 1 0 0 00		5
6		Cash	111		1 1 0 0 00	6
7		Owner's withdrawal				7
8						8

1. continued

GENERAL JOURNAL   PAGE **2**

	DATE	DESCRIPTION	POST. REF.	DEBIT	CREDIT	
9	24	Charitable Contributions Expense	557	1 0 0 00		9
10		Cash	111		1 0 0 00	10
11		Contribution to National				11
12		Multiple Sclerosis Society				12
13						13
14	27	Cash	111	2 0 0 0 00		14
15		Professional Fees	411		2 0 0 0 00	15
16		Received cash for services				16
17		rendered				17
18						18
19	28	Wages Expense	542	6 0 0 00		19
20		Cash	111		6 0 0 00	20
21		Paid temporary secretaries				21
22						22
23	29	Accounts Payable	216	1 0 0 00		23
24		Cash	111		1 0 0 00	24
25		Payment on account to Bowers				25
26		Office Supply				26

2.

GENERAL LEDGER

ACCOUNT: Cash   ACCOUNT NO. **111**

DATE		ITEM	POST. REF.	DEBIT	CREDIT	BALANCE	
						DEBIT	CREDIT
19-- Dec.	1		J1	20 0 0 0 00		20 0 0 0 00	
	3		J1		1 0 0 0 00	19 0 0 0 00	
	4		J1	2 5 0 0 00		21 5 0 0 00	
	6		J1		7 5 00	21 4 2 5 00	
	7		J1	2 0 0 0 00		23 4 2 5 00	
	12		J1		6 0 00	23 3 6 5 00	
	14		J1		6 0 0 00	22 7 6 5 00	
	20		J2		1 0 0 00	22 6 6 5 00	
	21		J2		1 1 0 0 00	21 5 6 5 00	
	24		J2		1 0 0 00	21 4 6 5 00	
	27		J2	2 0 0 0 00		23 4 6 5 00	
	28		J2		6 0 0 00	22 8 6 5 00	
	29		J2		1 0 0 00	22 7 6 5 00	

ACCOUNT: Office Supplies   ACCOUNT NO. 152

DATE	ITEM	POST. REF.	DEBIT	CREDIT	BALANCE DEBIT	BALANCE CREDIT
19-- Dec. 17		J1	2 8 0 00		2 8 0 00	

ACCOUNT: Accounts Payable   ACCOUNT NO. 216

DATE	ITEM	POST. REF.	DEBIT	CREDIT	BALANCE DEBIT	BALANCE CREDIT
19-- Dec. 17		J1		2 8 0 00		2 8 0 00
29		J2	1 0 0 00			1 8 0 00

ACCOUNT: George Fielding, Capital   ACCOUNT NO. 311

DATE	ITEM	POST. REF.	DEBIT	CREDIT	BALANCE DEBIT	BALANCE CREDIT
19-- Dec. 1		J1		20 0 0 0 00		20 0 0 0 00

ACCOUNT: George Fielding, Drawing   ACCOUNT NO. 312

DATE	ITEM	POST. REF.	DEBIT	CREDIT	BALANCE DEBIT	BALANCE CREDIT
19-- Dec. 21		J2	1 1 0 0 00		1 1 0 0 00	

ACCOUNT: Professional Fees   ACCOUNT NO. 411

DATE	ITEM	POST. REF.	DEBIT	CREDIT	BALANCE DEBIT	BALANCE CREDIT
19-- Dec. 4		J1		2 5 0 0 00		2 5 0 0 00
7		J1		2 0 0 0 00		4 5 0 0 00
27		J2		2 0 0 0 00		6 5 0 0 00

ACCOUNT: Rent Expense   ACCOUNT NO. 541

DATE	ITEM	POST. REF.	DEBIT	CREDIT	BALANCE DEBIT	BALANCE CREDIT
19-- Dec. 3		J1	1 0 0 0 00		1 0 0 0 00	

ACCOUNT: Wages Expense   ACCOUNT NO. 542

DATE	ITEM	POST. REF.	DEBIT	CREDIT	BALANCE DEBIT	BALANCE CREDIT
19-- Dec. 14		J1	6 0 0 00		6 0 0 00	
28		J2	6 0 0 00		1 2 0 0 00	

ACCOUNT: Telephone Expense   ACCOUNT NO. 545

DATE	ITEM	POST. REF.	DEBIT	CREDIT	BALANCE DEBIT	BALANCE CREDIT
19-- Dec. 20		J2	1 0 0 00		1 0 0 00	

ACCOUNT: Automobile Expense						ACCOUNT NO. 546	
DATE	ITEM	POST. REF.	DEBIT	CREDIT	BALANCE		
					DEBIT	CREDIT	
19-- Dec. 12		J1	6 0 00		6 0 00		

ACCOUNT: Utilities Expense						ACCOUNT NO. 555	
DATE	ITEM	POST. REF.	DEBIT	CREDIT	BALANCE		
					DEBIT	CREDIT	
19-- Dec. 6		J1	7 5 00		7 5 00		

ACCOUNT: Charitable Contributions Expense						ACCOUNT NO. 557	
DATE	ITEM	POST. REF.	DEBIT	CREDIT	BALANCE		
					DEBIT	CREDIT	
19-- Dec. 24		J2	1 0 0 00		1 0 0 00		

3.

George Fielding, Financial Planning Consultant
Trial Balance
December 31, 19--

ACCOUNT TITLE	ACCOUNT NO.	DEBIT BALANCE	CREDIT BALANCE
Cash	111	22 7 6 5 00	
Office Supplies	152	2 8 0 00	
Accounts Payable	216		1 8 0 00
George Fielding, Capital	311		20 0 0 0 00
George Fielding, Drawing	312	1 1 0 0 00	
Professional Fees	411		6 5 0 0 00
Rent Expense	541	1 0 0 0 00	
Wages Expense	542	1 2 0 0 00	
Telephone Expense	545	1 0 0 00	
Automobile Expense	546	6 0 00	
Utilities Expense	555	7 5 00	
Charitable Contributions Expense	557	1 0 0 00	
		26 6 8 0 00	26 6 8 0 00

SERIES A   EXERCISES

3 **EXERCISE 4A1 SOURCE DOCUMENTS**   Source documents trigger the analysis of events requiring an accounting entry. Match the following source documents with the type of information they provide.

1. Check stubs or check register

2. Purchase invoice from suppliers (vendors)

3. Sales tickets or invoices to customers

4. Receipts or cash register tapes

a. A good or service has been sold.

b. Cash has been received by the business.

c. Cash has been paid by the business.

d. Goods or services have been purchased by the business.

4 **EXERCISE 4A2 GENERAL JOURNAL ENTRIES** For each of the following transactions, list the account to be debited and the account to be credited in the general journal.

1. Invested cash in the business, $5,000
2. Paid office rent, $500.
3. Purchased office supplies on account, $300.
4. Received cash for services rendered (fees), $400.
5. Paid cash on account, $50.
6. Rendered services on account, $300.
7. Received cash for an amount owed by a customer, $100.

5 **EXERCISE 4A3 GENERAL LEDGER ACCOUNTS** Set up T accounts for each of the general ledger accounts needed for Exercise 4A2 and post debits and credits to the accounts.

4 **EXERCISE 4A4 GENERAL JOURNAL ENTRIES** Jean Jones has opened Jones Consulting. Journalize the following transactions that occurred during January of the current year. Use the following journal pages: January 1–10, page 1 and January 11–29, page 2. Use the chart of accounts provided below.

Chart of Accounts

Assets		Revenues	
111	Cash	411	Consulting Fees
121	Office Supplies		
131	Office Equipment	Expenses	
		511	Rent Expense
Liabilities		521	Wages Expense
211	Accounts Payable	531	Telephone Expense
		541	Utilities Expense
Owner's Equity		551	Miscellaneous Expense
311	Jean Jones, Capital		
312	Jean Jones, Drawing		

Jan. 1 Invested cash in the business, $10,000.
      2 Paid office rent, $500.
      3 Purchased office equipment on account, $1,500.
      5 Received cash for services rendered, $750.
      8 Paid telephone bill, $65.
     10 Paid for a magazine subscription, $15 (miscellaneous expense).
     11 Purchased office supplies on account, $300.
     15 Made a payment on account, $150 (see Jan. 3 transaction).
     18 Paid part-time employee, $500.
     21 Received cash for services rendered, $350.
     25 Paid utilities bill, $85.
     27 Withdrew cash for personal use, $100.
     29 Paid part-time employee, $500.

5 **EXERCISE 4A5 GENERAL LEDGER ACCOUNTS; TRIAL BALANCE**   Set up four-column general ledger accounts using the chart of accounts provided in Exercise 4A4. Post the transactions from Exercise 4A4 to the general ledger accounts and prepare a trial balance.

EXERCISE 4A6 FINANCIAL STATEMENTS   From the information in Exercises 4A4 and 4A5, prepare an income statement, a statement of owner's equity, and a balance sheet.

EXERCISE 4A7 FINANCIAL STATEMENTS   From the following trial balance taken after one month of operation, prepare an income statement, a statement of owner's equity, and a balance sheet. Assume that TJ Ulza made no additional investments in the business during the month.

TJ's Paint Service
Trial Balance
July 31, 19--

ACCOUNT TITLE	ACCOUNT NO.	DEBIT BALANCE	CREDIT BALANCE
Cash	101	4 3 0 0 00	
Accounts Receivable	111	1 1 0 0 00	
Supplies	121	8 0 0 00	
Paint Equipment	131	9 0 0 00	
Accounts Payable	201		2 1 5 0 00
TJ Ulza, Capital	311		3 2 0 5 00
TJ Ulza, Drawing	312	5 0 0 00	
Painting Fees	411		3 6 0 0 00
Rent Expense	511	2 5 0 00	
Telephone Expense	521	5 0 00	
Utilities Expense	531	7 0 00	
Transportation Expense	541	6 0 00	
Wages Expense	551	9 0 0 00	
Miscellaneous Expense	561	2 5 00	
		8 9 5 5 00	8 9 5 5 00

6 **EXERCISE 4A8 FINDING AND CORRECTING ERRORS**   Joe Adams bought $500 worth of office supplies on account. The following entry was recorded on May 17. Find the error(s) and correct it (them) using the ruling method.

14						14
15	19-- May	17	Office Equipment	4 0 0 00		15
16			Cash		4 0 0 00	16
17			Purchased copy paper			17

On May 25, after the transactions had been posted, Adams discovered that the following entry contains an error. The cash received represents a collection on account, rather than new service fees. Correct the error in the general journal using the correcting entry method.

22								22
23	19— May	23	Cash	111	1 0 0 0 00			23
24			Service Fees	411		1 0 0 0 00		24
25			Received cash for services					25
26			previously earned					26

SERIES A PROBLEMS

4/5 **PROBLEM 4A1 JOURNALIZING AND POSTING TRANSACTIONS**
Jim Andrews opened a delivery business in March. He rented a small office and has a part-time assistant. His trial balance (shown on the next page) shows accounts for the first three months of business. Andrews' transactions for the month of June are as follows:

June   1 Paid rent, $300.
2 Performed delivery service: $100 in cash and $200 on account.
4 Paid for newspaper advertising, $15.
6 Purchased office supplies on account, $180.
7 Received cash for delivery services rendered, $260.
9 Paid cash on account (truck payment), $200.
10 Purchased a copier (office equipment): paid $100 in cash and put $600 on account.
11 Made a contribution to the Red Cross (charitable contributions), $20.
12 Received cash for delivery services rendered, $380.
13 Received cash on account for services previously rendered, $100.
15 Paid a part-time worker, $200.
16 Paid electric bill, $36.
18 Paid telephone bill, $46.
19 Received cash on account for services previously rendered, $100.
20 Andrews withdrew cash for personal use, $200.
21 Paid for gas and oil, $32.
22 Made payment on account (for office supplies), $40.
24 Received cash for services rendered, $340.
26 Paid for a magazine subscription (miscellaneous expense), $15.
27 Received cash for services rendered, $180.
27 Received cash on account for services previously rendered, $100.
29 Paid for gasoline, $24.
30 Paid a part-time worker, $200.

REQUIRED

1. Journalize the transactions for June in a two-column general journal. Use the following journal pages: June 1–10: page 7; June 11–20: page 8; June 21–30: page 9.

Jim's Quick Delivery
Trial Balance
May 31, 19--

ACCOUNT TITLE	ACCOUNT NO.	DEBIT BALANCE		CREDIT BALANCE	
Cash	101	3 8 2 6	00		
Accounts Receivable	111	1 2 1 2	00		
Office Supplies	121	6 4 8	00		
Office Equipment	131	2 1 0 0	00		
Delivery Truck	151	8 0 0 0	00		
Accounts Payable	211			6 0 0 0	00
Jim Andrews, Capital	311			4 4 7 8	00
Jim Andrews, Drawing	312	1 8 0 0	00		
Delivery Fees	411			9 8 8 0	00
Rent Expense	511	9 0 0	00		
Wages Expense	523	1 2 0 0	00		
Telephone Expense	542	1 2 6	00		
Electricity Expense	546	9 8	00		
Gas and Oil Expense	551	1 8 6	00		
Advertising Expense	562	9 0	00		
Charitable Contributions Expense	571	6 0	00		
Miscellaneous Expense	592	1 1 2	00		
		20 3 5 8	00	20 3 5 8	00

2. Set up four-column general ledger accounts, entering the balances as of June 1. Post the entries from the general journal.

3. Prepare a trial balance.

4/5 **PROBLEM 4A2 JOURNALIZING AND POSTING TRANSACTIONS**
Annette Creighton opened Creighton Consulting. She rented a small office space and paid a part-time worker to answer the telephone and make deliveries. Her chart of accounts is as follows:

Chart of Accounts

Assets
101   Cash
111   Office Supplies
121   Office Equipment

Liabilities
211   Accounts Payable

Owner's Equity
311   Annette Creighton, Capital
312   Annette Creighton, Drawing

Revenues
411   Consulting Fees

Expenses
511   Rent Expense
522   Wages Expense
524   Telephone Expense
531   Utilities Expense
533   Transportation Expense
542   Advertising Expense
568   Miscellaneous Expense

Creighton's transactions for the first month of business are as follows:

Jan. 1 Creighton invested cash in the business, $10,000.
      1 Paid rent, $500.
      2 Purchased office supplies on account, $300.
      4 Purchased office equipment on account, $1,500.
      6 Received cash for services rendered, $580.
      7 Paid telephone bill, $42.
      8 Paid utilities bill, $38.
     10 Received cash for services rendered, $360.
     12 Made payment on account, $50.
     13 Paid for car rental while visiting an out-of-town client (transportation expense), $150.
     15 Paid part-time worker, $360.
     17 Received cash for services rendered, $420.
     18 Withdrew cash for personal use, $100.
     20 Paid for a newspaper ad, $26.
     22 Reimbursed part-time employee for cab fare incurred delivering materials to clients (transportation expense), $35.
     24 Paid for books on consulting practices (miscellaneous expense), $28.
     25 Received cash for services rendered, $320.
     27 Made payment on account for office equipment purchased, $150.
     29 Paid part-time worker, $360.
     30 Received cash for services rendered, $180.

REQUIRED
1. Journalize the transactions for January in a two-column general journal. Use the following journal page numbers: Jan 1–10, page 1; Jan 12–24, page 2; Jan 25–30, page 3.
2. Set up four-column general ledger accounts from the chart of accounts and post the transactions from the general journal.
3. Prepare a trial balance.
4. Prepare an income statement and a statement of owner's equity for the month of January, and a balance sheet as of January 31, 19--.

6 **PROBLEM 4A3 CORRECTING ERRORS**   Assuming that all entries have been posted, prepare correcting entries for each of the following errors:

1. The following entry was made to record the purchase of $500 in supplies on account:

Supplies	500	
Cash		500

2. The following entry was made to record the payment of $300 in wages:

Rent Expense	300	
Cash		300

3. The following entry was made to record a $200 payment to a supplier on account:

Supplies	100	
Cash		100

3   **EXERCISE 4B1 SOURCE DOCUMENTS**   What type of information is found on each of the following source documents?

1. Cash register tape
2. Sales ticket (issued to customer)
3. Purchase invoice (received from supplier or vendor)
4. Check stub

4   **EXERCISE 4B2 GENERAL JOURNAL ENTRIES**   For each of the following transactions, list the account to be debited and the account to be credited in the general journal.

1. Invested cash in the business, $1,000.
2. Performed services on account, $200.
3. Purchased office equipment on account, $500.
4. Received cash on account for services previously rendered, $200.
5. Made a payment on account, $100.

5   **EXERCISE 4B3 GENERAL LEDGER ACCOUNTS**   Set up T accounts for each general ledger account needed for Exercise 4B2 and post debits and credits to the accounts. Foot the accounts and enter the balances. Prove that total debits equal total credits.

4   **EXERCISE 4B4 GENERAL JOURNAL ENTRIES**   Sengel Moon opened The Bike Doctor. Journalize the following transactions that occurred during the month of October of the current year. Use the following journal pages: October 1–12, page 1 and October 14–29, page 2. Use the chart of accounts provided below.

Chart of Accounts

Assets	Revenues
111 Cash	411 Repair Fees
121 Office Supplies	
131 Bicycle Parts	Expenses
	511 Rent Expense
Liabilities	521 Wages Expense
211 Accounts Payable	531 Telephone Expense
	541 Utilities Expense
Owner's Equity	551 Miscellaneous Expense
311 Sengel Moon, Capital	
312 Sengel Moon, Drawing	

Oct.   1   Moon invested cash in the business, $15,000.
       2   Paid shop rental for the month, $300.
       3   Purchased bicycle parts on account, $2,000.
       5   Purchased office supplies on account, $250.
       8   Paid telephone bill, $38.
       9   Received cash for services, $140.

continued

Oct. 11 Paid a sports magazine subscription (miscellaneous expense), $15.
　　 12 Made payment on account (see Oct. 3 transaction), $100.
　　 14 Paid part-time employee, $300.
　　 15 Received cash for services, $350.
　　 16 Paid utilities bill, $48.
　　 19 Received cash for services, $250.
　　 23 Moon withdrew cash for personal use, $50.
　　 25 Made payment on account (see Oct. 5 transaction), $50.
　　 29 Paid part-time employee, $300.

5 **EXERCISE 4B5 GENERAL LEDGER ACCOUNTS; TRIAL BALANCE**
Set up four-column general ledger accounts. Post the transactions from
Exercise 4B4 to the general ledger accounts and prepare a trial balance.

EXERCISE 4B6 FINANCIAL STATEMENTS　From the information in
Exercises 4B4 and 4B5, prepare an income statement, a statement of
owner's equity, and a balance sheet.

EXERCISE 4B7 FINANCIAL STATEMENTS　From the following trial
balance taken after one month of operation, prepare an income statement, a
statement of owner's equity, and a balance sheet. Assume that no additional
investments were made during the month.

AT's Speaker's Bureau
Trial Balance
March 31, 19--

ACCOUNT TITLE	ACCOUNT NO.	DEBIT BALANCE	CREDIT BALANCE
Cash	101	6 6 0 0 00	
Accounts Receivable	111	2 8 0 0 00	
Office Supplies	121	1 0 0 0 00	
Office Equipment	131	1 5 0 0 00	
Accounts Payable	211		3 0 0 0 00
AT Speaker, Capital	311		6 0 9 8 00
AT Speaker, Drawing	312	8 0 0 00	
Speaking Fees	411		4 8 0 0 00
Rent Expense	511	2 0 0 00	
Telephone Expense	521	3 5 00	
Wages Expense	531	4 0 0 00	
Utilities Expense	541	8 8 00	
Travel Expense	551	4 5 0 00	
Miscellaneous Expense	561	2 5 00	
		13 8 9 8 00	13 8 9 8 00

6 **EXERCISE 4B8 FINDING AND CORRECTING ERRORS**　Mary Smith
purchased $350 worth of office equipment on account. The following entry

was recorded on April 6. Find the error(s) and correct it (them) using the ruling method.

	19--											
9	Apr.	6	Office Supplies			5 3 0	00					9
10			Cash						5 3 0	00		10
11			Purchased office equipment									11

On April 25, after the transactions had been posted, Smith discovered the following entry contains an error. When her customer received services, Cash was debited, but no cash was received. Correct the error in the journal using the correcting entry method.

	19--											
28	Apr.	21	Cash	111		3 0 0	00					28
29			Service Fees	411					3 0 0	00		29
30			Revenue earned from services									30

SERIES B PROBLEMS

4/5 **PROBLEM 4B1 JOURNALIZING AND POSTING TRANSACTIONS**
Ann Tailor owns a suit tailoring shop. She opened business in September. She rented a small work space and has an assistant to receive job orders and process claim tickets. Her trial balance shows her account balances for the first two months of business.

Tailor Tailoring
Trial Balance
October 31, 19--

ACCOUNT TITLE	ACCOUNT NO.	DEBIT BALANCE	CREDIT BALANCE
Cash	101	6 2 1 1 00	
Accounts Receivable	111	4 8 4 00	
Tailoring Supplies	121	1 0 0 0 00	
Tailoring Equipment	131	3 8 0 0 00	
Accounts Payable	211		4 1 2 5 00
Ann Tailor, Capital	311		6 1 3 0 00
Ann Tailor, Drawing	312	8 0 0 00	
Tailoring Fees	411		3 6 0 0 00
Rent Expense	511	6 0 0 00	
Wages Expense	522	8 0 0 00	
Telephone Expense	533	6 0 00	
Electricity Expense	555	4 4 00	
Advertising Expense	566	3 4 00	
Miscellaneous Expense	588	2 2 00	
		13 8 5 5 00	13 8 5 5 00

Tailor's transactions for November are as follows:

Nov.   1 Paid rent, $300.
       2 Purchased tailoring supplies on account, $150.
       3 Purchased a new button hole machine on account, $300.
       5 Earned first week's revenue: $100 in cash and $300 on account.
       8 Paid for newspaper advertising, $13.
       9 Paid telephone bill, $28.
      10 Paid electric bill, $21.
      11 Received cash on account from customers, $200.
      12 Earned second week's revenue: $200 in cash and $250 on account.
      15 Paid assistant, $400.
      16 Made payment on account, $100.
      17 Paid for magazine subscription (miscellaneous expense), $12.
      19 Earned third week's revenue: $300 in cash, $150 on account.
      23 Received cash on account from customers, $300.
      24 Paid for newspaper advertising, $13.
      26 Paid for postage (miscellaneous expense), $12.
      27 Earned fourth week's revenue: $200 in cash and $400 on account.
      30 Received cash on account from customers, $400.

REQUIRED

1. Journalize the transactions for November in a two-column general journal. Use the following journal page numbers: Nov. 1–11, page 7; Nov. 12–24, page 8; Nov. 26–30, page 9.
2. Set up four-column general ledger accounts, entering the balances as of November 1, 19--. Post the entries from the general journal.
3. Prepare a trial balance.

4/5   **PROBLEM 4B2 JOURNALIZING AND POSTING TRANSACTIONS**
Benito Mendez opened Mendez Appraisals. He rented office space and has a part-time secretary to answer the telephone and make appraisal appointments. His chart of accounts is as follows:

Assets
111   Cash
122   Accounts Receivable
133   Office Supplies
146   Office Equipment

Liabilities
211   Accounts Payable

Owner's Equity
311   Benito Mendez, Capital
312   Benito Mendez, Drawing

Revenues
411   Appraisal Fees

Expenses
512   Rent Expense
532   Advertising Expense
544   Telephone Expense
555   Electricity Expense
562   Wages Expense
577   Transportation Expense
592   Miscellaneous Expense

Mendez's transactions for the first month of business are as follows:

May   1 Invested cash in the business, $5,000.
      2 Paid rent, $500.

continued

May   3 Purchased office supplies, $100.
       4 Purchased office equipment on account, $2,000.
       5 Received cash for services rendered, $280.
       8 Paid telephone bill, $38.
       9 Paid electric bill, $42.
      10 Received cash for services rendered, $310.
      13 Paid part-time employee, $500.
      14 Paid car rental for out-of-town trip, $200.
      15 Paid for newspaper ad, $30.
      18 Received cash for services rendered, $620.
      19 Paid mileage reimbursement for part-time employee's use of personal car for business deliveries (transportation expense), $22.
      21 Withdrew cash for personal use, $50.
      23 Made payment on account for office equipment purchased earlier, $200.
      24 Earned appraisal fee, which will be paid in a week, $500.
      26 Paid for newspaper ad, $30.
      27 Paid for local softball team sponsorship (miscellaneous expense), $15.
      28 Paid part-time employee, $500.
      29 Received cash on account, $250.
      30 Received cash for services rendered, $280.
      31 Paid cab fare (transportation expense), $13.

REQUIRED

1. Journalize the transactions for May in a two-column general journal. Use the following journal page numbers: May 1–10, page 1; May 13–24, page 2; May 26–31, page 3.

2. Set up four-column general ledger accounts from the chart of accounts and post the transactions from the general journal.

3. Prepare a trial balance.

4. Prepare an income statement and a statement of owner's equity for the month of May, and a balance sheet as of May 31, 19--.

6 **PROBLEM 4B3 CORRECTING ERRORS**   Assuming that all entries have been posted, prepare correcting entries for each of the following errors:

1. The following entry was made to record the purchase of $400 in equipment on account:

Supplies	400	
Cash		400

2. The following entry was made to record the payment of $200 for advertising:

Repair Expense	200	
Cash		200

3. The following entry was made to record a $600 payment to a supplier on account:

Prepaid Insurance	400	
Cash		400

MASTERY PROBLEM

Barry Bird opened the Barry Bird Basketball Camp for children ages 10 through 18. Campers typically register for one week in June or July, arriving on Sunday and returning home the following Saturday. College players serve as cabin counselors and assist the local college and high school coaches who run the practice sessions. The registration fee includes a room, meals at a nearby restaurant, and basketball instruction. In the off-season, the facilities are used for weekend retreats and coaching clinics. Bird developed the following chart of accounts for his service business.

Assets
111   Cash
152   Office Supplies
182   Athletic Equipment
183   Basketball Facilities

Liabilities
216   Accounts Payable

Owner's Equity
311   Barry Bird, Capital
312   Barry Bird, Drawing

Revenues
411   Registration Fees

Expenses
532   Advertising Expense
542   Wages Expense
544   Food Expense
545   Telephone Expense
555   Utilities Expense
564   Postage Expense

The following transactions took place during the month of June.

June   1 Bird invested cash in business, $10,000.
       1 Purchased basketballs and other athletic equipment, $3,000.
       2 Paid Hite Advertising for fliers that had been mailed to prospective campers, $5,000.
       2 Collected registration fees, $15,000.
       2 Rogers Construction completed work on a new basketball court that cost $12,000. Arrangements were made to pay the bill in July.
       5 Purchased Office Supplies on account from Gordon Office Supplies, $300.
       6 Received bill from Magic's Restaurant for meals served to campers on account, $5,800.
       7 Collected registration fees, $16,200.
     10 Paid wages to camp counselors, $500.
     14 Collected registration fees, $13,500.
     14 Received bill from Magic's Restaurant for meals served to campers on account, $6,200.
     17 Paid wages to camp counselors, $500.
     18 Paid postage, $85.
     21 Collected registration fees, $15,200.
     22 Received bill from Magic's Restaurant for meals served to campers on account, $6,500.
     24 Paid wages to camp counselors, $500.
     28 Collected registration fees, $14,000.

continued

June 30 Received bill from Magic's Restaurant for meals served to campers on account, $7,200.

30 Paid wages to camp counselors, $500.

30 Paid Magic's Restaurant on account, $25,700.

30 Paid utility bill, $500.

30 Paid telephone bill, $120.

30 Barry Bird withdrew cash for personal use, $2,000.

REQUIRED

1. Enter the above transactions in a general journal. Use the following journal pages: June 1–6, page 1; June 7–22, page 2; June 24–30, page 3.

2. Post the entries to the general ledger.

3. Prepare a trial balance.

5

Adjusting Entries and the Work Sheet

Careful study of this chapter should enable you to:

LO1 Prepare end-of-period adjustments.

LO2 Prepare a work sheet.

LO3 Describe methods for finding errors on the work sheet.

LO4 Journalize adjusting entries.

LO5 Post adjusting entries to the general ledger.

After reviewing the trial balance, Betsy Ray, Quick Dunk's controller commented, "These accounts don't look right. Let's make a few adjustments before we issue the financial statements." Does it seem appropriate to make adjustments prior to issuing financial statements?

Up to this point, you have learned how to journalize business transactions, post to the ledger, and prepare a trial balance. Now, it is time to learn how to make end-of-period adjustments to the accounts listed in the trial balance. This chapter explains the need for adjustments and illustrates how they are made using a work sheet.

END-OF-PERIOD ADJUSTMENTS

LO1 Prepare end-of-period adjustments.

Throughout the accounting period, business transactions are entered in the accounting system. These transactions are based on exchanges between the business and other firms and individuals. During the accounting period, other changes occur that affect the firm's financial condition. For example, equipment is wearing out, prepaid insurance and supplies are being used up, and employees are earning wages that have not yet been paid.

 Matching revenues earned with expenses incurred as a result of efforts to produce those revenues offers the best measure of net income.

The **matching principle** in accounting requires the matching of revenues earned during an accounting period with the expenses incurred to produce the revenues. This approach offers the best measure of net income. The income statement reports earnings for a specific period of time and the balance sheet reports the assets, liabilities, and owner's equity on a specific date. Thus, to follow the matching principle, the accounts must be brought up to date before financial statements are prepared. This requires adjusting some of the accounts listed in the trial balance. Figure 5-1 lists reasons to adjust the trial balance.

FIGURE 5-1 Reasons to Adjust the Trial Balance

1. To report all revenues earned during the accounting period.
2. To report all expenses incurred to produce the revenues earned in this accounting period.
3. To accurately report the assets on the balance sheet date. Some may have been used up during the accounting period.
4. To accurately report the liabilities on the balance sheet date. Expenses may have been incurred but not yet paid.

Generally, adjustments are made and financial statements prepared at the end of a twelve-month period called a **fiscal year**. This period does not need to be the same as a calendar year. In fact, some businesses schedule their fiscal year-end for a time when business is slow. In this chapter we continue the illustration of Jessie Jane's Campus Delivery and will prepare adjustments at the end of the first month of operations. We will focus on the following accounts: Supplies, Prepaid Insurance, Delivery Equipment, and Wages Expense.

Supplies

> Since it is not practical to make a journal entry for supplies expense each time a supply, such as an envelope is used, one adjusting entry is made at the end of the accounting period.

During June, Jane purchased supplies consisting of paper, pens, and delivery envelopes for $80. *Since these supplies were expected to provide future benefits, Supplies, an asset, was debited at the time of the purchase.* No other entries were made to the supplies account during June. As reported on the trial balance in Figure 5-2, the $80 balance remains in the supplies account at the end of the month.

FIGURE 5-2 Trial Balance

Jessie Jane's Campus Delivery
Trial Balance
June 30, 19--

ACCOUNT TITLE	ACCOUNT NO.	DEBIT BALANCE	CREDIT BALANCE
Cash	111	3 7 0 00	
Accounts Receivable	131	5 0 0 00	
Supplies	151	8 0 00	
Prepaid Insurance	155	2 0 0 00	
Delivery Equipment	185	3 6 0 0 00	
Accounts Payable	216		1 8 0 0 00
Jessica Jane, Capital	311		2 0 0 0 00
Jessica Jane, Drawing	312	1 5 0 00	
Delivery Fees	411		2 0 0 0 00
Rent Expense	541	2 0 0 00	
Wages Expense	542	6 5 0 00	
Telephone Expense	545	5 0 00	
		5 8 0 0 00	5 8 0 0 00

As supplies are used, an expense is incurred. However, it is not practical to make a journal entry to recognize this expense and the reduction in the supplies account every time someone uses an envelope. It is more efficient to wait until the end of the accounting period to make one adjusting entry to reflect the expense incurred for the use of supplies for the entire month.

At the end of the month, an inventory, or physical count, of the remaining supplies is taken. The inventory shows that supplies costing $20 were still unused at the end of June. Since Jane bought supplies costing $80, and only $20 worth remain, supplies costing $60 must have been used ($80 − $20 = $60). Thus, supplies expense for the month is $60. (Trial balance is abbreviated TB in Figure 5-3 and other T account illustrations.)

> Abbreviations: Often debit and credit are abbreviated as:
>
> *Dr.* = *Debit*
> *Cr.* = *Credit*
> *(based on the Latin terms*
> *"debere" and "credere").*

FIGURE 5-3   Adjustment for Supplies

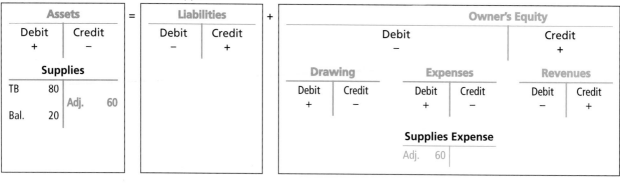

Since $60 worth of supplies have been used, Supplies Expense is debited and Supplies (asset) is credited for $60. Thus, as shown in Figure 5-4, supplies with a cost of $20 will be reported as an asset on the balance sheet and a supplies expense of $60 will be reported on the income statement. The adjusting entry affected an income statement account (Supplies Expense) and a balance sheet account (Supplies).

> By making an adjusting entry that debits Supplies Expense and credits Supplies, you are taking the amount of supplies used out of the Supplies account and putting it in Supplies Expense.

FIGURE 5-4   Effect of Adjusting Entry for Supplies on Financial Statements

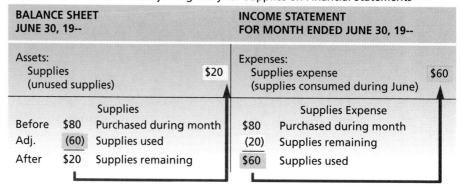

Prepaid Insurance

On June 18, Jane paid $200 for an eight-month liability insurance policy with coverage beginning on June 1. *Prepaid Insurance, an asset, was debit-*

ed because the insurance policy is expected to provide future benefits. The $200 balance is reported on the trial balance. As the insurance policy expires with the passage of time, the asset should be reduced and an expense recognized.

 **LEARNING KEY** The $200 premium covers eight months. The cost for June is $25 ($200 ÷ 8 months).

Since the $200 premium covers eight months, the cost of the expired coverage for June is $25 ($200 ÷ 8 months). As shown in Figure 5-5, the adjusting entry is to debit Insurance Expense for $25 and credit Prepaid Insurance for $25. Figure 5-6 shows that the unexpired portion of the insurance premium will be reported on the balance sheet as Prepaid Insurance of $175. The expired portion will be reported on the income statement as Insurance Expense of $25.

FIGURE 5-5   Adjustment for Expired Insurance

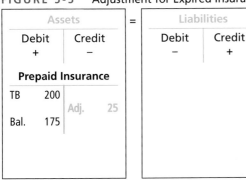
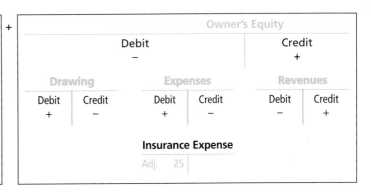

FIGURE 5-6   Effect of Adjusting Entry for Prepaid Insurance on Financial Statements

BALANCE SHEET JUNE 30, 19--			INCOME STATEMENT FOR MONTH ENDED JUNE 30, 19--		
Assets: Prepaid Insurance (unexpired premium)		$175	Expenses: Insurance expense (insurance expired during June)		$25
	Prepaid Insurance			Insurance Expense	
Before	$200	Premiums paid	$200	Premiums paid	
Adj.	(25)	Prepaid ins. expired	(175)	Prepaid ins. remaining	
After	$175	Prepaid ins. remaining	$25	Prepaid ins. expired	

Wages Expense

Jane paid her part-time employees $650 on June 26. Since then, they have earned an additional $50, but have not yet been paid. The additional wages expense must be recognized.

Since the employees have not been paid, Wages Payable, a liability, should be established. Thus, Wages Expense is debited and Wages Payable is credited for $50 in Figure 5-7. Note in Figure 5-8 that Wages Expense of $700 is reported on the income statement and Wages Payable of $50 is reported on the balance sheet.

FIGURE 5-7   Adjustment for Unpaid Wages

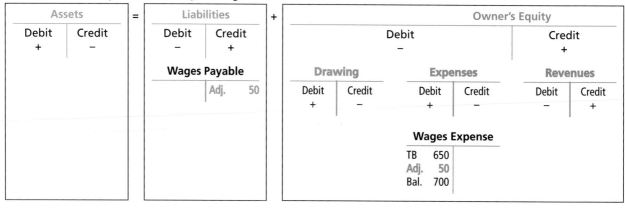

FIGURE 5-8   Effect of Adjusting Entry for Wages on Financial Statements

BALANCE SHEET JUNE 30, 19--		INCOME STATEMENT FOR MONTH ENDED JUNE 30, 19--	
Liabilities: Wages Payable (owed to employees)	$50	Expenses: Wages expense (incurred for June)	$700

Wages Payable		Wages Expense		
$700	Total wages expense incurred	Before	$650	Wages paid
$(650)	Paid to employees	Adj.	50	Wages owed
$50	Owed to employees	After	$700	Total wages expense

Depreciation Expense

> The historical cost principle is an important accounting concept. Assets are recorded at their actual cost. This historical cost is not adjusted for changes in market values.

During the month of June, Jane purchased three motor scooters. Since the scooters will provide future benefits, they were recorded as assets in the delivery equipment account. Under the **historical cost principle**, assets are recorded at their actual cost, in this case $3,600. This cost remains on the books as long as the business owns the asset. No adjustments are made for changes in the market value of the asset. It does not matter whether the firm got a "good buy" or paid "too much" when the asset was purchased.

The period of time that an asset is expected to help produce revenues is called its **useful life**. The asset's useful life expires as a result of wear and tear or because it no longer satisfies the needs of the business. For example, as Jane adds miles to her scooters, they will become less reliable and will eventually fail to run. As this happens, depreciation expense should be recognized and the value of the asset should be reduced. **Depreciation** is a method of *matching* an asset's original cost against the revenues produced over its useful life. There are many depreciation methods. In our example, we will use the **straight-line method**.

Let's assume that Jane's motor scooters have useful lives of three years and will have no salvage value at the end of that time period. **Salvage value** is the expected **market value** or selling price of the asset at the end of its useful life. Let's also assume that a full month's depreciation is recognized in the month in which an asset is purchased. The cost of the scooters that is subject to depreciation, called **depreciable cost**, is $3,600.

The depreciable cost is spread over 36 months (3 years x 12 months). Thus, the straight-line depreciation expense for the month of June is $100 ($3,600 ÷ 36 months).

Straight-Line Depreciation

Original Cost − Salvage Value = Depreciable Cost

$$\frac{\text{Depreciable Cost}}{\text{Estimated Useful Life}} = \frac{\$3,600}{36 \text{ months}} = \$100 \text{ per month}$$

LEARNING KEY Depreciable assets provide benefits over more than one year. Therefore, rather than directly crediting the asset to show that it has been depreciated, a *contra-asset* account is used.

When we made adjustments for supplies and prepaid insurance, the asset accounts were credited to show that they had been consumed. Assets expected to provide benefits over a longer period of time, called **plant assets**, require a different approach. The business maintains a record of the original cost and the amount of depreciation taken since the asset was acquired. By comparing these two amounts, the reader can estimate the relative age of the assets. Thus, instead of crediting Delivery Equipment for the amount of depreciation, a contra-asset account, Accumulated Depreciation—Delivery Equipment, is credited. A **contra-asset** has a credit balance and is deducted from the related asset account on the balance sheet.

As shown in Figure 5-9, the appropriate adjusting entry consists of a debit to Depreciation Expense—Delivery Equipment and a credit to Accumulated Depreciation—Delivery Equipment. Note the position of the accumulated depreciation account in the accounting equation. It is shown in the asset section, directly beneath Delivery Equipment. Contra-asset accounts should always be shown along with the related asset account. Therefore, Delivery Equipment and Accumulated Depreciation—Delivery Equipment are shown together.

The same concept is used on the balance sheet. Note in Figure 5-10 that Accumulated Depreciation is reported immediately beneath Delivery Equipment as a deduction. The difference between these accounts is known as the **book value**, or **undepreciated cost**, of the delivery equipment. Book value simply means the value carried on the books or in the accounting

FIGURE 5-9   Adjustment for Depreciation of Delivery Equipment

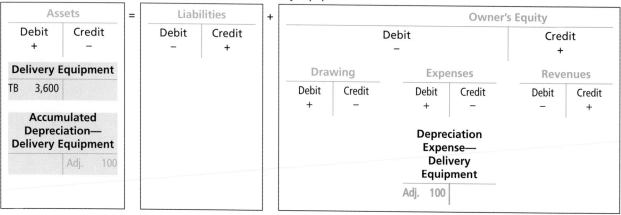

FIGURE 5-10   Effect of Adjusting Entry for Depreciation on Financial Statements for June

BALANCE SHEET JUNE 30, 19--			INCOME STATEMENT FOR MONTH ENDED JUNE 30, 19--	
Assets:			Expenses:	
Delivery equipment	$3,600		Depreciation expense	$100
Less: Accumulated depreciation	100	$3,500	(Expired cost for June)	
		(Book value)		

records. It does *not* represent the **market value**, or selling price, of the asset.

LEARNING KEY   Cost of Plant Assets – Accumulated Depreciation = Book Value

If no delivery equipment is bought or sold during the next month, the same adjusting entry would be made at the end of July. If an income statement for the month of July and a balance sheet as of July 31 were prepared, the amounts shown in Figure 5-11 would be reported for the delivery equipment.

FIGURE 5-11   Effect of Adjusting Entry for Depreciation on Financial Statements for July

BALANCE SHEET JULY 31, 19--			INCOME STATEMENT FOR MONTH ENDED JULY 31, 19--	
Assets:			Expenses:	
Delivery equipment	$3,600		Depreciation expense	$100
Less: Accumulated depreciation	200	$3,400	(Expired cost for July)	
		(Book value)		

The cost ($3,600) remains unchanged, but the accumulated depreciation has increased to $200. This represents *the depreciation that has accumulated* since the delivery equipment was purchased ($100 in June and $100 in

July). The depreciation expense for July is $100, the same as reported for June. Depreciation expense is reported for a specific time period. It does not accumulate across reporting periods.

Expanded Chart of Accounts

Several new accounts were needed to make the adjusting entries. New accounts are easily added to the chart of accounts, as shown in Figure 5-12. Note the close relationship between assets and contra-assets in the numbering of the accounts. Contra-accounts carry the same number as the related asset account with a ".1" suffix. For example, Delivery Equipment is account number 185 and the contra-asset account, Accumulated Depreciation—Delivery Equipment, is account number 185.1.

FIGURE 5-12   Expanded Chart of Accounts

Jessie Jane's Campus Delivery Chart of Accounts				
Assets			**Revenue**	
111	Cash		411	Delivery Fees
131	Accounts Receivable			
151	Supplies		**Expenses**	**(500–599)**
155	Prepaid Insurance		541	Rent Expense
185	Delivery Equipment		542	Wages Expense
185.1	*Accumulated Depr.—*		*543*	*Supplies Expense*
	Delivery Equipment		545	Telephone Expense
			547	*Depr. Expense—*
Liabilities				*Delivery Equipment*
216	Accounts Payable		*559*	*Insurance Expense*
219	*Wages Payable*			
Owner's Equity				
311	Jessica Jane, Capital			
312	Jessica Jane, Drawing			

THE WORK SHEET

LO2   Prepare a work sheet.

A **work sheet** pulls together all of the information needed to enter adjusting entries and prepare the financial statements. Work sheets are not financial statements and are not a formal part of the accounting system. Ordinarily, only the accountant uses a work sheet. For this reason, a work sheet is usually prepared in pencil or as a spreadsheet on a computer.

The Ten-Column Work Sheet

Although a work sheet can take several forms, a common format has a column for account titles and ten amount columns grouped into five pairs. The work sheet format and the five steps in preparing the work sheet are illustrated in Figure 5-13. As with financial statements, the work sheet has a heading consisting of the name of the company, name of the working paper, and the date of the accounting period just ended. The five major column headings for the work sheet are: Trial Balance, Adjustments, Adjusted Trial Balance, Income Statement, and Balance Sheet.

Preparing the Work Sheet

Let's apply the five steps required for the preparation of a work sheet to Jessie Jane's Campus Delivery.

STEP 1   **Prepare the Trial Balance.**   As shown in Figure 5-14, the first pair of amount columns is for the trial balance. The trial balance assures the equality of the debits and credits before the adjustment process begins. The columns should be double ruled to show that they are equal.

 You are already familiar with a trial balance. Here we are simply copying a trial balance to a different form, called a work sheet.

Note that all accounts listed in the expanded chart of accounts are included in the Trial Balance columns of the work sheet. This is done even though some accounts have zero balances. The accounts with zero balances could be added to the bottom of the list as they are needed for adjusting entries. However, it is easier to include them now, especially if preparing the work sheet on an electronic spreadsheet. Listing the accounts within their proper classifications (assets, liabilities, etc.) also makes it easier to extend the amounts to the proper columns.

STEP 2   **Prepare the Adjustments.**   As shown in Figure 5-15, the second pair of amount columns is used to prepare the adjusting entries. Enter the adjustments directly in these columns. When an account is debited or credited, the amount is entered on the same line as the name of the account and in the appropriate Adjustments Debit or Credit column. Each adjusting entry made on the work sheet is identified by a small letter in parentheses.

 For adjustments (a), (b), and (d), we are simply recognizing that assets have been used. When this happens, the asset must be decreased and an expense recognized. Note that the reported amount for delivery equipment is reduced by crediting a contra-asset.

FIGURE 5-13   Steps in Preparing the Work Sheet

Name of Company
Work Sheet
For Month Ended June 30, 19--

ACCOUNT TITLE	TRIAL BALANCE		ADJUSTMENTS		ADJUSTED TRIAL BALANCE		INCOME STATEMENT		BALANCE SHEET		
	DEBIT	CREDIT	DEBIT	CREDIT	DEBIT	CREDIT	DEBIT	CREDIT	DEBIT	CREDIT	
Insert ledger account titles	**STEP 1** Prepare the trial balance		**STEP 2** Prepare the adjustments		**STEP 3** Prepare the adjusted trial balance		**STEP 4** Extend adjusted account balances				1
	Assets										2
		Liabilities			Assets				Assets		3
		Capital				Liabilities				Liabilities	4
	Drawing					Capital				Capital	5
		Revenues			Drawing				Drawing		6
	Expenses					Revenues		Revenues			7
					Expenses		Expenses				8
											9
											10
											11
											12
											13
											14
											15
											16
							STEP 5 Complete the work sheet				17
							1. Sum columns				18
							2. Compute net income (loss)				19
											20
											21
											22
											23
											24
							Net Income	Net Loss	Net Loss	Net Income	25
											26
											27
											28
											29
											30

FIGURE 5-14   Step 1—Prepare the Trial Balance

Jessie Jane's Campus Delivery
Work Sheet
For Month Ended June 30, 19--

	ACCOUNT TITLE	TRIAL BALANCE DEBIT	TRIAL BALANCE CREDIT	ADJUSTMENTS DEBIT	ADJUSTMENTS CREDIT	ADJUSTED TRIAL BALANCE DEBIT	ADJUSTED TRIAL BALANCE CREDIT	INCOME STATEMENT DEBIT	INCOME STATEMENT CREDIT	BALANCE SHEET DEBIT	BALANCE SHEET CREDIT	
1	Cash	3 7 0 0 00										1
2	Accounts Receivable	5 0 0 00										2
3	Supplies	8 0 00										3
4	Prepaid Insurance	2 0 0 00										4
5	Delivery Equipment	3 6 0 0 00										5
6	Accum. Depr.—Del. Equip.											6
7	Accounts Payable		1 8 0 0 00									7
8	Wages Payable											8
9	Jessica Jane, Capital		2 0 0 0 00									9
10	Jessica Jane, Drawing	1 5 0 00										10
11	Delivery Fees		2 0 0 0 00									11
12	Rent Expense	2 0 0 00										12
13	Wages Expense	6 5 0 00										13
14	Supplies Expense											14
15	Telephone Expense	5 0 00										15
16	Depr. Expense—Del. Equip.											16
17	Insurance Expense											17
18		5 8 0 0 00	5 8 0 0 00									18
19												19
20												20
21												21
22												22
23												23
24												24
25												25
26												26
27												27
28												28
29												29
30												30

STEP 1

Preparing the Work Sheet

STEP 1

Prepare the Trial Balance.

- Write the heading, account titles, and the debit and credit amounts from the general ledger.
- Place a single rule across the Trial Balance columns and total the debit and credit amounts.
- Place a double rule under the columns to show that they are equal.

STEP 2

Prepare the Adjustments.

- Record the adjustments.
  Hint: Make certain that each adjustment is on the same line as the account name and in the appropriate column.
  Hint: Identify each adjusting entry by a letter in parentheses.
- Rule the Adjusted Trial Balance columns.
- Total the debit and credit columns and double rule the columns to show equality.

STEP 3

Prepare the Adjusted Trial Balance.

- Extend those debits and credits that are not adjusted directly to the appropriate Adjusted Trial Balance column.
- Enter the adjusted balances in the appropriate Adjusted Trial Balance column.
  Hint: If an account has a debit and a credit, sub-tract the adjustment. If an account has two debits or two credits, add the adjustment.
- Single rule the Adjusted Trial Balance columns. Total and double rule the debit and credit columns.

STEP 4

Extend Adjusted Balances to the Income Statement and Balance Sheet Columns.

- Extend all revenue accounts to the Income Statement Credit column.
- Extend all expense accounts to the Income Statement Debit column.
- Extend the asset and drawing accounts to the Balance Sheet Debit column.
- Extend the liability and owner's capital accounts to the Balance Sheet Credit column.

STEP 5

Complete the Work Sheet.

- Rule and total the Income Statement and Balance Sheet columns.
- Calculate the difference between the Income Statement Debit and Credit columns. Calculate the difference between the Balance Sheet Debit and Credit columns.
  Hint: If the Income Statement credits exceed debits, net income has occurred; otherwise a net loss has occurred. If the Balance Sheet debits exceed the credits, the differ-ence is net income; otherwise a net loss has occurred.
  Hint: The difference between the Balance Sheet columns and the difference between the Income Statement columns should be the same.
- Add the net income to the Income Statement Debit column or add the net loss to the Income Statement Credit column. Add the net income to the Balance Sheet Credit column or the net loss to the Balance Sheet Debit column.
- Total and double rule the columns.

ADJUSTMENT (a):

Supplies costing $60 were used during June.

	Debit	Credit
Supplies Expense	60	
Supplies		60

ADJUSTMENT (b):

One month's insurance premium has expired.

Insurance Expense	25	
Prepaid Insurance		25

ADJUSTMENT (c):

Employees earned $50 that has not yet been paid.

Wages Expense	50	
Wages Payable		50

> Adjustment (c) recognizes an economic event that has not required an actual transaction yet. Employees earned wages, but have not been paid. The adjustment recognizes an expense and a liability.

ADJUSTMENT (d):

Depreciation on the motor scooters is recognized.

Depreciation Expense—Delivery Equipment	100	
Accumulated Depreciation—Delivery Equipment		100

When all adjustments have been entered on the work sheet, each column should be totaled to assure that the debits equal the credits for all entries. After balancing the columns, they should be double ruled.

STEP 3   **Prepare the Adjusted Trial Balance.**   As shown in Figure 5-16, the third pair of amount columns of the work sheet are the **Adjusted Trial Balance Columns**. When an account balance is not affected by entries in the Adjustments columns, the amount in the Trial Balance columns is extended directly to the Adjusted Trial Balance columns. *When affected by an entry in the Adjustments columns, the balance to be entered in the Adjusted Trial Balance columns increases or decreases by the amount of the adjusting entry.*

For example, in Jessica Jane's business, Supplies is listed in the Trial Balance Debit column as $80. Since the entry of $60 is in the Adjustments Credit column, the amount extended to the Adjusted Trial Balance Debit column is $20 ($80 − $60).

Wages Expense is listed in the Trial Balance Debit column as $650. Since $50 is in the Adjustments Debit column, the amount extended to the Adjusted Trial Balance Debit column is $700 ($650 + $50).

After all extensions have been made, the Adjusted Trial Balance columns are totaled to prove the equality of the debits and the credits. Once balanced, the columns are double ruled.

STEP 4   **Extend Adjusted Balances to the Income Statement and Balance Sheet Columns.**   As shown in Figure 5-17, each account listed in the Adjusted Trial Balance must be extended to either the Income Statement or Balance Sheet columns. The **Income Statement columns** show the amounts that will be reported in the income statement. All revenue accounts are extended to the Income Statement Credit column and expense accounts are extended to the Income Statement Debit column.

 LEARNING KEY | The Balance Sheet columns show the amounts in both the balance sheet and the statement of owner's equity.

The asset, liability, drawing, and capital accounts are extended to the **Balance Sheet columns**. Although called the Balance Sheet columns, these columns of the work sheet show the amounts that will be reported in the balance sheet and the statement of owner's equity. The asset and drawing accounts are extended to the Balance Sheet Debit column. The liability and owner's capital accounts are extended to the Balance Sheet Credit column.

STEP 5   **Complete the Work Sheet.**   To complete the work sheet, first total the Income Statement columns. If the total of the credits (revenues) exceeds the total of the debits (expenses), the difference represents net income. If the total of the debits exceeds the total of the credits, the difference represents a net loss.

The Income Statement columns of Jane's work sheet in Figure 5-18 show total credits of $2,000 and total debits of $1,135. The difference, $865, is the net income for the month of June. This amount should be added to the debit column to balance the Income Statement columns and "Net Income" should be written on the same line in the Account Title column. If the business had a net loss, the amount of the loss would be added to the Income Statement Credit column and the words "Net Loss" would be written in the Account Title column. Once balanced, the columns should be double ruled.

Finally, the Balance Sheet columns are totaled. The difference between the totals of these columns also is the amount of net income or net loss for the accounting period. If the total debits exceed the total credits, the difference is net income. If the total credits exceed the total debits, the difference is a net loss. This difference should be the same as the difference we found for the Income Statement columns.

The Balance Sheet columns of Jane's work sheet show total debits of $4,815 and total credits of $3,950. The difference of $865 represents the amount of net income for the month. This amount is added to the credit column to balance the Balance Sheet columns. If the business had a net loss, this amount would be added to the Balance Sheet Debit column. Once balanced, the columns should be double ruled.

A trick for remembering the appropriate placement of the net income and net loss is the following: Net Income *apart*; Net Loss *together*. Figure 5-19 illustrates this learning aid.

FIGURE 5-19 Net Income Apart, Net Loss Together

| | Income Statement | | Balance Sheet | | | | Income Statement | | Balance Sheet | |
	Debit	Credit	Debit	Credit			Debit	Credit	Debit	Credit
	1,135	2,000	4,815	3,950			2,500	2,000	5,015	5,515
Net Income	865			865	Net Loss			500	500	
	2,000	2,000	4,815	4,815			2,500	2,500	5,515	5,515

Apart   Together

FINDING ERRORS ON THE WORK SHEET

LO3 Describe methods for finding errors on the work sheet.

If any of the columns on the work sheet do not balance, you must find the error before you continue. Once you are confident that the work sheet is accurate, you are ready to journalize the adjusting entries and prepare financial statements. Figure 5-20 offers tips for finding errors on the work sheet.

FIGURE 5-20 Finding Errors on the Work Sheet

TIPS FOR FINDING ERRORS ON THE WORK SHEET
1. Check the addition of all columns.
2. Check the addition and subtraction required when extending to the Adjusted Trial Balance columns.
3. Make sure the adjusted account balances have been extended to the appropriate columns.
4. Make sure that the net income or net loss has been added to the appropriate columns.

JOURNALIZING ADJUSTING ENTRIES

LO4 Journalize adjusting entries.

Keep in mind that the work sheet simply helps the accountant organize the end-of-period work. Writing the adjustments on the work sheet has no effect on the ledger accounts in the accounting system. The only way to change the balance of a ledger account is to make a journal entry. Once the adjustments have been entered on the work sheet, simply copy the adjustments from the work sheet to the journal.

Jane's adjusting entries are illustrated in Figure 5-21 as they would appear in a general journal. Note that the last day of the accounting period, June 30, has been entered in the date column and *"Adjusting Entries"* is written in the Description column prior to the first adjusting entry. No explanation is required in the Description column for individual adjusting entries. We simply label them as adjusting entries.

POSTING ADJUSTING ENTRIES

LO5   Post adjusting entries to the general ledger.

Adjusting entries are posted to the general ledger in the same manner as all other entries, except that *"Adjusting"* is written in the Item column of the general ledger. Figure 5-22 shows the posting of the adjusting entry for supplies.

FIGURE 5-21   Adjusting Entries

GENERAL JOURNAL   PAGE 3

	DATE		DESCRIPTION	POST. REF.	DEBIT	CREDIT	
1			Adjusting Entries				1
2	June 30		Supplies Expense	543	6 0 00		2
3			Supplies	151		6 0 00	3
4							4
5		30	Insurance Expense	548	2 5 00		5
6			Prepaid Insurance	155		2 5 00	6
7							7
8		30	Wages Expense	542	5 0 00		8
9			Wages Payable	219		5 0 00	9
10							10
11		30	Depr. Expense—Delivery Equip.	547	1 0 0 00		11
12			Accum. Depr.—Delivery Equip.	185.1		1 0 0 00	12

FIGURE 5-22   Posting the Adjusting Entry for Supplies

GENERAL LEDGER

ACCOUNT: Supplies   ACCOUNT NO. 151

DATE		ITEM	POST. REF.	DEBIT	CREDIT	BALANCE DEBIT	BALANCE CREDIT
June 16			J1	8 0 00		8 0 00	
	30	Adjusting	J3		6 0 00	2 0 00	

ACCOUNT: Supplies Expense   ACCOUNT NO. 543

DATE		ITEM	POST. REF.	DEBIT	CREDIT	BALANCE DEBIT	BALANCE CREDIT
June 30		Adjusting	J3	6 0 00		6 0 00	

KEY POINTS

1   End-of-period adjustments are necessary to bring the general ledger accounts up to date prior to preparing financial statements. Reasons to adjust the trial balance are:

1. To report all revenues earned during the accounting period.
2. To report all expenses incurred to produce the revenues.
3. To accurately report the assets on the balance sheet date. Some may have been used during the accounting period.
4. To accurately report the liabilities on the balance sheet date. Expenses may have been incurred, but not yet paid.

2 Steps in preparing the work sheet are:

1. Prepare the trial balance.
2. Prepare the adjustments.
3. Prepare the adjusted trial balance.
4. Extend the adjusted account balances to the Income Statement and Balance Sheet columns.
5. Total the Income Statement and Balance Sheet columns to compute the net income or net loss.

3 Tips for finding errors on the work sheet include:

1. Check the addition of all columns.
2. Check the addition and subtraction required when extending to the Adjusted Trial Balance columns.
3. Make sure the adjusted account balances have been extended to the appropriate columns.
4. Make sure that the net income or net loss has been added to the appropriate columns.

4 The adjustments are copied from the work sheet to the journal. The last day of the accounting period is entered in the Date column and "Adjusting Entries" is written in the Description column.

5 Adjusting entries are posted to the general ledger in the same manner as all other entries, except that "Adjusting" is written in the Item column of the general ledger.

KEY TERMS

Adjusted Trial Balance columns 132H   The third pair of amount columns of the work sheet.

Balance Sheet columns 133   The work sheet columns that show the amounts that will be reported in the balance sheet and the statement of owner's equity.

book value 129   The difference between the asset account and its related accumulated depreciation account. The value reflected by the accounting records.

contra-asset 129   An account with a credit balance that is deducted from the related asset account on the balance sheet.

depreciable cost 129   The cost of an asset that is subject to depreciation.

depreciation 129   A method of matching an asset's original cost against the revenues produced over its useful life.

fiscal year 124   A twelve-month period for which financial reports are prepared.

historical cost principle 128   Under this principle, assets are recorded at their actual cost.

Income Statement columns 133   The work sheet columns that show the amounts that will be reported in the income statement.

market value 129   The amount an item can be sold for under normal economic conditions.

matching principle 124   A principle that requires the matching of revenues earned during an accounting period with the expenses incurred to produce the revenues.

plant assets 129   Assets expected to provide benefits over a long period of time.

salvage value 129   The expected market value of an asset at the end of its useful life.

straight-line method 129   A depreciation method in which the depreciable cost is divided by the estimated useful life.

undepreciated cost 129   The difference between the asset account and its related accumulated depreciation account. Also known as book value.

useful life 128   The period of time that an asset is expected to help produce revenues.

work sheet 131   A form used to pull together all of the information needed to enter adjusting entries and prepare the financial statements.

REVIEW QUESTIONS

1. Explain the matching principle.
2. Explain the historical cost principle.
3. Describe a plant asset.
4. What is a contra-asset?
5. What is the useful life of an asset?
6. What is the purpose of depreciation?
7. What is an asset's depreciable cost?
8. What is the book value of an asset?
9. Explain the purpose of the work sheet.
10. Identify the five major column headings on a work sheet.
11. List the five steps taken in preparing a work sheet.
12. Describe four tips for finding errors on the work sheet.

MANAGING YOUR WRITING

Delia Alvarez, owner of Delia's Lawn Service, wants to borrow money to buy new lawn equipment. A local bank has asked for financial statements. Alvarez has asked you to prepare financial statements for the year ended December 31, 19--. You have been given the unadjusted trial balance shown on the next page and suspect that Alvarez expects you to base your statements on this information. You are concerned, however, that some of the account balances may need to be adjusted. Write a memo to Alvarez explaining what additional information you need before you can prepare the financial statements. Alvarez is not familiar with accounting issues.

Therefore, explain in your memo why you need this information, the potential impact of this information on the financial statements, and the importance of making these adjustments before approaching the bank for a loan.

Delia's Lawn Service
Trial Balance
December 31, 19--

ACCOUNT TITLE	ACCOUNT NO.	DEBIT BALANCE	CREDIT BALANCE
Cash		7 7 0 00	
Accounts Receivable		1 7 0 0 00	
Supplies		2 8 0 00	
Prepaid Insurance		4 0 0 00	
Lawn Equipment		13 8 0 0 00	
Accounts Payable			2 2 0 0 00
Delia Alvarez, Capital			3 0 0 0 00
Delia Alvarez, Drawing		3 5 0 00	
Lawn Cutting Fees			52 4 0 0 00
Rent Expense		1 2 0 0 00	
Wages Expense		35 8 5 0 00	
Gas and Oil Expense		3 2 5 0 00	
		57 6 0 0 00	57 6 0 0 00

DEMONSTRATION PROBLEM

Justin Park is a lawyer specializing in corporate tax law. He began his practice on January 1. A chart of accounts and trial balance taken on December 31, 19-1 are provided below.

Information for year-end adjustments:

(a) Office supplies on hand at year end amounted to $300.
(b) On January 1, 19-1, Park purchased office equipment costing $15,000 with an expected life of five years and no salvage value.
(c) Computer equipment costing $6,000 with an expected life of three years and no salvage value was purchased on July 1, 19-1. Assume that Park computes depreciation to the nearest full month.
(d) A premium of $1,200 for a one-year insurance policy was paid on December 1, 19-1.
(e) Wages earned by Park's part-time secretary, which have not yet been paid, amount to $300.

REQUIRED

1. Prepare the work sheet for the year ended December 31, 19-1.
2. Prepare adjusting entries in a general journal.

Justin Park Legal Services
Chart of Accounts

Assets		Revenues	
111	Cash	411	Client Fees
152	Office Supplies		
155	Prepaid Insurance	**Expenses**	
181	Office Equipment	541	Rent Expense
181.1	Accum. Depr.—	542	Wages Expense
	Office Equip.	543	Office Supp. Exp.
194	Computer Equip.	545	Telephone Expense
194.1	Accum. Depr.—	547	Depr. Expense—
	Computer Equip.		Office Equip.
		548	Depr. Expense—
Liabilities			Computer Equip.
216	Accounts Payable	555	Utilities Expense
218	Notes Payable	559	Insurance Expense
219	Wages Payable		
Owner's Equity			
311	Justin Park, Capital		
312	Justin Park, Drawing		

Justin Park Legal Services
Trial Balance
December 31, 19-1

ACCOUNT TITLE	ACCOUNT NO.	DEBIT BALANCE	CREDIT BALANCE
Cash		7 0 0 0 00	
Office Supplies		8 0 0 00	
Prepaid Insurance		1 2 0 0 00	
Office Equipment		15 0 0 0 00	
Computer Equipment		6 0 0 0 00	
Accounts Payable			5 0 0 00
Notes Payable			5 0 0 0 00
Justin Park, Capital			11 4 0 0 00
Justin Park, Drawing		5 0 0 0 00	
Client Fees			40 0 0 0 00
Rent Expense		5 0 0 0 00	
Wages Expense		12 0 0 0 00	
Telephone Expense		1 0 0 0 00	
Utilities Expense		3 9 0 0 00	
		56 9 0 0 00	56 9 0 0 00

SOLUTION 1.

Justin Park Legal Services
Work Sheet
For Year Ended December 31, 19-1

	ACCOUNT TITLE	TRIAL BALANCE		ADJUSTMENTS		ADJUSTED TRIAL BALANCE		INCOME STATEMENT		BALANCE SHEET	
		DEBIT	CREDIT	DEBIT	CREDIT	DEBIT	CREDIT	DEBIT	CREDIT	DEBIT	CREDIT
1	Cash	7000.00				7000.00				7000.00	
2	Office Supplies	800.00			(a) 500.00	300.00				300.00	
3	Prepaid Insurance	1200.00			(d) 100.00	1100.00				1100.00	
4	Office Equipment	15000.00				15000.00				15000.00	
5	Accum. Depr.—Office Equip.				(b) 300.00		300.00				300.00
6	Computer Equipment	6000.00				6000.00				6000.00	
7	Accum. Depr.—Computer Equip.				(c) 100.00		100.00				100.00
8	Accounts Payable		500.00				500.00				500.00
9	Notes Payable		500.00				500.00				500.00
10	Wages Payable				(e) 300.00		300.00				300.00
11	Justin Park, Capital		11400.00				11400.00				11400.00
12	Justin Park, Drawing	5000.00				5000.00				5000.00	
13	Client Fees		40000.00				40000.00		40000.00		
14	Rent Expense	5000.00				5000.00		5000.00			
15	Wages Expense	12000.00		(e) 300.00		12300.00		12300.00			
16	Office Supplies Expense			(a) 500.00		500.00		500.00			
17	Telephone Expense	1000.00				1000.00		1000.00			
18	Depr. Expense—Office Equip.			(b) 300.00		300.00		300.00			
19	Depr. Expense—Computer Equip.			(c) 100.00		100.00		100.00			
20	Utilities Expense	3900.00				3900.00		3900.00			
21	Insurance Expense			(d) 100.00		100.00		100.00			
22		56900.00	56900.00	4900.00	4900.00	61200.00	61200.00	26800.00	40000.00	34400.00	21200.00
23	Net Income							13200.00			13200.00
24								40000.00	40000.00	34400.00	34400.00

2.

GENERAL JOURNAL

PAGE **11**

	DATE		DESCRIPTION	POST. REF.	DEBIT	CREDIT	
1			Adjusting Entries				1
2	Dec.^19-1	31	Office Supplies Expense		5 0 0 00		2
3			Office Supplies			5 0 0 00	3
4							4
5		31	Depr. Expense—Office Equip.		3 0 0 0 00		5
6			Accum. Depr.—Office Equip.			3 0 0 0 00	6
7							7
8		31	Depr. Expense—Computer Equip.		1 0 0 0 00		8
9			Accum. Depr.—Computer Equip.			1 0 0 0 00	9
10							10
11		31	Insurance Expense		1 0 0 00		11
12			Prepaid Insurance			1 0 0 00	12
13							13
14		31	Wages Expense		3 0 0 00		14
15			Wages Payable			3 0 0 00	15

SERIES A   EXERCISES

1 **EXERCISE 5A1 ADJUSTMENT FOR SUPPLIES**   On December 31, the trial balance indicates that the supplies account has a balance, prior to the adjusting entry, of $320. A physical count of the supplies inventory shows that $90 of supplies remain. Analyze this adjustment for supplies using T accounts, and them formally enter this adjustment in the general journal.

1 **EXERCISE 5A2 ADJUSTMENT FOR INSURANCE**   On December 1, a six-month liability insurance policy was purchased for $900. Analyze the required adjustment as of December 31 using T accounts, and then formally enter this adjustment in the general journal.

1 **EXERCISE 5A3 ADJUSTMENT FOR WAGES**   On December 31, the trial balance shows wages expense of $600. An additional $200 of wages was earned by the employees, but has not yet been paid. Analyze this adjustment for wages, and then formally enter this adjustment in the general journal.

1 **EXERCISE 5A4 ADJUSTMENT FOR DEPRECIATION OF ASSET**   On December 1, delivery equipment was purchased for $7,200. The delivery equipment has an estimated useful life of 4 years (48 months) and no salvage value. Using the straight-line depreciation method, prepare the necessary adjusting entry as of December 31 (one month), and then formally enter this adjustment in the general journal.

1 **EXERCISE 5A5 CALCULATION OF BOOK VALUE** One June 1, 19--, a depreciable asset was acquired for $5,400. The asset has an estimated useful life of 5 years (60 months) and no salvage value. Using the straight-line depreciation method, calculate the book value as of December 31, 19--.

1 **EXERCISE 5A6 ANALYSIS OF ADJUSTING ENTRY FOR SUPPLIES** Analyze each situation and indicate the correct dollar amount for the adjusting entry. (Trial balance is abbreviated as TB.)

1. Ending inventory of supplies is $130.

(Balance Sheet) Supplies	(Income Statement) Supplies Expense
TB 460 Adj. _____	Adj. _____
Bal. _____	

2. Amount of supplies used is $320.

(Balance Sheet) Supplies	(Income Statement) Supplies Expense
TB 545 Adj. _____	Adj. _____
Bal. _____	

1 **EXERCISE 5A7 ANALYSIS OF ADJUSTING ENTRY FOR INSURANCE** Analyze each situation and indicate the correct dollar amount for the adjusting entry.

1. Amount of insurance expired is $900.

(Balance Sheet) Prepaid Insurance	(Income Statement) Insurance Expense
TB 1,300 Adj. _____	Adj. _____
Bal. _____	

2. Amount of unexpired insurance is $185.

(Balance Sheet) Prepaid Insurance	(Income Statement) Insurance Expense
TB 860 Adj. _____	Adj. _____
Bal. _____	

2 **EXERCISE 5A8 WORK SHEET AND ADJUSTING ENTRIES** A partial work sheet for Jim Jacob's Furniture Repair is shown as follows. The work sheet contains four adjusting entries. Indicate by letters (a) through (d) the four adjustments of the work sheet, properly matching each debit and credit. Complete the Adjustments columns.

Jim Jacob's Furniture Repair
Work Sheet (Partial)
For Year Ended December 31, 19--

	ACCOUNT TITLE	TRIAL BALANCE		ADJUSTMENTS		ADJUSTED TRIAL BALANCE		
		DEBIT	CREDIT	DEBIT	CREDIT	DEBIT	CREDIT	
1	Cash	1 0 0 00				1 0 0 00		1
2	Supplies	8 5 0 00				2 0 0 00		2
3	Prepaid Insurance	9 0 0 00				3 0 0 00		3
4	Delivery Equipment	3 6 0 0 00				3 6 0 0 00		4
5	Accum. Depr.—Del. Equip.		6 0 0 00				8 0 0 00	5
6	Wages Payable						1 0 0 00	6
7	Jim Jacobs, Capital		4 0 0 0 00				4 0 0 0 00	7
8	Repair Fees		1 6 5 0 00				1 6 5 0 00	8
9	Wages Expense	6 0 0 00				7 0 0 00		9
10	Advertising Expense	2 0 0 00				2 0 0 00		10
11	Supplies Expense					6 5 0 00		11
12	Depr. Exp.—Del. Equip.					2 0 0 00		12
13	Insurance Expense					6 0 0 00		13
14		6 2 5 0 00	6 2 5 0 00			6 5 5 0 00	6 5 5 0 00	14

4   **EXERCISE 5A9 JOURNALIZING ADJUSTING ENTRIES** From the Adjustments columns from Exercise 5A8, journalize the four adjusting entries, on December 31, in proper general journal format.

5   **EXERCISE 5A10 POSTING ADJUSTING ENTRIES**   Two adjusting entries are in the following general journal. Post these adjusting entries to the four general ledger accounts. The following account numbers were taken from the chart of accounts: 151, Supplies; 219, Wages Payable; 542, Wages Expense; and 543, Supplies Expense. If you are not using the working papers that accompany this text, enter the following balances before posting the entries: Supplies, $200 Dr.; Wages Expense, $1,200 Dr.

GENERAL JOURNAL   PAGE 9

	DATE		DESCRIPTION	POST. REF.	DEBIT	CREDIT	
1			Adjusting Entries				1
2	19-1 Dec.	31	Supplies Expense		8 5 00		2
3			Supplies			8 5 00	3
4							4
5		31	Wages Expense		2 2 0 00		5
6			Wages Payable			2 2 0 00	6

2   **EXERCISE 5A11 EXTENDING ADJUSTED BALANCES TO THE INCOME STATEMENT AND BALANCE SHEET COLUMNS**   Indicate with an "x" whether each account total should be extended to the Income

Statement Debit or Credit or to the Balance Sheet Debit or Credit columns on the work sheet.

	Income Statement		Balance Sheet	
	Debit	Credit	Debit	Credit
Cash	___	___	___	___
Accounts Receivable	___	___	___	___
Supplies	___	___	___	___
Prepaid Insurance	___	___	___	___
Delivery Equipment	___	___	___	___
Accum. Depr.—Delivery Equip.	___	___	___	___
Accounts Payable	___	___	___	___
Wages Payable	___	___	___	___
Owner, Capital	___	___	___	___
Owner, Drawing	___	___	___	___
Delivery Fees	___	___	___	___
Rent Expense	___	___	___	___
Wages Expense	___	___	___	___
Supplies Expense	___	___	___	___
Insurance Expense	___	___	___	___
Depr. Exp.—Delivery Equip.	___	___	___	___

2 **EXERCISE 5A12 ANALYSIS OF NET INCOME OR NET LOSS ON THE WORK SHEET**   Indicate with an "x" in which columns, Income Statement Debit or Credit or Balance Sheet Debit or Credit, a net income or a net loss would appear on a work sheet.

	Income Statement		Balance Sheet	
	Debit	Credit	Debit	Credit
Net Income	___	___	___	___
Net Loss	___	___	___	___

SERIES A PROBLEMS

1/2 **PROBLEM 5A1 ADJUSTMENTS AND WORK SHEET SHOWING NET INCOME**   The trial balance after one month of operation for Mason's Delivery Service as of September 30, 19--, is shown on the next page.

Data to complete the adjustments are as follows:
(a) Supplies inventory as of September 30, $165.
(b) Insurance expired, $800.
(c) Depreciation on delivery equipment, $400.
(d) Wages earned by employees, but not paid as of September 30, $225.

REQUIRED
1. Enter the adjustments in the Adjustments columns of the work sheet.
2. Complete the work sheet.

Mason's Delivery Service
Work Sheet
For Month Ended September 30, 19--

	ACCOUNT TITLE	TRIAL BALANCE		ADJUSTMENTS		
		DEBIT	CREDIT	DEBIT	CREDIT	
1	Cash	1 6 0 0 00				1
2	Accounts Receivable	9 4 0 00				2
3	Supplies	6 3 5 00				3
4	Prepaid Insurance	1 2 0 0 00				4
5	Delivery Equipment	6 4 0 0 00				5
6	Accum. Depr.—Del. Equip.					6
7	Accounts Payable		1 2 2 0 00			7
8	Wages Payable					8
9	Jill Mason, Capital		8 0 0 0 00			9
10	Jill Mason, Drawing	1 4 0 0 00				10
11	Delivery Fees		6 2 0 0 00			11
12	Rent Expense	8 0 0 00				12
13	Wages Expense	1 5 0 0 00				13
14	Supplies Expense					14
15	Telephone Expense	1 6 5 00				15
16	Oil and Gas Expense	9 0 00				16
17	Depr. Exp.—Del. Equip.					17
18	Insurance Expense					18
19	Advertising Expense	4 6 0 00				19
20	Repair Expense	2 3 0 00				20
21		15 4 2 0 00	15 4 2 0 00			21
22						22
23						23
24						24
25						25
26						26
27						27

2 **PROBLEM 5A2 ADJUSTMENTS AND WORK SHEET SHOWING A NET LOSS**   Jason Armstrong started a business called Campus Escort Service. After the first month of operations, the trial balance as of November 30, 19--, is shown on the next page.

REQUIRED

1. Analyze the following adjustments and enter them on the work sheet.
   (a) Ending inventory of supplies on November 30, $185.
   (b) Unexpired insurance as of November 30, $800.
   (c) Depreciation expense on van, $300.
   (d) Wages earned, but not paid as of November 30, $190.
2. Complete the work sheet.

Campus Escort Service
Work Sheet
For Month Ended November 30, 19--

	ACCOUNT TITLE	TRIAL BALANCE		ADJUSTMENTS		
		DEBIT	CREDIT	DEBIT	CREDIT	
1	Cash	9 8 0 00				1
2	Accounts Receivable	5 9 0 00				2
3	Supplies	5 7 5 00				3
4	Prepaid Insurance	1 3 0 0 00				4
5	Van	5 8 0 0 00				5
6	Accum. Depr.—Van					6
7	Accounts Payable		9 6 0 00			7
8	Wages Payable					8
9	Jason Armstrong, Capital		10 0 0 0 00			9
10	Jason Armstrong, Drawing	6 0 0 00				10
11	Escort Fees		2 6 0 0 00			11
12	Rent Expense	9 0 0 00				12
13	Wages Expense	1 8 0 0 00				13
14	Supplies Expense					14
15	Telephone Expense	2 2 0 00				15
16	Oil and Gas Expense	1 0 0 00				16
17	Depr. Exp.—Van					17
18	Insurance Expense					18
19	Advertising Expense	3 8 0 00				19
20	Repair Expense	3 1 5 00				20
21		13 5 6 0 00	13 5 6 0 00			21
22						22
23						23
24						24
25						25

4/5 **PROBLEM 5A3 JOURNALIZE AND POST ADJUSTING ENTRIES FROM THE WORK SHEET** Refer to Problem 5A2 and the following additional information.

Account Name	Account Number	Balance in Account Before Adjusting Entry
Supplies	151	$ 575
Prepaid Insurance	155	1,300
Accum. Depr.—Van	185.1	0
Wages Payable	219	0
Wages Expense	542	1,800
Supplies Expense	543	0
Depr. Expense—Van	547	0
Insurance Expense	548	0

REQUIRED

1. Journalize the adjusting entries on page 5 of the general journal.
2. Post the adjusting entries to the general ledger. (If you are not using the working papers that accompany this text, enter the balances provided on page 146 before posting adjusting entries.)

3 **PROBLEM 5A4 CORRECTING WORK SHEET WITH ERRORS**   A beginning accounting student tried to complete a work sheet for Joyce Lee's Tax Service. The following adjusting entries were to have been analyzed and entered onto the work sheet. The worksheet is shown on page 148.

(a) Ending inventory of supplies as of March 31, $160.
(b) Unexpired insurance as of March 31, $520.
(c) Depreciation of office equipment, $275.
(d) Wages earned, but not paid as of March 31, $110.

REQUIRED

The accounting student made a number of errors. Review the work sheet for addition mistakes, transpositions, and other errors and make all necessary corrections.

SERIES B   EXERCISES

1 **EXERCISE 5B1 ADJUSTMENT FOR SUPPLIES**   On July 31, the trial balance indicates that the supplies account has a balance, prior to the adjusting entry, of $430. A physical count of the supplies inventory shows that $120 of supplies remain. Analyze the adjustment for supplies using T accounts, and then formally enter this adjustment in the general journal.

1 **EXERCISE 5B2 ADJUSTMENT FOR INSURANCE**   On July 1, a six-month liability insurance policy was purchased for $750. Analyze the required adjustment as of July 31 using T accounts, and then formally enter this adjustment in the general journal.

1 **EXERCISE 5B3 ADJUSTMENT FOR WAGES**   On July 31, the trial balance shows wages expense of $800. An additional $150 of wages was earned by the employees but has not yet been paid. Analyze the required adjustment using T accounts, and then formally enter this adjustment in the general journal.

1 **EXERCISE 5B4 ADJUSTMENT FOR DEPRECIATION OF ASSET**   On July 1, delivery equipment was purchased for $4,320. The delivery equipment has an estimated useful life of 3 years (36 months) and no salvage value. Using the straight-line depreciation method, prepare the necessary adjusting entry as of July 31 (one month), and then formally enter this adjustment in the general journal.

Joyce Lee's Tax Service
Work Sheet
For Month Ended March 31, 19--

	ACCOUNT TITLE	TRIAL BALANCE DEBIT	TRIAL BALANCE CREDIT	ADJUSTMENTS DEBIT	ADJUSTMENTS CREDIT	ADJUSTED TRIAL BALANCE DEBIT	ADJUSTED TRIAL BALANCE CREDIT	INCOME STATEMENT DEBIT	INCOME STATEMENT CREDIT	BALANCE SHEET DEBIT	BALANCE SHEET CREDIT	
1	Cash	1725 00				1725 00				1725 00		1
2	Accounts Receivable	960 00				960 00				96 00		2
3	Supplies	525 00			(a) 160 00	365 00				365 00		3
4	Prepaid Insurance	930 00			(b) 410 00	540 00				540 00		4
5	Office Equipment	5450 00			(c) 275 00	5175 00				5175 00		5
6	Accum. Depr.—Office Equip.											6
7	Accounts Payable		480 00				480 00				480 00	7
8	Wages Payable				(d) 110 00		110 00		110 00			8
9	Joyce Lee, Capital		7500 00				750 00				7500 00	9
10	Joyce Lee, Drawing	1125 00				1125 00		1125 00				10
11	Professional Fees		5700 00				570 00		570 00			11
12	Rent Expense	700 00				700 00		700 00				12
13	Wages Expense	1420 00		(d) 110 00		1420 00		1420 00				13
14	Supplies Expense			(a) 160 00		160 00		160 00				14
15	Telephone Expense	130 00				130 00		130 00				15
16	Depr. Expense—Office Equip.			(c) 275 00		275 00		275 00				16
17	Insurance Expense			(b) 410 00		410 00		410 00				17
18	Utilities Expense	190 00				190 00		190 00				18
19	Advertising Expense	350 00				350 00		350 00				19
20	Miscellaneous Expense	175 00				175 00		175 00				20
21		13680 00	13680 00	955 00	955 00	13160 00	13790 00	4566 00	5810 00	9508 00	7980 00	21
22								1244 00			1528 00	22
23								5810 00	5810 00	9508 00	9508 00	23
24												24

This worksheet contains errors

1 **EXERCISE 5B5 CALCULATION OF BOOK VALUE**   On January 1, 19--, a depreciable asset was acquired for $5,760. The asset has an estimated useful life of 4 years (48 months) and no salvage value. Use the straight-line depreciation method to calculate the book value as of July 1, 19--.

1 **EXERCISE 5B6 ANALYSIS OF ADJUSTING ENTRY FOR SUPPLIES**   Analyze each situation and indicate the correct dollar amount for the adjusting entry.

1. Ending inventory of supplies is $95.

(Balance Sheet) Supplies	(Income Statement) Supplies Expense
TB 540 Adj. _____	Adj. _____
Bal. _____	

2. Amount of supplies used is $280.

(Balance Sheet) Supplies	(Income Statement) Supplies Expense
TB 330 Adj. _____	Adj. _____
Bal. _____	

1 **EXERCISE 5B7 ANALYSIS OF ADJUSTING ENTRY FOR INSURANCE**   Analyze each situation and indicate the correct dollar amount for the adjusting entry.

1. Amount of insurance expired is $830.

(Balance Sheet) Prepaid Insurance	(Income Statement) Insurance Expense
TB 960 Adj. _____	Adj. _____
Bal. _____	

2. Amount of unexpired insurance is $340.

(Balance Sheet) Prepaid Insurance	(Income Statement) Insurance Expense
TB 1,135 Adj. _____	Adj. _____
Bal. _____	

2 **EXERCISE 5B8 WORK SHEET AND ADJUSTING ENTRIES**   The following shows a partial work sheet for Jasmine Kah's Auto Detailing. The work sheet contains four adjusting entries. Indicate by letters (a) through (d) the four adjustments in the adjustment columns of the work sheet, properly matching each debit and credit. Complete the Adjustments columns.

Jasmine Kah's Auto Detailing
Work Sheet (Partial)
For Month Ended June 30, 19--

	ACCOUNT TITLE	TRIAL BALANCE DEBIT	TRIAL BALANCE CREDIT	ADJUSTMENTS DEBIT	ADJUSTMENTS CREDIT	ADJUSTED TRIAL BALANCE DEBIT	ADJUSTED TRIAL BALANCE CREDIT	
1	Cash	1 5 0 00				1 5 0 00		1
2	Supplies	5 2 0 00				9 0 00		2
3	Prepaid Insurance	7 5 0 00				2 0 0 00		3
4	Cleaning Equipment	5 4 0 0 00				5 4 0 0 00		4
5	Accum. Depr.—Clean. Equip.		8 5 0 00				1 1 5 0 00	5
6	Wages Payable						2 5 0 00	6
7	Jasmine Kah, Capital		4 6 0 0 00				4 6 0 0 00	7
8	Detailing Fees		2 2 2 0 00				2 2 2 0 00	8
9	Wages Expense	7 0 0 00				9 5 0 00		9
10	Advertising Expense	1 5 0 00				1 5 0 00		10
11	Supplies Expense					4 3 0 00		11
12	Depr. Exp—Clean. Equip.					3 0 0 00		12
13	Insurance Expense					5 5 0 00		13
14		7 6 7 0 00	7 6 7 0 00			8 2 2 0 00	8 2 2 0 00	14

4 **EXERCISE 5B9 JOURNALIZING ADJUSTING ENTRIES** From the Adjustments columns in Exercise 5B8, journalize the four adjusting entries as of June 30, in proper general journal format.

5 **EXERCISE 5B10 POSTING ADJUSTING ENTRIES** Two adjusting entries are shown in the following general journal. Post these adjusting entries to the four general ledger accounts. The following account numbers were taken from the chart of accounts: 155, Prepaid Insurance; 186.1, Accumulated Depreciation—Cleaning Equipment; 547, Depreciation Expense—Cleaning Equipment; and 548, Insurance Expense. If you are not using the working papers that accompany this text, enter the following balances before posting the entries: Prepaid Insurance, $960 Dr.; Accumulated Depr.—Cleaning Equip., $870 Cr.

GENERAL JOURNAL   PAGE 7

	DATE	DESCRIPTION	POST. REF.	DEBIT	CREDIT	
1		Adjusting Entries				1
2	19-1 July 31	Insurance Expense		3 2 0 00		2
3		Prepaid Insurance			3 2 0 00	3
4						4
5	31	Depr. Expense—Cleaning Equip.		1 4 5 00		5
6		Accum. Depr.—Cleaning Equip.			1 4 5 00	6
7						7

2 **EXERCISE 5B11 EXTENDING ADJUSTED BALANCES TO THE INCOME STATMENT AND BALANCE SHEET COLUMNS**   Indicate with an "x" whether each account total should be extended to the Income Statement Debit or Credit or to the Balance Sheet Debit or Credit columns on the work sheet.

	Income Statement		Balance Sheet	
	Debit	Credit	Debit	Credit
Cash	____	____	____	____
Accounts Receivable	____	____	____	____
Supplies	____	____	____	____
Prepaid Insurance	____	____	____	____
Automobile	____	____	____	____
Accum. Depr.—Automobile	____	____	____	____
Accounts Payable	____	____	____	____
Wages Payable	____	____	____	____
Owner, Capital	____	____	____	____
Owner, Drawing	____	____	____	____
Service Fees	____	____	____	____
Utilities Expense	____	____	____	____
Wages Expense	____	____	____	____
Supplies Expense	____	____	____	____
Insurance Expense	____	____	____	____
Depr. Exp.—Automobile	____	____	____	____

2 **EXERCISE 5B12 ANALYSIS OF NET INCOME OR NET LOSS ON THE WORK SHEET**   Insert the dollar amounts where the net income or net loss would appear on the work sheet.

	Income Statement		Balance Sheet	
	Debit	Credit	Debit	Credit
Net Income: $2,500	____	____	____	____
Net Loss: $1,900	____	____	____	____

SERIES B   PROBLEMS

2 **PROBLEM 5B1 ADJUSTMENTS AND WORK SHEET SHOWING NET INCOME**   Louie Long started a business called Louie's Lawn Service. After the first month of operation, the trial balance as of March 31 is shown on the next page.

REQUIRED

1. Analyze the following adjustments and enter them on a work sheet.
   (a) Ending supplies inventory as of March 31, $165.
   (b) Insurance expired, $100.
   (c) Depreciation of lawn equipment, $200.
   (d) Wages earned, but not paid as of March 31, $180.
2. Complete the work sheet.

Louie's Lawn Service
Work Sheet
For Month Ended March 31, 19--

	ACCOUNT TITLE	TRIAL BALANCE		ADJUSTMENTS		
		DEBIT	CREDIT	DEBIT	CREDIT	
1	Cash	1 3 7 5 00				1
2	Accounts Receivable	8 8 0 00				2
3	Supplies	4 9 0 00				3
4	Prepaid Insurance	8 0 0 00				4
5	Lawn Equipment	5 7 0 0 00				5
6	Accum. Depr.—Lawn Equip.					6
7	Accounts Payable		7 8 0 00			7
8	Wages Payable					8
9	Louie Long, Capital		6 5 0 0 00			9
10	Louie Long, Drawing	1 2 5 0 00				10
11	Lawn Service Fees		6 1 0 0 00			11
12	Rent Expense	7 2 5 00				12
13	Wages Expense	1 1 4 5 00				13
14	Supplies Expense					14
15	Telephone Expense	1 6 0 00				15
16	Miscellaneous Expense	6 5 00				16
17	Depr. Exp.—Lawn Equip.					17
18	Insurance Expense					18
19	Advertising Expense	5 4 0 00				19
20	Repair Expense	2 5 0 00				20
21		1 3 3 8 0 00	1 3 3 8 0 00			21
22						22
23						23
24						24
25						25
26						26
27						27

2 **PROBLEM 5B2 ADJUSTMENTS AND WORK SHEET SHOWING A NET LOSS** Val Nolan started a business called Nolan's Home Appraisals. After the first month of operations, the trial balance as of October 31 is shown on the following page.

REQUIRED
1. Analyze the following adjustments and enter them on the work sheet.
   (a) Supplies inventory as of October 31, $210.
   (b) Unexpired insurance as of October 31, $800.
   (c) Depreciation of automobile, $250.
   (d) Wages earned, but not paid as of October 31, $175.
2. Complete the work sheet.

Nolan's Home Appraisals
Work Sheet
For Month Ended October 31, 19--

	ACCOUNT TITLE	TRIAL BALANCE		ADJUSTMENTS		
		DEBIT	CREDIT	DEBIT	CREDIT	
1	Cash	8 3 0 00				1
2	Accounts Receivable	7 6 0 00				2
3	Supplies	6 2 5 00				3
4	Prepaid Insurance	9 5 0 00				4
5	Automobile	6 5 0 0 00				5
6	Accum. Depr.—Automobile					6
7	Accounts Payable		1 5 0 0 00			7
8	Wages Payable					8
9	Val Nolan, Capital		9 9 0 0 00			9
10	Val Nolan, Drawing	1 1 0 0 00				10
11	Appraisal Fees		3 0 0 0 00			11
12	Rent Expense	1 0 5 0 00				12
13	Wages Expense	1 5 6 0 00				13
14	Supplies Expense					14
15	Telephone Expense	2 5 5 00				15
16	Oil and Gas Expense	8 0 00				16
17	Depr. Exp.—Automobile					17
18	Insurance Expense					18
19	Advertising Expense	4 2 0 00				19
20	Repair Expense	2 7 0 00				20
21		14 4 0 0 00	14 4 0 0 00			21
22						22
23						23
24						24
25						25

4/5   **PROBLEM 5B3 JOURNALIZE AND POST ADJUSTING ENTRIES FROM THE WORK SHEET**   Refer to Problem 5B2 and the following additional information.

Account Name	Account Number	Balance in Account Before Adjusting Entry
Supplies	151	$ 625
Prepaid Insurance	155	950
Accum. Depr.—Automobile	185.1	0
Wages Payable	219	0
Wages Expense	542	1,560
Supplies Expense	543	0
Depr. Expense—Automobile	547	0
Insurance Expense	548	0

REQUIRED
1. Journalize the adjusting entries on page 3 of the general journal.
2. Post the adjusting entries to the general ledger. (If you are not using the working papers that accompany this text, enter the balances provided on page 153 before posting adjusting entries.)

3 PROBLEM 5B4 CORRECTING WORK SHEET WITH ERRORS   A beginning accounting student tried to complete a work sheet for Dick Ady's Bookkeeping Service. The following adjusting entries were to have been analyzed and entered in the work sheet.

(a) Ending inventory of supplies on July 31, $130.
(b) Unexpired insurance on July 31, $420.
(c) Depreciation of office equipment, $325.
(d) Wages earned, but not paid as of July 31, $95.

REQUIRED
Review the work sheet shown on page 155 for addition mistakes, transpositions, and other errors and make all necessary corrections.

MASTERY PROBLEM

Kristi Williams offers family counseling services specializing in financial and marital problems. A chart of accounts and a trial balance taken on December 31, 19-1, are provided below.

Kristi Williams Family Counseling Services Chart of Accounts			
Assets		**Revenue**	
111	Cash	411	Client Fees
152	Office Supplies		
155	Prepaid Insurance	**Expenses**	
181	Office Equipment	541	Rent Expense
181.1	Accum. Depr.—	542	Wages Expense
	Office Equip.	543	Office Supp. Exp.
194	Computer Equip.	547	Depr. Expense—
194.1	Accum. Depr.—		Office Equip.
	Computer Equip.	548	Depr. Expense—
			Computer Equip.
Liabilities		555	Utilities Expense
216	Accounts Payable	559	Insurance Expense
218	Notes Payable	592	Miscellaneous Exp.
Owner's Equity			
311	Kristi Williams, Capital		
312	Kristi Williams, Drawing		

Dick Ady's Bookkeeping Service
Work Sheet
For Month Ended July 31, 19--

ACCOUNT TITLE	TRIAL BALANCE DEBIT	TRIAL BALANCE CREDIT	ADJUSTMENTS DEBIT	ADJUSTMENTS CREDIT	ADJUSTED TRIAL BALANCE DEBIT	ADJUSTED TRIAL BALANCE CREDIT	INCOME STATEMENT DEBIT	INCOME STATEMENT CREDIT	BALANCE SHEET DEBIT	BALANCE SHEET CREDIT
1 Cash	1365 00				1365 00				1365 00	
2 Accounts Receivable	845 00				845 00			845 00		
3 Supplies	620 00			(a) 490 00	130 00				130 00	
4 Prepaid Insurance	1150 00			(b) 730 00	420 00				420 00	
5 Office Equipment	6400 00			(c) 325 00	6725 00				6725 00	
6 Accum. Depr.—Office Equip.										
7 Accounts Payable		735 00				735 00				735 00
8 Wages Payable				(d) 95 00		95 00				59 00
9 Dick Ady, Capital		7800 00				7800 00				7800 00
10 Dick Ady, Drawing	1200 00				1200 00				1200 00	
11 Professional Fees		6350 00				6350 00		6350 00		
12 Rent Expense	850 00				850 00		850 00			
13 Wages Expense	1495 00		(d) 95 00		1590 00		1590 00			
14 Supplies Expense			(a) 490 00		490 00		490 00			
15 Telephone Expense	205 00				205 00		250 00			
16 Depr. Expense—Office Equip.			(c) 325 00		325 00		325 00			
17 Insurance Expense			(b) 420 00		420 00		420 00			
18 Utilities Expense	285 00				285 00		285 00			
19 Advertising Expense	380 00				380 00		380 00			
20 Miscellaneous Expense	90 00				90 00		90 00			
21	14885 00	14885 00	1330 00	1330 00	15630 00	14980 00	4880 00	7195 00	10141 00	8594 00
22 Net Income							2315 00			1547 00
23							7195 00	7195 00	10141 00	10141 00

This worksheet contains errors

Kristi Williams Family Counseling Services
Trial Balance
December 31, 19-1

ACCOUNT TITLE	ACCOUNT NO.	DEBIT BALANCE	CREDIT BALANCE
Cash	111	8 7 3 0 00	
Office Supplies	152	7 0 0 00	
Prepaid Insurance	155	6 0 0 00	
Office Equipment	181	18 0 0 0 00	
Computer Equipment	194	6 0 0 0 00	
Accounts Payable	216		5 0 0 00
Notes Payable	218		8 0 0 0 00
Kristi Williams, Capital	311		11 4 0 0 00
Kristi Williams, Drawing	312	3 0 0 0 00	
Client Fees	411		35 8 0 0 00
Rent Expense	541	6 0 0 0 00	
Wages Expense	542	9 5 0 0 00	
Utilities Expense	555	2 1 7 0 00	
Miscellaneous Expense	592	1 0 0 0 00	
		55 7 0 0 00	55 7 0 0 00

Information for year-end adjustments:

(a) Office supplies on hand at year end amounted to $100.

(b) On January 1, 19-1, Williams purchased office equipment that cost $18,000. It has an expected useful life of ten years and no salvage value.

(c) On July 1, 19-1, Williams purchased computer equipment costing $6,000. It has an expected useful life of three years and no salvage value. Assume that Williams computes depreciation to the nearest full month.

(d) On December 1, 19-1, Williams paid a premium of $600 for a six-month insurance policy.

REQUIRED

1. Prepare the work sheet for the year ended December 31, 19-1.
2. Prepare adjusting entries in a general journal.

CHAPTER 5 APPENDIX

Depreciation Methods

Careful study of this appendix should enable you to:

LO1 Prepare a depreciation schedule using the straight-line method.

LO2 Prepare a depreciation schedule using the sum-of-the-years'-digits method.

LO3 Prepare a depreciation schedule using the double-declining-balance method.

LO4 Prepare a depreciation schedule for tax purposes using the Modified Accelerated Cost Recovery System.

In Chapter 5, we introduced the straight-line method of depreciation. Here, we will review this method and illustrate three others: sum-of-the-year's-digits; double-declining-balance; and, for tax purposes, the Modified Accelerated Cost Recovery System. For all illustrations, we will assume that a delivery van was purchased for $18,000. It has a five-year useful life and salvage value of $3,000.

STRAIGHT-LINE METHOD

LO1   Prepare a depreciation schedule using the straight-line method.

Under the straight-line method, an equal amount of depreciation will be taken each period. First, compute the depreciable cost by subtracting the salvage value from the cost of the asset. This is done because we expect to sell the asset for $3,000 at the end of its useful life. Thus, the total cost to be recognized as an expense over the five years is $15,000, not $18,000.

$$\text{Cost} - \text{Salvage Value} = \text{Depreciable Cost}$$
$$\$18,000 - \$3,000 = \$15,000$$

Next, we divide the depreciable cost by the expected life of the asset, 5 years.

$$\text{Depreciation Expense per Year} = \frac{\text{Depreciable Cost}}{\text{Years of Life}}$$

$$\$3,000 \text{ per year} = \frac{\$15,000}{5 \text{ years}}$$

When preparing a depreciation schedule, it is often convenient to use a depreciation rate per year. In this case it would be 20% (1 year ÷ 5 years of life). Figure 5A-1 shows the depreciation expense, accumulated depreciation, and book value for each of the five years.

FIGURE 5A-1 Depreciation Schedule Using Straight-Line Method

						ACCUMULATED	
YEAR	DEPRECIABLE COST[a]	x	RATE[b]	=	DEPRECIATION EXPENSE	DEPRECIATION (END OF YEAR)	BOOK VALUE[c] (END OF YEAR)
1	$15,000		20%		$3,000	$ 3,000	$15,000
2	15,000		20%		3,000	6,000	12,000
3	15,000		20%		3,000	9,000	9,000
4	15,000		20%		3,000	12,000	6,000
5	15,000		20%		3,000	15,000	3,000

[a]Depreciable Cost = Cost − Salvage Value ($18,000 − $3,000 = $15,000).
[b]Rate = 1 year ÷ 5 years of life x 100 = 20%.
[c]Book Value = Cost ($18,000) − Accumulated Depreciation.

SUM-OF-THE-YEARS'-DIGITS

LO2 Prepare a depreciation schedule using the sum-of-the-years'-digits method.

Under the sum-of-the-years'-digits method, depreciation is determined by multiplying the depreciable cost by a schedule of fractions. The numerator of the fraction for a specific year is the number of years of remaining useful life for the asset, measured from the beginning of the year. The denominator for all fractions is determined by adding the digits that represent the years of the estimated life of the asset. The calculation for our delivery van with a five-year useful life is shown below.

Sum-of-the-Years'-Digits = 5 + 4 + 3 + 2 + 1 = 15

A depreciation schedule using these fractions is shown in Figure 5A-2.

DOUBLE-DECLINING-BALANCE METHOD

LO3 Prepare a depreciation schedule using the double-declining-balance method.

Under this method, the book value is multiplied by a fixed rate, often double the straight-line rate. The van has a five year life, so the straight-line rate is 1 ÷ 5, or 20%. Double the straight-line rate is 2 ÷ 5, or 40%. The double-declining-balance depreciation schedule is shown in Figure 5A-3. Note that the rate is applied to the book value of the asset. Once the book value is reduced to the expected salvage value, $3,000, no more depreciation may be recognized.

FIGURE 5A-2   Depreciation Schedule Using Sum-of-the-Years'-Digits Method

						ACCUMULATED	
YEAR	DEPRECIABLE COST[a]	x	RATE[b]	=	DEPRECIATION EXPENSE	DEPRECIATION (END OF YEAR)	BOOK VALUE[c] (END OF YEAR)

SUM-OF-THE-YEARS'-DIGITS

YEAR	DEPRECIABLE COST[a]	x	RATE[b]	=	DEPRECIATION EXPENSE	ACCUMULATED DEPRECIATION (END OF YEAR)	BOOK VALUE[c] (END OF YEAR)
1	$15,000		5/15		$5,000	$ 5,000	$13,000
2	15,000		4/15		4,000	9,000	9,000
3	15,000		3/15		3,000	12,000	6,000
4	15,000		2/15		2,000	14,000	4,000
5	15,000		1/15		1,000	15,000	3,000

[a]Depreciable Cost = Cost − Salvage Value ($18,000 − $3,000 = $15,000).
[b]Rate = Number of Years of Remaining Useful Life ÷ Sum-of-the-Years'-Digits.
[c]Book Value = Cost ($18,000) − Accumulated Depreciation.

FIGURE 5A-3   Depreciation Schedule for Double-Declining-Balance Method

DOUBLE-DECLINING-BALANCE METHOD

YEAR	BOOK VALUE[a] (BEGINNING OF YEAR)	x	RATE[b]	=	DEPRECIATION EXPENSE	ACCUMULATED DEPRECIATION (END OF YEAR)	BOOK VALUE (END OF YEAR)
1	$18,000		40%		$7,200	$ 7,200	$10,800
2	10,800		40%		4,320	11,520	6,480
3	6,480		40%		2,592	14,112	3,888
4	3,888				888	15,000	3,000
5	3,000				0	15,000	3,000

[a]Book Value = Cost ($18,000) − Accumulated Depreciation.
[b]Rate = Double the straight-line rate (1/5 x 2 = 2/5 or 40%).

> **LEARNING KEY** Double means double the straight-line rate. Declining-balance means that the rate is multiplied by the *book value* (not depreciable cost) at the beginning of each year. This amount is *declining* each year.

MODIFIED ACCELERATED COST RECOVERY SYSTEM

LO4   Prepare a depreciation schedule for tax purposes using the Modified Accelerated Cost Recovery System.

For assets purchased since 1986, many firms use the Modified Accelerated Cost Recovery System (MACRS) for tax purposes. Under this method, the Internal Revenue Service (IRS) classifies various assets according to useful life and sets depreciation rates for each year of the asset's life. These rates are then multiplied by the cost of the asset. Even though the van is expected to have a useful life of five years, and a salvage value of $3,000, the IRS schedule, shown in Figure 5A-4, spreads the depreciation over a six-year period and assumes no salvage value.

FIGURE 5A-4 Depreciation Schedule for Modified Accelerated Cost Recovery System

					DEPRECIATION	ACCUMULATED DEPRECIATION	BOOK VALUE[b]
YEAR	COST	x	RATE[a]	=	EXPENSE	(END OF YEAR)	(END OF YEAR)
1	$18,000		20.00%		$3,600	$ 3,600	$14,400
2	18,000		32.00%		5,760	9,360	8,640
3	18,000		19.20%		3,456	12,816	5,184
4	18,000		11.52%		2,074	14,890	3,110
5	18,000		11.52%		2,074	16,964	1,036
6	18,000		5.76%		1,036	18,000	0

[a]Rates set by IRS.
[b]Book Value = Cost ($18,000) − Accumulated Depreciation.

SERIES A EXERCISES

1 **EXERCISE 5ApxA1 STRAIGHT-LINE DEPRECIATION** A small delivery truck was purchased on January 1 at a cost of $25,000. It has an estimated useful life of 4 years and an estimated salvage value of $5,000. Prepare a depreciation schedule showing the depreciation expense, accumulated depreciation, and book value for each year under the straight-line method.

2 **EXERCISE 5ApxA2 SUM-OF-THE-YEARS'-DIGITS DEPRECIATION** Using the information given in Exercise 5ApxA1, prepare a depreciation schedule showing the depreciation expense, accumulated depreciation, and book value for each year under the sum-of-the-years'-digits method.

3 **EXERCISE 5ApxA3 DOUBLE-DECLINING BALANCE DEPRECIATION** Using the information given in Exercise 5ApxA1, prepare a depreciation schedule showing the depreciation expense, accumulated depreciation, and book value for each year under the double-declining-balance method.

4 **EXERCISE 5ApxA4 MODIFIED ACCELERATED COST RECOVERY SYSTEM** Using the information given in Exercise 5ApxA1 and the rates shown in Figure 5A-4, prepare a depreciation schedule showing the depreciation expense, accumulated depreciation, and book value for each year under the Modified Accelerated Cost Recovery System. For tax purposes, assume that the truck has a useful life of 5 years.

SERIES B EXERCISES

1 **EXERCISE 5ApxB1 STRAIGHT-LINE DEPRECIATION** A computer was purchased on January 1 at a cost of $5,000. It has an estimated useful life of 5 years and an estimated salvage value of $500. Prepare a depreciation schedule showing the depreciation expense, accumulated depreciation, and book value for each year under the straight-line method.

2 **EXERCISE 5ApxB2 SUM-OF-THE-YEARS'-DIGITS DEPRECIATION**
Using the information given in Exercise 5ApxB1, prepare a depreciation schedule showing the depreciation expense, accumulated depreciation, and book value for each year under the sum-of-the-years'-digits method.

3 **EXERCISE 5ApxB3 DOUBLE-DECLINING BALANCE DEPRECIATION** Using the information given in Exercise 5ApxB1, prepare a depreciation schedule showing the depreciation expense, accumulated depreciation, and book value for each year under the double-declining-balance method.

4 **EXERCISE 5ApxB4 MODIFIED ACCELERATED COST RECOVERY SYSTEM** Using the information given in Exercise 5ApxB1 and the rates shown in Figure 5A-4, prepare a depreciation schedule showing the depreciation expense, accumulated depreciation, and book value for each year under the Modified Accelerated Cost Recovery System. For tax purposes, assume that the truck has a useful life of 5 years.

6

Financial Statements and the Closing Process

"Come on Carlota, let's get busy. We have to close the books before we go to the New Year's Eve party," said Ramon. But after seeing the disappointed look on Carlota's face, Ramon changed his mind. "What the heck. Let's do it on the 2nd, while we recover from watching all of those bowl games." "Great," said Carlota, "let's get out of here." Will Ramon and Carlota be in trouble for not closing the books before the end of the year?

The work sheet, introduced in Chapter 5, is used for three major end-of-period activities:

1. journalizing adjusting entries,
2. preparing financial statements, and
3. journalizing closing entries.

This chapter illustrates the use of the work sheet for preparing financial statements and closing entries. In addition, the post-closing trial balance will be explained and illustrated. All of these activities take place at the end of the firm's fiscal year. However, to continue our illustration of Jessie Jane's Campus Delivery, we will demonstrate these activities at the end of the first month of operations.

THE FINANCIAL STATEMENTS

LO1   Prepare financial statements with the aid of a work sheet.

Since Jane made no additional investments, the work sheet prepared in Chapter 5 supplies all of the information needed to prepare an income statement, a statement of owner's equity, and a balance sheet. The statements and work sheet columns from which they are derived for Jessie Jane's Campus Delivery are shown in Figures 6-1 and 6-2.

As you refer to the financial statements in Figures 6-1 and 6-2, notice the placement of dollar signs, single rulings, and double rulings. Dollar signs are placed at the top of each column and beneath rulings. Single rulings indicate addition or subtraction, and double rulings are placed under totals. Notice that each statement heading contains three lines: (1) company name, (2) statement title, and (3) period ended or date.

Working Together to Understand the Income Statement

In 1980, SRC, an engine remanufacturing subsidiary of International Harvester, was facing crippling financial difficulties. The company was taken private in a leveraged buyout organized by plant manager Jack Stack. Jack set out to "teach anyone who moved a broom or operated a grinder everything a bank lender knew. That way they could really understand how every nickel saved could make a difference."

Today, after extensive financial training, every employee can interpret the business' income statement. Weekly, employees meet in small groups to study the most current financial statements. Since their yearly bonus is based on meeting goals measured by numbers in these statements, employees take a keen interest in the numbers. Employees know how much it costs to make a photocopy or shut down a machine for repairs. They also look for ways to reduce costs and improve net income, the company's bottom line. One group of machinists recently chose to work overtime to cover an increased work load, rather than pay for the training of new employees. After studying the numbers, they decided the overtime would cost the company less.

Source: Jaclyn Fierman, "Winning Ideas from Maverick Managers" *Fortune* (February 6, 1995): 67–68.

FIGURE 6-1   The Work Sheet and the Income Statement

Jessie Jane's Campus Delivery
Work Sheet (Partial)
For Month Ended June 30, 19--

	ACCOUNT TITLE	INCOME STATEMENT DEBIT	INCOME STATEMENT CREDIT	BALANCE SHEET DEBIT	BALANCE SHEET CREDIT	
1	Cash					1
2	Accounts Receivable					2
3	Supplies					3
4	Prepaid Insurance					4
5	Delivery Equipment					5
6	Accum. Depr.—Del. Equip.					6
7	Accounts Payable					7
8	Wages Payable					8
9	Jessica Jane, Capital					9
10	Jessica Jane, Drawing					10
11	Delivery Fees		2 0 0 0 00			11
12	Rent Expense	2 0 0 00				12
13	Wages Expense	7 0 0 00				13
14	Supplies Expense	6 0 00				14
15	Telephone Expense	5 0 00				15
16	Depr. Exp.—Del. Equip.	1 0 0 00				16
17	Insurance Expense	2 5 00				17
18		1 1 3 5 00	2 0 0 0 00			18
19	Net Income	8 6 5 00				19
20		2 0 0 0 00	2 0 0 0 00			20
21						21
22						22

> Dollar signs are not used on the work sheet

The Income Statement

Figure 6-1 shows how the Income Statement columns of the work sheet provide the information needed to prepare an income statement. Revenue is shown first, followed by an itemized and totaled list of expenses. Then, net income is calculated to double check the accuracy of the work sheet. It is presented with a double ruling as the last item in the statement.

The expenses could be listed in the same order that they appear in the chart of accounts or in descending order by dollar amount. The second approach helps the reader identify the most important expenses.

LEARNING KEY   Multiple columns are used on the financial statements to make them easier to read. There are no debit or credit columns on the financial statements.

FIGURE 6-1   The Work Sheet and the Income Statement (continued)

Jessie Jane's Campus Delivery Income Statement For Month Ended June 30, 19--		
Revenue:		
Delivery fees		$2 0 0 0 00
Expenses:		
Rent expense	$ 2 0 0 00	
Wages expense	7 0 0 00	
Supplies expense	6 0 00	
Telephone expense	5 0 00	
Depreciation expense—delivery equipment	1 0 0 00	
Insurance expense	2 5 00	
Total expenses		1 1 3 5 00
Net income		$ 8 6 5 00

Name of company
Title of statement
Accounting period ended

Revenues listed first

Expenses listed second by amount (largest to smallest) or in chart of accounts order; amounts are itemized in left column, subtotaled in right column

Dollar signs used at top of columns and under rulings

Single rulings indicate addition or subtraction

Double rulings indicate totals

The Statement of Owner's Equity

Figure 6-2 shows that the Balance Sheet columns of the work sheet provide the information needed to prepare a statement of owner's equity. Jane's capital account balance and the drawing account balance are in the Balance Sheet columns of the work sheet. The net income for the year can be found either on the work sheet at the bottom of the Balance Sheet columns or on the income statement. With these three items of information, the statement of owner's equity can be prepared.

Be careful when using the capital account balance reported in the balance sheet columns of the work sheet. This account balance is the beginning balance *plus any additional investments made during the period.* Since Jane made no additional investments during June, the $2,000 balance may be used as the beginning balance on the statement of owner's equity.

The owner's capital account in the general ledger must be reviewed to determine if additional investments were made during the accounting period.

What if the owner of a business made additional investments during the accounting period? Then, we must review the owner's capital account in the general ledger to get the information needed to prepare the statement of owner's equity. Figure 6-3 illustrates this situation for another business, Ramon's Shopping Service. The $5,000 balance on July 1, 19--, in Ramon Balboa's general ledger capital account is used as the beginning balance on the statement of owner's equity. The additional investment of $3,000 made on July 5 and posted to Balboa's general ledger capital account is reported by writing "Add additional investments" on the line immediately after the beginning balance. The beginning balance plus the additional investment equals the total investment by the owner in the business. From this point,

FIGURE 6-2 Using the Balance Sheet Columns of the Work Sheet to Prepare Statements

Jessie Jane's Campus Delivery
Work Sheet (Partial)
For Month Ended June 30, 19--

	ACCOUNT TITLE			BALANCE SHEET		
				DEBIT	CREDIT	
1	Cash			3 7 0 00		1
2	Accounts Receivable			5 0 0 00		2
3	Supplies			2 0 00		3
4	Prepaid Insurance			1 7 5 00		4
5	Delivery Equipment			3 6 0 0 00		5
6	Accum. Depr.—Del. Equip.				1 0 0 00	6
7	Accounts Payable				1 8 0 0 00	7
8	Wages Payable				5 0 00	8
9	Jessica Jane, Capital				2 0 0 0 00	9
10	Jessica Jane, Drawing			1 5 0 00		10
11	Delivery Fees					11
12	Rent Expense					12
13	Wages Expense					13
14	Supplies Expense					14
15	Telephone Expense					15
16	Depr. Exp.—Del. Equip.					16
17	Insurance Expense					17
18				4 8 1 5 00	3 9 5 0 00	18
19	Net Income				8 6 5 00	19
20				4 8 1 5 00	4 8 1 5 00	20
21						21
22						22

the preparation of the statement is the same as for businesses without additional investments.

The Balance Sheet

As shown in Figure 6-2, the work sheet and the statement of owner's equity are used to prepare Jane's balance sheet. The asset and liability amounts can be found in the Balance Sheet columns of the work sheet. The ending balance in Jessica Jane, Capital has been computed on the statement of owner's equity. This amount should be copied from the statement of owner's equity to the balance sheet.

Two important features of the balance sheet in Figure 6-2 should be noted. First, it is a **report form of balance sheet,** which means that the liabilities and owner's equity sections are shown below the assets section. It differs from an **account form of balance sheet** in which the assets are on the left and the liabilities and owner's equity sections on the right. (See Jane's balance sheet illustrated in Figure 2-2 on page 28 in Chapter 2.)

FIGURE 6-2   Using the Balance Sheet Columns of the Work Sheet to Prepare Statements (concluded)

Jessie Jane's Campus Delivery
Statement of Owner's Equity
For Month Ended June 30, 19--

Jessica Jane, capital, June 1, 19--		$2 0 0 0 00
Net income for June	$ 8 6 5 00	
Less withdrawals for June	1 5 0 00	
Increase in capital		7 1 5 00
Jessica Jane, capital, June 30, 19--		$2 7 1 5 00

Name of company
Title of statement
Accounting period ended

Dollar signs used at top of columns and beneath rulings

Single rulings indicate addition or subtraction

Double rulings indicate totals

Jessie Jane's Campus Delivery
Balance Sheet
June 30, 19--

Assets		
Current assets:		
Cash	$ 3 7 0 00	
Accounts receivable	5 0 0 00	
Supplies	2 0 00	
Prepaid insurance	1 7 5 00	
Total current assets		$1 0 6 5 00
Property, plant, and equipment:		
Delivery equipment	$3 6 0 0 00	
Less accumulated depreciation	1 0 0 00	3 5 0 0 00
Total assets		$4 5 6 5 00
Liabilities		
Current liabilities:		
Accounts payable	$1 8 0 0 00	
Wages payable	5 0 00	
Total current liabilities		$1 8 5 0 00
Owner's Equity		
Jessica Jane, capital		2 7 1 5 00
Total liabilities and owner's equity		$4 5 6 5 00

Name of company
Title of statement
Date of statement

Report form of balance sheet

Current assets: cash and items that will be converted to cash or used up within a year

Property, plant, and equipment: assets that will help produce revenues for more than a year

Current liabilities: amounts owed that will be paid within a year (will require the use of current assets)

Ending capital is not taken from work sheet; it is computed on the statement of owner's equity

Second, it is a **classified balance sheet,** which means that similar items are grouped together on the balance sheet. Assets are classified as current assets and property, plant, and equipment. Similarly, liabilities are broken down into current and long-term sections. The following major balance sheet classifications are generally used.

Current Assets.   **Current assets** include cash and assets that will be converted into cash or consumed within either one year or the normal operating cycle of the business, whichever is longer. An **operating cycle** is the period of time required to purchase supplies and services and convert them back into cash.

FIGURE 6-3   Statement of Owner's Equity with Additional Investment

GENERAL LEDGER

ACCOUNT: Ramon Balboa, Capital   ACCOUNT NO. 311

DATE	ITEM	POST. REF.	DEBIT	CREDIT	BALANCE DEBIT	BALANCE CREDIT
July 1				5 0 0 0 00		5 0 0 0 00
5				3 0 0 0 00		8 0 0 0 00

Amount invested July 1

Amount reported on work sheet

Ramon's Shopping Service
Statement of Owner's Equity
For Month Ended July 31, 19--

Ramon Balboa, capital, July 1, 19--		$5 0 0 0 00
Add additional investments		3 0 0 0 00
Total investment		$8 0 0 0 00
Net income for July	$2 1 0 0 00	
Less withdrawals for July	2 5 0 00	
Increase in capital		1 8 5 0 00
Ramon Balboa, capital, July 31, 19--		$9 8 5 0 00

From general ledger

From work sheet

Property, Plant, and Equipment.   **Property, plant and equipment,** also called **plant assets** or **long-term assets,** represent assets that are expected to serve the business for many years.

Current Liabilities.   **Current liabilities** are liabilities that are due within either one year or the normal operating cycle of the business, whichever is longer, and that are to be paid out of current assets. Accounts payable and wages payable are classified as current liabilities.

Long-Term Liabilities.   **Long-term liabilities,** or **long-term debt,** are obligations that are not expected to be paid within a year and do not require the use of current assets. A mortgage on an office building is an example of a long-term liability. Jane has no long-term debts. If she did, they would be listed on the balance sheet in the long-term liabilities section immediately following the current liabilities.

THE CLOSING PROCESS

LO2   Journalize and post closing entries.

Assets, liabilities, and the owner's capital account accumulate information across accounting periods. Their balances are brought forward for each new period. For example, the amount of cash at the end of one accounting period must be the same as the amount of cash at the beginning of the next. Thus, the balance reported for Cash is a result of all cash transactions since the business first opened. This is true for all accounts reported on the balance sheet. For this reason, they are called **permanent accounts.**

 LEARNING KEY Permanent accounts contain the results of all transactions since the business started. Their balances are carried forward to each new accounting period.

Revenue, expense, and drawing accounts accumulate information *for a specific accounting period.* At the end of the fiscal year, these accounts must be *closed.* The **closing process** gives these accounts zero balances so they are prepared to accumulate new information for the next accounting period. Since these accounts do not accumulate information across accounting periods, they are called **temporary accounts.** The drawing account and all accounts reported on the income statement are temporary accounts and must be closed at the end of each accounting period.

 LEARNING KEY Temporary accounts contain information for one accounting period. These accounts are closed at the end of each accounting period.

The closing process is most clearly demonstrated by returning to the accounting equation and T accounts. As shown in Figure 6-4, revenues, expenses, and drawing impact owner's equity and should be considered "under the umbrella" of the capital account. The effect of these accounts on owner's equity is formalized at the end of the accounting period when the balances of the temporary accounts are transferred to the owner's capital account (a permanent account) during the closing process.

The four basic steps in the closing process are illustrated in Figure 6-4. As you can see, a new account, **Income Summary,** is used in the closing

FIGURE 6-4   The Closing Process

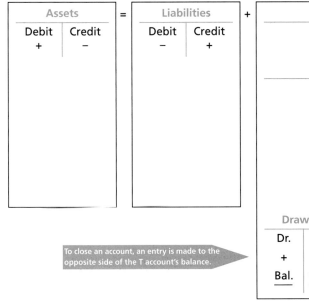
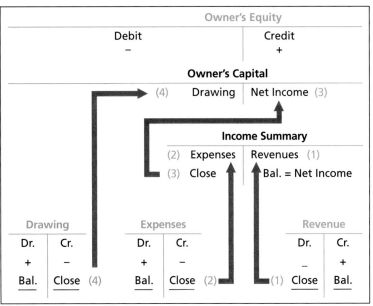

process. This account may also be called *Expense and Revenue Summary*. This temporary account summarizes the effects of all revenue and expense accounts. Income Summary is opened during the closing process. Then it is closed to the owner's capital account. It does not appear on any financial statement. The four steps in the closing process are explained below.

STEPS IN THE CLOSING PROCESS

STEP 1   **Close Revenue Accounts to Income Summary.**   Revenues have credit balances and increase owner's equity. Therefore, the revenue account is debited to create a zero balance. Income Summary is credited for the same amount.

STEP 2   **Close Expense Accounts to Income Summary.**   Expenses have debit balances and reduce owner's equity. Therefore, the expense accounts are credited to create a zero balance. Income Summary must be debited for the total of the expenses.

STEP 3   **Close Income Summary to Capital.**   The balance in Income Summary represents the net income (credit balance) or net loss (debit balance) for the period. This balance is transferred to the owner's capital account. If net income has been earned, Income Summary is debited to create a zero balance, and the owner's capital account is credited. If a net loss has been incurred, the owner's capital account is debited and Income Summary is credited to create a zero balance Figure 6-5 shows examples of Step 3 for net income and net loss.

FIGURE 6-5   Step 3: Closing Net Income and Closing Net Loss

NET INCOME				NET LOSS			
	Capital				Capital		
		1,000	STEP 3	STEP 3	2,000		
		(Net Income)			(Net Loss)		
	Income Summary				Income Summary		
(Exp.)	4,000	5,000	(Rev.)	(Exp.)	6,000	4,000	(Rev.)
STEP 3	1,000	____			____	2,000	STEP 3

STEP 4   **Close Drawing to Capital.**   Drawing has a debit balance and reduces owner's equity. Therefore, it is credited to create a zero balance. The owner's capital account is debited.

> The owner can make withdrawals from the business for any amount and at any time, as long as the assets are available. These withdrawals are for personal reasons and have nothing to do with measuring the profitability of the firm. Thus, they are closed directly to the owner's capital account.

Upon completion of these four steps, all temporary accounts have zero balances as indicated by the rules at the bottom of the T accounts. The earnings and withdrawals for the period have been transferred to the owner's capital account.

Journalize Closing Entries

Of course, to actually change the ledger accounts, the closing entries must be journalized and posted to the general ledger. As shown in Figure 6-6, the balances of the accounts to be closed are readily available from the Income Statement and Balance Sheet columns of the work sheet. These balances are used to illustrate the closing entries for Jessie Jane's Campus Delivery, in T account and general journal form, in Figures 6-7 and 6-8 respectively. Remember: closing entries are made at the end of the *fiscal year*. Closing entries at the end of June are illustrated here so you can see the completion of the accounting cycle for Jessie Jane's Campus Delivery.

FIGURE 6-6   Role of the Work Sheet in the Closing Process

Jessie Jane's Campus Delivery
Work Sheet (Partial)
For Month Ended June 30, 19--

	ACCOUNT TITLE	INCOME STATEMENT DEBIT	INCOME STATEMENT CREDIT	BALANCE SHEET DEBIT	BALANCE SHEET CREDIT	
1	Cash			3 7 0 00		1
2	Accounts Receivable			5 0 0 00		2
3	Supplies			2 0 00		3
4	Prepaid Insurance			1 7 5 00		4
5	Delivery Equipment			3 6 0 0 00		5
6	Accum. Depr.—Del. Equip.				1 0 0 00	6
7	Accounts Payable				1 8 0 0 00	7
8	Wages Payable		STEP 1		5 0 00	8
9	Jessica Jane, Capital	STEP 2			2 0 0 0 00	9
10	Jessica Jane, Drawing			1 5 0 00		10
11	Delivery Fees		2 0 0 0 00			11
12	Rent Expense	2 0 0 00				12
13	Wages Expense	7 0 0 00		STEP 4		13
14	Supplies Expense	6 0 00				14
15	Telephone Expense	5 0 00				15
16	Depr. Exp.—Del. Equip.	1 0 0 00				16
17	Insurance Expense	2 5 00				17
18		1 1 3 5 00	2 0 0 0 00	4 8 1 5 00	3 9 5 0 00	18
19	Net Income STEP 3	8 6 5 00			8 6 5 00	19
20		2 0 0 0 00	2 0 0 0 00	4 8 1 5 00	4 8 1 5 00	20

STEP 1 Close revenue accounts to Income Summary.

STEP 2 Close expense accounts to Income Summary.

STEP 3 Close Income Summary to the owner's capital account.

STEP 4 Close Drawing to the owner's capital account.

Like adjusting entries, the closing entries are made on the last day of the accounting period. "Closing Entries" is written in the description column before the first entry and no explanations are required. Note that it is best to make one compound entry to close the expense accounts.

FIGURE 6-7   Closing Entries in T Account Form

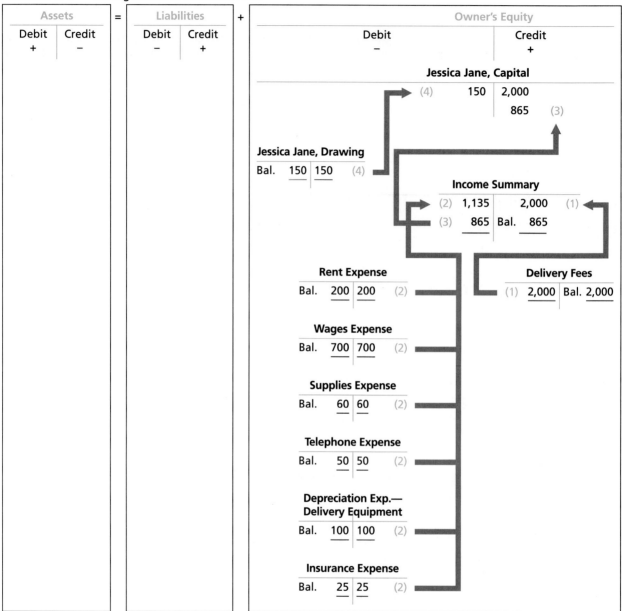

 LEARNING KEY   Each individual revenue, expense, and drawing account must be closed.

Post the Closing Entries

The account numbers have been entered in the Posting Reference column of the journal to show that the entries have been posted to the ledger

FIGURE 6-8 Closing Entries in General Journal

	DATE		DESCRIPTION	POST. REF.	DEBIT	CREDIT	
GENERAL JOURNAL						PAGE **4**	
1			Closing Entries				1
2	June 19--	30	Delivery Fees	411	2 0 0 0 00		2
3			Income Summary	313		2 0 0 0 00	3
4							4
5		30	Income Summary	313	1 1 3 5 00		5
6			Rent Expense	541		2 0 0 00	6
7			Wages Expense	542		7 0 0 00	7
8			Supplies Expense	543		6 0 00	8
9			Telephone Expense	545		5 0 00	9
10			Depr. Exp.—Del. Equip.	547		1 0 0 00	10
11			Insurance Expense	559		2 5 00	11
12							12
13		30	Income Summary	313	8 6 5 00		13
14			Jessica Jane, Capital	311		8 6 5 00	14
15							15
16		30	Jessica Jane, Capital	311	1 5 0 00		16
17			Jessica Jane, Drawing	312		1 5 0 00	17
18							18
19							19

STEP 1 (rows 2–3)
STEP 2 (rows 5–11)
Compound entry
STEP 3 (rows 13–14)
STEP 4 (rows 16–17)
No explanations are necessary

accounts illustrated in Figure 6-9. Note that "Closing" has been written in the Item column of each account to identify the closing entries. Zero account balances are recorded by drawing a line through both the debit and credit Balance columns.

 LEARNING KEY

Once the closing entries are posted, the general ledger account balances will agree with the amounts reported on the balance sheet.

FIGURE 6-9 Closing Entries Posted to the General Ledger

GENERAL LEDGER

ACCOUNT: Jessica Jane, Capital   ACCOUNT NO. 311

DATE		ITEM	POST. REF.	DEBIT	CREDIT	BALANCE DEBIT	BALANCE CREDIT
June 19--	1		J1		2 0 0 0 00		2 0 0 0 00
	30	Closing	J4		8 6 5 00		2 8 6 5 00
	30	Closing	J4	1 5 0 00			2 7 1 5 00

FIGURE 6-9 Closing Entries Posted to the General Ledger (continued)

ACCOUNT: Jessica Jane, Drawing   ACCOUNT NO. 312

DATE		ITEM	POST. REF.	DEBIT	CREDIT	BALANCE DEBIT	BALANCE CREDIT
19-- June	30		J2	1 5 0 00		1 5 0 00	
	30	Closing	J4		1 5 0 00	—	—

ACCOUNT: Income Summary   ACCOUNT NO. 313

DATE		ITEM	POST. REF.	DEBIT	CREDIT	BALANCE DEBIT	BALANCE CREDIT
19-- June	30	Closing	J4		2 0 0 0 00		2 0 0 0 00
	30	Closing	J4	1 1 3 5 00			8 6 5 00
	30	Closing	J4	8 6 5 00		—	—

ACCOUNT: Delivery Fees   ACCOUNT NO. 411

DATE		ITEM	POST. REF.	DEBIT	CREDIT	BALANCE DEBIT	BALANCE CREDIT
19-- June	6		J1		5 0 0 00		5 0 0 00
	15		J1		6 0 0 00		1 1 0 0 00
	30		J2		9 0 0 00		2 0 0 0 00
	30	Closing	J4	2 0 0 0 00		—	—

ACCOUNT: Rent Expense   ACCOUNT NO. 541

DATE		ITEM	POST. REF.	DEBIT	CREDIT	BALANCE DEBIT	BALANCE CREDIT
19-- June	7		J1	2 0 0 00		2 0 0 00	
	30	Closing	J4		2 0 0 00	—	—

ACCOUNT: Wages Expense   ACCOUNT NO. 542

DATE		ITEM	POST. REF.	DEBIT	CREDIT	BALANCE DEBIT	BALANCE CREDIT
19-- June	27		J2	6 5 0 00		6 5 0 00	
	30	Adjusting	J3	5 0 00		7 0 0 00	
	30	Closing	J4		7 0 0 00	—	

ACCOUNT: Supplies Expense   ACCOUNT NO. 543

DATE		ITEM	POST. REF.	DEBIT	CREDIT	BALANCE DEBIT	BALANCE CREDIT
19-- June	30	Adjusting	J3	6 0 00		6 0 00	
	30	Closing	J4		6 0 00	—	—

FIGURE 6-9 Closing Entries Posted to the General Ledger (concluded)

ACCOUNT: Telephone Expense   ACCOUNT NO. 545

DATE	ITEM	POST. REF.	DEBIT	CREDIT	BALANCE DEBIT	BALANCE CREDIT
June 15 (19--)		J1	5 0 00		5 0 00	
30	Closing	J4		5 0 00		

ACCOUNT: Depreciation Expense   ACCOUNT NO. 547

DATE	ITEM	POST. REF.	DEBIT	CREDIT	BALANCE DEBIT	BALANCE CREDIT
June 30 (19--)	Adjusting	J3	1 0 0 00		1 0 0 00	
30	Closing	J4		1 0 0 00		

ACCOUNT: Insurance Expense   ACCOUNT NO. 559

DATE	ITEM	POST. REF.	DEBIT	CREDIT	BALANCE DEBIT	BALANCE CREDIT
June 30 (19--)	Adjusting	J3	2 5 00		2 5 00	
30	Closing	J4		2 5 00		

POST-CLOSING TRIAL BALANCE

LO3 Prepare a post-closing trial balance.

After posting the closing entries, a **post-closing trial balance** should be prepared to prove the equality of the debit and credit balances in the general ledger accounts. The ending balance of each general ledger account that remains open at the end of the year is listed. Remember: only the permanent accounts remain open after the closing process is completed. Figure 6-10 shows the post-closing trial balance for Jane's ledger.

THE ACCOUNTING CYCLE

LO4 List and describe the steps in the accounting cycle.

The steps involved in accounting for all of the business activities during an accounting period are called the **accounting cycle.** The cycle begins with the analysis of source documents and ends with a post-closing trial balance. A brief summary of the steps in the cycle follows.

FIGURE 6-10   Post-Closing Trial Balance

Jessie Jane's Campus Delivery
Post-Closing Trial Balance
June 30, 19--

ACCOUNT TITLE	ACCOUNT NO.	DEBIT BALANCE	CREDIT BALANCE
Cash	111	3 7 0 00	
Accounts Receivable	131	5 0 0 00	
Supplies	151	2 0 00	
Prepaid Insurance	155	1 7 5 00	
Delivery Equipment	185	3 6 0 0 00	
Accumulated Depreciation—Delivery Equipment	185.1		1 0 0 00
Accounts Payable	216		1 8 0 0 00
Wages Payable	219		5 0 00
Jessica Jane, Capital	311		2 7 1 5 00
		4 6 6 5 00	4 6 6 5 00

STEPS IN THE ACCOUNTING CYCLE

During Accounting Period

STEP 1   Analyze source documents.

STEP 2   Journalize the transactions.

STEP 3   Post to the ledger accounts.

End of Accounting Period

STEP 4   Prepare a trial balance.

STEP 5   Determine and prepare the needed adjustments on the work sheet.

STEP 6   Complete an end-of-period work sheet.

STEP 7   Prepare an income statement, statement of owner's equity, and balance sheet.

STEP 8   Journalize and post the adjusting entries.

STEP 9   Journalize and post the closing entries.

STEP 10   Prepare a post-closing trial balance.

 Properly analyzing and journalizing transactions is very important. A mistake made in Step 1 is carried through the entire accounting cycle.

Steps (4) through (10) in the preceding list are performed *as of* the last day of the accounting period. This does not mean that they are actually done on the last day. The accountant may not be able to do any of these things until the first few days (sometimes weeks) of the next period. Nevertheless, the work sheet, statements, and entries are prepared as of the closing date.

KEY POINTS

1 The work sheet is a very useful tool. It is used as an aid in preparing the:

1. adjusting entries,
2. financial statements, and
3. closing entries.

The following classifications are used for accounts reported on the balance sheet.

- **Current assets** include cash and assets that will be converted into cash or consumed within either one year or the normal operating cycle of the business, whichever is longer. An **operating cycle** is the time required to purchase supplies and services and convert them back into cash.
- **Property, plant, and equipment,** also called **plant assets** or **long-term assets,** represent assets that are expected to serve the business for many years.
- **Current liabilities** are liabilities that are due within either one year or the normal operating cycle of the business, whichever is longer, and that are to be paid out of current assets.
- **Long-term liabilities,** or **long-term debt,** are obligations that are not expected to be paid within a year and do not require the use of current assets.

2 Steps in the closing process are:

1. Close revenue accounts to Income Summary.
2. Close expense accounts to Income Summary.
3. Close Income Summary to Capital.
4. Close Drawing to Capital.

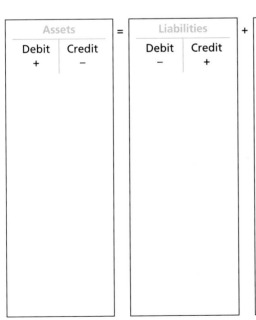
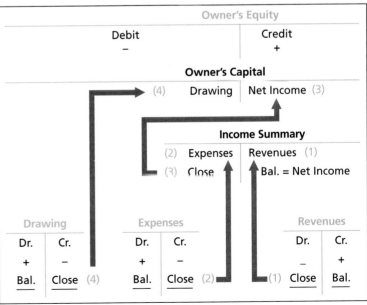

3 After posting the closing entries, a post-closing trial balance should be prepared to prove the equality of the debit and credit balances in the general ledger accounts. The accounts shown in the post-closing trial balance are the permanent accounts.

4 Steps in the accounting cycle are:

During Accounting Period

1. Analyze source documents.
2. Journalize the transactions.
3. Post to the ledger accounts.

End of Accounting Period

4. Prepare a trial balance.
5. Determine and prepare the needed adjustments on the work sheet.
6. Complete an end-of-period work sheet.
7. Prepare an income statement, statement of owner's equity, and balance sheet.
8. Journalize and post the adjusting entries.
9. Journalize and post the closing entries.
10. Prepare a post-closing trial balance.

KEY TERMS

account form of balance sheet 166 The assets are on the left and the liabilities and the owner's equity sections are on the right.

accounting cycle 175 The steps involved in accounting for all of the business activities during an accounting period.

classified balance sheet 167 Similar items are grouped together on the balance sheet.

closing process 169 The process of giving zero balances to the temporary accounts so that they can accumulate information for the next accounting period.

current assets 167 Cash and assets that will be converted into cash or consumed within either one year or the normal operating cycle of the business, whichever is longer.

current liabilities 168 Liabilities that are due within either one year or the normal operating cycle of the business, whichever is longer, and that are to be paid out of current assets.

Income Summary 169 A temporary account used in the closing process to summarize the effects of all revenue and expense accounts.

long-term assets 168 See property, plant, and equipment.

long-term debt 168 See long-term liabilities.

long-term liabilities 168 Obligations that are not expected to be paid within a year and do not require the use of current assets.

operating cycle 167 The period of time required to purchase supplies and services and convert them back into cash.

permanent accounts 169 All accounts reported on the balance sheet.

plant assets 168 See property, plant, and equipment.

post-closing trial balance 175   Prepared after posting the closing entries to prove the equality of the debit and credit balances in the general ledger accounts.

property, plant, and equipment 168   Assets that are expected to serve the business for many years. Also called plant assets or long-term assets.

report form of balance sheet 166   The liabilities and the owner's equity sections are shown below the assets section.

temporary accounts 169   Accounts that do not accumulate information across accounting periods but are closed, such as the drawing account and all income statement accounts.

REVIEW QUESTIONS

1. Identify the source of the information needed to prepare the income statement.
2. Describe two approaches to listing the expenses in the income statement.
3. Identify the sources of the information needed to prepare the statement of owner's equity.
4. If additional investments were made during the year, what information in addition to the work sheet would be needed to prepare the statement of owner's equity?
5. Identify the sources of the information needed to prepare the balance sheet.
6. What is a permanent account? On which financial statement are permanent accounts reported?
7. Name three types of temporary accounts.
8. List the four steps for closing the temporary accounts.
9. Describe the net effect of the four closing entries on the balance of the owner's capital account. Where else is this same amount calculated?
10. What is the purpose of the post-closing trial balance?
11. List the ten steps in the accounting cycle.

MANAGING YOUR WRITING

At lunch, two bookkeepers got into a heated discussion about whether closing entries should be made before or after preparing the financial statements. They have come to you to resolve this issue and have agreed to accept your position. Write a memo explaining the purpose of closing entries and whether they should be made before or after preparing the financial statements.

DEMONSTRATION PROBLEM

Timothy Chang owns and operates Hard Copy Printers. A work sheet for the year ended December 31, 19--, is provided on the next page. Chang made no additional investments during the year.

REQUIRED

1. Prepare financial statements.
2. Prepare closing entries.

Hard Copy Printers
Work Sheet
For Year Ended December 31, 19--

	TRIAL BALANCE		ADJUSTMENTS		ADJUSTED TRIAL BALANCE		INCOME STATEMENT		BALANCE SHEET	
ACCOUNT TITLE	DEBIT	CREDIT	DEBIT	CREDIT	DEBIT	CREDIT	DEBIT	CREDIT	DEBIT	CREDIT
1 Cash	1180 00				1180 00				1180 00	
2 Paper Supplies	3600 00			(a) 3550 00	50 00				50 00	
3 Prepaid Insurance	1000 00			(b) 505 00	495 00				495 00	
4 Printing Equipment	5800 00				5800 00				5800 00	
5 Accum. Depr.—Printing Equip.				(d) 1200 00		1200 00				1200 00
6 Accounts Payable		500 00				500 00				500 00
7 Wages Payable				(c) 30 00		30 00				30 00
8 Timothy Chang, Capital		10000 00				10000 00				10000 00
9 Timothy Chang, Drawing	1300 00				1300 00				1300 00	
10 Printing Fees		35100 00				35100 00		35100 00		
11 Rent Expense	7500 00				7500 00		7500 00			
12 Wages Expense	11970 00		(c) 30 00		12000 00		12000 00			
13 Paper Supplies Expense			(a) 3550 00		3550 00		3550 00			
14 Telephone Expense	550 00				550 00		550 00			
15 Depr. Expense—Printing Equip.			(d) 1200 00		1200 00		1200 00			
16 Utilities Expense	1000 00				1000 00		1000 00			
17 Insurance Expense			(b) 505 00		505 00		505 00			
18	45600 00	45600 00	5285 00	5285 00	46830 00	46830 00	26305 00	35100 00	20525 00	11730 00
19 Net Income							8795 00			8795 00
20							35100 00	35100 00	20525 00	20525 00
21										

SOLUTION

1.

Hard Copy Printers
Income Statement
For Year Ended December 31, 19--

Revenue:					
Printing fees				$35 1 0 0	00
Expenses:					
Rent expense	$ 7 5 0 0	00			
Wages expense	12 0 0 0	00			
Paper supplies expense	3 5 5 0	00			
Telephone expense	5 5 0	00			
Depreciation expense—printing equipment	1 2 0 0	00			
Utilities expense	1 0 0 0	00			
Insurance expense	5 0 5	00			
Total expenses				26 3 0 5	00
Net income				$ 8 7 9 5	00

Hard Copy Printers
Statement of Owner's Equity
For Year Ended December 31, 19--

Timothy Chang, capital, Jan. 1, 19--				$10 0 0 0	00
Net income for 19--	$ 8 7 9 5	00			
Less withdrawals for 19--	13 0 0 0	00			
Decrease in capital				(4 2 0 5	00)
Timothy Chang, capital, Dec. 31, 19--				$ 5 7 9 5	00

Hard Copy Printers
Balance Sheet
December 31, 19--

Assets					
Current assets:					
Cash	$1 1 8 0	00			
Paper supplies	5 0	00			
Prepaid insurance	4 9 5	00			
Total current assets				$1 7 2 5	00
Property, plant, and equipment:					
Printing equipment	$5 8 0 0	00			
Less accumulated depreciation	1 2 0 0	00	4 6 0 0	00	
Total assets				$6 3 2 5	00
Liabilities					
Current liabilities:					
Accounts payable	$ 5 0 0	00			
Wages payable	3 0	00			
Total current liabilities				$ 5 3 0	00
Owner's Equity					
Timothy Chang, capital				5 7 9 5	00
Total liabilities and owner's equity				$6 3 2 5	00

2.

			GENERAL JOURNAL									PAGE 4	
	DATE		DESCRIPTION	POST. REF.		DEBIT				CREDIT			
1			Closing Entries										1
2	Dec.¹⁹⁻⁻	31	Printing Fees		35	1	0	0	00				2
3			Income Summary							35	1	0 0 00	3
4													4
5		31	Income Summary		26	3	0	5	00				5
6			Rent Expense							7	5	0 0 00	6
7			Wages Expense							12	0	0 0 00	7
8			Paper Supplies Expense							3	5	5 0 00	8
9			Telephone Expense								5	5 0 00	9
10			Depr. Expense—Printing Equip.							1	2	0 0 00	10
11			Utilities Expense							1	0	0 0 00	11
12			Insurance Expense								5	0 5 00	12
13													13
14		31	Income Summary		8	7	9	5	00				14
15			Timothy Chang, Capital							8	7	9 5 00	15
16													16
17		31	Timothy Chang, Capital		13	0	0	0	00				17
18			Timothy Chang, Drawing							13	0	0 0 00	18
19													19
20													20
21													21
22													22

SERIES A EXERCISES

1 **EXERCISE 6A1 INCOME STATEMENT** From the partial work sheet for Case Advising on page 183, prepare an income statement.

1 **EXERCISE 6A2 STATEMENT OF OWNER'S EQUITY** From the partial work sheet in Exercise 6A1, prepare a statement of owner's equity, assuming no additional investment was made by the owner.

1 **EXERCISE 6A3 BALANCE SHEET** From the partial work sheet in Exercise 6A1, prepare a balance sheet.

2 **EXERCISE 6A4 CLOSING ENTRIES (NET INCOME)** Set up T accounts for Case Advising based on the work sheet and chart of accounts provided on page 183. Enter the existing balance for each account. Prepare closing entries in general journal form. Then post the closing entries to the T accounts.

Case Advising
Work Sheet (Partial)
For Month Ended January 31, 19--

ACCOUNT TITLE	INCOME STATEMENT DEBIT	INCOME STATEMENT CREDIT	BALANCE SHEET DEBIT	BALANCE SHEET CREDIT	
1 Cash			1212 00		1
2 Accounts Receivable			896 00		2
3 Supplies			482 00		3
4 Prepaid Insurance			900 00		4
5 Office Equipment			3000 00		5
6 Accum. Depr.—Off. Equip.				100 00	6
7 Accounts Payable				1000 00	7
8 Wages Payable				200 00	8
9 Bill Case, Capital				4000 00	9
10 Bill Case, Drawing			800 00		10
11 Advising Fees		3793 00			11
12 Rent Expense	500 00				12
13 Wages Expense	800 00				13
14 Supplies Expense	120 00				14
15 Telephone Expense	58 00				15
16 Depr. Exp.—Off. Equip.	100 00				16
17 Insurance Expense	30 00				17
18 Electricity Expense	44 00				18
19 Advertising Expense	80 00				19
20 Gas and Oil Expense	38 00				20
21 Miscellaneous Expense	33 00				21
22	1803 00	3793 00	7290 00	5300 00	22
23 Net Income	1990 00			1990 00	23
24	3793 00	3793 00	7290 00	7290 00	24

Chart of Accounts

Assets
111   Cash
131   Accounts Receivable
151   Supplies
155   Prepaid Insurance
181   Office Equipment
181.1   Accum. Depr.—Office Equip.

Liabilities
216   Accounts Payable
219   Wages Payable

Owner's Equity
311   Bill Case, Capital
312   Bill Case, Drawing
313   Income Summary

Revenues
411   Advising Fees

Expenses
541   Rent Expense
542   Wages Expense
543   Supplies Expense
545   Telephone Expense
547   Depr. Exp.—Office Equip.
548   Insurance Expense
549   Electricity Expense
551   Advertising Expense
552   Gas and Oil Expense
572   Miscellaneous Expense

2 **EXERCISE 6A5 CLOSING ENTRIES (NET LOSS)**   Using the following T accounts, prepare closing entries in general journal form dated January 31, 19--. Then post the closing entries to the T accounts.

Accum. Depr.— Del. Equip. 185.1	Rent Expense 541	Insurance Expense 548
Bal. 100	Bal. 500	Bal. 30

Wages Payable 219	Wages Expense 542	Electricity Expense 549
Bal. 200	Bal. 1,800	Bal. 44

Saburo Goto, Capital 311	Supplies Expense 543	Advertising Expense 551
Bal. 4,000	Bal. 120	Bal. 80

Saburo Goto, Drawing 312	Telephone Expense 545	Gas and Oil Expense 552
Bal. 800	Bal. 58	Bal. 38

Income Summary 313	Depr. Exp.— Del. Equip. 547	Miscellaneous Expense 572
	Bal. 100	Bal. 33

Delivery Fees 411
Bal. 2,200

SERIES A PROBLEMS

1 **PROBLEM 6A1 FINANCIAL STATEMENTS**   The following page shows a work sheet for Monte's Repairs. No additional investments were made by the owner during the month.

REQUIRED

1. Prepare an income statement.
2. Prepare a statement of owner's equity.
3. Prepare a balance sheet.

1 **PROBLEM 6A2 STATEMENT OF OWNER'S EQUITY**   The capital account for Autumn Chou, with an additional investment, and a partial work sheet are shown on page 186.

Monte's Repairs
Work Sheet
For Month Ended January 31, 19--

	Account Title	Trial Balance Debit	Trial Balance Credit	Adjustments Debit	Adjustments Credit	Adjusted Trial Balance Debit	Adjusted Trial Balance Credit	Income Statement Debit	Income Statement Credit	Balance Sheet Debit	Balance Sheet Credit	
1	Cash	3150 00				3150 00				3150 00		1
2	Accounts Receivable	1200 00				1200 00				1200 00		2
3	Supplies	800 00			(a) 200 00	600 00				600 00		3
4	Prepaid Insurance	900 00			(b) 100 00	800 00				800 00		4
5	Delivery Equipment	3000 00				3000 00				3000 00		5
6	Accum. Depr.—Delivery Equip.				(d) 30 00		30 00				30 00	6
7	Accounts Payable		1100 00				1100 00				1100 00	7
8	Wages Payable				(c) 150 00		150 00				150 00	8
9	Monte Eli, Capital		7000 00				7000 00				7000 00	9
10	Monte Eli, Drawing	1000 00				1000 00				1000 00		10
11	Repair Fees		4230 00				4230 00		4230 00			11
12	Rent Expense	420 00				420 00		420 00				12
13	Wages Expense	1650 00		(c) 150 00		1800 00		1800 00				13
14	Supplies Expense			(a) 200 00		200 00		200 00				14
15	Telephone Expense	49 00				49 00		49 00				15
16	Depr. Exp.—Delivery Equip.			(d) 30 00		30 00		30 00				16
17	Insurance Expense			(b) 100 00		100 00		100 00				17
18	Advertising Expense	100 00				100 00		100 00				18
19	Gas and Oil Expense	33 00				33 00		33 00				19
20	Miscellaneous Expense	28 00				28 00		28 00				20
21		12330 00	12330 00	480 00	480 00	12510 00	12510 00	2760 00	4230 00	9750 00	8280 00	21
22	Net Income							1470 00			1470 00	22
23								4230 00	4230 00	9750 00	9750 00	23

REQUIRED
Prepare a statement of owner's equity.

GENERAL LEDGER

ACCOUNT: Autumn Chou, Capital					ACCOUNT NO. 311	
DATE	**ITEM**	**POST. REF.**	**DEBIT**	**CREDIT**	**BALANCE DEBIT**	**BALANCE CREDIT**
19-- Jan. 1	Balance	✔				4 8 0 0 00
18		J1		1 2 0 0 00		6 0 0 0 00

Autumn's Home Designs
Work Sheet (Partial)
For Month Ended January 31, 19--

	ACCOUNT TITLE	INCOME STATEMENT DEBIT	INCOME STATEMENT CREDIT	BALANCE SHEET DEBIT	BALANCE SHEET CREDIT	
1	Cash			3 2 0 0 00		1
2	Accounts Receivable			1 6 0 0 00		2
3	Supplies			8 0 0 00		3
4	Prepaid Insurance			9 0 0 00		4
5	Office Equipment			2 5 0 0 00		5
6	Accum. Depr.—Office Equip.				5 0 00	6
7	Accounts Payable				1 9 5 0 00	7
8	Wages Payable				1 8 0 00	8
9	Autumn Chou, Capital				6 0 0 0 00	9
10	Autumn Chou, Drawing			1 0 0 0 00		10
11	Design Fees		4 8 6 6 00			11
12	Rent Expense	6 0 0 00				12
13	Wages Expense	1 9 0 0 00				13
14	Supplies Expense	2 0 0 00				14
15	Telephone Expense	8 5 00				15
16	Depr. Exp.—Office Equip.	5 0 00				16
17	Insurance Expense	6 0 00				17
18	Electricity Expense	4 8 00				18
19	Advertising Expense	2 1 00				19
20	Gas and Oil Expense	3 2 00				20
21	Miscellaneous Expense	5 0 00				21
22		3 0 4 6 00	4 8 6 6 00	1 0 0 0 0 00	8 1 8 0 00	22
23	Net Income	1 8 2 0 00			1 8 2 0 00	23
24		4 8 6 6 00	4 8 6 6 00	1 0 0 0 0 00	1 0 0 0 0 00	24

1/2/3 **PROBLEM 6A3 FINANCIAL STATEMENTS, CLOSING ENTRIES, POST-CLOSING TRIAL BALANCE** Refer to the work sheet in
SS Problem 6A1 for Monte's Repairs. The trial balance amounts (before adjustments) have been entered in the ledger accounts provided in the working

papers. If you are not using the working papers that accompany this book, set up ledger accounts and enter these balances as of January 31, 19--. A chart of accounts is provided below.

Monte's Repairs
Chart of Accounts

Assets
111   Cash
131   Accounts Receivable
151   Supplies
155   Prepaid Insurance
185   Delivery Equipment
185.1 Accum. Depr.—Delivery Equip.

Liabilities
216   Accounts Payable
219   Wages Payable

Owner's Equity
311   Monte Eli, Capital
312   Monte Eli, Drawing
313   Income Summary

Revenues
411   Repair Fees

Expenses
541   Rent Expense
542   Wages Expense
543   Supplies Expense
545   Telephone Expense
547   Depr. Exp.—Delivery Equip.
548   Insurance Expense
551   Advertising Expense
552   Gas and Oil Expense
572   Miscellaneous Expense

REQUIRED

1. Journalize (page 10) and post the adjusting entries.
2. Journalize (page 11) and post the closing entries.
3. Prepare a post-closing trial balance.

SERIES B EXERCISES

1 **EXERCISE 6B1 INCOME STATEMENT** From the partial work sheet for Adams' Shoe Shine shown on the next page, prepare an income statement.

1 **EXERCISE 6B2 STATEMENT OF OWNER'S EQUITY** From the partial work sheet in Exercise 6B1, prepare a statement of owner's equity, assuming no additional investment was made by the owner.

1 **EXERCISE 6B3 BALANCE SHEET** From the partial work sheet in Exercise 6B1, prepare a balance sheet for Adams' Shoe Shine.

2 **EXERCISE 6B4 CLOSING ENTRIES (NET INCOME)** Set up T accounts for Adams' Shoe Shine based on the work sheet and chart of accounts provided on page 188. Enter the existing balance for each account. Prepare closing entries in general journal form. Then, post the closing entries to the T accounts.

Adams' Shoe Shine
Work Sheet (Partial)
For Month Ended June 30, 19--

	ACCOUNT TITLE	INCOME STATEMENT		BALANCE SHEET		
		DEBIT	CREDIT	DEBIT	CREDIT	
1	Cash			3 2 6 2 00		1
2	Accounts Receivable			1 2 4 4 00		2
3	Supplies			8 0 0 00		3
4	Prepaid Insurance			6 4 0 00		4
5	Office Equipment			2 1 0 0 00		5
6	Accum. Depr.—Office Equip.				1 1 0 00	6
7	Accounts Payable				1 8 5 0 00	7
8	Wages Payable				2 6 0 00	8
9	Mary Adams, Capital				6 0 0 0 00	9
10	Mary Adams, Drawing			2 0 0 00		10
11	Service Fees		4 8 1 3 00			11
12	Rent Expense	9 0 0 00				12
13	Wages Expense	1 0 8 0 00				13
14	Supplies Expense	3 2 2 00				14
15	Telephone Expense	1 3 3 00				15
16	Depr. Exp.—Office Equip.	1 1 0 00				16
17	Insurance Expense	1 2 0 00				17
18	Utilities Expense	1 0 2 00				18
19	Advertising Expense	3 4 00				19
20	Gas and Oil Expense	8 8 00				20
21	Miscellaneous Expense	9 8 00				21
22		2 9 8 7 00	4 8 1 3 00	1 0 0 4 6 00	8 2 2 0 00	22
23	Net Income	1 8 2 6 00			1 8 2 6 00	23
24		4 8 1 3 00	4 8 1 3 00	1 0 0 4 6 00	1 0 0 4 6 00	24

Chart of Accounts

Assets
111 Cash
131 Accounts Receivable
151 Supplies
155 Prepaid Insurance
191 Office Equipment
191.1 Accum. Depr.—Office Equip.

Liabilities
216 Accounts Payable
219 Wages Payable

Owner's Equity
311 Mary Adams, Capital
312 Mary Adams, Drawing
313 Income Summary

Revenues
411 Service Fees

Expenses
541 Rent Expense
542 Wages Expense
543 Supplies Expense
545 Telephone Expense
547 Depr. Exp.—Office Equip.
548 Insurance Expense
549 Utilities Expense
551 Advertising Expense
552 Gas and Oil Expense
572 Miscellaneous Expense

2 EXERCISE 6B5 CLOSING ENTRIES (NET LOSS)   From the T accounts shown below, prepare closing entries in general journal form dated June 30, 19--. Then, post the closing entries to the T accounts.

Accum. Depr.—Office Equip. 191.1		Rent Expense 541		Insurance Expense 548	
	Bal. 110	Bal. 900		Bal. 120	

Wages Payable 219		Wages Expense 542		Utilities Expense 549	
	Bal. 260	Bal. 1,080		Bal. 102	

Raquel Zapata, Capital 311		Supplies Expense 543		Advertising Expense 551	
	Bal. 6,000	Bal. 322		Bal. 34	

Raquel Zapata, Drawing 312		Telephone Expense 545		Gas and Oil Expense 552	
Bal. 2,000		Bal. 133		Bal. 88	

Income Summary 313		Depr. Exp.—Office Equip. 547		Miscellaneous Expense 572	
		Bal. 110		Bal. 98	

Referral Fees 411	
	Bal. 2,813

SERIES B   PROBLEMS

1 PROBLEM 6B1 FINANCIAL STATEMENTS   A work sheet for Juanita's Consulting is shown on page 190. No additional investments were made by the owner this month.

REQUIRED

1. Prepare an income statement.
2. Prepare a statement of owner's equity.
3. Prepare a balance sheet.

Juanita's Consulting
Work Sheet
For Month Ended June 30, 19--

	ACCOUNT TITLE	TRIAL BALANCE DEBIT	TRIAL BALANCE CREDIT	ADJUSTMENTS DEBIT	ADJUSTMENTS CREDIT	ADJUSTED TRIAL BALANCE DEBIT	ADJUSTED TRIAL BALANCE CREDIT	INCOME STATEMENT DEBIT	INCOME STATEMENT CREDIT	BALANCE SHEET DEBIT	BALANCE SHEET CREDIT	
1	Cash	5 2 8 5 00				5 2 8 5 00				5 2 8 5 00		1
2	Accounts Receivable	1 0 7 5 00				1 0 7 5 00				1 0 7 5 00		2
3	Supplies	7 5 0 00			(a) 2 5 0 00	5 0 0 00				5 0 0 00		3
4	Prepaid Insurance	5 0 0 00			(b) 1 0 0 00	4 0 0 00				4 0 0 00		4
5	Office Equipment	2 2 0 0 00				2 2 0 0 00				2 2 0 0 00		5
6	Accum. Depr.—Office Equip.				(d) 1 1 0 00		1 1 0 00				1 1 0 00	6
7	Accounts Payable		1 5 0 0 00				1 5 0 0 00				1 5 0 0 00	7
8	Wages Payable				(c) 2 0 0 00		2 0 0 00				2 0 0 00	8
9	Juanita Alvarez, Capital		7 0 0 0 00				7 0 0 0 00				7 0 0 0 00	9
10	Juanita Alvarez, Drawing	8 0 0 00				8 0 0 00				8 0 0 00		10
11	Consulting Fees		4 2 0 4 00				4 2 0 4 00		4 2 0 4 00			11
12	Rent Expense	5 0 0 00				5 0 0 00		5 0 0 00				12
13	Wages Expense	1 4 0 0 00		(c) 2 0 0 00		1 6 0 0 00		1 6 0 0 00				13
14	Supplies Expense			(a) 2 5 0 00		2 5 0 00		2 5 0 00				14
15	Telephone Expense	4 6 00				4 6 00		4 6 00				15
16	Depr. Exp.—Office Equip.			(d) 1 1 0 00		1 1 0 00		1 1 0 00				16
17	Insurance Expense			(b) 1 0 0 00		1 0 0 00		1 0 0 00				17
18	Electricity Expense	3 9 00				3 9 00		3 9 00				18
19	Advertising Expense	6 0 00				6 0 00		6 0 00				19
20	Gas and Oil Expense	2 8 00				2 8 00		2 8 00				20
21	Miscellaneous Expense	2 1 00				2 1 00		2 1 00				21
22		1 2 7 0 4 00	1 2 7 0 4 00	6 6 0 00	6 6 0 00	1 3 0 1 4 00	1 3 0 1 4 00	2 7 5 4 00	4 2 0 4 00	1 0 2 6 0 00	8 8 1 0 00	22
23	Net Income							1 4 5 0 00			1 4 5 0 00	23
24								4 2 0 4 00	4 2 0 4 00	1 0 2 6 0 00	1 0 2 6 0 00	24
25												25
26												26
27												27
28												28
29												29
30												30
31												31
32												32

1   **PROBLEM 6B2 STATEMENT OF OWNER'S EQUITY**   The capital account for Minta's Editorial Services, with an additional investment and a partial work sheet are shown below.

GENERAL LEDGER

ACCOUNT: Minta Berry, Capital					ACCOUNT NO. 311	
DATE	ITEM	POST. REF.	DEBIT	CREDIT	BALANCE DEBIT	BALANCE CREDIT
Jan. 1	Balance	✔				3 6 0 0 00
22		J1		2 9 0 0 00		6 5 0 0 00

Minta's Editorial Services
Work Sheet (Partial)
For Month Ended January 31, 19--

	ACCOUNT TITLE	INCOME STATEMENT DEBIT	INCOME STATEMENT CREDIT	BALANCE SHEET DEBIT	BALANCE SHEET CREDIT	
1	Cash			3 8 0 0 00		1
2	Accounts Receivable			2 2 0 0 00		2
3	Supplies			1 0 0 0 00		3
4	Prepaid Insurance			9 5 0 00		4
5	Comp. Equipment			4 5 0 0 00		5
6	Accum. Depr.—Comp. Equip.				2 2 5 00	6
7	Accounts Payable				2 1 0 0 00	7
8	Wages Payable				1 5 0 00	8
9	Minta Berry, Capital				6 5 0 0 00	9
10	Minta Berry, Drawing			1 7 0 0 00		10
11	Editing Fees		7 0 1 2 00			11
12	Rent Expense	4 5 0 00				12
13	Wages Expense	6 0 0 00				13
14	Supplies Expense	2 8 8 00				14
15	Telephone Expense	4 4 00				15
16	Depr. Exp.—Comp. Equip.	2 2 5 00				16
17	Insurance Expense	1 2 5 00				17
18	Utilities Expense	3 8 00				18
19	Advertising Expense	4 9 00				19
20	Miscellaneous Expense	1 8 00				20
21		1 8 3 7 00	7 0 1 2 00	14 1 5 0 00	8 9 7 5 00	21
22	Net Income	5 1 7 5 00			5 1 7 5 00	22
23		7 0 1 2 00	7 0 1 2 00	14 1 5 0 00	14 1 5 0 00	23
24						24

REQUIRED

Prepare a statement of owner's equity.

1/2/3 **PROBLEM 6B3 FINANCIAL STATEMENTS, CLOSING ENTRIES, AND POST-CLOSING TRIAL BALANCE**   Refer to the work sheet for Juanita's Consulting in Problem 6B1. The trial balance amounts (before adjustments) have been entered in the ledger accounts provided in the working papers. If you are not using the working papers that accompany this book, set up ledger accounts and enter these balances as of June 30, 19--. A chart of accounts is provided below.

Juanita's Consulting
Chart of Accounts

Assets		Revenues	
111	Cash	411	Consulting Fees
131	Accounts Receivable		
151	Supplies		Expenses
155	Prepaid Insurance	541	Rent Expense
191	Office Equipment	542	Wages Expense
191.1	Accum. Depr.—Office Equip.	543	Supplies Expense
		545	Telephone Expense
Liabilities		547	Depr. Exp.—Office Equip.
216	Accounts Payable	548	Insurance Expense
219	Wages Payable	549	Electricity Expense
		551	Advertising Expense
Owner's Equity		552	Gas and Oil Expense
311	Juanita Alvarez, Capital	572	Miscellaneous Expense
312	Juanita Alvarez, Drawing		
313	Income Summary		

REQUIRED

1. Journalize (page 10) and post the adjusting entries.
2. Journalize (page 11) and post the closing entries.
3. Prepare a post-closing trial balance.

MASTERY PROBLEM

Elizabeth Soltis owns and operates Aunt Ibby's Styling Salon. A year-end work sheet is provided on the next page. Using this information, prepare financial statements and closing entries. Soltis made no additional investments during the year.

Aunt Ibby's Styling Salon
Work Sheet
For Year Ended December 31, 19--

	ACCOUNT TITLE	TRIAL BALANCE Debit	TRIAL BALANCE Credit	ADJUSTMENTS Debit	ADJUSTMENTS Credit	ADJUSTED TRIAL BALANCE Debit	ADJUSTED TRIAL BALANCE Credit	INCOME STATEMENT Debit	INCOME STATEMENT Credit	BALANCE SHEET Debit	BALANCE SHEET Credit
1	Cash	940 00				940 00				940 00	
2	Styling Supplies	1 500 00			(a) 1 450 00	50 00				50 00	
3	Prepaid Insurance	800 00			(b) 650 00	150 00				150 00	
4	Salon Equipment	4 500 00				4 500 00				4 500 00	
5	Accum. Depr.—Salon Equip.				(d) 900 00		900 00				900 00
6	Accounts Payable		225 00				225 00				225 00
7	Wages Payable				(c) 40 00		40 00				40 00
8	Elizabeth Soltis, Capital		2 765 00				2 765 00				2 765 00
9	Elizabeth Soltis, Drawing	12 000 00				12 000 00				12 000 00	
10	Styling Fees		32 000 00				32 000 00		32 000 00		
11	Rent Expense	6 000 00				6 000 00		6 000 00			
12	Wages Expense	8 000 00		(c) 40 00		8 040 00		8 040 00			
13	Styling Supplies Expense			(a) 1 450 00		1 450 00		1 450 00			
14	Telephone Expense	450 00				450 00		450 00			
15	Depr. Expense—Salon Equip.			(d) 900 00		900 00		900 00			
16	Utilities Expense	800 00				800 00		800 00			
17	Insurance Expense			(b) 650 00		650 00		650 00			
18		34 990 00	34 990 00	3 040 00	3 040 00	35 930 00	35 930 00	18 290 00	32 000 00	17 640 00	3 930 00
19	Net Income							13 710 00			13 710 00
20								32 000 00	32 000 00	17 640 00	17 640 00
21											

CHAPTER 6 APPENDIX

Statement of Cash Flows

Careful study of this appendix should enable you to:

LO1 Classify business transactions as operating, investing, or financing.

LO2 Prepare a statement of cash flows by analyzing and categorizing a series of business transactions.

Thus far, we have discussed three financial statements: the income statement, the statement of owner's equity, and the balance sheet. A fourth statement, the statement of cash flows, is also very important. It explains what the business did to generate cash and how the cash was used. This is done by categorizing all cash transactions into three types of activities: operating, investing, and financing.

TYPES OF BUSINESS ACTIVITIES

LO1 Classify business transactions as operating, investing, or financing.

There are three types of business activities: operating, investing, and financing.

Cash flows from **operating activities** are related to the revenues and expenses reported on the income statement. Examples include cash received for services performed and the payment of cash for expenses.

Investing activities are those transactions involving the purchase and sale of long-term assets, lending money, and collecting the principal on the related loans.

Financing activities are those transactions dealing with the exchange of cash between the business and its owners and creditors. Examples include cash received from the owner to finance the operations and cash paid to the owner as withdrawals. Financing activities also include borrowing cash and repaying the loan.

Lending money to another entity is an outflow of cash from investing activities. The collection of the principal when the loan is due is an inflow of cash from investing activities. Borrowing cash is an inflow from financing activities. Repayment of the loan is an outflow from financing activities.

194

Figure 6A-1 provides a review of the transactions for Jessie Jane's Campus Delivery for the month of June. The transactions are classified as operating, investing, or financing, and an explanation for the classification is provided.

FIGURE 6A-1   Summary of Transactions for Jessie Jane's Campus Delivery

SUMMARY OF TRANSACTIONS JESSIE JANE'S CAMPUS DELIVERY	TYPE OF TRANSACTION	EXPLANATION
(a) Jessica Jane invested cash in her business, $2,000.	Financing	Cash received from the owner is an inflow from financing activities. Don't be fooled by the word "invested." From Jane's point of view, this is an investment. From the firm's point of view, this is a way to *finance* the business.
(b) Purchased delivery equipment for cash, $1,200.	Investing	Purchases of long-term assets are investments.
(c) Purchased delivery equipment on account from Big Red Scooters, $900. (Note: Big Red has loaned Jane $900.)	No cash involved	This transaction will not affect the statement of cash flows.
(d) Paid first installment to Big Red Scooters, $300. (See transaction (c).)	Financing	Repayments of loans are financing activities.
(e) Received cash for delivery services rendered, $500.	Operating	Cash received as a result of providing services is classified as an operating activity.
(f) Paid cash for June office rent, $200.	Operating	Cash payments for expenses are classified as operating activities.
(g) Paid telephone bill, $50.	Operating	Cash payments for expenses are classified as operating activities.
(h) Made deliveries on account for a total of $600: $400 for the Accounting Department and $200 for the School of Optometry.	No cash involved	This transaction will not affect the statement of cash flows.
(i) Purchased supplies for cash, $80.	Operating	Cash payments for expenses are classified as operating activities. Most of these supplies were used up. Those that remain will be used in the near future. These are not long-term assets and, thus, do not qualify as investments.
(j) Paid for an eight-month liability insurance policy, $200. Coverage began on June 1.	Operating	Cash payments for expenses are classified as operating activities. Prepaid Insurance is not considered a long-term asset and, thus, does not qualify as an investment.
(k) Received $570 in cash for services performed earlier in transaction (h): $400 from the Accounting Department and $170 from the School of Optometry.	Operating	Cash received as a result of providing services is classified as an operating activity.

FIGURE 6A-1   Summary of Transactions for Jessie Jane's Campus Delivery (concluded)

SUMMARY OF TRANSACTIONS JESSIE JANE'S CAMPUS DELIVERY	TYPE OF TRANSACTION	EXPLANATION
(l) Purchased a third scooter from Big Red Scooters, $1,500. A down payment of $300 was made with the remaining payments expected over the next four months.	Investing	Purchases of long-term assets are investments. Only the $300 cash paid will be reported on the statement of cash flows.
(m) Paid part-time employees wages, $650.	Operating	Cash payments for expenses are classified as operating activities.
(n) Earned delivery fees for the remainder of the month amounting to $900: $430 for cash and $470 on account. Deliveries on account: $100 for the Accounting Department, and $370 for the Athletic Ticket Office.	Operating	Cash received ($430) as a result of providing services is classified as an operating activity.
(o) Jane withdrew cash for personal use, $150.	Financing	Cash payments to owners are classified as a financing activity.

PREPARING THE STATEMENT OF CASH FLOWS

LO2   Prepare a statement of cash flows by analyzing and categorizing a series of business transactions.

The classifications of the cash transactions for Jessie Jane's Campus Delivery are summarized in the expanded cash T account shown in Figure 6A-2. Using this information, we can prepare a statement of cash flows. As shown in Figure 6A-3, the heading is similar to that used for the income statement. Since the statement of cash flows reports on the flow of cash for a period of time, the statement is dated for the month ended June 30, 19--.

FIGURE 6A-2   Cash T Account for Jessie Jane's Campus Delivery with Classifications for Cash Transactions

Cash

Event	Classification	Amount	Amount	Classification	Event
(a) Investment by Jane.	Financing	2,000	1,200	Investing	Purchased delivery equipment. (b)
(e) Cash received for services.	Operating	500	300	Financing	Made payment on loan. (d)
(k) Cash received for services.	Operating	570	200	Operating	Paid office rent. (f)
(n) Cash received for services.	Operating	430	50	Operating	Paid telephone bill. (g)
		_3,500_	80	Operating	Purchased supplies. (i)
			200	Operating	Paid for insurance. (j)
			300	Investing	Purchased delivery equipment. (l)
			650	Operating	Paid wages. (m)
			150	Financing	Withdrawal by owner. (o)
			_3,130_		
	Bal.	370			

The main body of the statement is arranged in three sections: operating, investing, and financing activities. First, cash received from customers is listed under operating activities. Then, cash payments for operating activities are listed and totaled. The net amount is reported as net cash provided by operating activities. Since this is the main purpose of the business, it is important to be able to generate positive cash flows from operating activities.

The next two sections list the inflows and outflows from investing and financing activities. Debits to the cash account are inflows and credits are outflows. Note that there was an outflow from investing activities resulting from the purchase of the motor scooters. In addition, the business had a net inflow from financing activities because Jane's initial investment more than covered her withdrawal and the payment on the loan. These investing and financing activities are typical for a new business.

> **LEARNING KEY**
> To prove the accuracy of the statement of cash flows, compare the net increase or decrease reported on the statement with the change in the balance of the cash account.

The sum of the inflows and outflows from operating, investing, and financing activities equals the net increase (or decrease) in the cash account during the period. Since this is a new business, the cash account had a beginning balance of zero. The ending balance is $370. This agrees with the net increase in cash reported on the statement of cash flows of $370.

FIGURE 6A-3   Statement of Cash Flows for Jessie Jane's Campus Delivery

Jessie Jane's Campus Delivery
Statement of Cash Flows
For Month Ended June 30, 19--

Cash flows from operating activities:		
Cash received from customers for		
delivery services		$ 1 5 0 0 00
Cash paid for rent	$ (2 0 0 00)	
Cash paid for telephone	(5 0 00)	
Cash paid for supplies	(8 0 00)	
Cash paid for insurance	(2 0 0 00)	
Cash paid for wages	(6 5 0 00)	
Total cash paid for operations		(1 1 8 0 00)
Net cash provided by operating activities		$ 3 2 0 00
Cash flows from investing activities:		
Cash paid for delivery equipment	$(1 5 0 0 00)	
Net cash used for investing activities		(1 5 0 0 00)
Cash flows from financing activities:		
Cash investment by owner	$ 2 0 0 0 00	
Cash withdrawal by owner	(1 5 0 00)	
Payment made on loan	(3 0 0 00)	
Net cash provided by financing activities		1 5 5 0 00
Net increase in cash		$ 3 7 0 00

The purpose of this appendix was to introduce you to the purpose and format of the statement of cash flows. Here, we classified entries made to the cash account as operating, investing, or financing. These classifications were then used to prepare the statement. Large businesses have thousands of entries to the cash account. Thus, this approach to preparing the statement is not practical for large businesses. Other approaches to preparing the statement will be discussed in Chapter 24. However, the purpose and format of the statements are the same.

KEY POINTS

1 The purpose of the statement of cash flows is to report what the firm did to generate cash and how the cash was used. Business transactions are classified as operating, investing, and financing activities.

Operating activities are related to the revenues and expenses reported on the income statement.

Investing activities are those transactions involving the purchase and sale of long-term assets, lending money, and collecting the principal on the related loans.

Financing activities are those transactions dealing with the exchange of cash between the business and its owners and creditors.

2 The main body of the statement of cash flows consists of three sections: operating, investing, and financing activities.

Name of Business
Statement of Cash Flows
For Period Ended Date

Cash flows from operating activities:			
Cash received from customers			$ x x x x xx
List cash paid for various expenses		$ (x x x xx)	
Total cash paid for operations			(x x x x xx)
Net cash provided by (used for) operating activities			$ x x x xx
Cash flows from investing activities:			
List cash received from the sale of long-term assets			
and other investing activities	$ x x x x x xx		
List cash paid for the purchase of long-term assets			
and other investing activities	x x x x xx		
Net cash provided by (used for) investing			
activities			x x x x xx
Cash flows from financing activities:			
List cash received from owners and creditors	$ x x x x x xx		
List cash paid to owners and creditors	(x x x xx)		
Net cash provided by (used for) financing activities			x x x x xx
Net increase (decrease) in cash			$ x x x xx

KEY TERMS

financing activities 194   Those transactions dealing with the exchange of cash between the business and its owners and creditors.

investing activities 194   Those transactions involving the purchase and sale of long-term assets, lending money, and collecting the principal on the related loans.

operating activities 194   Those transactions related to the revenues and expenses reported on the income statement.

REVIEW QUESTIONS

1. Explain the purpose of the statement of cash flows.

2. Define and provide examples of the three types of business activities.

SERIES A   EXERCISE

1 **EXERCISE 6ApxA1 CLASSIFYING BUSINESS TRANSACTIONS** Dolores Lopez opened a new consulting business. The following transactions occurred during January of the current year. Classify each transaction as an operating, investing, or financing activity.

(a) Invested cash in the business, $10,000.

(b) Paid office rent, $500.

(c) Purchased office equipment. Paid $1,500 cash and agreed to pay the balance of $2,000 in four monthly installments.

(d) Received cash for services rendered, $900.

(e) Paid telephone bill, $65.

(f) Made payment on loan in transaction c, $500.

(g) Paid wages to part-time employee, $500.

(h) Received cash for services rendered, $800.

(i) Paid electricity bill, $85.

(j) Withdrew cash for personal use, $100.

(k) Paid wages to part-time employee, $500.

SERIES A   PROBLEM

2 **PROBLEM 6ApxA1 PREPARING A STATEMENT OF CASH FLOWS**   Prepare a statement of cash flows based on the transactions reported in Exercise A-1.

SERIES B   EXERCISE

1 **EXERCISE 6ApxB1 CLASSIFYING BUSINESS TRANSACTIONS** Bob Jacobs opened an advertising agency. The following transactions occurred during January of the current year. Classify each transaction as an operating, investing, or financing activity.

(a) Invested cash in the business, $5,000.
(b) Purchased office equipment. Paid $2,500 cash and agreed to pay the balance of $2,000 in four monthly installments.
(c) Paid office rent, $400.
(d) Received cash for services rendered, $600.
(e) Paid telephone bill, $95.
(f) Received cash for services rendered, $700.
(g) Made payment on loan in transaction b, $500.
(h) Paid wages to part-time employee, $800.
(i) Paid electricity bill, $100.
(j) Withdrew cash for personal use, $500.
(k) Paid wages to part-time employee, $600.

SERIES B PROBLEM

2 **PROBLEM 6ApxB1 PREPARING A STATEMENT OF CASH FLOWS**   Prepare a statement of cash flows based on the transactions reported in Exercise B-1.

COMPREHENSIVE PROBLEM 1: THE ACCOUNTING CYCLE

Bob Night opened "The General's Favorite Fishing Hole." The fishing camp is open from April through September and attracts many famous college basketball coaches during the off-season. Guests typically register for one week, arriving on Sunday afternoon and returning home the following Saturday afternoon. The registration fee includes room and board, the use of fishing boats, and professional instruction in fishing techniques. The chart of accounts for the camping operations is provided below.

The General's Favorite Fishing Hole
Chart of Accounts

Assets		Revenues	
111	Cash	411	Registration Fees
152	Office Supplies		
154	Food Supplies		Expenses
155	Prepaid Insurance	541	Rent Expense
185	Fishing Boats	542	Wages Expense
185.1	Accum. Depr.—Fishing Boats	543	Office Supplies Expense
		545	Telephone Expense
Liabilities		547	Depr. Exp.—Fishing Boats
216	Accounts Payable	548	Insurance Expense
219	Wages Payable	555	Utilities Expense
		556	Food Supplies Expense
Owner's Equity		564	Postage Expense
311	Bob Night, Capital		
312	Bob Night, Drawing		
313	Income Summary		

The following transactions took place during April 19--.

Apr. 1 Night invested cash in business, $90,000.
   1 Paid insurance premium for camping season, $9,000.
   2 Paid rent on lodge and campgrounds for the month of April, $40,000.
   2 Deposited registration fees, $35,000.
   2 Purchased ten fishing boats on account for $60,000. The boats have estimated useful lives of five years, at which time they will be donated to a local day camp. Arrangements were made to pay for the boats in July.
   3 Purchased food supplies from Acme Super Market on account, $7,000.
   5 Purchased office supplies from Gordon Office Supplies on account, $500.
   7 Deposited registration fees, $38,600.
   10 Purchased food supplies from Acme Super Market on account, $8,200.
   10 Paid wages to fishing guides, $10,000.
   14 Deposited registration fees, $30,500.

Apr. 16 Purchased food supplies from Acme Super Market on account, $9,000.
17 Paid wages to fishing guides, $10,000.
18 Paid postage, $150.
21 Deposited registration fees, $35,600.
24 Purchased food supplies from Acme Super Market on account, $8,500.
24 Paid wages to fishing guides, $10,000.
28 Deposited registration fees, $32,000.
29 Paid wages to fishing guides, $10,000.
30 Purchased food supplies from Acme Super Market on account, $6,000.
30 Paid Acme Super Market on account, $32,700.
30 Paid utility bill, $2,000.
30 Paid telephone bill, $1,200.
30 Bob Night withdrew cash for personal use, $6,000.

Adjustment information for the end of April is provided below:

(a) Office supplies remaining on hand, $100.
(b) Food supplies remaining on hand, $8,000.
(c) Insurance expired during the month of April, $1,500.
(d) Depreciation on the fishing boats for the month of April, $1,000.
(e) Wages earned, but not yet paid at the end of April, $500.

REQUIRED

1. Enter the above transactions in a general journal.
2. Post the entries to the general ledger. (If you are not using the working papers that accompany this text, you will need to enter the account titles and account numbers in the general ledger accounts.)
3. Prepare a trial balance on a work sheet.
4. Complete the work sheet.
5. Prepare the income statement.
6. Prepare the statement of owner's equity.
7. Prepare the balance sheet.
8. Journalize the adjusting entries.
9. Post the adjusting entries to the general ledger.
10. Journalize the closing entries.
11. Post the closing entries to the general ledger.
12. Prepare a post-closing trial balance.

PART

2

Specialized Accounting Procedures for Service Businesses and Proprietorships

7

Accounting for a Professional Service Business: The Combination Journal

You have just been hired to work in a doctor's office as a bookkeeper. You have been observing general office procedures and are a bit confused about when to record revenues. Some patients pay cash as they leave the office. Others submit forms that are filed with insurance companies. Sometimes the insurance companies pay the entire amount. Other times, only a portion of the bill is paid, with the balance being billed to the patient. Generally, the patients pay the balance, but occasionally they don't. Finally, there are some patients that never seem to pay. This all seems very confusing. When should revenues be recognized?

Throughout the first six chapters, the accrual basis of accounting for a service business was demonstrated. For simplicity, we used a general journal as the book of original entry. Not all businesses use the accrual basis of accounting and many use specialized journals. In this chapter we explain the cash basis and modified cash basis of accounting. In addition, we demonstrate the advantages of using a combination journal as the book of original entry.

ACCRUAL BASIS VERSUS CASH BASIS

LO1   Explain the cash, modified cash, and accrual bases of accounting.

Under the **accrual basis of accounting**, revenues are recorded when earned. Revenues are earned when a service is provided or a product sold, regardless of whether cash is received. If cash is not received, a receivable is set up. The accrual basis also assumes that expenses are recorded when incurred. Expenses are incurred when a service is received or an asset consumed, regardless of when cash is paid. If cash is not paid when a service is received, a payable is set up. When assets are consumed, prepaid assets are decreased or long-term assets are depreciated. Since the accrual basis accounts for long-term assets, prepaid assets, receivables, and payables, it is the best method of measuring income for the vast majority of businesses.

Accrual Basis

Accounting for Revenues and Expenses	**Assets and Liabilities**
Record revenue when earned.	Accounts receivable: Yes
Record expenses when incurred.	Accounts payable: Yes
	Prepaid assets: Yes
	Long-term assets: Yes

However, the **cash basis of accounting** is used by some small businesses and by most individuals for tax purposes. Under the cash basis of accounting, revenues are recorded when cash is received and expenses are recorded when cash is paid. This method does not account for long-term assets, prepaid assets, receivables, or payables. As shown in Figure 7-1, the cash and accrual bases can result in very different measures of net income.

Cash Basis

Accounting for Revenues and Expenses	**Assets and Liabilities**
Record revenue when cash is received.	Accounts receivable: No
Record expenses when cash is paid.	Accounts payable: No
	Prepaid assets: No
	Long-term assets: No

Accrual Basis:

Revenues
  recorded when
  earned

Expenses
  recorded when
  incurred

Cash Basis:

Revenues
  recorded when
  cash is received

Expenses
  recorded when
  cash is paid

FIGURE 7-1   Cash Versus Accrual Accounting

	ACCRUAL BASIS		CASH BASIS	
Entries Made for Expenses and Revenues				
	METHOD OF ACCOUNTING			
TRANSACTION	EXPENSE	REVENUE	EXPENSE	REVENUE
(a) Sold merchandise on account, $600.		600		
(b) Paid wages, $300.	300		300	
(c) Received cash for merchandise sold on account, $200.				200
(d) Received cleaning bill for month, $250	250			
(e) Paid on account for last month's advertising, $100			100	
	550	600	400	200
Revenue		$600		$200
Expense		550		400
Net Income (Loss)		$ 50		($200)
Revenues are recognized when:		earned		cash is received
Expenses are recognized when:		incurred		cash is paid

A third method of accounting combines aspects of the cash and accrual methods. With the **modified cash basis**, a firm uses the cash basis for recording revenues and most expenses. Exceptions are made when cash is paid for assets with useful lives greater than one accounting period. For example, under a strict cash basis, if cash is paid for equipment, buildings, supplies, or insurance, the amount is immediately recorded as an expense. This approach would cause major distortions when measuring net income. Under the modified cash basis, cash payments like these are recorded as assets, and adjustments are made each period as under the accrual basis.

Although similar to the accrual basis, the modified cash basis does not account for receivables or for payables for services received. Thus, the modified cash basis is a combination of the cash and accrual methods of accounting. The differences and similarities among the cash, modified cash, and accrual methods of accounting are demonstrated in Figure 7-2.

Modified Cash Basis

Accounting for Revenues and Expenses

Record revenue when cash is received. Record expenses when paid, except for assets with useful lives greater than one accounting period. Accrual accounting is used for prepaid assets (insurance and supplies) and long-term assets.

Assets and Liabilities

Accounts receivable: No
Accounts payable
  for purchase of assets: Yes
  for services received: No
Prepaid assets: Yes
Long-term assets: Yes

Shaded area shows that sometimes the modified cash basis is the same as the cash basis and sometimes it is the same as the accrual basis. For some transactions, all methods are the same.

FIGURE 7-2   Comparison of Cash, Modified Cash, and Accrual Methods

	Entries Made Under Each Accounting Method		
EVENT	**CASH**	**MODIFIED CASH**	**ACCRUAL**
Revenues: Perform services for cash	Cash Professional fees	Cash Professional fees	Cash Professional fees
Perform services on account	No entry	No entry	Accounts Receivable Professional fees
Expenses: Pay cash for operating expenses: wages advertising, rent, telephone, etc.	Expense Cash	Expense Cash	Expense Cash
Pay cash for prepaid items: insurance, supplies, etc.	Expense Cash	Prepaid Asset Cash	Prepaid Asset Cash
Pay cash for property, plant, and equipment (PP & E)	Expense Cash	PP & E Asset Cash	PP & E Asset Cash
End-of-period adjustments: Wages earned but not paid	No entry	No entry	Wages Expense Wages Payable
Prepaid items used	No entry	Expense Prepaid Asset	Expense Prepaid Asset
Depreciation on property, plant, and equipment	No entry	Depreciation Expense Accumulated Depreciation	Depreciation Expense Accumulated Depreciation
Other: Purchase of assets on account	No entry	Asset Accounts Payable	Asset Accounts Payable

ACCOUNTING FOR A PROFESSIONAL SERVICE BUSINESS

LO2   Describe special records for a professional service business using the modified cash basis.

Many small professional service businesses use the modified cash basis of accounting. Professional service businesses include law, dentistry, medicine, optometry, architecture, engineering, and accounting.

Look again at Figure 7-2. There are two primary differences between the accrual basis and the modified cash basis. First, under the modified cash basis, no adjusting entries are made for accrued wages expense. Second, under the modified cash basis, revenues from services performed on account are not recorded until cash is received. Thus, no accounts receivable are entered in the accounting system. This means that other records must be maintained to keep track of amounts owed by clients and patients. These records generally include an appointment record and a client or patient ledger record. These records are illustrated in Figures 7-3 and 7-4.

The appointment record is used to schedule appointments and to maintain a record of the services rendered, fees charged, and payments received. This information is copied to the patient ledger records, which show the amount owed by each client or patient for services performed. A copy of this record may also be used for billing purposes.

THE COMBINATION JOURNAL

LO3   Use the combination journal to record transactions of a professional service business.

The two-column general journal illustrated in Chapter 4 can be used to enter every transaction of a business. However, in most businesses, there are many similar transactions that involve the same account or accounts. Cash receipts and payments are good examples. Suppose that in a typical

Quality

Continuing education for professionals is one way to help improve the quality of service to consumers. Regulatory agencies now require continuing education for a wide variety of professionals including certified public accountants.

Requiring professionals to continue their education is one way to encourage professionals to keep up on changes in their profession. A specific number of continuing education hours is usually required every year or two years. Depending on the profession, CE credits can be earned in several ways. Professionals can take classes offered by colleges, universities, and professional organizations. There are also companies that are in business solely to provide continuing education through lectures, videotape presentations, and correspondence courses.

Reading professional journals is another avenue for earning continuing education credits. For example, members of the American Institute of CPAs can earn credits by reading selected articles in the *Journal of Accountancy*, completing study guides, and passing examinations.

In addition to continuing education required for licensing and certification, some professional organizations require CE to maintain membership. Some companies routinely provide continuing education for all levels of employees.

Whether it is a warehouse employee learning new techniques for handling hazardous chemicals, a surgeon learning new ways to use lasers, or an accountant learning about new accounting standards, continuing education is a key to quality.

FIGURE 7-3   Appointment Record

Date: 6/4/--

Time	Patient	Medical Service	Fees	Payments
8:00	Dennis Rogan	OV	40.00	40.00
15				
30	Rick Cosier	OV;EKG	120.00	
45				
9:00	George Hettenhouse	OV;MISC	50.00	
15				
30	Sam Frumer	OV;LAB	75.00	75.00
45				
10:00	Dan Dalton	OV	40.00	
15				
30	Louis Biagioni	OV;X	65.00	
45				
11:00	Mike Groomer	X	40.00	40.00
15				
30				
45				
12:00				
15				
30				
45				
1:00	Mike Tiller	OV;LAB	80.00	
15				
30	Peggy Hite	OV;PHYS	190.00	
45				
2:00				
15				
30				
45				
3:00	Vivian Winston	OV;MISC	40.00	
15				
30				
45				
4:00	Hank Davis	OV	40.00	40.00
15				
30				
45				
	Bill Sharp			150.00
	Phil Jones			80.00
	Diane Gallagher			200.00
			780.00	625.00

FIGURE 7-4   Client or Patient Ledger Account

Patient Name   Dennis Rogan
Address   1542 Hamilton Avenue Cincinnati, OH 45240
Phone Number   555-1683

Date	Service Rendered	Time	Debit	Credit	Balance
19-- June 4	Office visit	8:00	40.00		
4				40.00	----

month there are 30 transactions that result in an increase in cash and 40 transactions that cause a decrease in cash. In a two-column general journal, this would require entering the account "Cash" 70 times, using a journal line each time.

A considerable amount of time and space is saved if a journal contains **special columns** for cash debits and cash credits. At the end of the month, the special columns for cash debits and credits are totaled. The total of the Cash Debit column is posted as one amount to the debit side of the cash account and the total of the Cash Credit column is posted as one amount to the credit side of the cash account. Thus, instead of receiving 70 postings, Cash receives only two: one debit and one credit. This method requires much less time and reduces the risk of making posting errors.

 LEARNING KEY   The totals of special journal columns are posted as one amount to the account. This saves time and reduces the possibility of posting errors.

If other accounts are used frequently, special columns can be added for these accounts. When accounts are used infrequently, the only columns necessary are a **General Debit column** and a **General Credit column**. A journal with such special and general columns is called a **combination journal**.

Many small professional enterprises use a combination journal to record business transactions. To demonstrate the use of a combination journal, let's consider the medical practice of Dr. Ray Bonita. Bonita uses the modified cash basis of accounting. The chart of accounts for his medical practice is shown in Figure 7-5. The transactions for the month of June, his first month in practice, are provided in Figure 7-6.

 LEARNING KEY   Set up special columns for the most frequently used accounts.

A combination journal for Bonita's medical practice is illustrated in Figure 7-7 on page 213. Note that special columns were set up for Cash (Debit and Credit), Medical Fees (Credit), Wages Expense (Debit), Laboratory Expense (Debit), Medical Supplies (Debit), and Office Supplies (Debit). Special columns were set up for these accounts because they will be used frequently in this business. Other businesses might set up special

FIGURE 7-5   Chart of Accounts

Ray Bonita, M.D. Chart of Accounts			
Assets		**Revenues**	
111	Cash	411	Medical Fees
151	Medical Supplies		
152	Office Supplies	**Expenses**	
155	Prepaid Insurance	541	Rent Expense
185	Medical Equipment	542	Wages Expense
185.1	Accum. Depr.–Med. Equip.	543	Office Supplies Exp.
192	Office Furniture	544	Med. Supplies Exp.
192.1	Accum. Depr.—Office Furn.	545	Telephone Expense
Liabilities		546	Laboratory Expense
216	Accounts Payable	547	Depr. Exp.—Med. Equip.
		548	Depr. Exp.—Off. Furn.
Owner's Equity		559	Insurance Expense
311	Ray Bonita, Capital		
312	Ray Bonita, Drawing		
313	Income Summary		

columns for different accounts depending on the frequency of their use. Of course, General Debit and Credit columns for transactions affecting other accounts are also needed.

Journalizing in a Combination Journal

The following procedures were used to enter the transactions for Bonita for June.

General Columns.   Enter transactions in the *general columns* in a manner similar to that used for the *general journal.* Look at the entry for June 5 in Figure 7-7.

a. Enter the name of the debited account (Office Furniture) first at the extreme left of the Description column.
b. Enter the amount in the General Debit column.
c. Enter the name of the account credited (Accounts Payable—Bittle's Furniture) on the next line, indented about ½ inch.
d. Enter the amount in the General Credit column.

FIGURE 7-6 Summary of Transactions for Ray Bonita's Medical Practice

June	1	Ray Bonita invested cash to start a medical practice, $50,000.
	2	Paid for a one-year liability insurance policy, $6,000. Coverage began on June 1.
	3	Purchased medical equipment for cash, $22,000.
	4	Paid bill for laboratory work, $300.
	5	Purchased office furniture on credit from Bittle's Furniture, $9,000.
	6	Received cash from patients and insurance companies for medical services rendered, $5,000.
	7	Paid June office rent, $2,000.
	8	Paid part-time wages, $3,000.
	9	Purchased medical supplies for cash, $250.
	15	Paid telephone bill, $150.
	15	Received cash from patients and insurance companies for medical services rendered, $10,000.
	16	Paid bill for laboratory work, $280.
	17	Paid part-time wages, $3,000.
	19	Purchased office supplies for cash, $150.
	20	Received cash from patients and insurance companies for medical services rendered, $3,000.
	22	Paid the first installment to Bittle's Furniture, $3,000.
	23	Purchased medical supplies for cash, $200.
	24	Paid bill for laboratory work, $400.
	25	Purchased additional furniture from Bittle's Furniture, $3,500. A down payment of $500 was made, with the remaining payments expected over the next four months.
	27	Paid part-time wages, $2,500.
	30	Received cash from patients and insurance companies for medical services rendered, $7,000.
	30	Bonita withdrew cash for personal use, $10,000.

General and Special Accounts. Some transactions affect both a *general account and a special account.* Look at the entry for June 1 in Figure 7-7.

a. Enter the name of the general account in the Description column.
b. Enter the amount in the General Debit or Credit column.
c. Enter the amount of the debit or credit for the special account in the appropriate special column.

Enter all of this information on the same line.

FIGURE 7-7 Combination Journal

COMBINATION JOURNAL

PAGE 1

Date	Description	Post. Ref.	Cash Debit	Cash Credit	General Debit	General Credit	Medical Fees Credit	Wages Expense Debit	Laboratory Expense Debit	Medical Supplies Debit	Office Supplies Debit
19— June 1	Ray Bonita, Capital	311	50 000 00			50 000 00					
2	Prepaid Insurance	155		6 000 00	6 000 00						
3	Medical Equipment	185		22 000 00	22 000 00						
4		—		3 00 00					3 00 00		
5	Office Furniture	192			9 000 00						
	Accounts Payable—Bittle's Furn.	216				9 000 00					
6		—	5 000 00				5 000 00				
7	Rent Expense	541		2 000 00	2 000 00						
8		—		3 000 00				3 000 00			
9		—		2 50 00						2 50 00	
		—	10 000 00				10 000 00				
15	Telephone Expense	545		1 50 00	1 50 00						
		—		2 80 00					2 80 00		
		—		3 000 00				3 000 00			
		—		1 50 00							1 50 00
		—	3 000 00				3 000 00				
	Accounts Payable—Bittle's Furn.	216		3 000 00	3 000 00						
		—		2 00 00						2 00 00	
		—		4 00 00					4 00 00		
	Office Furniture	192		5 00 00	3 50 00						
	Accounts Payable—Bittle's Furn.	216				3 000 00					
		—		2 500 00				2 500 00			
30		—	7 000 00				7 000 00				
30	Ray Bonita, Drawing	312		10 000 00	10 000 00						
			75 000 00	53 730 00	55 650 00	62 000 00	25 000 00	8 500 00	9 80 00	4 50 00	1 50 00
			(111)	(111)	(✓)	(✓)	(411)	(542)	(546)	(151)	(152)

Proving the Combination Journal

Debit Columns		Credit Columns	
Cash	75,000	Cash	53,730
General	55,650	General	62,000
Wages Expense	8,500	Medical Fees	25,000
Laboratory Expense	980		140,730
Medical Supplies	450		
Office Supplies	150		
	140,730		

Special Accounts. Many transactions affect only *special accounts*. Look at the entry for June 6 in Figure 7-7.

a. Enter the amounts in the appropriate special debit and credit columns.
b. Do not enter anything in the Description column.
c. Place a dash in the Posting Reference column to indicate that this amount is not posted individually. It will be posted as part of the total of the special column at the end of the month. (The posting process is described later in this chapter.)

Description Column. In general, the **Description column** is used for the following:

a. To enter the account titles for the General Debit and General Credit columns.
b. To identify specific creditors when assets are purchased on account (see entry for June 5).
   NOTE: For firms using the accrual basis of accounting, this column also would be used to identify specific customers receiving services on account.
c. To identify amounts forwarded. When more than one page is required during an accounting period, amounts from the previous page are brought forward. In this situation, "Amounts Forwarded" is entered in the Description column on the first line.

Proving the Combination Journal

At the end of the accounting period, all columns of the combination journal should be totaled and ruled. The sum of the debit columns should be compared with the sum of the credit columns to verify that they are equal. The proving of Bonita's combination journal for the month of June is shown at the bottom of Figure 7-7 on page 213.

POSTING FROM THE COMBINATION JOURNAL

LO4 Post from the combination journal to the general ledger.

The procedures for posting a special column are different from the procedures used when posting a general column. Accounts debited or credited in the general columns are posted individually in the same manner as that followed for the general journal. A different procedure is used for special columns. Figure 7-8 describes the procedures to follow in posting from the combination journal.

> Amounts in the General column are posted individually. Only the totals of the special columns are posted.

The general ledger accounts for Cash, Accounts Payable, and Medical Fees are shown in Figure 7-9 to illustrate the effects of this posting process.

FIGURE 7-8   Posting from a Combination Journal

GENERAL COLUMNS	Since a combination journal is being used, enter "CJ" and the page number in each general ledger account's Posting Reference column. Once the amount has been posted to the general ledger account, the account number is entered in the **Posting Reference column** of the combination journal. Accounts in the general column should be posted daily. The check marks at the bottom of the General Debit and Credit columns indicate that these totals should not be posted.
SPECIAL COLUMNS	1. Post the totals of the special columns to the appropriate general ledger accounts. 2. Once posted, enter the account number (in parentheses) beneath the column.

FIGURE 7-9   The General Ledger After Posting

GENERAL LEDGER

ACCOUNT: **Cash**   ACCOUNT NO. 111

DATE		ITEM	POST. REF.	DEBIT	CREDIT	BALANCE	
						DEBIT	CREDIT
19-- June	30		CJ1	75 0 0 0 00		75 0 0 0 00	
	30		CJ1		53 7 3 0 00	21 2 7 0 00	

ACCOUNT: **Accounts Payable**   ACCOUNT NO. 216

DATE		ITEM	POST. REF.	DEBIT	CREDIT	BALANCE	
						DEBIT	CREDIT
19-- June	5		CJ1		9 0 0 0 00		9 0 0 0 00
	22		CJ1	3 0 0 0 00			6 0 0 0 00
	25		CJ1		3 0 0 0 00		9 0 0 0 00

ACCOUNT: **Medical Fees**   ACCOUNT NO. 411

DATE		ITEM	POST. REF.	DEBIT	CREDIT	BALANCE	
						DEBIT	CREDIT
19-- June	30		CJ1		25 0 0 0 00		25 0 0 0 00

To see the advantages of posting a combination journal compared with the general journal, simply compare the accounts in Figure 7-9 with the same accounts in Chapter 4, Figure 4-12. Note the number of postings required for the general journal and combination journal.

	Number of Postings		
	General Journal	Combination Journal	
Cash	13	2	(Special columns for cash)
Accounts Payable	3	3	(No special column)
Delivery/Medical Fees	3	1	(Special column for Medical Fees)

Clearly, using the combination journal can be quite efficient.

Determining the Cash Balance

	Beginning cash balance
+	Cash debits to date
−	Cash credits to date
	Current cash balance

The debits and credits to Cash are not posted until the end of the account-ing period. Therefore, the cash balance must be computed when this infor-mation is needed. The cash balance may be computed at any time during the month by taking the beginning balance, adding total cash debits and subtracting total cash credits to date. Figure 7-10 shows the calculation of Bonita's cash balance on June 15.

PERFORMING END-OF-PERIOD WORK FOR A PROFESSIONAL SERVICE BUSINESS

LO5 Prepare a work sheet, financial statements, and adjusting and closing entries for a professional service business.

Once the combination journal has been posted to the general ledger, the end-of-period work sheet is prepared in the same way as described in Chapter 5. Recall that financial statements are prepared and end-of-period work is normally performed at the end of the fiscal year. For illustration purposes, we will perform these activities at the end of Bonita's first month of operations.

Preparing the Work Sheet

Bonita's work sheet is illustrated in Figure 7-11. Adjustments were made for the following items:

(a) Medical supplies remaining on June 30, $350.
(b) Office supplies remaining on June 30, $100.
(c) Prepaid insurance expired during June, $500.
(d) Depreciation on medical equipment for June, $300.
(e) Depreciation on office furniture for June, $200.

Preparing Financial Statements

No additional investment was made by Bonita during June. Thus, as we saw in Chapter 6, the financial statements can be prepared directly from the

FIGURE 7-10 Determining the Cash Balance

COMBINATION JOURNAL PAGE 1

	DATE		CASH DEBIT	CASH CREDIT	DESCRIPTION	POST. REF.	GENERAL DEBIT	GENERAL CREDIT	MEDICAL FEES CREDIT	WAGES EXPENSE DEBIT	LABORATORY EXPENSE DEBIT	MEDICAL SUPPLIES DEBIT	OFFICE SUPPLIES DEBIT	
1	19-- June	1	50 000 00		Ray Bonita, Capital	311		50 000 00						1
2		2		6 000 00	Prepaid Insurance	155	6 000 00							2
3		3		22 000 00	Medical Equipment	185	22 000 00							3
4		4		300 00		—					300 00			4
5		5			Office Furniture	192	9 000 00							5
6					Accounts Payable—Bittle's Furn.	216		9 000 00						6
7		6	5 000 00			—			5 000 00					7
8		7		2 000 00	Rent Expense	541	2 000 00							8
9		8		3 000 00		—				3 000 00				9
10		9		250 00		—						250 00		10
11		15		150 00	Telephone Expense	545	150 00							11
12		15	10 000 00			—			10 000 00					12
13			65 000 00	33 700 00										13

Beginning balance	$ 0
Add cash debits	65,000
Total	65,000
Less cash credits	33,700
Cash balance, June 15	$31,300

FIGURE 7-11 Work Sheet for Ray Bonita, M.D.

Ray Bonita, M.D.
Work Sheet
For Month Ended June 30, 19--

	ACCOUNT TITLE	TRIAL BALANCE		ADJUSTMENTS		ADJUSTED TRIAL BALANCE		INCOME STATEMENT		BALANCE SHEET		
		DEBIT	CREDIT	DEBIT	CREDIT	DEBIT	CREDIT	DEBIT	CREDIT	DEBIT	CREDIT	
1	Cash	21,270.00				21,270.00				21,270.00		1
2	Medical Supplies	450.00			(a) 100.00	350.00				350.00		2
3	Office Supplies	150.00			(b) 50.00	100.00				100.00		3
4	Prepaid Insurance	6,000.00			(c) 500.00	5,500.00				5,500.00		4
5	Medical Equipment	22,000.00				22,000.00				22,000.00		5
6	Accum. Depr.—Medical Equip.				(d) 300.00		300.00				300.00	6
7	Office Furniture	12,500.00				12,500.00				12,500.00		7
8	Accum. Depr.—Office Furniture				(e) 200.00		200.00				200.00	8
9	Accounts Payable		9,000.00				9,000.00				9,000.00	9
10	Ray Bonita, Capital		50,000.00				50,000.00				50,000.00	10
11	Ray Bonita, Drawing	10,000.00				10,000.00				10,000.00		11
12	Medical Fees		25,000.00				25,000.00		25,000.00			12
13	Rent Expense	2,000.00				2,000.00		2,000.00				13
14	Wages Expense	8,500.00				8,500.00		8,500.00				14
15	Office Supplies Expense			(b) 50.00		50.00		50.00				15
16	Medical Supplies Expense			(a) 100.00		100.00		100.00				16
17	Telephone Expense	150.00				150.00		150.00				17
18	Laboratory Expense	980.00				980.00		980.00				18
19	Depr. Expense—Medical Equip.			(d) 300.00		300.00		300.00				19
20	Depr. Expense—Office Furniture			(e) 200.00		200.00		200.00				20
21	Insurance Expense			(c) 500.00		500.00		500.00				21
22		84,000.00	84,000.00	1,150.00	1,150.00	84,500.00	84,500.00	12,780.00	25,000.00	71,720.00	59,500.00	22
23	Net Income							12,220.00			12,220.00	23
24								25,000.00	25,000.00	71,720.00	71,720.00	24
25												25
26												26
27												27
28												28
29												29
30												30
31												31
32												32
33												33
34												34
35												35
36												36
37												37
38												38
39												39
40												40

Profiles in Accounting

AMY BUTLER, Office Manager

Amy Butler earned an Associate Degree in Travel/Hospitality Management. After completing her externship with the Clubhouse Inn, Amy worked for Design Coatings as a receptionist. After eight months, she accepted an office manager's position with EMI, a database consulting firm.

Amy's duties include accounts payable and receivable, payroll, word processing, filing, and supervising and training eight employees.

She considers being professional at all times the key to success.

work sheet. Recall that if Bonita had made an additional investment, this amount would be identified by reviewing Bonita's capital account and would need to be reported in the statement of owner's equity. Bonita's financial statements are illustrated in Figure 7-12.

FIGURE 7-12   Financial Statements for Ray Bonita, M.D.

Ray Bonita, M.D.
Income Statement
For Month Ended June 30, 19--

Revenue:		
Medical fees		$25 000 00
Expenses:		
Rent expense	$2 000 00	
Wages expense	8 500 00	
Office supplies expense	50 00	
Medical supplies expense	1 00 00	
Telephone expense	1 50 00	
Laboratory expense	9 80 00	
Depreciation expense—medical equipment	3 00 00	
Depreciation expense—office furniture	2 00 00	
Insurance expense	5 00 00	
Total expenses		12 780 00
Net income		$12 220 00

Ray Bonita, M.D.
Statement of Owner's Equity
For Month Ended June 30, 19--

Ray Bonita, capital, June 1, 19--		$50 000 00
Net income for June	$12 220 00	
Less withdrawals for June	10 000 00	
Increase in capital		2 220 00
Ray Bonita, capital, June 30, 19--		$52 220 00

FIGURE 7-12   Financial Statements for Ray Bonita, M.D. (continued)

Ray Bonita, M.D. Balance Sheet June 30, 19--			
Assets			
Current assets:			
Cash	$21 2 7 0 00		
Medical supplies	3 5 0 00		
Office supplies	1 0 0 00		
Prepaid insurance	5 5 0 0 00		
Total current assets		$27 2 2 0 00	
Property, plant, and equipment:			
Medical equipment	$22 0 0 0 00		
Less accumulated depreciation	3 0 0 00	21 7 0 0 00	
Office furniture	$12 5 0 0 00		
Less accumulated depreciation	2 0 0 00	12 3 0 0 00	
Total assets		$61 2 2 0 00	
Liabilities			
Current liabilities:			
Accounts payable		$ 9 0 0 0 00	
Owner's Equity			
Ray Bonita, capital		52 2 2 0 00	
Total liabilities and owner's equity		$61 2 2 0 00	

Preparing Adjusting and Closing Entries

Adjusting and closing entries are made in the combination journal in the same manner demonstrated for the general journal in Chapter 6. We simply use the Description and General Debit and Credit columns. These posted entries are illustrated in Figures 7-13 and 7-14.

FIGURE 7-13   Adjusting Entries

COMBINATION JOURNAL

	DATE		CASH DEBIT	CASH CREDIT	DESCRIPTION	POST. REF.	GENERAL DEBIT	GENERAL CREDIT	
1					Adjusting Entries				1
2	19-- June	30			Medical Supplies Expense	544	1 0 0 00		2
3					Medical Supplies	151		1 0 0 00	3
4		30			Office Supplies Expense	543	5 0 00		4
5					Office Supplies	152		5 0 00	5
6		30			Insurance Expense	559	5 0 0 00		6
7					Prepaid Insurance	155		5 0 0 00	7
8		30			Depreciation Expense—Medical Equipment	547	3 0 0 00		8
9					Accumulated Depreciation—Medical Equipment	185.1		3 0 0 00	9
10		30			Depreciation Expense—Office Furniture	548	2 0 0 00		10
11					Accumulated Depreciation—Office Furniture	192.1		2 0 0 00	11

FIGURE 7-14   Closing Entries

COMBINATION JOURNAL

	DATE		CASH DEBIT	CASH CREDIT	DESCRIPTION	POST. REF.	GENERAL DEBIT	GENERAL CREDIT	
12									12
13					Closing Entries				13
14	June	30			Medical Fees	411	25 0 0 0 00		14
15					Income Summary	313		25 0 0 0 00	15
16		30			Income Summary	313	12 7 8 0 00		16
17					Rent Expense	541		2 0 0 0 00	17
18					Wages Expense	542		8 5 0 0 00	18
19					Office Supplies Expense	543		5 0 00	19
20					Medical Supplies Expense	544		1 0 0 00	20
21					Telephone Expense	545		1 5 0 00	21
22					Laboratory Expense	546		9 8 0 00	22
23					Depreciation Expense—Medical Equipment	547		3 0 0 00	23
24					Depreciation Expense—Office Furniture	548		2 0 0 00	24
25					Insurance Expense	559		5 0 0 00	25
26		30			Income Summary	313	12 2 2 0 00		26
27					Ray Bonita, Capital	311		12 2 2 0 00	27
28		30			Ray Bonita, Capital	311	10 0 0 0 00		28
29					Ray Bonita, Drawing	312		10 0 0 0 00	29

KEY POINTS

1   There are three bases of accounting: cash, modified cash, and accrual. Differences in the recording of revenues, expenses, assets, and liabilities are listed below.

Recording revenues

Cash:	when cash is received
Modified cash:	when cash is received
Accrual:	when earned

Recording expenses

Cash:	when cash is paid
Modified cash:	when cash is paid, except for property, plant and equipment and prepaid items
Accrual:	when incurred

Recording assets and liabilities

	Cash Basis	Modified Cash Basis	Accrual Basis
Accounts receivable	No	No	Yes
Payables			
for purchase of assets	No	Yes	Yes
for services received (wages payable)	No	No	Yes
Prepaid assets	No	Yes	Yes
Long-term assets	No	Yes	Yes

2 Special records are required for a professional service business using the modified cash basis. Since accounts receivable are not entered in the accounting system, other records must be maintained to keep track of amounts owed by clients and patients. These records generally include an appointment record and a client or patient ledger record.

3 A combination journal is used by some businesses to improve the efficiency of recording and posting transactions. It includes general and special columns. The headings for a typical combination journal for a doctor's office are shown below.

	COMBINATION JOURNAL								PAGE 1

DATE	CASH		DESCRIPTION	POST. REF.	GENERAL		MEDICAL FEES CREDIT	WAGES EXPENSE DEBIT	LABORATORY EXPENSE DEBIT	MEDICAL SUPPLIES DEBIT	OFFICE SUPPLIES DEBIT
	DEBIT	CREDIT			DEBIT	CREDIT					

4 Rules for posting a combination journal:

1. Amounts entered in the general columns are posted individually to the general ledger on a daily basis.
2. The totals of the special columns are posted to the general ledger at the end of the month.

5 The work sheet, financial statements, adjusting entries, and closing entries are prepared in the same manner as discussed in Chapters 5 and 6. Remember, however, that under the modified cash basis, adjustments are made only for prepaid items and depreciation of plant and equipment.

KEY TERMS

accrual basis of accounting 205   A method of accounting under which revenues are recorded when earned and expenses are recorded when incurred.

cash basis of accounting 205   A method of accounting under which revenues are recorded when cash is received and expenses are recorded when cash is paid.

combination journal 210   A journal with special and general columns.

Description column 214   In the combination journal, this column is used to enter the account titles for the General Debit and General Credit columns, to identify specific creditors when assets are purchased on account, and to identify amounts forwarded.

General Credit column 210   In the combination journal, this column is used to credit accounts that are used infrequently.

General Debit column 210   In the combination journal, this column is used to debit accounts that are used infrequently.

modified cash basis 206   A method of accounting that combines aspects of the cash and accrual methods. It uses the cash basis for recording revenues and most expenses. Exceptions are made when cash is paid for assets with useful lives greater than one accounting period.

Posting Reference column 215   In the combination journal, the account number is entered in this column after posting.

special columns 210   Columns in journals for frequently used accounts.

REVIEW QUESTIONS

1. Explain when revenues are recorded under the cash basis, modified cash basis, and accrual basis of accounting.
2. Explain when expenses are recorded under the cash basis, modified cash basis, and accrual basis of accounting.
3. Explain the purpose of an appointment record.
4. Explain the purpose of a patient ledger account.
5. Explain the purpose of a special column in the combination journal.
6. Explain the purpose of the General columns in the combination journal.
7. How does the use of the combination journal save time and space in entering cash transactions?
8. Explain the purpose of the Description column in the combination journal.
9. What is the purpose of proving the totals in the combination journal?
10. When an entry is posted from the combination journal to a ledger account, what information is entered in the Posting Reference column of the combination journal? In the Posting Reference column of the ledger account?

MANAGING YOUR WRITING

Your friend is planning to start her own business and has asked you for advice. In particular, she is concerned about which method of accounting she should use. She has heard about the cash, modified cash, and accrual methods of accounting. However, she does not really understand the differences. Write a memo that explains each method and the type of business for which each method is most appropriate.

DEMONSTRATION PROBLEM

Maria Vietor is a financial planning consultant. She developed the following chart of accounts for her business.

Vietor Financial Planning
Chart of Accounts

Assets	Revenues
111 Cash	411 Professional Fees
152 Office Supplies	
	Expenses
Liabilities	541 Rent Expense
216 Accounts Payable	542 Wages Expense
	543 Office Supplies Expense
Owner's Equity	545 Telephone Expense
311 Maria Vietor, Capital	546 Automobile Expense
312 Maria Vietor, Drawing	555 Utilities Expense
313 Income Summary	557 Charitable Contributions Expense

Vietor completed the following transactions during the month of December of the current year:

Dec. 1   Vietor invested cash to start a consulting business, $20,000.
    3   Paid December office rent, $1,000.
    4   Received a check from Aaron Bisno, a client, for services, $2,500.
    6   Paid Union Electric for December heating and light, $75.
    7   Received a check from Will Carter, a client, for services $2,000.
    12   Paid Smith's Super Service for gasoline and oil purchases, $60.
    14   Paid Comphelp for temporary secretarial services obtained through them during the past two weeks, $600.
    17   Purchased office supplies from Cleat Office Supply on account, $280.
    20   Paid Cress Telephone Co. for local and long-distance business calls during the past month, $100.
    21   Vietor withdrew cash for personal use, $1,100.
    24   Made donation to the National Multiple Sclerosis Society, $100.
    27   Received a check from Ellen Thaler, a client, for services, $2,000.
    28   Paid Comphelp for temporary secretarial services obtained through them during the past two weeks, $600.
    29   Made payment on account to Cleat Office Supply, $100.

REQUIRED
REQUIRED

1. Enter the transactions in a combination journal. Establish special columns for Professional Fees, Wages Expense, and Automobile Expense. Vietor uses the modified cash basis of accounting. (Refer to the Chapter 4 Demonstration Problem to see how similar transactions were recorded in a general journal. Notice that the combination journal is much more efficient.)

2. Prove the combination journal.

3. Post these transactions to a general ledger.

4. Prepare a trial balance.

SOLUTION

1, 2   See page 226.

3.

GENERAL LEDGER

ACCOUNT: Cash   ACCOUNT NO. 111

DATE	ITEM	POST. REF.	DEBIT	CREDIT	BALANCE DEBIT	BALANCE CREDIT
19-- Dec. 31		CJ1	26 5 0 0 00		26 5 0 0 00	
31		CJ1		3 7 3 5 00	22 7 6 5 00	

ACCOUNT: Office Supplies   ACCOUNT NO. 152

DATE	ITEM	POST. REF.	DEBIT	CREDIT	BALANCE DEBIT	BALANCE CREDIT
19-- Dec. 17		CJ1	2 8 0 00		2 8 0 00	

ACCOUNT: Accounts Payable   ACCOUNT NO. 216

DATE	ITEM	POST. REF.	DEBIT	CREDIT	BALANCE DEBIT	BALANCE CREDIT
19-- Dec. 17		CJ1		2 8 0 00		2 8 0 00
29		CJ1	1 0 0 00			1 8 0 00

ACCOUNT: Maria Vietor, Capital   ACCOUNT NO. 311

DATE	ITEM	POST. REF.	DEBIT	CREDIT	BALANCE DEBIT	BALANCE CREDIT
19-- Dec. 1		CJ1		20 0 0 0 00		20 0 0 0 00

ACCOUNT: Maria Vietor, Drawing   ACCOUNT NO. 312

DATE	ITEM	POST. REF.	DEBIT	CREDIT	BALANCE DEBIT	BALANCE CREDIT
19-- Dec. 21		CJ1	1 1 0 0 00		1 1 0 0 00	

ACCOUNT: Income Summary   ACCOUNT NO. 313

DATE	ITEM	POST. REF.	DEBIT	CREDIT	BALANCE DEBIT	BALANCE CREDIT
19--						

COMBINATION JOURNAL

PAGE 1

	DATE	CASH DEBIT	CASH CREDIT	DESCRIPTION	POST. REF.	GENERAL DEBIT	GENERAL CREDIT	PROFESSIONAL FEES CREDIT	WAGES EXPENSE DEBIT	AUTOMOBILE EXPENSE DEBIT	
1	19-- Dec. 1	20 0 0 0 00		Maria Vietor, Capital	311		20 0 0 0 00				1
2	3		1 0 0 0 00	Rent Expense	541	1 0 0 0 00					2
3	4	2 5 0 0 00			—			2 5 0 0 00			3
4	6		7 5 00	Utilities Expense	555	7 5 00					4
5	7	2 0 0 0 00			—			2 0 0 0 00			5
6	12		6 0 00		—					6 0 00	6
7	14		6 0 0 00		—				6 0 0 00		7
8	17			Office Supplies	152	2 8 0 00					8
9				Accounts Payable—Cleat Office Supply	216		2 8 0 00				9
10	20		1 0 0 00	Telephone Expense	545	1 0 0 00					10
11	21		1 1 0 0 00	Maria Vietor, Drawing	312	1 1 0 0 00					11
12	24		1 0 0 00	Charitable Contributions Expense	557	1 0 0 00					12
13	27	2 0 0 0 00			—			2 0 0 0 00			13
14	28		6 0 0 00		—				6 0 0 00		14
15	29		1 0 0 00	Accounts Payable—Cleat Office Supply	216	1 0 0 00					15
16		26 5 0 0 00	3 7 3 5 00			2 7 5 5 00	20 2 8 0 00	6 5 0 0 00	1 2 0 0 00	6 0 00	16
17		(111)	(111)			(✓)	(✓)	(411)	(542)	(546)	17
18											18
19											19
20											20
21											21
22											22
23											23
24											24
25											25
26											26

Proving the Combination Journal

Debit Columns		Credit Columns	
Cash	26,500	Cash	3,735
General	2,755	General	20,280
Wages Expense	1,200	Professional Fees	6,500
Auto. Expense	60		30,515
	30,515		

ACCOUNT: Professional Fees   ACCOUNT NO. 411

DATE	ITEM	POST. REF.	DEBIT	CREDIT	BALANCE DEBIT	BALANCE CREDIT
19-- Dec. 31		CJ1		6 5 0 0 00		6 5 0 0 00

ACCOUNT: Rent Expense   ACCOUNT NO. 541

DATE	ITEM	POST. REF.	DEBIT	CREDIT	BALANCE DEBIT	BALANCE CREDIT
19-- Dec. 3		CJ1	1 0 0 0 00		1 0 0 0 00	

ACCOUNT: Wages Expense   ACCOUNT NO. 542

DATE	ITEM	POST. REF.	DEBIT	CREDIT	BALANCE DEBIT	BALANCE CREDIT
19-- Dec. 31		CJ1	1 2 0 0 00		1 2 0 0 00	

ACCOUNT: Office Supplies Expense   ACCOUNT NO. 543

DATE	ITEM	POST. REF.	DEBIT	CREDIT	BALANCE DEBIT	BALANCE CREDIT
19--						

ACCOUNT: Telephone Expense   ACCOUNT NO. 545

DATE	ITEM	POST. REF.	DEBIT	CREDIT	BALANCE DEBIT	BALANCE CREDIT
19-- Dec. 20		CJ1	1 0 0 00		1 0 0 00	

ACCOUNT: Automobile Expense   ACCOUNT NO. 546

DATE	ITEM	POST. REF.	DEBIT	CREDIT	BALANCE DEBIT	BALANCE CREDIT
19-- Dec. 31		CJ1	6 0 00		6 0 00	

ACCOUNT: Utilities Expense   ACCOUNT NO. 555

DATE	ITEM	POST. REF.	DEBIT	CREDIT	BALANCE DEBIT	BALANCE CREDIT
19-- Dec. 6		CJ1	7 5 00		7 5 00	

ACCOUNT: Charitable Contributions Expense   ACCOUNT NO. 557

DATE	ITEM	POST. REF.	DEBIT	CREDIT	BALANCE DEBIT	BALANCE CREDIT
19-- Dec. 24		CJ1	1 0 0 00		1 0 0 00	

4.

Vietor Financial Planning
Trial Balance
December 31, 19--

ACCOUNT TITLE	ACCOUNT NO.	DEBIT BALANCE	CREDIT BALANCE
Cash	111	22 7 6 5 00	
Office Supplies	152	2 8 0 00	
Accounts Payable	216		1 8 0 00
Maria Vietor, Capital	311		20 0 0 0 00
Maria Vietor, Drawing	312	1 1 0 0 00	
Professional Fees	411		6 5 0 0 00
Rent Expense	541	1 0 0 0 00	
Wages Expense	542	1 2 0 0 00	
Telephone Expense	545	1 0 0 00	
Automobile Expense	546	6 0 00	
Utilities Expense	555	7 5 00	
Charitable Contributions Expense	557	1 0 0 00	
		26 6 8 0 00	26 6 8 0 00

SERIES A   EXERCISES

1   **EXERCISE 7A1 CASH, MODIFIED CASH, AND ACCRUAL BASES OF ACCOUNTING**   Prepare the entry for each of the following transactions, using the (a) cash basis, (b) modified cash basis, and (c) accrual basis of accounting.

1. Purchase supplies on account.
2. Make payment on asset previously purchased.
3. Purchase supplies for cash.
4. Purchase insurance for cash.
5. Pay cash for wages.
6. Pay cash for telephone expense.
7. Pay cash for new equipment.

End-of-Period Adjusting Entries:

8. Wages earned but not paid.
9. Prepaid item purchased, partly used.
10. Depreciation on long-term assets.

1   **EXERCISE 7A2 JOURNAL ENTRIES**   Jean Akins opened a consulting business. Journalize the following transactions that occurred during the month of January of the current year using the modified cash basis and a combination journal. Set up special columns for consulting fees (credit) and wages expense (debit).

Jan. 1 Invested cash in the business, $10,000.
2 Paid office rent, $500.
3 Purchased office equipment from Business Machines, Inc., on account, $1,500.
5 Received cash for services rendered, $750.
8 Paid telephone bill, $65.
10 Paid for a magazine subscription (miscellaneous expense), $15.
11 Purchased office supplies from Leo's Office Supplies on account, $300.
15 Paid for one-year liability insurance policy, $150.
18 Paid part-time help, $500.
21 Received cash for services rendered, $350.
25 Paid electricity bill, $85.
27 Withdrew cash for personal use, $100.
29 Paid part-time help, $500.

1/3 **EXERCISE 7A3 JOURNAL ENTRIES** Bill Rackes opened a bicycle repair shop. Journalize the following transactions that occurred during the month of October of the current year. Use the modified cash basis and a combination journal with special columns for Repair Fees (credit) and Wages Expense (debit). Prove the combination journal.

Oct. 1 Invested cash in the business, $15,000.
2 Paid shop rental for the month, $300.
3 Purchased bicycle parts from Tracker's Bicycle Parts on account, $2,000.
5 Purchased office supplies from Downtown Office Supplies on account, $250.
8 Paid telephone bill, $38.
9 Received cash for services, $140.
11 Paid for a sports magazine subscription (miscellaneous expense), $15.
12 Made payment on account for parts previously purchased, $100.
14 Paid part-time help, $300.
15 Received cash for services, $350.
16 Paid electricity bill, $48.
19 Received cash for services, $250.
23 Withdrew cash for personal use, $50.
25 Made payment on account for office supplies previously purchased, $50.
29 Paid part-time help, $300.

SERIES A PROBLEMS

3/4/5 **PROBLEM 7A1 JOURNALIZING AND POSTING TRANS-ACTIONS AND PREPARING FINANCIAL STATEMENTS** Angela McWharton opened an on-call nursing services business. She rented a small office space and pays a part-time worker to answer the telephone. Her chart of accounts is shown on the next page.

Angela McWharton Nursing Services
Chart of Accounts

Assets
101   Cash
111   Office Supplies
121   Office Equipment

Liabilities
211   Accounts Payable

Owner's Equity
311   Angela McWharton, Capital
312   Angela McWharton, Drawing
313   Income Summary

Revenues
411   Nursing Care Fees

Expenses
511   Rent Expense
522   Wages Expense
524   Telephone Expense
531   Electricity Expense
533   Transportation Expense
542   Advertising Expense
568   Miscellaneous Expense

McWharton's transactions for the first month of business are as follows:

Jan.   1 Invested cash in the business, $10,000.
       1 Paid January rent, $500.
       2 Purchased office supplies from Crestline Office Supplies on account, $300.
       4 Purchased office equipment from Office Technology, Inc., on account, $1,500.
       6 Received cash for nursing services rendered, $580.
       7 Paid telephone bill, $42.
       8 Paid electricity bill, $38.
      10 Received cash for nursing services rendered, $360.
      12 Made payment on account for office supplies previously purchased, $50.
      13 Reimbursed part-time worker for use of personal automobile (transportation expense), $150.
      15 Paid part-time worker, $360.
      17 Received cash for nursing services rendered, $420.
      18 Withdrew cash for personal use, $100.
      20 Paid for newspaper advertising, $26.
      22 Paid for gas and oil, $35.
      24 Paid subscription for journal on nursing care practices (miscellaneous expense), $28.
      25 Received cash for nursing services rendered, $320.
      27 Made payment on account for office equipment previously purchased, $150.
      29 Paid part-time worker, $360.
      30 Received cash for nursing services rendered, $180.

REQUIRED

1. Journalize the transactions for January using the modified cash basis and page 1 in a combination journal. Set up special columns for Nursing Care Fees (credit), Wages Expense (debit), and Transportation Expense (debit).

2. Determine the cash balance as of January 12 (using the combination journal).
3. Prove the combination journal.
4. Set up four-column general ledger accounts from the chart of accounts and post the transactions from the combination journal.
5. Prepare a trial balance.

3/4/5   **PROBLEM 7A2 JOURNALIZING AND POSTING TRANS-ACTIONS AND PREPARING FINANCIAL STATEMENTS**   Sue Reyton owns a suit tailoring shop. She opened business in September. She rented a small work space and has an assistant to receive job orders and process claim tickets. Her trial balance shows her account balances for the first two months of business (September and October).

Sue Reyton Tailors
Trial Balance
October 31, 19--

ACCOUNT TITLE	ACCOUNT NO.	DEBIT BALANCE	CREDIT BALANCE
Cash	101	6 2 1 1 50	
Office Supplies	111	4 8 4 50	
Tailoring Supplies	121	1 0 0 0 00	
Prepaid Insurance	131	1 0 0 00	
Tailoring Equipment	141	3 8 0 0 00	
Accumulated Depreciation—Tailoring Equipment	141.1		8 0 0 00
Accounts Payable	211		4 1 2 5 00
Sue Reyton, Capital	311		5 4 3 0 00
Sue Reyton, Drawing	312	8 0 0 00	
Tailoring Fees	411		3 6 0 0 00
Rent Expense	511	6 0 0 00	
Wages Expense	522	8 0 0 00	
Telephone Expense	533	6 0 00	
Electricity Expense	555	4 4 00	
Advertising Expense	566	3 3 00	
Miscellaneous Expense	588	2 2 00	
		13 9 5 5 00	13 9 5 5 00

Reyton's transactions for November are as follows:

Nov.   1 Paid November rent, $300.
2 Purchased tailoring supplies from Sew Easy Supplies on account, $150.
3 Purchased a new button hole machine from Seam's Sewing Machines on account, $3,000.
5 Earned first week's revenue: $400 in cash.
8 Paid for newspaper advertising, $13.

Nov.   9 Paid telephone bill, $28.
       10 Paid electricity bill, $21.
       12 Earned second week's revenue: $200 in cash, $300 on account.
       15 Paid part-time worker, $400.
       16 Made payment on account for tailoring supplies, $100.
       17 Paid for magazine subscription (miscellaneous expense), $12.
       19 Earned third week's revenue: $450 in cash.
       21 Paid for prepaid insurance for the year, $500.
       23 Received cash from customers (previously owed), $300.
       24 Paid for newspaper advertising, $13.
       26 Paid for special delivery fee (miscellaneous expense), $12.
       29 Earned fourth week's revenue: $600 in cash.

Additional accounts needed are:

313   Income Summary
541   Tailoring Supplies Expense
542   Office Supplies Expense
543   Insurance Expense
544   Depreciation Expense—Tailoring Equipment

Nov. 30 Adjustments:

(a)   Tailoring supplies on hand, $450.
(b)   Office supplies on hand, $284.50.
(c)   Prepaid insurance expired over past three months, $150.
(d)   Depreciation on tailoring equipment for past three months, $300.

REQUIRED

1. Journalize the transactions for November using the modified cash basis and page 5 in a combination journal. Set up special columns for Tailoring Fees (credit), Wages Expense (debit), and Advertising Expense (debit).
2. Determine the cash balance as of November 12.
3. Prove the combination journal.
4. Set up four-column general ledger accounts, including the additional accounts listed above, entering the balances as of November 1, 19--. Post the entries from the combination journal.
5. Prepare a work sheet for the three months ended November 30, 19--.
6. Prepare an income statement, statement of owner's equity, and balance sheet as of November 30, 19--. (Assume that Reyton made an investment of $5,430 on September 1, 19--.)
7. Record the adjusting and closing entries on page 6 of the combination journal and post to the general ledger accounts.

SERIES B EXERCISES

1 **EXERCISE 7B1 CASH, MODIFIED CASH, AND ACCRUAL BASES OF ACCOUNTING**   For each journal entry shown below, indicate the accounting method(s) for which the entry would be appropriate. If the journal entry is not appropriate for a particular accounting method, explain the proper accounting treatment for that method.

1. Office Equipment
  Cash
   Purchased equipment for cash

2. Office Equipment
  Accounts Payable
   Purchased equipment on account

3. Cash
  Revenue
   Cash receipts for week

4. Accounts Receivable
  Revenue
   Services performed on account

5. Prepaid Insurance
  Cash
   Purchased prepaid asset

6. Supplies
  Accounts Payable
   Purchased prepaid asset

7. Telephone Expense
  Cash
   Paid telephone bill

8. Wages Expense
  Cash
   Paid wages for month

9. Accounts Payable
  Cash
   Payment on account

Adjusting Entries:

10. Supplies Expense
  Supplies

11. Wages Expense
  Wages Payable

12. Depreciation Expense—Office Equipment
  Accumulated Depreciation—Office Equipment

EXERCISE 7B2 JOURNAL ENTRIES Bill Miller opened a bookkeeping service business. Journalize the following transactions that occurred during the month of March of the current year. Use the modified cash basis and a combination journal with special columns for Bookkeeping Fees (credit) and Wages Expense (debit).

Mar. 1 Invested cash in the business, $7,500.
   3 Paid March office rent, $500.

Mar. 5 Purchased office equipment from Desk Top Office Equipment on account, $800.
6 Received cash for services rendered, $400.
8 Paid telephone bill, $48.
10 Paid for a magazine subscription (miscellaneous expense), $25.
11 Purchased office supplies, $200.
14 Received cash for services rendered, $520.
16 Paid for a one-year insurance policy, $200.
18 Paid part-time worker, $400.
21 Received cash for services rendered, $380.
22 Made payment on account for office equipment previously purchased, $100.
24 Paid electricity bill, $56.
27 Withdrew cash for personal use, $200.
29 Paid part-time worker, $400.
30 Received cash for services rendered, $600.

3 **EXERCISE 7B3 JOURNAL ENTRIES** Amy Anjelo opened a delivery service. Journalize the following transactions that occurred in January of the current year. Use the modified cash basis and a combination journal with special columns for Delivery Fees (credit) and Wages Expense (debit). Prove the combination journal.

Jan. 1 Invested cash in the business, $10,000.
2 Paid shop rental for the month, $400.
3 Purchased a delivery cart from Walt's Wheels on account, $1,000.
5 Purchased office supplies, $250.
6 Paid telephone bill, $51.
8 Received cash for delivery services, $428.
11 Paid electricity bill, $37.
12 Paid part-time employee, $480.
13 Paid for postage stamps (miscellaneous expense), $29.
15 Received cash for delivery services, $382.
18 Made payment on account for delivery cart previously purchased, $90.
21 Withdrew cash for personal use, $250.
24 Paid for a one-year liability insurance policy, $180.
26 Received cash for delivery services, $292.
29 Paid part-time employee, $480.

SERIES B PROBLEMS

3/4/5 **PROBLEM 7B1 JOURNALIZING AND POSTING TRANSACTIONS AND PREPARING FINANCIAL STATEMENTS** J.B. Hoyt opened a training center at the marina where he provides private waterskiing lessons. He rented a small building at the marina and has a part-time worker to assist him. His chart of accounts is shown on the next page.

Water Walking by Hoyt
Chart of Accounts

Assets
101   Cash
111   Office Supplies
121   Skiing Equipment

Liabilities
211   Accounts Payable

Owner's Equity
311   J.B. Hoyt, Capital
312   J.B. Hoyt, Drawing
313   Income Summary

Revenues
411   Training Fees

Expenses
511   Rent Expense
522   Wages Expense
524   Telephone Expense
531   Repair Expense
538   Electricity Expense
542   Transportation Expense
568   Miscellaneous Expense

Transactions for the first month of business are as follows:

July   1 Invested cash in the business, $5,000.
       2 Paid rent for the month, $250.
       3 Purchased office supplies, $150.
       4 Purchased skiing equipment from Water Fun, Inc., on account, $2,000.
       6 Paid telephone bill, $36.
       7 Received cash for skiing lessons, $200.
      10 Paid electricity bill, $28.
      12 Paid part-time worker, $250.
      14 Received cash for skiing lessons, $300.
      16 Paid for gas and oil (transportation expense), $60.
      17 Received cash for skiing lessons, $250.
      20 Paid for repair to ski rope, $20.
      21 Made payment on account for skiing equipment previously purchased, $100.
      24 Received cash for skiing lessons, $310.
      26 Paid for award certificates (miscellaneous expense), $18.
      28 Paid part-time worker, $250.
      30 Received cash for skiing lessons, $230.
      31 Paid for repair to life jacket, $20.

REQUIRED

1. Journalize the transactions for July using the modified cash basis and page 1 in a combination journal. Set up special columns for Training Fees (credit), Wages Expense (debit), and Repair Expense (debit).
2. Determine the cash balance as of July 14, 19--.
3. Prove the combination journal.
4. Set up four-column general ledger accounts from the chart of accounts and post the transactions from the combination journal.
5. Prepare a trial balance.

3/4/5   **PROBLEM 7B2 JOURNALIZING AND POSTING TRANS-
ACTIONS AND PREPARING FINANCIAL STATEMENTS**   Molly
Claussen owns a lawn care business. She opened her business in April. She
rented a small shop area where she stores her equipment and has an assistant to receive orders and process accounts. Her trial balance shows her
account balances for the first two months of business (April and May).

Transactions for June are as follows:

June 1 Paid shop rent, $200.
      2 Purchased office supplies, $230.
      3 Purchased new landscaping equipment from Earth Care, Inc., on
         account, $1,000.
      5 Paid telephone bill, $31.
      6 Received cash for lawn care fees, $640.
      8 Paid electricity bill, $31.
     10 Paid part-time worker, $300.
     11 Received cash for lawn care fees, $580.
     12 Paid for a one-year insurance policy, $200.
     14 Made payment on account for landscaping equipment previously
         purchased, $100.
     15 Paid for gas and oil, $40.
     19 Paid for mower repairs, $25.
     21 Received $310 cash for lawn care fees and earned $480 on account.
     24 Withdrew cash for personal use, $100.
     26 Paid for edging equipment repairs, $20.
     28 Received cash from customers (previously owed), $480.
     29 Paid part-time worker, $300.

Additional accounts needed are:

313 Income Summary
541 Lawn Care Supplies Expense
542 Office Supplies Expense
543 Insurance Expense
544 Depreciation Expense—Lawn Care Equipment

June 30 Adjustments:

(a) Office supplies on hand, $273.
(b) Lawn care supplies on hand, $300.
(c) Prepaid insurance expired over past three months, $100.
(d) Depreciation on lawn care equipment for past three months, $260.

REQUIRED

1. Journalize the transactions for June using the modified cash basis and
   page 5 in a combination journal. Set up special columns for Lawn Care
   Fees (credit), Repair Expense (debit), and Wages Expense (debit).
2. Determine the cash balance as of June 12.
3. Prove the combination journal.

Molly Claussen's Green Thumb
Trial Balance
May 31, 19--

ACCOUNT TITLE	ACCOUNT NO.	DEBIT BALANCE	CREDIT BALANCE
Cash	101	4 8 4 4 00	
Office Supplies	111	2 4 3 00	
Lawn Care Supplies	121	5 8 8 00	
Prepaid Insurance	131	1 5 0 00	
Lawn Care Equipment	144	2 4 0 8 00	
Accumulated Depreciation—Lawn Care Equip.	144.1		2 4 0 00
Accounts Payable	211		1 0 8 0 00
Molly Claussen, Capital	311		5 0 0 0 00
Molly Claussen, Drawing	312	8 0 0 00	
Lawn Care Fees	411		4 0 3 3 00
Rent Expense	511	4 0 0 00	
Wages Expense	522	6 0 0 00	
Telephone Expense	533	8 8 00	
Electricity Expense	555	6 2 00	
Gas and Oil Expense	566	1 2 0 00	
Repair Expense	588	5 0 00	
		10 3 5 3 00	10 3 5 3 00

4. Set up four-column general ledger accounts including the additional accounts listed above, entering balances as of June 1, 19--. Post the entries from the combination journal.
5. Prepare a work sheet for the three months ended June 30, 19--.
6. Prepare an income statement, statement of owner's equity, and balance sheet as of June 30, 19--. Assume that Claussen invested $5,000 on April 1, 19--.
7. Record the adjusting and closing entries on page 6 of the combination journal and post to the general ledger accounts.

MASTERY PROBLEM

John McRoe opened a tennis resort in June 19--. Most guests register for one week, arriving on Sunday afternoon and returning home the following Saturday afternoon. Guests stay at an adjacent hotel. Lunch and dinner are provided by the tennis resort. Dining and exercise facilities are provided in a building rented by McRoe. A dietitian, masseuse, physical therapist, and athletic trainers are on call to assure the proper combination of diet and exercise. The chart of accounts and transactions for the month of June are provided on the next page. McRoe uses the modified cash basis of accounting.

McRoe Tennis Resort
Chart of Accounts

Assets
111   Cash
152   Office Supplies
154   Food Supplies
183   Tennis Facilities
183.1 Accum. Depr.—Tennis Facilities
184   Exercise Equipment
184.1 Accum. Depr.—Exercise Equip.

Liabilities
216   Accounts Payable

Owner's Equity
311   John McRoe, Capital
312   John McRoe, Drawing
313   Income Summary

Revenues
411   Registration Fees

Expenses
541   Rent Expense
542   Wages Expense
543   Office Supplies Expense
544   Food Supplies Expense
545   Telephone Expense
547   Depr. Exp.—Tennis Facilities
548   Depr. Exp.—Exercise Equip.
555   Utilities Expense
559   Insurance Expense
564   Postage Expense

June 1 McRoe invested cash in the business, $90,000.
1 Paid for new exercise equipment, $9,000.
2 Deposited registration fees in the bank, $15,000.
2 Paid rent for month of June on building and land, $2,000.
2 Rogers Construction completed work on new tennis courts that cost $70,000. The estimated useful life of the facility is five years, at which time the courts will have to be resurfaced. Arrangements were made to pay the bill in July.
3 Purchased food supplies from Au Naturel Foods on account, $5,000.
5 Purchased office supplies on account from Gordon Office Supplies, $300.
7 Deposited registration fees in the bank, $16,200.
10 Purchased food supplies from Au Naturel Foods on account, $6,200.
10 Paid wages to staff, $500.
14 Deposited registration fees in the bank, $13,500.
16 Purchased food supplies from Au Naturel Foods on account, $4,000.
17 Paid wages to staff, $500.
18 Paid postage, $85.
21 Deposited registration fees in the bank, $15,200.
24 Purchased food supplies from Au Naturel Foods on account for $5,500.
24 Paid wages to staff, $500.
28 Deposited registration fees in the bank, $14,000.
30 Purchased food supplies from Au Naturel Foods on account, $6,000.
30 Paid wages to staff, $500.
30 Paid Au Naturel Foods on account, $28,700.

June   30 Paid utility bill, $500.
       30 Paid telephone bill, $120.
       30 McRoe withdrew cash for personal use, $2,000.

REQUIRED

1. Enter the transactions in a combination journal. Establish special columns for Registration Fees (credit), Wages Expense (debit), and Food Supplies (debit).
2. Prove the combination journal.
3. Post these transactions to a general ledger.
4. Prepare a trial balance as of June 30.

8

Accounting for Cash

*Careful study of this chapter
should enable you to:*

LO1 Describe how to open and use a checking account.

LO2 Prepare a bank reconciliation.

LO3 Describe how to operate a petty cash fund.

LO4 Use the cash short and over account.

Do you want to be able to pay your bills by mail? Then you need a checking account, because it is unsafe to mail cash. Do you want to avoid being fined for writing a check for more than you have in your account? Then you need to know how to keep track of your checking account balance. Do you want to know why your checkbook balance does not agree with the one on the bank statement? Then you need to know how to prepare a bank reconciliation.

Cash is an asset that is quite familiar and important to all of us. We generally think of **cash** as the currency and coins in our pockets and the money we have in our checking accounts. To a business, cash also includes checks received from customers, money orders, and bank cashier's checks.

Because it plays such a central role in operating a business, cash must be carefully managed and controlled. A business should have a system of **internal control**—a set of procedures designed to ensure proper accounting for transactions. For good internal control of cash transactions, all cash received should be deposited daily in a bank. All disbursements, except for payments from petty cash, should be made by check.

CHECKING ACCOUNT

LO1   Describe how to open and use a checking account.

The key documents and forms required in opening and using a checking account are the signature card, deposit tickets, checks, and bank statements.

Opening a Checking Account

To open a checking account, each person authorized to sign checks must complete and sign a **signature card** (Figure 8-1). The bank uses this card to verify the depositor's signature on any banking transactions. The depositor's social security number or employer identification number (EIN) is shown on the card to identify the depositor. An EIN can be obtained from the Internal Revenue Service.

FIGURE 8-1   Signature Card

LAST NAME, FIRST NAME, MIDDLE INITIAL	ACCT #	
	TYPE	
	DATE	INIT.
STREET ADDRESS TOWN	STATE ZIP	

I CERTIFY THAT THE NUMBER SHOWN ON THIS FORM IS MY CORRECT TAXPAYER IDENTIFICATION NUMBER AND THAT I AM NOT SUBJECT TO BACKUP WITHHOLDING.

SIGNATURE 1	DATE OF BIRTH	SOCIAL SECURITY NO.
SIGNATURE 2		
SIGNATURE 3		

Making Deposits

A **deposit ticket** (Figure 8-2) is a detailed listing of items being deposited. Currency, coins, and checks are listed separately. Sometimes each check is identified by its **ABA (American Bankers Association) Number.** This number is the small fraction printed in the upper right hand corner of each check. The number is used to sort and route checks throughout the banking system. Normally, only the numerator of the fraction is used in identifying checks on the deposit ticket.

FIGURE 8-2 Deposit Ticket

MAPLE CONSULTING
4112 WEBER ST.
ORLANDO, FL 32818-1123

63-1209 / 631

DEPOSIT TICKET

WIZARD BANK
3711 Buena Vista Dr.
Orlando, FL 32811-1314

DATE *October 13* 19 --

CHECKS AND OTHER ITEMS ARE RECEIVED FOR DEPOSIT SUBJECT TO THE TERMS AND CONDITIONS OF THIS FINANCIAL INSTITUTION'S ACCOUNT AGREEMENT.

SIGN HERE ONLY IF CASH RECEIVED FROM DEPOSIT

CURRENCY		934	00
COIN		42	63
CHECKS	4-21	320	80
	80-459	680	00
	4-5	590	00
TOTAL FROM OTHER SIDE			
SUB-TOTAL		2,567	43
LESS CASH RECEIVED			
TOTAL DEPOSIT		2,567	43

:063112094: 0001632475

The depositor delivers or mails the deposit ticket and all items being deposited to the bank. The bank then gives or mails a receipt to the depositor.

Endorsements. Each check being deposited must be endorsed by the depositor. The **endorsement** consists of stamping or writing the depositor's name and sometimes other information on the back of the check, near the left end. There are two basic types of endorsements.

Profiles in Accounting

LISA DAVIS, Legal Coordinator

Lisa Davis began working as a part-time legal secretary with Zegarelli Associates. Lisa continued her career with this company after earning an Associate Degree in Legal Office Management.

After graduation Lisa was hired as a legal assistant and later promoted to legal coordinator. Her duties include budgeting, accounts receivable, supervising two employees, coordinating schedules, researching, and dealing with clients on a daily basis.

According to Lisa, dependability, initiative, and loyalty lead to success. Lisa chose the legal field because she always had an interest in law and wanted to work in a fast-paced environment.

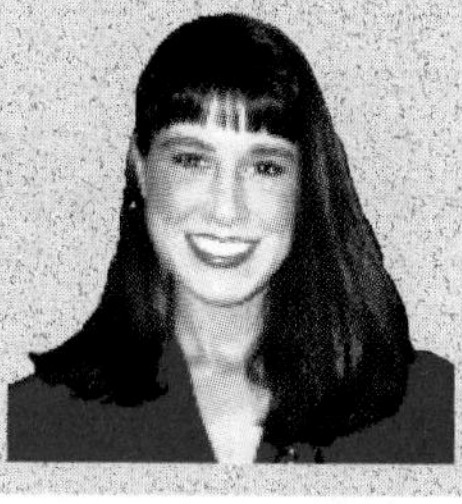

1. **Blank endorsement**—the depositor simply signs the back of the check. This makes the check payable to any bearer.
2. **Restrictive endorsement**—the depositor adds words such as "For deposit," "Pay to any bank," or "Pay to Daryl Beck only" to restrict the payment of the check.

Businesses commonly use a rubber stamp to endorse checks for deposit. The check shown in Figure 8-3 has been stamped with a restrictive endorsement.

FIGURE 8-3   Restrictive Endorsement

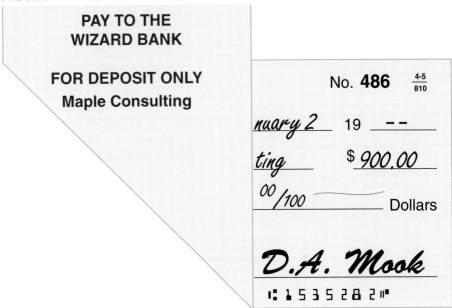

Automated Teller Machines.   Many banks now make **automated teller machines (ATM)** available at all times to depositors for making deposits or withdrawals. Each depositor has a plastic card (Figure 8-4) and a personal identification number (PIN). The depositor inserts the card into the machine and keys in the PIN, whether the transaction is a withdrawal or a deposit, and the amount. The machine has a drawer or door for the withdrawal or deposit.

Writing Checks

A **check** is a document ordering a bank to pay cash from a depositor's account. There are three parties to every check:

1. **Drawer**—the depositor who orders the bank to pay the cash.
2. **Drawee**—the bank on which the check is drawn.
3. **Payee**—the person being paid the cash.

Checks used by businesses are usually bound in the form of a book. In some checkbooks, each check is attached to a **check stub** (Figure 8-5) that contains space to record all relevant information about the check. Other

FIGURE 8-4   Automated Teller Machine Card

times the checkbook is accompanied by a small register book in which the relevant information is noted. If a financial computer software package is used, both the check and the register can be prepared electronically.

Use the following three steps in preparing a check.

STEP 1   Complete the check stub or register.

STEP 2   Enter the date, payee name, and amount on the check.

STEP 3   Sign the check.

The check stub should be completed first so that the drawer retains a record of each check issued. This information is needed to determine the proper journal entry for the transaction.

The payee name is entered on the first long line on the check, followed by the amount in figures. The amount in words is then entered on the second long line. If the amount in figures does not agree with the amount in words, the bank will either pay the amount in words, contact the drawer for the correct amount, or return the check unpaid.

The most critical point in preparing a check is signing it, and this should be done last. The signature authorizes the bank to pay cash from the drawer's account. The check signer should make sure that all other aspects of the check are correct before signing it.

Figure 8-5 shows properly completed checks and stubs.

Bank Statement

A statement of account issued by a bank to each depositor once a month is called a **bank statement**. Figure 8-6 is a bank statement for a checking account. The statement shows:

1. The balance at the beginning of the period.
2. Deposits and other amounts added during the period.
3. Checks and other amounts subtracted during the period.
4. The balance at the end of the period.

FIGURE 8-5   Checks and Check Stubs

NO. **107**	MAPLE CONSULTING 4112 WEBER ST. ORLANDO, FL 32818-1123		No. **107**	63-1209 / 631

DATE *April 3* 19 - -
TO *Linclay Corp.*
FOR *April Rent*

ACCT. *Rent Expense*

PAY TO THE ORDER OF *Linclay Corporation* $ *300.00*

FOR CLASSROOM USE ONLY

Three hundred 00/100 _____ Dollars

	DOLLARS	CENTS
BAL BRO'T FOR'D	3,625	41
AMT. DEPOSITED		
TOTAL		
AMT. THIS CHECK	300	00
BAL CAR'D FOR'D	3,325	41

WIZARD BANK 3711 Buena Vista Dr. Orlando, FL 32811-1314

MEMO _____ BY *James Maple*

⑆063112094⑆ 000163 2475⑈

NO. **108**	MAPLE CONSULTING 4112 WEBER ST. ORLANDO, FL 32818-1123		No. **108**	63-1209 / 631

DATE *April 4* 19 - -
TO *Continental Mfg. Co.*
FOR *Inv. March 31*

ACCT. *Accounts Payable*

PAY TO THE ORDER OF *Continental Mfg. Co.* $ *1,478.18*

FOR CLASSROOM USE ONLY

One thousand four hundred seventy-eight 18/100 Dollars

	DOLLARS	CENTS
BAL BRO'T FOR'D	3,325	41
AMT. DEPOSITED	1,694	20
TOTAL	5,019	61
AMT. THIS CHECK	1,478	18
BAL CAR'D FOR'D	3,541	43

WIZARD BANK 3711 Buena Vista Dr. Orlando, FL 32811-1314

MEMO _____ BY *James Maple*

⑆063112094⑆ 000163 2475⑈

Along with the bank statement, the bank sends to the depositor:

1. **Cancelled checks** (the depositor's checks paid by the bank during the period).
2. Any other forms representing items added to or subtracted from the account.

RECONCILING THE BANK STATEMENT

LO2   Prepare a bank reconciliation.

On any given day, the balance in the cash account on the depositor's books (the book balance) is unlikely to be the same as that on the bank's books (the bank balance). Although this may be the result of errors, it is most likely because of differences in when the transactions are recorded by the business and the bank.

Deposits

Suppose there are cash receipts of $600 on April 30. These cash receipts would be recorded on the depositor's books on April 30 and a deposit of $600 would be taken to the bank. The deposit would not be recognized by the bank, however, until at least the following day, May 1. This timing difference in recording the $600 of cash receipts is illustrated in Figure 8-7.

FIGURE 8-6   Bank Statement

Statement			WIZARD BANK		

Maple Consulting	Reference Number	16 3247 5	Page Number	1
4112 Weber St.	Statement Date	Nov. 21, 19--		
Orlando, FL 32818-1123	Statement Instructions			

Beginning Balance	No. of Deposits and Credits	We have added these deposits and credits totaling	No. of withdrawals and charges	We have subtracted these withdrawals and charges totaling	Resulting in a statement balance of
$2,721.51	2	$2,599.31	17	$3,572.73	$1,748.09
Document Count	Average daily balance this statement period		Minimum balance this statement period	Date	Amount

If your account does not balance, please see reverse side and report any discrepancy to our Customer Service Department.

Date	Description	Amount	Balance
10/20	Beginning Balance		2,721.51
10/27	Check No. 207	-242.00	2,479.51
10/28	Check No. 212	-68.93	2,410.58
10/28	Check No. 213	-58.00	2,352.58
10/29	Deposit	867.00	3,219.58
11/3	Deposit	1,732.31	4,951.89
11/3	Check No. 214	-18.98	4,932.91
11/3	Check No. 215	-229.01	4,703.90
11/3	Check No. 216	-452.13	4,251.77
11/3	Check No. 217	-94.60	4,157.17
11/10	Check No. 218	-1,800.00	2,357.17
11/10	DM: NSF	-200.00	2,157.17
11/10	Check No. 220	-32.42	2,124.75
11/10	Check No. 221	-64.08	2,060.67
11/10	Check No. 222	-110.87	1,949.80
11/13	ATM Withdrawal	-100.00	1,849.80
11/18	Check No. 223	-18.00	1,831.80
11/18	Check No. 225	-23.31	1,808.49
11/18	Check No. 226	-58.60	1,749.89
11/19	DM: Service Charge	-1.80	1,748.09

EC - Error Correction	NSF - Not Sufficient Funds	TR - Wire Transfer
CM - Credit Memo	ATM - Automated Teller Machine	
DM - Debit Memo		

Notice that on April 30, the balances in the depositor's books and in the bank's books differ.

Cash Payments

Similar timing differences occur with cash payments. Suppose a check for $350 is written on April 30. This cash payment would be recorded on the depositor's books on April 30 and the check mailed to the payee. The check probably would not be received by the payee until May 3. If the payee deposited the check promptly, it still would not clear the bank until May 4. This timing difference in recording the $350 cash payment is illustrated in Figure 8-8. Notice once again that on April 30, the balances in the depositor's books and the bank's books differ.

Reasons for Differences Between Bank and Book Balances

When the bank statement is received, the depositor examines the records to identify the items that explain the difference between the book and bank

FIGURE 8-7   Depositor and Bank Records—Deposits

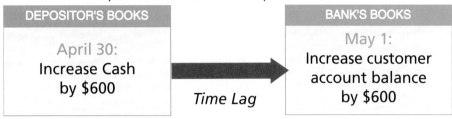

FIGURE 8-8   Depositor and Bank Records—Cash Payments

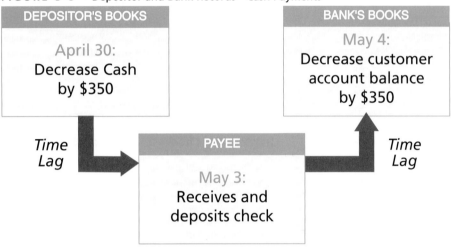

balances. This process of bringing the book and bank balances into agreement is called preparing a **bank reconciliation.**

The most common reasons for differences between the book and bank balances are the following:

1. **Outstanding checks.** Checks issued during the period that have not been presented to the bank for payment before the statement is prepared.
2. **Deposits in transit.** Deposits that have not reached or been recorded by the bank before the statement is prepared.
3. **Service charges.** Bank charges for services such as check printing and processing.
4. **Collections.** Collections of promissory notes or charge accounts made by the bank on behalf of the depositor.
5. **Not sufficient funds (NSF) checks.** Checks deposited by the depositor that are not paid because the drawer did not have sufficient funds.
6. **Errors.** Errors made by the bank or the depositor in recording cash transactions.

Steps in Preparing the Bank Reconciliation

Use the following three steps in preparing the bank reconciliation.

STEP 1   Identify deposits in transit and any related errors.

STEP 2   Identify outstanding checks and any related errors.

STEP 3   Identify additional reconciling items.

Deposits in Transit and Related Errors.   Follow these steps:

STEP 1   Compare deposits listed on the bank statement with deposits in transit on last month's bank reconciliation. All of last month's deposits in transit should appear on the current month's bank statement.

STEP 2   Compare the remaining deposits on the bank statement with deposits listed in the accounting records. Any deposits listed in the accounting records but not on the bank statement are deposits in transit on the current bank reconciliation.

STEP 3   Compare the individual deposit amounts on the bank statement and in the accounting records. If they differ, the error needs to be corrected.

Outstanding Checks and Related Errors.   Follow these steps:

STEP 1   Compare cancelled checks with the bank statement and the accounting records. If the amounts differ, the error needs to be corrected.

STEP 2   As each cancelled check is compared with the accounting records, place a check mark on the check stub or other accounting record to indicate that the check has cleared.

STEP 3   Any checks written that have not been checked off represent outstanding checks on the bank reconciliation.

Additional Reconciling Items.   Compare any additions and deductions on the bank statement that are not deposits or checks with the accounting records. Items that the bank adds to the account are called **credit memos**. Items that the bank deducts from the account are called **debit memos**. Any of these items not appearing in the accounting records represent additional items on the bank reconciliation.

Illustration of a Bank Reconciliation

A general format for a bank reconciliation is shown in Figure 8-9. Not every item shown in this illustration would be in every bank reconciliation, but this format is helpful in determining where to put items.

To illustrate the preparation of a bank reconciliation, we will use the Maple Consulting bank statement shown in Figure 8-6. That statement shows a balance of $1,748.09 as of November 21, 19--. The balance in Maple's check stubs and general ledger cash account is $2,393.23. The three steps listed at the top of this page were used to identify the following items, and the reconciliation in Figure 8-10 was prepared.

FIGURE 8-9   Bank Reconciliation Format

BANK RECONCILIATION		
Bank statement balance		$xxxx
Add: Deposits in transit	$xxxx	
Bank errors	xxxx	xxxx
Subtotal		$xxxx
Deduct: Outstanding checks	$xxxx	
Bank errors	xxxx	xxxx
Adjusted bank balance		$xxxx
Book balance		$xxxx
Add: Bank credit memos	$xxxx	
Book errors	xxxx	xxxx
Subtotal		$xxxx
Deduct: Bank debit memos	$xxxx	
Book errors	xxxx	xxxx
Adjusted book balance		$xxxx

1. A deposit of $637.02 on November 21 on the books had not been received by the bank. The deposit in transit is added to the bank statement balance. Maple has received the funds, but the amount has not yet been counted by the bank.

2. Check numbers 219, 224, and 227 are outstanding. The amount of these outstanding checks is subtracted from the bank statement balance. The funds have been disbursed by Maple, but have not yet been paid out by the bank.

3. Check number 214 was written for $18.98, but was entered on the check stub and on the books as $19.88. This $.90 error is added to the book balance because $.90 too much had been deducted from the book balance.

4. Maple made the ATM withdrawal of $100 on November 13 for personal use. This amount is deducted from the book balance. The bank has reduced Maple's balance by this amount but Maple had neglected to record the withdrawal.

5. The bank returned an NSF check of $200. This amount is deducted from the book balance. The bank has reduced Maple's balance by this amount but Maple has not yet recorded it.

6. The bank service charge was $1.80. This amount is deducted from the book balance. The bank has reduced Maple's balance by this amount, but Maple has not yet recorded it

Journal Entries

LEARNING KEY   Errors in the books and bank additions and deductions that are not in the accounting records require journal entries.

Only two kinds of items appearing on a bank reconciliation require journal entries:

FIGURE 8-10   Bank Reconciliation

Maple Consulting Bank Reconciliation November 21, 19--				
Bank statement balance, November 21				$1 7 4 8 09
Add deposit in transit				6 3 7 02
				$2 3 8 5 11
Deduct outstanding checks:				
No. 219	$ 2 0 0 00			
No. 224	2 5 00			
No. 227	6 7 78		2 9 2 78	
Adjusted bank balance			$2 0 9 2 33	
Book balance, November 21			$2 3 9 3 23	
Add error on check no. 214			90	
			$2 3 9 4 13	
Deduct:				
Unrecorded ATM withdrawal	$ 1 0 0 00			
NSF check	2 0 0 00			
Bank service charge	1 80		3 0 1 80	
Adjusted book balance			$2 0 9 2 33	

Requires journal entry → Add error on check no. 214

Require journal entries → Unrecorded ATM withdrawal / NSF check

Reconciled balances

1. Errors in the books.
2. Bank additions and deductions that do not already appear in the accounting records.

Note the four items in the lower portion of the bank reconciliation in Figure 8-10. A journal entry always is required for each item in this portion of the bank reconciliation.

The $.90 item is an error in the accounting records that occurred when the check amount was incorrectly entered. Assuming the $18.98 was in payment of an account payable, the entry to correct this error is:

4		Cash			90			4
5		Accounts Payable					90	5
6		Error in recording check						6

The $100 ATM withdrawal has been deducted from Maple's account by the bank. Maple has not yet recorded the withdrawal. Maple withdrew the funds for personal use, so the following journal entry is required.

8		James Maple, Drawing			1 0 0 00			8
9		Cash				1 0 0 00		9
10		Unrecorded ATM withdrawal						10

The $200 NSF check is a bank charge for a check deposited by Maple that proved to be worthless. This amount must be deducted from the book balance. Assuming the $200 check was received from a customer on account, the following journal entry is required.

12		Accounts Receivable	2 0 0 00			12
13		Cash		2 0 0 00		13
14		Record NSF check				14

The $1.80 bank service charge is a fee for bank services received by Maple. The bank has deducted this amount from Maple's account. Bank service charges are usually small and are charged to Miscellaneous Expense.

16		Miscellaneous Expense	1 80		16
17		Cash		1 80	17
18		Bank service charge			18

Electronic Funds Transfer

Electronic funds transfer (EFT) uses a computer rather than paper checks to complete transactions with the bank. This technique is being used increasingly today. Applications of EFT include payrolls, social security payments, retail purchases, and the ATM transactions described earlier in the chapter.

Heavy use of EFT can present a challenge in preparing bank reconciliations. Many of the documents handled in a purely manual environment disappear when EFT is used. Bank accounts are just one of many areas where computers require accountants to think in new ways. Regardless of what system is used, the key point to remember is that the accounting records must be correctly updated.

THE PETTY CASH FUND

LO3   Describe how to operate a petty cash fund.

For good control over cash, payments generally should be made by check. Unfortunately, payments of very small amounts by check can be both inconvenient and inefficient. For example, the time and cost required to write a check for $.70 to mail a letter might be greater than the cost of the postage. Therefore, businesses customarily establish a **petty cash fund** to pay for small items with cash. "Petty" means small, and both the amount of the fund and the maximum amount of any bill that can be paid from the fund are small.

Establishing a Petty Cash Fund

To establish a petty cash fund, a check is written to the petty cash custodian for the amount to be set aside in the fund. The amount may be $50, $100, $200, or any amount considered necessary. The journal entry to establish a petty cash fund of $100 would be as follows.

4		Petty Cash			1 0 0 00				4
5		Cash				1 0 0 00	5
6		Establish petty cash fund					6

Petty cash is an asset that is listed immediately below Cash on the balance sheet.

The custodian cashes the check and places the money in a petty cash box. For good control, the custodian should be the only person authorized to make payments from the fund. The custodian should be able to account for the full amount of the fund at any time.

Making Payments from a Petty Cash Fund

A receipt called a **petty cash voucher** (Figure 8-11) should be prepared for every payment from the fund. The voucher shows the name of the payee, the purpose of the payment, and the account to be charged for the payment. Each voucher should be signed by the custodian and by the person receiving the cash. The vouchers should be numbered consecutively so that all vouchers can be accounted for.

FIGURE 8-11   Petty Cash Voucher

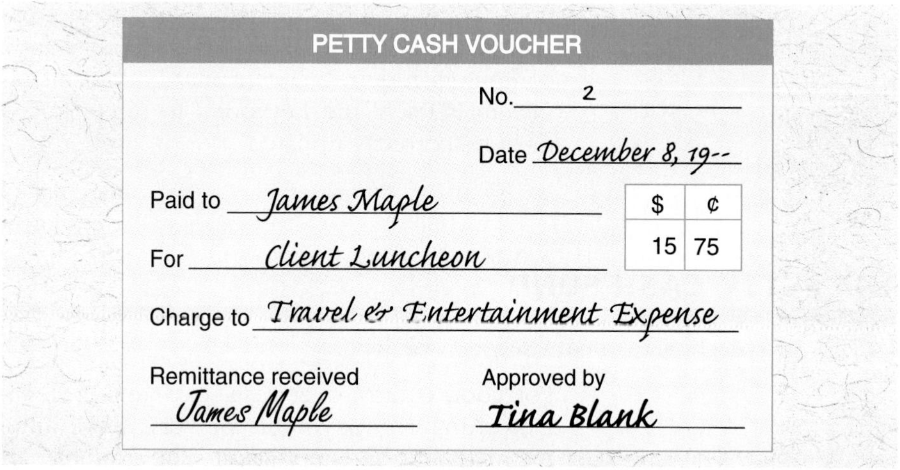

PETTY CASH VOUCHER

No. 2

Date _December 8, 19--_

Paid to _James Maple_ $ 15 ¢ 75

For _Client Luncheon_

Charge to _Travel & Entertainment Expense_

Remittance received   Approved by
James Maple   _Tina Blank_

Petty Cash Payments Record

When a petty cash fund is maintained, a formal record is often kept of all payments from the fund. The **petty cash payments record** (Figure 8-12) is a special multicolumn record that supplements the regular accounting records. It is not a journal. The headings of the Distribution of Payments columns may vary, depending on the types of expenditures.

The petty cash payments record of Maple Consulting is shown in Figure 8-12 on page 254. A narrative of the petty cash transactions shown in Figure 8-12 follows.

Dec. 1 Maple issued a check for $200.00 payable to Tina Blank, Petty Cash Custodian. Blank cashed the check and placed the money in a secure cash box.

A notation of the amount received is made in the Description column of the petty cash payments record. In addition, this transaction is entered in the journal as follows:

8	Dec. 1	Petty Cash		2 0 0 00		8
9		Cash			2 0 0 00	9
10		Establish petty cash fund				10

During the month of December, the following payments were made from the petty cash fund:

Dec. 5 Paid $32.80 to Jerry's Auto for servicing the company automobile. Voucher No. 1.

8 Reimbursed Maple $15.75 for the amount spent for lunch with a client. Voucher No. 2.

9 Gave Maple $30.00 for personal use. Voucher No. 3.

There is no special Distribution column for entering amounts withdrawn by the owner for personal use. Therefore this $30.00 payment is entered in the Amount column at the extreme right of the petty cash payments record.

15 Paid $28.25 for typewriter repairs. Voucher No. 4.

17 Reimbursed Maple $14.50 for travel expenses. Voucher No. 5.

19 Paid $8.00 to Big Red Car Care for washing the company automobile. Voucher No. 6.

22 Paid $9.50 for mailing a package. Voucher No. 7.

29 Paid $30.00 for postage stamps. Voucher No. 8.

Replenishing the Petty Cash Fund

The petty cash fund should be replenished whenever the fund runs low, and at the end of each accounting period, so that the accounts are brought up to date. The amount columns of the petty cash payments record are totaled to verify that the total of the Total Amount column equals the total of the Distribution columns. The amount columns are then ruled as shown in Figure 8-12.

The information in the petty cash payments record is used to replenish the petty cash fund. On December 31, a check for $168.80 is issued to the petty cash custodian. The journal entry to record the replenishment of the fund is as follows:

FIGURE 8-12 Maple Consulting's Petty Cash Payments Record

PETTY CASH PAYMENTS FOR THE MONTH OF December 19--

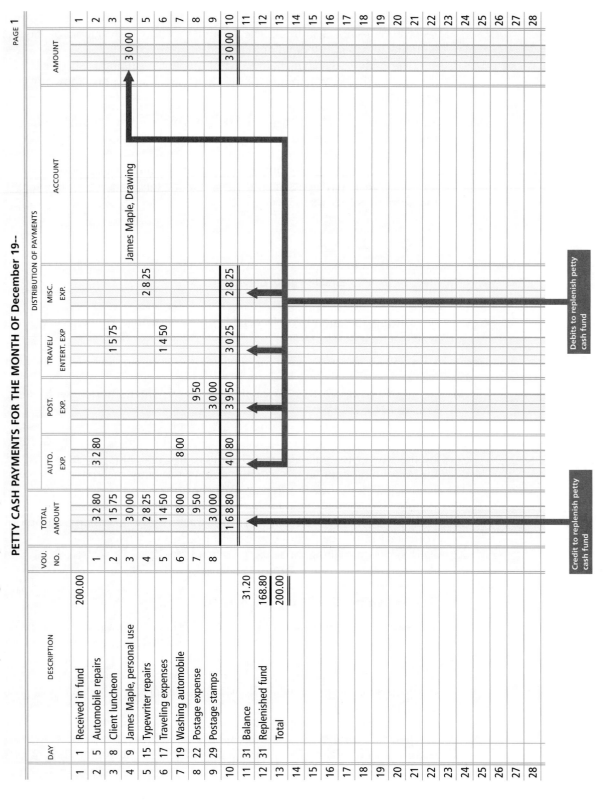

PAGE 1

	DAY		DESCRIPTION	VOU. NO.	TOTAL AMOUNT	AUTO. EXP.	POST. EXP.	TRAVEL/ ENTERT. EXP	MISC. EXP.	ACCOUNT	AMOUNT	
1	1	1	Received in fund		200.00							1
2	2	5	Automobile repairs	1	32 80	32 80						2
3	3	8	Client luncheon	2	15 75			15 75				3
4	4	9	James Maple, personal use	3	30 00					James Maple, Drawing	30 00	4
5	5	15	Typewriter repairs	4	28 25				28 25			5
6	6	17	Traveling expenses	5	14 50			14 50				6
7	7	19	Washing automobile	6	8 00	8 00						7
8	8	22	Postage expense	7	9 50		9 50					8
9	9	29	Postage stamps	8	30 00		30 00					9
10	10				168 80	40 80	39 50	30 25	28 25		30 00	10
11	11	31	Balance		31.20							11
12	12	31	Replenished fund		168.80							12
13	13		Total		200.00							13
14	14											14
15	15											15
16	16											16
17	17											17
18	18											18
19	19											19
20	20											20
21	21											21
22	22											22
23	23											23
24	24											24
25	25											25
26	26											26
27	27											27
28	28											28

DISTRIBUTION OF PAYMENTS

Credit to replenish petty cash fund

Debits to replenish petty cash fund

18	Dec. 31	Automobile Expense					4	0	80						18
19		Postage Expense					3	9	50						19
20		Travel and Entertainment Expense					3	0	25						20
21		Miscellaneous Expense					2	8	25						21
22		James Maple, Drawing					3	0	00						22
23		Cash									1	6	8	80	23
24		Replenishment of petty cash fund													24
25															25

> **LEARNING KEY**   Once the petty cash fund is established, no further entries are made to Petty Cash unless the amount of the fund is being changed. No posting is done from the petty cash payments record.

Note two important aspects of the functioning of a petty cash fund.

1. Once the fund is established by debiting Petty Cash and crediting Cash, no further entries are made to Petty Cash. Notice in the journal entry to replenish the fund that the debits are to appropriate expense accounts and the credit is to the cash account. Only if the amount of the fund itself is being changed would there be a debit or credit to Petty Cash.
2. The petty cash payments record is strictly a supplement to the regular accounting records. Because it is not a journal, no posting is done from this record.

CASH SHORT AND OVER

LO4   Use the cash short and over account.

Businesses generally must be able to make change when customers pay for goods or services received. An unavoidable part of this change-making process is that errors can occur. It is important to know whether such errors have occurred and how to account for them.

Businesses commonly use cash registers with tapes that accumulate a record of the day's receipts. The amount of cash according to the tapes can be compared with the amount of cash in the register to determine the existence and amount of any error. For example, assume a cash shortage is identified for June 19.

Receipts per register tapes	$963
Cash count	961
Cash shortage	$ 2

Similarly, assume a cash overage is identified for June 20.

Receipts per register tapes	$814
Cash count	815
Cash overage	$ 1

We account for such errors by using an account called Cash Short and Over. The register tapes on June 19 showed receipts of $963, but only $961 in cash was counted. The journal entry on June 19 to record the revenues and cash shortage would be:

18	June 19	Cash			9 6 1 00					18
19		Cash Short and Over			2 00					19
20		Service Fees					9 6 3 00			20
21		Record cash shortage								21

The entry on June 20 to record the revenues and cash overage would be:

23	20	Cash			8 1 5 00					23
24		Service Fees					8 1 4 00			24
25		Cash Short and Over					1 00			25
26		Record cash overage								26

The cash short and over account is used to accumulate cash shortages and overages throughout the accounting period. At the end of the period, a debit balance in the account (a net shortage) is treated as an expense. A credit balance in the account (a net overage) is treated as revenue.

KEY POINTS

1 Three steps to follow in preparing a check are:

1. Complete the check stub or register.
2. Enter the date, payee name, and amount on the check.
3. Sign the check.

2 The most common reasons for differences between the book and bank cash balances are:

1. Outstanding checks
2. Deposits in transit
3. Bank service charges
4. Bank collections for the depositor
5. NSF checks
6. Errors by the bank or the depositor

Three steps to follow in preparing a bank reconciliation are:

1. Identify deposits in transit and any related errors.
2. Identify outstanding checks and any related errors.
3. Identify additional reconciling items.

Only two kinds of items on a bank reconciliation require journal entries:

1. Errors on the depositor's books.
2. Bank additions and deductions that do not already appear in the accounting records.

3 Two important aspects of the functioning of a petty cash fund are:

1. Once the fund is established, subsequent entries do not affect the petty cash account balance, unless the size of the fund itself is being changed.
2. The petty cash payments record is supplemental to the regular accounting records. No posting is done from this record.

4 Cash shortages and overages are accounted for using the cash short and over account. A debit balance in this account represents expense; a credit balance represents revenue.

KEY TERMS

ABA (American Bankers Association) Number 242   The small fraction printed in the upper right hand corner of each check.

automated teller machines (ATM) 243   Machines used by depositors to make withdrawals or deposits at any time.

bank reconciliation 247   Bringing the book and bank balances into agreement.

bank statement 244   A statement of account issued by a bank to each depositor once a month.

blank endorsement 243   The depositor signs on the back of the check, making the check payable to any bearer.

cancelled checks 245   The depositor's checks paid by the bank during the period.

cash 241   To a business, cash includes currency, coins, checks received from customers, money orders, and bank cashier's checks.

check 243   A document ordering a bank to pay cash from a depositor's account.

check stub 243   In some checkbooks, each check is attached to a stub that contains space for relevant information.

credit memos 248   Items that the bank adds to the account.

debit memos 248   Items that the bank deducts from the account.

deposit ticket 241   A detailed listing of items being deposited.

deposits in transit 247   Deposits that have not reached or been recorded by the bank before the statement is prepared.

drawee 243   The bank on which the check is drawn.

drawer 243   The depositor who orders the bank to pay the cash.

electronic funds transfer (EFT) 251   Using a computer rather than paper checks to complete transactions with the bank.

endorsement 242   Stamping or writing the depositor's name and sometimes other information on the back of the check.

internal control 241   A set of procedures designed to ensure proper accounting for transactions.

not sufficient funds (NSF) checks 247 Checks deposited by the depositor that are not paid because the drawer did not have sufficient funds.

outstanding checks 247 Checks issued during the period that have not been presented to the bank for payment before the statement is prepared.

payee 243 The person being paid the cash.

petty cash fund 251 A fund established to pay for small items.

petty cash payments record 252 A special multicolumn record that supplements the regular accounting records.

petty cash voucher 252 A receipt that is prepared for every payment from the petty cash fund.

restrictive endorsement 243 The depositor adds words such as "For deposit" to restrict the payment of the check.

service charges 247 Bank charges for services such as check printing and processing.

signature card 241 A card that is completed and signed by each person authorized to sign checks.

REVIEW QUESTIONS

1. Why must a signature card be filled out and signed to open a checking account?
2. Explain the difference between a blank endorsement and a restrictive endorsement.
3. Who are the three parties to every check?
4. What are the three steps to follow in preparing a check?
5. What are the most common reasons for differences between the book and bank cash balances?
6. What are the three steps to follow in preparing a bank reconciliation?
7. What two kinds of items on a bank reconciliation require journal entries?
8. Name four applications of electronic funds transfer in current use.
9. What is the purpose of a petty cash fund?
10. What should be prepared every time a petty cash payment is made?
11. At what two times should the petty cash fund be replenished?
12. From what source is the information obtained for issuing a check to replenish the petty cash fund?
13. What does a debit balance in the cash short and over account represent? What does a credit balance in this account represent?

MANAGING YOUR WRITING

The current month's bank statement for your account arrives in the mail. In reviewing the statement, you notice a deposit listed for $400 that you did not make. It has been credited in error to your account. Write a memo discussing whether you have an ethical or legal obligation to inform the bank of the error. What action should you take?

DEMONSTRATION PROBLEM

Jason Kuhn's check stubs for Kuhn's Wilderness Outfitters indicated a balance of $4,673.12 on March 31, 19--. This included a record of a deposit of $926.10 mailed to the bank on March 30, but not credited to Kuhn's account until April 1. In addition, the following checks were outstanding on March 31.

No. 462, $524.26
No. 465, $213.41
No. 473, $543.58
No. 476, $351.38
No. 477, $197.45

The bank statement showed a balance of $5,419.00 as of March 31. The bank statement included a service charge of $4.10 dated March 29. In matching the cancelled checks and record of deposits with the stubs, you discovered that check no. 456, to Office Suppliers, Inc., for $93 was erroneously recorded on the stub for $39. This caused the bank balance on that stub and those following to be $54 too large. You also discovered that an ATM withdrawal of $100 for personal use was not recorded on the books.

Kuhn maintains a $200.00 petty cash fund. His petty cash payments record showed the following totals at the end of March of the current year.

Automobile expense	$ 32.40
Postage expense	27.50
Charitable contributions expense	35.00
Telephone expense	6.20
Travel and entertainment expense	38.60
Miscellaneous expense	17.75
Jason Kuhn, Drawing	40.00
Total	$197.45

This left a balance of $2.55 in the petty cash fund.

REQUIRED

1. Prepare a bank reconciliation for Kuhn's Wilderness Outfitters as of March 31, 19--.
2. Journalize the entries that should be made for Kuhn's Wilderness Outfitters on the books as of March 31, 19--: (a) as a result of the bank reconciliation and (b) to replenish the petty cash fund.
3. Show proof that, after these entries, the total of the cash and petty cash account balances equals $4,715.02.

SOLUTION

1.

Kuhn's Wilderness Outfitters
Bank Reconciliation
March 31, 19--

Bank statement balance, March 31						$5	4	1	9	00
Add deposit in transit							9	2	6	10
						$6	3	4	5	10
Deduct outstanding checks:										
No. 462	$	5	2	4	26					
No. 465		2	1	3	41					
No. 473		5	4	3	58					
No. 476		3	5	1	38					
No. 477		1	9	7	45	1	8	3	0	08
Adjusted bank balance						$4	5	1	5	02
Book balance, March 31						$4	6	7	3	12
Deduct: Bank service charge	$			4	10					
Error on check no. 456			5	4	00					
Unrecorded ATM withdrawal		1	0	0	00		1	5	8	10
Adjusted book balance						$4	5	1	5	02

3											3
2.a. 4	Mar.	31	Miscellaneous Expense					4	10		4
5			Accounts Payable—Office Supp., Inc.				5	4	00		5
6			Jason Kuhn, Drawing			1	0	0	00		6
7			Cash							1 5 8 10	7
8			Bank transactions for March								8
9											9
b. 10		31	Automobile Expense				3	2	40		10
11			Postage Expense				2	7	50		11
12			Charitable Contributions Expense				3	5	00		12
13			Telephone Expense					6	20		13
14			Travel and Entertainment Expense				3	8	60		14
15			Miscellaneous Expense				1	7	75		15
16			Jason Kuhn, Drawing				4	0	00		16
17			Cash							1 9 7 45	17
18			Replenishment of petty cash								18
19			fund								19
20											20
21											21

3. Cash in bank:

Check stub balance, March 31	$4,673.12
Less bank charges	158.10
Adjusted cash in bank	$4,515.02

Cash on hand:

Petty cash fund	$ 2.55
Add replenishment	197.45
Adjusted cash on hand	$ 200.00
Total cash in bank and petty cash on hand	$4,715.02

SERIES A EXERCISES

1 **EXERCISE 8A1 CHECKING ACCOUNT TERMS** Match the following words with their definitions.

1. An endorsement where the depositor simply signs on the back of the check
2. An endorsement that contains words like "For Deposit Only" together with the signature
3. A card filled out and signed by each person authorized to sign checks on an account
4. The depositor who orders the bank to pay cash from the depositor's account
5. The bank on which the check is drawn
6. The person being paid the cash
7. A check that has been paid by the bank and is being returned to the depositor

a. signature card
b. cancelled check
c. blank endorsement
d. drawer
e. restrictive endorsement
f. drawee
g. payee

1 **EXERCISE 8A2 PREPARE DEPOSIT TICKET** Based on the following information, prepare a deposit ticket.

Date:		January 15, 19--
Currency:		$334.00
Coin:		26.00
Checks:	No. 4-11	311.00
	No. 80-322	108.00
	No. 3-9	38.00

1 **EXERCISE 8A3 PREPARE CHECK AND STUB** Based on the following information, prepare a check and stub.

Date:	January 15, 19--
Balance brought forward:	$2,841.50
Deposit:	(From Exercise 8A2)
Check to:	J.M. Suppliers
Amount:	$150.00
For:	Office Supplies
Signature:	Sign your name

2 **EXERCISE 8A4 BANK RECONCILIATION TERMINOLOGY** In a format similar to the following, indicate whether the action at the left will result in an addition to (+) or subtraction from (–) the ending bank balance or the ending checkbook balance.

	Ending Bank Balance	Ending Checkbook Balance
1. Deposits in transit to the bank	_____	_____
2. Error in checkbook: check recorded as $32 but was actually for $23	_____	_____
3. Service fee charged by bank	_____	_____
4. Outstanding checks	_____	_____
5. NSF check deposited earlier	_____	_____
6. Error in checkbook: check recorded as $22 but was actually for $220	_____	_____
7. Bank credit memo advising they collected a note for us	_____	_____

2 **EXERCISE 8A5 PREPARE JOURNAL ENTRIES FOR BANK RECONCILIATION** Based on the bank reconciliation information shown on the next page, prepare the journal entries.

3 **EXERCISE 8A6 PETTY CASH JOURNAL ENTRIES** Based on the following petty cash information, prepare (a) the journal entry to establish a petty cash fund, and (b) the journal entry to replenish the petty cash fund.

On January 1, 19--, a check was written in the amount of $200 to establish a petty cash fund. During January, the following vouchers were written for cash removed from the petty cash drawer:

Voucher No.	Account Debited	Amount
1	Telephone Expense	$17.50
2	Automobile Expense	33.00
3	Joseph Levine, Drawing	70.00
4	Postage Expense	12.50
5	Charitable Contributions Expense	15.00
6	Miscellaneous Expense	49.00

Lisa Choy Associates
Bank Reconciliation
July 31, 19--

Bank statement balance, July 31			$2 7 6 4 40
Add deposits in transit	$2 5 0 00		
	9 8 00	3 4 8 00	
		$3 1 1 2 40	
Deduct outstanding checks:			
No. 387	$3 5 3 50		
No. 393	1 7 80		
No. 398	3 3 20	4 0 4 50	
Adjusted bank balance			$2 7 0 7 90
Book balance, July 31			$3 1 3 0 90
Deduct: Error on check no. 394*	$ 2 3 00		
NSF check	3 9 0 00		
Bank service charge	1 0 00	4 2 3 00	
Adjusted book balance			$2 7 0 7 90
*Accounts Payable was debited in original entry.			

4 **EXERCISE 8A7 CASH SHORT AND OVER ENTRIES** Based on the following information, prepare the weekly entries for cash receipts from service fees and cash short and over.

Date	Cash Register Receipt Amount	Actual Cash Counted
April 2	$268.50	$266.50
9	237.75	233.50
16	309.25	311.00
23	226.50	224.00
30	318.00	322.00

SERIES A PROBLEMS

2 **PROBLEM 8A1 BANK RECONCILIATION AND RELATED JOUR-** **NAL ENTRIES** The balance in the checking account of Violette Enterprises as of October 31 is $4,765.00. The bank statement shows an ending balance of $4,235.00. The following information is discovered by comparing checks deposited and written and noting service charges and other debit and credit memos shown on the bank statement.

Deposits in transit: 10/26 $175.00
                                       10/28   334.00

Outstanding checks:	No. 1764	$ 47.00
	No. 1767	146.00
	No. 1781	369.00

Unrecorded ATM withdrawal*:	180.00
Bank service charge:	43.00
NSF check:	370.00

Error on check no. 1754	Checkbook shows it was for $72, but was actually written for $62. Accounts Payable was debited.

*Funds were withdrawn by Guy Violette for personal use.

REQUIRED
1. Prepare a bank reconciliation as of October 31, 19--.
2. Prepare the required journal entries.

3   **PROBLEM 8A2 PETTY CASH RECORD AND JOURNAL ENTRIES**
On May 1 a petty cash fund was established for $150. The following vouchers were issued during May:

Date	Voucher No.	Purpose	Amount
May 1	1	postage due	$ 3.50
3	2	office supplies	11.00
5	3	auto repair (miscellaneous)	22.00
7	4	drawing (Joy Adams)	25.00
11	5	donation (Red Cross)	10.00
15	6	travel expenses	28.00
22	7	postage stamps	3.50
26	8	telephone call	5.00
30	9	donation (Boy Scouts)	30.00

REQUIRED
1. Prepare the journal entry to establish the petty cash fund.
2. Record the vouchers in the petty cash record. Total and rule the petty cash record.
3. Prepare the journal entry to replenish the petty cash fund. Make the appropriate entry in the petty cash record.

4   **PROBLEM 8A3 CASH SHORT AND OVER ENTRIES**   Listed below are the weekly cash register tape amounts for service fees and the related cash counts during the month of July.

Date	Cash Register Receipt Amount	Actual Cash Counted
July 2	$289.50	$287.00
9	311.50	311.50
16	306.00	308.50
23	317.50	315.00
30	296.00	299.50

REQUIRED

1. Prepare the journal entries to record the cash service fees and cash short and over for each of the five weeks.
2. Post to the cash short and over account (use account no. 573).
3. Determine the ending balance of the cash short and over account. Does it represent an expense or revenue?

SERIES B EXERCISES

1 **EXERCISE 8B1 CHECKING ACCOUNT TERMS**   Match the following words with their definitions.

1. Banking number used to identify checks for deposit tickets
2. A card filled out to open a checking account
3. A machine from which withdrawals can be taken or deposits made to accounts
4. A place where relevant information is recorded about a check
5. A set of procedures designed to ensure proper accounting for transactions
6. A statement of account issued to each depositor once a month
7. A detailed listing of items being deposited to an account

a. bank statement
b. deposit ticket
c. signature card
d. internal control
e. check stub
f. ATM
g. ABA number

1 **EXERCISE 8B2 PREPARE DEPOSIT TICKET**   Based on the following information, prepare a deposit ticket.

Date:		November 15, 19--
Currency:		$283.00
Coin:		19.00
Checks:	No. 3-22	201.00
	No. 19-366	114.00
	No. 3-2	28.00

1 **EXERCISE 8B3 PREPARE CHECK AND STUB**   Based on the following information, prepare a check and stub.

Date: November 15,19--
Balance brought forward: $3,181.00
Deposit: (from Exercise 8B2)
Check to: R.J. Smith Co.
Amount: $120.00
For: Payment on account
Signature: Sign your name

2 **EXERCISE 8B4 BANK RECONCILIATION TERMINOLOGY**   In a format similar to the following, indicate whether the action at the left will result in an addition to (+) or subtraction from (–) the ending bank balance or the ending checkbook balance.

	Ending Bank Balance	Ending Checkbook Balance
1. Service fee of $12 charged by bank		
2. Outstanding checks		
3. Error in checkbook: check recorded as $36 was actually for $28		
4. NSF check deposited earlier		
5. Bank credit memo advising they collected a note for us		
6. Deposits in transit to the bank		
7. Error in checkbook: check recorded as $182 was actually for $218		

2 **EXERCISE 8B5 PREPARE JOURNAL ENTRIES FOR BANK RECONCILIATION**   Based on the following bank reconciliation information, prepare the journal entries.

Regina D'Alfonso Associates
Bank Reconciliation
July 31, 19--

Bank statement balance, July 31		$1 7 8 4 00
Add deposits in transit	$ 4 1 8 50	
	1 0 0 50	5 1 9 00
		$2 3 0 3 00
Deduct outstanding checks:		
No. 185	$ 2 0 6 50	
No. 203	3 1 7 40	
No. 210	5 6 10	5 8 0 00
Adjusted bank balance		$1 7 2 3 00
Book balance, July 31		$1 7 9 4 00
Add error on check no. 191*		1 0 00
		$1 8 0 4 00
Deduct: NSF check	$ 6 6 00	
Bank service charge	1 5 00	8 1 00
Adjusted book balance		$1 7 2 3 00
*Accounts Payable was debited in original entry.		

3 **EXERCISE 8B6 PETTY CASH JOURNAL ENTRIES** Based on the following petty cash information, prepare (a) the journal entry to establish a petty cash fund, and (b) the journal entry to replenish the petty cash fund.

On October 1, 19--, a check was written in the amount of $200 to establish a petty cash fund. During October, the following vouchers were written for cash taken from the petty cash drawer:

Voucher No.	Account Debited	Amount
1	Postage Expense	$13.00
2	Miscellaneous Expense	17.00
3	John Flanagan, Drawing	45.00
4	Telephone Expense	36.00
5	Charitable Contributions Expense	50.00
6	Automobile Expense	29.00

4 **EXERCISE 8B7 CASH SHORT AND OVER ENTRIES** Based on the following information, prepare the weekly entries for cash receipts from service fees and cash short and over.

Date	Cash Register Receipt Amount	Actual Cash Counted
June 1	$330.00	$333.00
8	297.00	300.00
15	233.00	231.00
22	302.00	296.50
29	316.00	312.00

SERIES B PROBLEMS

2 **PROBLEM 8B1 BANK RECONCILIATION AND RELATED JOURNAL ENTRIES** The balance in the checking account of Kyros Enterprises as of November 30, is $3,004.00. The bank statement shows an ending balance of $2,525.00. The following information is discovered by comparing checks deposited and written and noting service charges and other debit and credit memos shown on the bank statement.

Deposits in transit:	11/21	$125.00
	11/26	200.00
Outstanding checks:	No. 322	17.00
	No. 324	105.00
	No. 327	54.00
Unrecorded ATM withdrawal*:		100.00
Bank service charge:		25.00
NSF check:		185.00

Error on check no. 321   Checkbook shows is was for $44, but was actually written for $64. Accounts Payable was debited.

*Funds were withdrawn by Steve Kyros for personal use.

REQUIRED
1. Prepare a bank reconciliation as of November 30, 19--.
2. Prepare the required journal entries.

3   **PROBLEM 8B2 PETTY CASH RECORD AND JOURNAL ENTRIES**
On July 1, a petty cash fund was established for $100. The following vouchers were issued during July:

Date	Voucher No.	Purpose	Amount
July 1	1	office supplies	$ 3.00
3	2	donation (Goodwill)	15.00
5	3	travel expenses	5.00
7	4	postage due	2.00
8	5	office supplies	4.00
11	6	postage due	3.50
15	7	telephone call	5.00
21	8	travel expenses	11.00
25	9	withdrawal by owner (L. Bean)	20.00
26	10	copier repair (miscellaneous)	18.50

REQUIRED
1. Prepare the journal entry to establish the petty cash fund.
2. Record the vouchers in the petty cash record. Total and rule the petty cash record.
3. Prepare the journal entry to replenish the petty cash fund. Make the appropriate entry in the petty cash record.

4   **PROBLEM 8B3 CASH SHORT AND OVER ENTRIES**   Listed below are the weekly cash register tape amounts for service fees and the related cash counts during the month of July.

Date	Cash Register Receipt Amount	Actual Cash Counted
Aug. 1	$292.50	$295.00
8	305.00	301.50
15	286.00	286.00
22	330.25	332.75
29	298.50	295.00

REQUIRED
1. Prepare the journal entries to record the cash service fees and cash short and over for each of the five weeks.
2. Post to the cash short and over account. (Use account no. 573.)
3. Determine the ending balance of the cash short and over account. Does it represent an expense or revenue?

MASTERY PROBLEM

Turner Excavation maintains a checking account and has decided to open a petty cash fund. The following petty cash fund transactions occurred during July.

July 2 Established a petty cash fund by issuing check no. 301 for $100.00.
   5 Paid $25.00 from the petty cash fund for postage. Voucher no. 1.
   7 Paid $30.00 from the petty cash fund for delivery of flowers for the secretaries (miscellaneous expense). Voucher no. 2.
   8 Paid $20.00 from the petty cash fund to repair a tire on the company truck. Voucher no. 3.
   12 Paid $22.00 from the petty cash fund for a newspaper advertisement. Voucher no. 4.
   13 Issued check no. 303 to replenish the petty cash fund. (Total and rule the petty cash payments record. Record the balance and the amount needed to replenish the fund in the Description column of the petty cash payments record.)
   20 Paid $26.00 from the petty cash fund to reimburse an employee for expenses incurred to repair the company truck. Voucher no. 5.
   24 Paid $12.50 from the petty cash fund for telephone calls made from a phone booth. Voucher no. 6.
   28 Paid $25.00 from the petty cash fund as a contribution to the YMCA. Voucher no. 7.
   31 Issued check no. 308 to replenish the petty cash fund. (Total and rule the petty cash payments record. Record the balance and the amount needed to replenish the fund in the Description column of the petty cash payments record.)

The following additional transactions occurred during July.

July 5 Issued check no. 302 to pay office rent, $650.00.
   15 Issued check no. 304 for the purchase of office equipment, $525.00.
   17 Issued check no. 305 for the purchase of supplies, $133.00.
   18 Issued check no. 306 to pay attorney fees, $1,000.
   30 Issued check no. 307 to pay newspaper for an advertisement, $200.20.

REQUIRED

1. Record the petty cash transactions in a petty cash payments record. Use the following Distribution of Payments column headings: Truck Expense, Postage Expense, Charitable Contributions Expense, Telephone Expense, Advertising Expense, and Miscellaneous Expense. Total and rule the petty cash record.
2. Make all required general journal entries for cash transactions. (Note: The petty cash fund was established and replenished twice during July.)
3. The bank statement shown in Figure 8-13 was received in the mail. Deposits were made on July 6 for $3,500.00 and on July 29 for $2,350.00.

FIGURE 8-13 Bank Statement

Statement					Merchant's National Bank	

Turner Excavation
220 Main Street
Oakhurst, NJ 07755-1461

Reference Number	16 3247 5	Page Number
Statement Date	July 31, 19--	
Statement Instructions		

Beginning Balance	No. of Deposits and Credits	We have added these deposits and credits totaling	No. of withdrawals and charges	We have subtracted these withdrawals and charges totaling	Resulting in a statement balance of
$1,250.25	1	$3,500.00	6	$1,512.50	$3,237.75
Document Count	Average Daily balance this statement period		Minimum balance this statement period	Date	Amount

If your account does not balance, please see reverse side and report any discrepancy to our Customer Service Department.

Date	Description	Amount	Balance
7/1	Beginning Balance		1,250.25
7/5	Check No. 301	-100.00	1,150.25
7/8	Check No. 302	-655.00	495.25
7/9	Deposit	3,500.00	3,995.25
7/15	Check No. 303	-97.00	3,898.25
7/20	Check No. 304	-525.00	3,373.25
7/28	Check No. 305	-133.00	3,240.25
7/31	Sevice Charge	-2.50	3,237.75

EC-Error Correction   OD-Overdrawn   RC-Return Check Charge
ATM-Automated Teller Machine   TR-Wire Transfer   D/N-Day/Night

Depositor agrees and Bank accepts business upon the terms and conditions of Bank's rules and regulations now in effect or as may be hereafter adopted.

The checkbook balance on July 31 is $4,331.55. Notice the discrepancy in check no. 302 that cleared the bank for $655.00. This check was written on July 5 for rent expense, but was incorrectly entered on the check stub and in the journal as $650.00. Prepare a bank reconciliation and make any necessary journal entries as of July 31.

9

Payroll Accounting: Employee Earnings and Deductions

You work 40 hours at $6 an hour to earn $240. So why is your paycheck so much less than $240? What does your employer do with all that money deducted from your paycheck? Are the right amounts being deducted? To answer these questions, you need to know about employee payroll accounting.

The only contact most of us have with payroll is receiving a paycheck. Few of us have seen the large amount of record keeping needed to produce that paycheck.

Employers maintain complete payroll accounting records for two reasons. First, payroll costs are major expenditures for most companies. Payroll accounting records provide data useful in analyzing and controlling these expenditures. Second, federal, state, and local laws require employers to keep payroll records. Companies must accumulate payroll data both for the business as a whole and for each employee.

EMPLOYEES AND INDEPENDENT CONTRACTORS

LO1 Distinguish between employees and independent contractors.

Not every person who performs services for a business is considered an employee. An **employee** works under the control and direction of an employer. Examples include secretaries, maintenance workers, salesclerks, and plant supervisors. In contrast, an **independent contractor** performs a service for a fee and does not work under the control and direction of the company paying for the service. Examples of independent contractors include public accountants, real estate agents, and lawyers.

The distinction between an employee and an independent contractor is very important for payroll purposes. Government laws and regulations regarding payroll are much more complex for employees than for independent contractors. Employers must deduct certain taxes, maintain payroll records, and file numerous reports for all employees. Only one form must be filed for independent contractors. The payroll accounting procedures described in this chapter apply only to employer/employee relationships.

EMPLOYEE EARNINGS AND DEDUCTIONS

LO2 Calculate employee earnings and deductions.

Three steps are required to determine how much to pay an employee for a pay period.

1. Calculate total earnings.
2. Determine the amounts of deductions.
3. Subtract deductions from total earnings to compute net pay.

Salaries and Wages

Compensation for managerial or administrative services usually is called **salary.** A salary normally is expressed in biweekly (every two weeks), monthly, or annual terms. Compensation for skilled or unskilled labor usually is referred to as **wages.** Wages ordinarily are expressed in terms of hours, weeks, or units produced. The terms "salaries" and "wages" often are used interchangeably in practice.

The **Fair Labor Standards Act (FLSA)** requires employers to pay overtime at $1^1/_2$ times the regular rate to any hourly employee who works over 40 hours in a week. Some companies pay a higher rate for hours worked on Saturday or Sunday, but this is not required by the FLSA. Some salaried employees are exempt from the FLSA rules and are not paid overtime.

Computing Total Earnings

Compensation usually is based on the time worked during the payroll period. Sometimes earnings are based on sales or units of output during the period. When compensation is based on time, a record must be kept of the time worked by each employee. Time cards (Figure 9-1) are helpful for this purpose. In large businesses with computer-based timekeeping systems, plastic cards or badges with special barcodes (Figure 9-2) can be used.

To illustrate the computation of total earnings, look at Helen Kuzmik's time card in Figure 9-1. The card shows that Kuzmik worked 55 hours for the week.

FIGURE 9-1 Time Card

Westly, Inc.
Time Card - Hourly Payroll

Period Ending	Mo. Dec.	Day 19	Yr. 19--
Name of Dept.	Sales		
NAME (Print)	Last: Kuzmik	First: Helen	
Payroll No.	25-1	Section A	

1st. wk.	M	T	W	Th	F	Sa	Su	Totals
Reg. Sched.	8	8	8	8	8			40
Over-time	1	1	1	1	1	6		11
Dbl. Time							4	4
1st. wk.	**M**	**T**	**W**	**Th**	**F**	**Sa**	**Su**	**Totals**
Reg. Sched.								
Over-time								

Remarks

I certify that to the best of my knowledge the above is a true report of the attendence of the employee named.

T.M.
Department Head

FIGURE 9-2   Barcode Time Card

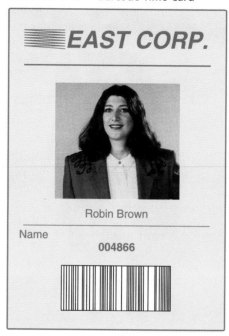

Kuzmik's regular rate of pay is $12 per hour. She is paid $1\frac{1}{2}$ times the regular rate for hours worked in excess of 40 per week, and twice the regular rate for hours worked on Sunday. Kuzmik's total earnings for the week ended December 19 are computed as follows:

Regular hours	40 hours
Overtime	11
Double time	4
Total hours worked	55 hours

40 hours × $12	$480
11 hours × $18 ($1\frac{1}{2}$ × $12 = $18)	198
4 hours (on Sunday) × $24 (2 × $12 = $24)	96
Total earnings for the week	$774

An employee who is paid a salary may also be entitled to premium pay for overtime. If this is the case, it is necessary to compute the regular hourly rate of pay before computing the overtime rate. To illustrate, assume that Linda Swaney has a salary of $2,288 a month plus $1\frac{1}{2}$ times the regular hourly rate for hours worked in excess of 40 per week. Swaney's overtime rate of pay is computed as follows:

$2,288 × 12 months	$27,456 annual pay
$27,456 ÷ 52 weeks	$528.00 pay per week
$528.00 ÷ 40 hours	$13.20 pay per regular hour
$13.20 × $1\frac{1}{2}$	$19.80 overtime pay per hour

If Swaney worked 50 hours during the week ended December 19, her total earnings for the week would be computed as follows:

40 hours × $13.20	$528.00
10 hours × $19.80	198.00
Total earnings for the week	$726.00

Deductions from Total Earnings

An employee's total earnings are called **gross pay.** Various deductions are made from gross pay to yield take-home or **net pay.** Deductions from gross pay fall into three major categories:

1. Federal (and possibly state and city) income tax withholding
2. Employees **FICA tax** withholding
3. Voluntary deductions

Employees Income Tax Withholding.   Federal law requires employers to withhold certain amounts from the total earnings of each employee. These withholdings are applied toward the payment of the employee's federal income tax. Four factors determine the amount to be withheld from an employee's gross pay each pay period.

1. Total earnings
2. Marital status
3. Number of withholding allowances claimed
4. Length of the pay period

Withholding Allowances.   Each employee is required to furnish the employer with an Employee's Withholding Allowance Certificate, Form W-4 (Figure 9-3). The marital status of the employee and the number of allowances claimed on Form W-4 determine the dollar amount of earnings subject to withholding. A **withholding allowance** exempts a specific dollar amount of an employee's gross pay from federal income tax withholding. In general, each employee is permitted one personal withholding allowance, one for a spouse who does not also claim an allowance, and one for each dependent.

An allowance certificate completed by Ken Istone is shown on page 276. Istone is married, has a spouse who does not claim an allowance, and has four dependent children. On line 5 of the W-4 form, Istone claims 6 allowances, calculated as follows:

Personal allowance	1
Spouse allowance	1
Allowances for dependents	4
Total withholding allowances	6

Wage-Bracket Method.   Employers may use the **wage-bracket method** to determine the amount of tax to be withheld from an employee's pay. The employee's gross pay for a specific time period is traced into the

FIGURE 9-3 Employee's Withholding Allowance Certificate (Form W-4)

------------------------- Cut here and give the certificate to your employer. Keep the top portion for your records. -------------------------

Form **W-4** Department of the Treasury Internal Revenue Service	**Employee's Withholding Allowance Certificate** ▶ For Privacy Act and Paperwork Reduction Act Notice, see reverse.		OMB No. 1545-0010 19**95**
1 Type or print your first name and middle initial *Ken M.*	Last name *Istone*		2 Your social security number 393 58 8194

3 ☐ Single ☒ Married ☐ Married, but withhold at higher Single rate.
Home address (number and street or rural route) *1546 Swallow Drive*
Note: *If married, but legally separated, or spouse is a nonresident alien, check the Single box.*

City or town, state, and ZIP code *St. Louis, MO 63144-4752*
4 If your last name differs from that on your social security card, check here and call 1-800-772-1213 for a new card . . . . . ▶ ☐

| 5 | Total number of allowances you are claiming (from line G above or from the worksheets on page 2 if they apply) . | 5 | *6* |
| 6 | Additional amount, if any, you want withheld from each paycheck . . . . | 6 | $ |

7 I claim exemption from withholding for 1995 and I certify that I meet **BOTH** of the following conditions for exemption:
 • Last year I had a right to a refund of **ALL** Federal income tax withheld because I had **NO** tax liability; **AND**
 • This year I expect a refund of **ALL** Federal income tax withheld because I expect to have **NO** tax liability.
 If you meet both conditions, enter "EXEMPT" here . . . . ▶ | 7 |

Under penalties of perjury, I certify that I am entitled to the number of withholding allowances claimed on this certificate or entitled to claim exempt status.

Employee's signature ▶ *Ken M. Istone*   Date ▶ *January 3*, 19--

8	Employer's name and address (Employer: Complete 8 and 10 only if sending to the IRS)	9 Office code (optional)	10 Employer identification number

Cat. No. 10220Q

appropriate wage-bracket table provided by the Internal Revenue Service (IRS). These tables cover various time periods, and there are separate tables for single and married taxpayers. Copies are provided in *Circular E—Employer's Tax Guide*, which may be obtained from any local IRS office.

Portions of weekly income tax wage-bracket withholding tables for single (not married) and married persons are illustrated in Figure 9-4. Assume that Ken Istone (who claims 6 allowances) had gross earnings of $545 for the week ended December 19, 19--. The table for married persons is used as follows:

> 1. Find the row for wages.
> 2. Find the column for withholding allowances.
> 3. Find the amount where they cross.

1. Find the row for wages of "at least $540, but less than $550."
2. Find the column headed "6 withholding allowances."
3. Where the row and column cross, $20 is given as the amount to be withheld.

For state or city income taxes, withholding generally is handled in one of two ways: (1) forms and tables similar to those provided by the IRS are used, or (2) an amount equal to a percentage of the federal withholding amount is withheld.

Employees FICA Tax Withholding. The Federal Insurance Contributions Act requires employers to withhold FICA taxes from employees' earnings. FICA taxes include amounts for both Social Security and Medicare programs. **Social Security taxes** provide pensions and disability benefits. **Medicare taxes** provide health insurance.

FIGURE 9-4   Federal Withholding Tax Table: Unmarried Persons

SINGLE Persons—**WEEKLY** Payroll Period

(For Wages Paid in 1995)

If the wages are—		And the number of withholding allowances claimed is—										
At least	But less than	0	1	2	3	4	5	6	7	8	9	10
		The amount of income tax to be withheld is—										
$300	$310	38	31	24	17	9	2	0	0	0	0	0
310	320	40	33	25	18	11	4	0	0	0	0	0
320	330	41	34	27	20	12	5	0	0	0	0	0
330	340	43	36	28	21	14	7	0	0	0	0	0
340	350	44	37	30	23	15	8	1	0	0	0	0
350	360	46	39	31	24	17	10	2	0	0	0	0
360	370	47	40	33	26	18	11	4	0	0	0	0
370	380	49	42	34	27	20	13	5	0	0	0	0
380	390	50	43	36	29	21	14	7	0	0	0	0
390	400	52	45	37	30	23	16	8	1	0	0	0
400	410	53	46	39	32	24	17	10	3	0	0	0
410	420	55	48	40	33	26	19	11	4	0	0	0
420	430	56	49	42	35	27	20	13	6	0	0	0
430	440	58	51	43	36	29	22	14	7	0	0	0
440	450	59	52	45	38	30	23	16	9	2	0	0
450	460	61	54	46	39	32	25	17	10	3	0	0
460	470	62	55	48	41	33	26	19	12	5	0	0
470	480	64	57	49	42	35	28	20	13	6	0	0
480	490	66	58	51	44	36	29	22	15	8	0	0
490	500	69	60	52	45	38	31	23	16	9	2	0
500	510	72	61	54	47	39	32	25	18	11	3	0
510	520	75	63	55	48	41	34	26	19	12	5	0
520	530	78	64	57	50	42	35	28	21	14	6	0
530	540	80	67	58	51	44	37	29	22	15	8	1
540	550	83	70	60	53	45	38	31	24	17	9	2
550	560	86	73	61	54	47	40	32	25	18	11	4
560	570	89	75	63	56	48	41	34	27	20	12	5
570	580	92	78	65	57	50	43	35	28	21	14	7
580	590	94	81	68	59	51	44	37	30	23	15	8
590	600	97	84	70	60	53	46	38	31	24	17	10
600	610	100	87	73	62	54	47	40	33	26	18	11
610	620	103	89	76	63	56	49	41	34	27	20	13
620	630	106	92	79	65	57	50	43	36	29	21	14
630	640	108	95	82	68	59	52	44	37	30	23	16
640	650	111	98	84	71	60	53	46	39	32	24	17
650	660	114	101	87	74	62	55	47	40	33	26	19
660	670	117	103	90	76	63	56	49	42	35	27	20
670	680	120	106	93	79	66	58	50	43	36	29	22
680	690	122	109	96	82	69	59	52	45	38	30	23
690	700	125	112	98	85	71	61	53	46	39	32	25
700	710	128	115	101	88	74	62	55	48	41	33	26
710	720	131	117	104	90	77	64	56	49	42	35	28
720	730	134	120	107	93	80	66	58	51	44	36	29
730	740	136	123	110	96	83	69	59	52	45	38	31
740	750	139	126	112	99	85	72	61	54	47	39	32
750	760	142	129	115	102	88	75	62	55	48	41	34
760	770	145	131	118	104	91	78	64	57	50	42	35
770	780	148	134	121	107	94	80	67	58	51	44	37
780	790	150	137	124	110	97	83	70	60	53	45	38
790	800	153	140	126	113	99	86	72	61	54	47	40
800	810	156	143	129	116	102	89	75	63	56	48	41
810	820	159	145	132	118	105	92	78	65	57	50	43
820	830	162	148	135	121	108	94	81	67	59	51	44
830	840	164	151	138	124	111	97	84	70	60	53	46
840	850	167	154	140	127	113	100	86	73	62	54	47
850	860	170	157	143	130	116	103	89	76	63	56	49
860	870	173	159	146	132	119	106	92	79	65	57	50
870	880	176	162	149	135	122	108	95	81	68	59	52
880	890	178	165	152	138	125	111	98	84	71	60	53
890	900	181	168	154	141	127	114	100	87	74	62	55
900	910	184	171	157	144	130	117	103	90	76	63	56
910	920	187	173	160	146	133	120	106	93	79	66	58
920	930	190	176	163	149	136	122	109	95	82	68	59
930	940	192	179	166	152	139	125	112	98	85	71	61
940	950	195	182	168	155	141	128	114	101	88	74	62
950	960	198	185	171	158	144	131	117	104	90	77	64
960	970	201	187	174	160	147	134	120	107	93	80	66
970	980	204	190	177	163	150	136	123	109	96	82	69
980	990	206	193	180	166	153	139	126	112	99	85	72
990	1,000	209	196	182	169	155	142	128	115	102	88	75
1,000	1,010	212	199	185	172	158	145	131	118	104	91	77
1,010	1,020	215	201	188	174	161	148	134	121	107	94	80
1,020	1,030	218	204	191	177	164	150	137	123	110	96	83
1,030	1,040	222	207	194	180	167	153	140	126	113	99	86
1,040	1,050	225	210	196	183	169	156	142	129	116	102	89
1,050	1,060	228	213	199	186	172	159	145	132	118	105	91
1,060	1,070	231	216	202	188	175	162	148	135	121	108	94
1,070	1,080	234	219	205	191	178	164	151	137	124	110	97
1,080	1,090	237	222	208	194	181	167	154	140	127	113	100
1,090	1,100	240	225	210	197	183	170	156	143	130	116	103
1,100	1,110	243	228	213	200	186	173	159	146	132	119	105
1,110	1,120	246	231	216	202	189	176	162	149	135	122	108
1,120	1,130	249	235	220	205	192	178	165	151	138	124	111
1,130	1,140	253	238	223	208	195	181	168	154	141	127	114
1,140	1,150	256	241	226	211	197	184	170	157	144	130	117
1,150	1,160	259	244	229	214	200	187	173	160	146	133	119
1,160	1,170	262	247	232	217	203	190	176	163	149	136	122
1,170	1,180	265	250	235	220	206	192	179	165	152	138	125
1,180	1,190	268	253	238	223	209	195	182	168	155	141	128
1,190	1,200	271	256	241	226	211	198	184	171	158	144	131
1,200	1,210	274	259	244	229	215	201	187	174	160	147	133
1,210	1,220	277	262	247	233	218	204	190	177	163	150	136
1,220	1,230	280	266	251	236	221	206	193	170	166	152	139
1,230	1,240	284	269	254	239	224	209	196	182	169	155	142
1,240	1,250	287	272	257	242	227	212	198	185	172	158	145

$1,250 and over   Use Table 1(a) for a **SINGLE person** on page 32. Also see the instructions on page 30.

FIGURE 9-4   Federal Withholding Tax Table (continued): Married Persons

MARRIED Persons—**WEEKLY** Payroll Period

(For Wages Paid in 1995)

If the wages are—		And the number of withholding allowances claimed is—										
At least	But less than	0	1	2	3	4	5	6	7	8	9	10
		The amount of income tax to be withheld is—										
$290	$300	26	19	11	4	0	0	0	0	0	0	0
300	310	27	20	13	6	0	0	0	0	0	0	0
310	320	29	22	14	7	0	0	0	0	0	0	0
320	330	30	23	16	9	1	0	0	0	0	0	0
330	340	32	25	17	10	3	0	0	0	0	0	0
340	350	33	26	19	12	4	0	0	0	0	0	0
350	360	35	28	20	13	6	0	0	0	0	0	0
360	370	36	29	22	15	7	0	0	0	0	0	0
370	380	38	31	23	16	9	2	0	0	0	0	0
380	390	39	32	25	18	10	3	0	0	0	0	0
390	400	41	34	26	19	12	5	0	0	0	0	0
400	410	42	35	28	21	13	6	0	0	0	0	0
410	420	44	37	29	22	15	8	1	0	0	0	0
420	430	45	38	31	24	16	9	2	0	0	0	0
430	440	47	40	32	25	18	11	4	0	0	0	0
440	450	48	41	34	27	19	12	5	0	0	0	0
450	460	50	43	35	28	21	14	7	0	0	0	0
460	470	51	44	37	30	22	15	8	1	0	0	0
470	480	53	46	38	31	24	17	10	2	0	0	0
480	490	54	47	40	33	25	18	11	4	0	0	0
490	500	56	49	41	34	27	20	13	5	0	0	0
500	510	57	50	43	36	28	21	14	7	0	0	0
510	520	59	52	44	37	30	23	16	8	1	0	0
520	530	60	53	46	39	31	24	17	10	3	0	0
530	540	62	55	47	40	33	26	19	11	4	0	0
540	550	63	56	49	42	34	27	20	13	6	0	0
550	560	65	58	50	43	36	29	22	14	7	0	0
560	570	66	59	52	45	37	30	23	16	9	1	0
570	580	68	61	53	46	39	32	25	17	10	3	0
580	590	69	62	55	48	40	33	26	19	12	4	0
590	600	71	64	56	49	42	35	28	20	13	6	0
600	610	72	65	58	51	43	36	29	22	15	7	0
610	620	74	67	59	52	45	38	31	23	16	9	2
620	630	75	68	61	54	46	39	32	25	18	10	3
630	640	77	70	62	55	48	41	34	26	19	12	5
640	650	78	71	64	57	49	42	35	28	21	13	6
650	660	80	73	65	58	51	44	37	29	22	15	8
660	670	81	74	67	60	52	45	38	31	24	16	9
670	680	83	76	68	61	54	47	40	32	25	18	11
680	690	84	77	70	63	55	48	41	34	27	19	12
690	700	86	79	71	64	57	50	43	35	28	21	14
700	710	87	80	73	66	58	51	44	37	30	22	15
710	720	89	82	74	67	60	53	46	38	31	24	17
720	730	90	83	76	69	61	54	47	40	33	25	18
730	740	92	85	77	70	63	56	49	41	34	27	20
740	750	93	86	79	72	64	57	50	43	36	28	21
750	760	95	88	80	73	66	59	52	44	37	30	23
760	770	96	89	82	75	67	60	53	46	39	31	24
770	780	98	91	83	76	69	62	55	47	40	33	26
780	790	99	92	85	78	70	63	56	49	42	34	27
790	800	101	94	86	79	72	65	58	50	43	36	29
800	810	102	95	88	81	73	66	59	52	45	37	30
810	820	104	97	89	82	75	68	61	53	46	39	32
820	830	105	98	91	84	76	69	62	55	48	40	33
830	840	108	100	92	85	78	71	64	56	49	42	35
840	850	111	101	94	87	79	72	65	58	51	43	36
850	860	113	103	95	88	81	74	67	59	52	45	38
860	870	116	104	97	90	82	75	68	61	54	46	39
870	880	119	106	98	91	84	77	70	62	55	48	41
880	890	122	108	100	93	85	78	71	64	57	49	42
890	900	125	111	101	94	87	80	73	65	58	51	44
900	910	127	114	103	96	88	81	74	67	60	52	45
910	920	130	117	104	97	90	83	76	68	61	54	47
920	930	133	119	106	99	91	84	77	70	63	55	48
930	940	136	122	109	100	93	86	79	71	64	57	50
940	950	139	125	112	102	94	87	80	73	66	58	51
950	960	141	128	114	103	96	89	82	74	67	60	53
960	970	144	131	117	105	97	90	83	76	69	61	54
970	980	147	133	120	107	99	92	85	77	70	63	56
980	990	150	136	123	109	100	93	86	79	72	64	57
990	1,000	153	139	126	112	102	95	88	80	73	66	59
1,000	1,010	155	142	128	115	103	96	89	82	75	67	60
1,010	1,020	158	145	131	118	105	98	91	83	76	69	62
1,020	1,030	161	147	134	121	107	99	92	85	78	70	63
1,030	1,040	164	150	137	123	110	101	94	86	79	72	65
1,040	1,050	167	153	140	126	113	102	95	88	81	73	66
1,050	1,060	169	156	142	129	115	104	97	89	82	75	68
1,060	1,070	172	159	145	132	118	105	98	91	84	76	69
1,070	1,080	175	161	148	135	121	108	100	92	85	78	71
1,080	1,090	178	164	151	137	124	110	101	94	87	79	72
1,090	1,100	181	167	154	140	127	113	103	95	88	81	74
1,100	1,110	183	170	156	143	129	116	104	97	90	82	75
1,110	1,120	186	173	159	146	132	119	106	98	91	84	77
1,120	1,130	189	175	162	149	135	122	108	100	93	85	78
1,130	1,140	192	178	165	151	138	124	111	101	94	87	80
1,140	1,150	195	181	168	154	141	127	114	103	96	88	81
1,150	1,160	197	184	170	157	143	130	117	104	97	90	83
1,160	1,170	200	187	173	160	146	133	119	106	99	91	84
1,170	1,180	203	189	176	163	149	136	122	109	100	93	86
1,180	1,190	206	192	179	165	152	138	125	111	102	94	87
1,190	1,200	209	195	182	168	155	141	128	114	103	96	89
1,200	1,210	211	198	184	171	157	144	131	117	105	97	90
1,210	1,220	214	201	187	174	160	147	133	120	106	99	92
1,220	1,230	217	203	190	177	163	150	136	123	109	100	93
1,230	1,240	220	206	193	179	166	152	139	125	112	102	95
1,240	1,250	223	209	196	182	169	155	142	128	115	103	96
1,250	1,260	225	212	198	185	171	158	145	131	118	105	98
1,260	1,270	228	215	201	188	174	161	147	134	120	107	99
1,270	1,280	231	217	204	191	177	164	150	137	123	110	101
1,280	1,290	234	220	207	193	180	166	153	139	126	113	102

Congress has frequently changed the tax rates and the maximum amounts of earnings subject to FICA taxes. For 1995, the Social Security rate is 6.2% on maximum earnings of $61,200. The Medicare rate is 1.45% on all earnings; there is no maximum.

To illustrate the calculation of FICA taxes, assume the following earnings for Sarah Cadrain:

	Earnings	
Pay Period	Week	Year-to-Date
Dec. 6–12	$1,200	$60,540
Dec. 13–19	$1,260	$61,800

For the week of December 6–12, FICA taxes on Cadrain's earnings would be:

Gross Pay	x	Tax Rate	=	Tax
$1,200		Social Security 6.2%		$74.40
		Medicare 1.45%		17.40
				$91.80

During the week of December 13–19, Cadrain's earnings for the calendar year went over the $61,200 Social Security maximum by $600 ($61,800 – $61,200). Therefore, $600 of her $1,260 earnings for the week would not be subject to the Social Security tax.

Year-to-date earnings	$61,800
Social Security maximum.	61,200
Amount not subject to Social Security tax	$ 600

The Social Security tax on Cadrain's December 13–19 earnings would be:

Gross pay	$1,260.00
Amount not subject to Social Security tax	600.00
Amount subject to Social Security tax	660.00
Tax rate	6.2%
Social Security tax	$ 40.92

Since there is no Medicare maximum, all of Cadrain's December 13–19 earnings would be subject to the Medicare tax.

Gross pay	$1,260.00
Tax rate	1.45%
Medicare tax	$ 18.27

The total FICA tax would be:

Social Security tax	$40.92
Medicare tax	18.27
Total FICA tax	$59.19

For the remainder of the calendar year, Cadrain's earnings would be subject only to Medicare taxes.

Voluntary Deductions. In addition to the mandatory deductions from employee earnings for income and FICA taxes, many other deductions are possible. These deductions are usually voluntary and depend on specific agreements between the employee and employer. Examples of voluntary deductions are:

1. United States savings bond purchases
2. Health insurance premiums
3. Credit union deposits
4. Pension plan payments
5. Charitable contributions

Computing Net Pay

To compute an employee's net pay for the period, subtract all tax withholdings and voluntary deductions from the gross pay. Ken Istone's net pay for the week ended December 19 would be calculated as follows.

Gross pay		$545.00
Deductions:		
Federal income tax withholding	$20.00	
Social Security tax withholding	33.79	
Medicare tax withholding	7.90	
Health insurance premiums	10.00	
Total deductions		71.69
Net pay		$473.31

PAYROLL RECORDS

LO3   Prepare payroll records.

Payroll records should provide the following information for each employee:

1. Name, address, occupation, Social Security number, marital status, and number of withholding allowances.
2. Gross amount of earnings, date of payment, and period covered by each payroll.
3. Gross amount of earnings accumulated for the year.
4. Amounts of taxes and other items withheld.

Three types of payroll records are used to accumulate this information.

1. The payroll register
2. The payroll check with earnings statement attached
3. The employee's earnings record

These records can be prepared by either manual or automated methods. The illustrations in this chapter are based on a manual system. The forms and procedures illustrated are equally applicable to both manual and automated systems.

Payroll Register

A **payroll register** is a form used to assemble the data required at the end of each payroll period. Figure 9-5 illustrates Westly, Inc.'s, payroll register for the payroll period ended December 19, 19--. Detailed information on earnings, taxable earnings, deductions, and net pay is provided for each employee. Column headings for deductions may vary, depending on which deductions are commonly used by a particular business. The sources of key information in the register are indicated in Figure 9-5.

Westly, Inc., has eight employees. The first $61,200 of each employee's earnings is subject to Social Security tax. The Cumulative Total column, under the Earnings category, shows that Sarah Cadrain has exceeded this limit during the period. Thus, only $660 of her earnings for this pay period is subject to Social Security tax, as shown in the Taxable Earnings columns. The Taxable Earnings columns are needed for determining the Social Security tax and the employer's payroll taxes. Employers must pay unemployment tax on the first $7,000 of employee earnings and Social Security tax on the first $61,200. Employer payroll taxes are discussed in Chapter 10.

Regular deductions are made from employee earnings for federal income tax and Social Security and Medicare taxes. In addition, voluntary deductions are made for health insurance and United Way contributions, based on agreements with individual employees.

After the data for each employee have been entered, the amount columns in the payroll register should be totaled and the totals verified as follows:

Regular earnings		$4,743.00
Overtime earnings		692.00
Gross earnings		$5,435.00
Deductions:		
Federal income tax	$633.00	
Social Security tax	299.77	
Medicare tax	78.81	
Health insurance premiums	46.00	
United Way	40.00	1,097.58
Net amount of payroll		$4,337.42

In a computerized accounting system, the payroll software performs this proof. An error in the payroll register could cause the payment of an incorrect amount to an employee. It also could result in sending an incorrect amount to the government or other agencies for whom funds are withheld.

Payroll Check

Employees may be paid in cash or by check. In some cases, the employee does not even handle the paycheck. Rather, payment is made by **direct**

FIGURE 9-5   Payroll Register (Left Half)

PAYROLL

	NAME	ALLOW-ANCES	MARITAL STATUS	EARNINGS				TAXABLE EARNINGS		
				REGULAR	OVERTIME	TOTAL	CUMULATIVE TOTAL	UNEMPLOY. COMPENSATION	SOCIAL SECURITY	
1	Cadrain, Sarah	4	M	1 1 0 0 00	1 6 0 00	1 2 6 0 00	61 8 0 0 00		6 6 0 00	1
2	Guder, James	1	S	8 6 0 00	4 0 00	9 0 0 00	43 4 0 0 00		9 0 0 00	2
3	Istone, Ken	6	M	5 4 5 00		5 4 5 00	27 0 2 5 00		5 4 5 00	3
4	Kuzmik, Helen	2	M	4 8 0 00	2 9 4 00	7 7 4 00	31 0 0 0 00		7 7 4 00	4
5	Lee, Hoseoup	3	M	4 4 0 00		4 4 0 00	22 3 4 0 00		4 4 0 00	5
6	Swaney, Linda	2	S	5 2 8 00	1 9 8 00	7 2 6 00	27 5 0 0 00		7 2 6 00	6
7	Tucci, Paul	5	M	4 9 0 00		4 9 0 00	25 0 5 0 00		4 9 0 00	7
8	Wiles, Harry	1	S	3 0 0 00		3 0 0 00	6 3 0 00	3 0 0 00	3 0 0 00	8
9				4 7 4 3 00	6 9 2 00	5 4 3 5 00	244 4 1 5 00	3 0 0 00	4 8 3 5 00	9

↑ Time cards, pay rates   ↑ Prior period total + current period earnings   ↑ Current below $7,000 cumul. total   ↑ Current below $61,200 cumul. total

FIGURE 9-5   Payroll Register (Right Half)

REGISTER—WEEK ENDED 12/19/--

	FEDERAL INCOME TAX	SOCIAL SEC. TAX	MEDICARE TAX	HEALTH INSURANCE	UNITED WAY	OTHER	TOTAL	NET PAY	CHECK NO.	
1	1 7 4 00	4 0 92	1 8 27				2 3 3 19	1 0 2 6 81	409	1
2	1 7 1 00	5 5 80	1 3 05		2 0 00		2 5 9 85	6 4 0 15	410	2
3	2 0 00	3 3 79	7 90	1 0 00			7 1 69	4 7 3 31	411	3
4	8 3 00	4 7 99	1 1 22	1 3 00	2 0 00		1 7 5 21	5 9 8 79	412	4
5	2 7 00	2 7 28	6 38	1 3 00			7 3 66	3 6 6 34	413	5
6	1 0 7 00	4 5 01	1 0 53				1 6 2 54	5 6 3 46	414	6
7	2 0 00	3 0 38	7 11	1 0 00			6 7 49	4 2 2 51	415	7
8	3 1 00	1 8 60	4 35				5 3 95	2 4 6 05	416	8
9	6 3 3 00	2 9 9 77	7 8 81	4 6 00	4 0 00		1 0 9 7 58	4 3 3 7 42		9

↑ Withholding Tax Table   ↑ 6.2% x Social Security taxable earnings   ↑ 1.45% x total earnings   ↑ Specific employer–employee agreements   ↑ Total earnings – Total deductions

deposit or electronic funds transfer (EFT) by the employer to the employee's bank. The employee receives the earnings statement from the check and a nonnegotiable copy of the check indicating that the deposit has been made. Payment by check or direct deposit provides better internal accounting control than payment by cash.

Data needed to prepare a paycheck for each employee are contained in the payroll register. In a computer-based system, the paychecks and payroll register normally are prepared at the same time. The employer furnishes a statement of payroll deductions to each employee along with each paycheck. Paychecks with detachable earnings statements, like the one for Ken Istone illustrated in Figure 9-6, are widely used for this purpose. Before the check is deposited or cashed, the employee should detach the stub and keep it.

Employees Earnings Record

A separate record of each employee's earnings is called an **employees earnings record.** An employees earnings record for Ken M. Istone for a portion of the last quarter of the calendar year is illustrated in Figure 9-7.

FIGURE 9-6   Paycheck and Earnings Statement

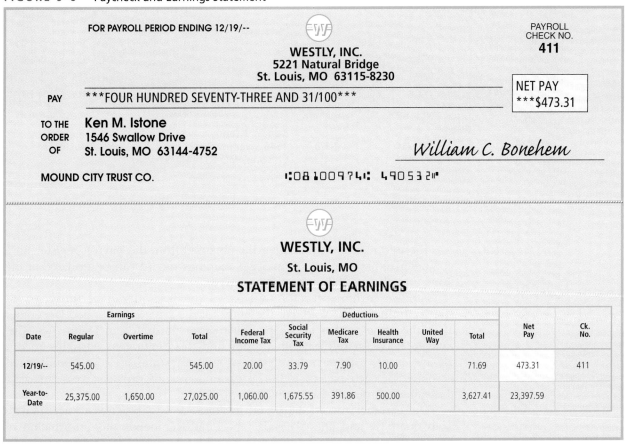

	Earnings			Deductions						Net Pay	Ck. No.
Date	Regular	Overtime	Total	Federal Income Tax	Social Security Tax	Medicare Tax	Health Insurance	United Way	Total		
12/19/--	545.00		545.00	20.00	33.79	7.90	10.00		71.69	473.31	411
Year-to-Date	25,375.00	1,650.00	27,025.00	1,060.00	1,675.55	391.86	500.00		3,627.41	23,397.59	

FIGURE 9-7   Employees Earnings Record (Left Half)

EMPLOYEES EARNINGS RECORD

19-- PERIOD ENDED	EARNINGS				TAXABLE EARNINGS	
	REGULAR	OVERTIME	TOTAL	CUMULATIVE TOTAL	UNEMPLOY. COMP.	SOCIAL SECURITY
11/28	5 4 5 00	7 5 00	6 2 0 00	25 2 4 0 00		6 2 0 00
12/5	5 4 5 00	7 5 00	6 2 0 00	25 8 6 0 00		6 2 0 00
12/12	5 4 5 00	7 5 00	6 2 0 00	26 4 8 0 00		6 2 0 00
12/19	5 4 5 00		5 4 5 00	27 0 2 5 00		5 4 5 00

GENDER		DEPARTMENT	OCCUPATION	SOC. SEC. NO.	MARITAL STATUS	ALLOWANCES
M	F					
✓		Maint.	Service	393-58-8194	M	6

FIGURE 9-7   Employees Earnings Record (Right Half)

FOR PERIOD ENDED   19--

	DEDUCTIONS								
FEDERAL INCOME TAX	SOCIAL SEC. TAX	MEDICARE TAX	HEALTH INSURANCE	UNITED WAY	OTHER		TOTAL	CHECK NO.	AMOUNT
3 2 00	3 8 44	8 99	1 0 00				8 9 43	387	5 3 0 57
3 2 00	3 8 44	8 99	1 0 00				8 9 43	395	5 3 0 57
3 2 00	3 8 44	8 99	1 0 00				8 9 43	403	5 3 0 57
2 0 00	3 3 79	7 90	1 0 00				7 1 69	411	4 7 3 31

PAY RATE	DATE OF BIRTH	DATE HIRED	NAME/ADDRESS	EMPLOYEE NUMBER
$545/wk	8/17/64	1/3/87	Ken M. Istone 1546 Swallow Drive St. Louis, MO 63144-4752	3

The information in this record is obtained from the payroll register. In a computerized system, the employees earnings record can be updated at the same time the payroll register is prepared.

Istone's earnings for four weeks of the last quarter of the year are shown on this form. Note that the entry for the pay period ended December 19 is the same as that in the payroll register illustrated in Figure 9-5. This linkage between the payroll register and the employees earnings record always exists. The payroll register provides a summary of all employees' earnings for each pay period. The earnings record provides a summary of the annual earnings of an individual employee.

The earnings record illustrated in Figure 9-7 is designed to accumulate both quarterly and annual totals. The employer needs this information to prepare several reports. These reports will be discussed in Chapter 10.

ACCOUNTING FOR EMPLOYEE EARNINGS AND DEDUCTIONS

LO4   Account for employee earnings and deductions.

The payroll register described in the previous section provides complete payroll data for each pay period. But, the payroll register is not a journal. We still need to make a journal entry for payroll.

Journalizing Payroll Transactions

The totals at the bottom of the columns of the payroll register in Figure 9-5 show the following information.

Regular earnings		$4,743.00
Overtime earnings		692.00
Gross earnings		$5,435.00
Deductions:		
Federal income tax	$633.00	
Social Security tax	299.77	
Medicare tax	78.81	
Health insurance premiums	46.00	
United Way contributions	40.00	1,097.58
Net amount of payroll		$4,337.42

The payroll register column totals thus provide the basis for the following journal entry:

5	Dec.¹⁹⁻⁻	19	Wages and Salaries Expense	5 4 3 5 00		5
6			Employees Income Tax Payable		6 3 3 00	6
7			Social Security Tax Payable		2 9 9 77	7
8			Medicare Tax Payable		7 8 81	8
9			Health Ins. Premiums Payable		4 6 00	9
10			United Way Contrib. Payable		4 0 00	10
11			Cash		4 3 3 7 42	11
12			Payroll for week ended			12
13			Dec. 19			13

Employee paychecks can be written from the regular bank account or from a special payroll bank account. Large businesses with many employees commonly use a payroll bank account. If Westly uses a payroll bank account, a single check for $4,337.42 is written to "Payroll Cash." Individual checks are then drawn on that account for the amount due to each employee. Otherwise, individual checks totaling $4,337.42 are written to the employees from the regular bank account.

LEARNING KEY   Wages and Salaries Expense is debited for the gross pay. A separate account is kept for each earnings deduction. Cash is credited for the net pay.

Notice two important facts about the payroll entry. First, Wages and Salaries Expense is debited for the gross pay of the employees. The expense to the employer is the gross pay, not the employees' net pay after deductions. Second, a separate account is kept for each deduction.

The accounts needed in entering deductions depend on the deductions involved. To understand the accounting for these deductions, consider what the employer is doing. By deducting amounts from employees' earnings, the employer is simply serving as an agent for the government and other groups. Amounts that are deducted from an employee's gross earnings must be paid by the employer to these groups. Therefore, a separate account should be kept for the liability for each type of deduction.

To help you understand the journal entry for payroll, let's examine the accounts involved. The seven accounts affected by the payroll entry shown above are as follows.

ACCOUNT	CLASSIFICATION
Wages and Salaries Expense	Expense
Employees Income Tax Payable	Liability
Social Security Tax Payable	Liability
Medicare Tax Payable	Liability
Health Insurance Premiums Payable	Liability
United Way Contributions Payable	Liability
Cash (or Payroll Cash)	Asset

Wages and Salaries Expense

This account is debited for the gross pay of all employees for each pay period. Sometimes, separate expense accounts are kept for the employees of different departments. Thus, separate accounts may be kept for Office Salaries Expense, Sales Salaries Expense, and Factory Wages Expense.

Wages and Salaries Expense

Debit	Credit
gross pay of employees for each pay period	

Employees Income Tax Payable

This account is credited for the total federal income tax withheld from employees' earnings. The account is debited for amounts paid to the IRS. When all of the income taxes withheld have been paid, the account will have a zero balance. A state or city income tax payable account is used in a similar manner.

Employees Income Tax Payable

Debit	Credit
payment of income tax previously withheld	federal income tax withheld from employees' earnings

Social Security and Medicare Taxes Payable

These accounts are credited for (1) the Social Security and Medicare tax withheld from employees' earnings and (2) the Social Security and Medicare taxes imposed on the employer. Social Security and Medicare taxes imposed on the employer are discussed in Chapter 10. The accounts are debited for amounts paid to the IRS. When all of the Social Security and Medicare taxes have been paid, the accounts will have zero balances.

Social Security Tax Payable

Debit	Credit
payment of Social Security tax previously withheld or imposed	Social Security taxes (1) withheld from employees' earnings and (2) imposed on the employer

Medicare Tax Payable

Debit	Credit
payment of Medicare tax previously withheld or imposed	Medicare taxes (1) withheld from employees' earnings and (2) imposed on the employer

Other Deductions

Health Insurance Premiums Payable is credited for health insurance contributions deducted from an employee's pay. The account is debited for the subsequent payment of these amounts to the health insurer. United Way Contributions Payable is handled in a similar manner.

PAYROLL RECORD-KEEPING METHODS

LO5   Describe various payroll record-keeping methods.

You probably noticed that the same information appears in several places in the payroll records—in the payroll register, paycheck and stub, and employees earnings records. If all records are prepared by hand (a **manual system**), the same information would be recorded several times. Unless an employer has only a few employees, this can be very inefficient. Various approaches are available to make payroll accounting more efficient and accurate.

Both medium- and large-size businesses commonly use two approaches for payroll record keeping: payroll processing centers and electronic systems. A **payroll processing center** is a business that sells payroll record-keeping services. The employer provides the center with all basic employee data and each period's report of hours worked. The processing center maintains all payroll records and prepares each period's payroll checks. Payroll processing center fees tend to be much less than it would cost an employer to handle payroll internally.

An **electronic system** is a computer system based on a software package that performs all payroll record keeping and prepares payroll checks. In this system, only the employee number and hours worked need to be entered into a computer each pay period, as shown in Figure 9-8. All other payroll data needed to prepare the payroll records can be stored in the computer. The computer uses the employee number and hours worked to determine the gross pay, deductions, and net pay. The payroll register, checks, and employees earnings records are provided as outputs.

FIGURE 9-8   Electronic Payroll System

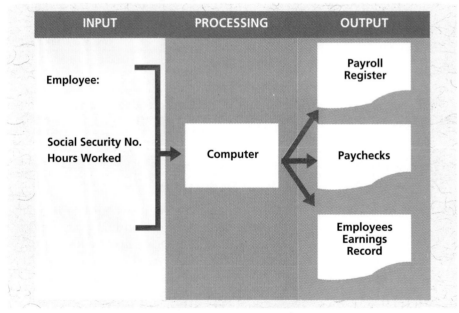

The same inputs and outputs are required in all payroll systems. Even with a computer, the data required for payroll processing have to be entered into the system at some point. The outputs—the payroll register, paychecks, and employees earnings records—are basically the same under each system.

KEY POINTS

1 Payroll accounting procedures apply only to employees, not to independent contractors.

2 Three steps are required to determine how much to pay an employee for a pay period:

1. Calculate total earnings.
2. Determine the amounts of deductions.
3. Subtract deductions from total earnings to compute net pay.

Deductions from gross pay fall into three categories:

1. Employees income tax withholding
2 Employees Social Security and Medicare taxes withholding
3. Voluntary deductions

Four factors determine the amount to be withheld from an employee's gross pay each pay period for federal income tax:

1. Total earnings
2. Marital status
3. Number of withholding allowances claimed
4. Length of the pay period

3 The payroll register and the employees earnings record are linked. The payroll register provides a summary of earnings of all employees for each pay period. The earnings record provides a summary of the annual earnings of an individual employee.

4 The totals at the bottom of the columns of the payroll register provide the basis for the journal entry for payroll.

Amounts withheld or deducted by the employer from employee earnings are credited to liability accounts. The employer must pay these amounts to the proper government groups and other appropriate groups.

5 In a manual payroll system, the same information may need to be recorded several times. An electronic payroll system is much more efficient.

KEY TERMS

direct deposit 281   The employee does not handle the paycheck; payment is made by the employer directly to the employee's bank.

electronic system 288   A computer system based on a software package that performs all payroll record keeping and prepares payroll checks.

employee 272   Person who works under the control and direction of an employer.

employees earnings record 283   A separate record of each employee's earnings.

Fair Labor Standards Act (FLSA) 273 Requires employers to pay overtime at 1½ times the regular rate to any hourly employee who works over 40 hours in a week.

FICA taxes 275 Payroll taxes withheld to provide Social Security and Medicare benefits.

gross pay 275 An employee's total earnings.

independent contractor 272 Person who performs a service for a fee and does not work under the control and direction of the company paying for the service.

manual system 287 Payroll system in which all records are prepared by hand.

Medicare taxes 276 Payroll taxes that are intended to provide health insurance benefits.

net pay 275 Gross pay less mandatory and voluntary deductions.

payroll processing center 288 A business that sells payroll record-keeping services.

payroll register 280 A form used to assemble the data required at the end of each payroll period.

salary 272 Compensation for managerial or administrative services.

Social Security taxes 276 Payroll taxes that are intended to provide pensions and disability benefits.

wage-bracket method 275 Employers determine the amount to withhold from an employee's gross pay for a specific time period from the appropriate wage-bracket table provided by the IRS.

wages 272 Compensation for skilled or unskilled labor.

withholding allowance 275 Exempts a specific dollar amount of an employee's gross pay from federal income tax withholding.

REVIEW QUESTIONS

1. Why is it important for payroll accounting purposes to distinguish between an employee and an independent contractor?
2. Name three major categories of deductions from an employee's gross pay.
3. Identify the four factors that determine the amount of federal income tax that is withheld from an employee's pay each pay period.
4. In general, an employee is entitled to withholding allowances for what purposes?
5. Identify the three payroll records usually needed by an employer.
6. Describe the information contained in the payroll register.
7. Why is it important to total and verify the totals of the payroll register after the data for each employee have been entered?
8. Distinguish between the payroll register and the employee earnings record.
9. Explain what an employer does with the amounts withheld from an employee's pay.
10. Explain why payroll processing centers and electronic systems are commonly used in payroll accounting.

MANAGING YOUR WRITING

The minimum wage originally was only $.25 an hour. Today it is $4.25 an hour. Assume that Congress is considering raising the minimum wage again and your United States representative is asking for public opinion on this issue. Write two letters to your representative, one with arguments for and the other with arguments against a higher minimum wage.

DEMONSTRATION PROBLEM

Carole Vohsen operates a pet grooming salon called Canine Coiffures. She has five employees, all of whom are paid on a weekly basis. Canine Coiffures uses a payroll register, individual employees earnings records, a journal, and a general ledger.

The payroll data for each employee for the week ended January 21, 19--, are given below. Employees are paid $1\frac{1}{2}$ times the regular rate for work over 40 hours a week and double time for work on Sunday.

Name	Employee No.	No. of Allowances	Marital Status	Total Hours Worked Jan. 15–21	Rate	Total Earnings Jan. 1–14
DeNourie, Katie	1	2	S	44	$11.50	$1,058.00
Garriott, Pete	2	1	M	40	12.00	1,032.00
Martinez, Sheila	3	3	M	39	12.50	987.50
Parker, Nancy	4	4	M	42	11.00	957.00
Shapiro, John	5	2	S	40	11.50	931.50

Sheila Martinez is the manager of the Shampooing Department. Her Social Security number is 500-88-4189, and she was born April 12, 1969. She lives at 46 Darling Crossing; Norwich, CT 06360. Martinez was hired September 1 of last year.

Canine Coiffures uses a federal income tax withholding table. A portion of this weekly table is provided in Figure 9-4 on pages 277 and 278. Social Security tax is withheld at the rate of 6.2% of the first $61,200 earned, Medicare tax is withheld at the rate of 1.45%, and city earnings tax at the rate of 1%, both applied to gross pay. Garriott and Parker each have $14.00 and DeNourie and Martinez each have $4.00 withheld for health insurance. DeNourie, Martinez, and Shapiro each have $15.00 withheld to be invested in the groomers' credit union. Garriott and Shapiro each have $18.75 withheld under a savings bond purchase plan.

Canine Coiffures' payroll is met by drawing checks on its regular bank account. This week, the checks were issued in sequence, beginning with no. 811.

REQUIRED

1. Prepare a payroll register for Canine Coiffures for the week ended January 21, 19--. (In the Taxable Earnings/Unemployment Compensation column, enter the same amounts as in the Social Security column.) Total the amount columns, verify the totals, and rule with single and double lines.
2. Prepare an employees earnings record for Sheila Martinez for the week ended January 21, 19--.
3. Assuming that the wages for the week ended January 21 were paid on January 23, prepare the journal entry for the payment of this payroll.
4. Post the entry in requirement 3 to the affected accounts in the ledger of Canine Coiffures. Do not enter any amounts in the Balance columns. Use account numbers as follows: Cash—111; Employees Income Tax Payable—211; Social Security Tax Payable—212; Medicare Tax Payable—213; City Earnings Tax Payable—215; Health Insurance Premiums Payable—227; Credit Union Payable—228; Savings Bond Deductions Payable—261; Wages and Salaries Expense—542.

SOLUTION

1.

PAYROLL

	NAME	EMPLOYEE NO.	ALLOW-ANCES	MARITAL STATUS	EARNINGS				TAXABLE EARNINGS		
					REGULAR	OVERTIME	TOTAL	CUMULATIVE TOTAL	UNEMPLOY. COMPENSATION	SOCIAL SECURITY	
1	DeNourie, Katie	1	2	S	460 00	69 00	529 00	1587 00	529 00	529 00	1
2	Garriott, Pete	2	1	M	480 00		480 00	1512 00	480 00	480 00	2
3	Martinez, Sheila	3	3	M	487 50		487 50	1475 00	487 50	487 50	3
4	Parker, Nancy	4	4	M	440 00	33 00	473 00	1430 00	473 00	473 00	4
5	Shapiro, John	5	2	S	460 00		460 00	1391 50	460 00	460 00	5
6					2327 50	102 00	2429 50	7395 50	2429 50	2429 50	6
7											7

REGISTER—WEEK ENDED January 21, 19--

	DEDUCTIONS								NET PAY	CHECK NO.	
	FEDERAL INCOME TAX	SOCIAL SEC. TAX	MEDICARE TAX	CITY TAX	HEALTH INSURANCE	CREDIT UNION	OTHER	TOTAL			
1	57 00	32 80	7 67	5 29	4 00	15 00		121 76	407 24	811	1
2	47 00	29 76	6 96	4 80	14 00		US Sav. Bond 18 75	121 27	358 73	812	2
3	33 00	30 23	7 07	4 88	4 00	15 00		94 18	393 32	813	3
4	24 00	29 33	6 86	4 73	14 00			78 92	394 08	814	4
5	48 00	28 52	6 67	4 60		15 00	US Sav. Bond 18 75	121 54	338 46	815	5
6	209 00	150 64	35 23	24 30	36 00	45 00	37 50	537 67	1891 83		6
7											7

2.

EMPLOYEES EARNINGS RECORD

19--PERIOD ENDED	EARNINGS				TAXABLE EARNINGS	
	REGULAR	OVERTIME	TOTAL	CUMULATIVE TOTAL	UNEMPLOY. COMP.	SOCIAL SECURITY
1/7						
1/14						
1/21	4 8 7 50		4 8 7 50	1 4 7 5 00	4 8 7 50	4 8 7 50
1/28						

GENDER		DEPARTMENT	OCCUPATION	SOC. SEC. NO.	MARITAL STATUS	EXEMPTIONS
M	F					
	✓	Shampooing	Manager	500-88-4189	M	3

FOR PERIOD ENDED   19--

DEDUCTIONS								CHECK NO.	AMOUNT
FEDERAL INCOME TAX	SOCIAL SEC. TAX	MEDICARE TAX	CITY TAX	HEALTH INSURANCE	CREDIT UNION	OTHER	TOTAL		
3 3 00	3 0 23	7 07	4 88	4 00	1 5 00		9 4 18	813	3 9 3 32

PAY RATE	DATE OF BIRTH	DATE HIRED	NAME/ADDRESS	EMPLOYEE NUMBER
$12.50	4/12/69	9/1/--	Sheila Martinez 46 Darling Crossing Norwich, CT 06360	3

3.

GENERAL JOURNAL   PAGE 1

	DATE		DESCRIPTION	POST. REF.	DEBIT	CREDIT	
1	19--Jan.	23	Wages and Salaries Expense	542	2 4 2 9 50		1
2			Employees Income Tax Payable	211		2 0 9 00	2
3			Social Security Tax Payable	212		1 5 0 64	3
4			Medicare Tax Payable	213		3 5 23	4
5			City Earnings Tax Payable	215		2 4 30	5
6			Health Insurance Prem. Payable	227		3 6 00	6
7			Credit Union Payable	228		4 5 00	7
8			Savings Bond Deductions Payable	261		3 7 50	8
9			Cash	111		1 8 9 1 83	9
10			Payroll for week ended Jan. 21.				10

GENERAL LEDGER

ACCOUNT: Cash   **ACCOUNT NO.** 111

DATE	ITEM	POST. REF.	DEBIT	CREDIT	BALANCE DEBIT	BALANCE CREDIT
Jan. 23		J1		1 89 1 83		

ACCOUNT: Employees Income Tax Payable   **ACCOUNT NO.** 211

DATE	ITEM	POST. REF.	DEBIT	CREDIT	BALANCE DEBIT	BALANCE CREDIT
Jan. 23		J1		2 09 00		

ACCOUNT: Social Security Tax Payable   **ACCOUNT NO.** 212

DATE	ITEM	POST. REF.	DEBIT	CREDIT	BALANCE DEBIT	BALANCE CREDIT
Jan. 23		J1		1 50 64		

ACCOUNT: Medicare Tax Payable   **ACCOUNT NO.** 213

DATE	ITEM	POST. REF.	DEBIT	CREDIT	BALANCE DEBIT	BALANCE CREDIT
Jan. 23		J1		3 5 23		

ACCOUNT: City Earnings Tax Payable   **ACCOUNT NO.** 215

DATE	ITEM	POST. REF.	DEBIT	CREDIT	BALANCE DEBIT	BALANCE CREDIT
Jan. 23		J1		2 4 30		

ACCOUNT: Health Insurance Premiums Payable   **ACCOUNT NO.** 227

DATE	ITEM	POST. REF.	DEBIT	CREDIT	BALANCE DEBIT	BALANCE CREDIT
Jan. 23		J1		3 6 00		

ACCOUNT: Credit Union Payable   **ACCOUNT NO.** 228

DATE	ITEM	POST. REF.	DEBIT	CREDIT	BALANCE DEBIT	BALANCE CREDIT
Jan. 23		J1		4 5 00		

ACCOUNT: Savings Bond Deductions Payable   **ACCOUNT NO.** 261

DATE	ITEM	POST. REF.	DEBIT	CREDIT	BALANCE DEBIT	BALANCE CREDIT
Jan. 23		J1		3 7 50		

ACCOUNT: Wages and Salaries Expense   **ACCOUNT NO.** 542

DATE	ITEM	POST. REF.	DEBIT	CREDIT	BALANCE DEBIT	BALANCE CREDIT
Jan. 23		J1	2 4 29 50			

SERIES A   EXERCISES

2 **EXERCISE 9A1 COMPUTING NET PAY**   Mary Sue Guild works for a company that pays its employees 1¹/₂ times the regular rate for all hours worked in excess of 40 per week. Guild's pay rate is $10.00 per hour. Her wages are subject to deductions for federal income tax, Social Security tax, and Medicare tax. She is married and claims 4 withholding allowances. Guild has a ¹/₂-hour lunch break during an 8¹/₂-hour day. Her time card is shown below.

Name	Mary Sue Guild					
Week Ending	March 30, 19--					
					Hours Worked	
Day	**In**	**Out**	**In**	**Out**	**Regular**	**Overtime**
M	7:57	12:05	12:35	4:33	8	
T	7:52	12:09	12:39	5:05	8	1/2
W	7:59	12:15	12:45	5:30	8	1
T	8:00	12:01	12:30	6:31	8	2
F	7:56	12:05	12:34	4:30	8	
S	8:00	10:31				2 1/2

Complete the following:
(a) _____ regular hours × $10.00 per hour $_____
(b) _____ overtime hours × $15.00 per hour $_____
(c) Total gross wages $_____
(d) Federal income tax withholding (from tax tables in
        Figure 9-4, pages 277 and 278) $_____
(e) Social Security withholding at 6.2% $_____
(f) Medicare withholding at 1.45% $_____
(g) Total withholding $_____
(h) Net pay $_____

2 **EXERCISE 9A2 COMPUTING WEEKLY GROSS PAY**   Ryan Lawrence's regular hourly rate is $15.00. He receives 1¹/₂ times the regular rate for any hours worked over 40 a week and double the rate for work on Sunday. During the past week, Lawrence worked 8 hours each day Monday through Thursday, 10 hours on Friday, and 5 hours on Sunday. Compute Lawrence's gross pay for the past week.

2 **EXERCISE 9A3 COMPUTING OVERTIME RATE OF PAY AND GROSS WEEKLY PAY**   Artis Wilson receives a regular salary of $2,600 a month and is paid 1¹/₂ times the regular hourly rate for hours worked in excess of 40 per week.
(a) Calculate Wilson's overtime rate of pay.
(b) Calculate Wilson's total gross weekly pay if he works 45 hours during the week.

2 **EXERCISE 9A4 COMPUTING FEDERAL INCOME TAX**   Using the table in Figure 9-4 on pages 277 and 278, determine the amount of federal income tax an employer should withhold weekly for employees with the following marital status, earnings, and withholding allowances.

	Marital Status	Total Weekly Earnings	Number of Allowances	Amount of Withholding
(a)	S	$327.90	2	_____
(b)	S	$410.00	1	_____
(c)	M	$438.16	5	_____
(d)	S	$518.25	0	_____
(e)	M	$603.98	6	_____

2 **EXERCISE 9A5 CALCULATING SOCIAL SECURITY AND MEDICARE TAXES**   Assume a Social Security tax rate of 6.2% is applied to maximum earnings of $61,200 and a Medicare tax rate of 1.45% is applied to all earnings. Calculate the Social Security and Medicare tax for the following situations.

Cumul. Pay Before Current Weekly Payroll	Current Gross Pay	Year-to-Date Earnings	Soc. Sec. Maximum	Amount Over Max. Soc. Sec.	Amount Subject to Soc. Sec.	Soc. Sec. Tax Withheld	Medicare Tax Withheld
$22,000	$1,200	_____	$61,200	_____	_____	_____	_____
$54,000	$4,200	_____	$61,200	_____	_____	_____	_____
$58,600	$3,925	_____	$61,200	_____	_____	_____	_____
$60,600	$4,600	_____	$61,200	_____	_____	_____	_____

4 **EXERCISE 9A6 PAYROLL TRANSACTIONS**   On December 31, the payroll register of Hamstreet Associates indicated the following information:

Wages and Salaries Expense	$8,700.00
Employees Income Tax Payable	920.00
United Way Contributions Payable	200.00
Earnings subject to Social Security tax	8,000.00

Determine the amount of Social Security and Medicare taxes to be withheld and record the journal entry for the payroll, crediting Cash for the net pay.

4 **EXERCISE 9A7 PAYROLL JOURNAL ENTRY**   Journalize the following data taken from the payroll register of University Printing as of April 15, 19--.

Regular earnings	$5,418.00
Overtime earnings	824.00
Deductions:	
Federal income tax	593.00
Social Security tax	387.00
Medicare tax	90.51
Pension plan	90.00
Health insurance premiums	225.00
United Way contributions	100.00

SERIES A PROBLEMS

2/4 **PROBLEM 9A1 GROSS PAY, DEDUCTIONS, AND NET PAY**
Donald Chin works for Northwest Supplies. His rate of pay is $8.50 per hour and he is paid 1¹/₂ times the regular rate for all hours worked in excess of 40 per week. During the last week of January of the current year he worked 48 hours. Chin is married and claims 4 withholding allowances on his W-4 form. His weekly wages are subject to the following deductions.

(a) Employees income tax (use Figure 9-4 on pages 277 and 278)
(b) Social Security tax at 6.2%
(c) Medicare tax at 1.45%
(d) Health insurance premium, $85.00
(e) Credit union, $125.00
(f) United Way contribution, $10.00

REQUIRED

1. Compute Chin's regular pay, overtime pay, gross pay, and net pay.
2. Journalize the payment of his wages for the week ended January 31, crediting Cash for the net amount.

2/3/4 **PROBLEM 9A2 PAYROLL REGISTER AND PAYROLL JOURNAL**
ENTRY   Don McCullum operates a travel agency called Don's Luxury Travel. He has five employees, all of whom are paid on a weekly basis. The travel agency uses a payroll register, individual employees earnings records, and a general journal.

Don's Luxury Travel uses a weekly federal income tax withholding table. The payroll data for each employee for the week ended March 22, 19--, are given below. Employees are paid 1¹/₂ times the regular rate for working over 40 hours a week.

Name	No. of Allowances	Marital Status	Total Hours Worked Mar. 16–22	Rate	Total Earnings Jan. 1–Mar. 15
Ali, Loren	4	M	45	$11.00	$5,280.00
Carson, Judy	1	S	40	12.00	5,760.00
Ellis, Susan	3	M	43	9.50	4,560.00
Knox, Wayne	1	S	39	11.00	5,125.50
Puglione, Jim	2	M	40	10.50	4,720.50

Social Security tax is withheld from the first $61,200 of earnings at the rate of 6.2%. Medicare tax is withheld at the rate of 1.45%, and city earnings tax at the rate of 1%, both applied to gross pay. Ali and Knox have $15 withheld and Carson and Ellis have $5 withheld for health insurance. Ali and Knox have $20 withheld to be invested in the travel agencies' credit union. Carson has $38.75 withheld and Ellis $18.75 withheld under a savings bond purchase plan.

Don's Luxury Travel's payroll is met by drawing checks on its regular bank account. The checks were issued in sequence, beginning with check no. 423.

continued

REQUIRED

1. Prepare a payroll register for Don's Luxury Travel for the week ended March 22, 19--. (In the Taxable Earnings/Unemployment compensation column, enter the same amounts as in the Social Security column.) Total the amount columns, verify the totals, and rule with single and double lines.

2. Assuming that the wages for the week ended March 22 were paid on March 24, prepare the journal entry for the payment of the payroll.

3 **PROBLEM 9A3 EMPLOYEES EARNINGS RECORD**   Don's Luxury Travel in Problem 9A2 keeps employee earnings records. Judy Carson, employee number 62, is employed as a manager in the ticket sales department. She was born on May 8, 1959, and was hired on June 1 of last year. Her Social Security number is 544-67-1283. She lives at 28 Quarry Drive, Vernon, CT 06066.

REQUIRED

For the week ended March 22, complete an employees earnings record for Judy Carson. (Insert earnings data only for the week of March 22.)

SERIES B   EXERCISES

2 **EXERCISE 9B1 COMPUTING NET PAY**   Tom Hallinan works for a company that pays its employees 1½ times the regular rate for all hours worked in excess of 40 per week. Hallinan's pay rate is $12.00 per hour. His wages are subject to deductions for federal income tax, Social Security tax, and Medicare tax. He is married and claims 5 withholding allowances. Hallinan has a ½-hour lunch break during an 8½-hour day. His time card is shown below.

Name	Tom Hallinan					
Week Ending	March 30, 19--					
					Hours Worked	
Day	In	Out	In	Out	Regular	Overtime
M	7:55	12:02	12:32	5:33	8	1
T	7:59	12:04	12:34	6:05	8	1 1/2
W	7:59	12:05	12:35	4:30	8	
T	8:00	12:01	12:30	5:01	8	1/2
F	7:58	12:02	12:31	5:33	8	1
S	7:59	9:33				1 1/2

Complete the following:

(a) _____ regular hours × $12.00 per hour $_____
(b) _____ overtime hours × $18.00 per hour $_____
(c) Total gross wages $_____

continued

    (d) Federal income tax withholding (from tax tables in
Figure 9-4, pages 277 and 278) $\$$_____

    (e) Social Security withholding at 6.2% $\$$_____

    (f) Medicare withholding at 1.45% $\$$_____

    (g) Total withholding $\$$_____

    (h) Net pay $\$$_____

2   **EXERCISE 9B2 COMPUTING WEEKLY GROSS PAY**   William Brown's regular hourly rate is $12.00. He receives 1½ times the regular rate for hours worked in excess of 40 a week and double the rate for work on Sunday. During the past week, Brown worked 8 hours each day Monday through Thursday, 11 hours on Friday, and 6 hours on Sunday. Compute Brown's gross pay for the past week.

2   **EXERCISE 9B3 COMPUTING OVERTIME RATE OF PAY AND GROSS WEEKLY PAY**   Mike Fritz receives a regular salary of $3,250 a month and is paid 1½ times the regular hourly rate for hours worked in excess of 40 per week.

    (a) Calculate Fritz's overtime rate of pay. (Compute to the nearest half cent.)

    (b) Calculate Fritz's total gross weekly pay if he works 46 hours during the week.

2   **EXERCISE 9B4 COMPUTING FEDERAL INCOME TAX**   Using the table in Figure 9-4 on pages 277 and 278, determine the amount of federal income tax an employer should withhold weekly for employees with the following marital status, earnings, and withholding allowances.

	Marital Status	Total Weekly Earnings	Number of Allowances	Amount of Withholding
(a)	M	$346.32	4	_____
(b)	M	$390.00	3	_____
(c)	S	$461.39	2	_____
(d)	M	$522.88	6	_____
(e)	S	$612.00	0	_____

2   **EXERCISE 9B5 CALCULATING SOCIAL SECURITY AND MEDICARE TAXES**   Assume a Social Security tax rate of 6.2% is applied to maximum earnings of $61,200 and a Medicare tax rate of 1.45% is applied to all earnings. Calculate the Social Security and Medicare tax for the following situations.

Cumul. Pay Before Current Weekly Payroll	Current Gross Pay	Year-to-Date Earnings	Soc. Sec. Maximum	Amount Over Max. Soc. Sec.	Amount Subject to Soc. Sec.	Soc. Sec. Tax Withheld	Medicare Tax Withheld
$31,000	$1,500	_____	$61,200	_____	_____	_____	_____
$53,000	$2,860	_____	$61,200	_____	_____	_____	_____
$58,300	$3,140	_____	$61,200	_____	_____	_____	_____
$60,600	$2,920	_____	$61,200	_____	_____	_____	_____

4   **EXERCISE 9B6 JOURNALIZING PAYROLL TRANSACTIONS**   On
November 30, the payroll register of Webster & Smith indicated the following information:

Wages and Salaries Expense	$9,400.00
Employees Income Tax Payable	985.00
United Way Contributions Payable	200.00
Earnings subject to Social Security tax	9,400.00

Determine the amount of Social Security and Medicare taxes to be withheld
and record the journal entry for the payroll, crediting Cash for the net pay.

4   **EXERCISE 9B7 PAYROLL JOURNAL ENTRY**   Journalize the following data taken from the payroll register of Himes Bakery as of June 12, 19--.

Regular earnings	$6,520.00
Overtime earnings	950.00
Deductions:	
Federal income tax	782.00
Social Security tax	463.14
Medicare tax	108.32
Pension plan	80.00
Health insurance premiums	190.00
United Way contributions	150.00

SERIES B   PROBLEMS

2/4   **PROBLEM 9B1 GROSS PAY, DEDUCTIONS, AND NET PAY**

Elyse Lin works for Columbia Industries. Her rate of pay is $9.00 per hour
and she is paid 1$\frac{1}{2}$ times the regular rate for all hours worked in excess of
40 per week. During the last week of January of the current year she
worked 46 hours. Lin is married and claims 5 withholding allowances on
her W-4 form. Her weekly wages are subject to the following deductions.

(a)   Employees income tax (use Figure 9-4 on pages 277 and 278)
(b)   Social Security tax at 6.2%
(c)   Medicare tax at 1.45%
(d)   Health insurance premium, $92.00
(e)   Credit union, $110.00
(f)   United Way contribution, $5.00

REQUIRED
1.   Compute Lin's regular pay, overtime pay, gross pay, and net pay.
2.   Journalize the payment of her wages for the week ended January 31,
crediting Cash for the net amount.

2/3/4   **PROBLEM 9B2 PAYROLL REGISTER AND PAYROLL JOURNAL
ENTRY**   Karen Jolly operates a bakery called Karen's Cupcakes. She has five
employees, all of whom are paid on a weekly basis. Karen's Cupcakes uses a
payroll register, individual employees earnings records, and a general journal.

continued

Karen's Cupcakes uses a weekly federal income tax withholding table. The payroll data for each employee for the week ended February 15, 19--, are given below. Employees are paid 1¹/₂ times the regular rate for working over 40 hours a week.

Name	No. of Allowances	Marital Status	Total Hours Worked Feb. 9–15	Rate	Total Earnings Jan. 1–Feb. 15
Barone, William	1	S	40	$10.00	$2,400.00
Hastings, Gene	4	M	45	12.00	3,360.00
Ridgeway, Ruth	3	M	46	8.75	2,935.00
Smith, Judy	4	M	42	11.00	2,745.00
Tarshis, Dolores	1	S	39	10.50	2,650.75

Social Security tax is withheld from the first $61,200 of earnings at the rate of 6.2%, Medicare tax is withheld at the rate of 1.45%, and city earnings tax at the rate of 1%, both applied to gross pay. Hastings and Smith have $35 withheld and Ridgeway and Tarshis have $15 withheld for health insurance. Ridgeway and Tarshis have $25 withheld to be invested in the bakers' credit union. Hastings has $18.75 withheld and Smith $43.75 withheld under a savings bond purchase plan.

Karen's Cupcakes payroll is met by drawing checks on its regular bank account. The checks were issued in sequence, beginning with no. 365.

REQUIRED

1. Prepare a payroll register for Karen's Cupcakes for the week ended February 15, 19--. (In the Taxable Earnings/Unemployment Compensation column, enter the same amounts as in the Social Security column.) Total the amount columns, verify the totals, and rule with single and double lines.
2. Assuming that the wages for the week ended February 15 were paid on February 17, prepare the journal entry for the payment of this payroll.

3   PROBLEM 9B3 EMPLOYEES EARNINGS RECORD   Karen's Cupcakes in Problem 9B2 keeps employees earnings records. William Barone, employee number 19, is employed as a baker in the desserts department. He was born on August 26, 1969, and was hired on October 1 of last year. His Social Security number is 342-73-4681. He lives at 30 Timber Lane, Willington, CT 06279.

REQUIRED

For the week ended February 15, complete an employees earnings record for William Barone. (Insert earnings data only for the week of February 15.)

MASTERY PROBLEM

Abigail Trenkamp owns and operates the Trenkamp Collection Agency. Listed below are the name, number of allowances claimed, marital status, information from time cards on hours worked each day, and the hourly rate of each employee. All hours worked in excess of 8 hours on weekdays are paid at $1\frac{1}{2}$ times the regular rate. All weekend hours are paid at double the regular rate.

Trenkamp uses a weekly federal income tax withholding table (see Figure 9-4 on pages 277 and 278). Social Security tax is withheld at the rate of 6.2% for the first $61,200 earned. Medicare tax is withheld at 1.45% and state income tax at 3.5%. Each employee has $5.00 withheld for health insurance. All employees use payroll deduction to the credit union for varying amounts as listed below.

Trenkamp Collection Agency
Payroll Information for the Week Ended November 18,19--

Name	Employee No.	No. of Allowances	Marital Status	Regular Hours Worked							Hourly Rate	Credit Union Deposit	Total Earnings 1/1–11/18
				S	S	M	T	W	T	F			
Berling, James	1	3	M	2	2	9	8	8	9	10	$12.00	$149.60	$24,525.00
Merz, Linda	2	4	M	4	3	8	8	8	8	11	10.00	117.00	20,480.00
Goetz, Ken	3	5	M	0	0	6	7	8	9	10	11.00	91.30	21,500.00
Menick, Judd	4	2	M	8	8	0	0	8	8	9	11.00	126.50	22,625.00
Morris, Ruth	5	3	M	0	0	8	8	8	6	8	13.00	117.05	24,730.00
Heimbrock, Jacob	6	2	S	0	0	8	8	8	8	8	30.00	154.25	60,400.00
Townsley, Sarah	7	2	M	4	0	6	6	6	6	4	9.00	83.05	21,425.00
Salzman, Ben	8	4	M	6	2	8	8	6	6	6	11.00	130.00	6,635.00
Layton, Esther	9	4	M	0	0	8	8	8	8	8	11.00	88.00	5,635.00
Thompson, David	10	5	M	0	2	10	9	7	7	10	11.00	128.90	21,635.00
Wissman, Celia	11	2	S	8	0	4	8	8	8	9	13.00	139.11	24,115.00

The Trenkamp Collection Agency follows the practice of drawing a single check for the net amount of the payroll and depositing the check in a special payroll account at the bank. Individual checks issued were numbered consecutively, beginning with no. 331.

REQUIRED

1. Prepare a payroll register for Trenkamp Collection Agency for the week ended November 18, 19--. (In the Taxable Earnings/ Unemployment Compensation column, enter $365 for Salzman and $440 for Layton. Leave this column blank for all other employees.) Total the amount columns, verify the totals, and rule with single and double lines.

2. Assuming that the wages for the week ended November 18 were paid on November 21, prepare the journal entry for the payment of this payroll.

3. The current employees earnings record for Ben Salzman is provided in the working papers. Update Salzman's earnings record to reflect the November 18 payroll. Although this information should have been entered earlier, complete the required information on the earnings record. The necessary information is provided below.

Name	Ben F. Salzman
Address	12 Windmill Lane
	Trumbull, CT 06611

continued

Employee No.	8
Gender	Male
Department	Administration
Occupation	Office Manager
Social Security No.	446-46-6321
Marital Status	Married
Allowances	4
Pay Rate	$11.00 per hour
Date of Birth	4/5/64
Date Hired	7/22/--

10

Payroll Accounting: Employer Taxes and Reports

Careful study of this chapter should enable you to:

LO1 Describe and calculate employer payroll taxes.

LO2 Account for employer payroll taxes expense.

LO3 Describe employer reporting and payment responsibilities.

LO4 Describe and account for workers' compensation insurance.

You have worked the same job for nine months at $6 an hour and think you deserve a raise. When you approach your boss, you are told the business can't afford it. Besides, the boss says you already cost the business *more than* $6 an hour. How can this be? You know that in your paychecks you always take home *less than* $6 an hour. Is your boss being honest with you? To answer these questions, you need to know about employer payroll accounting.

The taxes we discussed in Chapter 9 had one thing in common—they all were levied on the employee. The employer withheld them from employees' earnings and paid them to the government. They did not add anything to the employer's payroll expenses.

In this chapter, we will examine several taxes that are imposed directly on the employer. All of these taxes represent additional payroll expenses.

EMPLOYER PAYROLL TAXES

LO1   Describe and calculate employer payroll taxes.

Most employers must pay FICA taxes, FUTA (Federal Unemployment Tax Act) taxes, and SUTA (State Unemployment Tax) taxes.

Employer FICA Taxes

Employer FICA taxes are levied on employers at the same rates and on the same earnings bases as the employee FICA taxes. As explained in Chapter 9, for 1995 the Social Security component is 6.2% on maximum earnings of $61,200 for each employee. The Medicare component is 1.45% on all earnings.

 LEARNING KEY   Use the information contained in the payroll register to compute employer payroll taxes.

The payroll register we saw in Chapter 9 is a key source of information for computing employer payroll taxes. That payroll register is reproduced in Figure 10-1. The Taxable Earnings Social Security column shows that $4,835 of employee earnings were subject to Social Security tax for the pay period. The employer's Social Security tax on these earnings is computed as follows:

Social Security Taxable Earnings	x	Tax Rate	=	Tax
$4,835		6.2%		$299.77

The Medicare tax applies to the total earnings of $5,435. The employer's Medicare tax on these earnings is computed as follows:

Total Earnings	x	Tax Rate	=	Tax
$5,435		1.45%		$78.81

These amounts plus the employees' Social Security and Medicare taxes withheld must be paid by the employer to the Internal Revenue Service (IRS).

Self-Employment Tax

Individuals who own and run their own business are considered self-employed. These individuals can be viewed as both employer and employee. They do not receive salary or wages from the business, but they do have earnings in the form of the business net income. **Self-employment income** is the net income of a trade or business run by an individual.

FIGURE 10-1 Payroll Register (Left Half)

PAYROLL

	NAME	ALLOW-ANCES	MARITAL STATUS	EARNINGS				TAXABLE EARNINGS		
				REGULAR	OVERTIME	TOTAL	CUMULATIVE TOTAL	UNEMPLOY. COMPENSATION	SOCIAL SECURITY	
1	Cadrain, Sarah	4	M	1 1 0 0 00	1 6 0 00	1 2 6 0 00	61 8 0 0 00		6 6 0 00	1
2	Guder, James	1	S	8 6 0 00	4 0 00	9 0 0 00	43 4 0 0 00		9 0 0 00	2
3	Istone, Ken	6	M	5 4 5 00		5 4 5 00	27 0 2 5 00		5 4 5 00	3
4	Kuzmik, Helen	2	M	4 8 0 00	2 9 4 00	7 7 4 00	31 0 0 0 00		7 7 4 00	4
5	Lee, Hoseoup	3	M	4 4 0 00		4 4 0 00	22 3 4 0 00		4 4 0 00	5
6	Swaney, Linda	2	S	5 2 8 00	1 9 8 00	7 2 6 00	27 5 0 0 00		7 2 6 00	6
7	Tucci, Paul	5	M	4 9 0 00		4 9 0 00	25 0 5 0 00		4 9 0 00	7
8	Wiles, Harry	1	S	3 0 0 00		3 0 0 00	6 3 0 0 00	3 0 0 00	3 0 0 00	8
9				4 7 4 3 00	6 9 2 00	5 4 3 5 00	244 4 1 5 00	3 0 0 00	4 8 3 5 00	9

Time cards, pay rates

Prior period total + current period earnings

Current below $7,000 cumul. total

Current below $61,200 cumul. total

Currently, persons earning self-employment income of $400 or more must pay a **self-employment tax**. Self-employment tax is a contribution to the FICA program. The tax rates are about double the Social Security and Medicare rates. They are applied to the same income bases as are used for the Social Security and Medicare taxes.

One half of the self-employment tax is a personal expense of the owner of the business. The other half is similar to the employer Social Security and Medicare taxes paid for each employee. This portion of the tax is considered a business expense and is debited to Self-Employment Tax.

Employer's FUTA Tax

The **FUTA (Federal Unemployment Tax Act) tax** is levied only on employers. It is not deducted from employees' earnings. The purpose of this tax is to raise funds to administer the combined federal/state unemployment compensation program. The maximum amount of earnings subject to the FUTA tax and the tax rate can be changed by Congress. The current rate is 6.2% applied to maximum earnings of $7,000 for each employee. But, employers are allowed a credit of up to 5.4% for participation in state unemployment programs. Thus, the effective federal rate is commonly 0.8%.

Gross FUTA rate	6.2%
Credit for SUTA (state unemployment taxes)	5.4%
Net FUTA rate	0.8%

FIGURE 10-1   Payroll Register (Right Half)

REGISTER—WEEK ENDED 12/19/--

	FEDERAL INCOME TAX	SOCIAL SEC. TAX	MEDICARE TAX	HEALTH INSURANCE	UNITED WAY	OTHER	TOTAL	NET PAY	CHECK NO.	
1	174 00	40 92	18 27				233 19	1026 81	409	1
2	171 00	55 80	13 05		20 00		259 85	640 15	410	2
3	20 00	33 79	7 90	10 00			71 69	473 31	411	3
4	83 00	47 99	11 22	13 00	20 00		175 21	598 79	412	4
5	27 00	27 28	6 38	13 00			73 66	366 34	413	5
6	107 00	45 01	10 53				162 54	563 46	414	6
7	20 00	30 38	7 11	10 00			67 49	422 51	415	7
8	31 00	18 60	4 35				53 95	246 05	416	8
9	633 00	299 77	78 81	46 00	40 00		1097 58	4337 42		9

Federal Income Tax: Withholding Tax Table
Social Sec. Tax: 6.2% x Social Security taxable earnings
Medicare Tax: 1.45% x total earnings
Health Insurance / United Way: Specific employer–employee agreements

To illustrate the computation of the FUTA tax, refer to Figure 10-1. The Taxable Earnings Unemployment Compensation column shows that only $300 of employee earnings were subject to the FUTA tax. This amount is so low because the payroll period is late in the calendar year (December 19, 19--). It is common for most employees to exceed the $7,000 earnings limit by this time. The FUTA tax is computed as shown in Figure 10-2.

FIGURE 10-2   Computation of FUTA Tax

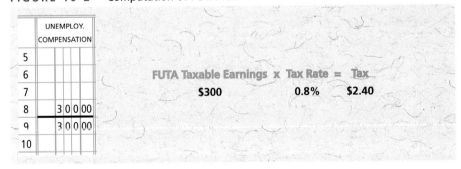

	UNEMPLOY. COMPENSATION
5	
6	
7	
8	300 00
9	300 00
10	

FUTA Taxable Earnings x Tax Rate = Tax
$300   0.8% $2.40

Employer's State Unemployment Tax

The **state unemployment tax (SUTA)** is also levied only on employers in most states. The purpose of this tax is to raise funds to pay unemployment benefits. Tax rates and unemployment benefits vary among the states. The most common rate is 5.4% applied to maximum earnings of $7,000 for each

Tax Cheats Worldwide

Each year the U.S. Government collects billions of dollars from tax-payers—individuals and corporations. For tax year 1994 the Internal Revenue Service collected an estimated $555 billion dollars. It is also estimated that $150 billion will not be collected because of cheating.

There is no profile of the typical tax cheat, but one thing that most cheats have in common is the opportunity to cheat. Full-time salaried employees with only one employer have much less opportunity to cheat than individuals who are self-employed. It is relatively easy for independent contractors, sole proprietors, and others who are self-employed to fail to report a portion of their income.

Many cheaters are not caught, but those who are face back taxes, interest on back taxes, fines and penalties, legal fees, and prison. In an effort to catch cheaters and collect additional taxes, the budget for audits in 1995 allows the IRS to target an additional half million returns.

The United States is not the only country where individuals and companies cheat on their taxes. In Argentina the government recently got tough with corporate tax cheats. Tax officials publicly named 150 large- and medium-sized companies suspected of underpaying taxes. The companies were given one week to pay their tax debt or face prosecution. It is estimated that these 150 companies underpaid their taxes by approximately $1 billion.

Source: Jonathan Friedland, "Argentina's Tax Collector Names Names," *The Wall Street Journal*, April 13, 1995.
Teresa Tritch, "The $150 Billion Tax Cheats," *Money*, April 1995.

employee. Most states have a **merit-rating system** to encourage employers to provide regular employment to workers. If an employer has very few former employees receiving unemployment compensation, the employer qualifies for a lower state unemployment tax rate. If an employer qualifies for a lower state rate, the full credit of 5.4% would still be allowed in computing the federal unemployment tax due.

Refer again to the payroll register in Figure 10-1. As we saw with the FUTA tax, only $300 of employee earnings for this pay period are subject to the state unemployment tax. The tax is computed as shown in Figure 10-3.

FIGURE 10-3   Computation of SUTA Tax

	UNEMPLOY. COMPENSATION
5	
6	
7	
8	3 0 0 00
9	3 0 0 00
10	

State Unemployment Taxable Earnings × Tax Rate = Tax

$300   5.4% $16.20

ACCOUNTING FOR EMPLOYER PAYROLL TAXES

LO2   Account for employer payroll taxes expense.

Now that we have computed the employer payroll taxes, we need to journalize them. It is common to debit all employer payroll taxes to a single account—Payroll Taxes Expense. However, we usually credit separate liability accounts for Social Security, Medicare, FUTA, and SUTA taxes payable.

Journalizing Employer Payroll Taxes

The employer payroll taxes computed in the previous section can be summarized as follows:

Employer's Social Security tax	$299.77
Employer's Medicare tax	78.81
FUTA tax	2.40
SUTA tax	16.20
Total employer payroll taxes	$397.18

These amounts provide the basis for the following journal entry:

5	Dec. 19	Payroll Taxes Expense		3 9 7 18			5
6		Social Security Tax Payable			2 9 9 77		6
7		Medicare Tax Payable			7 8 81		7
8		FUTA Tax Payable			2 40		8
9		SUTA Tax Payable			1 6 20		9
10		Employer payroll taxes for					10
11		week ended December 19					11

The steps needed to prepare this journal entry for employer payroll taxes are as follows.

STEP 1   Obtain the taxable earnings amounts from the Taxable Earnings columns of the payroll register. In this case, Social Security taxable earnings were $4,835; unemployment compensation taxable earnings were $300.

STEP 2   Compute the amount of employer Social Security tax by multiplying the total Social Security taxable earnings by 6.2%.

STEP 3   Compute the amount of Medicare tax by multiplying total earnings by 1.45%.

STEP 4   Compute the amount of FUTA tax by multiplying the total unemployment taxable earnings by 0.8%.

STEP 5   Compute the amount of SUTA tax by multiplying the total unemployment taxable earnings by 5.4%.

STEP 6   Prepare the appropriate journal entry using the amounts computed in steps 2 through 5.

To understand the journal entry for employer payroll taxes, let's examine the accounts involved.

Payroll Taxes Expense

The Social Security, Medicare, FUTA, and SUTA taxes imposed on the employer are expenses of doing business. Each of the employer taxes is debited to Payroll Taxes Expense.

Payroll Taxes Expense

Debit	Credit
Social Security, Medicare, FUTA, and SUTA taxes imposed on the employer	

Social Security and Medicare Taxes Payable

These are the same liability accounts used in Chapter 9 to record the Social Security and Medicare taxes withheld from employees' earnings. The accounts are credited to enter the Social Security and Medicare taxes imposed on the employer. They are debited when the taxes are paid to the IRS. When all of the Social Security and Medicare taxes have been paid, the accounts will have zero balances.

 LEARNING KEY Social Security Tax Payable and Medicare Tax Payable for employer FICA taxes are the same liability accounts used to record the FICA taxes withheld from employees' earnings.

Social Security Tax Payable

Debit	Credit
payment of Social Security tax	Social Security taxes (1) withheld from employees' earnings and (2) imposed on the employer

Medicare Tax Payable

Debit	Credit
payment of Medicare tax	Medicare taxes (1) withheld from employees' earnings and (2) imposed on the employer

FUTA Tax Payable

A separate liability account entitled FUTA Tax Payable is kept for the employer's FUTA tax. This account is credited for the tax imposed on employers under the Federal Unemployment Tax Act. The account is debited when this tax is paid. When all of the FUTA taxes have been paid, the account will have a zero balance.

FUTA Tax Payable

Debit	Credit
payment of FUTA tax	FUTA tax imposed on the employer

SUTA Tax Payable

A separate liability account entitled SUTA Tax Payable is kept for the state unemployment tax. This account is credited for the tax imposed on employers under the state unemployment compensation laws. The account is debited when these taxes are paid. When all of the state unemployment taxes have been paid, the account will have a zero balance.

SUTA Tax Payable

Debit	Credit
state unemployment tax paid	state unemployment tax imposed on the employer

Total Payroll Cost of an Employee

It is interesting to note what it really costs to employ a person. The employer must, of course, pay the gross wages of an employee. In addition, the employer must pay payroll taxes on employee earnings up to certain dollar limits.

To illustrate, assume that an employee earns $26,000 a year. The total cost of this employee to the employer is calculated as follows.

Gross wages	$26,000
Employer Social Security tax (6.2% of $26,000)	1,612
Employer Medicare tax (1.45% of $26,000)	377
SUTA tax (5.4% of $7,000)	378
FUTA tax (0.8% of $7,000)	56
	$28,423

Thus, the total payroll cost of employing a person whose stated compensation is $26,000 is $28,423. Employer payroll taxes clearly are a significant cost of doing business.

REPORTING AND PAYMENT RESPONSIBILITIES

LO3   Describe employer reporting and payment responsibilities.

Employer payroll reporting and payment responsibilities fall into five areas:

1. Federal income tax withholding and Social Security and Medicare taxes
2. FUTA taxes
3. SUTA taxes
4. Employee Wage and Tax Statement (Form W-2)
5. Summary of employee wages and taxes

Federal Income Tax Withholding and Social Security and Medicare Taxes

Three important aspects of employer reporting and payment responsibilities for federal income tax withholding and Social Security and Medicare taxes are:

1. Determining when payments are due
2. Use of Form 8109, Federal Tax Deposit Coupon
3. Use of Form 941, Employer's Quarterly Federal Tax Return

When Payments Are Due. The date by which federal income tax withholding and Social Security and Medicare taxes must be paid depends on the amount of these taxes. Figure 10-4 summarizes the deposit rules stated in *Circular E—Employer's Tax Guide.* In general, the larger the amount that needs to be deposited, the more frequently payments must be made. For simplicity, we will assume that deposits must be made 15 days after the end of each month.

FIGURE 10-4   Summary of Deposit Rules

DEPOSIT AMOUNT	DEPOSIT DUE
1. Less than $500 at the end of the current quarter	1. Pay with Form 941 at end of the month following end of the quarter
2. $500 or more at the end of the current quarter and $50,000 or less in total during the lookback period*	2. Deposit 15 days after end of the month
3. $500 or more at the end of the current quarter and more than $50,000 in total during the lookback period*	3. Deposit every other Wednesday or Friday, depending on the day of the week payroll payments are made
4. $100,000 or more on any day during current quarter	4. Deposit by the end of the next banking day

*The lookback period is the four quarters beginning July 1, two years ago, and ending June 30, one year ago.

Form 8109. Deposits are made at a Federal Reserve Bank or other authorized commercial bank using Form 8109, Federal Tax Deposit Coupon (Figure 10-5). The **Employer Identification Number (EIN)** shown on this

FIGURE 10-5   Federal Tax Deposit Coupon (Form 8109)

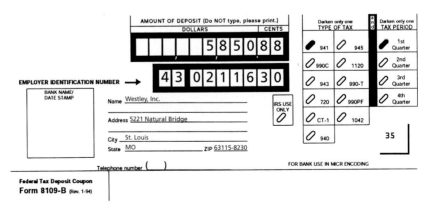

form is obtained by the employer from the IRS. This number identifies the employer and must be shown on all payroll forms and reports filed with the IRS.

The $5,850.88 deposit shown in Figure 10-5 for Westly was for the following taxes:

Employees' income tax withheld from wages		$2,526.80
Social Security tax:		
Withheld from employees' wages	$1,346.24	
Imposed on employer	1,346.24	2,692.48
Medicare tax:		
Withheld from employees' wages	$ 315.80	
Imposed on employer	315.80	631.60
Amount of check		$5,850.88

The journal entry for this deposit would be:

5		Employees Income Tax Payable	2 5 2 6 80	5
6		Social Security Tax Payable	2 6 9 2 48	6
7		Medicare Tax Payable	6 3 1 60	7
8		Cash	5 8 5 0 88	8
9		Deposit of employee federal		9
10		income tax and Social Security		10
11		and Medicare taxes		11

Paying a Worldwide Work Force

 As companies enter the global marketplace they face new opportunities and challenges. Employee compensation is one of these challenges.

Just getting payroll checks to employees requires developing and implementing new procedures. One of the first things to consider is what currency will be used for payment. Employees who live and work in Japan during times when the U.S. dollar is falling against the Japanese yen will lose buying power if they are being paid in dollars. On the other hand, employees living and working in Mexico when the value of the peso is weak gain buying power if they are paid in dollars.

It is also important to decide exactly how wages are going to get from the company's bank to the employee. Waiting for international mail is not usually a good option. Electronic funds transfer is often a better choice.

Health insurance is often part of a compensation package. A health maintenance organization (HMO) that provides health care for local employees through a network of local physicians and hospitals is not appropriate for employees living halfway around the world.

These are not the only challenges to compensating employees in a global economy. Most companies seek advice from accounting and legal professionals who specialize in employee compensation.

Form 941.   Form 941, Employer's Quarterly Federal Tax Return, must be filed with the IRS at the end of the month following each calendar quarter. This form is a report of employee federal income tax and Social Security and Medicare tax withholding and employer Social Security and Medicare taxes for the quarter. A completed form for Westly for the first quarter of the calendar year is shown in Figure 10-6. Instructions for completing the form are provided with the form and in *Circular E*.

FUTA Taxes

Federal unemployment taxes must be calculated on a quarterly basis. If the accumulated liability exceeds $100, the total must be paid to a Federal Reserve Bank or other authorized commercial bank. The total is due by the end of the month following the close of the quarter. If the liability is $100 or less, no deposit is necessary. The amount is simply added to the amount to be deposited for the next quarter. FUTA taxes are deposited using Form 8109 (Figure 10-5).

Assume that Westly's accumulated FUTA tax liability for the first quarter of the calendar year is $408. Westly would use Form 8109 to deposit this amount on April 30. The journal entry for this transaction would be as follows:

15	19-- Apr.	30	FUTA Tax Payable			4 0 8 00			15
16			Cash				4 0 8 00		16
17			Paid federal unemployment						17
18			tax						18

Form 940.   In addition to making quarterly deposits, employers are required to file an annual report of federal unemployment tax on Form 940. This form must be filed with the IRS by January 31 following the end of the calendar year. Figure 10-7 shows a completed Form 940 for Westly. Instructions for completing the form are provided with the form and in *Circular E*.

SUTA Taxes

Deposit rules and forms for state unemployment taxes vary among the states. Deposits usually are required on a quarterly basis. Assume that Westly's accumulated state unemployment liability for the first quarter of the calendar year is $2,754. The journal entry for the deposit of this amount with the state on April 30 would be:

15	19-- Apr.	30	SUTA Tax Payable			2 7 5 4 00			15
16			Cash				2 7 5 4 00		16
17			Paid state unemployment tax						17

FIGURE 10-6 Employer's Quarterly Federal Tax Return (Form 941)

Form **941** (Rev. April 1994) Department of the Treasury Internal Revenue Service

4141

Employer's Quarterly Federal Tax Return

▶ See separate instructions for information on completing this return.

Please type or print.

Enter state code for state in which deposits made ▶ M O (see page 2 of instructions).

Name (as distinguished from trade name)	Date quarter ended March 30,19--	OMB No. 1545-0029
Trade name, if any Westley, Inc.	Employer identification number 43-0211630	T FF FD
Address (number and street) 5221 Natural Bridge	City, state, and ZIP code St. Louis, Mo 63115-8230	FP I T

If address is different from prior return, check here ▶ ☐ — IRS Use

If you do not have to file returns in the future, check here ▶ ☐ and enter date final wages paid ▶

If you are a seasonal employer, see **Seasonal employers** on page 2 and check here (see instructions) ▶ ☐

Line	Description			Amount
1	Number of employees (except household) employed in the pay period that includes March 12th ▶			8
2	Total wages and tips subject to withholding, plus other compensation			65,160 00
3	Total income tax withheld from wages, tips, and sick pay			7,595 80
4	Adjustment of withheld income tax for preceding quarters of calendar year			0
5	Adjusted total of income tax withheld (line 3 as adjusted by line 4—see instructions)			7,595 80
6a	Taxable social security wages	$ 65,160 00	× 12.4% (.124) =	8,079 84
6b	Taxable social security tips	$ 0	× 12.4% (.124) =	0
7	Taxable Medicare wages and tips	$ 65,160 00	× 2.9% (.029) =	1,889 64
8	Total social security and Medicare taxes (add lines 6a, 6b, and 7). Check here if wages are not subject to social security and/or Medicare tax ▶ ☐			9,969 48
9	Adjustment of social security and Medicare taxes (see instructions for required explanation) Sick Pay $ ____ ± Fractions of Cents $ ____ ± Other $ ____ =			0
10	Adjusted total of social security and Medicare taxes (line 8 as adjusted by line 9—see instructions)			9,969 48
11	**Total taxes** (add lines 5 and 10)			17,565 28
12	Advance earned income credit (EIC) payments made to employees, if any			
13	Net taxes (subtract line 12 from line 11). **This should equal line 17, column (d) below** (or line D of Schedule B (Form 941))			17,565 28
14	Total deposits for quarter, including overpayment applied from a prior quarter			17,565 28
15	**Balance due** (subtract line 14 from line 13). Pay to Internal Revenue Service			
16	**Overpayment,** if line 14 is more than line 13, enter excess here ▶ $ ____ and check if to be: ☐ Applied to next return OR ☐ Refunded.			

- **All filers.** If line 13 is less than $500, you need not complete line 17 or Schedule B.
- **Semiweekly depositors:** Complete Schedule B and check here ▶ ☐
- **Monthly depositors:** Complete line 17, columns (a) through (d) and check here ▶ ☒

17 Monthly Summary of Federal Tax Liability.

(a) First month liability	(b) Second month liability	(c) Third month liability	(d) Total liability for quarter
5,850.88	5,690.77	6,023.63	17,565.28

Sign Here Under penalties of perjury, I declare that I have examined this return, including accompanying schedules and statements, and to the best of my knowledge and belief, it is true, correct, and complete.

Signature ▶ William P. Jones Print Your Name and Title ▶ Treasurer Date ▶ 4/30/--

For Paperwork Reduction Act Notice, see page 1 of separate instructions. Cat. No. 17001Z Form **941** (Rev. 4-94)

Printed on recycled paper

FIGURE 10-7 Employer's Annual Federal Unemployment (FUTA) Tax Return (Form 940)

Form **940**

Department of the Treasury
Internal Revenue Service

Employer's Annual Federal Unemployment (FUTA) Tax Return

▶ **For Paperwork Reduction Act Notice, see separate instructions.**

OMB No. 1545-0028

1994

T	
FF	
FD	
FP	
I	
T	

Name (as distinguished from trade name) — Calendar year

Trade name, if any
Westley, Inc.

Address and ZIP code
5221 Natural Bridge
St. Louis, MO 63115-8230

Employer identification number
43 0211630

A Are you required to pay unemployment contributions to only one state? (If no, skip questions B and C.) . . ☒ **Yes** ☐ **No**

B Did you pay all state unemployment contributions by January 31, 1995? (If a 0% experience rate is granted, check "Yes.") (If no, skip question C.) . . . ☒ **Yes** ☐ **No**

C Were all wages that were taxable for FUTA tax also taxable for your state's unemployment tax? . . . ☒ **Yes** ☐ **No**

If you answered "No" to any of these questions, you must file Form 940. If you answered "Yes" to all the questions, you may file Form 940-EZ, which is a simplified version of Form 940. You can get Form 940-EZ by calling 1-800-TAX-FORM (1-800-829-3676).

If you will not have to file returns in the future, check here, complete, and sign the return . . . ▶ ☐
If this is an Amended Return, check here . . . ▶ ☐

Computation of Taxable Wages

		Amount paid		
1	Total payments (including exempt payments) during the calendar year for services of employees		1	258,954 00
2	Exempt payments. (Explain each exemption shown, attach additional sheets if necessary.) ▶	2		
3	Payments of more than $7,000 for services. Enter only amounts over the first $7,000 paid to each employee. Do not include payments from line 2. The $7,000 amount is the Federal wage base. Your state wage base may be different. **Do not use the state wage limitation**	3 203,254 00		
4	Total exempt payments (add lines 2 and 3) . . .		4	203,254 00
5	**Total taxable wages** (subtract line 4 from line 1) . . . ▶		5	55,700 00

Be sure to complete both sides of this return and sign in the space provided on the back. Cat. No. 11234O Form **940** (1994)

Employee Wage and Tax Statement

By January 31 of each year, employers must furnish each employee with a Wage and Tax Statement, Form W-2 (Figure 10-8). This form shows the total amount of wages paid to the employee and the amounts of taxes withheld during the preceding tax year. The employee's earnings record contains the information needed to complete this form.

Multiple copies of Form W-2 are needed for the following purposes:

- Copy A—Employer sends to Social Security Administration.
- Copy B—Employee attaches to federal income tax return.
- Copy C—Employee retains for personal records.

FIGURE 10-7 (continued)   Employer's Annual Federal Unemployment (FUTA) Tax Return (Form 940)

Form 940 (1994)   Page **2**

███████   **Tax Due or Refund**

1	Gross FUTA tax. Multiply the wages in Part I, line 5, by .062	**1**	3,453 40
2	Maximum credit. Multiply the wages in Part I, line 5, by .054 . . . | **2** | 3,007 80		

3   **Computation of tentative credit (Note:** *All taxpayers must complete the applicable columns.*)

(a) Name of state	(b) State reporting number(s) as shown on employer's state contribution returns	(c) Taxable payroll (as defined in state act)	(d) State experience rate period From	(d) State experience rate period To	(e) State experience rate	(f) Contributions if rate had been 5.4% (col. (c) x .054)	(g) Contributions payable at experience rate (col. (c) x col. (e))	(h) Additional credit (col. (f) minus col.(g)). If 0 or less, enter -0-.	(i) Contributions actually paid to state
MO	36112	55,700.00	1/1/--	12/31/--	.054	3,007.80	3,007.80	-0-	3,007.80
3a Totals . . . ▶		55,700.00							

3b	**Total tentative credit** (add line 3a, columns (h) and (i) only—see instructions for limitations on late payments) ▶		3,007 80
4	██		
5			
6	**Credit:** Enter the smaller of the amount in Part II, line 2, or line 3b	**6**	3,007 80
7	**Total FUTA tax** (subtract line 6 from line 1)	**7**	445 60
8	Total FUTA tax deposited for the year, including any overpayment applied from a prior year . .	**8**	427 60
9	**Balance due** (subtract line 8 from line 7). This should be $100 or less. Pay to the Internal Revenue Service. See page 3 of the Instructions for Form 940 for details . . . . ▶	**9**	18 00
10	**Overpayment** (subtract line 7 from line 8). Check if it is to be: ☐ **Applied to next return,** or ☐ **Refunded** . . . . ▶	**10**	

███████   **Record of Quarterly Federal Unemployment Tax Liability** (Do not include state liability)

Quarter	First	Second	Third	Fourth	Total for year
Liability for quarter	408.00	26.00	5.60	6.00	445.60

Under penalties of perjury, I declare that I have examined this return, including accompanying schedules and statements, and to the best of my knowledge and belief, it is true, correct, and complete, and that no part of any payment made to a state unemployment fund claimed as a credit was or is to be deducted from the payments to employees.

Signature ▶ *William P. Jones*   Title (Owner, etc.) ▶ *Treasurer*   Date ▶ *1/31/--*

- Copy D—Employer retains for business records.
- Copy 1—Employer sends to state or local tax department.
- Copy 2—Employee attaches to state or local income tax return.

Summary of Employee Wages and Taxes

Employers send Form W-3, Transmittal of Wage and Tax Statements (Figure 10-9), with Copy A of Forms W-2 to the Social Security Administration. Form W-3 must be filed by the last day of February following the end of each tax year. This form summarizes the employee earnings and tax information presented on Forms W-2 for the year. Information needed to complete Form W-3 is contained in the employees earnings records.

Summary of Reports and Payments

Keeping track of the many payroll reports, deposits, and due dates can be a challenge for an employer. Figure 10-10 shows a calendar that highlights the

FIGURE 10-8   Wage and Tax Statement (Form W-2)

a Control number		OMB No. 1545-0008		
b Employer's identification number 43-0211630		1 Wages, tips, other compensation 27,645.00	2 Federal income tax withheld 1,088.00	
c Employer's name, address, and ZIP code Westley, Inc. 5221 Natural Bridge St. Louis, MO 63115-8230		3 Social security wages 27,645.00	4 Social security tax withheld 1,713.99	
		5 Medicare wages and tips 27,645.00	6 Medicare tax withheld 400.85	
		7 Social security tips	8 Allocated tips	
d Employee's social security number 393-58-8194		9 Advance EIC payment	10 Dependent care benefits	
e Employee's name, address, and ZIP code Ken M. Istone 1546 Swallow Dr. St. Louis, MO 63144-4752		11 Nonqualified plans	12 Benefits included in box 1	
		13 See Instrs. for Form W-2	14 Other	
		15 Statutory employee ☐ Deceased ☐ Pension plan ☐ Legal rep. ☐ 942 emp. ☐ Subtotal ☐ Deferred compensation ☐		

16 State	Employer's state I.D. No.	17 State wages, tips, etc.	18 State income tax	19 Locality name	20 Local wages, tips, etc.	21 Local income tax

Department of the Treasury—Internal Revenue Service

Form **W-2** Wage and Tax Statement **1994**

Copy D For Employer

For Paperwork Reduction Act Notice, see separate instructions.

FIGURE 10-9   Transmittal of Wage and Tax Statements (Form W-3)

a Control number		OMB No. 1545-0008		
b Kind of Payer	941 ☒ Military ☐ 943 ☐ CT-1 ☐ 942 ☐ Medicare govt. emp. ☐	1 Wages, tips, other compensation 249,815.00	2 Federal income tax withheld 29,100.00	
		3 Social security wages 247,955.00	4 Social security tax withheld 15,373.21	
c Total number of statements 8	d Establishment number	5 Medicare wages and tips 249,815.00	6 Medicare tax withheld 3,622.32	
e Employer's identification number 43-0211630		7 Social security tips	8 Allocated tips	
f Employer's name Westley, Inc.		9 Advance EIC payments	10 Dependent care benefits	
5221 Natural Bridge St. Louis, MO 63115-8230 YOUR COPY		11 Nonqualified plans	12 Deferred compensation	
		13 Adjusted total social security wages and tips 247,955.00		
		14 Adjusted total Medicare wages and tips 249,815.00		
g Employer's address and ZIP code				
h Other EIN used this year		15 Income tax withheld by third-party payer		
i Employer's state I.D. No. 21686001				

Form **W-3** Transmittal of Wage and Tax Statements **1994**   Department of the Treasury Internal Revenue Service

due dates for the various reports and deposits. The calendar assumes the following for an employer:

1. Undeposited FIT (federal income tax) and Social Security and Medicare taxes of $500 at the end of each quarter and less than $50,000 during the lookback period.

FIGURE 10-10   Payroll Calendar

| January |
| S M T W T F S |
| 1 2 3 4 |
| 5 6 7 8 9 10 11 |
| 12 13 14 15 16 17 18 |
| 19 20 21 22 23 24 25 |
| 26 27 28 29 30 31 |

| February |
| S M T W T F S |
| 1 |
| 2 3 4 5 6 7 8 |
| 9 10 11 12 13 14 15 |
| 16 17 18 19 20 21 22 |
| 23 24 25 26 27 28 29 |

| March |
| S M T W T F S |
| 1 2 3 4 5 6 7 |
| 8 9 10 11 12 13 14 |
| 15 16 17 18 19 20 21 |
| 22 23 24 25 26 27 28 |
| 29 30 31 |

| April |
| S M T W T F S |
| 1 2 3 4 |
| 5 6 7 8 9 10 11 |
| 12 13 14 15 16 17 18 |
| 19 20 21 22 23 24 25 |
| 26 27 28 29 30 |

| May |
| S M T W T F S |
| 1 2 |
| 3 4 5 6 7 8 9 |
| 10 11 12 13 14 15 16 |
| 17 18 19 20 21 22 23 |
| 24 25 26 27 28 29 30 |
| 31 |

| June |
| S M T W T F S |
| 1 2 3 4 5 6 |
| 7 8 9 10 11 12 13 |
| 14 15 16 17 18 19 20 |
| 21 22 23 24 25 26 27 |
| 28 29 30 |

| July |
| S M T W T F S |
| 1 2 3 4 |
| 5 6 7 8 9 10 11 |
| 12 13 14 15 16 17 18 |
| 19 20 21 22 23 24 25 |
| 26 27 28 29 30 31 |

| August |
| S M T W T F S |
| 1 |
| 2 3 4 5 6 7 8 |
| 9 10 11 12 13 14 15 |
| 16 17 18 19 20 21 22 |
| 23 24 25 26 27 28 29 |
| 30 31 |

| September |
| S M T W T F S |
| 1 2 3 4 5 |
| 6 7 8 9 10 11 12 |
| 13 14 15 16 17 18 19 |
| 20 21 22 23 24 25 26 |
| 27 28 29 30 |

| October |
| S M T W T F S |
| 1 2 3 |
| 4 5 6 7 8 9 10 |
| 11 12 13 14 15 16 17 |
| 18 19 20 21 22 23 24 |
| 25 26 27 28 29 30 31 |

| November |
| S M T W T F S |
| 1 2 3 4 5 6 7 |
| 8 9 10 11 12 13 14 |
| 15 16 17 18 19 20 21 |
| 22 23 24 25 26 27 28 |
| 29 30 |

| December |
| S M T W T F S |
| 1 2 3 4 5 |
| 6 7 8 9 10 11 12 |
| 13 14 15 16 17 18 19 |
| 20 21 22 23 24 25 26 |
| 27 28 29 30 31 |

File Forms 940, 941, state unemployment tax report, and send W-2 to employees.

File Form W-3 with Copy A of W-2s.

File Form 941 and state unemployment tax report.

Deposit FIT and Social Security and Medicare taxes from previous month.

2. Undeposited FUTA taxes of more than $100 at the end of each quarter.
3. SUTA taxes deposited quarterly.

WORKERS' COMPENSATION INSURANCE

LO4   Describe and account for workers' compensation insurance.

Most states require employers to carry workers' compensation insurance. **Workers' compensation insurance** provides insurance for employees who suffer a job-related illness or injury.

The employer usually pays the entire cost of workers' compensation insurance. The cost of the insurance depends on the number of employees, riskiness of the job, and the company's accident history. For example, the insurance premium for workers in a chemical plant could be higher than that for office workers. Employers generally can obtain the insurance either from the state in which they operate or from a private insurance company.

The employer usually pays the premium at the beginning of the year, based on the estimated payroll for the year. At the end of the year, after the actual amount of payroll is known, an adjustment is made. If the employer has overpaid, a credit is received from the state or insurance company. If the employer has underpaid, an additional premium is paid.

To illustrate the accounting for workers' compensation insurance, assume that Lockwood Co. expects its payroll for the year to be $210,000. If Lockwood's insurance premium rate is 0.2%, its payment for workers' compensation insurance at the beginning of the year would be $420:

Estimated Payroll x Rate = Estimated Insurance Premium

$210,000   0.2% $420

The journal entry for the payment of this $420 premium would be:

7		Workers' Compensation Insur. Exp.		4 2 0 00		7
8		Cash			4 2 0 00	8
9		Paid insurance premium				9

If Lockwood's actual payroll for the year is $220,000, Lockwood would owe an additional premium of $20 at year end:

Actual Payroll   x   Rate = Insurance Premium

$220,000   0.2% $440.00
Less estimated premium paid   420.00
Additional premium due $ 20.00

The adjusting entry at year end for this additional expense would be:

11		Workers' Compensation Insur. Exp.		2 0 00		11
12		Workers' Compensation Insur. Pay.			2 0 00	12
13		Adjustment for insurance				13
14		premium				14

In T account form, the total Workers' Compensation Insurance Expense of $440.00 would look like this.

Workers' Compensation Insurance Expense

Debit	Credit
420.00	
20.00	
440.00	

If Lockwood's actual payroll for the year is only $205,000, Lockwood would be due a refund of $10:

Actual Payroll	x	Rate	=	Insurance Premium
$205,000		0.2%		$410.00
Less estimated premium paid				420.00
Refund				$(10.00)

The adjusting entry at year end for this refund due would be:

16		Insurance Refund Receivable			1 0 00				16
17		Workers' Compensation Insur. Exp.					1 0 00		17
18		Adjustment for insurance							18
19		premium							19

In T account form, the total Workers' Compensation Insurance Expense of $410 would look like this.

Workers' Compensation Insurance Expense

Debit	Credit
420.00	10.00
410.00	

KEY POINTS

1/2 Employer payroll taxes represent additional payroll expenses of the employer. The journal entry for payroll taxes is:

8		Payroll Taxes Expense			x x x xx				8
9		Social Security Tax Payable					x x x xx		9
10		Medicare Tax Payable					x x x xx		10
11		FUTA Tax Payable					x x x xx		11
12		SUTA Tax Payable					x x x xx		12

The steps to be followed in preparing this journal entry are as follows.

STEP 1   Obtain the taxable earnings amounts from the Taxable Earnings columns of the payroll register.

STEP 2   Compute the amount of employer Social Security tax by multiplying the Social Security taxable earnings by 6.2%.

STEP 3   Compute the amount of Medicare tax by multiplying total earnings by 1.45%.

STEP 4   Compute the amount of FUTA tax by multiplying the unemployment taxable earnings by 0.8%.

STEP 5   Compute the amount of SUTA tax by multiplying the unemployment taxable earnings by 5.4%.

STEP 6   Prepare the appropriate journal entry using the amounts computed in Steps 2 through 5.

3 Employer payroll reporting and payment responsibilities fall into five areas:

1. Federal income tax withholding and Social Security and Medicare taxes
2. FUTA taxes
3. SUTA taxes
4. Employee Wage and Tax Statement (Form W-2)
5. Summary of employee wages and taxes

Key forms needed in reporting and paying employer payroll taxes are:

1. Form 8109, Federal Tax Deposit Coupon
2. Form 941, Employer's Quarterly Federal Tax Return
3. Form 940, Employer's Annual Federal Unemployment Tax Return

By January 31 of each year, employers must provide each employee with a Wage and Tax Statement, Form W-2.

By February 28 of each year, employers must file Form W-3 and Copy A of Forms W-2 with the Social Security Administration.

4 Employers generally are required to carry and pay the entire cost of workers' compensation insurance.

KEY TERMS

employer FICA taxes 305   Taxes levied on employers at the same rates and on the same earnings bases as the employee FICA taxes.

Employer Identification Number (EIN) 312   A number that identifies the employer on all payroll forms and reports filed with the IRS.

FUTA (Federal Unemployment Tax Act) tax 306   A tax levied on employers to raise funds to administer the federal/state unemployment compensation program.

merit-rating system 308   A system to encourage employers to provide regular employment to workers.

self-employment income 305   The net income of a trade or business run by an individual.

self-employment tax 306   A contribution to the FICA program.

state unemployment tax (SUTA) 307   A tax levied on employers to raise funds to pay unemployment benefits.

workers' compensation insurance 319   Provides insurance for employees who suffer a job related illness or injury.

REVIEW QUESTIONS

1. Why do employer payroll taxes represent an additional expense to the employer, whereas the various employee payroll taxes do not?
2. At what rate and on what earnings base is the employer's Social Security tax levied?
3. What is the purpose of the FUTA tax and who must pay it?
4. What is the purpose of the state unemployment tax and who must pay it?

5. What accounts are affected when employer payroll tax expenses are properly recorded?

6. Identify all items that are debited or credited to the (1) Social Security tax payable account and (2) Medicare tax payable account.

7. Explain why an employee whose gross salary is $20,000 costs an employer more than $20,000 to employ.

8. What is the purpose of Form 8109, Federal Tax Deposit Coupon?

9. What is the purpose of Form 941, Employer's Quarterly Federal Tax Return?

10. What is the purpose of Form 940, Employer's Annual Federal Unemployment Tax Return?

11. What information appears on Form W-2, the employee's Wage and Tax Statement?

12. What is the purpose of workers' compensation insurance and who must pay for it?

MANAGING YOUR WRITING

The Director of the Art Department, Wilson Watson, wants to hire new office staff. His boss tells him that to do so he must find in his budget not only the base salary for this position but an additional 30% for "fringe benefits." Watson explodes: "How in the world can fringe benefits cost 30% extra?" Write a memo to Watson explaining the costs that probably make up these fringe benefits.

DEMONSTRATION PROBLEM

The totals line from Hart Company's payroll register for the week ended December 31, 19--, is as follows:

(Left half)   **PAYROLL**

| | NAME | EMPLOYEE NO. | ALLOW-ANCES | MARITAL STATUS | EARNINGS | | | | TAXABLE EARNINGS | | |
					REGULAR	OVERTIME	TOTAL	CUMULATIVE TOTAL	UNEMPLOY. COMPENSATION	SOCIAL SECURITY	
1	Totals				3 5 0 0 00	3 0 0 00	3 8 0 0 00	197 6 0 0 00	4 0 0 00	3 8 0 0 00	1

REGISTER—PERIOD ENDED December 31, 19--   **(Right half)**

| | DEDUCTIONS | | | | | | | NET PAY | CHECK NO. |
	FEDERAL INCOME TAX	SOCIAL SEC. TAX	MEDICARE TAX	HEALTH INSURANCE	UNITED WAY	OTHER	TOTAL		
1	3 8 0 00	2 3 5 60	5 5 10	5 0 00	1 0 0 00		8 2 0 70	2 9 7 9 30	1

Payroll taxes are imposed as follows: Social Security, 6.2%; Medicare, 1.45%; FUTA, 0.8%; and SUTA, 5.4%.

REQUIRED

1. a. Prepare the journal entry for payment of this payroll on December 31, 19--.

b. Prepare the journal entry for the employer's payroll taxes for the period ended December 31, 19--.

2. Hart Company had the following balances in its general ledger *after* the entries for requirement (1) were made:

Employees Income Tax Payable	$1,520.00
Social Security Tax Payable	1,847.00
Medicare Tax Payable	433.00
FUTA Tax Payable	27.20
SUTA Tax Payable	183.60

a. Prepare the journal entry for payment of the liabilities for employees federal income taxes and Social Security and Medicare taxes on January 15, 19--.

b. Prepare the journal entry for payment of the liability for FUTA tax on January 31, 19--.

c. Prepare the journal entry for payment of the liability for SUTA tax on January 31, 19--.

3. Hart Company paid a premium of $280 for workers' compensation insurance based on estimated payroll as of the beginning of the year. Based on actual payroll as of the end of the year, the premium is $298. Prepare the adjusting entry to reflect the underpayment of the insurance premium.

SOLUTION

1, 2, 3.

GENERAL JOURNAL   PAGE 1

	DATE	DESCRIPTION	POST. REF.	DEBIT	CREDIT	
1	Dec. 31	Wages and Salaries Expense		3 8 0 0 00		1
2		Employees Income Tax Payable			3 8 0 00	2
3		Social Security Tax Payable			2 3 5 60	3
4		Medicare Tax Payable			5 5 10	4
5		Health Insurance Premiums Pay.			5 0 00	5
6		United Way Contributions Pay.			1 0 0 00	6
7		Cash			2 9 7 9 30	7
8		To record Dec. 31 payroll				8
9						9
10	Dec. 31	Payroll Taxes Expense		3 1 5 50		10
11		Social Security Tax Payable			2 3 5 60	11
12		Medicare Tax Payable			5 5 10	12
13		FUTA Tax Payable			3 20	13
14		SUTA Tax Payable			2 1 60	14
15		Employer payroll taxes for				15
16		week ended Dec. 31				16

	Date		Description	Debit	Credit	
18	Jan.	15	Employees Income Tax Payable	1 5 2 0 00		18
19			Social Security Tax Payable	1 8 4 7 00		19
20			Medicare Tax Payable	4 3 3 00		20
21			Cash		3 8 0 0 00	21
22			Paid employees federal income,			22
23			Social Security, and Medicare			23
24			taxes			24
25						25
26	Jan.	31	FUTA Tax Payable	2 7 20		26
27			Cash		2 7 20	27
28			Paid FUTA tax			28
29						29
30	Jan.	31	SUTA Tax Payable	1 8 3 60		30
31			Cash		1 8 3 60	31
32			Paid SUTA tax			32
33						33
34	Jan.	31	Workers' Compensation Insur. Exp.	1 8 00		34
35			Workers' Compensation Insur. Pay.		1 8 00	35
36			Adjustment for insurance			36
37			premium			37

SERIES A   EXERCISES

1/2 **EXERCISE 10A1 JOURNAL ENTRY FOR EMPLOYER PAYROLL TAXES**   Portions of the payroll register for Barney's Bagels for the week ended July 15 are shown below. The SUTA tax rate is 5.4% and the FUTA tax rate is 0.8%, both of which are levied on the first $7,000 of earnings. The Social Security tax rate is 6.2% on the first $61,200 of earnings. The Medicare rate is 1.45% on gross earnings.

Barney's Bagels
Payroll Register

Total Earnings	Total Taxable Earnings of All Employees	
	Unemployment Compensation	Social Security
$12,200	$10,500	$12,200

Calculate the employer's payroll taxes expense and prepare the journal entry to record the employer's payroll taxes expense for the week ended July 15, of the current year.

1/2 **EXERCISE 10A2 EMPLOYER PAYROLL TAXES**   Earnings for several employees for the week ended March 12, 19--, are as follows:

| Employee Name | Total Earnings | Taxable Earnings | |
		Unemployment Compensation	Social Security
Aus, Glenn E.	$ 700	$200	$ 700
Diaz, Charles K.	350	350	350
Knapp, Carol S.	1,200	—	1,200
Mueller, Deborah F.	830	125	830
Yeager, Jackie R.	920	35	920

Calculate the employer's payroll taxes expense and prepare the journal entry as of March 12, 19--, assuming that FUTA tax is 0.8%, SUTA tax is 5.4%, Social Security tax is 6.2%, and Medicare tax is 1.45%.

1/2 **EXERCISE 10A3 TAXABLE EARNINGS AND EMPLOYER'S PAYROLL TAXES JOURNAL ENTRY**   Selected information from the payroll register of Raynette's Boutique for the week ended September 14, 19--, is as follows. Social Security tax is 6.2% on the first $61,200 of earnings for each employee. Medicare tax is 1.45% of gross earnings. FUTA tax is 0.8% and SUTA tax is 5.4% on the first $7,000 of earnings.

| Employee Name | Cumulative Pay Before Current Earnings | Current Gross Pay | Taxable Earnings | |
			Unemployment Compensation	Social Security
Adams, John R.	$ 6,800	$1,250		
Ellis, Judy A.	6,300	1,100		
Lewis, Arlene S.	54,200	2,320		
Mason, Jason W.	53,900	2,270		
Yates, Ruby L.	27,650	1,900		
Zielke, Ronald M.	59,330	2,680		

Calculate the amount of taxable earnings for unemployment, Social Security, and Medicare taxes, and prepare the journal entry to record the employer's payroll taxes as of September 14, 19--.

3 **EXERCISE 10A4 JOURNAL ENTRY FOR PAYMENT OF EMPLOYER'S PAYROLL TAXES**   Bruce Brown owns a business called Brown Construction Co. He does his banking at Citizens National Bank in Portland, Oregon. The amounts in his general ledger for payroll taxes and the employees' withholding of Social Security, Medicare, and Federal income tax payable as of April 15 of the current year are as follows:

Social Security tax payable (includes both employer and employee)	$3,750
Medicare tax payable (includes both employer and employee)	875
FUTA tax payable	200
SUTA tax payable	1,350
Employees income tax payable	2,275

continued

Journalize the payment of the Form 941 deposit (i.e. Social Security, Medicare, and federal income tax) to Citizens National Bank and the payment of the SUTA tax to the state of Oregon as of April 15, 19--.

1 **EXERCISE 10A5 TOTAL COST OF EMPLOYEE**   J.B. Kenton employs Sharla Knox at a salary of $32,000 a year. Kenton is subject to employer Social Security taxes at a rate of 6.2% and Medicare taxes at a rate of 1.45% on Sharla's salary. In addition, Kenton must pay SUTA tax at a rate of 5.4% and FUTA tax at a rate of 0.8% on the first $7,000 of Knox's salary.
Compute the total cost to Kenton of employing Knox for the year.

4 **EXERCISE 10A6 WORKERS' COMPENSATION INSURANCE AND ADJUSTMENT**   General Manufacturing estimated that its total payroll for the coming year would be $425,000. The workers' compensation insurance premium rate is 0.2%.

REQUIRED

1. Calculate the estimated workers' compensation insurance premium and prepare the journal entry for the payment as of January 2, 19--.
2. Assume that General Manufacturing's actual payroll for the year is $432,000. Calculate the total insurance premium owed and prepare a journal entry as of December 31, 19--, to record the adjustment for the underpayment. The actual payment of the additional premium will take place in January of the next year.

SERIES A   PROBLEMS

1/2 **PROBLEM 10A1 CALCULATING PAYROLL TAXES EXPENSE AND PREPARING JOURNAL ENTRY**   Selected information from the payroll register of Anderson's Dairy for the week ended May 7, 19--, is shown below. SUTA tax is withheld at the rate of 5.4% and the FUTA tax at the rate of 0.8%, both on the first $7,000 of earnings. Social Security tax on the employer is 6.2% on the first $61,200 of earnings and Medicare tax is 1.45% on gross earnings.

| | Cumulative Pay Before Current Earnings | Current Weekly Earnings | Taxable Earnings | |
| | | | Unemployment Compensation | Social Security |
Employee Name				
Barnum, Alex	$ 6,750	$ 820		
Duel, Richard	6,340	725		
Hunt, J.B.	23,460	1,235		
Larson, Susan	6,950	910		
Mercado, Denise	59,850	2,520		
Swan, Judy	15,470	1,125		
Yates, Keith	28,675	1,300		

continued

REQUIRED
1. Calculate the total employer payroll taxes for these employees.
2. Prepare the journal entry to record the employer payroll taxes as of May 7, 19--.

2 PROBLEM 10A2 JOURNALIZING AND POSTING PAYROLL ENTRIES

The Cascade Company has four employees. All are paid on a monthly basis. The fiscal year of the business is July 1 to June 30. Payroll taxes are imposed as follows.

1. Social Security tax of 6.2% withheld from employees' wages on the first $61,200 of earnings and Medicare tax withheld at 1.45% of gross earnings.
2. Social Security tax of 6.2% imposed on the employer on the first $61,200 of earnings and Medicare tax of 1.45% on gross earnings.
3. SUTA tax of 5.4% imposed on the employer on the first $7,000 of earnings.
4. FUTA tax of 0.8% imposed on the employer on the first $7,000 of earnings.

The accounts kept by Cascade include the following:

Account Number	Title	Balance on July 1
111	Cash	$50,200
211	Employees Income Tax Payable	1,015
212	Social Security Tax Payable	1,458
213	Medicare Tax Payable	342
221	FUTA Tax Payable	164
222	SUTA Tax Payable	810
261	Savings Bond Deductions Payable	350
542	Wages and Salaries Expense	0
552	Payroll Taxes Expense	0

The following transactions relating to payrolls and payroll taxes occurred during July and August.

July 15 Paid $2,815 covering the following June taxes:

Social Security tax	$ 1,458
Medicare tax	342
Employees income tax withheld	1,015
Total	$ 2,815

31 July payroll:

Total wages and salaries expense		$12,000
Less amounts withheld:		
Social Security tax	$ 744	
Medicare tax	174	
Employees income tax	1,020	
Savings bond deductions	350	2,288
Net amount paid		$ 9,712

continued

July   31 Purchased savings bonds for employees,
$700

31 Data for completing employer's payroll
taxes expense for July:

Social Security taxable wages	$12,000
Unemployment taxable wages	3,000

Aug.   15 Paid $2,856 covering the following July
taxes:

Social Security tax	$ 1,488
Medicare tax	348
Employees income tax withheld	1,020
Total	$ 2,856

15 Paid SUTA tax for the quarter, $972
15 Paid FUTA tax, $188

REQUIRED

1. Journalize the preceding transactions using a general journal.
2. Open T accounts for the payroll expenses and liabilities. Enter the beginning balances and post the transactions recorded in the journal.

4 **PROBLEM 10A3 WORKERS' COMPENSATION INSURANCE AND ADJUSTMENT**   Willamette Manufacturing estimated that its total payroll for the coming year would be $650,000. The workers' compensation insurance premium rate is 0.3%.

REQUIRED

1. Calculate the estimated workers' compensation insurance premium and prepare the journal entry for the payment as of January 2, 19--.
2. Assume that Willamette Manufacturing's actual payroll for the year was $672,000. Calculate the total insurance premium owed and prepare a journal entry as of December 31, 19--, to record the adjustment for the underpayment. The actual payment of the additional premium will take place in January of the next year.
3. Assume instead that Willamette Manufacturing's actual payroll for the year was $634,000. Prepare a journal entry as of December 31, 19--, for the total amount that should be refunded. The refund will not be received until the next year.

SERIES B   EXERCISES

1/2 **EXERCISE 10B1 JOURNAL ENTRY FOR EMPLOYER PAYROLL TAXES**   Portions of the payroll register for Kathy's Cupcakes for the week ended June 21 are on the next page. The SUTA tax rate is 5.4% and the FUTA tax rate is 0.8%, both on the first $7,000 of earnings. The Social Security tax rate is 6.2% on the first $61,200 of earnings. The Medicare rate is 1.45% on gross earnings.   *continued*

Kathy's Cupcakes
Payroll Register

Total Taxable Earnings of All Employees		
Total Earnings	Unemployment Compensation	Social Security
$15,680	$12,310	$15,680

Calculate the employer's payroll taxes expense and prepare the journal entry to record the employer's payroll taxes expense for the week ended June 21 of the current year.

1/2 **EXERCISE 10B2 EMPLOYER PAYROLL TAXES**   Earnings for several employees for the week ended April 7, 19--, are as follows:

		Taxable Earnings	
Employee Name	**Total Earnings**	**Unemployment Compensation**	**Social Security**
Boyd, Glenda, L.	$ 850	$300	$ 850
Evans, Sheryl N.	970	225	970
Fox, Howard J.	830	830	830
Jacobs, Phyllis J.	1,825	—	1,825
Roh, William R.	990	25	990

Calculate the employer's payroll taxes expense and prepare the journal entry as of April 7, 19--, assuming that FUTA tax is 0.8%, SUTA tax is 5.4%, Social Security tax is 6.2%, and Medicare tax is 1.45%.

1/2 **EXERCISE 10B3 TAXABLE EARNINGS AND EMPLOYER'S PAYROLL TAXES JOURNAL ENTRY**   Selected information from the payroll register of Howard's Cutlery for the week ended October 7, 19--, is presented below. Social Security tax is 6.2% on the first $61,200 of earnings for each employee. Medicare tax is 1.45% on gross earnings. FUTA tax is 0.8% and SUTA tax is 5.4% on the first $7,000 of earnings.

	Cumulative Pay Before Current Earnings	Current Gross Pay	Taxable Earnings	
Employee Name			**Unemployment Compensation**	**Social Security**
Carlson, David J.	$ 6,635	$ 950		
Davis, Patricia S.	6,150	1,215		
Lewis, Arlene S.	54,375	2,415		
Nixon, Robert R.	53,870	1,750		
Shippe, Lance W.	24,830	1,450		
Watts, Brandon Q.	59,800	2,120		

Calculate the amount of taxable earnings for unemployment, Social Security, and Medicare taxes, and prepare the journal entry to record the employer's payroll taxes as of October 7, 19--.

3 **EXERCISE 10B4 JOURNAL ENTRY FOR PAYMENT OF EMPLOYER'S PAYROLL TAXES**   Francis Baker owns a business called Baker Construction Co. She does her banking at the American National Bank in Seattle, Washington. The amounts in her general ledger for payroll taxes and employees' withholding of Social Security, Medicare, and federal income tax payable as of July 15 of the current year are as follows:

Social Security tax payable (includes both employer and employee) $6,375
Medicare tax payable (includes both employer and employee)   1,500
FUTA tax payable   336
SUTA tax payable   2,268
Employees federal income tax payable   4,830

Journalize the payment of the Form 941 deposit (i.e., Social Security, Medicare, and federal income tax) to the American National Bank and the payment of the state unemployment tax to the state of Washington as of July 15, 19--.

1 **EXERCISE 10B5 TOTAL COST OF EMPLOYEE**   B.F. Goodson employs Eduardo Gonzales at a salary of $46,000 a year. Goodson is subject to employer Social Security taxes at a rate of 6.2% and Medicare taxes at a rate of 1.45% on Eduardo's salary. In addition, Goodson must pay SUTA tax at a rate of 5.4% and FUTA tax at a rate of 0.8% on the first $7,000 of Gonzales' salary.

Compute the total cost to Goodson of employing Gonzales for the year.

4 **EXERCISE 10B6 WORKERS' COMPENSATION INSURANCE AND ADJUSTMENT**   Columbia Industries estimated that its total payroll for the coming year would be $385,000. The workers' compensation insurance premium rate is 0.2%.

REQUIRED
1. Calculate the estimated workers' compensation insurance premium and prepare the journal entry for the payment as of January 2, 19--.
2. Assume that Columbia Industries' actual payroll for the year is $396,000. Calculate the total insurance premium owed and prepare a journal entry as of December 31, 19--, to record the adjustment for the underpayment. The actual payment of the additional premium will take place in January of the next year.

SERIES B   PROBLEMS

 1/2 **PROBLEM 10B1 CALCULATING PAYROLL TAXES EXPENSE AND PREPARING JOURNAL ENTRY**   Selected information from the payroll register of Wray's Drug Store for the week ended July 7, 19--, is shown on the next page. SUTA tax is withheld at the rate of 5.4% and FUTA tax at the rate of 0.8%, both on the first $7,000 of earnings. Social Security tax on the employer is 6.2% on the first $61,200 of earnings and Medicare tax is 1.45% on gross earnings.

	Cumulative Pay Before Current Earnings	Current Weekly Earnings	Taxable Earnings	
Employee Name			**Unemployment Compensation**	**Social Security**
Ackers, Alice	$ 6,460	$ 645		
Conley, Dorothy	27,560	1,025		
Davis, James	6,850	565		
Lawrence, Kevin	52,850	2,875		
Rawlings, Judy	16,350	985		
Tester, Leonard	22,320	835		
Vadillo, Raynette	59,360	2,540		

REQUIRED

1. Calculate the total employer payroll taxes for these employees.
2. Prepare the journal entry to record the employer payroll taxes as of July 7, 19--.

2 **PROBLEM 10B2 JOURNALIZING AND POSTING PAYROLL ENTRIES** The Oxford Company has five employees. All are paid on a monthly basis. The fiscal year of the business is June 1 to May 31. Payroll taxes are imposed as follows:

1. Social Security tax of 6.2% to be withheld from employees' wages on the first $61,200 of earnings and Medicare tax of 1.45% on gross earnings.
2. Social Security tax of 6.2% imposed on the employer on the first $61,200 of earnings and Medicare tax of 1.45% on gross earnings.
3. SUTA tax of 5.4% imposed on the employer on the first $7,000 of earnings.
4. FUTA tax of 0.8% imposed on the employer on the first $7,000 of earnings.

The accounts kept by the Oxford Company include the following:

Account Number	Title	Balance on June 1
111	Cash	$48,650
211	Employees Income Tax Payable	1,345
212	Social Security Tax Payable	1,823
213	Medicare Tax Payable	427
221	FUTA Tax Payable	360
222	SUTA Tax Payable	920
261	Savings Bond Deductions Payable	525
542	Wages and Salaries Expense	0
552	Payroll Taxes Expense	0

The following transactions relating to payrolls and payroll taxes occurred during June and July.

June 15 Paid $3,595.00 covering the
following May taxes:

Social Security tax	$ 1,823.00
Medicare tax	427.00
Employees income tax withheld	1,345.00
Total	$ 3,595.00

30 June payroll:

Total wages and salaries expense		$14,700.00
Less amounts withheld:		
Social Security tax	$ 911.40	
Medicare tax	213.15	
Employees income tax	1,280.00	
Savings bond deductions	525.00	2,929.55
Net amount paid		$11,770.45

30 Purchased savings bonds for
employees, $1,050.00

30 Data for completing employer's
payroll taxes expense for June:

Social Security taxable wages	$14,700.00
Unemployment taxable wages	4,500.00

July 15 Paid $3,529.10 covering the
following June taxes:

Social Security tax	$ 1,822.80
Medicare tax	426.30
Employees income tax withheld	1,280.00
Total	$ 3,529.10

15 Paid SUTA tax, $1,163.00
15 Paid FUTA tax, $396.00

REQUIRED

1. Journalize the preceding transactions using a general journal.
2. Open T accounts for the payroll expenses and liabilities. Enter the beginning balances and post the transactions recorded in the journal.

PROBLEM 10B3 WORKERS' COMPENSATION INSURANCE AND ADJUSTMENT   Multnomah Manufacturing estimated that its total payroll for the coming year would be $540,000. The workers' compensation insurance premium rate is 0.2%.

REQUIRED

1. Calculate the estimated workers' compensation insurance premium and prepare the journal entry for the payment as of January 2, 19--.
2. Assume that Multnomah Manufacturing's actual payroll for the year was $562,000. Calculate the total insurance premium owed and prepare a journal entry as of December 31, 19--, to record the adjustment for the underpayment. The actual payment of the additional premium will take place in January of the next year.   *continued*

3. Assume instead that Multnomah Manufacturing's actual payroll for the year was $532,000. Prepare a journal entry as of December 31, 19--, for the total amount that should be refunded. The refund will not be received until the next year.

MASTERY PROBLEM

The totals line from Nix Company's payroll register for the week ended March 31, 19--, is as follows:

(Left half)   **PAYROLL REGISTER**

| | NAME | EMPLOYEE NO. | ALLOW-ANCES | MARITAL STATUS | EARNINGS | | | | TAXABLE EARNINGS | |
					REGULAR	OVERTIME	TOTAL	CUMULATIVE TOTAL	UNEMPLOY. COMPENSATION	SOCIAL SECURITY
1	Totals				5 4 0 0 00	1 0 0 00	5 5 0 0 00	71 5 0 0 00	5 0 0 0 00	5 5 0 0 00	1

FOR PERIOD ENDED   March 31, 19--   **(Right half)**

| | DEDUCTIONS | | | | | | | | NET PAY | CHECK NO. |
	FEDERAL INCOME TAX	SOCIAL SEC. TAX	MEDICARE TAX	HEALTH INSURANCE	LIFE INSURANCE	OTHER		TOTAL		
1	5 0 0 00	3 4 1 00	7 9 75	1 6 5 00	2 0 0 00			1 2 8 5 75	4 2 1 4 25	1

Payroll taxes are imposed as follows: Social Security tax, 6.2%; Medicare tax, 1.45%; FUTA tax, 0.8%, and SUTA tax, 5.4%.

REQUIRED

1. **a.** Prepare the journal entry for payment of this payroll on March 31, 19--.
   b. Prepare the journal entry for the employer's payroll taxes for the period ended March 31, 19--.
2. Nix Company had the following balances in its general ledger *before* the entries for requirement (1) were made:

Employees income tax payable	$2,500
Social Security tax payable	2,008
Medicare tax payable	470
FUTA tax payable	520
SUTA tax payable	3,510

   a. Prepare the journal entry for payment of the liabilities for federal income taxes and Social Security and Medicare taxes on April 15, 19--.
   b. Prepare the journal entry for payment of the liability for FUTA tax on April 30, 19--.
   c. Prepare the journal entry for payment of the liability for SUTA tax on April 30, 19--.
3. Nix Company paid a premium of $420 for workers' compensation insurance based on the estimated payroll as of the beginning of the year. Based on actual payroll as of the end of the year, the premium is only $400. Prepare the adjusting entry to reflect the overpayment of the insurance premium at the end of the year (December 31, 19--).

11

Accounting for Sales and Cash Receipts

About a month ago you ordered three software packages from a mail order supplier you had not dealt with before. After some delay, two of the three packages arrived. The next day you received a bill for all three packages. You complained to the supplier, who said this was simply a "paper work" error that would be corrected. How could this happen? Was this company trying to cheat you?

Over the last ten chapters, we have learned how to account for a service business. We are now ready to consider accounting for a different kind of business—merchandising. A **merchandising business** purchases merchandise, such as clothing, furniture, or computers, and sells that merchandise to customers.

This chapter examines how to account for the sale of merchandise using the accrual basis of accounting. We will learn how to use four new accounts, two special journals, and a subsidiary ledger.

MERCHANDISE SALES TRANSACTIONS

LO1 Describe merchandise sales transactions.

A **sale** is a transfer of merchandise from one business or individual to another in exchange for cash or a promise to pay cash. Sales procedures and documents vary greatly, depending on the nature and size of the business.

Retailer

Retail businesses generally sell to customers who enter the store, select the merchandise they want, and bring it to a salesclerk. The salesclerk enters the sale in some type of electronic cash register that generates a receipt for the customer. A copy of the receipt is retained in the register. Most registers can print a summary of the day's sales activity, like the one in Figure 11-1. This summary can be used to journalize sales in the accounting records.

FIGURE 11-1   Cash Register Tape Summary

```
                (1)
            CASH SALES          327.79 *
                (3)
            MCARD/VISA          550.62 *
                (6)
            LAYAWAY              79.50 *
            TOTAL CASH          957.91 *
                (2)
            CHARGE SALES        543.84 *
                (5)
            APPROVAL            126.58 *
            TOTAL CHARGE        670.42 *

            TOTAL SALES       1,628.33 G*
            SALES TAX            81.42 *
                                 81.42 *

            REC'D ON ACCT.      324.51 *
                                324.51 *

            PAID OUT             76.51 *
                                 76.51 *

            NO SALE               0.00 *
                                  0.00 *

            *     SUB-TOTAL
            G*    GRAND TOTAL
```

An additional document often created as evidence of a sale in a retail business is a **sales ticket** (Figure 11-2). One copy of the sales ticket is given to the customer and the other copy is sent to accounting.

FIGURE 11-2   Sales Ticket

NORTHERN MICRO   134C

1099 E. Louisiana, Indianapolis, IN 46217-3322

Account No.	Sold by	Date
		4/10/--

Sold to *Brenda Myers*
Address *581 Acorn Way*
City *Zionsville*   State *IN* Zip *46077-2154*

Send to *same*
Address
City   State   Zip

Rec'd on Acct. ☐   Charge Sale ☒   Sales Ret/Allow ☐

Quantity	Articles	Amount
1	JD Laser Printer	$440.00
	Tax	22.00
		$462.00

Brenda Myers
CUSTOMER'S SIGNATURE

All claims & returned goods MUST be accompanied by this bill.

Wholesaler

Figure 11-3 shows how the wholesaler plays a different role than the retailer in the marketing chain. Retailers usually sell to final consumers, whereas wholesalers tend to sell to retailers. This causes the wholesale sales transaction process to differ, as shown in Figure 11-4.

FIGURE 11-3   Marketing Chain

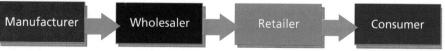

Manufacturer → Wholesaler → Retailer → Consumer

FIGURE 11-4   Wholesale Sales Transaction Process

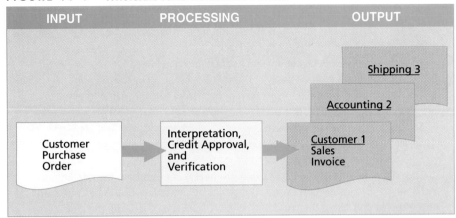

Customers commonly send in written orders to buy merchandise from wholesalers. When the customer purchase order arrives, the customer name and items being ordered are determined. Since wholesalers typically make sales on account, credit approval is needed. Three copies of a **sales invoice** are then generated. One is sent to the customer as a bill for the merchandise, one is sent to accounting to record the sale, and one is shipped with the merchandise. Figure 11-5 shows the customer copy of a sales invoice for Alladin Electric Supply.

FIGURE 11-5   Sales Invoice

Sales Invoice .   NO. 513

Alladin Electric Supply

204 Main St., Hartford, CT 06103

CUSTOMER:		DATE:	May 5, 19--	
Crafters Builders P.O. Box 502 Storrs, CT 06268		TERMS:	2/10, n/30	

QUANTITY	DESCRIPTION	UNIT PRICE	AMOUNT
6	#DC-26-AB Fixtures	$25	$150.00
5	#HPS-50-P Fixtures	$50	250.00
TOTAL			$400.00

Global Merchandising

Each year more and more consumer products cross national borders and enter the global marketplace. Many companies are speaking new languages as they package and label their wares for international sale.

It is not unusual for the label on a can of hair spray to contain the following information:

Styling mist for hold and control
Spray de coiffage pour tenue et controle
Spray fijador para dar volumen y control

The carton for a telephone answering machine is likely to be printed in English and Spanish. The installation instructions might be printed on both sides of a card. At the top of one side is the word "installation." On the other side, the reader sees "instalación."

In addition to multilingual labeling, manufacturers are using photographs, icons, and illustrations to identify products, to provide assembly and use instructions, and to caution consumers about safety concerns. The care instructions sewn into many garments are written in one or two languages, but the tag also includes icons that indicate how the garment is to be washed, dried, and ironed.

Creating labels and packages that are appropriate for consumers who speak different languages can reduce total packaging cost. It can also simplify the warehousing, inventory, and shipping processes.

Credit Memo

Both retailers and wholesalers sometimes have customers return goods or seek price reductions for damaged goods. Merchandise returned by the customer for a refund is called a **sales return**. Price reductions granted by the seller because of defects or other problems with the merchandise are called **sales allowances**. When credit is given for merchandise returned or for an allowance, a **credit memo** is issued for the amount involved. One copy is given to the customer and one copy is sent to accounting. Figure 11-6 shows a credit memo issued by Northern Micro for merchandise returned by a customer.

MERCHANDISE SALES ACCOUNTS

LO2 Describe and use merchandise sales accounts.

To account for merchandise sales transactions, we will use four new accounts.

1. Sales
2. Sales Tax Payable
3. Sales Returns and Allowances
4. Sales Discounts

FIGURE 11-6   Credit Memo

N NORTHERN MICRO
1099 E. Louisiana, Indianapolis, IN 46217-3322

CREDIT 72
MEMO

Date *April 2, 19--*

Name *Susan Chang*

Address *337 Elm Street*

City *Noblesville* State *IN* Zip *46060-3377*

Sales Number				OK	
Cash Refunn	Mdse. Order	Charge ✓	Gift		Amount *$42.00*

Quantity	Articles	Amount
2	*Printer Ribbons*	*$40.00*
	Tax	*2.00*
		$42.00

Forty-two ⁰⁰/₁₀₀ —————————— Dollars

Reason   *Not needed*

Rec'd. Stock By   *Laura Murphy*

x *Susan Chang*
Customer's Signature

Sales Account

The sales account is a revenue account used to record sales of merchandise. The account is credited for the selling price of merchandise sold during the period.

Sales	
Debit	Credit
	to enter the selling price of merchandise sold

If a $100 sale is made for cash, the following entry is made.

5			Cash			1 0 0 00				5
6			Sales				1 0 0 00			6
7			Made cash sale							7

If the same sale is made on account, the following entry is made.

5		Accounts Receivable/Customer			1 0 0 00					5
6		Sales					1 0 0 00			6
7		Made credit sale								7

Accounts Receivable is followed by a slash and the name of the specific customer who now owes money on account.

Sales Tax Payable Account

When sales tax is imposed on merchandise sold, a separate account for Sales Tax Payable is kept. This is a liability account that is credited for the taxes imposed on sales. The account is debited for sales taxes paid to the proper taxing authority or for sales taxes on merchandise returned by customers. A credit balance in the account indicates the amount owed to the taxing authority for taxes collected.

Sales Tax Payable	
Debit	**Credit**
to enter payment of tax to taxing authority or adjustment of tax on merchandise returned by customers	to enter tax imposed on sales

If a cash sale for $100 plus 5% sales tax ($100 × 5% = $5) occurs, the following entry is made.

10		Cash			1 0 5 00					10
11		Sales					1 0 0 00			11
12		Sales Tax Payable						5 00		12
13		Made cash sale								13

If the same sale is made on account, the following entry is made.

10		Accounts Receivable/Customer			1 0 5 00					10
11		Sales					1 0 0 00			11
12		Sales Tax Payable						5 00		12
13		Made credit sale								13

The debit to Accounts Receivable indicates that the amount owed by customers to the firm has increased. Since the buyer has accepted the merchandise and promised to pay for it, revenue is recognized by crediting the sales account. Sales Tax Payable is credited because the amount of sales tax owed to the taxing authority has increased.

Sales Returns and Allowances Account

Sales Returns and Allowances is a contra-revenue account to which sales returns and sales allowances are debited. As shown in Figure 11-7, this account is reported as a deduction from Sales on the income statement. Returns and allowances are debited to a separate account rather than directly to Sales so that the business can more readily keep track of this activity.

Sales Returns and Allowances

Debit	Credit
to enter returns and allowances	

Look at the credit memo in Figure 11-6 on page 341. The entry for the return of these printer ribbons by Susan Chang would be as follows.

19		Sales Returns and Allowances		4 0 00			19
20		Sales Tax Payable		2 00			20
21		Accounts Receivable/Susan Chang				4 2 00	21
22		Issued credit memo for					22
23		returned merchandise					23

Note carefully the parts of this entry. Sales Returns and Allowances is debited for the amount of the sale, *excluding* the sales tax. Sales Tax Payable is debited separately for the sales tax on the original sale amount. Accounts Receivable is credited for the total amount originally billed to Chang.

 LEARNING KEY | Debit Sales Returns and Allowances for the amount of the sale excluding the sales tax.

FIGURE 11-7   Net Sales on the Income Statement

Sales		$38,500.00
Less: Sales returns and allowances	$200.00	
Sales discounts	140.00	340.00
Net sales		$38,160.00

Sales Discounts Account

Some businesses offer **cash discounts** to encourage prompt payment by customers who buy merchandise on account. Some possible credit terms are shown in Figure 11-8.

To the seller, cash discounts are considered **sales discounts**. The sales discounts account is a contra-revenue account to which cash discounts allowed are debited. Like Sales Returns and Allowances, this account is reported as a deduction from Sales on the income statement (Figure 11-7).

FIGURE 11-8   Credit Terms

TERMS	MEANING
2/10, n/30*	2% discount off sales price if paid within 10 days Total amount due within 30 days
1/10, n/30	Same as 2/10, n/30, except 1% discount instead of 2%
2/eom, n/60	2% discount if paid before end of month Total amount due within 60 days
3/10 eom, n/60	3% discount if paid within 10 days after end of month Total amount due within 60 days

*See Figure 11-5. A discount of $8 (2% x $400) is allowed if this invoice is paid by May 15 (invoice date of May 5 + 10 days).

Sales Discounts

Debit	Credit
to enter cash discounts	

If merchandise is sold for $100 with credit terms of 2/10, n/30, and cash is received within the discount period, the following entries are made.

At time of sale:

26		Accounts Receivable/Customer		1 0 0 00			26
27		Sales			1 0 0 00		27
28		Made sale on account					28

At time of collection:

30		Cash		9 8 00			30
31		Sales Discounts		2 00			31
32		Accounts Receivable/Customer			1 0 0 00		32
33		Received cash on account					33

JOURNALIZING AND POSTING SALES TRANSACTIONS

LO3 Describe and use the sales journal and accounts receivable ledger.

To illustrate the journalizing and posting of sales transactions, we use Northern Micro, a retail computer business. Assume that the following sales transactions occurred during April 19--.

Apr. 4   Made sale no. 133C on account to Enrico Lorenzo, $1,520 plus $76 sales tax.
     10   Made sale no. 134C on account to Brenda Myers, $440 plus $22 sales tax.
     18   Made sale no. 105D on account to Edith Walton, $980 plus $49 sales tax.

Apr. 21 Made sale no. 202B on account to Susan Chang, $620 plus $31 sales tax.
     24 Made sale no. 162A on account to Heidi Schwitzer, $1,600 plus $80 sales tax.

These transactions could be entered in a general journal as shown in Figure 11-9.

FIGURE 11-9   Sales Entered in General Journal

4	Apr.	4	Accounts Receivable/E. Lorenzo	1 5 9 6 00		4
5			Sales		1 5 2 0 00	5
6			Sales Tax Payable		7 6 00	6
7			Sale No. 133C			7
8						8
9		10	Accounts Receivable/B. Myers	4 6 2 00		9
10			Sales		4 4 0 00	10
11			Sales Tax Payable		2 2 00	11
12			Sale No. 134C			12
13						13
14		18	Accounts Receivable/E. Walton	1 0 2 9 00		14
15			Sales		9 8 0 00	15
16			Sales Tax Payable		4 9 00	16
17			Sale No. 105D			17
18						18
19		21	Accounts Receivable/S. Chang	6 5 1 00		19
20			Sales		6 2 0 00	20
21			Sales Tax Payable		3 1 00	21
22			Sale No. 202B			22
23						23
24		24	Accounts Receivable/H. Schwitzer	1 6 8 0 00		24
25			Sales		1 6 0 0 00	25
26			Sales Tax Payable		8 0 00	26
27			Sale No. 162A			27

Notice that each of these five entries involved the same three accounts. The same account titles were recorded five times. Similarly, to post these entries to the general ledger, five separate postings would be made to each of the three accounts, a total of fifteen postings.

This repetition is inefficient. Fortunately, there is a much more efficient way to record sales on account. This is done by using a **special journal** designed for recording only certain kinds of transactions.

Sales Journal

A **sales journal** is a special journal used to record only sales on account. By using a sales journal, we streamline the journalizing and posting of sales on account.

LEARNING KEY	Use a sales journal to streamline journalizing and posting of sales on account.

To illustrate, reconsider the five sales made on account by Northern Micro. They are entered in the sales journal in Figure 11-10. The sales journal provides separate columns for Accounts Receivable Debit, Sales Credit, and Sales Tax Payable Credit, the three accounts used repeatedly in the general journal in Figure 11-9. A sale is recorded in the sales journal by entering the following information.

1. Date
2. Sale number
3. Customer
4. Dollar amounts

There is no need to enter any general ledger account titles.

FIGURE 11-10   Northern Micro Sales Journal

SALES JOURNAL   PAGE 6

	DATE	SALE NO.	TO WHOM SOLD	POST. REF.	ACCOUNTS RECEIVABLE DEBIT	SALES CREDIT	SALES TAX PAYABLE CREDIT	
1	19-- Apr. 4	133C	Enrico Lorenzo		1 5 9 6 00	1 5 2 0 00	7 6 00	1
2	10	134C	Brenda Myers		4 6 2 00	4 4 0 00	2 2 00	2
3	18	105D	Edith Walton		1 0 2 9 00	9 8 0 00	4 9 00	3
4	21	202B	Susan Chang		6 5 1 00	6 2 0 00	3 1 00	4
5	24	162A	Heidi Schwitzer		1 6 8 0 00	1 6 0 0 00	8 0 00	5

The sales journal in Figure 11-10 is designed for a company, like Northern Micro, that charges sales tax. For a wholesaler or any other company that does not charge sales tax, a sales journal like that in Figure 11-11 would be sufficient. In this case, there is only a single amount column headed Accounts Receivable Debit/Sales Credit. With no sales tax, the Accounts Receivable Debit and Sales Credit amounts are identical for each sale. Thus, only a single column is needed.

FIGURE 11-11   Sales Journal Without Sales Tax

SALES JOURNAL   PAGE 1

	DATE	SALE NO.	TO WHOM SOLD	POST. REF.	ACCOUNTS RECEIVABLE DEBIT/ SALES CREDIT	

Posting from the Sales Journal

Posting from the sales journal also is very efficient. Each general ledger account used in the sales journal requires only one posting each period. Figure 11-12 illustrates the general ledger posting process for Northern Micro's sales journal for the month of April.

The following steps are used to post from the sales journal to the general ledger at the end of each month, as indicated in Figure 11-12.

FIGURE 11-12   Posting the Sales Journal to the General Ledger

		SALES JOURNAL				Page 6
Date	Sale No.	To Whom Sold	Post Ref.	Accounts Receivable Debit	Sales Credit	Sales Tax Payable Credit
19--						
Apr. 4	133C	Enrico Lorenzo		1,596.00	1,520.00	76.00
10	134C	Brenda Myers		462.00	440.00	22.00
18	105D	Edith Walton		1,029.00	980.00	49.00
21	202B	Susan Chang		651.00	620.00	31.00
24	162A	Heidi Schwitzer		1,680.00	1,600.00	80.00
				5,418.00	5,160.00	258.00	**1**
				(131)	(411)	(225)	**4**

2

GENERAL LEDGER (Partial)

ACCOUNT Accounts Receivable   **ACCOUNT NO.** 131

Date	Item	Post. Ref.	Debit	Credit	Balance Debit	Balance Credit
19--						
Apr. 1	Bal.	✓			12,000.00	
30		S6	5,418.00		17,418.00	

3

1 Debit total:	**$5,418**			

ACCOUNT Sales Tax Payable   **ACCOUNT NO.** 225

Date	Item	Post. Ref.	Debit	Credit	Balance Debit	Balance Credit
19--						
Apr. 30		S6		258.00		258.00

3

Credit total:	**$5,160**
	258
	$5,418

ACCOUNT Sales   **ACCOUNT NO.** 411

Date	Item	Post. Ref.	Debit	Credit	Balance Debit	Balance Credit
19--						
Apr. 1	Bal.	✓				27,000.00
30		S6		5,160.00		32,160.00

3

STEP 1   Total the amount columns, verify that the total of the debit column equals the total of the credit columns, and rule the columns.

STEP 2   Post the column totals to the general ledger accounts indicated in the column headings.

STEP 3   Insert the date in the Date column and the initial "S" and the sales journal page number in the Posting Reference column of each ledger account.

STEP 4   Insert the general ledger account numbers immediately below the column totals.

The sales and accounts receivable accounts in the general ledger are now up to date. However, at this point Northern Micro has no complete record of the account receivable from *individual customers*. To run the business properly, Northern Micro needs this information.

A common approach to keeping a record of each customer's account receivable is to use a subsidiary **accounts receivable ledger**. This is a separate ledger containing an individual account receivable for each customer. If there are many customer accounts, it is good practice to assign each customer an account number. The subsidiary ledger accounts are kept in either alphabetical or numerical order, depending on whether customer accounts are identified by number. A summary accounts receivable account, called a **controlling account**, is still maintained in the general ledger. The accounts receivable ledger is "subsidiary" to this account.

Figure 11-13 illustrates the use of the accounts receivable ledger. The accounts receivable ledger is posted *daily* so that current information is available for each customer at all times. The following steps are used to post from the sales journal to the accounts receivable ledger, as shown in Figure 11-13.

STEP 1 Post the individual sale amount to the customer's account on the date the sale occurs.

STEP 2 Insert the date in the Date column and the initial "S" and the sales journal page number in the Posting Reference column of each customer account.

STEP 3 Insert a check mark (✓) in the Posting Reference column of the sales journal to indicate that the amount has been posted.

 The total of the accounts receivable ledger balances equals the Accounts Receivable balance in the general ledger.

Note the relationship between the sales journal, accounts receivable subsidiary ledger, and general ledger. All individual entries in the sales journal are posted to the accounts receivable ledger. The totals of all entries in the sales journal are posted to the general ledger accounts. After the posting of the accounts receivable ledger and the general ledger is completed, the total of the accounts receivable ledger balances should equal the Accounts Receivable balance in the general ledger. Remember, the accounts receivable ledger is simply a detailed listing of the same information that is summarized in Accounts Receivable in the general ledger.

Sales Returns and Allowances

 Enter sales returns and allowances in the general journal.

If a customer returns merchandise or is given an allowance for damaged merchandise, a general journal entry is required. Remember, the sales journal can be used only to enter sales on account. On May 5, Susan Chang returned two printer ribbons costing $40 plus $2 sales tax (Figure 11-6, page 341). Figure 11-14 shows the general journal entry, general ledger posting, and accounts receivable ledger posting for this transaction.

FIGURE 11-13   Posting the Sales Journal to the Accounts Receivable Ledger

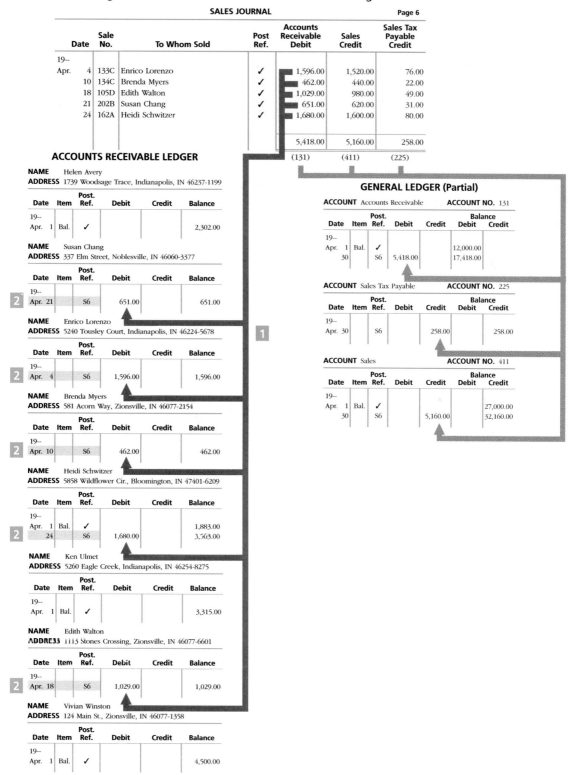

FIGURE 11-14   Accounting for Sales Returns and Allowances

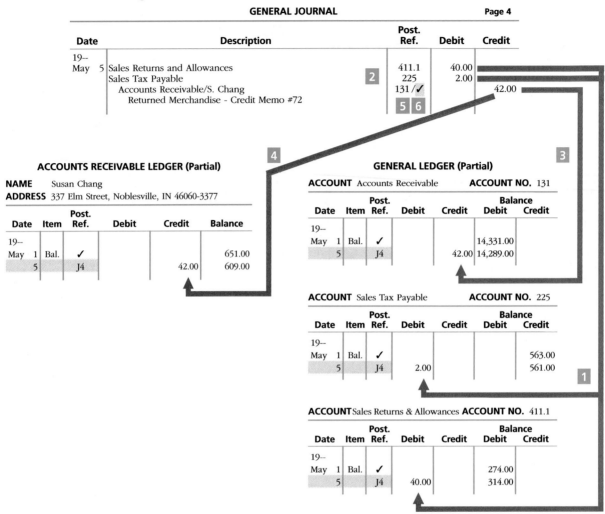

The general journal entry is made in the usual manner. The postings are made daily using the following steps.

STEP 1   Post the Sales Returns and Allowances and Sales Tax Payable debits to the general ledger accounts. Insert the date in the Date column and the general journal posting reference (J4) in the Posting Reference column of each ledger account.

STEP 2   Insert the general ledger account numbers in the Posting Reference column of the general journal.

Posting the Accounts Receivable credit requires special attention, as follows.

STEP 3   Post the Accounts Receivable credit to the general ledger account and insert the date in the Date column and the general journal posting reference (J4) in the Posting Reference column.

STEP 4 Post the same amount to the customer account in the accounts receivable ledger and insert the same date in the Date column and posting reference (J4) in the Posting Reference column.

STEP 5 To indicate that the general ledger has been posted, insert the account number (131) and a slash (/) in the Posting Reference column of the general journal.

STEP 6 To indicate that the customer account has been posted, insert a check mark (✓) following the slash in the Posting Reference column of the general journal.

JOURNALIZING AND POSTING CASH RECEIPTS

LO4 Describe and use the cash receipts journal and accounts receivable ledger.

Like sales transactions, cash receipt transactions occur frequently in most businesses. Sales on account lead to cash receipts, which could be entered in the general journal. For example, assume that Northern Micro receives cash from Enrico Lorenzo for sale no. 133C on April 14. The transaction could be recorded in the general journal as follows.

25	Apr.	14	Cash		1 5 9 6 00			25
26			Accounts Receivable/E. Lorenzo			1 5 9 6 00		26
27			Received cash on account					27

Most businesses also regularly make cash sales. A general journal can be used to record cash sales. The following entry shows cash sales of $500 recorded in the general journal on May 5.

3	May	5	Cash		5 0 0 00			3
4			Sales			5 0 0 00		4
5			Made cash sales					5

In addition, an increasing number of sales today are made using bank credit cards. Bank credit card sales are similar to cash sales because the cash is available to the business as soon as the credit card slips are deposited in the bank. But not all of the cash is available. The bank charges a fee to the business for processing the credit card items. The fee is based on the gross amount of the sale, including the sales tax. Thus, on a sale of $100, the bank might charge a fee of $4 (4%). The following entry shows this credit card sale recorded on May 6.

8	May	6	Cash		9 6 00			8
9			Bank Credit Card Expense		4 00			9
10			Sales			1 0 0 00		10
11			Made credit card sale					11

Note two important features of the three journal entries illustrated above.

1. Each involves a debit to Cash.
2. Each would occur quite frequently in a business.

If the general journal were used to record all such transactions, the journalizing and posting process would be repetitive and inefficient.

The previous section of this chapter showed how sales on account could be journalized and posted more efficiently by using a sales journal. Using a special journal to record cash receipts transactions also increases efficiency.

Cash Receipts Journal

 Use a cash receipts journal to streamline journalizing and posting of cash receipts.

A **cash receipts journal** is a special journal used to record only cash receipt transactions. To illustrate its use, we continue with the transactions of Northern Micro. Northern Micro's cash receipts journal for the month of April is shown in Figure 11-15, with the following transactions.

Apr. 14   Received cash on account from Enrico Lorenzo for sale no. 133C, $1,596.
    20   Received cash on account from Brenda Myers for sale no. 134C, $462.
    28   Received cash on account from Edith Walton for sale no. 105D, $1,029.
    30   Cash sales for the month, $3,600 plus tax of $180.
    30   Bank credit card sales for the month, $2,500 plus tax of $125. Bank credit card expenses on these sales, $100.
    30   Received cash for rent revenue, $600.
    30   Borrowed cash from the bank by signing a note, $3,000.

Northern Micro's cash receipts journal provides separate columns for Accounts Receivable Credit, Sales Credit, Sales Tax Payable Credit, Bank

FIGURE 11-15   Northern Micro Cash Receipts Journal

CASH RECEIPTS JOURNAL

	DATE		ACCOUNT CREDITED	POST. REF.	GENERAL CREDIT		
1	Apr. 19--	14	Enrico Lorenzo				1
2		20	Brenda Myers				2
3		28	Edith Walton				3
4		30					4
5		30					5
6		30	Rent Revenue		6 0 0 00		6
7		30	Notes Payable		3 0 0 0 00		7
8							8

Credit Card Expense Debit, and Cash Debit. These are the accounts most frequently affected by Northern Micro's cash receipts transactions. In addition, a General Credit column is provided for credits to any other accounts affected by cash receipts transactions.

A cash receipt is recorded in the cash receipts journal by entering the following information:

1. Date
2. Account credited (if applicable)
3. Dollar amounts

The Account Credited column is used for two purposes:

1. To identify the customer name for any collection on account. This column is used whenever the Accounts Receivable Credit column is used.
2. To enter the appropriate account name whenever the General Credit column is used.

The Account Credited column is left blank whenever the entry is for cash sales or bank credit card sales.

The cash receipts journal in Figure 11-15 is designed for a company, like Northern Micro, that charges sales tax, makes bank credit card sales, and offers no cash discounts. For a wholesaler who does not charge sales tax, makes no bank credit card sales, but does offer cash discounts, a cash receipts journal like the one in Figure 11-16 would be used. Recall that a special journal should be designed with column headings for frequently used accounts. Thus, the cash receipts journal in Figure 11-16 has no Sales Tax Payable Credit or Bank Credit Card Expense Debit columns. Instead, a Sales Discount Debit column is provided. In this way, the common cash receipts transactions of the wholesaler can be easily and efficiently recorded.

Posting from the Cash Receipts Journal

Figure 11-17 illustrates the general ledger posting process for Northern Micro's cash receipts journal.

FIGURE 11-15 (continued)   Northern Micro Cash Receipts Journal

PAGE 7

	ACCOUNTS RECEIVABLE CREDIT	SALES CREDIT	SALES TAX PAYABLE CREDIT	BANK CREDIT CARD EXPENSE DEBIT	CASH DEBIT	
1	1 5 9 6 00				1 5 9 6 00	1
2	4 6 2 00				4 6 2 00	2
3	1 0 2 9 00				1 0 2 9 00	3
4		3 6 0 0 00	1 8 0 00		3 7 8 0 00	4
5		2 5 0 0 00	1 2 5 00	1 0 0 00	2 5 2 5 00	5
6					6 0 0 00	6
7					3 0 0 0 00	7
8						8

FIGURE 11-16   Cash Receipts Journal Without Sales Tax

	DATE	ACCOUNT CREDITED	POST. REF.	GENERAL CREDIT	ACCOUNTS RECEIVABLE CREDIT	SALES CREDIT	SALES DISCOUNT DEBIT	CASH DEBIT	
1									1

CASH RECEIPTS JOURNAL — PAGE 1

On a daily basis:

STEP 1   Post each amount in the General Credit column to the appropriate general ledger account.

STEP 2   Insert the date in the Date column and the initials "CR" and the cash receipts journal page number in the Posting Reference column of each ledger account.

STEP 3   Insert the general ledger account numbers in the Posting Reference column of the cash receipts journal.

At the end of each month:

STEP 4   Total the amount columns, verify that the total of the debit columns equals the total of the credit columns, and rule the columns.

STEP 5   Post each column total except the General Credit column to the general ledger account indicated in the column headings.

STEP 6   Insert the date in the Date column and the initials "CR" and the cash receipts journal page number in the Posting Reference column of each ledger account.

STEP 7   Insert the general ledger account numbers immediately below each column total except the General Credit column.

STEP 8   Insert a check mark (✓) in the Posting Reference column of the cash receipts journal for the cash sales and bank credit card sales, and immediately below the General Credit column.

The general ledger accounts affected by the cash receipts transactions are now up to date. Postings to the accounts receivable ledger also must be made. These postings are made daily. Figure 11-18 illustrates the posting procedures, as follows.

STEP 1   Post the individual cash receipt to the customer's account on the date the receipt occurs.

STEP 2   Insert the date in the Date column and the initials "CR" and the cash receipts journal page number in the Posting Reference column of each customer account.

STEP 3   Insert a check mark (✓) in the Posting Reference column of the cash receipts journal to indicate that the amount has been posted.

FIGURE 11-17   Posting the Cash Receipts Journal to the General Ledger

CASH RECEIPTS JOURNAL   Page 7

Date	Account Credited	Post. Ref.	General Credit	Accounts Receivable Credit	Sales Credit	Sales Tax Payable Credit	Bank Credit Card Expense Debit	Cash Debit
19--								
Apr. 4	Enrico Lorenzo	8		1,596.00				1,596.00
10	Brenda Myers			462.00				462.00
18	Edith Walton			1,029.00				1,029.00
30		✓			3,600.00	180.00		3,780.00
30		✓			2,500.00	125.00	100.00	2,525.00
30	Rent Revenue	451	600.00					600.00
30	Notes Payable	218	3,000.00					3,000.00
		3	3,600.00	3,087.00	6,100.00	305.00	100.00	12,992.00
			(✓)	(131)	(411)	(225)	(553)	(111)

Debit total: $ 100
                        12,992
                     $13,092

Credit total: $ 3,600
                        3,087
                        6,100
                         305
                     $13,092

GENERAL LEDGER (Partial)

ACCOUNT Cash   **ACCOUNT NO.** 111

Date	Item	Post. Ref.	Debit	Credit	Balance Debit	Balance Credit
19--						
Apr. 1	Bal.	✓			20,000.00	
30		CR7	12,992.00		32,992.00	

ACCOUNT Accounts Receivable   **ACCOUNT NO.** 131

Date	Item	Post. Ref.	Debit	Credit	Balance Debit	Balance Credit
19--						
Apr. 1	Bal.	✓			12,000.00	
30		S6	5,418.00		17,418.00	
30		CR7		3,087.00	14,331.00	

ACCOUNT Notes Payable   **ACCOUNT NO.** 218

Date	Item	Post. Ref.	Debit	Credit	Balance Debit	Balance Credit
19--						
Apr. 1	Bal.	✓				6,000.00
30		CR7		3,000.00		9,000.00

ACCOUNT Sales Tax Payable   **ACCOUNT NO.** 225

Date	Item	Post. Ref.	Debit	Credit	Balance Debit	Balance Credit
19--						
Apr. 30		S6		258.00		258.00
30		CR7		305.00		563.00

ACCOUNT Sales   **ACCOUNT NO.** 411

Date	Item	Post. Ref.	Debit	Credit	Balance Debit	Balance Credit
19--						
Apr. 1	Bal.	✓				27,000.00
30		S6		5,160.00		32,160.00
30		CR7		6,100.00		38,260.00

ACCOUNT Rent Revenue   **ACCOUNT NO.** 451

Date	Item	Post. Ref.	Debit	Credit	Balance Debit	Balance Credit
19--						
Apr. 1	Bal.	✓				1,800.00
30		CR7		600.00		2,400.00

ACCOUNT Bank Credit Card Expense   **ACCOUNT NO.** 553

Date	Item	Post. Ref.	Debit	Credit	Balance Debit	Balance Credit
19--						
Apr. 1	Bal.	✓			430.00	
30		CR7	100.00		530.00	

FIGURE 11-18   Posting the Cash Receipts Journal to the Accounts Receivable Ledger

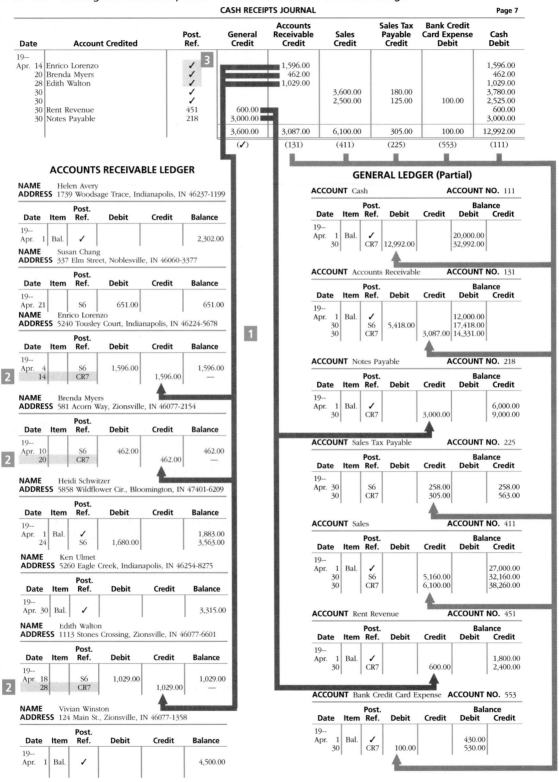

SCHEDULE OF ACCOUNTS RECEIVABLE

LO5 Prepare a schedule of accounts receivable.

All postings to the general ledger and accounts receivable ledger are now complete. At this point, the Accounts Receivable balance in the general ledger should equal the sum of the customer balances in the accounts receivable ledger.

To verify that the sum of the accounts receivable ledger balances equals the Accounts Receivable balance, a **schedule of accounts receivable** is prepared. This is a listing of customer accounts and balances, usually prepared at the end of the month. The schedule of accounts receivable for Northern Micro as of April 30 is illustrated in Figure 11-19.

FIGURE 11-19   Schedule of Accounts Receivable

Northern Micro
Schedule of Accounts Receivable
April 30, 19--

Helen Avery	$ 2 3 0 2 00
Susan Chang	6 5 1 00
Heidi Schwitzer	3 5 6 3 00
Ken Ulmet	3 3 1 5 00
Vivian Winston	4 5 0 0 00
Total	$14 3 3 1 00

International Sales Terms

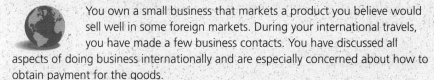

You own a small business that markets a product you believe would sell well in some foreign markets. During your international travels, you have made a few business contacts. You have discussed all aspects of doing business internationally and are especially concerned about how to obtain payment for the goods.

You normally offer your best customers terms of 2/10, n/30. However, you require new customers to pay cash on delivery of the goods. Since all your foreign customers would be new, you would like to receive payment in full before you ship your product. However, you have found no buyers willing to accept such terms. What other options do you have?

The most common form of payment in international trade is a letter of credit. Such letters are promises from banks to make payment based on the terms written in the letter.[1] For example, the bank would guarantee to wire payment to your business account when the goods have been received and inspected by the buyer. A letter of credit contains a guarantee from the bank, as well as the buyer, that payment will be made.

---

[1] Patricia M. Carey, "Trade Q&A," *Your Company* (Winter 1995): 12.

This schedule is prepared from the list of customer accounts in the accounts receivable ledger. The total calculated in the schedule is compared with the balance in Accounts Receivable in the general ledger. Note that the $14,331 total listed in the schedule equals the Accounts Receivable balance shown in Figure 11-18. If the schedule total and the Accounts Receivable balance do not agree, the error must be located and corrected. To find the error, use the following procedures.

STEP 1   Verify the total of the schedule.

STEP 2   Verify the postings to the accounts receivable ledger.

STEP 3   Verify the totals in the sales and cash receipts journals.

STEP 4   Verify the postings to Accounts Receivable in the general ledger.

KEY POINTS

1   A merchandising business buys and sells merchandise. Retailers generally make sales in the store. Important accounting documents are cash register tapes and sales tickets. Wholesalers generally ship merchandise to retailers. A key accounting document is the sales invoice. When customers return merchandise or obtain price adjustments, a credit memo is issued.

2   Four accounts are used in accounting for merchandise sales transactions:

1. Sales
2. Sales Tax Payable
3. Sales Returns and Allowances
4. Sales Discounts

3   A sales journal is a special journal for recording sales on account. A sale is recorded by entering the:

1. Date
2. Sale number
3. Customer
4. Dollar amounts

To post from the sales journal to the general ledger:

1. Total, verify the equality of, and rule the amount columns.
2. Post column totals to the general ledger accounts.
3. Insert the date and posting reference in the ledger accounts.
4. Insert the account numbers below the column totals in the sales journal.

To post from the sales journal to the accounts receivable ledger:

1. Post individual sale amounts to customer accounts.
2. Insert the date and posting reference in the customer accounts.
3. Insert a check mark (✓) in the Posting Reference column of the sales journal.

Sales returns and allowances are recorded in the general journal.

4 A cash receipts journal is a special journal for recording cash receipts. A cash receipt is recorded by entering the:

1. Date
2. Account credited (if applicable)
3. Dollar amounts

To post from the cash receipts journal to the general ledger:

On a daily basis:

1. Post General Credit column amounts to the general ledger.
2. Insert the date and posting reference in the accounts.
3. Insert the account numbers in the Posting Reference column of the cash receipts journal.

At the end of each month:

4. Total, verify the equality of, and rule the amount columns.
5. Post specific account column totals to the general ledger.
6. Insert the date and posting reference in the accounts.
7. Insert the account numbers below the specific account column totals.
8. Insert a check mark (✓) in the Posting Reference column for the cash sales and bank credit card sales and below the General Credit column.

To post from the cash receipts journal to the accounts receivable ledger:

1. Post individual cash receipts to customer accounts.
2. Insert the date and posting reference in the customer accounts.
3. Insert a check mark (✓) in the Posting Reference column of the cash receipts journal.

5 The schedule of accounts receivable is used to verify that the sum of the accounts receivable ledger balances equals the Accounts Receivable balance.

KEY TERMS

accounts receivable ledger 348   A separate ledger containing an individual account receivable for each customer, kept in either alphabetical or numerical order.

cash discounts 343   A discount to encourage prompt payment by customers who buy merchandise on account.

cash receipts journal 352   A special journal used to record only cash receipt transactions.

controlling account 348   A summary account maintained in the general ledger with a subsidiary ledger (for example, the accounts receivable ledger).

credit memo 340   A document issued when credit is given for merchandise returned or for an allowance.

merchandising business 337   A business that purchases merchandise, such as clothing, furniture, or computers, and sells that merchandise to its customers.

sale 337   A transfer of merchandise from one business or individual to another in exchange for cash or a promise to pay cash.

sales allowances 340   Reductions in the price of merchandise granted by the seller because of defects or other problems with the merchandise.

sales discounts 343   To the seller, cash discounts are considered sales discounts.

sales invoice 339   A document that is generated to bill the customer who made the purchase.

sales journal 345   A special journal used to record only sales on account.

sales return 340   Merchandise returned by the customer for a refund.

sales ticket 338   An additional document often created as evidence of a sale in a retail business.

schedule of accounts receivable 357   A listing of customer accounts and balances, usually prepared at the end of the month.

special journal 345   A journal designed for recording only certain kinds of transactions.

REVIEW QUESTIONS

1. Identify the sales documents commonly used in retail and wholesale businesses.
2. What is the purpose of a credit memo?
3. Describe how each of the following accounts is used: (1) Sales, (2) Sales Tax Payable, (3) Sales Returns and Allowances, and (4) Sales Discounts.
4. List four items of information about each sale entered in the sales journal.
5. What steps are followed in posting from the sales journal to the general ledger?
6. What steps are followed in posting from the sales journal to the accounts receivable ledger?
7. How is the posting of Sales Returns and Allowances from the general journal to the general ledger and accounts receivable ledger different from the normal posting process?
8. List three items of information about each cash receipt entered in the cash receipts journal.
9. What steps are followed in posting from the cash receipts journal to the general ledger?
10. What steps are followed in posting from the cash receipts journal to the accounts receivable ledger?
11. If the total of the schedule of accounts receivable does not agree with the Accounts Receivable balance, what procedures should be used to search for the error?

MANAGING YOUR WRITING

You and your spouse have separate charge accounts at a local department store. When you tried to use your card last week, you were told that you were over the credit limit. This puzzled you because you had paid the entire account balance several weeks ago. When the monthly statements arrived yesterday, the error was clear. The store had credited your payment to your spouse's account.

Your account was treated as over the limit, and the store had charged you interest on the unpaid balance. You suspect that part of the problem is that you and your spouse use the same last name (Morales) and have similar first names (Carmen and Carmelo).

Write a letter to the store requesting correction of your accounts and suggesting a way to identify your accounts so that this error does not happen again.

DEMONSTRATION PROBLEM

Karen Hunt operates Hunt's Audio-Video Store. The books include a sales journal, a cash receipts journal, and a general journal. The following transactions related to sales on account and cash receipts occurred during April.

April 3 Sold merchandise on account to Susan Haberman, $159.50 plus tax of $11.17. Sale no. 41.

4 Sold merchandise on account to Glenn Kelly, $299.95 plus tax of $21.00. Sale no. 42.

6 Received payment from Tera Scherrer on account, $69.50.

7 Issued a credit memo to Kenneth Watt for merchandise returned that had been sold on account, $42.75 including tax of $2.80.

10 Received payment from Kellie Cokley on account, $99.95.

11 Sold merchandise on account to Victor Cardona, $499.95 plus tax of $35.00. Sale no. 43.

14 Received payment from Kenneth Watt in full settlement of account, $157.00.

17 Sold merchandise on account to Susan Haberman, $379.95 plus tax of $26.60. Sale no. 44.

19 Sold merchandise on account to Tera Scherrer, $59.95 plus tax of $4.20. Sale no. 45.

21 Issued a credit memo to Glenn Kelly for merchandise returned that had been sold on account, $53.45 including tax of $3.50.

24 Received payment from Victor Cardona on account, $299.95.

25 Sold merchandise on account to Kellie Cokley, $179.50 plus tax of $12.57. Sale no. 46.

26 Received payment from Susan Haberman on account, $250.65.

28 Sold merchandise on account to Kenneth Watt, $49.95 plus tax of $3.50. Sale no. 47.

April 30   Bank credit card sales for the month, $1,220.00 plus tax of $85.40. Bank credit card expense on these sales, $65.27.

30   Cash sales for the month, $2,000.00 plus tax of $140.00.

Hunt had the following general ledger account balances as of April 1.

Account Title	Account No.	General Ledger Balance on April 1
Cash	111	$5,000.00
Accounts Receivable	131	1,208.63
Sales Tax Payable	225	72.52
Sales	411	8,421.49
Sales Returns and Allowances	411.1	168.43
Bank Credit Card Expense	553	215.00

Hunt also had the following accounts receivable ledger account balances as of April 1:

Customer	Accounts Receivable Balance
Victor Cardona 6300 Washington Blvd. St. Louis, MO 63130-9523	$299.95
Kellie Cokley 4220 Kingsbury Blvd. St. Louis, MO 63130-1645	$99.95
Susan Haberman 9421 Garden Ct. Kirkwood, MO 63122-1878	$79.98
Glenn Kelly 6612 Arundel Pl. Clayton, MO 63150-9266	$379.50
Tera Scherrer 315 W. Linden St. Webster Groves, MO 63119-9881	$149.50
Kenneth Watt 11742 Fawnridge Dr. St. Louis, MO 63131-1726	$199.75

REQUIRED

1. Open four-column general ledger accounts and three-column accounts receivable ledger accounts for Hunt's Audio-Video Store as of April 1 of the current year. Enter the April 1 balance in each of the accounts.

2. Enter each transaction either in a three-column sales journal (page 5), a six-column cash receipts journal (page 8), or a general journal (page 7).
3. Post directly from each of the three journals to the proper customers' accounts in the accounts receivable ledger. Each subsidiary ledger account should show the initials "S," "CR," or "J," followed by the appropriate journal page number as a posting reference for each transaction.
4. Enter the totals and rule the sales journal and the cash receipts journal. Complete the summary posting of the cash receipts and sales journals and the individual posting of the general journal to the proper general ledger accounts. Each general ledger account should show the initials "S," "CR," or "J," followed by the appropriate journal page number as a posting reference for each transaction.
5. Prove the balance of the summary accounts receivable account by preparing a schedule of accounts receivable as of April 30, based on the accounts receivable ledger.

SOLUTION

1, 3, 4.

ACCOUNTS RECEIVABLE LEDGER

NAME: Victor Cardona

DATE		ITEM	POST. REF.	DEBIT	CREDIT	BALANCE
Apr.^19--	1	Bal.	✓			2 9 9 95
	11		S5	5 3 4 95		8 3 4 90
	24		CR8		2 9 9 95	5 3 4 95

NAME: Kellie Cokley

DATE		ITEM	POST. REF.	DEBIT	CREDIT	BALANCE
Apr.^19--	1	Bal.	✓			9 9 95
	10		CR8		9 9 95	—
	25		S5	1 9 2 07		1 9 2 07

NAME: Susan Haberman

DATE		ITEM	POST. REF.	DEBIT	CREDIT	BALANCE
Apr.^19--	1	Bal.	✓			7 9 98
	3		S5	1 7 0 67		2 5 0 65
	17		S5	4 0 6 55		6 5 7 20
	26		CR8		2 5 0 65	4 0 6 55

1, 3, 4. (continued)

NAME: Glenn Kelly

DATE		ITEM	POST. REF.	DEBIT	CREDIT	BALANCE
Apr.	1	Bal.	✓			3 7 9 50
	4		S5	3 2 0 95		7 0 0 45
	21		J7		5 3 45	6 4 7 00

NAME: Tera Scherrer

DATE		ITEM	POST. REF.	DEBIT	CREDIT	BALANCE
Apr.	1	Bal.	✓			1 4 9 50
	6		CR8		6 9 50	8 0 00
	19		S5	6 4 15		1 4 4 15

NAME: Kenneth Watt

DATE		ITEM	POST. REF.	DEBIT	CREDIT	BALANCE
Apr.	1	Bal.	✓			1 9 9 75
	7		J7		4 2 75	1 5 7 00
	14		CR8		1 5 7 00	—
	28		S5	5 3 45		5 3 45

GENERAL LEDGER

ACCOUNT: Cash   ACCOUNT NO. 111

DATE		ITEM	POST. REF.	DEBIT	CREDIT	BALANCE DEBIT	BALANCE CREDIT
Apr.	1	Bal.	✓			5 0 0 0 00	
	30		CR8	4 2 5 7 18		9 2 5 7 18	

ACCOUNT: Accounts Receivable   ACCOUNT NO. 131

DATE		ITEM	POST. REF.	DEBIT	CREDIT	BALANCE DEBIT	BALANCE CREDIT
Apr.	1	Bal.	✓			1 2 0 8 63	
	7		J7		4 2 75	1 1 6 5 88	
	21		J7		5 3 45	1 1 1 2 43	
	30		S5	1 7 4 2 79		2 8 5 5 22	
	30		CR8		8 7 7 05	1 9 7 8 17	

1, 3, 4. (continued)

ACCOUNT: **Sales Tax Payable**   ACCOUNT NO. 225

DATE		ITEM	POST. REF.	DEBIT	CREDIT	BALANCE DEBIT	BALANCE CREDIT
Apr.^19--	1	Bal.	✓				7 2 52
	7		J7	2 80			6 9 72
	21		J7	3 50			6 6 22
	30		S5		1 1 4 04		1 8 0 26
	30		CR8		2 2 5 40		4 0 5 66

ACCOUNT: **Sales**   ACCOUNT NO. 411

DATE		ITEM	POST. REF.	DEBIT	CREDIT	BALANCE DEBIT	BALANCE CREDIT
Apr.^19--	1	Bal.	✓				8 4 2 1 49
	30		S5		1 6 2 8 75		10 0 5 0 24
	30		CR8		3 2 2 0 00		13 2 7 0 24

ACCOUNT: **Sales Returns and Allowances**   ACCOUNT NO. 411.1

DATE		ITEM	POST. REF.	DEBIT	CREDIT	BALANCE DEBIT	BALANCE CREDIT
Apr.^19--	1	Bal.	✓			1 6 8 43	
	7		J7	3 9 95		2 0 8 38	
	21		J7	4 9 95		2 5 8 33	

ACCOUNT: **Bank Credit Card Expense**   ACCOUNT NO. 553

DATE		ITEM	POST. REF.	DEBIT	CREDIT	BALANCE DEBIT	BALANCE CREDIT
Apr.^19--	1	Bal.	✓			2 1 5 00	
	30		CR8	6 5 27		2 8 0 27	

2.

GENERAL JOURNAL   PAGE 7

	DATE		DESCRIPTION	POST. REF.	DEBIT	CREDIT	
1	Apr.^19--	7	Sales Returns and Allowances	411.1	3 9 95		1
2			Sales Tax Payable	225	2 80		2
3			Accounts Receivable/K. Watt	131/✓		4 2 75	3
4							4
5		21	Sales Returns and Allowances	411.1	4 9 95		5
6			Sales Tax Payable	225	3 50		6
7			Accounts Receivable/G. Kelly	131/✓		5 3 45	7

2, 3, 4.

CASH RECEIPTS JOURNAL

	DATE		ACCOUNT CREDITED	POST. REF.	GENERAL CREDIT	
1	19-- Apr.	6	Tera Scherrer	✓		1
2		10	Kellie Cokley	✓		2
3		14	Kenneth Watt	✓		3
4		24	Victor Cardona	✓		4
5		26	Susan Haberman	✓		5
6		30		✓		6
7		30		✓		7
8						8
9						9
10						10

2, 3, 4.

SALES JOURNAL   PAGE 5

	DATE		SALE NO.	TO WHOM SOLD	POST. REF.	ACCOUNTS RECEIVABLE DEBIT	SALES CREDIT	SALES TAX PAYABLE CREDIT	
1	19-- Apr.	3	41	Susan Haberman	✓	1 7 0 67	1 5 9 50	1 1 17	1
2		4	42	Glenn Kelly	✓	3 2 0 95	2 9 9 95	2 1 00	2
3		11	43	Victor Cardona	✓	5 3 4 95	4 9 9 95	3 5 00	3
4		17	44	Susan Haberman	✓	4 0 6 55	3 7 9 95	2 6 60	4
5		19	45	Tera Scherrer	✓	6 4 15	5 9 95	4 20	5
6		25	46	Kellie Cokley	✓	1 9 2 07	1 7 9 50	1 2 57	6
7		28	47	Kenneth Watt	✓	5 3 45	4 9 95	3 50	7
8						1 7 4 2 79	1 6 2 8 75	1 1 4 04	8
9						(131)	(411)	(225)	9

5.

Hunt's Audio-Video Store
Schedule of Accounts Receivable
April 30, 19--

Victor Cardona	5 3 4 95
Kellie Cokley	1 9 2 07
Susan Haberman	4 0 6 55
Glenn Kelly	6 4 7 00
Tera Scherrer	1 4 4 15
Kenneth Watt	5 3 45
Total	1 9 7 8 17

PAGE 8

	ACCOUNTS RECEIVABLE CREDIT	SALES CREDIT	SALES TAX PAYABLE CREDIT	BANK CREDIT CARD EXPENSE DEBIT	CASH DEBIT	
1	6 9 50				6 9 50	1
2	9 9 95				9 9 95	2
3	1 5 7 00				1 5 7 00	3
4	2 9 9 95				2 9 9 95	4
5	2 5 0 65				2 5 0 65	5
6		1 2 2 0 00	8 5 40	6 5 27	1 2 4 0 13	6
7		2 0 0 0 00	1 4 0 00		2 1 4 0 00	7
8	8 7 7 05	3 2 2 0 00	2 2 5 40	6 5 27	4 2 5 7 18	8
9	(131)	(411)	(225)	(553)	(111)	9
10						10

SERIES A EXERCISES

1 **EXERCISE 11A1 SALES DOCUMENTS** For each document or procedure listed below, indicate whether it would be used for a retail business or a wholesale business, as described in the chapter.

1. sales ticket

2. sales invoice

3. credit approval

4. cash register tape summary

5. credit memo

6. customer purchase order

2 **EXERCISE 11A2 SALES TRANSACTIONS AND ACCOUNTS** Using T accounts for Cash, Accounts Receivable, Sales Tax Payable, Sales, Sales Returns and Allowances, and Sales Discounts, enter the following sales transactions. Use a new set of accounts for each part, 1–5.

1. No sales tax.
   (a) Merchandise is sold for $300 cash.
   (b) Merchandise is sold on account for $285.
   (c) Payment is received for merchandise sold on account.

2. 5% sales tax.
   (a) Merchandise is sold for $300 cash plus sales tax.
   (b) Merchandise is sold on account for $285 plus sales tax.
   (c) Payment is received for merchandise sold on account.

3. Cash and credit sales, with returned merchandise.
   (a) Merchandise is sold for $325 cash.
   (b) $25 of merchandise sold for $325 is returned for refund.
   (c) Merchandise is sold on account for $350.
   (d) $35 of merchandise sold for $350 is returned for a credit.
   (e) Payment is received for balance owed on merchandise sold on account.

4. 5% sales tax, with returned merchandise.
   (a) Merchandise is sold on account for $400 plus sales tax.
   (b) Merchandise totaling $40 is returned for a credit.
   (c) Balance on account is paid in cash.
   (d) Merchandise is sold for $280 cash plus sales tax.
   (e) $20 of merchandise sold for $280 cash is returned for refund.
5. Sales on account, with 2/10, n/30 cash discount.
   (a) Merchandise is sold on account for $350.
   (b) The balance is paid within the discount period.

2 **EXERCISE 11A3 COMPUTING NET SALES** Based on the following information, compute net sales.

Gross sales	$3,580
Sales returns and allowances	428
Sales discounts	73

3 **EXERCISE 11A4 JOURNALIZING SALES TRANSACTIONS**
Enter the following transactions (a) in a general journal and (b) in a sales journal. Use a 6% sales tax rate.

May 1 Sold merchandise on account to J. Adams, $2,000 plus sales tax. Sale no. 488.

   4 Sold merchandise on account to B. Clark, $1,800 plus sales tax. Sale no. 489.

   8 Sold merchandise on account to A. Duck, $1,500 plus sales tax. Sale no. 490.

   11 Sold merchandise on account to E. Hill, $1,950 plus sales tax. Sale no. 491.

3 **EXERCISE 11A5 JOURNALIZING SALES RETURNS AND ALLOWANCES** Enter the following transactions in a general journal and post them to the appropriate general ledger and accounts receivable ledger accounts. Use account numbers as shown in the chapter. Beginning balance in Accounts Receivable is $4,200. Beginning balances in customer accounts are: Abramowitz, $850; Perez, $1,018; and Gruder, $428.

June 1 John B. Abramowitz returned merchandise previously purchased on account (sale no. 329), $73.

   6 Marie L. Perez returned merchandise previously purchased on account (sale no. 321), $44.

   8 L. B. Gruder returned merchandise previously purchased on account (sale no. 299), $24.

4 **EXERCISE 11A6 JOURNALIZING CASH RECEIPTS** Enter the following transactions (a) in a general journal and (b) in a cash receipts journal.

July 3 James Adler made payment on account, $643.
   10 Cash sales for the week, $2,320.

continued

July 14 Betty Havel made payment on account, $430.
15 J. L. Borg made payment on account, $117.
18 Cash sales for the week, $2,237.

5 **EXERCISE 11A7 SCHEDULE OF ACCOUNTS RECEIVABLE**
From the accounts receivable ledger shown, prepare a schedule of accounts receivable for Pheng Co. as of August 31, 19--.

ACCOUNTS RECEIVABLE LEDGER

NAME B & G Distributors

ADDRESS 2628 Burlington Avenue, Chicago, IL 60604

DATE	ITEM	POST. REF.	DEBIT	CREDIT	BALANCE
Aug. 3		S1		1 3 8 0 00	1 3 8 0 00
8		J1	1 4 0 00		1 2 4 0 00

NAME P. L. Davis

ADDRESS 1422 SW Pacific, Chicago, IL 60603

DATE	ITEM	POST. REF.	DEBIT	CREDIT	BALANCE
Aug. 5		S1		2 1 3 6 00	2 1 3 6 00
11		CR1	2 1 3 6 00		—

NAME B. J. Hinschliff & Co.

ADDRESS 133 College Blvd., Des Plaines, IL 60611

DATE	ITEM	POST. REF.	DEBIT	CREDIT	BALANCE
Aug. 15		S1		1 1 0 6 00	1 1 0 6 00
21		S1		3 8 4 00	1 4 9 0 00

NAME Sally M. Pitts

ADDRESS 213 East 29th Place, Chicago, IL 60601

DATE	ITEM	POST. REF.	DEBIT	CREDIT	BALANCE
Aug. 21		S1		8 3 8 00	8 3 8 00

NAME Trendsetter, Inc.

ADDRESS 28 Industrial Way, Chicago, IL 60600

DATE	ITEM	POST. REF.	DEBIT	CREDIT	BALANCE
Aug. 28		S1		1 0 1 8 00	1 0 1 8 00

3 **PROBLEM 11A1 SALES JOURNAL** J. K. Bijan owns a retail business and made the following sales during the month of August 19--. There is a 6% sales tax on all sales.

Aug. 1 Sale no. 213 to Jung Manufacturing Co., $1,200 plus sales tax.
 3 Sale no. 214 to Hassad Co., $3,600 plus sales tax.
 7 Sale no. 215 to Helsinki, Inc., $1,400 plus sales tax. (Open a new account for this customer. Address is 125 Fishers Dr., Noblesville, IN 47870-8867.)
 11 Sale no. 216 to Ardis Myler, $1,280 plus sales tax.
 18 Sale no. 217 to Hassad Co., $4,330 plus sales tax.
 22 Sale no. 218 to Jung Manufacturing Co., $2,000 plus sales tax.
 30 Sale no. 219 to Ardis Myler, $1,610 plus sales tax.

REQUIRED

1. Record the transactions in the sales journal. Total and verify the column totals and rule the columns.
2. Post from the sales journal to the general ledger accounts and to the accounts receivable ledger accounts. Use account numbers as shown in the chapter.

4 **PROBLEM 11A2 CASH RECEIPTS JOURNAL** Zebra Imaginarium, a retail business, had the following cash receipts during December 19--. The sales tax is 6%.

Dec. 1 Received payment on account from Michael Anderson, $1,360.
 2 Received payment on account from Ansel Manufacturing, $382.
 7 Cash sales for the week, $3,160 plus tax. Bank credit card sales for the week, $1,000 plus tax. Bank credit card fee is 3%.
 8 Received payment on account from W. J. Beemer, $880.
 11 Michael Anderson returned merchandise for a credit, $60 plus tax.
 14 Cash sales for the week, $2,800 plus tax. Bank credit card sales for the week, $800 plus tax. Bank credit card fee is 3%.
 20 Received payment on account from Tom Wilson, $1,110.
 21 Ansel Manufacturing returned merchandise for a credit, $22 plus tax.
 22 Cash sales for the week, $3,200 plus tax.
 24 Received payment on account from Rachel Carson, $2,000.

Beginning general ledger account balances were:
Cash $9,862
Accounts Receivable 9,352

Beginning customer account balances were:

M. Anderson $2,480
Ansel Manufacturing 982
W. J. Beemer 880
R. Carson 3,200
T. Wilson 1,810

continued

1. Record the transactions in the cash receipts journal. Total and verify column totals and rule the columns. Use the general journal to record sales returns and allowances.
2. Post the journals to the general ledger and to the accounts receivable ledger accounts. Use account numbers as shown in the chapter.

3/4

SS

PROBLEM 11A3 SALES JOURNAL, CASH RECEIPTS JOURNAL, AND GENERAL JOURNAL

Owens Distributors is a retail business. The following sales, returns, and cash receipts occurred during March 19--. There is an 8% sales tax. Beginning general ledger account balances were: Cash, $9,741.00; and Accounts Receivable, $1,058.25. Beginning customer account balances were: Thompson Group, $1,058.25.

March 1 Sale no. 33C to Able & Co., $1,800 plus sales tax.
3 Sale no. 33D to R. J. Kalas, Inc., $2,240 plus sales tax.
5 Able & Co. returned merchandise from sale no. 33C for a credit (credit memo no. 66), $30 plus sales tax.
7 Cash sales for the week, $3,160 plus sales tax.
10 Received payment from Able & Co. for sale no. 33C less credit memo no. 66.
11 Sale no. 33E to Blevins Bakery, $1,210 plus sales tax.
13 Received payment from R. J. Kalas for sale no. 33D.
14 Cash sales for the week, $4,200 plus sales tax.
16 Blevins Bakery returned merchandise from sale no. 33E for a credit (credit memo no. 67), $44 plus sales tax.
18 Sale no. 33F to R. J. Kalas, Inc., $2,620 plus sales tax.
20 Received payment from Blevins Bakery for sale no. 33E less credit memo no. 67.
21 Cash sales for the week, $2,400 plus sales tax.
25 Sale no. 33G to Blevins Bakery, $1,915 plus sales tax.
27 Sale no. 33H to Thompson Group, $2,016 plus sales tax.
28 Cash sales for the week, $3,500 plus sales tax.

1. Record the transactions in the sales journal, the cash receipts journal, and the general journal. Total, verify, and rule the columns where appropriate at the end of the month.
2. Post from the journals to the general ledger and accounts receivable ledger accounts. Use account numbers as shown in the chapter.

5

PROBLEM 11A4 SCHEDULE OF ACCOUNTS RECEIVABLE

Based on the information provided in Problem 11A3, prepare a schedule of accounts receivable for Owens Distributors as of March 31, 19--. Verify that the accounts receivable account balance in the general ledger agrees with the schedule of accounts receivable total.

SERIES B EXERCISES

1

EXERCISE 11B1 SALES DOCUMENTS

Indicate whether the following documents and procedures are for a retail business or for a wholesale business, as described in the chapter.

1. A cash register receipt is given to the customer.
2. Credit approval is required since sales are almost always "on account."
3. Three copies of the sales invoice are prepared: one for shipping, one for the customer (as a bill), and one for accounting.
4. A sales ticket is given to a customer and another copy goes to accounting.
5. The sales process begins with a customer purchase order.
6. The sales invoice itemizes what is sold, its cost, and the total amount owed.

2 **EXERCISE 11B2 SALES TRANSACTIONS AND ACCOUNTS**
Using T accounts for Cash, Accounts Receivable, Sales Tax Payable, Sales, Sales Returns and Allowances, and Sales Discounts, enter the following sales transactions. Use a new set of accounts for each part, 1-5.

1. No sales tax.
   (a) Merchandise is sold for $250 cash.
   (b) Merchandise is sold on account for $225.
   (c) Payment is received for merchandise sold on account.
2. 6% sales tax.
   (a) Merchandise is sold for $250 cash plus sales tax.
   (b) Merchandise is sold on account for $225 plus sales tax.
   (c) Payment is received for merchandise sold on account.
3. Cash and credit sales, with returned merchandise.
   (a) Merchandise is sold for $481 cash.
   (b) $18 of merchandise sold for $481 is returned for a refund.
   (c) Merchandise is sold on account for $388.
   (d) $24 of merchandise sold for $388 is returned for a credit.
   (e) Payment is received for balance owed on merchandise sold on account.
4. 6% sales tax, with returned merchandise.
   (a) Merchandise is sold on account for $480 plus sales tax.
   (b) Merchandise totaling $30 is returned.
   (c) The balance on the account is paid in cash.
   (d) Merchandise is sold for $300 cash plus sales tax.
   (e) $30 of merchandise sold for $300 cash is returned for a refund.
5. Sales on account, with 2/10, n/30 cash discount.
   (a) Merchandise is sold on account for $280.
   (b) The balance is paid within the discount period.

2 **EXERCISE 11B3 COMPUTING NET SALES** Based on the following information, compute net sales.

Gross sales	$2,880
Sales returns and allowances	322
Sales discounts	56

3 **EXERCISE 11B4 JOURNALIZING SALES TRANSACTIONS**
Enter the following transactions (a) in a general journal, and (b) in a sales journal. Use a 5% sales tax rate.

Sept.   1 Sold merchandise on account to K. Smith, $1,800 plus sales tax. Sale no. 228.
3 Sold merchandise on account to J. Arnes, $3,100 plus sales tax. Sale no. 229.
5 Sold merchandise on account to M. Denison, $2,800 plus sales tax. Sale no. 230.
7 Sold merchandise on account to B. Marshall, $1,900 plus sales tax. Sale no. 231.

3 **EXERCISE 11B5 JOURNALIZING SALES RETURNS AND ALLOWANCES**   Enter the following transactions in a general journal and post them to the appropriate general ledger and accounts receivable ledger accounts. Use account numbers as shown in the chapter. Beginning balance in Accounts Receivable is $3,900. Beginning balances in customer accounts are: Phillips, $1,018; Adams, $850; and Green, $428.

June   1 Marie L. Phillips returned merchandise previously purchased on account (sale no. 33), $43.
11 John B. Adams returned merchandise previously purchased on account (sale no. 34), $59.
15 L. B. Greene returned merchandise previously purchased on account (sale no. 35), $21.

4 **EXERCISE 11B6 JOURNALIZING CASH RECEIPTS**   Enter the following transactions (a) in the general journal and (b) in a cash receipts journal.

Nov.   1 Jean Haghighat made payment on account, $750.
12 Marc Antonoff made payment on account, $464.
15 Cash sales, $3,763.
18 Will Mossein made payment on account, $241.
25 Cash sales, $2,648.

5 **EXERCISE 11B7 SCHEDULE OF ACCOUNTS RECEIVABLE** From the accounts receivable ledger shown, prepare a schedule of accounts receivable for Gelph Co. as of November 30, 19--.

ACCOUNTS RECEIVABLE LEDGER

NAME   James L. Adams Co.

ADDRESS   24481 McAdams Road, Dallas, TX 77001

DATE	ITEM	POST. REF.	DEBIT	CREDIT	BALANCE
19-- Nov. 1		S11		3 1 8 0 00	3 1 8 0 00
5		J8	1 8 0 00		3 0 0 0 00
7		S11		2 0 0 00	3 2 0 0 00

NAME	Trish Berens					
ADDRESS	34 West 55th Avenue, Fort Worth, TX 76310					

DATE	ITEM	POST. REF.	DEBIT	CREDIT	BALANCE
19-- Nov. 3		S11		1 3 6 0 00	1 3 6 0 00

NAME	M and T Jenkins, Inc.					
ADDRESS	100 NW Richfield, Austin, TX 78481					

DATE	ITEM	POST. REF.	DEBIT	CREDIT	BALANCE
19-- Nov. 5		S11		2 6 2 8 00	2 6 2 8 00
12		CR11	2 6 2 8 00		—

NAME	R & J Travis					
ADDRESS	288 Beacon Street, Dallas, TX 79301					

DATE	ITEM	POST. REF.	DEBIT	CREDIT	BALANCE
19-- Nov. 22		S11		1 8 4 2 00	1 8 4 2 00

SERIES B   PROBLEMS

3 **PROBLEM 11B1 SALES JOURNAL**   T. M. Maxwell owns a retail business and made the following sales during the month of July 19--. There is a 5% sales tax on all sales.

July   1 Sale no. 101 to Saga, Inc., $1,200 plus sales tax.
         8 Sale no. 102 to Vinnie Ward, $2,100 plus sales tax.
        15 Sale no. 103 to Dvorak Manufacturing, $4,300 plus sales tax.
        21 Sale no. 104 to Vinnie Ward, $1,800 plus sales tax.
        24 Sale no. 105 to Zapata Co., $1,600 plus sales tax. (Open a new account for this customer. Address is 789 N. Stafford Dr., Bloomington, IN 47401-6201.)
        29 Sale no. 106 to Saga, Inc., $1,450 plus sales tax.

REQUIRED
1. Record the transactions in the sales journal. Total and verify the column totals and rule the columns.
2. Post the sales journal to the general ledger accounts and to the accounts receivable ledger accounts. Use account numbers as shown in the chapter.

4 **PROBLEM 11B2 CASH RECEIPTS JOURNAL**   Color Florists, a retail business, had the following cash receipts during January 19--. The sales tax is 5%.

Jan.   1 Received payment on account from Ray Boyd, $880.
        3 Received payment on account from Clint Hassell, $271.
        5 Cash sales for the week, $2,800 plus tax. Bank credit card sales for
           the week, $1,200 plus tax. Bank credit card fee is 3%.
        8 Received payment on account from Jan Sowada, $912.
       11 Ray Boyd returned merchandise for a credit, $40 plus tax.
       12 Cash sales for the week, $3,100 plus tax. Bank credit card sales for
           the week, $1,900 plus tax. Bank credit card fee is 3%.
       15 Received payment on account from Robert Zehnle, $1,100.
       18 Robert Zehnle returned merchandise for a credit, $31 plus tax.
       19 Cash sales for the week, $2,230 plus tax.
       25 Received payment on account from Dazai Manufacturing, $318.

Beginning general ledger account balances were:

Cash $2,890.75
Accounts Receivable   6,300.00

Beginning customer account balances were:

R. Boyd $1,400
Dazai Manufacturing   318
C. Hassell   815
J. Sowada   1,481
R. Zehnle   2,286

REQUIRED

1. Record the transactions in the cash receipts journal. Total and verify the
column totals and rule the columns. Use the general journal to record
sales returns and allowances.

2. Post the journals to the general ledger and to the accounts receivable
ledger accounts. Use account numbers as shown in the chapter.

3/4

**PROBLEM 11B3 SALES JOURNAL, CASH RECEIPTS JOURNAL,
GENERAL JOURNAL**   Paul Jackson owns a retail business. The following sales, returns, and cash receipts are for April 19--. There is a 7% sales
tax.

April   1 Sale no. 111 to O. L. Meyers, $2,100 plus sales tax.
        3 Sale no. 112 to Andrew Plaa, $1,000 plus sales tax.
        6 O. L. Meyers returned merchandise from sale no. 111 for a credit
           (credit memo no. 42), $50 plus sales tax.
        7 Cash sales for the week, $3,240 plus sales tax.
        9 Received payment from O. L. Meyers for sale no. 111 less credit
           memo 42.
       12 Sale no. 113 to Melissa Richfield, $980 plus sales tax.
       14 Cash sales for the week, $2,180 plus sales tax.
       17 Melissa Richfield returned merchandise from sale no. 113 for a
           credit (credit memo no. 43), $40 plus sales tax.
       19 Sale no. 114 to Kelsay Munkres, $1,020 plus sales tax.
       21 Cash sales for the week, $2,600 plus sales tax.
       24 Sale no. 115 to O. L. Meyers, $920 plus sales tax.

continued

April 27 Sale no. 116 to Andrew Plaa, $1,320 plus sales tax.
       28 Cash sales for the week, $2,800 plus sales tax.

Beginning general ledger account balances were:

Cash	$2,864.54
Accounts Receivable	2,726.25

Beginning customer account balances were:

O. L. Meyers	$2,186.00
K. Munkres	482.00
M. Richfield	58.25

REQUIRED

1. Record the transactions in the sales journal, the cash receipts journal, and the general journal. Total, verify, and rule the columns where appropriate at the end of the month.
2. Post from the journals to the general ledger and accounts receivable ledger accounts. Use account numbers as shown in the chapter.

5 **PROBLEM 11B4 SCHEDULE OF ACCOUNTS RECEIVABLE**

Based on the information provided in Problem 11B3, prepare a schedule of accounts receivable for Paul Jackson as of April 30, 19--. Verify that the accounts receivable account balance in the general ledger agrees with the schedule of accounts receivable total.

MASTERY PROBLEM

Geoff and Sandy Harland own and operate Wayward Kennel and Pet Supply. Their motto is "If your pet is not becoming to you, he should be coming to us." The Harlands maintain a sales tax payable account throughout the month to account for the 6% sales tax. They use a sales journal, a cash receipts journal, and a general journal. The following sales and cash collections took place during the month of September.

Sept. 1 Sold a fish aquarium on account to Ken Shank, $125.00 plus tax of $7.50, terms n/30. Sale no. 101.
       3 Sold dog food on account to Nancy Truelove, $68.25 plus tax of $4.10, terms n/30. Sale no. 102.
       5 Sold a bird cage on account to Jean Warkentin, $43.95 plus tax of $2.64, terms n/30. Sale no. 103.
       8 Cash sales for the week, $2,332.45 plus tax of $139.95.
     10 Received cash for boarding and grooming services, $625.00 plus tax of $37.50.
     11 Jean Warkentin stopped by the store to point out a minor defect in the bird cage purchased in sale no. 103. The Harlands offered a sales allowance of $10.00 plus tax on the price of the cage which satisfied Warkentin.
     12 Sold a cockatoo on account to Tully Shaw, $1,200.00 plus tax of $72.00, terms n/30. Sale no. 104.

continued

Sept. 14 Received cash on account from Jayne Brown, $256.00
15 Jayne Brown returned merchandise, $93.28 including tax of $5.28.
16 Received cash on account from Nancy Truelove, $58.25.
17 Cash sales for the week, $2,656.85 plus tax of $159.41.
18 Received cash for boarding and grooming services, $535.00 plus tax of $32.10.
19 Received cash on account from Ed Cochran, $63.25.
20 Sold pet supplies on account to Susan Hays, $83.33 plus tax of $5.00, terms n/30. Sale no. 105.
21 Sold three Labrador Retriever puppies to All American Day Camp, $375.00 plus tax of $22.50, terms n/30. Sale no. 106.
22 Cash sales for the week, $3,122.45 plus tax of $187.35.
23 Received cash for boarding and grooming services, $515.00 plus tax of $30.90.
25 Received cash on account from Ken Shank, $132.50.
26 Received cash on account from Nancy Truelove, $72.35.
27 Received cash on account from Joe Gloy, $273.25.
28 Borrowed cash to purchase a pet limousine, $11,000.00.
29 Cash sales for the week, $2,835.45 plus tax of $170.13.
30 Received cash for boarding and grooming services, $488.00 plus tax of $29.28.

Wayward had the following general ledger account balances as of September 1.

Account Title	Account No.	General Ledger Balance on Sept. 1
Cash	111	$23,500.25
Accounts Receivable	131	850.75
Notes Payable	218	2,500.00
Sales Tax Payable	225	909.90
Sales	411	13,050.48
Sales Returns and Allowances	411.1	86.00
Boarding and Grooming Revenue	412	2,115.00

Wayward also had the following accounts receivable ledger balances as of September 1.

Customer	Accounts Receivable Balance
Jayne Brown 2541 East 2nd Street Bloomington, IN 47401-5356	$456.00
Ed Cochran 2669 Windcrest Drive Bloomington, IN 47401-5446	$63.25

continued

Customer	Accounts Receivable Balance
Joe Gloy 1458 Parnell Avenue Muncie, IN 47304-2682	$273.25
Nancy Truelove 2300 E. National Road Cumberland, IN 46229-4824	$58.25

New customers opening accounts during September were:

All American Day Camp
3025 Old Mill Run
Bloomington, IN 47408-1080

Susan Hays
1424 Jackson Creek Road
Nashville, IN 47448-2245

Ken Shank
6422 E. Bender Road
Bloomington, IN 47401-7756

Tully Shaw
3315 Longview Avenue
Bloomington, IN 47401-7223

Jean Warkentin
1813 Deep Well Court
Bloomington, IN 47401-5124

REQUIRED

1. Enter the transactions for the month of September in the proper journals.
2. Enter the totals and rule the journals where appropriate.
3. Post the entries to the general and subsidiary ledgers. Open new accounts for any customers who did not have a balance as of September 1.
4. Prepare a schedule of accounts receivable.
5. Compute the net sales for the month of September.

12

Accounting for Purchases and Cash Payments

Several months ago, you purchased an acoustic guitar for $800 at a local music store. While on vacation in Tennessee two months later, you found that you could purchase the same guitar direct from the manufacturer for only $500. Were you "ripped off" by the local store? What costs might explain the substantial price difference?

Chapter 11 demonstrated how to account for sales in a merchandising business. This chapter continues the study of the merchandising business by examining how to account for merchandise purchases. We will learn how to use four new accounts, two more special journals, and another subsidiary ledger.

MERCHANDISE PURCHASES TRANSACTIONS

LO1 Define merchandise purchases transactions.

In everyday language, purchases can refer to almost anything we have bought. For a merchandising business, however, **purchases** refers to merchandise acquired for resale. These are the goods a business buys for the sole purpose of selling them to its customers.

Purchasing procedures and documents vary, depending on the nature and size of a business. For example, in a small business, the owner or an employee might do the buying on a part-time basis. In a large business, there might be a separate purchasing department with a full-time manager and staff. In addition, the procedures and documents used can be affected by whether purchases are made on account or for cash.

The flowchart in Figure 12-1 shows some of the major documents used in the purchasing process of a merchandising business. In discussing the purchasing process, we will assume that the business makes purchases on account and has a purchasing department.

FIGURE 12-1   Purchasing Process Documents

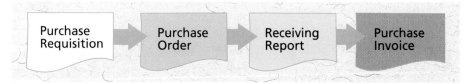

Purchase Requisition

A **purchase requisition** is a form used to request the purchase of merchandise or other property. Any authorized person or department can prepare this form and submit it to the purchasing department. Figure 12-2 shows a purchase requisition used by Northern Micro. One copy of this form is sent to the purchasing department, one to the accounting department, and one is kept by the department that prepared the requisition.

Purchase Order

The purchasing department reviews and approves the purchase requisition and prepares a purchase order. A **purchase order** is a written order to buy goods from a specific vendor (supplier). Figure 12-3 shows a purchase order prepared by Northern Micro based on the purchase requisition in Figure 12-2. One copy of the purchase order is sent to the vendor to order

FIGURE 12-2   Purchase Requisition

NORTHERN MICRO	PURCHASE REQUISITION NO. **A-106**
1099 E. Louisiana, Indianapolis, IN 46217-3322	

Date Issued February 24, 19--	Order From
Date Required March 12, 19--	TTA Products
Required For Department Computer Software	6439 E. Broad St.
Deliver To Gary L. Fishel	Columbus, OH 43223-9892

Quantity	Description
3	WordRight, No. F20386
4	Spellchecker, No. N10367

Purchasing Department Memorandum

Placed By *Emily Green*	Date February 26, 19--
Approved By *Chris Lynders*	Issued To TTA Products
Purchase Order No. 312	6439 E. Broad St.
	Columbus, OH 43223-9892

the goods, one to the accounting department, and one copy is kept in the purchasing department. Other copies can be sent to the department that prepared the purchase requisition and to the receiving area.

FIGURE 12-3   Purchase Order

NORTHERN MICRO	PURCHASE ORDER NO. **312**
1099 E. Louisiana, Indianapolis, IN 46217-3322	

Date February 26, 19--	TTA Products
Deliver By March 12, 19--	6439 E. Broad St.
Ship By Ajax Transfer Co.	Columbus, OH 43223-9892
FOB Columbus	

Quantity	Description	Unit Price	Total
3	WordRight, No. F20386	$180.00	$540.00
4	Spellchecker, No. N10367	75.00	300.00
	Total		$840.00

Chris Lynders

Receiving Report and Purchase Invoice

When the merchandise is received, a **receiving report** indicating what has been received is prepared. The receiving report can be a separate form or one can be created from the vendor's purchase invoice. Figure 12-4 shows a vendor invoice on which a rubber stamp has been used to imprint a type of receiving report. The receiving clerk has indicated on the form the date and condition of the goods received.

FIGURE 12-4   Purchase Invoice

An **invoice** is a document prepared by the seller as a bill for the merchandise shipped. To the seller, this is a sales invoice, as explained in Chapter 11. To the buyer, this is a **purchase invoice.** Figure 12-4 shows an invoice sent by TTA Products to Northern Micro for the goods ordered with the purchase order in Figure 12-3.

The accounting department compares the purchase invoice with the purchase requisition, purchase order, and receiving report. If the invoice is for the goods ordered and the correct price, the invoice is paid by the due date.

Cash and Trade Discounts

Notice that the invoice in Figure 12-4 shows terms of 2/10, n/30. These are the same credit terms discussed in Chapter 11. A discount is available if the bill is paid within the discount period. The only difference is that we are now looking from the buyer's point of view rather than the seller's. We will see how to account for these discounts later in the chapter.

Another type of discount, called a **trade discount,** is often offered by manufacturers and wholesalers. This discount is a reduction from the list or catalog price offered to different classes of customers. By simply adjusting the trade discount percentages, companies can avoid the cost of reprinting catalogs every time there is a change in prices. Trade discounts are usually shown as a deduction from the total amount of the invoice. For example, the invoice in Figure 12-5 includes a trade discount of 10%. The amount to be entered in the accounting records for this invoice is $756, the net amount after deducting the trade discount of $84. Trade discounts represent a reduction in the price of the merchandise and should not be entered in the accounts of either the seller or the buyer.

FIGURE 12-5   Purchase Invoice with Trade Discount

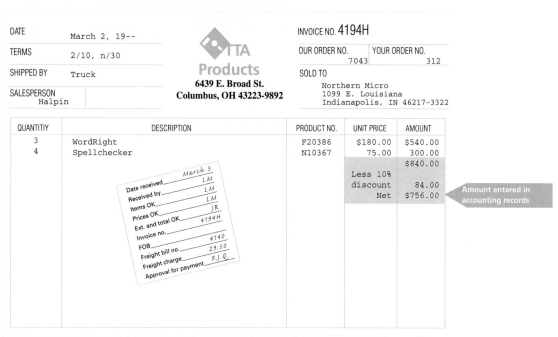

We need to be careful in computing the cash discount when an invoice has both cash and trade discounts. The cash discount applies to the *net amount* after deducting the trade discount. For example, the cash discount and amount to be paid on the invoice in Figure 12-5 would be calculated as follows:

Gross amount	$840.00
Less 10% trade discount	84.00
Net amount	$756.00
Less 2% cash discount	15.12
Amount to be paid	$740.88

MERCHANDISE PURCHASES ACCOUNTS

LO2 Describe and use merchandise purchases accounts.

To account for merchandise purchases transactions, we will use four new accounts.

1. Purchases
2. Purchases Returns and Allowances
3. Purchases Discounts
4. Freight-In

Purchases Account

The purchases account is used to record the cost of merchandise purchased.

Purchases	
Debit	Credit
to enter the cost of merchandise purchased	

If a $100 purchase is made for cash, the following entry is made.

9		Purchases			1 0 0 00			9
10		Cash				1 0 0 00		10
11		Made cash purchase						11

If the same purchase is made on account, the entry is:

9		Purchases			1 0 0 00			9
10		Accounts Payable				1 0 0 00		10
11		Made purchase on account						11

Purchases Returns and Allowances Account

Purchases Returns and Allowances is a contra-purchases account used to record purchases returns and purchases allowances. It is reported as a deduction from Purchases on the income statement.

Purchases returns and allowances are similar to the sales returns and allowances we discussed in Chapter 11. We are simply looking at returns and allowances from the buyer's point of view. If merchandise is returned to a supplier, or the supplier grants a price reduction because of defects or other problems with merchandise purchased, Purchases Returns and Allowances is credited.

Purchases Returns and Allowances	
Debit	Credit
	to enter returns and allowances

If merchandise that was purchased on account for $200 is defective and is returned to the supplier, the following entry is made:

9		Accounts Payable	2 0 0 00		9
10		Purchases Returns and Allowances		2 0 0 00	10
11		Returned merchandise			11

If the same merchandise is retained but the supplier grants a price reduction of $45 because of the defects, the entry is:

9		Accounts Payable	4 5 00		9
10		Purchases Returns and Allowances		4 5 00	10
11		Allowance for defective			11
12		merchandise			12

Purchases Discounts Account

Purchases Discounts is a contra-purchases account used to record cash discounts allowed on purchases. Like Purchases Returns and Allowances, it is reported as a deduction from Purchases on the income statement.

Purchases Discounts	
Debit	Credit
	for cash discounts taken

If merchandise is purchased for $100 on account, with credit terms of 2/10, n/30, the following entry is made.

14		Purchases	1 0 0 00		14
15		Accounts Payable		1 0 0 00	15
16		Made purchase on account			16

If payment for the merchandise is subsequently made within the discount period, the entry is:

18		Accounts Payable	1 0 0 00		18
19		Cash		9 8 00	19
20		Purchases Discounts		2 00	20
21		Made payment on account			21

Note the parts of this entry. Accounts Payable is debited for $100, the full amount of the invoice, because the entire debt has been satisfied. Cash is credited for only $98 because that is all that was required to pay the debt.

The difference of \$2 (\$100 − \$98) is credited to Purchases Discounts, which represents a reduction in the purchase price of the merchandise. That is why Purchases Discounts is deducted from Purchases on the income statement.

Freight-In Account

Freight-In is an adjunct-purchases account used to record transportation charges on merchandise purchases. It is added to Purchases on the income statement.

Freight-In	
Debit	**Credit**
for transportation charges on merchandise purchases	

Transportation charges are expressed in FOB (free on board) terms that indicate who is responsible for paying the freight costs. **FOB shipping point** means that transportation charges are paid by the buyer. **FOB destination** means that transportation charges are paid by the seller.

When the terms are FOB shipping point, either the freight charges will be listed separately on the purchase invoice or a separate freight bill will be sent. Assume Northern Micro receives an invoice for \$400 plus freight charges of \$38. The entry for this purchase is:

25	Purchases	4 0 0 00			25
26	Freight-In	3 8 00			26
27	Accounts Payable		4 3 8 00		27
28	Made purchase on account				28

Assume instead that Northern Micro receives an invoice for \$400 for the same merchandise, shipped FOB shipping point. Northern Micro then receives a separate bill from the transportation company for \$38. These two transactions are entered as follows.

30	Purchases	4 0 0 00			30
31	Accounts Payable		4 0 0 00		31
32	Made purchase on account				32
33					33
34	Freight-In	3 8 00			34
35	Accounts Payable		3 8 00		35
36	Freight charges on				36
37	merchandise purchase				37

When the terms are FOB destination, generally no freight charges appear on the purchase invoice. The buyer simply records the purchase at the amount of the invoice. The freight-in account is not used in recording this purchase.

Computation of Gross Profit

An important step in determining net income for a merchandising business is the calculation of its gross profit. **Gross profit** (also called **gross margin**) is the difference between net sales and cost of goods sold. **Cost of goods sold** (also called **cost of merchandise sold**) is the difference between the merchandise available for sale and the ending inventory. It indicates the cost of the goods sold during the period. Gross profit provides very important information. It tells management the amount of sales dollars available to cover expenses, after covering the cost of the goods sold.

LEARNING KEY   Gross profit is the difference between net sales and cost of goods sold.

To compute gross profit, we use two of the four new accounts described in Chapter 11, the four new accounts described above, and the merchandise inventory balances. Assume that Northern Micro has the following sales, purchases, and merchandise inventory balances for the year ended December 31, 19--.

From Chapter 11	Sales	$200,500
	Sales returns and allowances	1,200
	Purchases	105,000
	Purchases returns and allowances	800
From Chapter 12	Purchases discounts	1,000
	Freight-In	300
	Merchandise inventory, January 1, 19--	26,000
	Merchandise inventory, December 31, 19--	18,000

Profiles in Accounting

Figure 12-6 uses these balances to compute net sales, net purchases, cost of goods sold, and gross profit. The following four steps in computing gross profit are labeled in the figure.

STEP 1   Compute net sales.
(Sales − sales returns and allowances)

STEP 2   Compute goods available for sale.
(Beginning inventory + cost of goods purchased)

STEP 3   Compute cost of goods sold.
(Goods available for sale − ending inventory)

STEP 4   Compute gross profit.
(Net sales − cost of goods sold)

FIGURE 12-6   Computation of Gross Profit

Sales			$200 500 00	
Less: Sales returns and allowances			1 200 00	
1 **Net sales**				$199 300 00
Cost of goods sold:				
Merchandise inventory, Jan. 1			$ 26 000 00	
Purchases		$105 000 00		
Less: Purchases returns and allowances	$ 8 00 00			
Purchases discounts	1 000 00	1 800 00		
Net purchases		$103 200 00		
Add: Freight-in		300 00		
Cost of goods purchased			103 500 00	
2 **Goods available for sale**			$129 500 00	
Less: Merchandise inventory, Dec. 31			18 000 00	
3 **Cost of goods sold**				111 500 00
4 **Gross profit**				$ 87 800 00

JOURNALIZING AND POSTING PURCHASES TRANSACTIONS

LO3 Describe and use the purchases journal and accounts payable ledger.

To illustrate the journalizing and posting of purchases transactions, we will continue with the transactions of Northern Micro. Assume the following purchases on account occurred during the month of April.

Apr. 4   Purchased merchandise from Compucraft, $3,300. Invoice no. 631, dated Apr. 2, terms, n/30.

   8   Purchased merchandise from Datasoft, $2,500. Invoice no. 927D, dated Apr. 6, terms, n/30.

Apr. 11 Purchased merchandise from EZX, $8,700. Invoice no. 804, dated Apr. 9, terms, 1/15, n/30.

17 Purchased merchandise from Printpro, $800. Invoice no. 611, dated Apr. 16, terms, n/30.

23 Purchased merchandise from Televax, $5,300. Invoice no. 1465, dated Apr. 22, terms, 1/10, n/30.

These transactions could be entered in a general journal as shown in Figure 12-7.

FIGURE 12-7   Purchases Entered in General Journal

GENERAL JOURNAL   PAGE 1

	DATE		DESCRIPTION	POST. REF.	DEBIT	CREDIT	
1	Apr. 19--	4	Purchases		3 3 0 0 00		1
2			Accounts Payable/Compucraft			3 3 0 0 00	2
3			Invoice no. 631				3
4							4
5		8	Purchases		2 5 0 0 00		5
6			Accounts Payable/Datasoft			2 5 0 0 00	6
7			Invoice no. 927D				7
8							8
9		11	Purchases		8 7 0 0 00		9
10			Accounts Payable/EZX			8 7 0 0 00	10
11			Invoice no. 804				11
12							12
13		17	Purchases		8 0 0 00		13
14			Accounts Payable/Printpro			8 0 0 00	14
15			Invoice no. 611				15
16							16
17		23	Purchases		5 3 0 0 00		17
18			Accounts Payable/Televax			5 3 0 0 00	18
19			Invoice no. 1465				19

The same problem occurs with this approach to recording purchases that occurred in Chapter 11 with recording sales transactions. The same account titles had to be recorded five times to make these five entries. Similarly, to post these entries to the general ledger, five separate postings would have to be made to each of the two accounts, a total of ten postings.

Fortunately, there is a more efficient way to record purchases on account. A purchases journal is used.

Purchases Journal

A **purchases journal** is a special journal used to record only purchases of merchandise on account. By using a purchases journal, both journalizing and posting of purchases on account is much more efficient.

LEARNING KEY Using a purchases journal can make both journalizing and posting much more efficient.

To illustrate, reconsider Northern Micro's five purchases on account. They are entered in the purchases journal in Figure 12-8. Northern Micro's purchases journal has a single column for Purchases Debit/Accounts Payable Credit, the two accounts used repeatedly in the general journal in Figure 12-7. A purchase is recorded in the purchases journal by entering the following information:

1. Date
2. Invoice number
3. Supplier (from whom purchased)
4. Dollar amount

There is no need to enter any general ledger account titles since they appear in the column heading.

FIGURE 12-8   Northern Micro Purchases Journal

						PURCHASES	
	DATE	INVOICE NO.	FROM WHOM PURCHASED	POST. REF.		DEBIT/ACCOUNTS PAYABLE CREDIT	
1	19-- Apr. 4	631	Compucraft, Inc.			3 3 0 0 00	1
2	8	927D	Datasoft			2 5 0 0 00	2
3	11	804	EZX Corp.			8 7 0 0 00	3
4	17	611	Printpro Corp.			8 0 0 00	4
5	23	1465	Televax, Inc.			5 3 0 0 00	5
6						20 6 0 0 00	6

PURCHASES JOURNAL   PAGE **8**

The purchases journal in Figure 12-8 is designed for a company, like Northern Micro, whose suppliers generally pay freight charges. For a company that frequently pays freight charges as part of the purchase price of merchandise, a purchases journal like the one in Figure 12-9 would be used. In this case, there are three columns: (1) Purchases Debit, (2) Freight-In Debit, and (3) Accounts Payable Credit. Each special journal should be designed for the particular needs of the company using it.

FIGURE 12-9   Purchases Journal with Freight-In Column

PURCHASES JOURNAL

DATE	INVOICE NO.	FROM WHOM PURCHASED	POST. REF.	PURCHASES DEBIT	FREIGHT-IN DEBIT	ACCOUNTS PAYABLE CREDIT

Posting the Purchases Journal

Each general ledger account used in the purchases journal requires only one posting each period. Figure 12-10 illustrates the general ledger posting process for Northern Micro's purchases journal for the month of April.

FIGURE 12-10   Posting the Purchases Journal to the General Ledger

PURCHASES JOURNAL   Page 8

Date	Invoice No.	From Whom Purchased	Post. Ref.	Purchases Debit/ Accounts Payable Credit
19--				
Apr. 4	631	Compucraft, Inc.		3,300.00
8	927D	Datasoft		2,500.00
11	804	EZX Corp.		8,700.00
17	611	Printpro Corp.		800.00
23	1465	Televax, Inc.		5,300.00
				20,600.00 **1**
				(511) (216) **3**

1

GENERAL LEDGER (Partial)

ACCOUNT Accounts Payable   ACCOUNT NO. 216

Date	Item	Post. Ref.	Debit	Credit	Balance Debit	Balance Credit
19--						
Apr. 1	Bal.	✓				4,800.00
2 30		P8		20,600.00		25,400.00

ACCOUNT Purchases   ACCOUNT NO. 511

Date	Item	Post. Ref.	Debit	Credit	Balance Debit	Balance Credit
19--						
Apr. 1	Bal.	✓			17,400.00	
2 30		P8	20,600.00		38,000.00	

The following three steps are used to post from the purchases journal to the general ledger at the end of each month, as indicated in Figure 12-10.

STEP 1   Total and rule the amount column and post the total to the purchases and accounts payable accounts in the general ledger.

STEP 2   Insert the date in the Date column and the initial "P" and the purchases journal page number in the Posting Reference column of each ledger account.

STEP 3   Insert the purchases and accounts payable account numbers in parentheses immediately below the column total in the purchases journal.

The Purchases and Accounts Payable resulting from merchandise purchases on account are now up to date in the general ledger. A record can be kept of the amount owed to each supplier by using a subsidiary **accounts payable ledger.** This is a separate ledger containing an individual account payable for each supplier. If there are many supplier accounts, it is a good practice to assign each supplier an account number. The subsidiary ledger accounts are kept in either alphabetical or numerical order, depending on how the supplier accounts are identified. A summary accounts

Teamwork

 Teamwork is at the core of Rubbermaid's continuing success. During 1994, Rubbermaid announced plans to double its profits over the next five years. That translates into $4 billion by 1998. To help achieve this goal the company will reduce costs by $335 million in the next two years through a value improvement process.

Teamwork is already playing a significant role in the process. Manufacturing teams have increased production and cut costs through scrap reduction, faster mold changes, and more rapid color changes. Teams initiated product development improvements that lowered costs and reduced the time between the concept and manufacturing stages. These improvements make a big difference to a company that introduces a new product almost every day.

Another team focused their efforts on reducing the number of color hues from 426 to less than 100. Using fewer color variations simplifies the manufacturing process and reduces the number of suppliers and costs. As an added benefit, sharing this information throughout the company means more color choices are available to each product group.

The Rubbermaid name is found on laundry baskets, food storage containers, trash cans, tool boxes, spatulas, playground systems, and dustpans—the company's first housewares product introduced in 1934.

Source: Rubbermaid 1994 Annual Report. Contact: Investor Relations Department, Rubbermaid Incorporated, 1147 Akron Road, Wooster, OH 44691-6000.

---

payable account called a controlling account is maintained in the general ledger. The accounts payable ledger is "subsidiary" to this account.

Figure 12-11 illustrates the use of the accounts payable ledger. The following three steps are used to post from the purchases journal to the accounts payable ledger, as shown in Figure 12-11.

STEP 1   Post the individual purchase amount to the supplier's account on the date the purchase occurs.

STEP 2   Insert the date in the Date column and the initial "P" and the purchases journal page number in the Posting Reference column of each supplier account.

STEP 3   Insert a check mark (✓) in the Posting Reference column of the purchases journal to indicate that the amount has been posted.

After the posting of the accounts payable ledger and general ledger is completed, the total of the accounts payable ledger balances should equal the Accounts Payable balance in the general ledger.

Purchases Returns and Allowances

If a buyer returns merchandise or is given an allowance for damaged merchandise, a general journal entry is required. Remember, the purchases

FIGURE 12-11   Posting the Purchases Journal to the Accounts Payable Ledger

PURCHASES JOURNAL   Page 8

Date	Invoice No.	From Whom Purchased	Post. Ref.	Purchases Debit/ Accounts Payable Credit
19--				
Apr. 4	631	Compucraft, Inc.	✓	3,300.00
8	927D	Datasoft	✓	2,500.00
11	804	EZX Corp.	✓	8,700.00
17	611	Printpro Corp.	✓	800.00
23	1465	Televax, Inc.	✓	5,300.00
			3	20,600.00
				(511) (216)

ACCOUNTS PAYABLE LEDGER

NAME   B. B. Small
ADDRESS 2323 High Street, Gurnee, IL 60031

Date	Item	Post. Ref.	Debit	Credit	Balance
19--					
Apr. 1	Bal.	✓			4,800.00

NAME   Compucraft, Inc.
ADDRESS 2100 West Main Street, Muncie, IN 47304

Date	Item	Post. Ref.	Debit	Credit	Balance
19--					
Apr. 4		P8		3,300.00	3,300.00

NAME   Datasoft
ADDRESS 210 Kirkwood, Bloomington, IN 47408

Date	Item	Post. Ref.	Debit	Credit	Balance
19--					
Apr. 8		P8		2,500.00	2,500.00

NAME   EZX Corp.
ADDRESS 2989 Rhodes Ave., Indianapolis, IN 46201

Date	Item	Post. Ref.	Debit	Credit	Balance
19--					
Apr. 11		P8		8,700.00	8,700.00

NAME   Printpro Corp.
ADDRESS 1200 Chambers Pike, Lincolnwood, IL 60648

Date	Item	Post. Ref.	Debit	Credit	Balance
19--					
Apr. 17		P8		800.00	000.00

NAME   Televax, Inc.
ADDRESS 1500 North Walnut Street, Addison, IL 60101

Date	Item	Post. Ref.	Debit	Credit	Balance
19--					
Apr. 23		P8		5,300.00	5,300.00

GENERAL LEDGER (Partial)

ACCOUNT Accounts Payable   **ACCOUNT NO.** 216

Date	Item	Post. Ref.	Debit	Credit	Balance Debit	Balance Credit
19--						
Apr. 1	Bal.	✓				4,800.00
30		P8		20,600.00		25,400.00

ACCOUNT Purchases   **ACCOUNT NO.** 511

Date	Item	Post. Ref.	Debit	Credit	Balance Debit	Balance Credit
19--						
Apr. 1	Bal.	✓			17,400.00	
30		P8	20,600.00		38,000.00	

journal can only be used to enter purchases on account. Assume that on May 4, Northern Micro returns $200 of merchandise to Televax. These goods were part of the purchase made on April 23. Figure 12-12 shows the general journal entry, general ledger posting, and accounts payable ledger posting for this transaction.

LEARNING KEY   Enter purchases returns and allowances in the general journal.

FIGURE 12-12   Accounting for Purchases Returns and Allowances

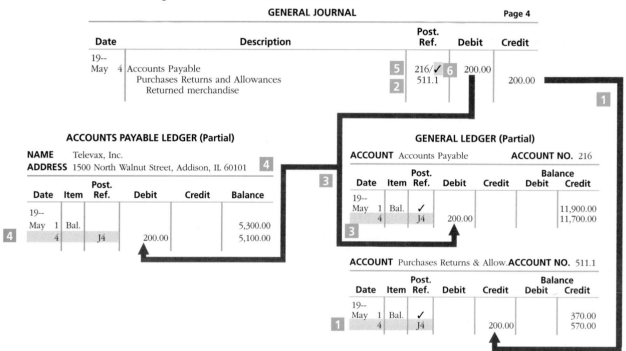

The general journal entry is made in the usual manner. The postings are made daily, using the following six steps.

STEP 1   Post the Purchases Returns and Allowances credit to the general ledger account. Insert the date in the Date column and the general journal reference (J4) in the Posting Reference column.

STEP 2   Insert the general ledger account number in the Posting Reference column of the general journal.

The Accounts Payable debit requires special attention, as follows.

STEP 3   Post the Accounts Payable debit to the general ledger account and insert the date in the Date column and the general journal posting reference (J4) in the Posting Reference column.

STEP 4   Post the same amount to the supplier account in the accounts payable ledger and insert the same date in the Date column and posting reference (J4) in the Posting Reference column.

STEP 5   To indicate that the general ledger has been posted, insert the account number (216) and a slash (/) in the Posting Reference column of the general journal.

STEP 6   To indicate that the supplier account has been posted, insert a check mark (✓) following the slash in the Posting Reference column of the general journal.

JOURNALIZING AND POSTING CASH PAYMENTS

LO4 Describe and use the cash payments journal and accounts payable ledger.

Chapter 11 demonstrated how a cash receipts journal can be used to efficiently record cash receipts transactions. Cash payments transactions generally occur just as frequently as do cash receipts transactions, so a special journal for cash payments also can be quite useful.

Cash Payments Journal

A **cash payments journal** is a special journal used to record only cash payments transactions. To illustrate its use, we will record the cash payments transactions of Northern Micro. Northern Micro's cash payments journal for the month of April is shown in Figure 12-13. Five types of cash payments transactions are shown.

1. Payment of an expense (April 2)
2. Cash purchase (April 4)
3. Payment of an account payable (April 10 and 24)
4. Payment of a note payable (April 14)
5. Withdrawal by the owner (April 22)

LEARNING KEY   Use a cash payments journal to streamline journalizing and posting of cash payments.

Northern Micro's cash payments journal provides separate columns for Accounts Payable Debit, Purchases Debit, Purchases Discounts Credit, and Cash Credit. These are the accounts most frequently affected by Northern Micro's cash payments transactions. In addition, a General Debit column is provided for debits to any other accounts affected by cash payments transactions. For good internal control over cash payments, all payments (except those out of petty cash) should be made by check. Therefore, the cash payments journal also includes a Check Number column.

A cash payment is recorded in the cash payments journal by entering the following information:

1. Date
2. Check number
3. Account debited (if applicable)
4. Dollar amounts

FIGURE 12-13 Northern Micro Cash Payments Journal

CASH PAYMENTS JOURNAL

	DATE	CK. NO.	ACCOUNT DEBITED	POST. REF.	GENERAL DEBIT	
1	Apr. 2	307	Rent Expense		2 4 0 0 00	1
2	4	308				2
3	10	309	B.B. Small			3
4	14	310	Notes Payable		2 0 0 0 00	4
5	22	311	Gary Fishel, Drawing		1 6 0 0 00	5
6	24	312	EZX Corp.			6
7					6 0 0 0 00	7

The Account Debited column is used for two purposes.

1. To identify the supplier name for any payment on account. This column is used whenever the Accounts Payable Debit column is used.
2. To enter the appropriate account name whenever the General Debit column is used.

Note that the column is left blank if the entry is for cash purchases.

Posting the Cash Payments Journal

Figure 12-14 illustrates the general ledger posting process for Northern Micro's cash payments journal.

ON A DAILY BASIS:

STEP 1 Post each amount in the General Debit column to the appropriate general ledger account.

STEP 2 Insert the date in the Date column and the initials "CP" and the cash payments journal page number in the Posting Reference column of each ledger account.

STEP 3 Insert the general ledger account numbers in the Posting Reference column of the cash payments journal.

AT THE END OF EACH MONTH:

STEP 4 Total the amount columns, verify that the total of the debit columns equals the total of the credit columns, and rule the columns.

STEP 5 Post each column total except the General Debit column to the general ledger account indicated in the column headings.

STEP 6 Insert the date in the Date column and the initials "CP" and the cash payments journal page number in the Posting Reference column of each ledger account.

STEP 7 Insert the general ledger account numbers below each column total except the General Debit column.

	ACCOUNTS PAYABLE DEBIT	PURCHASES DEBIT	PURCHASES DISCOUNTS CREDIT	CASH CREDIT	
1				2 4 0 0 00	1
2		1 4 0 0 00		1 4 0 0 00	2
3	4 8 0 0 00			4 8 0 0 00	3
4				2 0 0 0 00	4
5				1 6 0 0 00	5
6	8 7 0 0 00		8 7 00	8 6 1 3 00	6
7	13 5 0 0 00	1 4 0 0 00	8 7 00	20 8 1 3 00	7

PAGE 12

STEP 8 Insert a check mark (✓) in the Posting Reference column for the cash purchases and below the General Debit column.

Postings from the cash payments journal to the accounts payable ledger also must be made. These postings are made daily. Posting procedures are as follows, as shown in Figure 12-15.

STEP 1 Post the individual cash payment to the supplier's account on the date the payment occurs.

STEP 2 Insert the date in the Date column and the initials "CP" and the cash payments journal page number in the Posting Reference column of each supplier account.

STEP 3 Insert a check mark (✓) in the Posting Reference column of the cash payments journal to indicate that the amount has been posted.

SCHEDULE OF ACCOUNTS PAYABLE

LO5 Prepare a schedule of accounts payable.

All postings to the general ledger and accounts payable ledger are now complete. At this point, the Accounts Payable balance in the general ledger should equal the sum of the supplier balances in the accounts payable ledger.

To verify that the sum of the accounts payable ledger balances equals the Accounts Payable balance, a **schedule of accounts payable** is prepared. This is a listing of supplier accounts and balances, usually prepared at the end of the month. Note that suppliers whose account balance is zero are not included. Figure 12-16 shows the schedule of accounts payable for Northern Micro as of April 30.

This schedule is prepared from the list of supplier accounts in the accounts payable ledger. The total calculated in the schedule is compared with the balance in Accounts Payable in the general ledger. Note that the $11,900 total listed in the schedule equals the Accounts Payable balance

FIGURE 12-14 Posting the Cash Payments Journal to the General Ledger

CASH PAYMENTS JOURNAL Page 12

Date	Check No.	Account Credited	Post. Ref.	General Debit	Accounts Payable Debit	Purchases Debit	Purchases Discounts Credit	Cash Credit
19--								
Apr. 2	307	Rent Expense	541	2,400.00				2,400.00
4	308		✓			1,400.00		1,400.00
10	309	B.B. Small			4,800.00			4,800.00
14	310	Notes Payable	218	2,000.00				2,000.00
22	311	Gary Fishel, Drawing	312	1,600.00				1,600.00
24	312	EZX Corp.			8,700.00		87.00	8,613.00
				6,000.00	13,500.00	1,400.00	87.00	20,813.00
				(✓)	(216)	(511)	(511.2)	(111)

4 Debit total:
$ 6,000
13,500
1,400
$20,900

Credit total:
$ 87
20,813
$20,900

GENERAL LEDGER (Partial)

ACCOUNT Cash   **ACCOUNT NO.** 111

Date	Item	Post. Ref.	Debit	Credit	Balance Debit	Balance Credit
19--						
Apr. 1	Bal.	✓			20,000.00	
30		CR7	12,992.00		32,992.00	
30		CP12		20,813.00	12,179.00	

ACCOUNT Accounts Payable   **ACCOUNT NO.** 216

Date	Item	Post. Ref.	Debit	Credit	Balance Debit	Balance Credit
19--						
Apr. 1	Bal.	✓				4,800.00
30		P8		20,600.00		25,400.00
30		CP12	13,500.00			11,900.00

ACCOUNT Notes Payable   **ACCOUNT NO.** 218

Date	Item	Post. Ref.	Debit	Credit	Balance Debit	Balance Credit
19--						
Apr. 1	Bal.	✓				6,000.00
14		CP12	2,000.00			4,000.00

ACCOUNT Gary L. Fishel, Drawing   **ACCOUNT NO.** 312

Date	Item	Post. Ref.	Debit	Credit	Balance Debit	Balance Credit
19--						
Apr. 1	Bal.	✓			4,500.00	
22		CP12	1,600.00		6,100.00	

ACCOUNT Purchases   **ACCOUNT NO.** 511

Date	Item	Post. Ref.	Debit	Credit	Balance Debit	Balance Credit
19--						
Apr. 1	Bal.	✓			17,400.00	
30		P8	20,600.00		38,000.00	
30		CP12	1,400.00		39,400.00	

ACCOUNT Purchases Discounts   **ACCOUNT NO.** 511.2

Date	Item	Post. Ref.	Debit	Credit	Balance Debit	Balance Credit
19--						
Apr. 1	Bal.	✓				330.00
30		CP12		87.00		417.00

ACCOUNT Rent Expense   **ACCOUNT NO.** 541

Date	Item	Post. Ref.	Debit	Credit	Balance Debit	Balance Credit
19--						
Apr. 1	Bal.	✓			6,600.00	
2		CP12	2,400.00		9,000.00	

FIGURE 12-15   Posting the Cash Payments Journal to the Accounts Payable Ledger

CASH PAYMENTS JOURNAL   Page 12

Date	Check No.	Account Debited	Post. Ref.	General Debit	Accounts Payable Debit	Purchases Debit	Purchases Discounts Credit	Cash Credit
19--								
Apr. 2	307	Rent Expense	541	2,400.00				2,400.00
4	308		✓			1,400.00		1,400.00
10	309	B.B. Small	✓		4,800.00			4,800.00
14	310	Notes Payable	218	2,000.00				2,000.00
22	311	Gary Fishel, Drawing	312	1,600.00				1,600.00
24	312	EZX Corp.	✓		8,700.00		87.00	8,613.00
				6,000.00	13,500.00	1,400.00	87.00	20,813.00
				(✓)	(216)	(511)	(511.2)	(111)

ACCOUNTS PAYABLE LEDGER (Partial)

NAME   B.B. Small
ADDRESS   2323 High Street, Gurnee, IL 60031

Date	Item	Post. Ref.	Debit	Credit	Balance
19--					
Apr. 1	Bal.	✓			4,800.00
10		CP12	4,800.00		—

NAME   Compucraft, Inc.
ADDRESS   2100 West Main Street, Muncie, IN 47304

Date	Item	Post. Ref.	Debit	Credit	Balance
19--					
Apr. 4		P8		3,300.00	3,300.00

NAME   Datasoft
ADDRESS   210 Kirkwood, Bloomington, IN 47408

Date	Item	Post. Ref.	Debit	Credit	Balance
19--					
Apr. 8		P8		2,500.00	2,500.00

NAME   EZX Corp.
ADDRESS   2989 Rhodes Ave., Indianapolis, IN 46201

Date	Item	Post. Ref.	Debit	Credit	Balance
19--					
Apr. 11		P8		8,700.00	8,700.00
24		CP12	8,700.00		—

NAME   Printpro Corp.
ADDRESS   1200 Chambers Pike, Lincolnwood, IL 60648

Date	Item	Post. Ref.	Debit	Credit	Balance
19--					
Apr. 17		P8		800.00	800.00

NAME   Televax, Inc.
ADDRESS   1500 North Walnut Street, Addison, IL 60101

Date	Item	Post. Ref.	Debit	Credit	Balance
19--					
Apr. 23		P8		5,300.00	5,300.00

GENERAL LEDGER (Partial)

ACCOUNT   Cash   ACCOUNT NO.   111

Date	Item	Post. Ref.	Debit	Credit	Balance Debit	Balance Credit
19--						
Apr. 1	Bal.	✓			20,000.00	
30		CR7	12,992.00		32,992.00	
30		CP12		20,813.00	12,179.00	

ACCOUNT   Accounts Payable   ACCOUNT NO.   216

Date	Item	Post. Ref.	Debit	Credit	Balance Debit	Balance Credit
19--						
Apr. 1	Bal.	✓				4,800.00
30		P8		20,600.00		25,400.00
30		CP12	13,500.00			11,900.00

ACCOUNT   Notes Payable   ACCOUNT NO.   218

Date	Item	Post. Ref.	Debit	Credit	Balance Debit	Balance Credit
19--						
Apr. 1	Bal.	✓				6,000.00
14		CP12	2,000.00			4,000.00

ACCOUNT   Gary L. Fishel, Drawing   ACCOUNT NO.   312

Date	Item	Post. Ref.	Debit	Credit	Balance Debit	Balance Credit
19--						
Apr. 1	Bal.	✓			4,500.00	
22		CP12	1,600.00		6,100.00	

ACCOUNT   Purchases   ACCOUNT NO.   511

Date	Item	Post. Ref.	Debit	Credit	Balance Debit	Balance Credit
19--						
Apr. 1	Bal.	✓			17,400.00	
30		P8	20,600.00		38,000.00	
30		CP12	1,400.00		39,400.00	

ACCOUNT   Purchases Discounts   ACCOUNT NO.   511.2

Date	Item	Post. Ref.	Debit	Credit	Balance Debit	Balance Credit
19--						
Apr. 1	Bal.	✓				330.00
30		CP12		87.00		417.00

ACCOUNT   Rent Expense   ACCOUNT NO.   541

Date	Item	Post. Ref.	Debit	Credit	Balance Debit	Balance Credit
19--						
Apr. 1	Bal.	✓			6,600.00	
2		CP12	2,400.00		9,000.00	

FIGURE 12-16   Schedule of Accounts Payable

Northern Micro
Schedule of Accounts Payable
April 30, 19--

Compucraft, Inc.	$ 3 3 0 0 00
Datasoft	2 5 0 0 00
Printpro Corp.	8 0 0 00
Televax, Inc.	5 3 0 0 00
	$11 9 0 0 00

shown in Figure 12-15. If the schedule total and the Accounts Payable balance do not agree, the error must be located and corrected. To find the error, use the following procedures.

STEP 1   Verify the total of the schedule.

STEP 2   Verify the postings to the accounts payable ledger.

STEP 3   Verify the totals in the Purchases and Cash Payments Journals.

STEP 4   Verify the postings to Accounts Payable in the general ledger.

KEY POINTS

1   For a merchandising business, purchases refers to merchandise acquired for resale. Major documents used in the purchasing process are the purchase requisition, purchase order, receiving report, and purchase invoice.

2   Four accounts are used in accounting for merchandise purchases transactions:

1. Purchases
2. Purchases Returns and Allowances
3. Purchases Discounts
4. Freight-In

3   A purchases journal is a special journal for recording purchases on account. A purchase is recorded by entering the:

1. Date
2. Invoice number
3. Supplier
4. Dollar amount

To post from the purchases journal to the general ledger:

1. Total and rule the amount column.
2. Insert the date and posting reference in the accounts.
3. Insert the Purchases and Accounts Payable account numbers below the column total.

To post from the purchases journal to the accounts payable ledger:

1. Post individual purchase amounts to supplier accounts.
2. Insert the date and posting reference in the customer accounts.
3. Insert a check mark (✓) in the Posting Reference column of the purchases journal.

Purchases returns and allowances are recorded in the general journal.

4 A cash payments journal is a special journal for recording cash payments. A cash payment is recorded by entering the:

1. Date
2. Check number
3. Account debited (if applicable)
4. Dollar amounts

To post from the cash payments journal to the general ledger:

On a daily basis:

1. Post General Debit column amounts to the general ledger.
2. Insert the date and posting reference in the accounts.
3. Insert the account numbers in the Posting Reference column of the cash payments journal.

At the end of each month:

4. Foot, verify the equality of, and rule the amount columns.
5. Post account column totals to the appropriate general ledger accounts.
6. Insert the date and posting reference in the accounts.
7. Insert the account numbers below the specific account column totals.
8. Insert a check mark (✓) in the Posting Reference column for the cash purchases and below the General Debit column.

To post from the cash payments journal to the accounts payable ledger:

1. Post individual cash payments to supplier accounts.

2. Insert the date and posting reference in the customer accounts.

3. Insert a check mark (✓) in the Posting Reference column of the cash payments journal.

5 The schedule of accounts payable is used to verify that the sum of the accounts payable ledger balances equals the Accounts Payable balance.

KEY TERMS

accounts payable ledger 391   A separate ledger containing an individual account payable for each supplier.

cash payments journal 395   A special journal used to record only cash payments transactions.

cost of goods sold 387 The difference between the goods available for sale and the ending inventory.

cost of merchandise sold 387 See cost of goods sold.

FOB destination 386 Transportation charges are paid by the seller.

FOB shipping point 386 Transportation charges are paid by the buyer.

gross margin 387 See gross profit.

gross profit 387 The difference between net sales and cost of merchandise sold.

invoice 382 A document prepared by the seller as a bill for the merchandise shipped. To the seller, this is a sales invoice. To the buyer, this is a purchase invoice.

purchase invoice 382 A document prepared by the seller as a bill for the merchandise shipped. To the buyer, this is a purchase invoice.

purchase order 380 A written order to buy goods from a specific vendor (supplier).

purchase requisition 380 A form used to request the purchasing department to purchase merchandise.

purchases 380 Merchandise acquired by a merchandising business for resale to customers.

purchases journal 389 A special journal used to record only purchases on account.

receiving report 382 A report indicating what has been received.

schedule of accounts payable 397 A listing of supplier accounts and balances, usually prepared at the end of the month.

trade discount 383 A reduction from the list or catalog price offered to different classes of customers.

REVIEW QUESTIONS

1. Identify the major documents commonly used in the purchasing process.
2. Distinguish between a cash discount and a trade discount.
3. Describe how each of the following accounts is used: (1) Purchases, (2) Purchases Returns and Allowances, (3) Purchases Discounts, and (4) Freight-In.
4. How are cost of goods sold and gross profit computed?
5. List four items of information about each purchase entered in the purchases journal.
6. What steps are followed in posting from the purchases journal to the general ledger?
7. What steps are followed in posting from the purchases journal to the accounts payable ledger?
8. What steps are used to post Purchases Returns and Allowances from the general journal to the general ledger and accounts payable ledger?
9. List four items of information about each cash payment entered in the cash payments journal.
10. What steps are followed in posting from the cash payments journal to the general ledger?

11. What steps are followed in posting from the cash payments journal to the accounts payable ledger?
12. If the total of the schedule of accounts payable does not agree with the Accounts Payable balance, what procedures should be used to search for the error?

MANAGING YOUR WRITING

You have a part-time job as a bookkeeper at a local office supply store. The accounting records consist of a general journal and general ledger. The manager is concerned about efficiency and feels that too much time is spent recording transactions. In addition, there sometimes is difficulty determining the amount owed to specific suppliers. The manager knows you are an accounting student and asks for your suggestions to improve the accounting function. Write a memo to the manager describing how to increase efficiency and accuracy by using different accounting records.

DEMONSTRATION PROBLEM

Jodi Rutman operates a retail pharmacy called Rutman Pharmacy. The books of original entry include a purchases journal in which purchases of merchandise on account are entered, a cash payments journal in which all cash payments (except petty cash) are entered, and a general journal in which entries such as purchases returns and allowances are made. A subsidiary ledger is used for accounts payable. The following are the transactions related to purchases and cash payments for the month of June.

June 1 Purchased merchandise from Sullivan Co. on account, $234.20. Invoice no. 71 dated June 1, terms 2/10, n/30.
     2 Issued check no. 536 for payment of June rent (Rent Expense), $1,000.00.
     5 Purchased merchandise from Amfac Drug Supply on account, $562.40. Invoice no. 196 dated June 2, terms 1/15, n/30.
     7 Purchased merchandise from University Drug Co. on account, $367.35. Invoice no. 914A dated June 5, terms 3/10 eom, n/30.
     9 Issued check no. 537 to Sullivan Co. in payment of invoice no. 71 less 2% discount.
    12 Received a credit memo from Amfac Drug Supply for merchandise returned that was purchased on June 5, $46.20.
    14 Purchased merchandise from Mutual Drug Co. on account, $479.40. Invoice no. 745 dated June 14, terms 2/10, n/30.
    15 Received a credit memo from University Drug Co. for merchandise returned that was purchased on June 7, $53.70.

June 16   Issued check no. 538 to Amfac Drug Supply in payment of invoice no. 196 less the credit memo of June 12 and less 1% discount.

23   Issued check no. 539 to Mutual Drug Co. in payment of invoice no. 745 less 2% discount.

27   Purchased merchandise from Flites Pharmaceuticals on account, $638.47. Invoice no. 675 dated June 27, terms 2/10 eom, n/30.

29   Issued check no. 540 to Dolgin Candy Co. for a cash purchase of merchandise, $270.20.

30   Issued check no. 541 to Vashon Medical Supply in payment of invoice no. 416, $1,217.69. No discount allowed.

REQUIRED

1. Enter the transactions in a purchases journal, a five-column cash payments journal, and a general journal. Total and rule the purchases and cash payments journals. Prove the cash payments journal.
2. Post from the journals to the general ledger accounts and the accounts payable ledger. Then, update the account balances.
3. Prepare a schedule of accounts payable from the accounts payable ledger in the problem. Verify that the total of accounts payable in the schedule equals the June 30 balance of Accounts Payable in the general ledger.

SOLUTION

1,2.

Proof of Cash Payments Journal:

Debit total:	$1,000.00	Credit total:	$ 19.43
	2,447.49		3,698.26
	270.20		$3,717.69
	$3,717.69		

Cash Payments Journal (left side)

CASH PAYMENTS JOURNAL

	DATE		CK. NO.	ACCOUNT DEBITED	POST. REF.	GENERAL DEBIT	
1	19-- June	2	536	Rent Expense	541	1 0 0 0 00	1
2		9	537	Sullivan Co.	✓		2
3		16	538	Amfac Drug Supply	✓		3
4		23	539	Mutual Drug Co.	✓		4
5		29	540		✓		5
6		30	541	Vashon Medical Supply	✓		6
7						1 0 0 0 00	7
8						(✓)	8

PURCHASES JOURNAL

PAGE 2

	DATE	INVOICE NO.		FROM WHOM PURCHASED	POST. REF.	PURCHASES DEBIT/ACCOUNTS PAYABLE CREDIT	
1	June 19-- 1	71		Sullivan Co.	✓	2 3 4 20	1
2	5	196		Amfac Drug Supply	✓	5 6 2 40	2
3	7	914A		University Drug Co.	✓	3 6 7 35	3
4	14	745		Mutual Drug Co.	✓	4 7 9 40	4
5	27	675		Flites Pharmaceuticals	✓	6 3 8 47	5
6						2 2 8 1 82	6
7						(511) (216)	7

GENERAL JOURNAL

PAGE 4

	DATE	DESCRIPTION	POST. REF.	DEBIT	CREDIT	
1	June 19-- 12	Accts. Payable/Amfac Drug Supply	216/✓	4 6 20		1
2		Purchases Returns and Allow.	511.1		4 6 20	2
3		Returned merchandise				3
4						4
5	15	Accts. Payable/University Drug Co.	216/✓	5 3 70		5
6		Purchases Returns and Allow.	511.1		5 3 70	6
7		Returned merchandise				7

Cash Payments Journal (right side)

PAGE 4

	ACCOUNTS PAYABLE DEBIT	PURCHASES DEBIT	PURCHASES DISCOUNTS CREDIT	CASH CREDIT	
1				1 0 0 0 00	1
2	2 3 4 20		4 68	2 2 9 52	2
3	5 1 6 20		5 16	5 1 1 04	3
4	4 7 9 40		9 59	4 6 9 81	4
5		2 7 0 20		2 7 0 20	5
6	1 2 1 7 69			1 2 1 7 69	6
7	2 4 4 7 49	2 7 0 20	1 9 43	3 6 9 8 26	7
8	(216)	(511)	(511.2)	(111)	8

2.

GENERAL LEDGER

ACCOUNT: Cash   ACCOUNT NO. 111

DATE		ITEM	POST. REF.	DEBIT	CREDIT	BALANCE DEBIT	BALANCE CREDIT
19-- June	1	Balance	✓			9 1 8 0 00	
	30		CP4		3 6 9 8 26	5 4 8 1 74	

ACCOUNT: Accounts Payable   ACCOUNT NO. 216

DATE		ITEM	POST. REF.	DEBIT	CREDIT	BALANCE DEBIT	BALANCE CREDIT
19-- June	1	Balance	✓				1 2 1 7 69
	12		J4	4 6 20			1 1 7 1 49
	15		J4	5 3 70			1 1 1 7 79
	30		P2		2 2 8 1 82		3 3 9 9 61
	30		CP4	2 4 4 7 49			9 5 2 12

ACCOUNT: Purchases   ACCOUNT NO. 511

DATE		ITEM	POST. REF.	DEBIT	CREDIT	BALANCE DEBIT	BALANCE CREDIT
19-- June	1	Balance	✓			13 8 2 6 25	
	30		P2	2 2 8 1 82		16 1 0 8 07	
	30		CP4	2 7 0 20		16 3 7 8 27	

ACCOUNT: Purchases Returns and Allowances   ACCOUNT NO. 511.1

DATE		ITEM	POST. REF.	DEBIT	CREDIT	BALANCE DEBIT	BALANCE CREDIT
19-- June	1	Balance	✓				3 1 2 63
	12		J4		4 6 20		3 5 8 83
	15		J4		5 3 70		4 1 2 53

ACCOUNT: Purchases Discounts   ACCOUNT NO. 511.2

DATE		ITEM	POST. REF.	DEBIT	CREDIT	BALANCE DEBIT	BALANCE CREDIT
19-- June	1	Balance	✓				2 1 1 45
	30		CP4		1 9 43		2 3 0 88

ACCOUNT: Rent Expense   ACCOUNT NO. 541

DATE		ITEM	POST. REF.	DEBIT	CREDIT	BALANCE DEBIT	BALANCE CREDIT
19-- June	1	Balance	✓			5 0 0 0 00	
	2		CP4	1 0 0 0 00		6 0 0 0 00	

2. (cont.)

ACCOUNTS PAYABLE LEDGER

NAME: Amfac Drug Supply

DATE	ITEM	POST. REF.	DEBIT	CREDIT	BALANCE
June 5		P2		5 6 2 40	5 6 2 40
12		J4	4 6 20		5 1 6 20
16		CP4	5 1 6 20		—

NAME: Flites Pharmaceuticals

DATE	ITEM	POST. REF.	DEBIT	CREDIT	BALANCE
June 27		P2		6 3 8 47	6 3 8 47

NAME: Mutual Drug Co.

DATE	ITEM	POST. REF.	DEBIT	CREDIT	BALANCE
June 14		P2		4 7 9 40	4 7 9 40
23		CP4	4 7 9 40		—

NAME: Sullivan Co.

DATE	ITEM	POST. REF.	DEBIT	CREDIT	BALANCE
June 1		P2		2 3 4 20	2 3 4 20
9		CP4	2 3 4 20		—

NAME: University Drug Co.

DATE	ITEM	POST. REF.	DEBIT	CREDIT	BALANCE
June 7		P2		3 6 7 35	3 6 7 35
15		J4	5 3 70		3 1 3 65

NAME: Vashon Medical Supply

DATE	ITEM	POST. REF.	DEBIT	CREDIT	BALANCE
June 1	Balance	✓			1 2 1 7 69
30		CP4	1 2 1 7 69		

3.

Rutman Pharmacy
Schedule of Accounts Payable
June 30, 19--

Flites Pharmaceuticals	$	6 3 8 47
University Drug Co.		3 1 3 65
	$	9 5 2 12
Proof		
Balance of Accounts Payable, June 30	$	9 5 2 12

1 EXERCISE 12A1 PURCHASING DOCUMENTS AND FLOW CHART LABELING   A partially completed flowchart showing some of the major documents commonly used in the purchasing function of a merchandise business is presented below. Identify documents 1, 3, and 4.

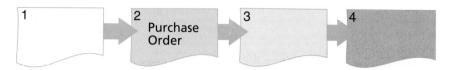

1 EXERCISE 12A2 TRADE DISCOUNT AND CASH DISCOUNTS   Merchandise was purchased on account from Jacob's Distributors on May 17, 19--. The purchase price was $2,000, subject to a 10% trade discount and credit terms of 2/10, n/30.

1. Calculate the net amount to record the invoice, subject to the 10% trade discount.
2. Calculate the amount to be paid on this invoice within the discount period.
3. Journalize the purchase of the merchandise on May 17 in a general journal. Journalize the payment on May 27 (within the discount period).

2 EXERCISE 12A3 PURCHASE TRANSACTIONS AND T ACCOUNTS   Using T accounts for Cash, Accounts Payable, Purchases, Purchases Returns and Allowances, Purchases Discounts, and Freight-In, enter the following purchase transactions. Identify each transaction with its corresponding letter. Use a new set of T accounts for each set of transactions, 1-4.

1. Purchase of merchandise with cash.
   (a) Merchandise is purchased for cash, $1,500.
   (b) Merchandise listed at $3,500, subject to a trade discount of 15%, is purchased for cash.
2. Purchase of merchandise on account with credit terms.
   (a) Merchandise is purchased on account, credit terms 2/10, n/30, $2,000.
   (b) Merchandise is purchased on account, credit terms 3/10, n/30, $1,200.
   (c) Payment is made on invoice (a) within the discount period.
   (d) Payment is made on invoice (b) too late to receive the cash discount.
3. Purchase of merchandise on account with return of merchandise.
   (a) Merchandise is purchased on account, credit terms 2/10, n/30, $4,000.
   (b) Merchandise is returned for credit before payment is made, $500.
   (c) Payment is made within the discount period.

4. Purchase of merchandise with freight-in.

　(a) Merchandise is purchased on account, $2,500 plus freight charges of $100. Terms of the sale were FOB shipping point.

　(b) Payment is made for the cost of merchandise and the freight charge.

2 **EXERCISE 12A4 COST OF GOODS SOLD**　The following data were taken from the accounts of Delhi Hardware, a small retail business. Determine the cost of goods sold.

Merchandise inventory, January 1	$34,000
Purchases during the period	76,000
Purchases returns and allowances during the period	4,000
Purchases discounts taken during the period	3,000
Freight-in on merchandise purchased during the period	1,500
Merchandise inventory, December 31	30,000

3 **EXERCISE 12A5 JOURNALIZING TRANSACTIONS IN PURCHASES JOURNAL AND GENERAL JOURNAL**

1. Journalize the following transactions in a general journal.

May　3　Purchased merchandise from Cintron, $6,500. Invoice no. 321, dated May 1, terms n/30.

　　9　Purchased merchandise from Mitsui, $2,300. Invoice no. 614, dated May 8, terms 2/10, n/30.

　18　Purchased merchandise from Aloha Distributors, $4,200. Invoice no. 180, dated May 15, terms 1/15, n/30.

　23　Purchased merchandise from Soto, $6,300. Invoice no. 913, dated May 22, terms 1/10, n/30.

2. Journalize the transactions in a purchases journal like the one below.

		PURCHASES JOURNAL		PAGE 5
DATE	INVOICE NO.	FROM WHOM PURCHASED	POST. REF.	PURCHASES DEBIT/ACCOUNTS PAYABLE CREDIT

3 **EXERCISE 12A6 JOURNALIZE PURCHASES RETURNS AND ALLOWANCES AND POST TO GENERAL LEDGER AND ACCOUNTS PAYABLE LEDGER**　Using page 3 of a general journal and the following general ledger and accounts payable ledger accounts, journalize and post the following transactions.

July　7　Merchandise returned to Starcraft Industries, $700.

　15　Merchandise returned to XYZ, Inc., $450.

　27　Merchandise returned to Datamagic, $900.

General Ledger

Account No.	Account	Balance July 1, 19--
216	Accounts Payable	$10,650
511.1	Purchases Returns and Allowances	

continued

Accounts Payable Ledger

Name	Balance	July 1, 19--
Datamagic	$2,600	
Starcraft Industries	4,300	
XYZ, Inc.	3,750	

4 **EXERCISE 12A7 CASH PAYMENTS JOURNAL** Landmark Industries uses a cash payments journal. Prepare a cash payments journal using the same format and account titles as illustrated in the chapter. Record the following payments for merchandise purchased.

Sept. 5 Issued check no. 318 to Clinton Corp. for merchandise purchased August 28, $6,000, terms 2/10, n/30. Payment is made within the discount period.

12 Issued check no. 319 to Mitchell Company for merchandise purchased September 2, $7,500, terms 1/10, n/30. Received a credit memo from Mitchell Company for merchandise returned, $500. Payment is made within the discount period after deduction for the return dated September 8.

19 Issued check no. 320 to Expert Systems for merchandise purchased August 19, $4,100, terms n/30.

27 Issued check no. 321 to Graphic Data for merchandise purchased September 17, $9,000, terms 2/10, n/30. Payment is made within the discount period.

5 **EXERCISE 12A8 PREPARATION OF SCHEDULE OF ACCOUNTS PAYABLE** Ryan's Express, a retail business, had the following beginning balances and purchases and payments activity in its accounts payable ledger during October. Prepare a schedule of accounts payable for Ryan's Express as of October 31, 19--.

Accounts Payable Ledger

Name	Balance Oct. 1, 19--	Purchases	Payments
Columbia Products	$4,350	$3,060	$2,060
Favorite Fashions	4,910	1,970	2,600
Rustic Legends	5,130	2,625	3,015

SERIES A PROBLEMS

3 **PROBLEM 12A1 PURCHASES JOURNAL** J. B. Speck, owner of Speck's Galleria, made the following purchases of merchandise on account during the month of September 19--.

Sept. 3 Purchase invoice no. 415, $2,650, from Smith Distributors.
   8 Purchase invoice no. 132, $3,830, from Michaels Wholesaler.
   11 Purchase invoice no. 614, $3,140, from J. B. Sanders & Co.
   18 Purchase invoice no. 329, $2,250, from Bateman & Jones, Inc.
   23 Purchase invoice no. 167, $4,160, from Smith Distributors.

continued

Sept. 27 Purchase invoice no. 744, $1,980, from Anderson Company.
     30 Purchase invoice no. 652, $2,780, from Michaels Wholesaler.

REQUIRED

1. Record the transactions in the purchases journal. Total and rule the journal.
2. Post from the purchases journal to the general ledger accounts and to the accounts payable ledger accounts. Use account numbers as shown in the chapter.

3 **PROBLEM 12A2 PURCHASES JOURNAL, GENERAL LEDGER, AND ACCOUNTS PAYABLE LEDGER** The purchases journal of Kevin's Kettle, a small retail business, is as follows.

PURCHASES JOURNAL   PAGE 1

	DATE	INVOICE NO.	FROM WHOM PURCHASED	POST. REF.	PURCHASES DEBIT/ACCOUNTS PAYABLE CREDIT	
1	19-- Jan. 2	101	Ruiz Imports		3 0 0 0 00	1
2	3	621	Helmut's Hair Supply		2 4 8 0 00	2
3	7	195	Viola's Boutique		4 3 6 0 00	3
4	12	267	Royal Flush		1 9 5 0 00	4
5	18	903	Maria's Melodies		4 7 0 0 00	5
6	25	680	Helmut's Hair Supply		1 7 6 0 00	6
7					18 2 5 0 00	7

REQUIRED

1. Post the total of the purchases journal to the appropriate general ledger accounts. Use account numbers as shown in the chapter.
2. Post the individual purchase amounts to the accounts payable ledger.

4 **PROBLEM 12A3 CASH PAYMENTS JOURNAL, ACCOUNTS PAYABLE LEDGER, AND GENERAL LEDGER** Sam Santiago operates a retail variety store. The books include a cash payments journal and an accounts payable ledger. All cash payments (except petty cash) are entered in the cash payments journal.

Selected account balances on May 1 are as follows:

General Ledger

Cash	$40,000
Accounts Payable	20,000

Accounts Payable Ledger

Fantastic Toys	$5,200
Goya Outlet	3,800
Mueller's Distributors	3,600
Van Kooning	5,500

continued

The following are the transactions related to cash payments for the month of May.

May   1 Issued check no. 426 in payment of May rent (Rent Expense), $2,400.

       3 Issued check no. 427 to Mueller's Distributors in payment of merchandise purchased on account, $3,600 less a 3% discount. Check was written for $3,492.

       7 Issued check no. 428 to Van Kooning for payment of merchandise purchased on account, $5,500. A cash discount was not allowed.

      12 Issued check no. 429 to Fantastic Toys for merchandise purchased on account, $5,200, less a 1% discount. Check was written for $5,148.

      15 Issued check no. 430 to City Power and Light (Utilities Expense), $1,720.

      18 Issued check no. 431 to A-1 Warehouse for a cash purchase of merchandise, $4,800.

      26 Issued check no. 432 to Goya Outlet for merchandise purchased on account, $3,800, less a 2% discount. Check was written for $3,724.

      30 Issued check no. 433 to Mercury Transit Company for freight charges on merchandise purchased (Freight-In), $1,200.

      31 Issued check no. 434 to Town Merchants for a cash purchase of merchandise, $3,000.

REQUIRED

1. Enter the transactions in a cash payments journal. Total, rule, and prove the cash payments journal.

2. Post from the cash payments journal to the general ledger and the accounts payable ledger. Use general ledger account numbers as shown in the chapter.

3/4
SS

PROBLEM 12A4 PURCHASES JOURNAL, CASH PAYMENTS JOURNAL, GENERAL JOURNAL, GENERAL LEDGER, AND ACCOUNTS PAYABLE LEDGER   Freddy Flint owns a small retail business called Flint's Fantasy. The cash account has a balance of $20,000 on July 1. The following transactions occurred during July 19--.

July   1 Issued check no. 414 in payment of July rent, $1,500.

        1 Purchased merchandise on account from Tang's Toys, invoice no. 311, $2,700, terms 2/10, n/30.

        3 Purchased merchandise on account from Smith & Company, invoice no. 812, $3,100, terms 1/10, n/30.

        5 Returned merchandise purchased from Tang's Toys, receiving a credit memo on the amount owed, $500.

        8 Purchased merchandise on account from Daisy's Dolls, invoice no. 139, $1,900, terms 2/10, n/30.

       11 Issued check no. 415 to Tang's Toys for merchandise purchased on account, less return of July 5 and less 2% discount.

continued

July 13 Issued check no. 416 to Smith & Company for merchandise purchased on account, less 1% discount.

15 Returned merchandise purchased from Daisy's Dolls, receiving a credit memo on the amount owed, $400.

18 Issued check no. 417 to Daisy's Dolls for merchandise purchased on account, less return of July 15 and less 2% discount.

25 Purchased merchandise on account from Allied Business, invoice no. 489, $2,450, terms n/30.

26 Purchased merchandise on account from Tang's Toys, invoice no. 375, $1,980, terms 2/10, n/30.

29 Purchased merchandise on account from Smith & Company, invoice no. 883, $3,460, terms 1/10, n/30.

31 Freddy Flint withdrew cash for personal use, $2,000. Issued check no. 418.

31 Issued check no. 419 to Glisan Distributors for a cash purchase of merchandise, $975.

REQUIRED

1. Enter the transactions in a purchases journal, a cash payments journal, and a general journal. Total and rule the purchases and cash payments journals. Prove the cash payments journal.

2. Post from the journals to the general ledger and accounts payable ledger accounts. Use general ledger account numbers as shown in the chapter.

5 **PROBLEM 12A5 SCHEDULE OF ACCOUNTS PAYABLE** Based on the information provided in Problem 12A4, prepare a schedule of accounts payable for Flint's Fantasy as of July 31, 19--. Verify that the accounts payable account balance in the general ledger agrees with the schedule of accounts payable total.

SERIES B EXERCISES

1 **EXERCISE 12B1 PURCHASING DOCUMENTS AND FLOW CHART LABELING** A flowchart showing some of the major documents commonly used in the purchasing function of a merchandise business is presented below. Briefly describe each document.

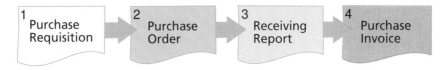

1
Purchase
Requisition

2
Purchase
Order

3
Receiving
Report

4
Purchase
Invoice

1 **EXERCISE 12B2 TRADE DISCOUNT AND CASH DISCOUNTS** Merchandise was purchased on account from Grant's Distributors on June 12, 19--. The purchase price was $5,000, subject to a 10% trade discount and credit terms of 3/10, n/30.

1. Calculate the net amount to record the invoice, subject to the 10% trade discount.

2. Calculate the amount to be paid on this invoice within the discount period.
3. Journalize the purchase of the merchandise on June 12 and the payment on June 22 (within the discount period) in a general journal.

2 **EXERCISE 12B3 PURCHASE TRANSACTIONS AND T ACCOUNTS**   Using T accounts for Cash, Accounts Payable, Purchases, Purchases Returns and Allowances, Purchases Discounts, and Freight-In, enter the following purchase transactions. Identify each transaction with its corresponding letter. Use a new set of T accounts for each set of transactions, 1–4.

1. Purchase of merchandise with cash.
   (a) Merchandise is purchased for cash, $2,300.
   (b) Merchandise listed at $4,000, subject to a trade discount of 10%, is purchased for cash.
2. Purchase of merchandise on account with credit terms.
   (a) Merchandise is purchased on account, credit terms 2/10, n/30, $4,000.
   (b) Merchandise is purchased on account, credit terms 3/10, n/30, $2,800.
   (c) Payment is made on invoice (a) within the discount period.
   (d) Payment is made on invoice (b) too late to receive the cash discount.
3. Purchase of merchandise on account with return of merchandise.
   (a) Merchandise is purchased on account, credit terms 2/10, n/30, $5,600.
   (b) Merchandise is returned for credit before payment is made, $600.
   (c) Payment is made within the discount period.
4. Purchase of merchandise with freight-in.
   (a) Merchandise is purchased on account, $3,800 plus freight charges of $200. Terms of the sale were FOB shipping point.
   (b) Payment is made for the cost of merchandise and the freight charge.

2 **EXERCISE 12B4 COST OF GOODS SOLD**   The following data were taken from the accounts of Burnside Bedknobs, a retail business. Determine the cost of goods sold.

Merchandise inventory, January 1	$ 30,000
Purchases during the period	100,000
Purchases returns and allowances during the period	2,000
Purchases discounts taken during the period	2,800
Freight-in on merchandise purchased during the period	1,500
Merchandise inventory, December 31	50,000

3 **EXERCISE 12B5 JOURNALIZING TRANSACTIONS IN PURCHASES JOURNAL AND GENERAL JOURNAL**

1. Journalize the following transactions in a general journal.

Jan.   3 Purchased merchandise from Feng, $6,000. Invoice no. 416, dated January 1, terms 2/10, n/30.
       12 Purchased merchandise from Miranda, $9,000. Invoice no. 624, dated January 10, terms n/30.
       19 Purchased merchandise from J.B. Barba, $6,400. Invoice no. 190, dated January 18, terms 1/10, n/30.
       26 Purchased merchandise from Ramirez, $3,700. Invoice no. 923, dated January 25, terms 1/15, n/30.

2. Journalize the transactions in a purchases journal like the one below.

	PURCHASES JOURNAL			PAGE 5
DATE	INVOICE NO.	FROM WHOM PURCHASED	POST. REF.	PURCHASES DEBIT/ACCOUNTS PAYABLE CREDIT

3   **EXERCISE 12B6 JOURNALIZE PURCHASES RETURNS AND ALLOWANCES AND POST TO GENERAL LEDGER AND ACCOUNTS PAYABLE LEDGER**   Using page 3 of a general journal and the following general ledger accounts and accounts payable ledger accounts, journalize and post the following transactions.

Mar.   5 Merchandise returned to Tower Industries, $500.
       11 Merchandise returned to A & D Arms, $625.
       23 Merchandise returned to Mighty Mansion, $275.

General Ledger

Account No.	Account	Balance Mar. 1, 19--
216	Accounts Payable	$8,350
511.1	Purchases Returns and Allowances	

Accounts Payable Ledger

Name	Balance	Mar. 1, 19--
A & D Arms	$2,300	
Mighty Mansion	1,450	
Tower Industries	4,600	

4   **EXERCISE 12B7 ENTRIES IN A CASH PAYMENTS JOURNAL**
Sandcastles Northwest uses a cash payments journal. Prepare a cash payments journal using the same format and account titles as illustrated in the chapter. Record the following payments for merchandise purchased.

April   5 Issued check no. 429 to Standard Industries for merchandise purchased April 3, $8,000, terms 2/10, n/30. Payment is made within the discount period.
       19 Issued check no. 430 to Finest Company for merchandise purchased April 10, $5,300, terms 1/10, n/30. Received a credit memo from Finest Company for merchandise returned, $300. Payment is made within the discount period after deduction for the return dated April 12.

continued

April 21 Issued check no. 431 to Funny Follies for merchandise purchased March 21, $3,250, terms n/30.

29 Issued check no. 432 to Classic Data for merchandise purchased April 20, $7,000, terms 2/10, n/30. Payment is made within the discount period.

5 **EXERCISE 12B8 PREPARATION OF SCHEDULE OF ACCOUNTS PAYABLE**   Crystal's Candles, a retail business, had the following balances and purchases and payments activity in its accounts payable ledger during November. Prepare a schedule of accounts payable for Crystal's Candles as of November 30, 19--.

Accounts Payable Ledger

Name	Balance Nov. 1, 19--	Purchases	Payments
Carl's Candle Wax	$4,135	$ 955	$1,610
Handy Supplies	3,490	1,320	1,850
Wishy Wicks	3,300	1,905	1,080

SERIES B PROBLEMS

3 **PROBLEM 12B1 PURCHASES JOURNAL**   Ann Benton, owner of Benton's Galleria, made the following purchases of merchandise on account during the month of October 19--.

Oct.   2 Purchase invoice no. 321, $1,950, from Boggs Distributors.
7 Purchase invoice no. 152, $2,915, from Wolfs Wholesaler.
10 Purchase invoice no. 634, $3,565, from Kennington & Co.
16 Purchase invoice no. 349, $2,845, from Fritz & McCord, Inc.
24 Purchase invoice no. 187, $3,370, from Boggs Distributors.
26 Purchase invoice no. 764, $2,240, from Sanderson Company.
31 Purchase invoice no. 672, $1,630, from Wolfs Wholesaler.

REQUIRED
1. Record the transactions in the purchases journal. Total and rule the journal.
2. Post from the purchases journal to the general ledger accounts and to the accounts payable ledger accounts. Use account numbers as shown in the chapter.

3 **PROBLEM 12B2 PURCHASES JOURNAL, GENERAL LEDGER, AND ACCOUNTS PAYABLE LEDGER**   The purchases journal of Ryan's Rats Nest, a small retail business, is shown on the next page.

REQUIRED
1. Post the total of the purchases journal to the appropriate general ledger accounts. Use account numbers as shown in the chapter.
2. Post the individual purchase amounts to the accounts payable subsidiary ledger.

PURCHASES JOURNAL PAGE 1

	DATE	INVOICE NO.	FROM WHOM PURCHASED	POST. REF.	PURCHASES DEBIT/ACCOUNTS PAYABLE CREDIT	
1	19-- Jan. 3	121	Sandra's Sweets		4 4 9 0 00	1
2	5	641	Amelia & Vincente		5 9 2 0 00	2
3	9	215	Nobuko's Nature Store		2 6 8 0 00	3
4	15	227	Smith and Johnson Company		6 5 6 0 00	4
5	21	933	Hidemi Inc.		1 3 0 0 00	5
6	30	650	Amelia & Vincente		1 8 9 0 00	6
7					22 8 4 0 00	7

4 **PROBLEM 12B3 CASH PAYMENTS JOURNAL, ACCOUNTS PAYABLE LEDGER, AND GENERAL LEDGER**   Kay Zembrowski operates a retail variety store. The books include a cash payments journal and an accounts payable ledger. All cash payments (except petty cash) are entered in the cash payments journal. Selected account balances on May 1 are as follows:

General Ledger

Cash	$40,000
Accounts Payable	20,000

Accounts Payable Ledger

Cortez Distributors	$4,200
Indra & Velga	6,200
Toy Corner	4,600
Troutman Outlet	4,400

The following are the transactions related to cash payments for the month of May.

May 1 Issued check no. 326 in payment of May rent (Rent Expense), $2,600.

4 Issued check no. 327 to Cortez Distributors in payment of merchandise purchased on account, $4,200 less a 3% discount. Check was written for $4,074.

7 Issued check no. 328 to Indra & Velga in payment of merchandise purchased on account, $6,200. A cash discount was not allowed.

11 Issued check no. 329 to Toy Corner for merchandise purchased on account, $4,600 less a 1% discount. Check was written for $4,554.

15 Issued check no. 330 to County Power and Light (Utilities Expense), $1,500.

19 Issued check no. 331 to Builders Warehouse for a cash purchase of merchandise, $3,500.

continued

May 25 Issued check no. 332 to Troutman Outlet for merchandise purchased on account, $4,400 less a 2% discount. Check was written for $4,312.

30 Issued check no. 333 to Rapid Transit Company for freight charges on merchandise purchased (Freight-In), $800.

31 Issued check no. 334 to City Merchants for a cash purchase of merchandise, $2,350.

REQUIRED

1. Enter the transactions in a cash payments journal. Total, rule, and prove the cash payments journal.

2. Post from the cash payments journal to the general ledger and the accounts payable ledger.

3/4   **PROBLEM 12B4 PURCHASES JOURNAL, CASH PAYMENTS JOURNAL, GENERAL JOURNAL, GENERAL LEDGER, AND**

SS   **ACCOUNTS PAYABLE LEDGER**   Debbie Mueller owns a small retail business called Debbie's Doll House. The cash account has a balance of $20,000 on July 1. The following transactions occurred during July 19--.

July 1 Issued check no. 314 for July rent, $1,400.

1 Purchased merchandise on account from Topper's Toys, invoice no. 211, $2,500, terms 2/10, n/30.

3 Purchased merchandise on account from Jones & Company, invoice no. 812, $2,800, terms 1/10, n/30.

5 Returned merchandise purchased from Topper's Toys receiving a credit memo on the amount owed, $400.

8 Purchased merchandise on account from Downtown Merchants, invoice no. 159, $1,600, terms 2/10, n/30.

11 Issued check no. 315 to Topper's Toys for merchandise purchased on account, less return of July 5 and less 2% discount.

13 Issued check no. 316 to Jones & Company for merchandise purchased on account, less 1% discount.

15 Returned merchandise purchased from Downtown Merchants receiving a credit memo on the amount owed, $600.

18 Issued check no. 317 to Downtown Merchants for merchandise purchased on account, less return of July 15 and less 2% discount.

25 Purchased merchandise on account from Columbia Products, invoice no. 468, $3,200, terms n/30.

26 Purchased merchandise on account from Topper's Toys, invoice no. 395, $1,430, terms 2/10, n/30.

29 Purchased merchandise on account from Jones & Company, invoice no. 853, $2,970, terms 1/10, n/30.

31 Mueller withdrew cash for personal use, $2,500. Issued check no. 318.

31 Issued check no. 319 to Burnside Warehouse for a cash purchase of merchandise, $1,050.

1. Enter the transactions in a purchases journal, a cash payments journal, and a general journal. Total and rule the purchases and cash payments journals. Prove the cash payments journal.
2. Post from the journals to the general ledger and accounts payable ledger accounts. Use general ledger account numbers as shown in the chapter.

5 **PROBLEM 12B5 SCHEDULE OF ACCOUNTS PAYABLE** Based on the information provided in Problem 12B4, prepare a schedule of accounts payable for Debbie's Doll House as of July 31, 19--. Verify that the accounts payable account balance in the general ledger agrees with the schedule of accounts payable total.

MASTERY PROBLEM

Michelle French owns and operates Books and More, a retail book store. Selected account balances on June 1 are as follows:

General Ledger

Cash	$32,200.00
Accounts Payable	2,000.00
Michelle French, Drawing	18,000.00
Purchases	67,021.66
Purchases Returns and Allowances	2,315.23
Purchases Discounts	905.00
Freight-In	522.60
Rent Expense	3,125.00
Utilities Expense	1,522.87

Accounts Payable Ledger

North-Eastern Publishing Co.	$2,000.00

The following purchases and cash payment transactions took place during the month of June:

June 1 Purchased books on account from Irving Publishing Company, $2,100. Invoice no. 101, terms 2/10, n/30, FOB destination.
2 Issued check no. 300 to North-Eastern Publishing Company for goods purchased on May 23, terms 2/10, n/30, $1,960 (the $2,000 invoice amount less the 2% discount.)
3 Purchased books on account from Broadway Publishing, Inc., $2,880. Invoice no. 711, subject to 20% trade discount, and invoice terms of 3/10, n/30, FOB shipping point.
3 Issued check no. 301 to Mayday Shipping for delivery from Broadway Publishing Company, $250.
4 Issued check no. 302 for June rent, $625.
8 Purchased books on account from North-Eastern Publishing Company, $5,825. Invoice no. 268, terms 2/eom, n/60, FOB destination.

continued

June 10 Received a credit memo from Irving Publishing Company, $550. Books had been returned because the covers were on upside down.

13 Issued check no. 304 to Broadway Publishing, Inc., for the purchase made on June 3. (Check no. 303 was voided because an error was made in preparing it.)

28 Made the following purchases:

Invoice No.	Company	Amount	Terms
579	Broadway Publishing, Inc.	$2,350	2/10, n/30 FOB destination
406	North-Eastern Publishing Co.	4,200	2/eom, n/60 FOB destination
964	Riley Publishing Co.	3,450	3/10, n/30 FOB destination

June 30 Issued check no. 305 to Taylor County Utility Co., for June utilities, $325.

30 French withdrew cash for personal use, $4,500. Issued check no. 306.

30 Issued check no. 307 to Irving Publishing Company for purchase made on June 1 less returns made on June 10.

30 Issued check no. 308 to North-Eastern Publishing Company for purchase made on June 8.

30 Issued check no. 309 for books purchased at an auction, $1,328.

REQUIRED

1. Enter the above transactions in the appropriate journals.
2. Total and rule the purchases journal and cash payments journal. Prove the cash payments journal.
3. Post from the journals to the general ledger accounts and the accounts payable ledger.
4. Prepare a schedule of accounts payable.
5. If merchandise inventory was $35,523 on January 1 and $42,100 as of June 30, prepare the cost of goods sold section of the income statement for the six months ended June 30, 19--.

The Net-Price Method of Recording Purchases

Careful study of this appendix should enable you to:

LO1 Describe the net-price method of recording purchases.

LO2 Record purchases and cash payments using the net-price method.

In chapter 12, purchases were recorded using the *gross-price method*. Under this method, purchases are recorded at the gross amount, regardless of available cash discounts. This appendix illustrates the **net-price method**, an alternative approach to accounting for purchases. Under this method, purchases are recorded at the net amount, assuming that all available cash discounts will be taken.

To compare the two methods, reconsider the purchase for $100 on account, with credit terms of 2/10, n/30, on page 385. At the time of the purchase, the following entries are made under the two methods:

GROSS-PRICE			NET-PRICE		
Purchases	100.00		Purchases	98.00*	
Accounts Payable		100.00	Accounts Payable		98.00
			* $100 − $2 (2% cash discount)		

If payment for the merchandise is made within the discount period, the entries are:

GROSS-PRICE			NET-PRICE		
Accounts Payable	100.00		Accounts Payable	98.00	
Cash		98.00	Cash		98.00
Purchases Discounts		2.00			

If payment for the merchandise is not made until after the discount period, the entries are:

GROSS-PRICE			NET-PRICE		
Accounts Payable	100.00		Accounts Payable	98.00	
Cash		100.00	Purchases Discounts Lost	2.00	
			Cash		100.00

Note that under the net-price method a new account, Purchases Discounts Lost, is used. Purchases Discounts Lost is a temporary owners' equity account used to record cash discounts lost on purchases.

Purchases Discounts Lost

Debit	Credit
for discounts lost because of late payment of invoices	

Purchases Discounts Lost represents a finance charge for postponing the payment for merchandise. If the balance in this account is large relative to the amount of gross purchases, management should review its cash payment procedures. Purchases Discounts Lost is reported as an expense on the income statement.

EXERCISES

2 **EXERCISE 12ApxA1 PURCHASES TRANSACTIONS—GROSS-PRICE AND NET-PRICE METHODS**   Romero's Heating and Cooling had the following transactions during April.

April 2 Purchased merchandise on account from Alanon Valve, $1,000, terms 2/10, n/30.
  5 Purchased merchandise on account from Leon's Garage, $1,400, terms 1/10, n/30.
  11 Paid the amount due to Alanon Valve for the purchase on April 2.
  25 Paid the amount due to Leon's Garage for the purchase on April 5.

1. Prepare general journal entries for these transactions using the gross-price method.
2. Prepare general journal entries for these transactions using the net-price method.

2 **EXERCISE 12ApxB1 PURCHASES TRANSACTIONS—GROSS-PRICE AND NET-PRICE METHODS**   Gloria's Repair Shop had the following transactions during May.

May 2 Purchased merchandise on account from Delgado's Supply, $900, terms 2/10, n/30.
  6 Purchased merchandise on account from Goro's Auto Care, $1,200, terms 1/10, n/30.

continued

May   11 Paid the amount due to Delgado's Supply for the purchase on May 2.

         27 Paid the amount due to Goro's Auto Care for the purchase on May 6.

1. Prepare general journal entries for these transactions using the gross-price method.

2. Prepare general journal entries for these transactions using the net-price method.

13

The Voucher System

Your friend is very excited about her new job in the purchasing department of a major department store. She is responsible for ordering merchandise from suppliers. She has always liked buying things, so from that standpoint the job is ideal. In addition, she figures that since she is authorized to order merchandise, she will order some for herself as well as for the business. Since the business will then pay for the merchandise, this will provide her with a nice "bonus." Will she be able to do this?

Chapter 12 demonstrated how merchandise purchased on account can be efficiently recorded in a purchases journal. In this chapter, we will learn to use a special journal for recording all purchases of assets and services of any kind. Chapter 12 also demonstrated how cash payments can be efficiently recorded in a cash payments journal. In this chapter, we will learn to use another type of journal for recording cash payments.

The two new journals introduced in this chapter provide more than an efficient way to record transactions. These journals are an important part of what is called a voucher system.

INTERNAL CONTROL OF EXPENDITURES

LO1 Describe how a voucher system is used to control expenditures.

To be successful, management must have adequate control of the operations of the business. When we think of controlling business operations, most of us tend to emphasize ways to control revenues. In fact, it is equally as important to control the expenditure process.

Management needs to see that expenditures are being made only for goods and services needed by the business and at a fair price. In a small business, management does so by direct involvement with the expenditure process. But, as a business grows larger, management cannot continue such direct involvement. Instead, in medium- and large-size businesses, management controls expenditures by using an appropriate internal control system.

Elements of Internal Control

Internal controls are the set of procedures used to ensure that there is proper accounting for all the activities of the business. A full discussion of internal controls is a subject for an advanced text. Our attention will be limited to three elements of internal control that are particularly important for expenditures.

1. Segregation of duties
2. Authorization procedures and related responsibilities
3. Accounting procedures

Segregation of duties means that:

1. Different employees should be responsible for different parts of a transaction; and
2. Employees who account for transactions should not also have custody of the assets.

For example, one employee should be responsible for ordering goods and another responsible for issuing the check to pay for them. Similarly, one employee should be responsible for recording the purchase of goods and another responsible for storing them. This segregation of duties provides a built-in check by one employee on another. One employee cannot obtain goods for personal use without being caught by another employee.

Authorization procedures and related responsibilities means that every business activity should be properly authorized. In addition, it should be possible to identify who is responsible for every activity that has occurred. For example, to acquire new equipment, a signed document should authorize the purchase. After the purchase is made, this signed document shows who is responsible for the action.

Accounting procedures means that accounting documents and records should be used so that all business transactions are recorded. For example, every purchase that occurs should be supported by a document. These documents should be prenumbered, used in sequence, and subsequently accounted for. In this way, the business can be sure that it has made a record of each transaction.

Voucher System

The three elements of internal control described above can be combined to control expenditures by using a voucher system. A **voucher system** is a control technique that requires that every acquisition and subsequent payment be supported by an approved voucher. A **voucher** is a document that shows that an acquisition is proper and that payment is authorized.

Figure 13-1 is a simplified illustration of how the purchasing portion of a voucher system operates. The purchase requisition, purchase order, receiving report, and purchase invoice were explained and illustrated in Chapter 12. Recall that an authorized person or department prepares a purchase requisition to indicate the need for goods. The purchasing department reviews and approves the purchase requisition and prepares a purchase order to send to the supplier. When the goods are received, a receiving report is prepared. A copy of each of these documents is sent to the vouchers payable section in the accounting department.

When the purchase invoice (Figure 13-2) arrives, it is compared with the purchase requisition, purchase order, and receiving report. If the purchase invoice is:

- for the goods ordered (purchase requisition and purchase order),
- at the correct price (purchase order),
- and for the correct quantity (receiving report),

then a voucher (Figure 13-3) is prepared. This is the first key control provided by the voucher system. If any aspect of the purchase is improper, it will be noticed when the voucher is prepared.

After the voucher is prepared and approved, it is entered in a special journal called a voucher register. It then is filed by due date.

The completed voucher provides the basis for paying the supplier's invoice on the due date. This is the second key control provided by the voucher system. No payment may be made without an approved voucher. The payment process will be discussed later in this chapter.

> The voucher system contains elements of internal control such as segregation of duties, authorization to order the goods and prepare the voucher, and accounting procedures that require prenumbering and accounting for the supporting documents.

FIGURE 13-1   Voucher System—Purchasing Process

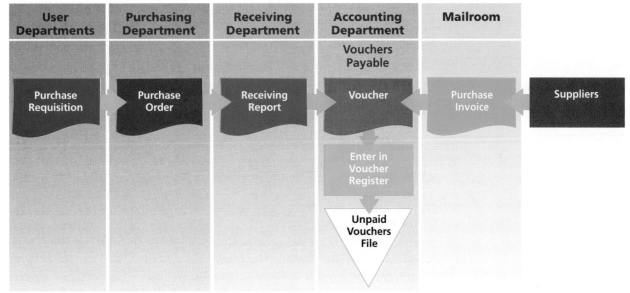

Notice how the three elements of internal control can be seen in this system. (1) *Duties are segregated* because different employees order, receive, and record the purchases. (2) *Authorization* is required to order the goods and to prepare the voucher. (3) The *accounting procedures* require prenumbering and accounting for the purchase requisitions, purchase orders, receiving reports, and vouchers. This means that every recorded purchase is supported by the following five documents:

1. Voucher
2. Purchase invoice
3. Receiving report
4. Purchase order
5. Purchase requisition

This provides management with strong assurance that purchasing activities are properly controlled.

PREPARING A VOUCHER

LO2 Prepare a voucher.

To illustrate the preparation of a voucher and how a voucher system works, we extend the Northern Micro transactions from Chapter 12. In this chapter, we assume that Northern Micro uses a voucher system. Note that several new transactions have been added.

When a purchase invoice (Figure 13-2) is received from a supplier, the following procedures are performed in the vouchers payable section.

STEP 1 Compare the invoice with the purchase requisition, purchase order, and receiving report to determine that:

(a) the quantity was requisitioned (purchase requisition), ordered (purchase order), and received (receiving report)

(b) the price and credit terms are proper (purchase order)

STEP 2 Judge whether the purchase is appropriate for the business.

STEP 3 Verify all computations on the invoice (quantity × price, and any discounts).

Note how personnel in the vouchers payable section thus provide a final, independent check on the entire purchasing process. If any aspect is improper, it can be caught before payment is made.

After performing these procedures, the voucher is prepared. Many acceptable formats for vouchers can be used. Figure 13-3 illustrates a commonly used form. This voucher was prepared based on the purchase invoice in Figure 13-2.

The front of the voucher usually shows the voucher number, date, supplier, and what was purchased. The back indicates the accounts to be debited and the payment date, check number, and amount.

The prenumbered voucher in Figure 13-3 was prepared using the following steps.

STEP 1 On the front of the voucher, insert

a. voucher date
b. invoice terms
c. due date
d. supplier name and address
e. invoice date
f. description of items purchased
g. invoice amount

STEP 2 On the back, insert the accounts and amounts to be debited.

After these steps are completed, the voucher clerk (B. Zimmer) signs the voucher and has it approved by the vouchers payable section supervisor (J. Jensen). On the back of the voucher, the "Distribution" (the accounts to which the expenditure is charged) is approved by the accounting supervisor (J.G.). The "Payment" approval is not completed until the voucher is paid on the due date. The $87 purchases discount will be recorded when the voucher is paid.

VOUCHER REGISTER

LO3 Describe and use a voucher register.

 A voucher register is used to record purchases of all types of assets and services.

FIGURE 13-2   Purchase Invoice

EZX corp

Invoice No. 4973

2989 RHODES AVE., CHICAGO, IL 60658

Sold to:
Northern Micro
1099 E. Louisiana
Indianapolis, IN 46217-3322

Date: 4/9/--
Your Order No: 319
Terms: 1/15, n/30

Quantity	Description	Unit Price	Total
3	P75 Computers	$1,900.00	$5,700.00
3	Q19 Laser Printers	1,000.00	3,000.00
			$8,700.00

FIGURE 13-3   Voucher

N NORTHERN MICRO
1099 E. Louisiana, Indianapolis, IN 46217-3322

Voucher No. **111**

Date 4/11/-- Terms 1/15, n/30   Due 4/24/--
To: EZX Corp.
    2989 Rhodes Ave.
    Chicago, IL 60658

Invoice Date	Invoice No.	Description	Amount
4/9/--	4973	P75 Computers-3	$5,700.00
		Q19 Laser Printers-3	3,000.00
			$8,700.00

Autorization   _J. Jensen_   (Supervisor)   Prepared by _B. Zimmer_   (Clerk)

Voucher No. **111**

Account Debited	Account No.	Amount	Summary	
Purchases	511	$8,700.00	Invoice	$8,700.00
			Discount	87.00
			Net	$8,613.00

Payment: Date 4/24/--   Check No. 437   Amount $8,613.00

Approved: Distribution _J.G._   Payment _____

After the voucher is completed and approved, it is entered in a voucher register. A **voucher register** is a special journal used to record purchases of all types of assets and services. You can think of a voucher register as an expanded purchases journal like the one we saw in Chapter 12. In fact, if a voucher register is used, it replaces the purchases journal.

Figure 13-4 illustrates Northern Micro's voucher register. It has four debit columns—for Purchases, Supplies, Wages Expense, and General Debit—and a credit column for Vouchers Payable. The General Debit column is used for transactions affecting account titles other than those with special column headings. The voucher register also has a "Payment" column that is used when the voucher is paid. As with any special journal, the exact number and types of debit and credit columns used depends on the nature of the business.

A voucher is recorded in the voucher register by entering the following information:

1. Date
2. Voucher number
3. Person or business to whom the voucher is issued
4. Dollar amounts of debits and credits

The entry for voucher no. 111 (Figure 13-3) was made on April 11.

Filing Unpaid Vouchers

After the voucher is entered in the voucher register, the voucher and supporting documents (purchase requisition, purchase order, receiving report, and purchase invoice) are stapled together. This "voucher packet" is then filed in an **unpaid vouchers file,** normally by due date. Alternatively, vouchers can be filed by supplier name. Filing by due date is preferred because this helps management plan for cash needs. It also helps ensure that vouchers are paid on the due date and that cash discounts are taken.

FIGURE 13-4 Voucher Register

VOUCHER REGISTER

	DATE	VOUCHER NO.	ISSUED TO	PURCHASES DEBIT	
1	4/2/--	106	Triumph Leasing		1
2	4/4/--	107	Sam's Cyberware	1 4 0 0 00	2
3	4/4/--	108	Compucraft, Inc.	3 3 0 0 00	3
4	4/8/--	109	Datasoft	2 5 0 0 00	4
5	4/9/--	110	Bemon Office Supply		5
6	4/11/--	111	EZX Corp.	8 7 0 0 00	6
7	4/15/--	112	Payroll		7
15				20 6 0 0 00	15

LEARNING KEY The unpaid vouchers file is like an accounts payable ledger grouped by due date rather than supplier.

The unpaid vouchers file functions as an accounts payable ledger. However, payables are grouped by due date rather than by supplier.

Posting from the Voucher Register

Both individual and summary postings are required from the voucher register to the general ledger. Figure 13-5 illustrates the posting process for Northern Micro's voucher register for April, as follows.

ON A DAILY BASIS:

STEP 1   Post each amount from the General Debit column to the appropriate general ledger account. (Note that only the first half of the month is shown in Figure 13-5. The rest of the month would be posted in a similar manner.)

STEP 2   Insert the date in the Date column and the initials "VR" and the voucher register page number in the Posting Reference column of each general ledger account.

STEP 3   Insert the general ledger account numbers in the Posting Reference column of the General Debit column of the voucher register.

AT THE END OF EACH MONTH:

STEP 4   Total the amount columns, verify that the total of the debit columns equals the total of the credit column, and rule the columns.

STEP 5   Post each column total except the General Debit column to the general ledger account indicated in the column headings.

STEP 6   Insert the date in the Date column and the initials "VR" and the voucher register page number in the Posting Reference column of each ledger account.

PAGE **4**

	SUPPLIES DEBIT	WAGES EXPENSE DEBIT	GENERAL DEBIT			VOUCHERS PAYABLE CREDIT	PAYMENT		
			ACCOUNT	POST. REF.	AMOUNT		DATE	CHECK NO.	
1			Rent Exp.		2 4 0 0 00	2 4 0 0 00	4/2/--	421	1
2						1 4 0 0 00	4/4/--	423	2
3						3 3 0 0 00			3
4						2 5 0 0 00			4
5	1 6 0 00					1 6 0 00	4/25/--	438	5
6						8 7 0 0 00	4/24/--	437	6
7		8 3 0 00				8 3 0 00	4/15/--	430	7
15	2 8 0 00	1 7 0 0 00			3 7 6 0 00	26 3 4 0 00			15

FIGURE 13-5 Posting Voucher Register to General Ledger

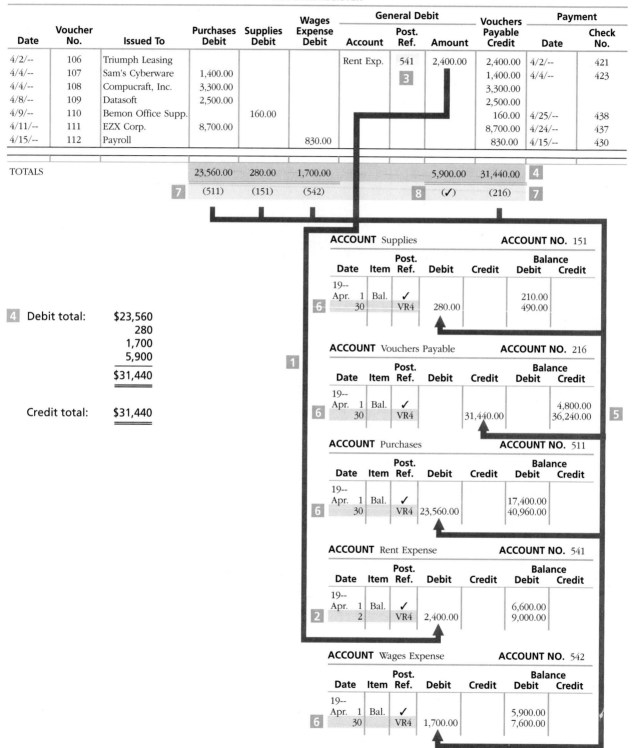

VOUCHER REGISTER

Date	Voucher No.	Issued To	Purchases Debit	Supplies Debit	Wages Expense Debit	General Debit			Vouchers Payable Credit	Payment	
						Account	Post. Ref.	Amount		Date	Check No.
4/2/--	106	Triumph Leasing				Rent Exp.	541	2,400.00	2,400.00	4/2/--	421
4/4/--	107	Sam's Cyberware	1,400.00						1,400.00	4/4/--	423
4/4/--	108	Compucraft, Inc.	3,300.00						3,300.00		
4/8/--	109	Datasoft	2,500.00						2,500.00		
4/9/--	110	Bemon Office Supp.		160.00					160.00	4/25/--	438
4/11/--	111	EZX Corp.	8,700.00						8,700.00	4/24/--	437
4/15/--	112	Payroll			830.00				830.00	4/15/--	430
TOTALS			23,560.00	280.00	1,700.00				5,900.00	31,440.00	
			(511)	(151)	(542)				(✓)	(216)	

4 Debit total: $23,560
                     280
                   1,700
                   5,900
                 ─────────
                 $31,440

Credit total: $31,440

STEP 7   Insert the general ledger account numbers immediately below each column total except the General Debit column.

STEP 8   Insert a check mark (✓) immediately below the General Debit column.

Note that the payables account in Figure 13-5 can be called either Vouchers Payable or Accounts Payable. Even with a voucher system, many businesses still use the Accounts Payable title. On the balance sheet, the Accounts Payable title is almost always used.

No posting to an accounts payable ledger is necessary for Northern Micro. They use the unpaid vouchers file as their accounts payable ledger. The unpaid vouchers file was updated when the vouchers were filed after being entered in the voucher register.

THE PAYMENT PROCESS USING A VOUCHER SYSTEM

LO4 Describe the payment process using a voucher system.

Figure 13-6 illustrates the payment process when a voucher system is used. On the due date, the voucher is pulled from the unpaid vouchers file. The voucher is given to the person responsible for preparing and signing checks (for Northern Micro, the cashier). The cashier reviews each voucher and supporting documents to see that the expenditure is proper. The cashier then prepares and signs the check and sends it to the supplier. It is important for internal control that no check be prepared without a supporting voucher and that the check be mailed as soon as it is signed.

Ordinary checks may be used to make payments, but under the voucher system, voucher checks often are used. A **voucher check** is a check with space for entering data about the voucher being paid. Figure 13-7 shows Northern Micro's voucher check to pay voucher no. 111 (Figure 13-3).

The voucher check has two parts:

1. The check itself, which is similar to an ordinary check, and
2. A statement attached that indicates the invoice being paid and any deductions.

In addition, the voucher check stub identifies the voucher number being paid.

After the voucher has been paid, the cashier completes (initials) the "Payment" approval on the back of the voucher. The voucher and supporting documents are then canceled to indicate payment. The canceling can be done with a rubber stamp, by perforating, or by simply writing "paid" on all relevant documents. This prevents a voucher from being processed again to create a duplicate payment. The canceled voucher and supporting documents are then returned to the vouchers payable section. They are filed either numerically or by supplier in a **paid vouchers file**. In either case, the numerical sequence should be accounted for to identify possible missing or duplicate vouchers.

FIGURE 13-6 Voucher System—Payment Process

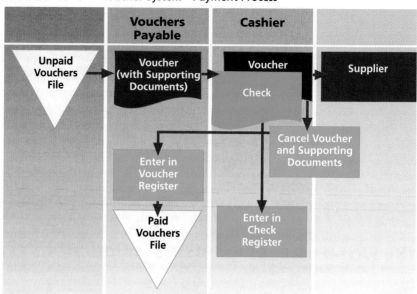

FIGURE 13-7 Voucher Check

No. **437**
Date *April 24, 19--*
To *EZX Corp.*

Voucher No. *111*
Amount of Voucher $ *8,700.00*
Discount $ *87.00*
Amount of Check $ *8,613.00*
Remarks

NORTHERN MICRO
1099 E. Louisiana, Indianapolis, IN 46217-3322

3-4/740
No. **437**

Date *April 24* 19*--*

Pay to the order of *EZX Corporation* $ *8,613.00*
Eight thousand six hundred thirteen 00/100 Dollars

First National Bank
Indianapolis, Indiana

Gary Fishel

⑆0740000091⑆ 9264181⑈

Detach this statement before depositing check

Date *April 24, 19--*

Attached voucher check is full settlement of the following:

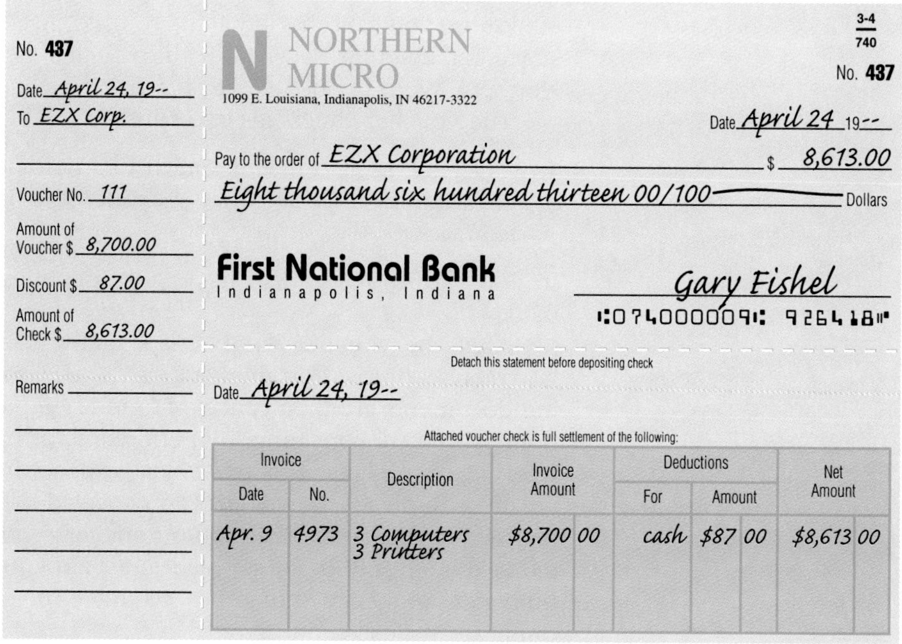

Invoice		Description	Invoice Amount	Deductions		Net Amount
Date	No.			For	Amount	
Apr. 9	*4973*	*3 Computers 3 Printers*	*$8,700 00*	*cash*	*$87 00*	*$8,613 00*

CHECK REGISTER

LO5 Describe and use a check register.

A copy of the check is used to enter the payment in a check register. A **check register** is a special journal used to record all checks written in a voucher system. Figure 13-8 illustrates Northern Micro's check register.

FIGURE 13-8   Check Register

	DATE	CHECK NO.	PAYEE	VOUCHERS PAYABLE DR. NO.	VOUCHERS PAYABLE DR. AMOUNT	PURCHASES DISCOUNT CREDIT	CASH CREDIT	
			CHECK REGISTER				PAGE 4	
1	4/1/--	420	Payroll	105	8 7 0 0 00		8 7 0 0 00	1
2	4/2/--	421	Triumph Leasing	106	2 4 0 0 00		2 4 0 0 00	2
6	4/24/--	437	EZX Corp.	111	8 7 0 0 00	8 7 00	8 6 1 3 00	6
7	4/25/--	438	Bemon Office Supplies	110	1 6 0 0 00		1 6 0 0 00	7
8	4/29/--	443	TTA Products	115	1 5 0 0 00		1 5 0 0 00	8
9	TOTALS				24 2 0 0 00	1 7 9 00	24 0 2 1 00	9

> **LEARNING KEY** A check register is similar to a cash payments journal except that only three amount columns are used—Vouchers Payable Debit, Purchases Discounts Credit, and Cash Credit.

A check register is similar to the cash payments journal we saw in Chapter 12 (Figure 12-13). A key difference is that the check register has only three amount columns—Vouchers Payable Debit, Purchases Discounts Credit, and Cash Credit. Recall that in a voucher system, every purchase of assets or services must be supported by a voucher. This means that every purchase has been recorded in a voucher register before any payment can be made. Thus, the only possible debit in the check register is to Vouchers Payable, and the only possible credits are to Purchases Discounts and Cash. When a business uses the voucher system and a voucher register, the check register replaces the cash payments journal.

A check is recorded in the check register by entering the following information:

1. Date
2. Check number
3. Payee
4. Voucher number
5. Dollar amounts

The entry on April 24 in Figure 13-8 is for the voucher check in Figure 13-7.

The check entering process also affects the voucher register. As shown in the diagram in Figure 13-6, the canceled voucher is used to enter the payment of the vouchers in the voucher register. A portion of the voucher register in Figure 13-4 is reproduced in Figure 13-9, with the Payment

FIGURE 13-9   Voucher Register

	DATE	VOUCHER NO.	ISSUED TO	PURCHASES DEBIT	
5	4/11/--	111	EZX Corp.	8 7 0 0 00	5
6					6
7					7

column filled in for voucher no. 111. Both the date of payment and the check number are inserted to indicate that the voucher has been paid.

Posting from the Check Register

Only monthly summary postings are required from the check register to the general ledger. Figure 13-10 illustrates the posting process for Northern Micro's check register at the end of April, as follows.

STEP 1   Total the amount columns, verify that the total of the debit column equals the total of the credit columns, and rule the columns.

STEP 2   Post each column total to the general ledger account indicated in the column headings.

STEP 3   Insert the date in the Date column and the initials "CK" and the check register page number in the Posting Reference column of each ledger account.

STEP 4   Insert the general ledger account numbers immediately below each column total.

Schedule of Vouchers Payable

It was explained earlier that most businesses that use a voucher system do not keep an accounts payable ledger. It is still desirable, however, to verify each month that the sum of the individual amounts owed to creditors equals the Vouchers Payable balance. For this purpose, a schedule of vouchers payable (Figure 13-11) is prepared. Note that the $11,900 total listed in the schedule equals the Vouchers Payable balance shown in Figure 13-10.

This schedule is prepared from either the voucher register or the unpaid vouchers file. Every blank in the Payment column of the voucher register represents an unpaid voucher to include in the schedule. Similarly, each voucher in the unpaid vouchers should be included in the schedule.

If the schedule total and the Vouchers Payable balance do not agree, the error must be located and corrected. To find the error, use the following procedures.

STEP 1   Verify the total of the schedule.

STEP 2   Review the voucher register or the unpaid vouchers file to be sure none were missed or counted twice.

PAGE **4**

			SUPPLIES DEBIT	WAGES EXPENSE DEBIT	GENERAL DEBIT			VOUCHERS PAYABLE CREDIT	PAYMENT		
					ACCOUNT	POST. REF.	AMOUNT		DATE	CHECK NO.	
5								8 7 0 0 00	4/24/--	437	5
6											6
7											7

FIGURE 13-10   Posting Check Register to General Ledger

CHECK REGISTER   PAGE **4**

Date	Check No.	Payee	Vouchers Payable Debit		Purchases Discounts Credit	Cash Credit
			No.	Amount		
4/1/--	420	Payroll	105	870.00		870.00
4/2/--	421	Triumph Leasing	106	2,400.00		2,400.00
4/24/--	437	EZX Corp.	111	8,700.00	87.00	8,613.00
4/25/--	438	Bemon Office Supp.	110	160.00		160.00
4/29/--	443	TTA Products	115	1,500.00		1,500.00
TOTALS				24,340.00	179.00	24,161.00	**1**
				(216)	(511.2)	(111)	**4**

2

1 Debit total: $24,340

Credit total: $ 179
                  24,161
                  $24,340

ACCOUNT Cash   **ACCOUNT NO.** 111

Date	Item	Post. Ref.	Debit	Credit	Balance Debit	Balance Credit
19--						
Apr. 1	Bal.	✓			20,000.00	
30		CR7	12,992.00		32,992.00	
3 30		CK4		24,161.00	8,831.00	

ACCOUNT Vouchers Payable   **ACCOUNT NO.** 216

Date	Item	Post. Ref.	Debit	Credit	Balance Debit	Balance Credit
19--						
Apr. 1	Bal.	✓				4,800.00
30		VR4		31,440.00		36,240.00
3 30		CK4	24,340.00			11,900.00

ACCOUNT Purchases Discounts   **ACCOUNT NO.** 511.2

Date	Item	Post. Ref.	Debit	Credit	Balance Debit	Balance Credit
19--						
Apr. 1	Bal.	✓				330.00
3 30		CK4		179.00		509.00

FIGURE 13-11   Schedule of Vouchers Payable

Northern Micro
Schedule of Vouchers Payable
April 30, 19--

Compucraft, Inc.	$ 3 3 0 0 00
Datasoft	2 5 0 0 00
Printpro Corp.	8 0 0 00
Televax, Inc.	5 3 0 0 00
	$11 9 0 0 00

STEP 3   Verify the totals in the voucher register and check register.

STEP 4   Verify the postings to Vouchers Payable in the general ledger.

Accounting for Returns, Allowances, and Partial Payments

For a voucher system to provide good control of expenditures, vouchers must be carefully handled and recorded. This includes both the initial creation and recording of the voucher as well as its subsequent payment. Because the voucher is such an important control device, special procedures are needed when the amount of the voucher needs to be changed.

Purchases Returns and Allowances.   If a complete return is made of merchandise costing $670 and a credit memo is received from the supplier, the following procedures are performed.

1. Note the return on the voucher, attach the credit memo, and place the voucher in the paid vouchers file.
2. Note the return in the Payment column of the voucher register by inserting the date of the return and an R in the Check No. column.

	DATE	VOUCHER NO.	ISSUED TO	PURCHASES DEBIT	VOUCHERS PAYABLE CREDIT	PAYMENT DATE	CHECK NO.
1	5/6/--	121	Compumax	6 7 0 00	6 7 0 00	5/9/--	R

3. Make a general journal entry to record the return.

5		Vouchers Payable/Compumax	6 7 0 00		5
6		Purchases Returns and Allowances		6 7 0 00	6
7		Returned merchandise			7

If a partial return is made of $250 of merchandise costing $670 and a credit memo is received, the following procedures are performed:

1. Note the return on the voucher, attach the credit memo, and return the voucher to the unpaid vouchers file.
2. Note the return in the voucher register in the Payment column, as follows:

	DATE	VOUCHER NO.	ISSUED TO	PURCHASES DEBIT	VOUCHERS PAYABLE CREDIT	PAYMENT DATE	CHECK NO.
1	5/6/--	121	Compumax	6 7 0 00	6 7 0 00	5/9/--	R/250

Notice that both the return and the dollar amount are indicated. This distinguishes the partial return from a complete return.

3. Make a general journal entry to record the return.

8		Vouchers Payable/Compumax	2 5 0 00		8
9		Purchases Returns and Allowances		2 5 0 00	9
10		Returned merchandise			10

4. When the voucher is paid for the original amount less the return, note the payment in the Payment column of the voucher register, as follows:

	DATE	VOUCHER NO.	ISSUED TO	PURCHASES DEBIT	VOUCHERS PAYABLE CREDIT	PAYMENT DATE	CHECK NO.
1	5/6/--	121	Compumax	6 7 0 00	6 7 0 00	5/9/-- 5/21/--	R/250 451

Partial Payments. If partial payments (installments) are planned at the time a purchase is made, a separate voucher is prepared for each payment. Each voucher and payment is then recorded in the voucher register and check register in the normal manner.

If a partial payment is made after a voucher is created and entered, the original voucher is canceled and new vouchers are created. Assume that merchandise is purchased for $600. Subsequently, a partial payment of only $200 is made. The following procedures are used to account for these events.

1. Make a general journal entry to cancel the original voucher.

12		Vouchers Payable/PC-Time	6 0 0 00		12
13		Purchases		6 0 0 00	13
14		Canceled voucher			14

2. Make a notation in the Payment column of the voucher register as follows:

	DATE	VOUCHER NO.	ISSUED TO	PURCHASES DEBIT	VOUCHERS PAYABLE CREDIT	PAYMENT DATE	CHECK NO.
1	5/3/--	118	PC-Time	6 0 0 00	6 0 0 00	5/7/--	V122/ 123

3. Prepare two new vouchers for $200 and $400 and enter them in the voucher register. Note the payment of the $200 voucher in the Payment column.

	DATE	VOUCHER NO.	ISSUED TO	PURCHASES DEBIT	VOUCHERS PAYABLE CREDIT	PAYMENT	
						DATE	CHECK NO.
1	5/7/--	122	PC-Time	200 00	200 00	5/7--	447
2	5/7/--	123	PC-Time	400 00	400 00		

KEY POINTS

1 The three elements of internal control that are combined to control expenditures in a voucher system are:

1. Segregation of duties
2. Authorization procedures and related responsibilities
3. Accounting procedures

2 In a voucher system, every acquisition and subsequent payment must be supported by a voucher.

When a purchase invoice arrives, the voucher section verifies the quantity, price, and computations on the invoice. In addition, the appropriateness of the purchase is evaluated before preparing the voucher.

3 A voucher is recorded in a voucher register by entering the following information:

1. Date
2. Voucher number
3. Person or business to whom the voucher is issued
4. Dollar amounts of debits and credits

After entry in the voucher register, vouchers are filed in an unpaid vouchers file, normally by due date.

The voucher register is posted to the general ledger as follows:

On a daily basis,
1. Post General Debit amounts to the general ledger.
2. Insert the date and posting reference in the accounts.
3. Insert the account numbers in the Posting Reference column of the voucher register.

At the end of each month,
4. Total, verify the equality of, and rule the amount columns.
5. Post specific account column totals to the general ledger.
6. Insert the date and posting reference in the accounts.
7. Insert the account numbers below the specific account column totals in the voucher register.
8. Insert a check mark below the General Debit column.

4 After a voucher is paid, the voucher and supporting documents should be canceled to prevent processing them again to create a duplicate payment.

A check is recorded in the check register by entering the following information:

1. Date
2. Check number
3. Payee
4. Voucher number
5. Dollar amounts

5 The check register is posted to the general ledger as follows:

1. Total, verify the equality of, and rule the amount columns.
2. Post column totals to the general ledger accounts.
3. Insert the date and posting reference in the accounts.
4. Insert the account numbers below the column totals in the check register.

To verify that the sum of the individual amounts owed to creditors equals the Vouchers Payable balance, a schedule of unpaid vouchers is prepared.

Special procedures are required when purchases returns and allowances or partial payments occur in a voucher system.

KEY TERMS

check register 435   A special journal used to record all checks written in a voucher system.

internal controls 425   Sets of procedures used to ensure that there is proper accounting for all activities of the business.

paid vouchers file 433   Contains vouchers paid and canceled and filed either numerically or by supplier.

unpaid vouchers file 430   Vouchers and supporting documents stapled together and filed either by due date (preferred) or by supplier until paid.

voucher 426   A document that shows that an acquisition is proper and that payment is authorized.

voucher check 433   A check with space for entering data about the voucher being paid.

voucher register 430   A special journal used to record purchases of all types of assets and services.

voucher system 426   A control technique that requires that every acquisition and subsequent payment be supported by an approved voucher.

REVIEW QUESTIONS

1. What three elements of internal control are particularly important for controlling expenditures?
2. What two key controls over expenditures are provided by the voucher system?

3. When a purchase invoice is received from a supplier, what procedures are performed by the voucher section?
4. List four items of information about each voucher entered in the voucher register.
5. Why is it desirable to file unpaid vouchers by due date?
6. What steps are followed in posting from the voucher register to the general ledger?
7. After a voucher is paid, what should be done with the voucher and supporting documents? Why?
8. List five items of information about each check entered in the check register.
9. What steps are followed in posting from the check register to the general ledger?
10. If the total of the schedule of vouchers payable does not equal the Vouchers Payable balance, what procedures should be used to search for the error?
11. If a partial return of merchandise is made, what procedures are used in a voucher system?
12. If a partial payment is made after a voucher has been created and entered for the full amount of a purchase, what procedures are used in a voucher system?

MANAGING YOUR WRITING

The major fund raiser for a local youth center traditionally has been a variety show put on by the members of the center. Tickets for the show are sold primarily by the members. The tickets are available in boxes at the center, and members simply take a bunch as needed. Money is then turned in for whatever tickets are sold. The new manager of the center is concerned about whether all of the money from ticket sales is being turned in and is seeking your advice. Write a memo to the manager explaining how to control the tickets and money to ensure that both are being accounted for properly.

DEMONSTRATION PROBLEM

Harpo, Inc., is a retail novelty store. The following transactions relate to operations for the month of March.

March 2 Issued voucher no. 313 to Tremont Rental for March rent, $500.
     2 Issued check no. 450 to Tremont Rental, $500. Voucher no. 313.
     3 Purchased merchandise from Gail's Gags, $550, terms 2/15, n/60. Voucher no. 314.
     4 Purchased merchandise from Silly Sam's, $200, terms 2/10, n/60. Voucher no. 315.
    10 Issued check no. 451 to Jerry's Jokes, $500 less $10 discount. Voucher no. 310.

March 12   Received a credit memo from Silly Sam's for returned merchandise that was purchased on March 4, $100.

14   Issued check no. 452 to Resource Supplies, $250. Voucher no. 311.

16   Purchased merchandise from Giggles, $700, terms 2/10, n/30. Voucher no. 316.

18   Issued check no. 453 to Gail's Gags for purchase made on March 3 less 2% discount. Voucher no. 314.

19   Issued check no. 454 to Donnelly's, $750. Voucher no. 312.

21   Purchased merchandise from Creations, $870, terms 3/15, n/60. Voucher no. 317.

25   Purchased supplies from Hal's Supply, $120, terms 3/10, n/30. Voucher no. 318.

31   Issued check no. 455 to Silly Sam's for purchase made on March 4 less returns made on March 12. Voucher no. 315.

31   Issued voucher no. 319 to Payroll in payment of March wages, $1,250.

31   Issued check no. 456 to Payroll, $1,250. Voucher no. 319.

REQUIRED

Selected general ledger accounts and their opening balances as well as a portion of the voucher register for February are shown below.

1. Enter the transactions in the voucher register, check register, and general journal. Total, rule, and prove the voucher register and check register.
2. Post the transactions to the general ledger accounts.
3. Prepare a schedule of vouchers payable and compare the March 31 balance to the balance of Vouchers Payable in the general ledger.

GENERAL LEDGER

ACCOUNT: **Cash**   ACCOUNT NO. **111**

DATE	ITEM	POST. REF.	DEBIT	CREDIT	BALANCE DEBIT	BALANCE CREDIT
19-- Mar. 1	Balance	✓			6 0 0 0 00	

ACCOUNT: **Supplies**   ACCOUNT NO. **151**

DATE	ITEM	POST. REF.	DEBIT	CREDIT	BALANCE DEBIT	BALANCE CREDIT
19-- Mar. 1	Balance	✓			4 0 0 00	

ACCOUNT: **Vouchers Payable**   ACCOUNT NO. **216**

DATE	ITEM	POST. REF.	DEBIT	CREDIT	BALANCE DEBIT	BALANCE CREDIT
19-- Mar. 1	Balance	✓				1 5 0 0 00

ACCOUNT: **Purchases**   ACCOUNT NO. **511**

DATE	ITEM	POST. REF.	DEBIT	CREDIT	BALANCE DEBIT	BALANCE CREDIT
Mar. 1	Balance	✓			4 2 5 0 00	

ACCOUNT: **Purchases Returns and Allowances**   ACCOUNT NO. **511.1**

DATE	ITEM	POST. REF.	DEBIT	CREDIT	BALANCE DEBIT	BALANCE CREDIT
Mar. 1	Balance	✓				1 0 0 00

ACCOUNT: **Purchases Discounts**   ACCOUNT NO. **511.2**

DATE	ITEM	POST. REF.	DEBIT	CREDIT	BALANCE DEBIT	BALANCE CREDIT
Mar. 1	Balance	✓				5 0 00

VOUCHER REGISTER

	DATE	VOUCHER NO.	ISSUED TO	PURCHASES DEBIT	
1	2/24/--	310	Jerry's Jokes	5 0 0 00	1
2	2/26/--	311	Resource Supplies		2
3	2/26/--	312	Donnelly's	7 5 0 00	3
4					4
5					5

SOLUTION

1.

VOUCHER REGISTER

	DATE	VOUCHER NO.	ISSUED TO	PURCHASES DEBIT	
1	2/24/--	310	Jerry's Jokes	5 0 0 00	1
2	2/26/--	311	Resource Supplies		2
3	2/26/--	312	Donnelly's	7 5 0 00	3
4					4
5					5

ACCOUNT: Rent Expense   ACCOUNT NO. 541

DATE		ITEM	POST. REF.	DEBIT	CREDIT	BALANCE	
						DEBIT	CREDIT
Mar.¹⁹⁻⁻	1	Balance	✓			1 0 0 0 00	

ACCOUNT: Wages Expense   ACCOUNT NO. 542

DATE		ITEM	POST. REF.	DEBIT	CREDIT	BALANCE	
						DEBIT	CREDIT
Mar.¹⁹⁻⁻	1	Balance	✓			2 5 0 0 00	

PAGE 6

	SUPPLIES DEBIT	WAGES EXPENSE DEBIT	GENERAL DEBIT			VOUCHERS PAYABLE CREDIT	PAYMENT		
			ACCOUNT	POST. REF.	AMOUNT		DATE	CHECK NO.	
1						5 0 0 00			1
2	2 5 0 00					2 5 0 00			2
3						7 5 0 00			3
4									4
5									5

PAGE 6

	SUPPLIES DEBIT	WAGES EXPENSE DEBIT	GENERAL DEBIT			VOUCHERS PAYABLE CREDIT	PAYMENT		
			ACCOUNT	POST. REF.	AMOUNT		DATE	CHECK NO.	
1						5 0 0 00	3/10/--	451	1
2	2 5 0 00					2 5 0 00	3/14/--	452	2
3						7 5 0 00	3/19/--	454	3
4									4
5									5

1. (cont.)

VOUCHER REGISTER

	DATE	VOUCHER NO.	ISSUED TO	PURCHASES DEBIT	
1	3/2/--	313	Tremont Rental		1
2	3/3/--	314	Gail's Gags	5 5 0 00	2
3	3/4/--	315	Silly Sam's	2 0 0 00	3
4	3/16/--	316	Giggles	7 0 0 00	4
5	3/21/--	317	Creations	8 7 0 00	5
6	3/25/--	318	Hal's Supply		6
7	3/31/--	319	Payroll		7
8				2 3 2 0 00	8
9				(511)	9
10					10

CHECK REGISTER   PAGE 6

	DATE	CHECK NO.	PAYEE	VOUCHERS PAYABLE DR. NO.	VOUCHERS PAYABLE DR. AMOUNT	PURCHASES DISCOUNT CREDIT	CASH CREDIT	
1	3/2/--	450	Tremont Rental	313	5 0 0 00		5 0 0 00	1
2	3/10/--	451	Jerry's Jokes	310	5 0 0 00	1 0 00	4 9 0 00	2
3	3/14/--	452	Resource Supplies	311	2 5 0 00		2 5 0 00	3
4	3/18/--	453	Gail's Gags	314	5 5 0 00	1 1 00	5 3 9 00	4
5	3/19/--	454	Donnelly's	312	7 5 0 00		7 5 0 00	5
6	3/31/--	455	Silly Sam's	315	1 0 0 00		1 0 0 00	6
7	3/31/--	456	Payroll	319	1 2 5 0 00		1 2 5 0 00	7
8					3 9 0 0 00	2 1 00	3 8 7 9 00	8
9					(216)	(511.2)	(111)	9

GENERAL JOURNAL   PAGE 3

	DATE		DESCRIPTION	POST. REF.	DEBIT	CREDIT	
1	Mar.	12	Vouchers Payable/Silly Sam's	216	1 0 0 00		1
2			Purchases Returns & Allowances	511.1		1 0 0 00	2
3			Received credit memo from				3
4			Silly Sam's				4
5							5
6							6
7							7
8							8
9							9
10							10

PAGE 7

	SUPPLIES DEBIT	WAGES EXPENSE DEBIT	GENERAL DEBIT			VOUCHERS PAYABLE CREDIT	PAYMENT		
			ACCOUNT	POST. REF.	AMOUNT		DATE	CHECK NO.	
1			Rent Exp.	541	5 0 0 00	5 0 0 00	3/2/--	450	1
2						5 5 0 00	3/18/--	453	2
3						2 0 0 00	3/12/-- 3/31/--	R/100 455	3
4						7 0 0 00			4
5						8 7 0 00			5
6	1 2 0 00					1 2 0 00			6
7		1 2 5 0 00				1 2 5 0 00	3/31/--	456	7
8	1 2 0 00	1 2 5 0 00			5 0 0 00	4 1 9 0 00			8
9	(151)	(542)			(✓)	(216)			9
10									10

2.

GENERAL LEDGER

ACCOUNT: **Cash**   ACCOUNT NO. **111**

DATE		ITEM	POST. REF.	DEBIT	CREDIT	BALANCE	
						DEBIT	CREDIT
Mar.19--	1	Balance	✓			6 0 0 0 00	
	31		CK6		3 8 7 9 00	2 1 2 1 00	

ACCOUNT: **Supplies**   ACCOUNT NO. **151**

DATE		ITEM	POST. REF.	DEBIT	CREDIT	BALANCE	
						DEBIT	CREDIT
Mar.19--	1	Balance	✓			4 0 0 00	
	31		VR7	1 2 0 00		5 2 0 00	

ACCOUNT: **Vouchers Payable**   ACCOUNT NO. **216**

DATE		ITEM	POST. REF.	DEBIT	CREDIT	BALANCE	
						DEBIT	CREDIT
Mar.19--	1	Balance	✓				1 5 0 0 00
	12		J3	1 0 0 00			1 4 0 0 00
	31		VR7		4 1 9 0 00		5 5 9 0 00
	31		CK6	3 9 0 0 00			1 6 9 0 00

ACCOUNT: **Purchases**   ACCOUNT NO. **511**

DATE		ITEM	POST. REF.	DEBIT	CREDIT	BALANCE	
						DEBIT	CREDIT
Mar.19--	1	Balance	✓			4 2 5 0 00	
	31		VR7	2 3 2 0 00		6 5 7 0 00	

ACCOUNT: Purchases Returns and Allowances   ACCOUNT NO. 511.1

DATE		ITEM	POST. REF.	DEBIT	CREDIT	BALANCE	
						DEBIT	CREDIT
Mar.¹⁹⁻⁻	1	Balance	✓				1 0 0 00
	12		J3		1 0 0 00		2 0 0 00

ACCOUNT: Purchases Discounts   ACCOUNT NO. 511.2

DATE		ITEM	POST. REF.	DEBIT	CREDIT	BALANCE	
						DEBIT	CREDIT
Mar.¹⁹⁻⁻	1	Balance	✓				5 0 00
	31		CK6		2 1 00		7 1 00

ACCOUNT: Rent Expense   ACCOUNT NO. 541

DATE		ITEM	POST. REF.	DEBIT	CREDIT	BALANCE	
						DEBIT	CREDIT
Mar.¹⁹⁻⁻	1	Balance	✓			1 0 0 0 00	
	2		VR7	5 0 0 00		1 5 0 0 00	

ACCOUNT: Wages Expense   ACCOUNT NO. 542

DATE		ITEM	POST. REF.	DEBIT	CREDIT	BALANCE	
						DEBIT	CREDIT
Mar.¹⁹⁻⁻	1	Balance	✓			2 5 0 0 00	
	31		VR7	1 2 5 0 00		3 7 5 0 00	

3.

Harpo, Inc.
Schedule of Vouchers Payable
March 31, 19--

Giggles	$ 7 0 0 00
Creations	8 7 0 00
Hal's Supply	1 2 0 00
	$1 6 9 0 00

SERIES A EXERCISES

1 **EXERCISE 13A1 PURCHASING PROCESS USING A VOUCHER SYSTEM**   In the flow chart below, identify the documents and records that illustrate the voucher process.

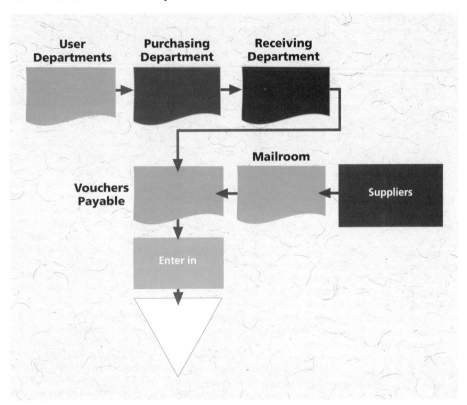

2 **EXERCISE 13A2 PREPARING A VOUCHER**   Prepare voucher no. 164 on May 8, similar to the one shown in Figure 13-3 in the chapter, from the purchase invoice shown on the next page.

The supplier, Sportime Corp., sent 12 Prince Spectrum rackets with a unit price of $130 and 2 DuraLink nets with a unit price of $110. Assume that the cash discount will be taken. Indicate that the voucher was prepared by you and authorized by J. Jenkins and that distribution was approved by B. Zimmer.

3 **EXERCISE 13A3 VOUCHER REGISTER**   Enter the following vouchers and payments into a voucher register.

Date	Voucher No.	Issued To	Amount	Purpose
6/1	331	Middleton Assoc.	$1,200	June rent
6/5	332	Guzman Distributors	960	Merchandise on account
6/9	333	MicroLabs, Inc.	1,400	Merchandise on account

continued

Sportime Corp.
6825 Kentucky Ave.
Louisville, KY 40258-4111

Invoice No. **163**

Sold to
Mitchell & Jenkins Sporting Goods
12191 E. Washington St.
Indianapolis, IN 46201-3216

Date May 6, 19--

Terms 2/10, n/30

Quantity	Description	Unit Price	Total
12	Prince Spectrum racket	$130.00	$1,560.00
2	DuraLink net	110.00	220.00
			$1,780.00

Received by *S. Miller*

Date *5/7/--*

Date	Voucher No.	Issued To	Amount	Purpose
6/11	334	Miller Office Supply	$ 244	Prepaid office supplies
6/13	335	Bradham Products	1,604	Merchandise on account
6/15	336	Payroll	6,000	Bimonthly paychecks
6/21	337	Guzman Distributors	1,700	Merchandise on account

The following vouchers were paid:

Date Paid	Voucher No.	Check No.
6/10	331	498
6/14	332	499
6/15	336	500
6/18	333	501
6/20	335	502
6/30	337	503

4 **EXERCISE 13A4 PAYMENT PROCESS USING A VOUCHER SYSTEM** In the flow chart on the next page, identify the documents and records that illustrate the payment process using a voucher system.

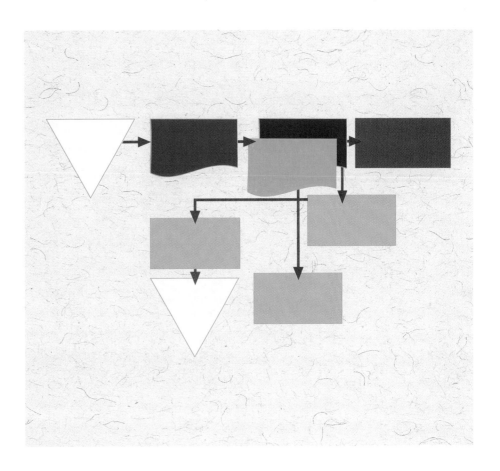

5 **EXERCISE 13A5 CHECK REGISTER**   The following information, taken from the voucher register, is evidenced by unpaid vouchers. Enter the appropriate information into a check register. The discount amounts shown should be deducted from the voucher amounts. Total and rule the register.

Date	Voucher No.	Pay To	Amount	Check No.	Purpose	Discount Amount
8/5	111	Armos Bros.	$1,600	406	Merchandise on account	$16.00
8/7	108	H & L Realty	1,000	407	August rent	
8/11	113	Excel Products	760	408	Merchandise on account	15.20
8/13	109	Bell & Mason	1,280	409	Merchandise on account	25.60
8/15	115	Payroll	4,000	410	Bimonthly paychecks	
8/19	117	C.P. Delgado	1,776	411	Merchandise on account	35.52
8/25	119	Office Pro, Inc.	500	412	Office Supplies	
8/31	120	Payroll	4,000	413	Bimonthly paychecks	

3 **EXERCISE 13A6 SCHEDULE OF VOUCHERS PAYABLE**   Prepare a schedule of vouchers payable for Randalls Appliances, based on information found in the register on page 452.

Voucher Register—Left Side

VOUCHER REGISTER

	DATE	VOUCHER NO.	ISSUED TO	PURCHASES DEBIT	
1	1/1/--	101	Alomar, Inc.	6 0 0 00	1
2	1/3/--	102	Bremer Office Supplies		2
3	1/6/--	103	Kettles and Kabrus	2 8 0 00	3
4	1/7/--	104	Moore & Johnson		4
5	1/11/--	105	Kitchen Kaboodle	3 0 0 00	5
6	1/13/--	106	Alomar, Inc.	3 7 5 00	6
7	1/16/--	107	Payroll		7
8	1/21/--	108	Rich & Associates	4 0 0 00	8
9	1/29/--	109	Darin Elwood Co.	2 1 9 00	9
10				2 1 7 4 00	10

Voucher Register—Right Side

PAGE 1

	SUPPLIES DEBIT	WAGES EXPENSE DEBIT	GENERAL DEBIT			VOUCHERS PAYABLE CREDIT	PAYMENT		
			ACCOUNT	POST. REF.	AMOUNT		DATE	CHECK NO.	
1						6 0 0 00	1/11/--	2	1
2	1 1 8 00					1 1 8 00			2
3						2 8 0 00	1/24/--	4	3
4			Rent Exp.	511	5 0 0 00	5 0 0 00	1/7/--	1	4
5						3 0 0 00			5
6						3 7 5 00			6
7		1 0 0 0 00				1 0 0 0 00	1/16/--	3	7
8						4 0 0 00			8
9						2 1 9 00			9
10	1 1 8 00	1 0 0 0 00			5 0 0 00	3 7 9 2 00			10

3   **EXERCISE 13A7 RETURN OF MERCHANDISE AND PARTIAL PAYMENTS**   Enter the following merchandise returns and partial payments in a general journal and in the voucher register on page 453, as appropriate.

Sept. 10 Merchandise purchased from XYZ Co. for $800, voucher no. 203, is returned. A credit memo is received, attached to the voucher, and the voucher is placed in the paid vouchers file.

     20 A partial return of merchandise purchased from Trizon Suppliers is made for $200, voucher no. 206. A credit memo is received, attached to the voucher, and the voucher is returned to the unpaid vouchers file.

     24 A partial payment for merchandise purchased from F.B. Jones Co. is made for $300 on voucher no. 208, that was for $600. Plan to pay the remaining $300 in two weeks (new vouchers are issued). Check no. 682.

continued

Sept. 28 A partial return of merchandise purchased form Arbiters, Inc. is made for $80, voucher no. 204. A credit memo is received, attached to the voucher, and the voucher is returned to the unpaid vouchers file.

Voucher Register—Left Side

VOUCHER REGISTER

	DATE	VOUCHER NO.	ISSUED TO	PURCHASES DEBIT	
1	9/6/--	202	Briggs Store	6 0 0 00	1
2	9/8/--	203	XYZ Co.	8 0 0 00	2
3	9/10/--	204	Arbiters, Inc.	7 0 0 00	3
4	9/11/--	205	Paper Traders		4
5	9/15/--	206	Trizon Suppliers	3 5 0 00	5
6	9/16/--	207	Payroll		6
7	9/18/--	208	F.B. Jones Co.	6 0 0 00	7
8					8

Voucher Register—Right Side

PAGE

	SUPPLIES DEBIT	WAGES EXPENSE DEBIT	GENERAL DEBIT			VOUCHERS PAYABLE CREDIT	PAYMENT		
			ACCOUNT	POST. REF.	AMOUNT		DATE	CHECK NO.	
1						6 0 0 00	9/8/--	681	1
2						8 0 0 00			2
3						7 0 0 00			3
4	1 8 6 00					1 8 6 00			4
5						3 5 0 00			5
6		1 2 0 0 00				1 2 0 0 00			6
7						6 0 0 00			7
8									8

SERIES A PROBLEMS

3 **PROBLEM 13A1 VOUCHER REGISTER AND POSTING TO GENERAL LEDGER**   Escribano Electronics had the following transactions for the month of July 19--.

Date	Voucher No.	Issued To	Amount	Purpose	Date Paid	Check No.
7/1	206	Parkhouse, Inc.	$ 600	July rent	7/1	318
7/3	207	G.B. Fiorucci	1,700	Merchandise	7/18	320
7/5	208	Richardson's	240	Office supplies		
7/9	209	Soto Supply	1,800	Merchandise	7/19	321
7/15	210	Payroll	2,000	Paychecks	7/15	319
7/21	211	Pressman's	1,160	Merchandise		
7/28	212	T.R. Canady Co.	1,240	Merchandise		

continued

Date	Voucher No.	Issued To	Amount	Purpose	Date Paid	Check No.
7/30	213	Excelsior Ltd.	656	Merchandise		
7/31	214	Payroll	2,000	Paychecks	7/31	322

REQUIRED

1. Enter the transactions for July 19-- on page 7 of the voucher register. Total, rule, and prove the register.
2. Post the voucher register to the general ledger. Use account numbers as shown in the chapter.
3. Prepare a schedule of vouchers payable.

5 **PROBLEM 13A2 CHECK REGISTER AND POSTING TO GENERAL LEDGER** The following transactions occurred during August 19--. A voucher register is used. Assume terms of 2/10, n/30 for purchases on account and assume that all discounts are taken. General ledger account balances on August 1 were: Cash, $9,862; and Vouchers Payable, $8,482.

Date	Check No.	Pay To	Voucher No.	Amount	Purpose
8/3	111	M. Pearson	108	$ 800	August rent
8/5	112	K.B. Adams Co.	109	550	Merchandise on account
8/8	113	Quality Paper	111	300	Office supplies
8/11	114	Paulson Group	113	600	Merchandise on account
8/15	115	Payroll	115	2,000	Bimonthly payroll
8/17	116	Peerson, Inc.	116	720	Merchandise on account
8/22	117	K.B. Adams Co.	118	380	Merchandise on account
8/25	118	Wilson's	121	440	Merchandise on account
8/31	119	Payroll	123	2,000	Bimonthly payroll

REQUIRED

1. Enter the transactions for August 19--, in the check register (page 8). Total, rule, and prove the register.
2. Post the check register totals to the general ledger. Use account numbers in the chapter.

PROBLEM 13A3 VOUCHER REGISTER, CHECK REGISTER, POSTING, AND SCHEDULE OF VOUCHERS PAYABLE Betty Classic owns the Classic Candle Shop. The following transactions occurred during April 19--. The Classic Candle Shop uses a voucher register, a check register, and a general ledger. Unpaid vouchers are filed and listed at the end of the month. General ledger account balances on April 1 were: Cash, $5,189; and Supplies, $408.

Date	Voucher No.	Issued To	Amount	Purpose	Terms
4/1	1101	Landmark Realty	$ 500	April rent	
4/3	1102	Wax House	280	Merchandise	2/10, n/30
4/5	1103	Designs West	490	Merchandise	2/10, n/30
4/9	1104	Crane Stationers	180	Office Supplies	
4/11	1105	Magic Solutions	$ 600	Merchandise	2/10, n/30
4/15	1106	Payroll	1,500	Bimonthly payroll	
4/23	1107	Wax House	510	Merchandise	1/10, n/30

continued

Date	Voucher No.	Issued To	Amount	Purpose	Terms
4/25	1108	Baskets & More	440	Merchandise	2/10, n/30
4/28	1109	Magic Solutions	450	Merchandise	2/10, n/30
4/30	1110	Payroll	1,500	Bimonthly payroll	

Checks issued:

Date	Check No.	Payee	Voucher No.	Amount
4/1	928	Landmark Realty	1101	$ 500
4/9	929	Crane Stationers	1104	180
4/11	930	Wax House	1102	280
4/15	931	Payroll	1106	1,500
4/19	932	Designs West	1103	490
4/30	933	Payroll	1110	1,500

REQUIRED

1. Enter the transactions for April in the voucher register. Total, rule, and prove the register. Update the Payment column when vouchers are paid.
2. Enter the transactions for April in the check register. Be sure to take discounts where appropriate. Total, rule, and prove the register.
3. Post the voucher register and the check register to the general ledger. Use account numbers as shown in the chapter.
4. Prepare a schedule of vouchers payable.

3/4/5   **PROBLEM 13A4 VOUCHER REGISTER, CHECK REGISTER, AND GENERAL JOURNAL (RETURNS AND PARTIAL PAYMENTS)**
Richard Harris owns Harris's Appliance Store. The following transactions occurred during May 19--. Harris's Appliance Store uses a voucher register, a check register, and a general journal.

May 1 Issued voucher no. 208 to McPherson's Co. for May rent, $800.
     1 Issued check no. 411 to McPherson's Co., $800. Voucher no. 208.
     3 Purchased merchandise from Welding Supply Co., $280, terms 2/10, n/30. Voucher no. 209.
     5 Received a credit memo from Welding Supply Co. for returned merchandise that was purchased on May 3, $40.
     7 Purchased supplies from Quality Office Supply, $118. Voucher no. 210.
     7 Issued check no. 412 to Quality Office Supply, $118. Voucher no. 210.
    10 Purchased merchandise from Piper's, Inc., $440, terms 2/10, n/30. Voucher no. 211.
    10 Received a credit memo from Piper's, Inc., for returned merchandise that was purchased on May 10, $440.
    11 Issued check no. 413 to Welding Supply Co. for purchase made on May 3, less return made on May 5 less 2% discount. Voucher no. 209.
    12 Purchased merchandise from Manley's Wholesale, $620, terms 2/10, n/30. Voucher no. 212.
    15 Issued voucher no. 213 to Payroll in payment of bimonthly wages, $1,000.
    15 Issued check no. 414 to Payroll, $1,000. Voucher no. 213.

continued

May 19 Purchased merchandise from Welding Supply Co., $860, terms 2/10, n/30. Voucher no. 214.

21 Issued check no. 415 to Welding Supply Co. in partial payment of goods purchased on May 19, $430 less 2% discount. Voucher no. 214. Issued new vouchers no. 215 and 216.

22 Purchased supplies from Quality Office Supply, $210. Voucher no. 217.

23 Issued check no. 416 to Manley's Wholesale, $620. Voucher no. 212.

25 Purchased merchandise from Regional Distributors, $460, terms 1/10, n/30. Voucher no. 218.

28 Purchased merchandise from Pringle's & Co., $600, terms 2/10, n/30. Voucher no. 219.

31 Issued voucher no. 220 to Payroll in payment of bimonthly wages, $1,000.

31 Issued check no. 417 to Payroll, $1,000. Voucher no. 220.

REQUIRED

Enter the transactions in a voucher register (page 5), check register (page 5), or general journal (page 5), as appropriate. Total, rule, and prove the voucher register and check register.

SERIES B   EXERCISES

1   EXERCISE 13B1 PURCHASING PROCESS USING A VOUCHER SYSTEM   In the following flow chart, identify the departments and other sources of the documents and records that illustrate the voucher process.

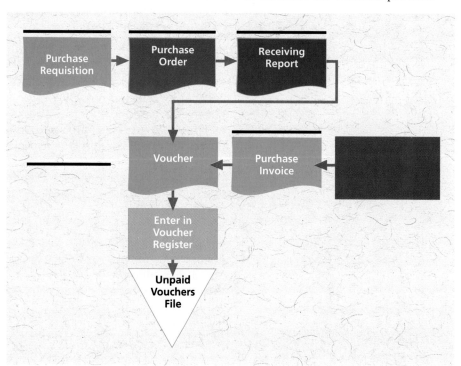

2 **EXERCISE 13B2 PREPARING A VOUCHER**   Prepare voucher no. 193 on May 18, similar to the one shown in Figure 13-3 in the chapter, from the purchase invoice shown below.

The supplier, Sportime Corp., sent 33 cases of Sport tennis balls at $30 a case and 14 Wilke racket covers at $25 each. Assume that the cash discount will be taken. Indicate that the voucher was prepared by you and authorized by J. Jenkins and that distribution was approved by B. Zimmer.

Sportime Corp.
6825 Kentucky Ave.
Louisville, KY 40258-4111

Invoice No. **169**

Sold to
Mitchell & Jenkins Sporting Goods
12191 E. Washington St.
Indianapolis, IN 46201-3216

Date   May 16, 19--

Terms   2/10, n/30

Quantity	Description	Unit Price	Total
33 cases	Sport tennis balls	$30.00	$ 990.00
14	Wilke racket covers	25.00	350.00
			$1340.00

Received by *S. Miller*
Date *5/17/--*

---

3 **EXERCISE 13B3 VOUCHER REGISTER**   Enter the following vouchers and payments into a voucher register.

Date	Voucher No.	Issued To	Amount	Purpose
7/1	431	Katz Management	$ 200	July rent
7/5	432	Garcia Distributors	340	Merchandise on account
7/9	433	Mirror Labs, Inc.	150	Merchandise on account
7/11	434	Owens Office Supply	55	Prepaid office supplies
7/13	435	Richards Products	176	Merchandise on account
7/15	436	Payroll	1,250	Bimonthly paychecks
7/21	437	Garcia Distributors	175	Merchandise on account

The following vouchers were paid:

Date Paid	Voucher No.	Check No.
7/10	431	598
7/14	432	599

continued

Date Paid	Voucher No.	Check No.
7/15	436	600
7/18	433	601
7/20	435	602

4 **EXERCISE 13B4 PAYMENT PROCESS USING A VOUCHER SYSTEM** The following flow chart illustrates the payment process using a voucher system. Briefly describe each document and file.

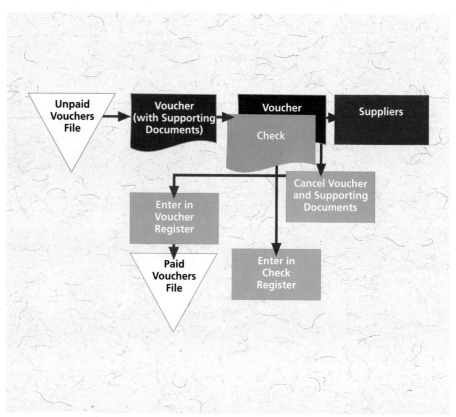

5 **EXERCISE 13B5 CHECK REGISTER** The following information, taken from the voucher register, is evidenced by unpaid vouchers. Enter the appropriate information into a check register. The discount amounts shown should be deducted from the voucher amounts. Total and rule the register.

Date	Voucher No.	Pay To	Amount	Check No.	Purpose	Discount Amount
9/5	1111	Mendel Bros.	$ 300	2814	Merchandise on account	$3.00
9/7	1108	B & J Realty	200	2815	September rent	
9/11	1113	Trycl Products	140	2816	Merchandise on account	$2.80
9/13	1114	Myro & Smith	270	2817	Merchandise on account	$5.40
9/15	1109	Payroll	1,100	2818	Bimonthly paychecks	
9/19	1117	T.M. Kingley	244	2819	Merchandise on account	$2.44
9/25	1123	Bly Stationers	75	2820	Office supplies	
9/30	1120	Payroll	1,100	2821	Bimonthly paychecks	

3 EXERCISE 13B6 SCHEDULE OF VOUCHERS PAYABLE
Prepare a schedule of vouchers payable for M.B. Jacobs, based on information found in the following voucher register.

Voucher Register—Left Side

VOUCHER REGISTER

	DATE	VOUCHER NO.	ISSUED TO	PURCHASES DEBIT	
1	3/1/--	306	Richland Associates		1
2	3/4/--	307	Carlson & Daughter	8 0 0 00	2
3	3/6/--	308	Wilson Office Supplies		3
4	3/9/--	309	Black & Brewer	6 0 0 00	4
5	3/12/--	310	Kreklow Company	3 8 0 00	5
6	3/16/--	311	Payroll		6
7	3/21/--	312	Anderson Enterprises	2 6 0 00	7
8	3/24/--	313	Carlson & Daughter	4 1 0 00	8
9	3/28/--	314	Wilson Office Supplies		9
10	3/31/--	315	Payroll		10
11				2 4 5 0 00	11

Voucher Register—Right Side

PAGE 3

	SUPPLIES DEBIT	WAGES EXPENSE DEBIT	GENERAL DEBIT ACCOUNT	POST. REF.	AMOUNT	VOUCHERS PAYABLE CREDIT	PAYMENT DATE	CHECK NO.	
1			Rent Exp.		3 0 0 00	3 0 0 00	3/2/--	806	1
2						8 0 0 00	3/11/--	808	2
3	1 8 0 00					1 8 0 00	3/8/--	807	3
4						6 0 0 00			4
5						3 8 0 00	3/18/--	810	5
6		1 0 0 0 00				1 0 0 0 00	3/16/--	809	6
7						2 6 0 00			7
8						4 1 0 00			8
9	9 8 00					9 8 00			9
10		1 0 0 0 00				1 0 0 0 00	3/31/--	811	10
11	2 7 8 00	2 0 0 0 00			3 0 0 00	5 0 2 8 00			11

3 EXERCISE 13B7 RETURN OF MERCHANDISE AND PARTIAL PAYMENTS   Enter the following merchandise returns and partial payments in a general journal and in the voucher register on page 460, as appropriate.

Sept. 15 Merchandise purchased from Arbiters, Inc. for $700, voucher no. 204, is returned. A credit memo is received, attached to the voucher, and the voucher is placed in the paid vouchers file.

continued

Sept. 20 A partial return of merchandise purchased from XYZ Co. is made for $300, voucher no. 203. A credit memo is received, attached to the voucher, and the voucher is returned to the unpaid vouchers file.

25 A partial payment for merchandise purchased from Trizon Suppliers is made for $150 on voucher no. 206, which was for $350. Plan to pay the remaining $200 in two weeks (new vouchers are issued). Check no. 682.

30 A partial return of merchandise purchased from F.B. Jones Co. is made for $20, voucher no. 208. A credit memo is received, attached to the voucher, and the voucher is returned to the unpaid vouchers file.

Voucher Register—Left Side

VOUCHER REGISTER

	DATE	VOUCHER NO.	ISSUED TO	PURCHASES DEBIT	
1	9/6/--	202	Briggs Store	6 0 0 00	1
2	9/8/--	203	XYZ Co.	8 0 0 00	2
3	9/10/--	204	Arbiters, Inc.	7 0 0 00	3
4	9/11/--	205	Paper Traders		4
5	9/15/--	206	Trizon Suppliers	3 5 0 00	5
6	9/16/--	207	Payroll		6
7	9/18/--	208	F.B. Jones Co.	6 0 0 00	7
8					8

Voucher Register—Right Side

PAGE

	SUPPLIES DEBIT	WAGES EXPENSE DEBIT	GENERAL DEBIT			VOUCHERS PAYABLE CREDIT	PAYMENT		
			ACCOUNT	POST. REF.	AMOUNT		DATE	CHECK NO.	
1						6 0 0 00	9/8/--	681	1
2						8 0 0 00			2
3						7 0 0 00			3
4	1 8 6 00					1 8 6 00			4
5						3 5 0 00			5
6		1 2 0 0 00				1 2 0 0 00			6
7						6 0 0 00			7
8									8

SERIES B PROBLEMS

3 **PROBLEM 13B1 VOUCHER REGISTER AND POSTING TO GENERAL LEDGER** Stodolski Sounds had the following transactions for the month of July 19--.

Date	Voucher No.	Issued To	Amount	Purpose	Date Paid	Check No.
7/1	771	Milltown Realty	$1,000	July rent	7/1	330
7/4	772	Khalaf Electronics	1,700	Merchandise	7/11	332
7/7	773	Phak's	640	Office Supplies	7/8	331
7/11	774	Breck Sound Supply	760	Merchandise	7/21	334
7/15	775	Payroll	3,000	Bimonthly paychecks	7/15	333
7/21	776	Clear Tone Disks	1,360	Merchandise		
7/28	777	Khalaf Electronics	820	Merchandise		
7/29	778	Phak's	456	Office supplies		
7/31	779	Payroll	3,000	Bimonthly paychecks	7/31	335

REQUIRED

1. Enter the transactions for July 19-- in the voucher register (page 7). Total, rule, and prove the voucher register.
2. Post the voucher register to the general ledger. Use account numbers as shown in the chapter.
3. Prepare a schedule of vouchers payable.

5 **PROBLEM 13B2 CHECK REGISTER AND POSTING TO GENERAL LEDGER**   The following transactions were for the month of August 19--. A voucher register is used. Assume terms of 2/10, n/30 for purchases on account, and assume that all discounts are taken. General ledger account balances on August 1 were: Cash, $9,862; and Vouchers Payable, $8,482.

Date	Check No.	Pay To	Voucher No.	Amount	Purpose
8/2	211	Realty Co.	108	$600	August rent
8/5	212	Tri-Cities Co.	111	238	Merchandise on account
8/8	213	Miller's	112	412	Merchandise on account
8/10	214	A&E Office Co.	115	108	Office supplies
8/15	215	Payroll	114	900	Bimonthly payroll
8/18	216	Blythe Mill	118	620	Merchandise on account
8/22	217	Tri-Cities Co.	119	512	Merchandise on account
8/27	218	Miller's	122	816	Merchandise on account
8/31	219	Payroll	123	900	Bimonthly payroll

REQUIRED

1. Enter the transactions for August 19-- in the check register (page 8). Total, rule, and prove the register.
2. Post the check register totals to the general ledger. Use account numbers as shown in the chapter.

3/4/5 **PROBLEM 13B3 VOUCHER REGISTER, CHECK REGISTER, POSTING, AND SCHEDULE OF VOUCHERS PAYABLE**   Jane Hledik is owner of Hledik Lawn Supply. The following transactions occurred during April 19--. Hledik Lawn Supply uses a voucher register, a check register, and a general ledger. Unpaid vouchers are filed and listed at the end of the month. General ledger account balances on April 1 were: Cash, $5,189; and Supplies, $408.

continued

Vouchers issued:

Date	Voucher No.	Issued To	Amount	Purpose	Terms
4/2	662	Brenner's	$600	April rent	
4/4	663	Lawn Care Wholesale	300	Merchandise	2/10, n/30
4/7	664	Southern Supply	128	Office supplies	
4/10	665	Clay's Chemicals	420	Merchandise	1/20, n/30
4/13	666	Mendel & Son	530	Merchandise	2/10, n/30
4/15	667	Payroll	950	Bimonthly payroll	
4/19	668	Lawn Care Wholesale	570	Merchandise	1/10, n/30
4/27	669	Southern Supply	99	Office supplies	
4/29	670	Lakeside Fertilizer	280	Merchandise	2/10, n/30
4/30	671	Payroll	950	Bimonthly payroll	

Checks issued:

Date	Check No.	Payee	Voucher No.	Amount
4/2	748	Brenner's	662	$600
4/7	749	Southern Supply	664	128
4/11	750	Lawn Care Wholesale	663	300
4/15	751	Payroll	667	950
4/20	752	Mendel & Son	666	530
4/30	753	Payroll	671	950

REQUIRED

1. Enter the transactions for April in the voucher register. Total, rule, and prove the register. Update the Payment column when vouchers are paid.
2. Enter the transactions for April in the check register. Be sure to take discounts where appropriate. Total, rule, and prove the register.
3. Post the voucher register and the check register to the general ledger. Use account numbers as shown in the chapter.
4. Prepare a schedule of vouchers payable.

3/4/5 **PROBLEM 13B4 VOUCHER REGISTER, CHECK REGISTER, AND GENERAL JOURNAL (RETURNS AND PARTIAL PAYMENTS)**
Michael Blake owns Blake's Appliance Store. The following transactions occurred during May 19--. Blake's Appliance Store uses a voucher register, a check register, and a general journal.

May 1 Issued voucher no. 308 to Johnson & Smith for May rent, $500.
1 Issued check no. 411 to Johnson & Smith in payment of May rent, $500. Voucher no. 308.
3 Purchased merchandise from Wilson Supply Co., $380, terms 2/10, n/30. Voucher no. 309.
5 Received a credit memo from Wilson Supply Co. for returned merchandise that was purchased May 3, $50.
7 Purchased supplies from B & J Office Supply, $138. Voucher no. 310.
7 Issued check no. 412 to B & J Office Supply, $138. Voucher no. 310.

continued

May 10 Purchased merchandise from P.T. Benkley Co., $540, terms 2/10, n/30. Voucher no. 311.

11 Received a credit memo from P.T. Benkley Co. for returned merchandise that was purchased May 10, $540.

11 Issued check no. 413 to Wilson Supply Co. for purchase made on May 3 less returns made on May 5 less 2% discount. Voucher no. 309.

12 Purchased merchandise from Wesley's Wholesale, $720, terms 2/10, n/30. Voucher no. 312.

15 Issued voucher no. 313 to Payroll in payment of bimonthly wages, $1,000.

15 Issued check no. 414 to Payroll, $1,000. Voucher no. 313.

19 Purchased merchandise from Wilson Supply Co., $660, terms 2/10, n/30. Voucher no. 314.

21 Issued check no. 415 to Wilson Supply Co. in partial payment for goods purchased on May 19, $330 less 2% discount. Voucher no. 314. Issued new vouchers no. 315 and 316.

22 Purchased supplies from B & J Office Supply, $120. Voucher no. 317.

23 Issued check no. 416 to Wesley's Wholesale, $720. Voucher no. 312.

25 Purchased merchandise from Eastern Distributors, $360, terms 1/10, n/30. Voucher no. 318.

28 Purchased merchandise from Tremble & Co., $400, terms 2/10, n/30. Voucher no. 319.

31 Issued voucher no. 320 to Payroll in payment of bimonthly wages, $1,000.

31 Issued check no. 417 to Payroll, $1,000. Voucher no. 320.

REQUIRED

Enter the transactions in a voucher register (page 5), check register (page 5), or general journal (page 5), as appropriate. Total, rule, and prove the voucher register and check register.

MASTERY PROBLEM

Sunshine Flower Shop began operations in the month of July. The following transactions occurred during the first month of business.

July 1 Purchased merchandise from Thorny Wholesale, $600. Voucher no. 1.

2 Issued check no. 1 to Strongs Rental for July rent, $1,000. Voucher no. 2

3 Purchased merchandise from Flowerbed, Inc., $470, terms 2/15, n/60, FOB shipping point. Voucher no. 3.

7 Issued check no. 2 to Thorny Wholesale in partial payment for goods purchased on July 1, $300. Voucher no. 1. Issued new vouchers no. 4 and 5.

continued

July 9 Issued check no. 3 to Charlie's Trucking for shipping charges, $20. Voucher no. 6.

15 Issued check no. 4 to Payroll for wages, $600. Voucher no. 7.

16 Purchased merchandise from Petals Co., $377, terms 2/15, n/30. Voucher no. 8.

17 Purchased merchandise from Weeds Plus, $436, terms 3/15, n/60. Voucher no. 9.

18 Issued check no. 5 to Flowerbed, Inc., for goods purchased on July 3 less discount. Voucher no. 3.

23 Purchased supplies from Staples Supply, $150. Voucher no. 10.

25 Received a credit memo from Weeds Plus for returned merchandise that was purchased on July 17, $80.

31 Issued check no. 6 to Petals Co. for goods purchased on July 16 less discount. Voucher no. 8.

31 Issued check no. 7 to Payroll for wages, $600. Voucher no. 11.

REQUIRED

The general ledger accounts are listed below. The $6,000 with which the Flower Shop began business is entered in the cash account. Only this account has a beginning balance.

Cash	111
Supplies	151
Vouchers Payable	216
Purchases	511
Purchases Returns and Allowances	511.1
Purchases Discounts	511.2
Freight-In	512
Rent Expense	541
Wages and Salaries Expense	542

1. Enter all transactions in the voucher register, check register, and general journal. Total, rule, and prove the voucher register and check register.
2. Post the transactions to the general ledger.
3. Prepare a schedule of vouchers payable and compare the July 31 total to the balance of Vouchers Payable in the general ledger.

14

Adjustments and the Work Sheet for a Merchandising Business

Careful study of this chapter should enable you to:

LO1 Prepare an adjustment for merchandise inventory.

LO2 Prepare an adjustment for unearned revenue.

LO3 Prepare a work sheet for a merchandising firm.

LO4 Journalize adjusting entries for a merchandising firm.

Often we are expected to pay in advance for goods and services. This is true for season tickets for sporting events, magazine subscriptions, or tickets for popular operas or rock concerts. In return, we expect to receive the goods or services. How are cash receipts of this kind treated by the business?

In Chapters 11 through 13, we learned how to account for the day-to-day transactions of a merchandising business. In this chapter, we focus on end-of-period adjustments and the preparation of the work sheet. Finally, in Chapter 15, we will complete the accounting cycle by preparing financial statements and closing entries.

A work sheet for a merchandising firm is similar to the work sheet prepared for a service business (Chapter 5). It is used to prepare adjustments for supplies, prepaid insurance, wages earned but not paid, depreciation, and other necessary year-end adjustments. A merchandising firm must also make an adjustment to properly report the amount of merchandise inventory held at the end of the accounting period. While revisiting the work sheet, we will also introduce a new adjustment for unearned revenue.

ADJUSTMENT FOR MERCHANDISE INVENTORY

LO1 Prepare an adjustment for merchandise inventory.

Figure 14-1 provides a review of the entries made when a business buys and sells merchandise. Note that the merchandise inventory account is never debited or credited during the year.

FIGURE 14-1   Review of Entries for Purchase and Sale of Merchandise

TRANSACTION	ENTRY		
Purchase of merchandise	Purchases	xxx	
	Accounts Payable or Cash		xxx
Sale of merchandise	Accounts Receivable or Cash	xxx	
	Sales		xxx

Since sales and purchases have taken place during the year, the beginning balance of the merchandise inventory account no longer provides an accurate picture of the inventory held at the end of the year. Thus, an adjustment must be made to remove the beginning inventory and enter the ending inventory in the merchandise inventory account. The quantity of inventory on hand at the end of the accounting period is determined by taking a physical count of the goods on hand. This process is referred to as a **physical inventory**. The cost of these goods is determined by reviewing the accounting records. Of course, this year's ending inventory becomes next year's beginning inventory.

To illustrate the adjustment for merchandise inventory, let's assume that Ponder's Bike Parts had a beginning merchandise inventory of $25,000. During the year, the entries shown in Figure 14-1 were made as merchandise was purchased and sold. At the end of the accounting period, a physical inventory of the merchandise determined that merchandise costing $30,000 was still on hand. This indicates that the cost of the merchandise purchased exceeded cost of goods sold by $5,000.

As shown in Figure 14-2, the inventory adjustment is made in two steps.

 To adjust the merchandise inventory account, take out the old and bring in the new.

STEP 1   In adjustment (a), the beginning inventory ($25,000) is removed by crediting Merchandise Inventory. Income Summary is debited because this amount is used in the calculation of cost of goods sold. "Cost of goods sold" is an expense on the income statement.

STEP 2   In adjustment (b), the ending inventory ($30,000) is entered by debiting Merchandise Inventory. Income Summary is credited because this amount also is used in the calculation of cost of goods sold. After making the second adjustment, the balance of $30,000 in Merchandise Inventory reflects the inventory on hand at the end of the accounting period.

LEARNING KEY   Income Summary is used to adjust Merchandise Inventory. It is also used when closing the temporary owner's equity accounts.

FIGURE 14-2   Two-Step Adjustment for Merchandise Inventory

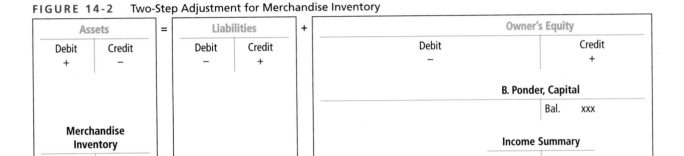

The two-step adjustment process is a bit unusual. Perhaps the best way to explain the reason for this approach is by illustrating how these adjustments are made on the work sheet and how the work sheet information is used to prepare the income statement. Figure 14-3 illustrates a partial work sheet for Ponder's Bike Parts and the cost of goods sold section of the income statement.

The inventory adjustments are made following the two-step process described above.

Step 1	Income Summary	25,000	
	Merchandise Inventory		25,000
Step 2	Merchandise Inventory	30,000	
	Income Summary		30,000

Both the debit of $25,000 and the credit of $30,000 made to the income summary account are extended to the Adjusted Trial Balance and Income Statement columns. *This is the only time that the individual figures, rather than the net amount, are extended on the work sheet.* It is done in this case because the individual amounts are needed for the calculation of cost of goods sold on the income statement. As shown in Figure 14-3, all of the information

FIGURE 14-3 Calculation of Cost of Goods Sold Using Information in the Income Statement Columns of the Work Sheet

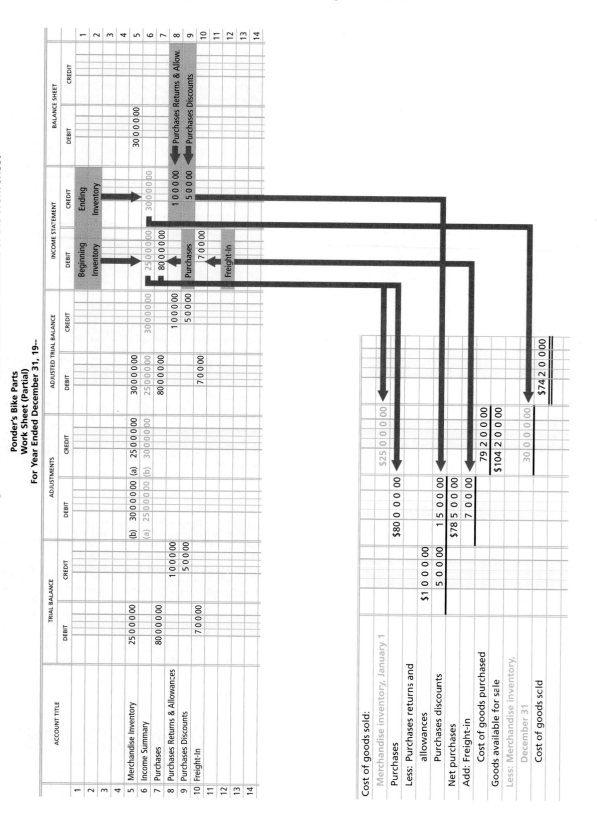

needed for the preparation of the income statement is in the Income Statement columns of the work sheet. This is the result of using the two-step adjustment process for inventory and extending both the debit and credit made to Income Summary.

> By extending both income summary amounts to the Income Statement columns, the amounts for the beginning and ending inventory are available in the Income Statement columns for preparation of the income statement. The amount in the debit column is the beginning inventory. The amount in the credit column is the ending inventory.

ADJUSTMENT FOR UNEARNED REVENUE

LO2 Prepare an adjustment for unearned revenue.

Some businesses require payment before delivering a product or performing a service. Examples include insurance companies, magazine publishers, apartment complexes, college food services, and theater companies that sell season tickets. The cash received in advance is called **unearned revenue**. Since the cash has been received in advance, the company owes the customers the product or service, or must refund their money. Thus, unearned revenue is reported as a *liability* on the balance sheet.

> Remember, under the accrual basis of accounting, revenue is recorded when *earned* regardless of when cash is received.

To illustrate, let's assume that the Brown County Playhouse sells season tickets for five plays produced throughout the year. Tickets sell for $10 each and a maximum of 1,000 seats can be sold for each play. For simplicity, let's assume that all shows sell out during the first week that season tickets are available for sale. As shown below and in Figure 14-4, the sale of the tickets would be recorded as follows:

8	(1)	Cash	50 0 0 0 00		8
9		Unearned Ticket Revenue		50 0 0 0 00	9
10		Season ticket sales			10
11		($10 x 1,000 seats x 5 shows)			11

To prepare financial statements following production of the third show, an adjusting entry is needed to recognize that $30,000 ($10 × 1,000 seats × 3 shows) in ticket revenue has been earned. To do this, the following adjusting entry is made.

13		Adjusting Entries			13
14		Unearned Ticket Revenue	30 0 0 0 00		14
15		Ticket Revenue		30 0 0 0 00	15

The remaining balance of $20,000 in Unearned Ticket Revenue is reported as a current liability on the balance sheet.

FIGURE 14-4 Entries for Unearned Revenue

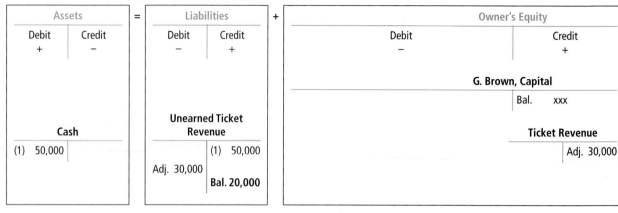

Expanded Chart of Accounts

Let's take a look at where the new accounts for a merchandising firm fit into a chart of accounts. Recall that the chart of accounts follows the form of the accounting equation (Assets = Liabilities + Owner's Equity + Revenues − Expenses). A chart of accounts for Northern Micro is provided in Figure 14-5. Note the classification of the new accounts introduced in Chapters 11 and 12 for a merchandising firm.

Merchandise Inventory is listed as a current asset, Unearned Subscriptions Revenue is listed as a current liability, and Subscriptions Revenue is listed as a revenue. Sales Returns and Allowances and Sales Discounts are **contra-revenue accounts**. Recall, however, that Northern Micro does not offer sales discounts.

Purchases, Purchases Returns and Allowances, Purchases Discounts, and Freight-In are used to compute cost of goods sold. Thus, they are listed under this heading. Purchases Returns and Allowances and Purchases Discounts are often called **contra-cost accounts** or contra-purchases accounts.

Interest Expense is classified as "Other Expense" instead of being listed under Operating Expenses. This is because it represents the expense of obtaining money to do business, rather than an expense directly associated with operating the business.

PREPARING A WORK SHEET FOR A MERCHANDISING FIRM

LO3 Prepare a work sheet for a merchandising firm.

The work sheet for a merchandising firm is similar to the one shown in Chapter 5 for a service business. Recall the five steps taken to prepare a work sheet:

FIGURE 14-5   Chart of Accounts for Northern Micro

Northern Micro Chart of Accounts			
Assets		**Revenue**	
Current Assets		411	Sales
111	Cash	*411.1*	*Sales Returns and*
131	Accounts Receivable		*Allowances*
141	*Merchandise Inventory*	**Other Revenue**	
151	Supplies	*421*	*Subscriptions Revenue*
155	Prepaid Insurance	*431*	*Interest Revenue*
Property, Plant, and Equipment		*451*	*Rent Revenue*
161	Land	**Cost of Goods Sold**	
171	Building	*511*	*Purchases*
171.1	Accumulated Depreciation—	*511.1*	*Purchases Returns and*
	Building		*Allowances*
181	Store Equipment	*511.2*	*Purchases Discounts*
181.1	Accumulated Depreciation—	*512*	*Freight-In*
	Store Equipment	**Operating Expenses**	
Liabilities		532	Advertising Expense
Current Liabilities		541	Rent Expense
216	Accounts Payable	542	Wages Expense
218	Notes Payable	543	Supplies Expense
219	Wages Payable	545	Telephone Expense
225	Sales Tax Payable	547	Depreciation Expense—
230	*Unearned Subscriptions Revenue*		Building
Long-Term Liabilities		548	Depreciation Expense—
262	Mortgage Payable		Store Equipment
Owner's Equity		553	Bank Credit Card
311	Gary L. Fishel, Capital		Expense
312	Gary L. Fishel, Drawing	555	Utilities Expense
313	Income Summary	559	Insurance Expense
		592	Miscellaneous Expense
		Other Expenses	
		595	Interest Expense

STEP 1 Prepare the trial balance.

STEP 2 Prepare the adjustments.

STEP 3 Prepare the adjusted trial balance.

STEP 4 Extend the adjusted trial balance to the Income Statement and Balance Sheet columns.

STEP 5 Total the Income Statement and Balance Sheet columns to compute the net income or net loss.

The work sheet format and the five steps taken when preparing the work sheet are illustrated in Figure 14-6. Note that the new accounts introduced for a merchandising firm and the unearned revenue account are highlighted so that you can see their proper placement and extensions. (The abbreviation BI stands for beginning inventory; EI stands for ending inventory.) Pay particular attention to the extension of Income Summary. Both the debit and credit amounts for this account must be extended.

Adjustments For Northern Micro

Before preparing a work sheet for Northern Micro, let's review the preparation of adjustments in T account form. Figure 14-7 provides year-end adjustment information for Northern Micro. Figure 14-8 shows adjusting entries based on this information.

Preparing A Work Sheet For Northern Micro

Let's prepare a work sheet for Northern Micro following the five steps illustrated in Figure 14-6.

STEP 1 In Figure 14-9, the Trial Balance columns are completed by copying the balances of all accounts from the general ledger (not shown).

STEP 2 In Figure 14-10, the adjustments are entered. These entries are exactly the same as those made in T account form in Figure 14-8.

STEP 3 In Figure 14-11, extensions are made to the Adjusted Trial Balance columns. Note that both the debit and credit amounts for Income Summary are extended.

STEP 4 In Figure 14-12, the adjusted trial balances are extended to the Income Statement and Balance Sheet columns.

STEP 5 In Figure 14-12, the work sheet is completed by totaling the Income Statement and Balance Sheet columns. The difference between the debits and credits for each pair of columns represents the net income or net loss.

ADJUSTING ENTRIES

LO4 Journalize adjusting entries for a merchandising firm.

Recall that making the adjustments on the work sheet has no effect on the actual accounts in the general ledger. Journal entries must be made to enter

FIGURE 14-6 Overview of Work Sheet for a Merchandising Firm

Name of Company
Work Sheet
For Month Ended June 30, 19--

ACCOUNT TITLE	TRIAL BALANCE		ADJUSTMENTS		ADJUSTED TRIAL BALANCE		INCOME STATEMENT		BALANCE SHEET		
	DEBIT	CREDIT	DEBIT	CREDIT	DEBIT	CREDIT	DEBIT	CREDIT	DEBIT	CREDIT	
‑‑‑‑‑‑‑‑‑‑‑	Step 1:		Step 2:		Step 3:		Step 4:				1
‑‑‑‑‑‑‑‑‑‑‑	Prepare a		Prepare the		Prepare the		Extend Adjusted				2
(Insert Ledger Account Title)	Trial Balance		Adjustments		Adjusted Trial Balance		Account Balances				3
	Assets						Assets				4
	Mdse. Inv. (BI)		EI	BI	Mdse. Inv. (EI)				Mdse. Inv. (EI)		5
		Liabilities				Liabilities				Liabilities	6
		Unearned				Unearned				Unearned	7
		Revenues				Revenues				Revenues	8
											9
		Capital				Capital				Capital	10
	Drawing				Drawing				Drawing		11
											12
Income Summary			BI	EI	BI	EI	BI	EI			13
‑‑‑‑‑‑‑‑‑‑‑											14
		Revenues				Revenues		Revenues			15
		Sales				Sales		Sales			16
	Sales R&A				Sales R&A		Sales R&A				17
	Sales Discounts				Sales Discounts		Sales Discounts				18
											19
	Expenses				Expenses		Expenses				20
	Purchases				Purchases		Purchases				21
		Purch. R&A				Purch. R&A		Purch. R&A			22
		Purch. Discounts				Purch. Discounts		Purch. Discounts			23
	Freight-In				Freight-In		Freight-In				24
							Step 5:				25
							Complete the work sheet				26
							1) Sum Columns				27
							2) Compute Net Income (Loss)				28
											29
							Net	Net	Net	Net	30
							Income	Loss	Loss	Income	31
											32

BI = Beginning Inventory
EI = Ending Inventory

FIGURE 14-7 Year-End Adjustment Data for Northern Micro

YEAR-END ADJUSTMENT DATA FOR NORTHERN MICRO	
(a, b)	A physical count showed that merchandise inventory costing $18,000 is on hand as of December 31.
(c)	Supplies remaining at the end of the year, $400.
(d)	Unexpired insurance on December 31, $600.
(e)	Depreciation expense on the building for 19--, $4,000.
(f)	Depreciation expense on the store equipment for 19--, $3,000.
(g)	Wages earned but not paid as of December 31, $450.
(h)	Northern Micro publishes a computer magazine. Subscribers pay in advance. Unearned subscriptions revenue as of December 31, $2,000.

FIGURE 14-8 Adjusting Entries for Northern Micro

Assets = Liabilities + Owner's Equity

Assets (Debit +, Credit −)

Merchandise Inventory	
Bal. 26,000	
	(a) 26,000
(b) 18,000	
Bal. 18,000	

Supplies	
Bal. 1,800	
	(c) 1,400
Bal. 400	

Prepaid Insurance	
Bal. 2,400	
	(d) 1,800
Bal. 600	

Accum. Deprec.—Building	
	Bal. 16,000
	(e) 4,000
	Bal. 20,000

Accum. Deprec.—Store Equipment	
	Bal. 15,000
	(f) 3,000
	Bal. 18,000

Liabilities (Debit −, Credit +)

Wages Payable	
	(g) 450

Unearned Subscriptions Revenue	
	Bal. 12,000
(h) 10,000	
	Bal. 2,000

Owner's Equity (Debit −, Credit +)

G. Fishel, Capital	
	Bal. XXX

Income Summary	
(a) 26,000	
	(b) 18,000

Supplies Expense	
(c) 1,400	

Insurance Expense	
(d) 1,800	

Deprec. Expense—Building	
(e) 4,000	

Deprec. Expense—Store Equipment	
(f) 3,000	

Wages Expense	
(g) 450	

Subscriptions Revenue	
	(h) 10,000

FIGURE 14-9   Step 1: Completion of the Trial Balance Columns

Northern Micro
Work Sheet
For Year Ended December 31, 19--

	ACCOUNT TITLE	TRIAL BALANCE DEBIT	TRIAL BALANCE CREDIT	ADJUSTMENTS DEBIT	ADJUSTMENTS CREDIT	ADJUSTED TRIAL BALANCE DEBIT	ADJUSTED TRIAL BALANCE CREDIT	INCOME STATEMENT DEBIT	INCOME STATEMENT CREDIT	BALANCE SHEET DEBIT	BALANCE SHEET CREDIT	
1	Cash	20 0 0 0 00										1
2	Accounts Receivable	15 0 0 0 00										2
3	Merchandise Inventory	26 0 0 0 00										3
4	Supplies	1 8 0 0 00										4
5	Prepaid Insurance	2 4 0 0 00										5
6	Land	10 0 0 0 00										6
7	Building	90 0 0 0 00										7
8	Accum. Deprec.—Building		16 0 0 0 00									8
9	Store Equipment	50 0 0 0 00										9
10	Accum. Deprec.—Store Equip.		15 0 0 0 00									10
11	Accounts Payable		10 0 0 0 00									11
12	Notes Payable		5 0 0 0 00									12
13	Wages Payable											13
14	Sales Tax Payable		1 5 0 0 00									14
15	Unearned Subscriptions Revenue		12 0 0 0 00									15
16	Mortgage Payable		30 0 0 0 00									16
17	Gary L. Fishel, Capital		114 4 0 0 00									17
18	Gary L. Fishel, Drawing	20 0 0 0 00										18
19	Income Summary											19
20	Sales		214 0 0 0 00									20
21	Sales Returns and Allowances	1 2 0 0 00										21
22	Subscriptions Revenue											22
23	Interest Revenue		9 0 0 00									23
24	Rent Revenue		8 0 0 00									24
25	Purchases	105 0 0 0 00										25
26	Purchases Returns & Allowances		8 0 0 00									26
27	Purchases Discounts		1 0 0 0 00									27
28	Freight-In	3 0 0 00										28
29	Advertising Expense	2 5 0 0 00										29
30	Rent Expense	20 0 0 0 00										30
31	Wages Expense	42 0 0 0 00										31
32	Supplies Expense											32
33	Telephone Expense	3 5 0 0 00										33
34	Deprec. Expense—Building											34
35	Deprec. Expense—Store Equip											35
36	Bank Credit Card Expense	1 5 0 0 00										36
37	Utilities Expense	12 0 0 0 00										37
38	Insurance Expense											38
39	Miscellaneous Expense	2 2 5 0 00										39
40	Interest Expense	3 1 5 0 00										40
41		428 6 0 0 00	428 6 0 0 00									41
42	Net Income											42

STEP 1

FIGURE 14-10   Step 2: Preparation of the Adjustments

Northern Micro
Work Sheet
For Year Ended December 31, 19--

	ACCOUNT TITLE	TRIAL BALANCE DEBIT	TRIAL BALANCE CREDIT	ADJUSTMENTS DEBIT	ADJUSTMENTS CREDIT	ADJUSTED TRIAL BALANCE DEBIT	ADJUSTED TRIAL BALANCE CREDIT	INCOME STATEMENT DEBIT	INCOME STATEMENT CREDIT	BALANCE SHEET DEBIT	BALANCE SHEET CREDIT	
1	Cash	20 0 0 0 00										1
2	Accounts Receivable	15 0 0 0 00										2
3	Merchandise Inventory	26 0 0 0 00		(b) 18 0 0 0 00	(a) 26 0 0 0 00							3
4	Supplies	1 8 0 0 00			(c) 1 4 0 00							4
5	Prepaid Insurance	2 4 0 00			(d) 1 8 0 00							5
6	Land	10 0 0 0 00										6
7	Building	90 0 0 0 00										7
8	Accum. Deprec.—Building		16 0 0 0 00		(e) 4 0 0 00							8
9	Store Equipment	50 0 0 0 00										9
10	Accum. Deprec.—Store Equip.		15 0 0 0 00		(f) 3 0 0 00							10
11	Accounts Payable		10 0 0 0 00									11
12	Notes Payable		5 0 0 0 00									12
13	Wages Payable				(g) 4 5 00							13
14	Sales Tax Payable		1 5 0 00									14
15	Unearned Subscriptions Revenue		12 0 0 0 00	(h) 10 0 0 0 00								15
16	Mortgage Payable		30 0 0 0 00									16
17	Gary L. Fishel, Capital		114 4 0 0 00									17
18	Gary L. Fishel, Drawing	20 0 0 0 00										18
19	Income Summary			(a) 26 0 0 0 00	(b) 18 0 0 0 00							19
20	Sales		214 0 0 0 00									20
21	Sales Returns and Allowances	1 2 0 0 00										21
22	Subscriptions Revenue				(h) 10 0 0 0 00							22
23	Interest Revenue		9 0 0 00									23
24	Rent Revenue		8 0 0 00									24
25	Purchases	105 0 0 0 00										25
26	Purchases Returns & Allowances		8 0 0 00									26
27	Purchases Discounts		1 0 0 0 00									27
28	Freight-In	3 0 0 00										28
29	Advertising Expense	2 5 0 0 00										29
30	Rent Expense	20 0 0 0 00										30
31	Wages Expense	42 0 0 0 00		(g) 4 5 00								31
32	Supplies Expense			(c) 1 4 0 00								32
33	Telephone Expense	3 5 0 00										33
34	Deprec. Expense—Building			(e) 4 0 0 00								34
35	Deprec. Expense—Store Equip.			(f) 3 0 0 00								35
36	Bank Credit Card Expense	1 5 0 00										36
37	Utilities Expense	1 2 0 0 00										37
38	Insurance Expense			(d) 1 8 0 00								38
39	Miscellaneous Expense	2 2 5 00										39
40	Interest Expense	3 1 5 00										40
41		428 6 0 0 00	428 6 0 0 00	64 6 5 0 00	64 6 5 0 00							41
42	Net Income											42

STEP 1   STEP 2

F I G U R E 14-11   Step 3: Extensions to the Adjusted Trial Balance Columns

Northern Micro
Work Sheet
For Year Ended December 31, 19--

	TRIAL BALANCE		ADJUSTMENTS		ADJUSTED TRIAL BALANCE		INCOME STATEMENT		BALANCE SHEET	
ACCOUNT TITLE	DEBIT	CREDIT	DEBIT	CREDIT	DEBIT	CREDIT	DEBIT	CREDIT	DEBIT	CREDIT
1 Cash	20 0 0 0 00				20 0 0 0 00					
2 Accounts Receivable	15 0 0 0 00				15 0 0 0 00					
3 Merchandise Inventory	26 0 0 0 00		(b) 18 0 0 0 00	(a) 26 0 0 0 00	18 0 0 0 00					
4 Supplies	1 8 0 0 00			(c) 1 4 0 0 00	4 0 0 00					
5 Prepaid Insurance	2 4 0 0 00			(d) 1 8 0 0 00	6 0 0 00					
6 Land	10 0 0 0 00				10 0 0 0 00					
7 Building	90 0 0 0 00				90 0 0 0 00					
8 Accum. Deprec.—Building		16 0 0 0 00		(e) 4 0 0 0 00		20 0 0 0 00				
9 Store Equipment	50 0 0 0 00				50 0 0 0 00					
10 Accum. Deprec.—Store Equip.		15 0 0 0 00		(f) 3 0 0 0 00		18 0 0 0 00				
11 Accounts Payable		10 0 0 0 00				10 0 0 0 00				
12 Notes Payable		5 0 0 0 00				5 0 0 0 00				
13 Wages Payable				(g) 4 5 0 00		4 5 0 00				
14 Sales Tax Payable		1 5 0 0 00				1 5 0 0 00				
15 Unearned Subscriptions Revenue		12 0 0 0 00	(h) 10 0 0 0 00			2 0 0 0 00				
16 Mortgage Payable		30 0 0 0 00				30 0 0 0 00				
17 Gary L. Fishel, Capital		114 4 0 0 00				114 4 0 0 00				
18 Gary L. Fishel, Drawing	20 0 0 0 00				20 0 0 0 00					
19 Income Summary			(a) 26 0 0 0 00	(b) 18 0 0 0 00	26 0 0 0 00	18 0 0 0 00				
20 Sales		214 0 0 0 00				214 0 0 0 00				
21 Sales Returns and Allowances	1 2 0 0 00				1 2 0 0 00					
22 Subscriptions Revenue				(h) 10 0 0 0 00		10 0 0 0 00				
23 Interest Revenue		9 0 0 00				9 0 0 00				
24 Rent Revenue		8 0 0 0 00				8 0 0 0 00				
25 Purchases	105 0 0 0 00				105 0 0 0 00					
26 Purchases Returns & Allowances		8 0 0 0 00				8 0 0 0 00				
27 Purchases Discounts		1 0 0 0 00				1 0 0 0 00				
28 Freight-In	3 0 0 00				3 0 0 00					
29 Advertising Expense	2 5 0 0 00				2 5 0 0 00					
30 Rent Expense	20 0 0 0 00				20 0 0 0 00					
31 Wages Expense	42 0 0 0 00		(g) 4 5 0 00		42 4 5 0 00					
32 Supplies Expense			(c) 1 4 0 0 00		1 4 0 0 00					
33 Telephone Expense	3 5 0 0 00				3 5 0 0 00					
34 Deprec. Expense—Building			(e) 4 0 0 0 00		4 0 0 0 00					
35 Deprec. Expense—Store Equip.			(f) 3 0 0 0 00		3 0 0 0 00					
36 Bank Credit Card Expense	1 5 0 0 00				1 5 0 0 00					
37 Utilities Expense	12 0 0 0 00				12 0 0 0 00					
38 Insurance Expense			(d) 1 8 0 0 00		1 8 0 0 00					
39 Miscellaneous Expense	2 2 5 0 00				2 2 5 0 00					
40 Interest Expense	3 1 5 0 00				3 1 5 0 00					
41	428 6 0 0 00	428 6 0 0 00	64 6 5 0 00	64 6 5 0 00	454 0 5 0 00	454 0 5 0 00				
42 Net Income										

Beginning Inventory

Both the debit and credit are extended

Ending Inventory

Ending Inventory

STEP 1   STEP 2   STEP 3

FIGURE 14-12   Step 4: Extensions to the Income Statement and Balance Sheet Columns
Step 5: Completing the Work Sheet and Computing Net Income

Northern Micro
Work Sheet
For Year Ended December 31, 19—

	Account Title	Trial Balance Debit	Trial Balance Credit	Adjustments Debit	Adjustments Credit	Adjusted Trial Balance Debit	Adjusted Trial Balance Credit	Income Statement Debit	Income Statement Credit	Balance Sheet Debit	Balance Sheet Credit	
1	Cash	20 000 00				20 000 00				20 000 00		1
2	Accounts Receivable	15 000 00				15 000 00				15 000 00		2
3	Merchandise Inventory	26 000 00		(b) 18 000 00	(a) 26 000 00	18 000 00				18 000 00		3
4	Supplies	1 800 00			(c) 1 400 00	400 00				400 00		4
5	Prepaid Insurance	2 400 00			(d) 1 800 00	600 00				600 00		5
6	Land	10 000 00				10 000 00				10 000 00		6
7	Building	9 000 00				9 000 00				9 000 00		7
8	Accum. Deprec.—Building		1 600 00		(e) 400 00		2 000 00				2 000 00	8
9	Store Equipment	5 000 00				5 000 00				5 000 00		9
10	Accum. Deprec.—Store Equip.		1 500 00		(f) 300 00		1 800 00				1 800 00	10
11	Accounts Payable		1 000 00				1 000 00				1 000 00	11
12	Notes Payable		500 00				500 00				500 00	12
13	Wages Payable				(g) 45 00		45 00				45 00	13
14	Sales Tax Payable		150 00				150 00				150 00	14
15	Unearned Subscriptions Revenue		1 200 00	(h) 1 000 00			200 00				200 00	15
16	Mortgage Payable		3 000 00				3 000 00				3 000 00	16
17	Gary L. Fishel, Capital		11 440 00				11 440 00				11 440 00	17
18	Gary L. Fishel, Drawing	2 000 00				2 000 00				2 000 00		18
19	Income Summary			(a) 26 000 00	(b) 18 000 00	26 000 00	18 000 00	26 000 00	18 000 00			19
20	Sales		21 400 00				21 400 00		21 400 00			20
21	Sales Returns and Allowances	1 200 00				1 200 00		1 200 00				21
22	Subscriptions Revenue				(h) 1 000 00		1 000 00		1 000 00			22
23	Interest Revenue		900 00				900 00		900 00			23
24	Rent Revenue		800 00				800 00		800 00			24
25	Purchases	10 500 00				10 500 00		10 500 00				25
26	Purchases Returns & Allowances		800 00				800 00		800 00			26
27	Purchases Discounts		1 000 00				1 000 00		1 000 00			27
28	Freight-In	300 00				300 00		300 00				28
29	Advertising Expense	2 500 00				2 500 00		2 500 00				29
30	Rent Expense	2 000 00				2 000 00		2 000 00				30
31	Wages Expense	4 200 00		(g) 45 00		4 245 00		4 245 00				31
32	Supplies Expense			(c) 1 400 00		1 400 00		1 400 00				32
33	Telephone Expense	350 00				350 00		350 00				33
34	Deprec. Expense—Building			(e) 400 00		400 00		400 00				34
35	Deprec. Expense—Store Equip.			(f) 300 00		300 00		300 00				35
36	Bank Credit Card Expense	150 00				150 00		150 00				36
37	Utilities Expense	1 200 00				1 200 00		1 200 00				37
38	Insurance Expense			(d) 1 800 00		1 800 00		1 800 00				38
39	Miscellaneous Expense	225 00				225 00		225 00				39
40	Interest Expense	315 00				315 00		315 00				40
41		42 860 00	42 860 00	6 465 00	6 465 00	45 405 00	45 405 00	23 005 00	25 270 00	22 400 00	20 135 00	41
42	Net Income							2 265 00			2 265 00	42
43								25 270 00	25 270 00	22 400 00	22 400 00	43

STEP 1 | STEP 2 | STEP 3 | STEPS 4 AND 5

the adjustments into the accounting system. Figure 14-13 shows the adjusting entries for Northern Micro.

 Recall that the work sheet is just a planning tool. The adjusting entries must be entered in the general journal.

FIGURE 14-13   Adjusting Entries for Northern Micro

GENERAL JOURNAL   PAGE 3

	DATE		DESCRIPTION	POST. REF.	DEBIT	CREDIT	
1	19--		**Adjusting Entries**				1
2	Dec.	31	Income Summary		26 0 0 0 00		2
3			Merchandise Inventory			26 0 0 0 00	3
4							4
5		31	Merchandise Inventory		18 0 0 0 00		5
6			Income Summary			18 0 0 0 00	6
7							7
8		31	Supplies Expense		1 4 0 0 00		8
9			Supplies			1 4 0 0 00	9
10							10
11		31	Insurance Expense		1 8 0 0 00		11
12			Prepaid Insurance			1 8 0 0 00	12
13							13
14		31	Deprec. Expense—Building		4 0 0 0 00		14
15			Accumulated Deprec.—Building			4 0 0 0 00	15
16							16
17		31	Deprec. Expense—Store Equipment		3 0 0 0 00		17
18			Accumulated Deprec.—Store				18
19			Equipment			3 0 0 0 00	19
20							20
21		31	Wages Expense		4 5 0 00		21
22			Wages Payable			4 5 0 00	22
23							23
24		31	Unearned Subscriptions Revenue		10 0 0 0 00		24
25			Subscriptions Revenue			10 0 0 0 00	25
26							26

KEY POINTS

1 Extra care is required for the end-of-period adjustment for merchandise inventory and the related extensions on the work sheet. The two-step adjustment process in T account form and the work sheet treatment for Northern Micro are reviewed in Figures 14-14 and 14-15 on pages 480 and 481.

FIGURE 14-14   Two-Step Adjustment for Merchandise Inventory in T Account Form

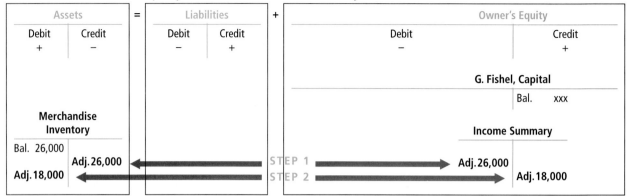

2 Some firms receive cash before providing a service or selling a product. This cash is considered a liability, unearned revenue, until earned.

3 Steps to follow when preparing a work sheet:
1. Prepare the trial balance.
2. Prepare the adjustments.
3. Prepare the adjusted trial balance.
4. Extend the adjusted trial balances to the Income Statement and Balance Sheet columns.
5. Total the Income Statement and Balance Sheet columns to compute the net income or net loss.

4 The worksheet is a useful tool when preparing end-of-period adjustments and financial statements. Remember: The work sheet is NOT a formal part of the accounting system. Adjustments made on the work sheet must be entered in a journal and posted to the ledger.

KEY TERMS

contra-cost accounts 470   Accounts that are deducted from the Purchases account when computing cost of goods sold—Purchases Returns and Allowances and Purchases Discounts.

contra-revenue accounts 470   Accounts that are deducted from Sales on the income statement—Sales Returns and Allowances and Sales Discounts.

physical inventory 466   Taking a physical count of the goods on hand.

unearned revenue 469   Cash received in advance of delivering a product or performing a service.

FIGURE 14-15   Work Sheet Adjustment and Extension for Merchandise Inventory and Calculation of Cost of Goods Sold Using Information in the Income Statement Columns of the Work Sheet

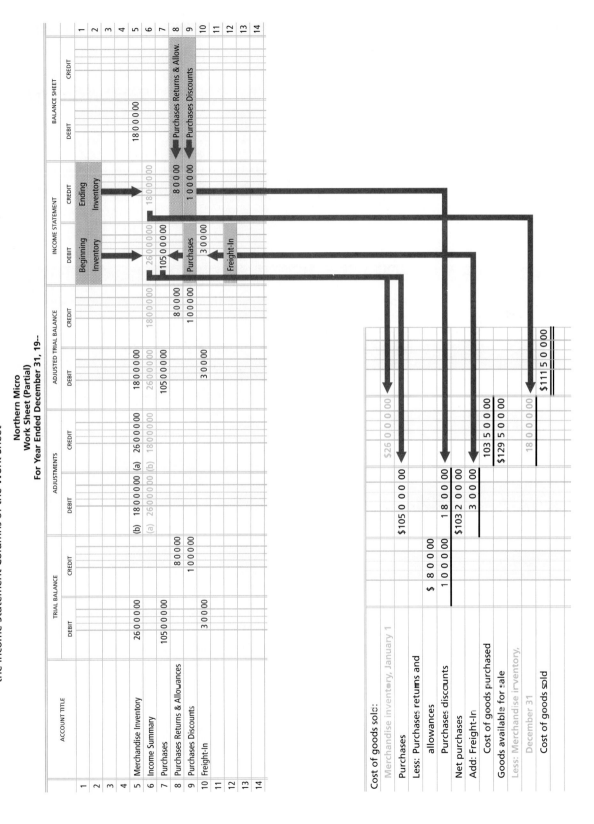

REVIEW QUESTIONS

1. What work sheet amounts are used to compute cost of goods sold?
2. Why are both the debit and credit amounts in the Adjustments columns on the Income Summary line of the work sheet extended to the Adjusted Trial Balance columns?
3. What is an unearned revenue?
4. Give three examples of unearned revenues.
5. List the five steps taken to prepare a work sheet.
6. What does the difference between the totals of the Income Statement columns represent? What does the difference between the Balance Sheet column totals represent?

MANAGING YOUR WRITING

A friend of yours recently opened Abracadabra, a sportswear shop specializing in monogrammed athletic gear. Most merchandise is special ordered for customers. However, a small inventory is on hand. Your friend does not understand why a physical inventory is necessary before preparing the financial statements. She knows how much she paid for all merchandise purchased. Why not simply use this amount for cost of goods sold? After all, it has been paid for. Write a brief memo explaining the purpose of the physical inventory and why she should not use the cost of purchases as cost of goods sold.

DEMONSTRATION PROBLEM

Aaron Patton owns and operates Patton's Bait Shop and Boat Rental. A year-end trial balance is shown on the next page.

Year-end adjustment data for Patton's Bait Shop and Boat Rental is as follows.

(a, b) A physical count shows that merchandise inventory costing $15,000 is on hand as of December 31, 19--.
(c) Supplies remaining at the end of the year, $200.
(d) Unexpired insurance on December 31, $300.
(e) Depreciation expense on the building for 19--, $2,000.
(f) Depreciation expense on the store equipment for 19--, $1,500.
(g) Wages earned but not paid as of December 31, $225.
(h) Unearned boat rental revenue as of December 31, $1,000.

REQUIRED
1. Prepare a year-end work sheet.
2. Journalize the adjusting entries.

Patton's Bait Shop and Boat Rental
Trial Balance
December 31, 19--

ACCOUNT TITLE	DEBIT BALANCE	CREDIT BALANCE
Cash	10 0 0 0 00	
Accounts Receivable	7 5 0 0 00	
Merchandise Inventory	19 0 0 0 00	
Supplies	9 0 0 00	
Prepaid Insurance	1 2 0 0 00	
Land	5 0 0 0 00	
Building	45 0 0 0 00	
Accumulated Depreciation—Building		8 0 0 0 00
Store Equipment	25 0 0 0 00	
Accumulated Depreciation—Store Equipment		7 5 0 0 00
Accounts Payable		5 0 0 0 00
Notes Payable		2 5 0 0 00
Wages Payable		
Unearned Boat Rental Revenue		11 0 0 0 00
Aaron Patton, Capital		77 9 0 0 00
Aaron Patton, Drawing	10 0 0 0 00	
Income Summary		
Sales		100 2 5 0 00
Sales Returns and Allowances	6 0 0 00	
Boat Rental Revenue		
Purchases	52 5 0 0 00	
Purchases Returns and Allowances		4 0 0 00
Purchases Discounts		5 0 0 00
Freight-In	1 5 0 00	
Advertising Expense	3 7 5 0 00	
Wages Expense	21 0 0 0 00	
Supplies Expense		
Telephone Expense	1 7 5 0 00	
Depreciation Expense—Building		
Depreciation Expense—Store Equipment		
Utilities Expense	6 0 0 0 00	
Insurance Expense		
Miscellaneous Expense	3 6 2 5 00	
Interest Expense	7 5 00	
	213 0 5 0 00	213 0 5 0 00

SOLUTION

1.

Patton's Bait Shop and Boat Rental
Work Sheet
For Year Ended December 31, 19--

	ACCOUNT TITLE	TRIAL BALANCE Debit	TRIAL BALANCE Credit	ADJUSTMENTS Debit	ADJUSTMENTS Credit	ADJUSTED TRIAL BALANCE Debit	ADJUSTED TRIAL BALANCE Credit	INCOME STATEMENT Debit	INCOME STATEMENT Credit	BALANCE SHEET Debit	BALANCE SHEET Credit	
1	Cash	10000 00				10000 00				10000 00		1
2	Accounts Receivable	7500 00				7500 00				7500 00		2
3	Merchandise Inventory	19000 00		(b) 15000 00	(a) 19000 00	15000 00				15000 00		3
4	Supplies	900 00			(c) 700 00	200 00				200 00		4
5	Prepaid Insurance	1200 00			(d) 900 00	300 00				300 00		5
6	Land	5000 00				5000 00				5000 00		6
7	Building	45000 00				45000 00				45000 00		7
8	Accum. Deprec.—Building		8000 00		(e) 2000 00		10000 00				10000 00	8
9	Store Equipment	25000 00				25000 00				25000 00		9
10	Accum. Deprec.—Store Equip.		7500 00		(f) 1500 00		9000 00				9000 00	10
11	Accounts Payable		5000 00				5000 00				5000 00	11
12	Notes Payable		2500 00				2500 00				2500 00	12
13	Wages Payable				(g) 225 00		225 00				225 00	13
14	Unearned Boat Rental Revenue		11000 00	(h) 10000 00			1000 00				1000 00	14
15	Aaron Patton, Capital		77900 00				77900 00				77900 00	15
16	Aaron Patton, Drawing	10000 00				10000 00				10000 00		16
17	Income Summary			(a) 19000 00	(b) 15000 00	19000 00	15000 00	19000 00	15000 00			17
18	Sales		100250 00				100250 00		100250 00			18
19	Sales Returns & Allowances	600 00				600 00		600 00				19
20	Boat Rental Revenue				(h) 10000 00		10000 00		10000 00			20
21	Purchases	52500 00				52500 00		52500 00				21
22	Purchases Returns & Allowances		400 00				400 00		400 00			22
23	Purchases Discounts		500 00				500 00		500 00			23
24	Freight-In	150 00				150 00		150 00				24
25	Advertising Expense	375 00				375 00		375 00				25
26	Wages Expense	21000 00		(g) 225 00		21225 00		21225 00				26
27	Supplies Expense			(c) 700 00		700 00		700 00				27
28	Telephone Expense	175 00				175 00		175 00				28
29	Deprec. Expense—Building			(e) 2000 00		2000 00		2000 00				29
30	Deprec. Expense—Store Equip.			(f) 1500 00		1500 00		1500 00				30
31	Utilities Expense	6000 00				6000 00		6000 00				31
32	Insurance Expense			(d) 900 00		900 00		900 00				32
33	Miscellaneous Expense	3625 00				3625 00		3625 00				33
34	Interest Expense	75 00				75 00		75 00				34
35		213050 00	213050 00	49325 00	49325 00	231775 00	231775 00	113775 00	126150 00	118000 00	105625 00	35
36	Net Income							12375 00			12375 00	36
37								126150 00	126150 00	118000 00	118000 00	37
38												38
39												39

2.

GENERAL JOURNAL   PAGE 3

	DATE	DESCRIPTION	POST. REF.	DEBIT	CREDIT	
1	19--	Adjusting Entries				1
2	Dec. 31	Income Summary		19 0 0 0 00		2
3		Merchandise Inventory			19 0 0 0 00	3
4						4
5	31	Merchandise Inventory		15 0 0 0 00		5
6		Income Summary			15 0 0 0 00	6
7						7
8	31	Supplies Expense		7 0 0 00		8
9		Supplies			7 0 0 00	9
10						10
11	31	Insurance Expense		9 0 0 00		11
12		Prepaid Insurance			9 0 0 00	12
13						13
14	31	Deprec. Expense—Building		2 0 0 0 00		14
15		Accumulated Deprec.—Building			2 0 0 0 00	15
16						16
17	31	Deprec. Expense—Store Equipment		1 5 0 0 00		17
18		Accumulated Deprec.—Store				18
19		Equipment			1 5 0 0 00	19
20						20
21	31	Wages Expense		2 2 5 00		21
22		Wages Payable			2 2 5 00	22
23						23
24	31	Unearned Boat Rental Revenue		10 0 0 0 00		24
25		Boat Rental Revenue			10 0 0 0 00	25

SERIES A EXERCISES

1 **EXERCISE 14A1 ADJUSTMENT FOR MERCHANDISING INVENTORY USING T ACCOUNTS**   Sam Baker owns a business called Sam's Sporting Goods. His beginning inventory as of January 1, 19--, was $47,000 and his ending inventory as of December 31, 19--, was $53,000. Set up T accounts for Merchandise Inventory and Income Summary and perform the year-end adjustment for merchandise inventory.

1 **EXERCISE 14A2 CALCULATION OF COST OF GOODS SOLD**
Prepare the cost of goods sold section for Adams Gift Shop. The following amounts are known:

Beginning merchandise inventory	$26,000
Ending merchandise inventory	23,000
Purchases	71,000
Purchases returns and allowances	3,500
Purchases discounts	5,500
Freight-in	200

2 **EXERCISE 14A3 ADJUSTMENT FOR UNEARNED REVENUES USING T ACCOUNTS**   Set up T accounts for Cash, Unearned Ticket Revenue, and Ticket Revenue. Post the following two transactions to the appropriate accounts indicating each transaction by letter.

(a) Sold 1,500 season tickets at $30 each, receiving cash of $45,000.
(b) An end-of-period adjustment is needed to recognize that $35,000 in ticket revenue has been earned.

3 **EXERCISE 14A4 WORK SHEET EXTENSIONS FOR MERCHANDISE INVENTORY ADJUSTMENTS**   The following partial work sheet is taken from Kevin's Gift Shop for the year ended December 31, 19--. The ending merchandise inventory is $50,000.

1. Complete the Adjustments columns for the merchandise inventory.
2. Extend the merchandise inventory to the Adjusted Trial Balance, Income Statement, and Balance Sheet columns.
3. Extend the remaining accounts to the Adjusted Trial Balance and Income Statement columns.
4. Prepare a cost of goods sold section from the partial work sheet.

Kevin's Gift Shop
Work Sheet (Partial)
For Year Ended December 31, 19--

	ACCOUNT TITLE	TRIAL BALANCE		ADJUSTMENTS		
		DEBIT	CREDIT	DEBIT	CREDIT	
1	Merchandise Inventory	40 0 0 0 00				1
12	Income Summary					12
13	Purchases	90 0 0 0 00				13
14	Purchases Returns & Allow.		2 0 0 0 00			14
15	Purchases Discounts		3 0 0 0 00			15
16	Freight-In	5 0 0 00				16
17						17
18						18

3 **EXERCISE 14A5 DETERMINING THE BEGINNING AND ENDING INVENTORY FROM A PARTIAL WORK SHEET**   From the following partial work sheet, indicate the dollar amount of beginning and ending merchandise inventory.

	ACCOUNT TITLE	TRIAL BALANCE		ADJUSTMENTS		
		DEBIT	CREDIT	DEBIT	CREDIT	
1	Merchandise Inventory			(b) 60 0 0 0 00	(a) 55 0 0 0 00	1
2	Income Summary			(a) 55 0 0 0 00	(b) 60 0 0 0 00	2

	ADJUSTED TRIAL BALANCE		INCOME STATEMENT		BALANCE SHEET		
	DEBIT	CREDIT	DEBIT	CREDIT	DEBIT	CREDIT	
1	60 0 0 0 00				60 0 0 0 00		1
2	55 0 0 0 00	60 0 0 0 00	55 0 0 0 00	60 0 0 0 00			2

5 **EXERCISE 14A6 JOURNALIZE ADJUSTING ENTRIES FOR A MERCHANDISING FIRM**   The following partial work sheet is taken from the books of Kelly's Kittens, a local pet kennel, for the year ended December 31, 19--. Journalize the adjustments in a general journal.

Kelly's Kittens
Work Sheet (Partial)
For Year Ended December 31, 19--

	ACCOUNT TITLE	TRIAL BALANCE		ADJUSTMENTS		
		DEBIT	CREDIT	DEBIT	CREDIT	
1	Merchandise Inventory	45 0 0 0 00		(b) 50 0 0 0 00	(a) 45 0 0 0 00	1
2	Supplies	10 0 0 0 00			(d) 7 0 0 0 00	2
3	Building	60 0 0 0 00				3
4	Accum. Deprec.—Building		15 0 0 0 00		(e) 5 0 0 0 00	4
5	Wages Payable				(f) 1 2 0 0 00	5
6	Unearned Deposit Fees		3 0 0 0 00	(c) 2 0 0 0 00		6
7	Income Summary			(a) 45 0 0 0 00	(b) 50 0 0 0 00	7
8	Deposit Fees Revenue		20 0 0 0 00		(c) 2 0 0 0 00	8
9	Wages Expense	37 0 0 0 00		(f) 1 2 0 0 00		9
10	Supplies Expense			(d) 7 0 0 0 00		10
11	Deprec. Expense—Building			(e) 5 0 0 0 00		11
12				110 2 0 0 00	110 2 0 0 00	12
13						13

SERIES A PROBLEMS

1/2/3/4 **PROBLEM 14A1 COMPLETION OF A WORK SHEET SHOWING A NET INCOME**   The trial balance for the Seaside Kite Shop, a business owned by Joyce Kennington, is shown on page 488. Year-end adjustment information is provided on page 489.

Seaside Kite Shop
Trial Balance
December 31, 19--

ACCOUNT TITLE	DEBIT BALANCE	CREDIT BALANCE
Cash	20 0 0 0 00	
Accounts Receivable	14 0 0 0 00	
Merchandise Inventory	25 0 0 0 00	
Supplies	8 0 0 0 00	
Prepaid Insurance	5 4 0 0 00	
Land	30 0 0 0 00	
Building	50 0 0 0 00	
Accumulated Depreciation—Building		20 0 0 0 00
Store Equipment	35 0 0 0 00	
Accumulated Depreciation—Store Equipment		14 0 0 0 00
Accounts Payable		9 6 0 0 00
Sales Tax Payable		5 9 0 0 00
Wages Payable		
Unearned Rent Revenue		8 9 0 0 00
Mortgage Payable		45 0 0 0 00
Joyce Kennington, Capital		65 4 1 0 00
Joyce Kennington, Drawing	26 0 0 0 00	
Income Summary		
Sales		118 0 0 0 00
Sales Returns and Allowances	1 7 0 0 00	
Rent Revenue		
Purchases	27 0 0 0 00	
Purchases Returns and Allowances		1 4 0 0 00
Purchases Discounts		1 8 0 0 00
Freight-In	2 1 0 0 00	
Wages Expense	32 0 0 0 00	
Supplies Expense		
Telephone Expense	1 3 5 0 00	
Depreciation Expense—Building		
Depreciation Expense—Store Equipment		
Insurance Expense		
Utilities Expense	8 0 0 0 00	
Advertising Expense	3 6 0 0 00	
Miscellaneous Expense	8 6 0 00	
	290 0 1 0 00	290 0 1 0 00

(a, b) Merchandise inventory costing $30,000 is on hand as of December 31, 19--.
(c) Supplies remaining at the end of the year, $2,700.
(d) Unexpired insurance on December 31, $2,900.
(e) Depreciation expense on the building for 19--, $5,000.
(f) Depreciation expense on the store equipment for 19--, $3,200.
(g) Unearned rent revenue as of December 31, $2,200.
(h) Wages earned but not paid as of December 31, $900.

REQUIRED
1. Complete the Adjustments columns, identifying each adjustment with its corresponding letter.
2. Complete the work sheet.
3. Enter the adjustments in a general journal.

1/2/3/4   **PROBLEM 14A2 COMPLETION OF A WORK SHEET SHOWING A NET LOSS**   The trial balance for Cascade Bicycle Shop, a business owned by David Lamond, is shown on page 490. Year-end adjustment information is provided below.

(a, b) Merchandise inventory costing $22,000 is on hand as of December 31, 19--.
(c) Supplies remaining at the end of the year, $2,400.
(d) Unexpired insurance on December 31, $1,750.
(e) Depreciation expense on the building for 19--, $4,000.
(f) Depreciation expense on the store equipment for 19--, $3,600.
(g) Unearned storage revenue as of December 31, $1,950.
(h) Wages earned but not paid as of December 31, $750.

REQUIRED
1. Complete the Adjustments columns, identifying each adjustment with its corresponding letter.
2. Complete the work sheet.
3. Enter the adjustments in the general journal.

1/2/4   **PROBLEM 14A3 WORKING BACKWARD FROM ADJUSTED TRIAL BALANCE TO DETERMINE ADJUSTING ENTRIES**   The partial work sheet shown on page 491 is taken from the books of Stark Street Computers, a business owned by Logan Cowart, for the year ended December 31, 19--.

REQUIRED
1. Determine the adjusting entries by analyzing the difference between the adjusted trial balance and the trial balance.
2. Journalize the adjusting entries in a general journal.

Cascade Bicycle Shop
Trial Balance
December 31, 19--

ACCOUNT TITLE	DEBIT BALANCE	CREDIT BALANCE
Cash	23 0 0 0 00	
Accounts Receivable	15 0 0 0 00	
Merchandise Inventory	31 0 0 0 00	
Supplies	7 2 0 0 00	
Prepaid Insurance	4 6 0 0 00	
Land	28 0 0 0 00	
Building	53 0 0 0 00	
Accumulated Depreciation—Building		17 0 0 0 00
Store Equipment	27 0 0 0 00	
Accumulated Depreciation—Store Equipment		9 0 0 0 00
Accounts Payable		3 8 0 0 00
Sales Tax Payable		3 0 5 0 00
Wages Payable		
Unearned Storage Revenue		5 6 0 0 00
Mortgage Payable		42 0 0 0 00
David Lamond, Capital		165 7 6 0 00
David Lamond, Drawing	33 0 0 0 00	
Income Summary		
Sales		51 0 0 0 00
Sales Returns and Allowances	2 4 0 0 00	
Storage Revenue		
Purchases	21 0 0 0 00	
Purchases Returns and Allowances		1 3 0 0 00
Purchases Discounts		1 9 0 0 00
Freight-In	1 8 0 0 00	
Wages Expense	35 0 0 0 00	
Supplies Expense		
Telephone Expense	2 2 0 0 00	
Depreciation Expense—Building		
Depreciation Expense—Store Equipment		
Insurance Expense		
Utilities Expense	9 6 0 0 00	
Advertising Expense	5 7 0 0 00	
Miscellaneous Expense	9 1 0 00	
	300 4 1 0 00	300 4 1 0 00

Stark Street Computers
Work Sheet (Partial)
For Year Ended December 31, 19--

	ACCOUNT TITLE	TRIAL BALANCE		ADJUSTMENTS		ADJUSTED TRIAL BALANCE		
		DEBIT	CREDIT	DEBIT	CREDIT	DEBIT	CREDIT	
1	Cash	18 0 0 0 00				18 0 0 0 00		1
2	Accounts Receivable	11 0 0 0 00				11 0 0 0 00		2
3	Merchandise Inventory	25 0 0 0 00				35 0 0 0 00		3
4	Supplies	8 0 0 0 00				2 8 2 0 00		4
5	Prepaid Insurance	5 4 0 0 00				1 2 2 5 00		5
6	Land	27 0 0 0 00				27 0 0 0 00		6
7	Building	48 0 0 0 00				48 0 0 0 00		7
8	Accum. Deprec.—Building		20 0 0 0 00				27 0 0 0 00	8
9	Store Equipment	33 0 0 0 00				33 0 0 0 00		9
10	Accum. Deprec.—Store Equip.		8 7 0 0 00				12 8 0 0 00	10
11	Accounts Payable		6 4 0 0 00				6 4 0 0 00	11
12	Sales Tax Payable		5 7 0 0 00				5 7 0 0 00	12
13	Wages Payable						1 3 0 0 00	13
14	Unearned Repair Revenue		8 2 0 0 00				1 8 0 0 00	14
15	Mortgage Payable		44 0 0 0 00				44 0 0 0 00	15
16	Logan Cowart, Capital		80 0 2 5 00				80 0 2 5 00	16
17	Logan Cowart, Drawing	35 0 0 0 00				35 0 0 0 00		17
18	Income Summary					25 0 0 0 00	35 0 0 0 00	18
19	Sales		122 0 0 0 00				122 0 0 0 00	19
20	Sales Returns & Allow.	2 2 5 0 00				2 2 5 0 00		20
21	Repair Revenue						6 4 0 0 00	21
22	Purchases	29 7 5 0 00				29 7 5 0 00		22
23	Purchases Returns & Allow.		1 8 5 0 00				1 8 5 0 00	23
24	Purchases Discounts		1 4 2 5 00				1 4 2 5 00	24
25	Freight-In	3 2 0 0 00				3 2 0 0 00		25
26	Wages Expense	37 0 0 0 00				38 3 0 0 00		26
27	Supplies Expense					5 1 8 0 00		27
28	Telephone Expense	1 6 5 0 00				1 6 5 0 00		28
29	Depr. Expense—Building					7 0 0 0 00		29
30	Depr. Expense—Store Equip.					4 1 0 0 00		30
31	Insurance Expense					4 1 7 5 00		31
32	Utilities Expense	9 1 5 0 00				9 1 5 0 00		32
33	Advertising Expense	4 1 2 5 00				4 1 2 5 00		33
34	Miscellaneous Expense	7 7 5 00				7 7 5 00		34
35		298 3 0 0 00	298 3 0 0 00			345 7 0 0 00	345 7 0 0 00	35
36								36
37								37
38								38
39								39

1/2/3   **PROBLEM 14A4 WORKING BACKWARD FROM THE INCOME STATEMENT AND BALANCE SHEET COLUMNS OF THE WORK SHEET TO DETERMINE ADJUSTED TRIAL BALANCE AND ADJUSTING ENTRIES**   The partially completed work sheet from the books of Lewis Music Store, a business owned by Hugo Lewis, for the year ended December 31, 19--, is shown on page 493.

REQUIRED

1. Analyze the work sheet and determine the adjusted trial balance and the adjusting entries by working backward from the Income Statement and Balance Sheet columns.
2. Journalize the adjusting entries in a general journal.
3. Prepare the cost of goods sold section of the income statement for Lewis Music Store.

SERIES B EXERCISES

1   **EXERCISE 14B1 ADJUSTMENT FOR MERCHANDISE INVENTORY USING T ACCOUNTS**   Sandra Owens owns a business called Sandra's Sporting Goods. Her beginning inventory as of January 1, 19--, was $33,000 and her ending inventory as of December 31, 19--, was $36,000. Set up T accounts for Merchandise Inventory and Income Summary and perform the year-end adjustment for merchandise inventory.

1   **EXERCISE 14B2 CALCULATION OF COST OF GOODS SOLD**   Prepare the cost of goods sold section for Havens Gift Shop. The following amounts are known:

Beginning merchandise inventory	$29,000
Ending merchandise inventory	27,000
Purchases	62,000
Purchases returns and allowances	2,800
Purchases discounts	3,400
Freight-in	300

2   **EXERCISE 14B3 ADJUSTMENT FOR UNEARNED REVENUES USING T ACCOUNTS**   Set up T accounts for Cash, Unearned Ticket Revenue, and Ticket Revenue. Post the following two transactions to the appropriate accounts indicating each transaction by letter.

(a)   Sold 1,200 season tickets at $20 each, receiving cash of $24,000.
(b)   An end-of-period adjustment is needed to recognize that $19,000 in ticket revenue has been earned.

3   **EXERCISE 14B4 WORK SHEET EXTENSIONS FOR MERCHANDISE INVENTORY ADJUSTMENTS**   The partial work sheet on page 494 is taken from Nicole's Gift Shop for the year ended December 31, 19--. The ending merchandise inventory is $37,000.

continued

PR14A4 (cont.)

Lewis Music Store
Work Sheet
For Year Ended December 31, 19--

	ACCOUNT TITLE	TRIAL BALANCE DEBIT	TRIAL BALANCE CREDIT	ADJUSTMENTS DEBIT	ADJUSTMENTS CREDIT	ADJUSTED TRIAL BALANCE DEBIT	ADJUSTED TRIAL BALANCE CREDIT	INCOME STATEMENT DEBIT	INCOME STATEMENT CREDIT	BALANCE SHEET DEBIT	BALANCE SHEET CREDIT	
1	Cash	27 000 00								27 000 00		1
2	Accounts Receivable	13 300 00								13 300 00		2
3	Merchandise Inventory	38 000 00								38 000 00		3
4	Supplies	5 300 00								1 500 00		4
5	Prepaid Insurance	6 100 00								1 785 00		5
6	Land	31 000 00								31 000 00		6
7	Building	52 000 00								52 000 00		7
8	Accum. Deprec.—Building		17 000 00								21 145 00	8
9	Store Equipment	39 000 00								39 000 00		9
10	Accum. Deprec.—Store Equip.		11 900 00								14 875 00	10
11	Accounts Payable		6 250 00								6 250 00	11
12	Sales Tax Payable		6 200 00								6 200 00	12
13	Wages Payable										875 00	13
14	Unearned Rent Revenue		7 400 00								3 175 00	14
15	Mortgage Payable		46 000 00								46 000 00	15
16	Hugo Lewis, Capital		111 620 00								111 620 00	16
17	Hugo Lewis, Drawing	37 000 00								37 000 00		17
18	Income Summary							34 000 00	38 000 00			18
19	Sales		136 000 00						136 000 00			19
20	Sales Returns and Allow.	3 500 00						3 500 00				20
21	Rent Revenue								4 225 00			21
22	Purchases	39 000 00						39 000 00				22
23	Purchases Returns and Allow.		2 530 00						2 530 00			23
24	Purchases Discounts		1 975 00						1 975 00			24
25	Freight-In	2 650 00						2 650 00				25
26	Wages Expense	42 000 00						42 875 00				26
27	Supplies Expense							3 800 00				27
28	Telephone Expense	1 980 00						1 980 00				28
29	Deprec. Expense—Building							4 145 00				29
30	Deprec. Expense—Store Equip.							2 975 00				30
31	Insurance Expense							4 315 00				31
32	Utilities Expense	7 945 00						7 945 00				32
33	Advertising Expense	4 175 00						4 175 00				33
34	Miscellaneous Expense	925 00						925 00				34
35		346 875 00	346 875 00					152 285 00	182 730 00	240 585 00	210 140 00	35
36	Net Income							30 445 00			30 445 00	36
37								182 730 00	182 730 00	240 585 00	240 585 00	37
38												38
39												39

EX14B4 (cont.)

Nicole's Gift Shop
Work Sheet (Partial)
For Year Ended December 31, 19--

	ACCOUNT TITLE	TRIAL BALANCE		ADJUSTMENTS		
		DEBIT	CREDIT	DEBIT	CREDIT	
1	Merchandise Inventory	30 0 0 0 00				1
12	Income Summary					12
13	Purchases	85 0 0 0 00				13
14	Purchases Returns & Allow.		2 2 0 0 00			14
15	Purchases Discounts		2 5 0 0 00			15
16	Freight-In	1 0 0 00				16
17						17
18						18

1. Complete the Adjustments columns for the merchandise inventory.
2. Extend the merchandise inventory to the Adjusted Trial Balance, Income Statement, and Balance Sheet columns.
3. Extend the remaining accounts to the Adjusted Trial Balance and Income Statement columns.
4. Prepare a cost of goods sold section from the partial work sheet.

3 **EXERCISE 14B5 DETERMINING THE BEGINNING AND ENDING INVENTORY FROM A PARTIAL WORK SHEET** From the following partial work sheet, indicate the dollar amount of beginning and ending merchandise inventory.

	ACCOUNT TITLE	TRIAL BALANCE		ADJUSTMENTS		
		DEBIT	CREDIT	DEBIT	CREDIT	
1	Merchandise Inventory			(b) 45 0 0 0 00	(a) 49 0 0 0 00	1
2	Income Summary			(a) 49 0 0 0 00	(b) 45 0 0 0 00	2

	ADJUSTED TRIAL BALANCE		INCOME STATEMENT		BALANCE SHEET		
	DEBIT	CREDIT	DEBIT	CREDIT	DEBIT	CREDIT	
1	45 0 0 0 00				45 0 0 0 00		1
2	49 0 0 0 00	45 0 0 0 00	49 0 0 0 00	45 0 0 0 00			2

5 **EXERCISE 14B6 JOURNALIZE ADJUSTING ENTRIES FOR A MERCHANDISING FIRM** The following partial work sheet is taken from the books of Carmen's Collies, a local pet kennel, for the year ended December 31, 19--. Journalize the adjustments in a general journal.

Carmen's Collies
Work Sheet (Partial)
For Year Ended December 31, 19--

	ACCOUNT TITLE	TRIAL BALANCE		ADJUSTMENTS		
		DEBIT	CREDIT	DEBIT	CREDIT	
1	Merchandise Inventory	35 0 0 0 00		(b) 30 0 0 0 00	(a) 35 0 0 0 00	1
2	Supplies	4 5 0 0 00			(d) 3 1 0 0 00	2
3	Building	50 0 0 0 00				3
4	Accum. Deprec.—Building		23 0 0 0 00		(e) 6 0 0 00	4
5	Wages Payable				(f) 1 3 0 0 00	5
6	Unearned Deposit Fees		7 0 0 0 00	(c) 5 5 0 0 00		6
7	Income Summary			(a) 35 0 0 0 00	(b) 30 0 0 0 00	7
8	Deposit Fees Revenue		24 0 0 0 00		(c) 5 5 0 0 00	8
9	Wages Expense	41 0 0 0 00		(f) 1 3 0 0 00		9
10	Supplies Expense			(d) 3 1 0 0 00		10
11	Deprec. Expense—Building			(e) 6 0 0 00		11
12				80 9 0 0 00	80 9 0 0 00	12
13						13

SERIES B   PROBLEMS

1/2/3/4 **PROBLEM 14B1 COMPLETION OF A WORK SHEET SHOWING A NET INCOME**   A trial balance for the Basket Corner, a business owned by Linda Palermo, is shown on page 496. Year-end adjustment information is provided below.

(a, b)   Merchandise inventory costing $24,000 is on hand as of December 31, 19--.
(c)   Supplies remaining at the end of the year, $2,100.
(d)   Unexpired insurance on December 31, $2,600.
(e)   Depreciation expense on the building for 19--, $5,300.
(f)   Depreciation expense on the store equipment for 19--, $3,800.
(g)   Unearned decorating fees as of December 31, $1,650.
(h)   Wages earned but not paid as of December 31, $750.

REQUIRED
1. Complete the Adjustments columns, identifying each adjustment with its corresponding letter.
2. Complete the work sheet.
3. Enter the adjustments in a general journal.

1/2/3/4 **PROBLEM 14B2 COMPLETION OF A WORK SHEET SHOWING A NET LOSS**   The trial balance for the Oregon Bike Company, a business owned by Craig Moody, is shown on page 497. Year-end adjustment information is provided on page 498.

PR 14B1 (cont.)

Basket Corner
Trial Balance
December 31, 19--

ACCOUNT TITLE	DEBIT BALANCE	CREDIT BALANCE
Cash	25 0 0 0 00	
Accounts Receivable	8 1 0 0 00	
Merchandise Inventory	32 0 0 0 00	
Supplies	7 1 0 0 00	
Prepaid Insurance	3 6 0 0 00	
Land	40 0 0 0 00	
Building	45 0 0 0 00	
Accumulated Depreciation—Building		16 0 0 0 00
Store Equipment	27 0 0 0 00	
Accumulated Depreciation—Store Equipment		5 5 0 0 00
Accounts Payable		3 6 0 0 00
Sales Tax Payable		6 2 0 0 00
Wages Payable		
Unearned Decorating Fees		6 3 0 0 00
Mortgage Payable		36 0 0 0 00
Linda Palermo, Capital		112 0 5 0 00
Linda Palermo, Drawing	31 0 0 0 00	
Income Summary		
Sales		125 0 0 0 00
Sales Returns and Allowances	2 6 0 0 00	
Decorating Fees		
Purchases	38 0 0 0 00	
Purchases Returns and Allowances		2 2 0 0 00
Purchases Discounts		1 7 0 0 00
Freight-In	1 9 0 0 00	
Wages Expense	38 0 0 0 00	
Supplies Expense		
Telephone Expense	1 8 7 0 00	
Depreciation Expense—Building		
Depreciation Expense—Store Equipment		
Insurance Expense		
Utilities Expense	8 4 0 0 00	
Advertising Expense	4 2 0 0 00	
Miscellaneous Expense	7 8 0 00	
	314 5 5 0 00	314 5 5 0 00

PR 14B2 (cont.)

Oregon Bike Company
Trial Balance
December 31, 19--

ACCOUNT TITLE	DEBIT BALANCE	CREDIT BALANCE
Cash	27 0 0 0 00	
Accounts Receivable	12 0 0 0 00	
Merchandise Inventory	39 0 0 0 00	
Supplies	6 2 0 0 00	
Prepaid Insurance	5 8 0 0 00	
Land	32 0 0 0 00	
Building	58 0 0 0 00	
Accumulated Depreciation—Building		27 0 0 0 00
Store Equipment	31 0 0 0 00	
Accumulated Depreciation—Store Equipment		14 0 0 0 00
Accounts Payable		4 9 0 0 00
Sales Tax Payable		2 9 0 0 00
Wages Payable		
Unearned Rent Revenue		6 1 0 0 00
Mortgage Payable		49 0 0 0 00
Craig Moody, Capital		169 5 0 0 00
Craig Moody, Drawing	36 0 0 0 00	
Income Summary		
Sales		58 0 0 0 00
Sales Returns and Allowances	3 3 0 0 00	
Rent Revenue		
Purchases	19 0 0 0 00	
Purchases Returns and Allowances		9 0 0 00
Purchases Discounts		1 4 5 0 00
Freight-In	8 0 0 00	
Wages Expense	47 0 0 0 00	
Supplies Expense		
Telephone Expense	1 8 6 0 00	
Depreciation Expense—Building		
Depreciation Expense—Store Equipment		
Insurance Expense		
Utilities Expense	8 1 0 0 00	
Advertising Expense	6 2 0 0 00	
Miscellaneous Expense	4 9 0 00	
	333 7 5 0 00	333 7 5 0 00

(a, b) Merchandise inventory costing $26,000 is on hand as of December 31, 19--.
(c)   Supplies remaining at the end of the year, $2,500.
(d)   Unexpired insurance on December 31, $1,820.
(e)   Depreciation expense on the building for 19--, $6,400.
(f)   Depreciation expense on the store equipment for 19--, $2,800.
(g)   Unearned rent revenue as of December 31, $2,350.
(h)   Wages earned but not paid as of December 31, $1,100.

REQUIRED

1. Complete the Adjustments columns, identifying each adjustment with its corresponding letter.
2. Complete the work sheet.
3. Enter the adjustments in a general journal.

`1/2/4` **PROBLEM 14B3 WORKING BACKWARD FROM ADJUSTED TRIAL BALANCE TO DETERMINE ADJUSTING ENTRIES**   The partial work sheet shown on page 499 is taken from the books of Burnside Auto Parts, a business owned by Barbara Davis, for the year ended December 31, 19--.

REQUIRED

1. Determine the adjusting entries by analyzing the difference between the adjusted trial balance and the trial balance.
2. Journalize the adjusting entries in a general journal.

`1/2/3` **PROBLEM 14B4 WORKING BACKWARD FROM THE INCOME STATEMENT AND BALANCE SHEET COLUMNS OF THE WORK SHEET TO DETERMINE ADJUSTED TRIAL BALANCE AND ADJUSTING ENTRIES**   The partial work sheet shown on page 500 is taken from the books of Diamond Music Store, a business owned by Ned Diamond, for the year ended December 31, 19--.

REQUIRED

1. Analyze the work sheet and determine the adjusted trial balance and the adjusting entries by working backward from the Income Statement and Balance Sheet columns.
2. Journalize the adjusting entries in a general journal.
3. Prepare the cost of goods sold section of the Income Statement for Diamond Music Store.

PR14B3 (cont.)

Burnside Auto Parts
Work Sheet (Partial)
For Year Ended December 31, 19--

	ACCOUNT TITLE	TRIAL BALANCE		ADJUSTMENTS		ADJUSTED TRIAL BALANCE		
		DEBIT	CREDIT	DEBIT	CREDIT	DEBIT	CREDIT	
1	Cash	21000 00				21000 00		1
2	Accounts Receivable	8300 00				8300 00		2
3	Merchandise Inventory	32000 00				36000 00		3
4	Supplies	6150 00				1865 00		4
5	Prepaid Insurance	5925 00				1835 00		5
6	Land	41750 00				41750 00		6
7	Building	43000 00				43000 00		7
8	Accum. Deprec.—Building		24000 00				27500 00	8
9	Store Equipment	25400 00				25400 00		9
10	Accum. Deprec.—Store Equip.		12400 00				14750 00	10
11	Accounts Payable		8100 00				8100 00	11
12	Sales Tax Payable		5200 00				5200 00	12
13	Wages Payable						980 00	13
14	Unearned Rent-A-Junk Revenue		7950 00				2350 00	14
15	Mortgage Payable		26000 00				26000 00	15
16	Barbara Davis, Capital		109130 00				109130 00	16
17	Barbara Davis, Drawing	40000 00				40000 00		17
18	Income Summary					32000 00	36000 00	18
19	Sales		123500 00				123500 00	19
20	Sales Returns & Allowances	2860 00				2860 00		20
21	Rent-A-Junk Revenue						5600 00	21
22	Purchases	32525 00				32525 00		22
23	Purchases Returns & Allow.		2150 00				2150 00	23
24	Purchases Discounts		2400 00				2400 00	24
25	Freight-In	3175 00				3175 00		25
26	Wages Expense	44175 00				45155 00		26
27	Supplies Expense					4285 00		27
28	Telephone Expense	2200 00				2200 00		28
29	Depr. Expense—Building					3500 00		29
30	Depr. Expense—Store Equip.					2350 00		30
31	Insurance Expense					4090 00		31
32	Utilities Expense	8250 00				8250 00		32
33	Advertising Expense	3275 00				3275 00		33
34	Miscellaneous Expense	845 00				845 00		34
35		320830 00	320830 00			363660 00	363660 00	35
36								36
37								37
38								38

PR14B4 (cont.)

Diamond Music Store
Work Sheet
For Year Ended December 31, 19—

	ACCOUNT TITLE	TRIAL BALANCE DEBIT	TRIAL BALANCE CREDIT	ADJUSTMENTS DEBIT	ADJUSTMENTS CREDIT	ADJUSTED TRIAL BALANCE DEBIT	ADJUSTED TRIAL BALANCE CREDIT	INCOME STATEMENT DEBIT	INCOME STATEMENT CREDIT	BALANCE SHEET DEBIT	BALANCE SHEET CREDIT	
1	Cash	31 000 00								31 000 00		1
2	Accounts Receivable	11 980 00								11 980 00		2
3	Merchandise Inventory	33 600 00							39 100 00	39 100 00		3
4	Supplies	7 140 00								1 965 00		4
5	Prepaid Insurance	5 985 00								1 235 00		5
6	Land	36 200 00								36 200 00		6
7	Building	51 850 00								51 850 00		7
8	Accum. Deprec.—Building		13 590 00								18 875 00	8
9	Store Equipment	32 675 00								32 675 00		9
10	Accum. Deprec.—Store Equip.		10 290 00								14 755 00	10
11	Accounts Payable		5 895 00								5 895 00	11
12	Sales Tax Payable		6 375 00								6 375 00	12
13	Wages Payable										1 250 00	13
14	Unearned Rent Revenue		8 850 00								2 930 00	14
15	Mortgage Payable		42 400 00								42 400 00	15
16	Ned Diamond, Capital		116 350 00								116 350 00	16
17	Ned Diamond, Drawing	39 500 00								39 500 00		17
18	Income Summary							33 600 00	39 100 00			18
19	Sales		148 000 00						148 000 00			19
20	Sales Returns and Allow.	2 800 00						2 800 00				20
21	Rent Revenue								5 920 00			21
22	Purchases	40 700 00						40 700 00				22
23	Purchases Returns and Allow.		2 775 00						2 775 00			23
24	Purchases Discounts		2 325 00						2 325 00			24
25	Freight-In	1 875 00						1 875 00				25
26	Wages Expense	47 000 00						48 250 00				26
27	Supplies Expense							5 175 00				27
28	Telephone Expense	2 250 00						2 250 00				28
29	Deprec. Expense—Building							5 285 00				29
30	Deprec. Expense—Store Equip.							4 465 00				30
31	Insurance Expense							4 750 00				31
32	Utilities Expense	6 825 00						6 825 00				32
33	Advertising Expense	4 695 00						4 695 00				33
34	Miscellaneous Expense	775 00						775 00				34
35		356 850 00	356 850 00					161 445 00	198 120 00	245 505 00	208 830 00	35
36	Net Income							36 675 00			36 675 00	36
37								198 120 00	198 120 00	245 505 00	245 505 00	37
38												38
39												39

MASTERY PROBLEM

John Neff owns and operates the Waikiki Surf Shop. A year-end trial balance is provided below. Year-end adjustment data for the Waikiki Surf Shop is shown on page 502.

Waikiki Surf Shop
Trial Balance
December 31, 19--

ACCOUNT TITLE	DEBIT BALANCE	CREDIT BALANCE
Cash	30 0 0 0 00	
Accounts Receivable	22 5 0 0 00	
Merchandise Inventory	57 0 0 0 00	
Supplies	2 7 0 0 00	
Prepaid Insurance	3 6 0 0 00	
Land	15 0 0 0 00	
Building	135 0 0 0 00	
Accumulated Depreciation—Building		24 0 0 0 00
Store Equipment	75 0 0 0 00	
Accumulated Depreciation—Store Equipment		22 5 0 0 00
Accounts Payable		15 0 0 0 00
Notes Payable		7 5 0 0 00
Wages Payable		
Unearned Boat Rental Revenue		33 0 0 0 00
John Neff, Capital		233 7 0 0 00
John Neff, Drawing	30 0 0 0 00	
Income Summary		
Sales		300 7 5 0 00
Sales Returns and Allowances	1 8 0 0 00	
Boat Rental Revenue		
Purchases	157 5 0 0 00	
Purchases Returns and Allowances		1 2 0 0 00
Purchases Discounts		1 5 0 0 00
Freight-In	4 5 0 00	
Advertising Expense	11 2 5 0 00	
Wages Expense	63 0 0 0 00	
Supplies Expense		
Telephone Expense	5 2 5 0 00	
Depreciation Expense—Building		
Depreciation Expense—Store Equipment		
Utilities Expense	18 0 0 0 00	
Insurance Expense		
Miscellaneous Expense	10 8 7 5 00	
Interest Expense	2 2 5 00	
	639 1 5 0 00	639 1 5 0 00

(a, b) A physical count shows merchandise inventory costing $45,000 on hand as of December 31, 19--.

(c) Supplies remaining at the end of the year, $600.

(d) Unexpired insurance on December 31, $900.

(e) Depreciation expense on the building for 19--, $6,000.

(f) Depreciation expense on the store equipment for 19--, $4,500.

(g) Wages earned but not paid as of December 31, $675.

(h) Unearned boat rental revenue as of December 31, $3,000.

REQUIRED

1. Prepare a year-end work sheet.

2. Journalize the adjusting entries.

Expense Method of Accounting for Prepaid Expenses

Careful study of this appendix should enable you to:

LO1 Use the expense method of accounting for prepaid expenses.

LO2 Make the appropriate adjusting entries when the expense method is used for prepaid expenses.

THE EXPENSE METHOD

LO1 Use the expense method of accounting for prepaid expenses.

Under the **expense method** of accounting for prepaid expenses, supplies and other prepaid items are entered as expenses when purchased. Under this method, we must adjust the accounts at the end of each accounting period to record the unused portions as assets. To illustrate, let's assume that the following entry was made when office supplies were purchased.

4		Office Supplies Expense	4 2 5 00		4
5		Cash		4 2 5 00	5
6		Purchased office supplies			6

ADJUSTING ENTRIES UNDER THE EXPENSE METHOD

LO2 Make the appropriate adjusting entries when the expense method is used for prepaid expenses.

Office Supplies Expense was debited for a total of $425 during the period. An inventory taken at the end of the period shows that supplies on hand amounted to $150. The following adjusting entry is made for supplies on hand:

8		Office Supplies	1 5 0 00		8
9		Office Supplies Expense		1 5 0 00	9
10					10

As shown in the T accounts below, after this entry is posted, the office supplies expense account has a debit balance of $275. This amount is reported on the income statement as an operating expense. The office supplies account has a debit balance of $150. It is reported on the balance sheet as a current asset.

Office Supplies		Office Supplies Expense	
			425
Adj. 150		Adj. 150	
		Bal. 275	

Let's consider another example of the use of the expense method. The following entry was made for the payment of $6,000 for a three-year insurance policy.

11		Insurance Expense		6 0 0 0 00		11
12		Cash			6 0 0 0 00	12
13		Paid insurance premium				13

At the end of the first year, one-third of the premium has expired and two-thirds remains. Thus, $2,000 for insurance expense should be reported on the income statement and $4,000 in prepaid insurance should be reported on the balance sheet. The following adjusting entry is made.

15		Prepaid Insurance		4 0 0 0 00		15
16		Insurance Expense			4 0 0 0 00	16
17						17

As shown in the T accounts below, after this entry is posted, the prepaid insurance account has a debit balance of $4,000. The insurance expense account has a debit balance of $2,000.

Prepaid Insurance		Insurance Expense	
		6,000	
Adj. 4,000		Adj. 4,000	
		Bal. 2,000	

The asset and expense methods of accounting for prepaid expenses give the same final result. In the **asset method,** the prepaid item is first debited to an asset account. At the end of each period, the amount consumed is debited to an expense account. In the **expense method,** the original amount is debited to an expense account. At the end of each accounting period, the portion not consumed is debited to an asset account.

EXERCISES

2 **EX14ApxA1 EXPENSE METHOD OF ACCOUNTING FOR PREPAID EXPENSES**   Davidson's Food Mart paid $1,200 in advance to the local newspaper for advertisements that will appear monthly. The following entry was made.

4		Advertising Expense		1 2 0 0 00			4
5		Cash			1 2 0 0 00		5
6		Paid prepaid advertising					6

At the end of the year, December 31, 19--, Davidson received notification that advertisements costing $800 had been run. Prepare the adjusting entry.

2 **EX14ApxB1 EXPENSE METHOD OF ACCOUNTING FOR PREPAID EXPENSES**   Ryan's Fish House purchased supplies costing $3,000 for cash. This amount was debited to the supplies expense account. At the end of the year, December 31, 19--, an inventory showed that supplies costing $500 remained. Prepare the entry for the purchase and year-end adjustment.

15

Financial Statements and Year-End Accounting for a Merchandising Business

Betty Jenkins has been in charge of payroll at Kreskies' Department Store for many years. In the past, she has always been very careful when making the first payroll entry for the new accounting period. She knows that those first paychecks for the year cover wages earned last year, but not yet paid, as well as wages earned this year. Thus, she has always checked with the chief accountant to get the proper allocation before recording the paychecks for the new year. Toward the end of last year, Isabel Hennis, the chief accountant, retired. Phil Mergo, a recent accounting graduate from the local university replaced Isabel. When Betty asked Phil about the proper allocation for the first payroll period of the new year, he said not to worry about it. "Just make the 'normal' entry by debiting Wages Expense and Crediting Cash," were his instructions. Betty is worried that this is a mistake, but does not want to question the "new kid" and risk embarrassment. Why is Phil not concerned about the proper allocation for the first payroll period?

The first six chapters of this text illustrated the accounting cycle for a service business. Chapter 7 demonstrated accounting procedures for a professional enterprise. In this chapter we complete the accounting cycle for a merchandising business.

In Chapter 14, we prepared the year-end work sheet and adjusting entries for Northern Micro. In this chapter, we will prepare financial statements, closing and reversing entries, and look briefly at financial statement analysis.

THE INCOME STATEMENT

LO1 Prepare a single-step and multiple-step income statement for a merchandising business.

As you know, a primary purpose of the work sheet is to serve as an aid in preparing the financial statements. Figure 15-1 shows the completed work sheet for Northern Micro. We will use it to prepare financial statements.

The purpose of an income statement is to summarize the results of operations during an accounting period. The income statement shows the sources of revenue, types of expenses, and the amount of the net income or net loss for the period. Two forms of the income statement commonly used are the single step and the multiple step. The **single-step income statement** lists all revenue items and their total first, followed by all expense items and their total. The difference, which is either net income or net loss, is then calculated. A single-step income statement for Northern Micro is illustrated in Figure 15-2.

The **multiple-step income statement** is commonly used for merchandising businesses. The term "multiple-step" is used because the final net income is calculated on a step-by-step basis. Gross sales is shown first, less sales returns and allowances and sales discounts. This difference is called **net sales**. (Many published income statements begin with the amount of net sales.) Cost of goods sold is subtracted next to arrive at **gross profit** (sometimes called **gross margin**).

Operating expenses are then listed and subtracted from the gross profit to compute **income from operations** (sometimes called **operating income**). Operating expenses are directly associated with providing the primary goods and services of the business. Some companies divide operating expenses into the following subcategories.

Selling expenses: Expenses directly associated with selling activities. Examples include:

- Sales Salaries Expense
- Sales Commissions Expense
- Delivery Expense
- Advertising Expense
- Bank Credit Card Expense
- Depreciation Expense—Store Equipment and Fixtures

FIGURE 15-1   Work Sheet for Northern Micro

Northern Micro
Work Sheet
For Year Ended December 31, 19--

#	Account Title	Trial Balance Debit	Trial Balance Credit	Adjustments Debit	Adjustments Credit	Adjusted Trial Balance Debit	Adjusted Trial Balance Credit	Income Statement Debit	Income Statement Credit	Balance Sheet Debit	Balance Sheet Credit
1	Cash	20 000 00				20 000 00				20 000 00	
2	Accounts Receivable	15 000 00				15 000 00				15 000 00	
3	Merchandise Inventory	26 000 00		(b) 18 000 00	(a) 26 000 00	18 000 00				18 000 00	
4	Supplies	1 800 00			(c) 1 400 00	400 00				400 00	
5	Prepaid Insurance	2 400 00			(d) 1 800 00	600 00				600 00	
6	Land	10 000 00				10 000 00				10 000 00	
7	Building	90 000 00				90 000 00				90 000 00	
8	Accum. Deprec.—Building		16 000 00		(e) 4 000 00		20 000 00				20 000 00
9	Store Equipment	50 000 00				50 000 00				50 000 00	
10	Accum. Deprec.—Store Equip.		15 000 00		(f) 3 000 00		18 000 00				18 000 00
11	Accounts Payable		10 000 00				10 000 00				10 000 00
12	Notes Payable		5 000 00				5 000 00				5 000 00
13	Wages Payable				(g) 450 00		450 00				450 00
14	Sales Tax Payable		1 500 00				1 500 00				1 500 00
15	Unearned Subscriptions Revenue		12 000 00	(h) 10 000 00			2 000 00				2 000 00
16	Mortgage Payable		30 000 00				30 000 00				30 000 00
17	Gary L. Fishel, Capital		114 400 00				114 400 00				114 400 00
18	Gary L. Fishel, Drawing	20 000 00				20 000 00				20 000 00	
19	Income Summary			(a) 26 000 00	(b) 18 000 00	26 000 00	18 000 00	26 000 00	18 000 00		
20	Sales		214 000 00				214 000 00		214 000 00		
21	Sales Returns and Allowances	1 200 00				1 200 00		1 200 00			
22	Subscriptions Revenue				(h) 10 000 00		10 000 00		10 000 00		
23	Interest Revenue		900 00				900 00		900 00		
24	Rent Revenue		8 000 00				8 000 00		8 000 00		
25	Purchases	105 000 00				105 000 00		105 000 00			
26	Purchases Returns & Allowances		800 00				800 00		800 00		
27	Purchases Discounts		1 000 00				1 000 00		1 000 00		
28	Freight-In	3 000 00				3 000 00		3 000 00			
29	Advertising Expense	2 500 00				2 500 00		2 500 00			
30	Rent Expense	20 000 00				20 000 00		20 000 00			
31	Wages Expense	42 000 00		(g) 450 00		42 450 00		42 450 00			
32	Supplies Expense			(c) 1 400 00		1 400 00		1 400 00			
33	Telephone Expense	3 500 00				3 500 00		3 500 00			
34	Deprec. Expense—Building			(e) 4 000 00		4 000 00		4 000 00			
35	Deprec. Expense—Store Equip.			(f) 3 000 00		3 000 00		3 000 00			
36	Bank Credit Card Expense	1 500 00				1 500 00		1 500 00			
37	Utilities Expense	12 000 00				12 000 00		12 000 00			
38	Insurance Expense			(d) 1 800 00		1 800 00		1 800 00			
39	Miscellaneous Expense	2 250 00				2 250 00		2 250 00			
40	Interest Expense	3 150 00				3 150 00		3 150 00			
41		428 600 00	428 600 00	64 650 00	64 650 00	454 050 00	454 050 00	230 050 00	252 700 00	224 000 00	201 350 00
42	Net Income							22 650 00			22 650 00
43								252 700 00	252 700 00	224 000 00	224 000 00

FIGURE 15-2   Single-Step Income Statement

Northern Micro
Income Statement
For Year Ended December 31, 19--

Revenues:			
Net sales	$212 8 0 0 00		
Subscriptions revenue	10 0 0 0 00		
Interest revenue	9 0 0 00		
Rent revenue	8 0 0 0 00		
Total revenues		$231 7 0 0 00	
Expenses:			
Cost of goods sold	$111 5 0 0 00		
Advertising expense	2 5 0 0 00		
Rent expense	20 0 0 0 00		
Wages expense	42 4 5 0 00		
Supplies expense	1 4 0 0 00		
Telephone expense	3 5 0 0 00		
Depreciation expense—building	4 0 0 0 00		
Depreciation expense—store equipment	3 0 0 0 00		
Bank credit card expense	1 5 0 0 00		
Utilities expense	12 0 0 0 00		
Insurance expense	1 8 0 0 00		
Miscellaneous expense	2 2 5 0 00		
Interest expense	3 1 5 0 00		
Total expenses		209 0 5 0 00	
Net income		$ 22 6 5 0 00	

General expenses: Expenses associated with administrative, office, or general operating activities. Examples include:

- Office Salaries Expense
- Office Supplies Expense
- Rent Expense
- Telephone Expense
- Depreciation Expense—Office Equipment
- Insurance Expense
- Utilities Expense

Finally, other revenues are added and other expenses are subtracted to arrive at net income (or net loss). A multiple-step income statement for Northern Micro is shown in Figure 15-3. Note that the operating expenses are arranged according to the order given in the chart of accounts. They could also be listed by descending amount, with Miscellaneous Expense last.

FIGURE 15-3   Multiple-Step Income Statement

Northern Micro
Income Statement
For Year Ended December 31, 19--

Revenue from sales:							
Sales					$214 0 0 0 00		
Less: Sales returns and allowances					1 2 0 0 00		
Net sales						$212 8 0 0 00	
Cost of goods sold:							
Merchandise inventory, January 1, 19--					$ 26 0 0 0 00		
Purchases			$105 0 0 0 00				
Less: Purchases returns and allowances	$ 8 0 0 00						
Purchases discounts	1 0 0 0 00		1 8 0 0 00				
Net purchases			$103 2 0 0 00				
Add: Freight-in			3 0 0 00				
Cost of goods purchased					103 5 0 0 00		
Goods available for sale					$129 5 0 0 00		
Less: Merchandise inventory, December 31, 19--					18 0 0 0 00		
Cost of goods sold						111 5 0 0 00	
Gross profit						$101 3 0 0 00	
Operating expenses:							
Advertising expense					$ 2 5 0 0 00		
Rent expense					20 0 0 0 00		
Wages expense					42 4 5 0 00		
Supplies expense					1 4 0 0 00		
Telephone expense					3 5 0 0 00		
Depreciation expense—building					4 0 0 0 00		
Depreciation expense—store equipment					3 0 0 0 00		
Bank credit card expense					1 5 0 0 00		
Utilities expense					12 0 0 0 00		
Insurance expense					1 8 0 0 00		
Miscellaneous expense					2 2 5 0 00		
Total operating expenses						94 4 0 0 00	
Income from operations						$ 6 9 0 0 00	
Other revenues:							
Subscriptions revenue					$ 10 0 0 0 00		
Interest revenue					9 0 0 00		
Rent revenue					8 0 0 0 00		
Total other revenues					$ 18 9 0 0 00		
Other expenses:							
Interest expense					3 1 5 0 00	15 7 5 0 00	
Net income						$ 22 6 5 0 00	

THE STATEMENT OF OWNER'S EQUITY

LO2 Prepare a statement of owner's equity.

The statement of owner's equity summarizes all changes in the owner's equity during the period. It includes the net income or loss and any additional investments or withdrawals by the owner. These changes result in the end-of-period balance shown on this statement and the balance sheet.

To prepare the statement of owner's equity for Northern Micro, two sources of information are needed: (1) the work sheet, and (2) Gary Fishel's capital account (no. 311) in the general ledger. The work sheet (Figure 15-1) shows net income of $22,650 and withdrawals of $20,000 during the year. Fishel's capital account (Figure 15-4) shows a beginning balance of $104,400. An additional $10,000 was invested in the business in February of the current year. The statement of owner's equity for Northern Micro for the year ended December 31, 19--, is shown in Figure 15-5.

FIGURE 15-4   Capital Account for Gary L. Fishel

ACCOUNT: Gary L. Fishel, Capital						ACCOUNT NO. 311	
DATE	ITEM	POST. REF.	DEBIT	CREDIT	BALANCE DEBIT	BALANCE CREDIT	
19-- Jan. 1	Balance	✓				104 4 0 0 00	
Feb. 12		CR7		10 0 0 0 00		114 4 0 0 00	

FIGURE 15-5   Statement of Owner's Equity

Northern Micro
Statement of Owner's Equity
For Year Ended December 31, 19--

Gary L. Fishel, capital, January 1, 19--		$104 4 0 0 00
Add: Additional investments		10 0 0 0 00
Total investment		$114 4 0 0 00
Net income for the year	$22 6 5 0 00	
Less withdrawals for the year	20 0 0 0 00	
Increase in capital		2 6 5 0 00
Gary L. Fishel, capital, December 31, 19--		$117 0 5 0 00

THE BALANCE SHEET

LO3 Prepare a classified balance sheet.

 Note the use of the ending balance for merchandise inventory. It is reported on the income statement as part of the calculation of cost of goods sold. It also is reported on the balance sheet as a current asset.

The report form of a classified balance sheet is illustrated in Figure 15-6. The balance sheet classifications used by Northern Micro are explained below.

Current Assets

Current assets include cash and all other assets expected to be converted into cash or consumed within one year or the normal operating cycle of the business, whichever is longer. The **operating cycle** is the length of time generally required for a firm to buy inventory, sell it, and collect the cash. This time period is generally less than a year. Thus, most firms use one year for classifying current assets. In a merchandising business, the current assets usually include cash, receivables (such as accounts receivable and notes receivable), and merchandise inventory. Since prepaid expenses, such as unused supplies and unexpired insurance, are likely to be consumed within a year, they also are reported as current assets.

Current assets are listed on the balance sheet from the most liquid to least liquid. **Liquidity** refers to the speed with which the asset can be converted to cash. Cash is the most liquid asset and is always listed first. It is often followed by Notes Receivable, Accounts Receivable, and Merchandise Inventory.

Property, Plant, and Equipment

Assets that are expected to be used for more than one year in the operation of a business are called **property, plant, and equipment**. Examples include land, buildings, office equipment, store equipment, and delivery equipment. Of these assets, only land is permanent; however, all of these assets have useful lives that are comparatively long. Typically, assets with longer useful lives are listed first.

The balance sheet of Northern Micro shows land, building, and store equipment. The accumulated depreciation amounts are shown as deductions from the costs of the building and store equipment. The difference represents the **undepreciated cost**, or **book value**, of the assets. This amount less any salvage value will be written off as depreciation expense in future periods.

Current Liabilities

Current liabilities include those obligations that are due within one year or the normal operating cycle of the business, whichever is longer, and will require the use of current assets. As of December 31, the current liabilities of Northern Micro consist of Notes Payable, Accounts Payable, Wages Payable, Sales Tax Payable, Unearned Subscriptions Revenue, and the portion of Mortgage Payable that is due within the next year.

Long-Term Liabilities

Long-term liabilities include those obligations that will extend beyond one year or the normal operating cycle, whichever is longer. A common long-term liability is a mortgage payable.

FIGURE 15-6   Balance Sheet for Northern Micro

Northern Micro
Balance Sheet
December 31, 19--

Assets					
Current assets:					
Cash			$20 0 0 0 00		
Accounts receivable			15 0 0 0 00		
Merchandise inventory			18 0 0 0 00		
Supplies			4 0 0 00		
Prepaid insurance			6 0 0 00		
Total current assets				$ 54 0 0 0 00	
Property, plant, and equipment:					
Land			$10 0 0 0 00		
Building	$90 0 0 0 00				
Less accumulated depreciation	20 0 0 0 00		70 0 0 0 00		
Store equipment	$50 0 0 0 00				
Less accumulated depreciation	18 0 0 0 00		32 0 0 0 00		
Total property, plant, and equipment				112 0 0 0 00	
Total assets				$166 0 0 0 00	
Liabilities					
Current liabilities:					
Accounts payable	$10 0 0 0 00				
Notes payable	5 0 0 0 00				
Wages payable	4 5 0 00				
Mortgage payable (current portion)	5 0 0 00				
Sales tax payable	1 5 0 0 00				
Unearned subscriptions revenue	2 0 0 0 00				
Total current liabilities			$19 4 5 0 00		
Long-term liabilities:					
Mortgage payable	$30 0 0 0 00				
Less: Current portion	5 0 0 00		29 5 0 0 00		
Total liabilities				$ 48 9 5 0 00	
Owner's Equity					
Gary L. Fishel, capital				117 0 5 0 00	
Total liabilities and owner's equity				$166 0 0 0 00	

A **mortgage** is a written agreement specifying that if the borrower does not repay a debt, the lender has the right to take over specific property to satisfy the debt. When the debt is paid, the mortgage becomes void. **Mortgage Payable** is an account that is used to reflect an obligation that is secured by a mortgage on certain property.

Owner's Equity

The permanent owner's equity accounts reported on the balance sheet are determined by the type of organization. The accounts for a sole proprietorship, a partnership, and a corporation differ. Northern Micro is a sole proprietorship and reports one owner's equity account, Gary L. Fishel, Capital. The balance of this account is taken from the statement of owner's equity. Partnerships are illustrated in Chapter 20 and corporations are discussed in Chapters 21 and 22.

FINANCIAL STATEMENT ANALYSIS

LO4 Compute standard financial ratios.

Both management and creditors are interested in using the financial statements to evaluate the financial condition and profitability of the firm. This can be done by making a few simple calculations.

Balance Sheet Analysis

Recall the following:

1. Current assets include cash, items that will be converted to cash, and items that will be used up within one year.
2. Current liabilities are obligations that will require the use of current assets.

Thus, the difference between current assets and current liabilities represents the amount of capital the firm has available for current operations. This is called **working capital**.

Working Capital = Current Assets − Current Liabilities

The balance sheet in Figure 15-6 shows that Northern Micro has current assets of $54,000 and current liabilities of $19,450. Thus, the working capital at year end is $34,550 ($54,000 − $19,450). This amount should be more than adequate to satisfy current operating requirements.

Two measures of the firm's ability to pay its current liabilities are the **current ratio** and **quick ratio**. The formulas for calculating these ratios are as follows.

Northern Micro

$$\text{Current Ratio} = \frac{\text{Current Assets}}{\text{Current Liabilities}} \quad \frac{\$54,000}{\$19,450} = 2.8 \text{ to } 1$$

$$\text{Quick Ratio} = \frac{\text{Quick Assets}}{\text{Current Liabilities}} \quad \frac{\$35,000}{\$19,450} = 1.8 \text{ to } 1$$

Northern Micro's current ratio of 2.8 to 1 is quite high, which indicates a favorable financial position. The traditional "rule of thumb" has been that a current ratio should be about 2 to 1, but many businesses operate successfully on a current ratio of 1.5 to 1. Although a rule of thumb is helpful, it is better to compare an individual company to industry averages, which are available in most public libraries.

> **LEARNING KEY**   Ratio analysis is most informative when the ratios are compared with past performance and with those of similar businesses.

Quick assets include cash and all other current assets that can be converted into cash quickly, such as accounts receivable and temporary investments. Temporary investments are discussed in more advanced textbooks. The balance sheet in Figure 15-6 shows total quick assets of $35,000 ($20,000 in cash + $15,000 in accounts receivable). This produces a quick ratio of 1.8 to 1. Quick assets appear to be more than adequate to meet current obligations. The traditional rule of thumb has been that a quick ratio should be about 1 to 1, but many businesses operate successfully on a quick ratio of 0.6 to 1.

Interstatement Analysis

Interstatement analysis provides a comparison of the relationships between selected income statement and balance sheet amounts. A good example of interstatement analysis is the ratio of net income to owner's equity in the business. This ratio is known as **return on owner's equity.**

$$\text{Return on Owner's Equity} = \frac{\text{Net Income}}{\text{Average Owner's Equity}} = \frac{\$22,650}{(\$104,400 + \$117,050) \div 2}$$

$$= \frac{\$22,650}{\$110,725}$$

$$= 20.5\%$$

Northern Micro

The statement of owner's equity in Figure 15-5 shows that the owner's equity of Northern Micro was $104,400 on January 1 and $117,050 on December 31. The net income for the year of $22,650 is 20.5% of the average owner's equity. A comparison of this ratio with the return on owner's equity in prior years should be of interest to the owner. It may also be of interest to compare the return on owner's equity of Northern Micro with the same ratio for other stores of comparable nature and size.

A second ratio involving both income statement and balance sheet accounts is the rate of **accounts receivable turnover.** This is the number of times the accounts receivable "turned over," or were collected, during the accounting period. This ratio is calculated as follows:

$$\text{Accounts Receivable Turnover} = \frac{\text{Net Credit Sales for the Period}}{\text{Average Accounts Receivable}}$$

The accounts receivable turnover for Northern Micro for the year ended December 31 is computed as follows.

Net *credit* sales for the year (determined from the
accounting records) $110,000
Accounts receivable balance, January 1, 19--
(taken from last year's balance sheet)   10,000
Accounts receivable balance, December 31, 19--   15,000

			Northern Micro
Average Accounts Receivable	$=$	$\dfrac{\text{Beginning Balance} + \text{Ending Balance}}{2}$	$\dfrac{\$10,000 + \$15,000}{2}$
			$= \$12,500$
Accounts Receivable Turnover	$=$	$\dfrac{\text{Net Credit Sales for the Period}}{\text{Average Accounts Receivable}}$	$\dfrac{\$110,000}{\$12,500}$
			$= 8.8$

The number of days in the year is divided by this rate of turnover to
determine the number of days credit customers take to pay for their purchases. Northern Micro's customers are taking about 42 days.

$$365 \text{ days} \div 8.8 = 41.5 \text{ days}$$

If Northern Micro allows credit terms of n/45, this means that customers
generally are paying on a timely basis.

A third ratio involving both income statement and balance sheet
accounts is the rate of **inventory turnover**. This is the number of times the
merchandise inventory turned over, or was sold, during the accounting period. This ratio is calculated as follows:

$$\text{Inventory Turnover} = \dfrac{\text{Cost of Goods Sold for the Period}}{\text{Average Inventory}}$$

If inventory is taken only at the end of each accounting period, the
average inventory for the period can be calculated by adding the beginning
and ending inventories and dividing their sum by two. Northern Micro's
turnover for the year ended December 31 is computed as follows:

Cost of goods sold for the period $111,500
Beginning inventory   26,000
Ending inventory   18,000

			Northern Micro
Average Inventory	$=$	$\dfrac{\text{Beginning Inventory} + \text{Ending Inventory}}{2}$	$\dfrac{\$26,000 + \$18,000}{2}$
			$= \$22,000$
Inventory Turnover	$=$	$\dfrac{\text{Cost of Goods Sold for the Period}}{\text{Average Inventory}}$	$\dfrac{\$111,500}{\$22,000}$
			$= 5.1$

The number of days in the year divided by the inventory turnover shows
that Northern Micro's inventory turned over about once every two months.

$$365 \text{ days} \div 5.1 = 71.6 \text{ days}$$

The higher the rate of inventory turnover, the smaller the profit required on each dollar of sales to produce a satisfactory total dollar amount of gross profit. This is because the increase in numbers of units sold offsets the smaller amount of gross profit earned per unit. Evaluation of Northern Micro's rate of inventory turnover would require comparison with prior years, other companies, or its industry.

CLOSING ENTRIES

LO5 Prepare closing entries for a merchandising business.

Closing entries for a service business were illustrated in Chapter 6. The process is essentially the same for a merchandising business. All revenues and expenses reported on the income statement must be closed to Income Summary. Then, the income summary and drawing accounts are closed to the owner's capital account. Keep in mind, however, that a few new accounts were needed for a merchandising business. These include Sales Returns and Allowances, Sales Discounts, Purchases Returns and Allowances, and Purchases Discounts. Since these are temporary accounts reported on the income statement, they also must be closed. The easiest way to accomplish this, as illustrated in Figure 15-7, is by using the work sheet to prepare the closing entries in four basic steps.

THE CLOSING PROCESS FOR A MERCHANDISING BUSINESS

Step 1	All income statement accounts with credit balances are debited, with an offsetting credit to Income Summary.
Step 2	All income statement accounts with debit balances are credited, with an offsetting debit to Income Summary.
Step 3	The resulting balance in Income Summary, which is the net income or loss for the period, is transferred to the owner's capital account.

ACCOUNT: **Income Summary**   ACCOUNT NO. **331**

DATE	ITEM	POST. REF.	DEBIT	CREDIT	BALANCE DEBIT	BALANCE CREDIT	
Dec. 31	Adjusting	J4	26 0 0 0 00		26 0 0 0 00		← Remove Beg. Inventory
31	Adjusting	J4		18 0 0 0 00	8 0 0 0 00		← Enter End. Inventory
31	Closing	J4		234 7 0 0 00		226 7 0 0 00	← Closing Step 1
31	Closing	J4	204 0 5 0 00			22 6 5 0 00	← Closing Step 2
31	Closing	J4	22 6 5 0 00				← Closing Step 3

| Step 4 | The balance in the owner's drawing account is transferred to the owner's capital account. |

FIGURE 15-7   Closing Entries for a Merchandising Business

Northern Micro
Work Sheet (Partial)
December 31, 19--

	ACCOUNT TITLE	INCOME STATEMENT DEBIT	INCOME STATEMENT CREDIT	BALANCE SHEET DEBIT	BALANCE SHEET CREDIT
17	Gary L. Fishel, Capital				114400 00
18	Gary L. Fishel, Drawing			2000 00	
19	Income Summary	26000 00	18000 00		
20	Sales		214000 00		
21	Sales Returns and Allow.	1200 00			
22	Subscriptions Revenue		10000 00		
23	Interest Revenue		900 00		
24	Rent Revenue		8000 00		
25	Purchases	105000 00			
26	Purchases Returns and Allow.		800 00		
27	Purchases Discounts		1000 00		
28	Freight-In	300 00			
29	Advertising Expense	2500 00			
30	Rent Expense	20000 00			
31	Wages Expense	4245 00			
32	Supplies Expense	1400 00			
33	Telephone Expense	3500 00			
34	Deprec. Exp.—Building	4000 00			
35	Deprec. Exp.—Store Equipment	3000 00			
36	Bank Credit Card Expense	1500 00			
37	Utilities Expense	12000 00			
38	Insurance Expense	1800 00			
39	Miscellaneous Expense	2250 00			
40	Interest Expense	3150 00			
41		230050 00	252700 00	224000 00	201350 00
42	Net Income	22650 00			22650 00
43		252700 00	252700 00	224000 00	224000 00

GENERAL JOURNAL PAGE 6

	DATE	DESCRIPTION	POST. REF.	DEBIT	CREDIT
1		Closing Entries			
2	19-- Dec. 31	Sales		214000 00	
3		Subscriptions Revenue		10000 00	
4		Interest Revenue		900 00	
5		Rent Revenue		8000 00	
6		Purchases Returns and Allowances		800 00	
7		Purchases Discounts		1000 00	
8		Income Summary			234700 00
9					
10	31	Income Summary		204050 00	
11		Sales Returns and Allowances			1200 00
12		Purchases			105000 00
13		Freight-In			300 00
14		Advertising Expense			2500 00
15		Rent Expense			20000 00
16		Wages Expense			4245 00
17		Supplies Expense			1400 00
18		Telephone Expense			3500 00
19		Depreciation Exp.—Building			4000 00
20		Depreciation Exp.—Store Equip.			3000 00
21		Bank Credit Card Expense			1500 00
22		Utilities Expense			12000 00
23		Insurance Expense			1800 00
24		Miscellaneous Expense			2250 00
25		Interest Expense			3150 00
26					
27	31	Income Summary		22650 00	
28		Gary L. Fishel, Capital			22650 00
29					
30	31	Gary L. Fishel, Capital		2000 00	
31		Gary L. Fishel, Drawing			2000 00
32					

Post-Closing Trial Balance

A trial balance of the general ledger accounts taken after the temporary owner's equity accounts have been closed is called a **post-closing trial balance**. The purpose of the post-closing trial balance is to prove that the general ledger is in balance at the beginning of a new accounting period, before any transactions for the new accounting period are entered. Figure 15-8 shows a post-closing trial balance for Northern Micro.

FIGURE 15-8   Post-Closing Trial Balance

Northern Micro
Post-Closing Trial Balance
December 31, 19--

ACCOUNT TITLE	ACCOUNT NO.	DEBIT BALANCE	CREDIT BALANCE
Cash	111	20 0 0 0 00	
Accounts Receivable	131	15 0 0 0 00	
Merchandise Inventory	141	18 0 0 0 00	
Supplies	151	4 0 0 00	
Prepaid Insurance	155	6 0 0 00	
Land	161	10 0 0 0 00	
Building	171	90 0 0 0 00	
Accumulated Depreciation—Building	171.1		20 0 0 0 00
Store Equipment	181	50 0 0 0 00	
Accumulated Depreciation—Store Equipment	181.1		18 0 0 0 00
Accounts Payable	216		10 0 0 0 00
Notes Payable	218		5 0 0 0 00
Wages Payable	219		4 5 0 00
Sales Tax Payable	225		1 5 0 0 00
Unearned Subscriptions Revenue	230		2 0 0 0 00
Mortgage Payable	262		30 0 0 0 00
Gary L. Fishel, Capital	311		117 0 5 0 00
		204 0 0 0 00	204 0 0 0 00

REVERSING ENTRIES

LO6 Prepare reversing entries.

Numerous adjusting entries are needed at the end of the accounting period to bring the account balances up to date for presentation in the financial statements. Although not required, some of these adjusting entries should be reversed at the beginning of the next accounting period. This is done to simplify the recording of transactions in the new accounting period. As its name implies, a **reversing entry** is the reverse or opposite of the adjusting entry.

ADJUSTING ENTRY

4	Dec.	31	Wages Expense		4 5 0 00				4
5			Wages Payable				4 5 0 00		5

REVERSING ENTRY (OPPOSITE)

7	Jan.	1	Wages Payable		4 5 0 00				7
8			Wages Expense				4 5 0 00		8

To see the advantage of using reversing entries, let's consider the effect of reversing Northern Micro's adjusting entry for wages earned, but not paid at the end of the year. Figure 15-9 shows that accrued wages on December 31 were $450. These wages are for work performed by the employees on the last three days of the accounting period ($150 \times 3 = \$450$). The employees will be paid on Friday, January 2, the normal payday.

Note that the adjusting and closing entries are the same, regardless of whether a reversing entry is made. However, the reversing entry on January 1 has an impact on the entry made when the employees are paid. *Without* a reversing entry, the payment on January 2, 19-2, must be split between reduction of the Wages Payable account for wages earned in 19-1 and Wages Expense for wages earned in 19-2. *With* a reversing entry, the bookkeeper simply debits Wages Expense and credits Cash, as is done on every other payday. Thus, the likelihood of error is reduced. Reversing entries are particularly important in large businesses where the individual recording the entry for wages may not even know what adjusting entries were made.

Not all adjusting entries should be reversed. To determine which adjusting entries to reverse, follow this rule:

Except for the first year of operation, reverse all adjusting entries that increase an asset or liability account from a zero balance.

 LEARNING KEY Reverse all adjusting entries that increase an asset or liability account from a zero balance.

Except for the first year of operation, merchandise inventory, and contra-assets like accumulated depreciation, will have existing balances. Thus, they should never be reversed. The adjusting entries for Northern Micro are shown in Figure 15-10. Note that only the adjustment for accrued wages is reversed in Figure 15-11.

KEY POINTS

1 The general format for a single-step and multiple-step income statement is shown on page 523.

FIGURE 15-9   Adjusting, Closing, and Reversing Entries for Wages

	12/29/-1 MONDAY	12/30/-1 TUESDAY	12/31/-1 WEDNESDAY	1/1/-2 THURSDAY	1/2/-2 FRIDAY
Wages Earned	150	150	150	150	150
Wages Paid	0	0	0	0	750
Total Earned			450		300
Total Paid			0		750
Accrued Wages on 12/31/-1			450		

DATE	WITHOUT REVERSING ENTRY	WITH REVERSING ENTRY

12/31/-1 Adj. Entry	Wages Expense 450
	    Wages Payable 450
		Wages Expense 450
		    Wages Payable 450

12/31/-1 Close. Entry	Income Summary 42,450
	    Wages Expense 42,450
		Income Summary 42,450
		    Wages Expense 42,450

1/1/-2 Rev. Entry	No Entry	Wages Payable 450 Wages Expense 450

1/2/-2 Payment of Payroll	Wages Expense 300
	Wages Payable 450
	    Cash 750
		Wages Expense 750
		    Cash 750

Description	Wages Expense	Description		Description	Wages Expense	Description
Bal.	42,000			Bal.	42,000	
12/31/-1 Adj.	450			12/31/-1 Adj.	450	
		42,450	12/31/-1 Close			42,450	12/31/-1 Close
1/2/-2 Payroll	300				450	1/1/-2 Reversing
				1/2/-2 Payroll	750	
				Bal.	300	

	Wages Payable				Wages Payable	
	450	12/31/-1 Adj.			450	12/31/-1 Adj.
1/2/-2 Payroll	450			1/1/-2 Rev.	450	

	Cash				Cash	
	750	1/2/-2 Payroll			750	1/2/-2 Payroll

FIGURE 15-10 Which Adjusting Entries to Reverse?

	DATE		DESCRIPTION	POST. REF.	DEBIT	CREDIT	
1			**Adjusting Entries**				1
2	19-1 Dec.	31	Income Summary		26 0 0 0 00		2
3			Merchandise Inventory			26 0 0 0 00	3
4							4
5		31	Merchandise Inventory		18 0 0 0 00		5
6			Income Summary			18 0 0 0 00	6
7							7
8		31	Supplies Expense		1 4 0 0 00		8
9			Supplies			1 4 0 0 00	9
10							10
11		31	Insurance Expense		1 8 0 0 00		11
12			Prepaid Insurance			1 8 0 0 00	12
13							13
14		31	Deprec. Exp.—Building		4 0 0 0 00		14
15			Accum. Deprec.—Building			4 0 0 0 00	15
16							16
17		31	Deprec. Exp.—Store Equipment		3 0 0 0 00		17
18			Accum. Deprec.—Store Equip.			3 0 0 0 00	18
19							19
20		31	Wages Expense		4 5 0 00		20
21			Wages Payable			4 5 0 00	21
22							22
23		31	Unearned Subscriptions Revenue		10 0 0 0 00		23
24			Subscriptions Revenue			10 0 0 0 00	24
25							25

GENERAL JOURNAL — PAGE 3

SHOULD THE ADJUSTMENT BE REVERSED?

Never reverse adjustments for merchandise inventory.

Never reverse adjustments for merchandise inventory.

No. No Asset or liability with a zero balance has been increased.

No. No asset or liability with a zero balance has been increased.

Never reverse adjustments for depreciation.

Never reverse adjustments for depreciation.

Yes. A liability account with a zero balance has been increased.

No. No asset or liability with a zero balance has been increased.

FIGURE 15-11 Reversing Entry for Northern Micro

GENERAL JOURNAL — PAGE 3

	DATE		DESCRIPTION	POST. REF.	DEBIT	CREDIT	
1			**Reversing Entries**				1
2	19-2 Jan.	1	Wages Payable		4 5 0 00		2
3			Wages Expense			4 5 0 00	3
4							4
5							5

Single-Step
Income Statement
For Year Ended December 31, 19--

Revenues:		
List all revenues	$xxx	
Total revenues		$xxx
Expenses:		
Cost of goods sold	$xxx	
List all other expenses	xxx	
Total expenses		xxx
Net income		$xxx

Multiple-Step
Income Statement
For Year Ended December 31, 19--

Revenue from sales:			
Sales		$xxx	
Less: Sales returns and allowances		xxx	
Net sales			$xxx
Cost of goods sold			xxx
Gross profit			$xxx
Operating expenses:			
List all operating expenses		$xxx	
Total operating expenses			xxx
Income from operations			$xxx
Other revenue:			
List all other revenue		$xxx	
Total other revenue		$xxx	
Other expenses:			
List all other expenses	$xxx		
Total other expenses		xxx	xxx
Net income			$xxx

2   A statement of owner's equity has the following format.

Business Name
Statement of Owner's Equity
For Year Ended December 31, 19--

Capital, January 1, 19--		$xxx
Add additional investments		xxx
Total investment		$xxx
Net income for the year	$xxx	
Less withdrawals	xxx	
Increase in capital		xxx
Capital, December 31, 19--		$xxx

3 A classified balance sheet has the following major headings.

Business Name
Balance Sheet
December 31, 19--

Assets

Current assets:			
All are listed		$xxx	
Total current assets			$xxx
Property, plant, and equipment:			
All are listed	$xxx		
Less: Accumulated depreciation (if appropriate)	xxx	$xxx	
Total property, plant, and equipment			xxx
Total assets			$xxx

Liabilities

Current liabilities:		
All are listed	$xxx	
Total current liabilities		$xxx
Long-term liabilities:		
All are listed	$xxx	
Total long-term liabilities		xxx
Total liabilities		$xxx

Owner's Equity

Owner's capital	xxx
Total liabilities and owner's equity	$xxx

4 The following measures of financial condition may be computed from financial statement information.

Working Capital = Current Assets – Current Liabilities

Current Ratio = Current Assets ÷ Current Liabilities

Quick Ratio = Quick Assets ÷ Current Liabilities

Return on Owner's Equity = Net Income ÷ Average Owner's Equity

$$\text{Accounts Receivable Turnover} = \frac{\text{Net Credit Sales for the Period}}{\text{Average Accounts Receivable}}$$

$$\text{Inventory Turnover} = \frac{\text{Cost of Goods Sold for the Period}}{\text{Average Inventory}}$$

5   There are four steps in the closing process for a merchandising business.

STEP 1   All income statement accounts with credit balances are debited, with an offsetting credit to Income Summary.

STEP 2   All income statement accounts with debit balances are credited, with an offsetting debit to Income Summary.

STEP 3   The resulting balance in Income Summary, which is the net income or loss for the period, is transferred to the owner's capital account.

STEP 4   The balance in the owner's drawing account is transferred to the owner's capital account.

6   Use the following rule to determine which adjusting entries to reverse:

Except for the first year of operation, reverse all adjusting entries that increase an asset or liability account from a zero balance.

KEY TERMS

accounts receivable turnover 515   The number of times the accounts receivable turned over, or were collected, during the accounting period. When 365 is divided by the turnover, this measure can be expressed in terms of the average number of days required to collect receivables.

book value 512   See undepreciated cost.

current assets 512   Cash and all other assets expected to be converted into cash or consumed within one year or the normal operating cycle of the business, whichever is longer.

current liabilities 512   Those obligations that are due within one year or the normal operating cycle of the business, whichever is longer, and will require the use of current assets.

current ratio 514   Current assets divided by current liabilities.

general expenses 509   Those expenses associated with administrative, office, or general operating activities.

gross margin 507   See gross profit.

gross profit 507   Net sales minus cost of goods sold.

income from operations 507   Gross profit minus operating expenses on a multiple-step income statement.

interstatement analysis 515   Compares the relationship between certain amounts in the income statement and balance sheet.

inventory turnover 516   The number of times the merchandise inventory turned over, or was sold, during the accounting period. When 365 is divided by the turnover, this measure can be expressed in terms of the average number of days required to sell inventory.

liquidity 512   Refers to the speed with which the asset can be converted to cash.

long-term liabilities 512   Those obligations that will extend beyond one year or the normal operating cycle, whichever is longer.

mortgage 513 A written agreement specifying that if the borrower does not repay a debt, the lender has the right to take over the property to satisfy the debt.

Mortgage Payable 513 An account that is used to reflect an obligation that is secured by a mortgage on certain property.

multiple-step income statement 507 This statement shows a step-by-step calculation of net sales, cost of goods sold, gross profit, operating expenses, income from operations, other revenues and expenses, and net income.

net sales 507 Gross sales less sales returns and allowances and discounts.

operating cycle 512 The length of time generally required for a business to buy inventory, sell it, and collect the cash.

operating income 507 See income from operations.

post-closing trial balance 519 A trial balance taken after the temporary owner's equity accounts have been closed.

property, plant, and equipment 512 Assets that are expected to be used for multiple years in the operation of a business.

quick assets 515 Cash and all other current assets that can be converted into cash quickly, such as accounts receivable and temporary investments.

quick ratio 514 Quick assets divided by current liabilities.

return on owner's equity 515 The ratio of net income to average owner's equity.

reversing entry 519 The opposite of the adjusting entry. It is made on the first day of the next accounting period and simplifies the recording of transactions in the new period.

selling expenses 507 Those expenses directly associated with selling activities.

single-step income statement 507 This statement lists all revenue items and their total first, followed by all expense items and their total.

undepreciated cost 512 Cost of plant and equipment less the accumulated depreciation amounts. Also called book value.

working capital 514 The difference between current assets and current liabilities, which represents the amount of capital the business has available for current operations.

REVIEW QUESTIONS

1. Describe the nature of the two forms of an income statement.
2. Name and describe the calculation of two measures that provide an indication of a firm's ability to pay current obligations.
3. Describe how to calculate the following ratios:
   a. return on owner's equity
   b. accounts receivable turnover
   c. inventory turnover
4. Where is the information obtained that is needed in journalizing the closing entries?

5. Explain the function of each of the four closing entries made by Northern Micro.
6. What is the purpose of a post-closing trial balance?
7. What is the primary purpose of reversing entries?
8. What is the customary date for reversing entries?
9. What adjusting entries should be reversed?

MANAGING YOUR WRITING

Go back and review the opening paragraph of the chapter about Betty Jenkins and Phil Mergo. Play the role of Phil (or Phyllis) Mergo and draft a brief memo to Betty explaining the change in accounting treatment.

DEMONSTRATION PROBLEM

Tom McKinney owns and operates McK's Home Electronics. He has a store where he sells and repairs televisions and stereo equipment. A completed work sheet for 19-3 is provided on the next page. McKinney made a $20,000 additional investment during 19-3. The current portion of Mortgage Payable is $1,000. Credit sales for 19-3 were $200,000, and the balance of Accounts Receivable on January 1 was $26,000.

REQUIRED

1. Prepare a multiple-step income statement.
2. Prepare a statement of owner's equity.
3. Prepare a balance sheet.
4. Compute the following measures of performance and financial condition for 19-3:
   a. current ratio
   b. quick ratio
   c. working capital
   d. return on owner's equity
   e. accounts receivable turnover and the average number of days required to collect receivables
   f. inventory turnover and the average number of days required to sell inventory
5. Prepare adjusting entries and indicate which should be reversed and why.
6. Prepare closing entries.
7. Prepare reversing entries for the adjustments where appropriate.

McK's Home Electronics
Work Sheet
For Year Ended December 31, 19-3

#	Account Title	Trial Balance Debit	Trial Balance Credit	Adjustments Debit	Adjustments Credit	Adjusted Trial Balance Debit	Adjusted Trial Balance Credit	Income Statement Debit	Income Statement Credit	Balance Sheet Debit	Balance Sheet Credit
1	Cash	10 000 00				10 000 00				10 000 00	
2	Accounts Receivable	22 500 00				22 500 00				22 500 00	
3	Merchandise Inventory	39 000 00		(b) 45 000 00	(a) 39 000 00	45 000 00				45 000 00	
4	Supplies	2 700 00			(c) 2 100 00	600 00				600 00	
5	Prepaid Insurance	3 600 00			(d) 2 700 00	900 00				900 00	
6	Land	15 000 00				15 000 00				15 000 00	
7	Building	135 000 00				135 000 00				135 000 00	
8	Accum. Deprec.—Building		24 000 00		(e) 6 000 00		30 000 00				30 000 00
9	Store Equipment	75 000 00				75 000 00				75 000 00	
10	Accum. Deprec.—Store Equip.		22 500 00		(f) 4 500 00		27 000 00				27 000 00
11	Accounts Payable		15 000 00				15 000 00				15 000 00
12	Notes Payable		7 500 00				7 500 00				7 500 00
13	Wages Payable				(g) 675 00		675 00				675 00
14	Sales Tax Payable		2 250 00				2 250 00				2 250 00
15	Unearned Repair Fees		18 000 00	(h) 15 000 00			3 000 00				3 000 00
16	Mortgage Payable		45 000 00				45 000 00				45 000 00
17	Tom McKinney, Capital		151 600 00				151 600 00				151 600 00
18	Tom McKinney, Drawing	30 000 00				30 000 00				30 000 00	
19	Income Summary			(a) 39 000 00	(b) 45 000 00	39 000 00	45 000 00	39 000 00	45 000 00		
20	Sales		300 750 00				300 750 00		300 750 00		
21	Sales Returns and Allowances	1 800 00				1 800 00		1 800 00			
22	Repair Fees										
23	Interest Revenue		1 350 00				1 350 00		1 350 00		
24	Purchases	157 500 00				157 500 00		157 500 00			
25	Purchases Returns and Allow.		1 200 00				1 200 00		1 200 00		
26	Purchases Discounts		1 500 00				1 500 00		1 500 00		
27	Freight-In	4 500 00				4 500 00		4 500 00			
28	Advertising Expense	3 750 00				3 750 00		3 750 00			
29	Wages Expense	63 000 00		(g) 675 00		63 675 00		63 675 00			
30	Supplies Expense			(c) 2 100 00		2 100 00		2 100 00			
31	Telephone Expense	5 250 00				5 250 00		5 250 00			
32	Deprec. Expense—Building			(e) 6 000 00		6 000 00		6 000 00			
33	Deprec. Expense—Store Equip.			(f) 4 500 00		4 500 00		4 500 00			
34	Utilities Expense	18 000 00				18 000 00		18 000 00			
35	Insurance Expense			(d) 2 700 00		2 700 00		2 700 00			
36	Miscellaneous Expense	3 375 00				3 375 00		3 375 00			
37	Interest Expense	4 725 00				4 725 00		4 725 00			
38		590 650 00	590 650 00	114 975 00	114 975 00	646 825 00	646 825 00	312 825 00	364 800 00	334 000 00	282 025 00
39	Net Income							51 975 00			51 975 00
40								364 800 00	364 800 00	334 000 00	334 000 00
42											

SOLUTION

1.

McK's Home Electronics
Income Statement
For Year Ended December 31, 19-3

Revenue from sales:				
Sales			$300 7 5 0 00	
Less: Sales returns and allowances			1 8 0 0 00	
Net sales				$298 9 5 0 00
Cost of goods sold:				
Merchandise inventory, January 1, 19-3			$ 39 0 0 0 00	
Purchases		$157 5 0 0 00		
Less: Purchases returns and allowances	$ 1 2 0 0 00			
Purchases discounts	1 5 0 0 00	2 7 0 0 00		
Net purchases		$154 8 0 0 00		
Add: Freight-in		4 5 0 00		
Cost of goods purchased			155 2 5 0 00	
Goods available for sale			$194 2 5 0 00	
Less merchandise inventory, December 31, 19-3			45 0 0 0 00	
Cost of goods sold				149 2 5 0 00
Gross profit				$149 7 0 0 00
Operating expenses:				
Advertising expense			$ 3 7 5 0 00	
Wages expense			63 6 7 5 00	
Supplies expense			2 1 0 0 00	
Telephone expense			5 2 5 0 00	
Depreciation expense—building			6 0 0 0 00	
Depreciation expense—store equipment			4 5 0 0 00	
Utilities expense			18 0 0 0 00	
Insurance expense			2 7 0 0 00	
Miscellaneous expense			3 3 7 5 00	
Total operating expenses				109 3 5 0 00
Income from operations				$ 40 3 5 0 00
Other revenues:				
Repair fees			$ 15 0 0 0 00	
Interest revenue			1 3 5 0 00	
Total other revenues			$ 16 3 5 0 00	
Other expenses:				
Interest expense			4 7 2 5 00	11 6 2 5 00
Net income				$ 51 9 7 5 00

2.

McK's Home Electronics
Statement of Owner's Equity
For Year Ended December 31, 19-3

Tom McKinney, capital, January 1, 19-3			$131 6 0 0 00
Add: Additional investments			20 0 0 0 00
Total investment			$151 6 0 0 00
Net income for the year	$51 9 7 5 00		
Less withdrawals	30 0 0 0 00		
Increase in capital			21 9 7 5 00
Tom McKinney, capital, December 31, 19-3			$173 5 7 5 00

3. See page 531.

4.

a. Current Ratio = Current Assets ÷ Current Liabilities
= $79,000 ÷ $29,425 = 2.68 to 1

b. Quick Ratio = Quick Assets ÷ Current Liabilities
= $32,500 ÷ $29,425 = 1.10 to 1

c. Working Capital = Current Assets − Current Liabilities
= $79,000 − $29,425 = $49,575

d. Return on Owner's Equity = Net Income ÷ Average Owner's Equity

$$= \frac{\$51,975}{(\$131,600 + \$173,575) \div 2}$$

= $51,975 ÷ $152,587.50

= 34%

e. Accounts Receivable Turnover = $\dfrac{\text{Net Credit Sales for the Period}}{\text{Average Accounts Receivable}}$

$$= \frac{\$200,000}{(\$26,000 + \$22,500) \div 2}$$

= $200,000 ÷ $24,250

= 8.25

Average number of days to collect an account receivable:
365 ÷ 8.25 = 44.24 days.

f. Inventory Turnover = $\dfrac{\text{Cost of Goods Sold for the Period}}{\text{Average Inventory}}$

$$= \frac{\$149,250}{(\$39,000 + \$45,000) \div 2}$$

= $149,250 ÷ $42,000

= 3.6

Average number of days to sell inventory:
365 ÷ 3.6 = 101.39 days.

3.

McK's Home Electronics
Balance Sheet
December 31, 19-3

Assets				
Current assets:				
Cash			$ 10 0 0 0 00	
Accounts receivable			22 5 0 0 00	
Merchandise inventory			45 0 0 0 00	
Supplies			6 0 0 00	
Prepaid insurance			9 0 0 00	
Total current assets				$ 79 0 0 0 00
Property, plant, and equipment:				
Land			$ 15 0 0 0 00	
Building	$135 0 0 0 00			
Less accumulated depreciation	30 0 0 0 00		105 0 0 0 00	
Store equipment	$75 0 0 0 00			
Less accumulated depreciation	27 0 0 0 00		48 0 0 0 00	
Total property, plant, and equipment				168 0 0 0 00
Total assets				$247 0 0 0 00
Liabilities				
Current liabilities:				
Accounts payable	$15 0 0 0 00			
Notes payable	7 5 0 0 00			
Wages payable	6 7 5 00			
Mortgage payable (current portion)	1 0 0 0 00			
Sales tax payable	2 2 5 0 00			
Unearned repair fees	3 0 0 0 00			
Total current liabilities			$ 29 4 2 5 00	
Long-term liabilities:				
Mortgage payable	$45 0 0 0 00			
Less current portion	1 0 0 0 00		44 0 0 0 00	
Total liabilities				$ 73 4 2 5 00
Owner's Equity				
Tom McKinney, capital				173 5 7 5 00
Total liabilities and owner's equity				$247 0 0 0 00

5.

GENERAL JOURNAL   PAGE 3

	DATE		DESCRIPTION	POST. REF.	DEBIT	CREDIT	
1			Adjusting Entries				1
2	19-3 Dec.	31	Income Summary		39 0 0 0 00		2
3			Merchandise Inventory			39 0 0 0 00	3
4							4
5		31	Merchandise Inventory		45 0 0 0 00		5
6			Income Summary			45 0 0 0 00	6
7							7
8		31	Supplies Expense		2 1 0 0 00		8
9			Supplies			2 1 0 0 00	9
10							10
11		31	Insurance Expense		2 7 0 0 00		11
12			Prepaid Insurance			2 7 0 0 00	12
13							13
14		31	Deprec. Exp.—Building		6 0 0 0 00		14
15			Accum. Deprec.—Building			6 0 0 0 00	15
16							16
17		31	Deprec. Exp.—Store Equip.		4 5 0 0 00		17
18			Accum. Deprec.—Store Equip.			4 5 0 0 00	18
19							19
20		31	Wages Expense		6 7 5 00		20
21			Wages Payable			6 7 5 00	21
22							22
23		31	Unearned Repair Fees		15 0 0 0 00		23
24			Repair Fees			15 0 0 0 00	24
25							25

SHOULD THE ADJUSTMENT BE REVERSED?

Never reverse adjustments for merchandise inventory.

Never reverse adjustments for merchandise inventory.

No. No asset or liability with a zero balance has been increased.

No. No asset or liability with a zero balance has been increased.

Never reverse adjustments for depreciation.

Never reverse adjustments for depreciation.

Yes. A liability account with a zero balance has been increased.

No. No asset or liability with a zero balance has been increased.

6.

GENERAL JOURNAL   PAGE 4

	DATE		DESCRIPTION	POST. REF.	DEBIT	CREDIT	
1			Closing Entries				1
2	19-3 Dec.	31	Sales		300 7 5 0 00		2
3			Repair Fees		15 0 0 0 00		3
4			Interest Revenue		1 3 5 0 00		4
5			Purchases Returns and Allowances		1 2 0 0 00		5
6			Purchases Discounts		1 5 0 0 00		6
7			Income Summary			319 8 0 0 00	7
8							8

6. (cont.)

					Debit					Credit				
9		31	Income Summary		273	8	2	5	00						9
10			Sales Returns and Allowances							1	8	0	0	00	10
11			Purchases							157	5	0	0	00	11
12			Freight-In								4	5	0	00	12
13			Advertising Expense							3	7	5	0	00	13
14			Wages Expense							63	6	7	5	00	14
15			Supplies Expense							2	1	0	0	00	15
16			Telephone Expense							5	2	5	0	00	16
17			Deprec. Expense—Building							6	0	0	0	00	17
18			Deprec. Expense—Store Equip.							4	5	0	0	00	18
19			Utilities Expense							18	0	0	0	00	19
20			Insurance Expense							2	7	0	0	00	20
21			Miscellaneous Expense							3	3	7	5	00	21
22			Interest Expense							4	7	2	5	00	22
23															23
24		31	Income Summary		51	9	7	5	00						24
25			Tom McKinney, Capital							51	9	7	5	00	25
26															26
27		31	Tom McKinney, Capital		30	0	0	0	00						27
28			Tom McKinney, Drawing							30	0	0	0	00	28
29															29

7.

GENERAL JOURNAL   PAGE 5

	DATE		DESCRIPTION	POST. REF.	DEBIT				CREDIT				
1			Reversing Entries										1
2	19-4 Jan.	1	Wages Payable		6	7	5	00					2
3			Wages Expense						6	7	5	00	3
4													4

SERIES A EXERCISES

1 **EXERCISE 15A1 REVENUE SECTION, MULTIPLE-STEP INCOME STATEMENT**   Based on the information that follows, prepare the revenue section of a multiple-step income statement.

Sales	$140,000
Sales Returns and Allowances	3,500
Sales Discounts	2,800

1 **EXERCISE 15A2 COST OF GOODS SOLD SECTION, MULTIPLE-STEP INCOME STATEMENT**   Based on the information that follows, prepare the cost of goods sold section of a multiple-step income statement.

Merchandise Inventory, January 1, 19--	$ 34,000
Purchases	102,000
Purchases Returns and Allowances	4,200
Purchases Discounts	2,040
Freight-In	800
Merchandise Inventory, December 31, 19--	28,000

1   **EXERCISE 15A3 MULTIPLE-STEP INCOME STATEMENT**   Based on the information that follows, prepare a multiple-step income statement including the revenue section and the cost of goods sold section, for Rau Office Supplies for the year ended December 31, 19--.

Sales	$148,300
Sales Returns and Allowances	1,380
Sales Discounts	2,166
Interest Revenue	240
Merchandise Inventory, January 1, 19--	26,500
Purchases	98,000
Purchases Returns and Allowances	2,180
Purchases Discounts	1,960
Freight-In	750
Merchandise Inventory, December 31,19--	33,250
Wages Expense	23,800
Utilities Expense	7,000
Depreciation Expense—Equipment	3,100
Telephone Expense	1,100
Insurance Expense	1,000
Supplies Expense	900
Miscellaneous Expense	720
Interest Expense	3,880

5   **EXERCISE 15A4 CLOSING ENTRIES**   From the work sheet on page 535, prepare closing entries for Gimbel's Gifts and Gadgets in a general journal.

6   **EXERCISE 15A5 REVERSING ENTRIES**   From the work sheet used in Exercise 15A4 identify the adjusting entry(ies) that should be reversed and prepare the reversing entry(ies).

4/5   **EXERCISE 15A6 ADJUSTING, CLOSING, AND REVERSING** Based on the information that follows, prepare two sets of entries—one that will have a reversing entry and the other without a reversing entry. Enter existing balances and post all entries to two sets of T accounts for Wages Expense and Wages Payable.

a.   Wages paid during 19-1 are $20,800.
b.   Wages earned but not paid (accrued) as of December 31, 19-1, are $300.
c.   On January 3, 19-2, payroll of $800 is paid, which includes the $300 of wages earned but not paid in December.

Gimbel's Gifts and Gadgets
Work Sheet
For Year Ended December 31, 19—

#	ACCOUNT TITLE	TRIAL BALANCE DEBIT	TRIAL BALANCE CREDIT	ADJUSTMENTS DEBIT	ADJUSTMENTS CREDIT	ADJUSTED TRIAL BALANCE DEBIT	ADJUSTED TRIAL BALANCE CREDIT	INCOME STATEMENT DEBIT	INCOME STATEMENT CREDIT	BALANCE SHEET DEBIT	BALANCE SHEET CREDIT
1	Cash	8214.00				8214.00				8214.00	
2	Accounts Receivable	6720.00				6720.00				6720.00	
3	Merchandise Inventory	14210.00		(b) 16800.00	(a) 14210.00	16800.00				16800.00	
4	Supplies	680.00			(c) 380.00	300.00				300.00	
5	Prepaid Insurance	800.00			(d) 200.00	600.00				600.00	
6	Building	80000.00				80000.00				80000.00	
7	Accum. Deprec.—Building		13600.00		(e) 4000.00		17600.00				17600.00
8	Accounts Payable		5280.00				5280.00				5280.00
9	Sales Tax Payable		3260.00				3260.00				3260.00
10	Wages Payable				(f) 280.00		280.00				280.00
11	J.M. Gimbel, Capital		87883.00				87883.00				87883.00
12	J.M. Gimbel, Drawing	8000.00				8000.00				8000.00	
13	Income Summary			(a) 14210.00	(b) 16800.00	14210.00	16800.00	14210.00	16800.00		
14	Sales		86000.00				86000.00		86000.00		
15	Sales Returns and Allowances	1840.00				1840.00		1840.00			
16	Purchases	54200.00				54200.00		54200.00			
17	Purchases Returns and Allow.		2813.00				2813.00		2813.00		
18	Purchases Discounts		1084.00				1084.00		1084.00		
19	Freight-In	800.00				800.00		800.00			
20	Wages Expense	16800.00		(f) 280.00		17080.00		17080.00			
21	Supplies Expense			(c) 380.00		380.00		380.00			
22	Telephone Expense	2100.00				2100.00		2100.00			
23	Deprec. Expense—Building			(e) 4000.00		4000.00		4000.00			
24	Insurance Expense			(d) 200.00		200.00		200.00			
25	Utilities Expense	1310.00				1310.00		1310.00			
26	Advertising Expense	784.00				784.00		784.00			
27	Miscellaneous Expense	386.00				386.00		386.00			
28	Interest Expense	142.00				142.00		142.00			
29		196986.00	196986.00	35870.00	35870.00	218066.00	218066.00	97432.00	106697.00	120634.00	111369.00
30	Net Income							9265.00			9265.00
31								106697.00	106697.00	120634.00	120634.00

3 **EXERCISE 15A7 FINANCIAL STATEMENT RATIOS** Based on the financial statements for Jackson Enterprises (income statement, statement of owner's equity, and balance sheet) shown below and on the next page, prepare the following financial statement ratios. All sales are credit sales. The Accounts Receivable balance on January 1, 19--, was $21,600.

1. Working capital
2. Current ratio
3. Quick ratio
4. Return on owner's equity
5. Accounts receivable turnover and average number of days required to collect receivables
6. Inventory turnover and average number of days required to sell inventory

Jackson Enterprises
Balance Sheet
December 31, 19--

Assets				
Current assets:				
Cash		$20 8 0 0 00		
Accounts receivable		18 9 0 0 00		
Merchandise inventory		28 1 7 7 00		
Supplies		1 3 2 3 00		
Prepaid insurance		9 0 0 00		
Total current assets			$ 70 1 0 0 00	
Property, plant, and equipment:				
Building	$90 0 0 0 00			
Less accumulated depreciation	28 0 0 0 00	$62 0 0 0 00		
Equipment	$33 0 0 0 00			
Less accumulated depreciation	7 5 0 0 00	25 5 0 0 00		
Total property, plant, and equipment			87 5 0 0 00	
Total assets			$157 6 0 0 00	
Liabilities				
Current liabilities:				
Accounts payable	$12 6 0 0 00			
Mortgage payable (current portion)	8 0 0 00			
Wages payable	5 0 0 00			
Sales tax payable	1 2 0 0 00			
Total current liabilities		$15 1 0 0 00		
Long-term liabilities:				
Mortgage payable	$39 1 0 0 00			
Less current portion	8 0 0 00	38 3 0 0 00		
Total liabilities			$ 53 4 0 0 00	
Owner's Equity				
J.B. Gray, capital			104 2 0 0 00	
Total liabilities and owner's equity			$157 6 0 0 00	

Jackson Enterprises
Income Statement
For Year Ended December 31, 19--

Revenue from sales:				
Sales			$184 2 0 0 00	
Less: Sales returns and allowances			2 1 0 0 00	
Net sales				$182 1 0 0 00
Cost of goods sold:				
Merchandise inventory, January 1, 19--			$ 31 3 0 0 00	
Purchases		$92 8 0 0 00		
Less: Purchases returns and allowances	$ 1 8 0 0 00			
Purchases discounts	1 8 5 6 00	3 6 5 6 00		
Net purchases		$89 1 4 4 00		
Add freight-in		9 3 3 00		
Cost of goods purchased			90 0 7 7 00	
Goods available for sale			$121 3 7 7 00	
Less merchandise inventory, December 31, 19--			28 1 7 7 00	
Cost of goods sold				93 2 0 0 00
Gross profit				$ 88 9 0 0 00
Operating expenses:				
Wages expense			$ 38 0 0 0 00	
Supplies expense			3 8 0 00	
Telephone expense			2 2 1 0 00	
Depreciation expense—building			4 0 0 0 00	
Depreciation expense—equipment			3 8 0 0 00	
Insurance expense			9 0 0 00	
Utilities expense			11 0 0 0 00	
Advertising expense			1 1 8 0 00	
Miscellaneous expense			5 3 0 00	
Total operating expenses				62 0 0 0 00
Income from operations				$ 26 9 0 0 00
Other revenues:				
Interest revenue			$ 1 8 0 0 00	
Other expenses:				
Interest expense			9 0 0 00	9 0 0 00
Net income				$ 27 8 0 0 00

Jackson Enterprises
Statement of Owner's Equity
For Year Ended December 31, 19--

J.B. Gray, capital, January 1, 19--			$ 88 0 0 0 00
Net income for the year	$27 8 0 0 00		
Less withdrawals for year	11 6 0 0 00		
Increase in capital			16 2 0 0 00
J.B. Gray, capital, December 31, 19--			$104 2 0 0 00

4/5   **PROBLEM 15A1 WORK SHEET, ADJUSTING, CLOSING, AND REVERSING ENTRIES**   Ellis Fabric Store shows the following trial balance as of December 31, 19--.

Ellis Fabric Store
Trial Balance
For Year Ended December 31, 19--

ACCOUNT TITLE	DEBIT BALANCE	CREDIT BALANCE
Cash	28 0 0 0 00	
Accounts Receivable	14 2 0 0 00	
Merchandise Inventory	33 0 0 0 00	
Supplies	1 6 0 0 00	
Prepaid Insurance	9 0 0 00	
Equipment	6 6 0 0 00	
Accumulated Depreciation—Equipment		1 0 0 0 00
Accounts Payable		16 6 2 0 00
Sales Tax Payable		8 5 0 00
Wages Payable		
W.P. Ellis, Capital		71 2 0 0 00
W.P. Ellis, Drawing	21 6 1 0 00	
Income Summary		
Sales		78 5 0 0 00
Sales Returns and Allowances	1 8 5 0 00	
Interest Revenue		1 2 0 00
Purchases	41 5 0 0 00	
Purchases Returns and Allowances		1 8 0 0 00
Purchases Discounts		8 3 0 00
Freight-In	6 6 0 00	
Wages Expense	14 8 8 0 00	
Supplies Expense		
Telephone Expense	1 2 1 0 00	
Depreciation Expense—Equipment		
Insurance Expense		
Utilities Expense	3 2 4 0 00	
Advertising Expense	8 1 0 00	
Miscellaneous Expense	9 2 0 00	
Interest Expense	1 0 2 0 00	
	172 0 0 0 00	172 0 0 0 00

At the end of the year, the following adjustments need to be made:

(a, b) Merchandise Inventory as of December 31, $28,900.
(c)   Unused supplies on hand, $1,350.
(d)   Insurance expired, $300.
(e)   Depreciation expense for the year, $500.
(f)   Wages earned but not paid (Wages Payable), $480.

REQUIRED
1. Prepare a work sheet.
2. Prepare adjusting entries.
3. Prepare closing entries.
4. Prepare a post-closing trial balance.
5. Prepare reversing entries.

`1/2/3`   **PROBLEM 15A2 INCOME STATEMENT, STATEMENT OF OWNER'S EQUITY, AND BALANCE SHEET**   Paulson's Pet Store completed the work sheet on page 540 for the year ended December 31, 19--. Owner's equity as of January 1, 19--, was $21,900. The current portion of Mortgage Payable is $500.

REQUIRED
1. Prepare a multiple-step income statement.
2. Prepare a statement of owner's equity.
3. Prepare a balance sheet.

`3`   **PROBLEM 15A3 FINANCIAL STATEMENT RATIOS**   Use the work sheet and financial statements prepared in Problem 15A2. All sales are credit sales. The Accounts Receivable balance on January 1, 19--, was $3,800.

REQUIRED
Prepare the following financial ratios:
a.   Working capital
b.   Current ratio
c.   Quick ratio
d.   Return on owner's equity
e.   Accounts receivable turnover and average number of days required to collect receivables
f.   Inventory turnover and average number of days required to sell inventory.

SERIES B   EXERCISES

`1`   **EXERCISE 15B1 REVENUE SECTION, MULTIPLE-STEP INCOME STATEMENT**   Based on the information that follows on page 541, prepare the revenue section of a multiple-step income statement.

PR15A2 and PR15A3 (cont.)

Paulson's Pet Store
Work Sheet
For Year Ended December 31, 19--

#	ACCOUNT TITLE	TRIAL BALANCE DEBIT	TRIAL BALANCE CREDIT	ADJUSTMENTS DEBIT	ADJUSTMENTS CREDIT	ADJUSTED TRIAL BALANCE DEBIT	ADJUSTED TRIAL BALANCE CREDIT	INCOME STATEMENT DEBIT	INCOME STATEMENT CREDIT	BALANCE SHEET DEBIT	BALANCE SHEET CREDIT
1	Cash	15 860 00				15 860 00				15 860 00	
2	Accounts Receivable	2 340 00				2 340 00				2 340 00	
3	Merchandise Inventory	15 000 00		(b) 16 500 00	(a) 15 000 00	16 500 00				16 500 00	
4	Supplies	800 00			(c) 2 00 00	600 00				600 00	
5	Prepaid Insurance	600 00			(d) 1 50 00	450 00				450 00	
6	Equipment	5 000 00				5 000 00				5 000 00	
7	Accum. Deprec.—Equipment		4 50 00		(e) 4 50 00		9 00 00				9 00 00
8	Accounts Payable		4 890 00				4 890 00				4 890 00
9	Sales Tax Payable		8 60 00				8 60 00				8 60 00
10	Wages Payable				(f) 3 00 00		3 00 00				3 00 00
11	Mortgage Payable		4 000 00				4 000 00				4 000 00
12	B. Paulson, Capital		23 900 00				23 900 00				23 900 00
13	B. Paulson, Drawing	1 200 00				1 200 00				1 200 00	
14	Income Summary			(a) 15 000 00	(b) 16 500 00	15 000 00	16 500 00	15 000 00	16 500 00		
15	Sales		71 510 00				71 510 00		71 510 00		
16	Sales Returns and Allow.	1 340 00				1 340 00		1 340 00			
17	Purchases	40 660 00				40 660 00		40 660 00			
18	Purchases Returns and Allow.		1 020 00				1 020 00		1 020 00		
19	Purchases Discounts		8 00 00				8 00 00		8 00 00		
20	Freight-In	400 00				400 00		4 00 00			
21	Wages Expense	22 300 00		(f) 3 00 00		22 600 00		22 600 00			
22	Supplies Expense			(c) 2 00 00		2 00 00		2 00 00			
23	Telephone Expense	6 84 00				6 84 00		6 84 00			
24	Deprec. Expense—Equipment			(e) 4 50 00		4 50 00		4 50 00			
25	Insurance Expense			(d) 1 50 00		1 50 00		1 50 00			
26	Utilities Expense	7 16 00				7 16 00		7 16 00			
27	Advertising Expense	3 00 00				3 00 00		3 00 00			
28	Miscellaneous Expense	1 50 00				1 50 00		1 50 00			
29	Interest Expense	80 00				80 00		80 00			
30		107 430 00	107 430 00	32 600 00	32 600 00	124 680 00	124 680 00	82 730 00	89 830 00	41 950 00	34 850 00
31	Net Income							7 100 00			7 100 00
32								89 830 00	89 830 00	41 950 00	41 950 00
33											

Sales	$86,200
Sales Returns and Allowances	2,280
Sales Discounts	1,724

1 **EXERCISE 15B2 COST OF GOODS SOLD SECTION, MULTIPLE-STEP INCOME STATEMENT** Based on the information that follows, prepare the cost of goods sold section of a multiple-step income statement.

Merchandise Inventory, January 1, 19--	$13,800
Purchases	71,300
Purchases Returns and Allowances	3,188
Purchases Discounts	1,460
Freight-In	390
Merchandise Inventory, December 31, 19--	21,400

1 **EXERCISE 15B3 MULTIPLE-STEP INCOME STATEMENT** Use the following information to prepare a multiple-step income statement, including the revenue section and the cost of goods sold section, for Aeito's Plumbing Supplies for the year ended December 31, 19--.

Sales	$166,000
Sales Returns and Allowances	1,620
Sales Discounts	3,320
Interest Revenue	3,184
Merchandise Inventory, January 1, 19--	33,200
Purchases	111,300
Purchases Returns and Allowances	3,600
Purchases Discounts	2,226
Freight-In	640
Merchandise Inventory, December 31, 19--	29,600
Wages Expense	22,000
Utilities Expense	9,000
Depreciation Expense—Building	4,600
Depreciation Expense—Equipment	2,800
Telephone Expense	1,100
Insurance Expense	1,000
Supplies Expense	650
Miscellaneous Expense	214
Interest Expense	1,126

5 **EXERCISE 15B4 CLOSING ENTRIES** From the work sheet on page 542, prepare closing entries for Balloons and Baubbles in a general journal.

6 **EXERCISE 15B5 REVERSING ENTRIES** From the work sheet in Exercise 15B4, identify the adjusting entry(ies) that should be reversed and prepare the reversing entry(ies).

EX15B4 and EX15B5 (cont.)

Balloons and Baubbles
Work Sheet
For Year Ended December 31, 19--

#	Account Title	Trial Balance Debit	Trial Balance Credit	Adjustments Debit	Adjustments Credit	Adjusted Trial Balance Debit	Adjusted Trial Balance Credit	Income Statement Debit	Income Statement Credit	Balance Sheet Debit	Balance Sheet Credit
1	Cash	2800.00				2800.00				2800.00	
2	Accounts Receivable	4200.00				4200.00				4200.00	
3	Merchandise Inventory	8600.00		(b) 7500.00	(a) 8600.00	7500.00				7500.00	
4	Supplies	7800.00			(c) 2800.00	5000.00				5000.00	
5	Prepaid Insurance	6200.00			(d) 1200.00	5000.00				5000.00	
6	Equipment	3000.00				3000.00				3000.00	
7	Accum. Deprec.—Equipment		600.00		(e) 300.00		900.00				900.00
8	Accounts Payable		1800.00				1800.00				1800.00
9	Sales Tax Payable		800.00				800.00				800.00
10	Wages Payable				(f) 200.00		200.00				200.00
11	L. Marlow, Capital		12200.00				12200.00				12200.00
12	L. Marlow, Drawing	2000.00				2000.00				2000.00	
13	Income Summary			(a) 8600.00	(b) 7500.00	8600.00	7500.00	8600.00	7500.00		
14	Sales		31000.00				31000.00		31000.00		
15	Sales Returns and Allowances	800.00				800.00		800.00			
16	Purchases	22000.00				22000.00		22000.00			
17	Purchases Returns and Allow.		1800.00				1800.00		1800.00		
18	Purchases Discounts		407.00				407.00		407.00		
19	Freight-In	2000.00				2000.00		2000.00			
20	Wages Expense	1200.00		(f) 200.00		1400.00		1400.00			
21	Supplies Expense			(c) 2800.00		2800.00		2800.00			
22	Telephone Expense	700.00				700.00		700.00			
23	Deprec. Expense—Equipment			(e) 300.00		300.00		300.00			
24	Insurance Expense			(d) 1200.00		1200.00		1200.00			
25	Utilities Expense	480.00				480.00		480.00			
26	Advertising Expense	300.00				300.00		300.00			
27	Miscellaneous Expense	110.00				110.00		110.00			
28	Interest Expense	97.00				97.00		97.00			
29		47887.00	47887.00	17000.00	17000.00	55887.00	55887.00	35387.00	40707.00	20500.00	15180.00
30	Net Income							5320.00			5320.00
31								40707.00	40707.00	20500.00	20500.00

5/6 **EXERCISE 15B6 ADJUSTING, CLOSING, AND REVERSING**
Based on the information that follows, prepare two sets of entries—one that will have a reversing entry and the other without a reversing entry. Enter existing balances and post all entries to two sets of T accounts for Wages Expense and Wages Payable.

Wages paid during 19-1 are $20,080.
Wages earned but not paid (accrued) as of December 31, 19-1 are $280.
On January 3, 19-2, payroll of $840 is paid, which includes the $280 of wages earned but not paid in December.

4 **EXERCISE 15B7 FINANCIAL STATEMENT RATIOS**   Based on the financial statements shown on pages 544 and 545 for McDonald Carpeting Co. (income statement, statement of owner's equity, and balance sheet), prepare the following financial statement ratios. All sales are credit sales. The balance of accounts receivable on January 1, 19--, was $6,800.

1. Working capital
2. Current ratio
3. Quick ratio
4. Return on owner's equity
5. Accounts receivable turnover and the average number of days required to collect receivables
6. Inventory turnover and the average number of days required to sell inventory

SERIES B   PROBLEMS

5/6 **PROBLEM 15B1 WORK SHEET, ADJUSTING, CLOSING, AND REVERSING ENTRIES**   The trial balance for Darby Kite Store as of December 31, 19-- is shown on page 546.

SS

At the end of the year, the following adjustments need to be made:

(a, b)   Merchandise inventory as of December 31, $23,600.
(c)   Unused supplies on hand, $1,050.
(d)   Insurance expired, $250.
(e)   Depreciation expense for the year, $400.
(f)   Wages earned but not paid (Wages Payable), $360.

REQUIRED

1. Prepare a work sheet.
2. Prepare adjusting entries.
3. Prepare closing entries.
4. Prepare a post-closing trial balance.
5. Prepare reversing entries.

EX15B7 (cont.)

McDonald Carpeting Co.
Income Statement
For Year Ended December 31, 19--

Revenue from sales:						
Sales				$122 8 0 0 00		
Less: Sales returns and allowances				1 1 0 0 00		
Net sales					$121 7 0 0 00	
Cost of goods sold:						
Merchandise inventory, January 1, 19--				$ 19 3 0 0 00		
Purchases			$62 8 0 0 00			
Less: Purchases returns and allowances	$ 2 8 0 0 00					
Purchases discounts	1 9 4 4 00		4 7 4 4 00			
Net purchases			$58 0 5 6 00			
Add freight-in			9 4 4 00			
Cost of goods purchased				59 0 0 0 00		
Goods available for sale				$78 3 0 0 00		
Less merchandise inventory, December 31, 19--				16 7 0 0 00		
Cost of goods sold					61 6 0 0 00	
Gross profit					$ 60 1 0 0 00	
Operating expenses:						
Wages expense				$ 18 0 0 0 00		
Supplies expense				3 2 0 00		
Telephone expense				1 2 0 0 00		
Depreciation expense—building				3 5 0 0 00		
Depreciation expense—equipment				2 5 0 0 00		
Insurance expense				8 0 0 00		
Utilities expense				8 0 0 0 00		
Advertising expense				9 8 0 00		
Miscellaneous expense				2 0 0 00		
Total operating expenses					35 5 0 0 00	
Income from operations					$ 24 6 0 0 00	
Other revenue:						
Interest revenue				$ 2 8 0 0 00		
Other expenses:						
Interest expense				2 1 0 0 00	7 0 0 00	
Net income					$ 25 3 0 0 00	

EX15B7 (cont.)

McDonald Carpeting Co.
Statement of Owner's Equity
For Year Ended December 31, 19--

C.S. McDonald, capital, January 1, 19--			$52 0 0 0 00
Net income for year	$25 3 0 0 00		
Less: Withdrawals for year	10 4 0 0 00		
Increase in capital			14 9 0 0 00
C.S. McDonald, capital, December 31, 19--			$66 9 0 0 00

McDonald Carpeting Co.
Balance Sheet
December 31, 19--

Assets				
Current assets:				
Cash			$10 4 0 0 00	
Accounts receivable			8 9 0 0 00	
Merchandise inventory			16 7 0 0 00	
Supplies			1 2 0 0 00	
Prepaid insurance			7 0 0 00	
Total current assets				$37 9 0 0 00
Property, plant, and equipment:				
Building	$60 0 0 0 00			
Less accumulated depreciation—building	18 0 0 0 00	$42 0 0 0 00		
Equipment	$22 0 0 0 00			
Less accumulated depreciation—equipment	6 2 0 0 00	15 8 0 0 00		
Total property, plant, and equipment				57 8 0 0 00
Total assets				$95 7 0 0 00
Liabilities				
Current liabilities:				
Accounts payable	$ 8 4 0 0 00			
Mortgage payable (current portion)	6 0 0 00			
Wages payable	3 0 0 00			
Sales tax payable	1 0 0 0 00			
Total current liabilities		$10 3 0 0 00		
Long-term liabilities:				
Mortgage payable	$19 1 0 0 00			
Less current portion	6 0 0 00	18 5 0 0 00		
Total liabilities				$28 8 0 0 00
Owner's Equity				
C.D. McDonald, capital				66 9 0 0 00
Total liabilities and owner's equity				$95 7 0 0 00

PR 15B1 (cont.)

Darby Kite Store
Trial Balance
For Year Ended December 31, 19--

ACCOUNT TITLE	DEBIT BALANCE	CREDIT BALANCE
Cash	11 7 0 0 00	
Accounts Receivable	11 2 0 0 00	
Merchandise Inventory	25 0 0 0 00	
Supplies	1 2 0 0 00	
Prepaid Insurance	8 0 0 00	
Equipment	5 4 0 0 00	
Accumulated Depreciation—Equipment		8 0 0 00
Accounts Payable		7 6 0 0 00
Sales Tax Payable		2 5 0 00
Wages Payable		
M.D. Akins, Capital		50 0 0 0 00
M.D. Akins, Drawing	10 5 0 0 00	
Income Summary		
Sales		57 9 9 0 00
Sales Returns and Allowances	1 4 5 0 00	
Purchases	34 5 0 0 00	
Purchases Returns and Allowances		1 1 0 0 00
Purchases Discounts		6 3 0 00
Freight-In	3 6 0 00	
Wages Expense	10 8 8 0 00	
Supplies Expense		
Telephone Expense	1 1 0 0 00	
Depreciation Expense—Equipment		
Insurance Expense		
Utilities Expense	2 3 0 0 00	
Advertising Expense	7 4 0 00	
Miscellaneous Expense	3 2 0 00	
Interest Expense	9 2 0 00	
	118 3 7 0 00	118 3 7 0 00

1/2/3 **PROBLEM 15B2 INCOME STATEMENT, STATEMENT OF OWNER'S EQUITY, AND BALANCE SHEET** Backlund Farm Supply completed the work sheet on page 547 for the year ended December 31, 19--. Owner's equity as of January 1, 19--, was $50,000. The current portion of Mortgage Payable is $1,000.

REQUIRED

1. Prepare a multiple-step income statement.
2. Prepare a statement of owner's equity.
3. Prepare a balance sheet.

PR15B2 (cont.)

Backlund Farm Supply
Work Sheet
For Year Ended December 31, 19--

ACCOUNT TITLE	TRIAL BALANCE DEBIT	TRIAL BALANCE CREDIT	ADJUSTMENTS DEBIT	ADJUSTMENTS CREDIT	ADJUSTED TRIAL BALANCE DEBIT	ADJUSTED TRIAL BALANCE CREDIT	INCOME STATEMENT DEBIT	INCOME STATEMENT CREDIT	BALANCE SHEET DEBIT	BALANCE SHEET CREDIT
1 Cash	10 1 8 0 00				10 1 8 0 00				10 1 8 0 00	
2 Accounts Receivable	26 4 2 0 00				26 4 2 0 00				26 4 2 0 00	
3 Merchandise Inventory	42 1 6 0 00		(b) 44 3 0 0 00	(a) 42 1 6 0 00	44 3 0 0 00				44 3 0 0 00	
4 Supplies	4 3 6 0 00			(c) 8 6 0 00	3 5 0 0 00				3 5 0 0 00	
5 Prepaid Insurance	3 0 0 0 00			(d) 7 5 0 00	2 2 5 0 00				2 2 5 0 00	
6 Equipment	38 0 0 0 00				38 0 0 0 00				38 0 0 0 00	
7 Accum. Deprec.—Equipment		6 0 0 0 00		(e) 9 0 0 00		6 9 0 0 00				6 9 0 0 00
8 Accounts Payable		41 2 0 0 00				41 2 0 0 00				41 2 0 0 00
9 Sales Tax Payable		8 0 0 00				8 0 0 00				8 0 0 00
10 Wages Payable				(f) 4 2 0 00		4 2 0 00				4 2 0 00
11 Mortgage Payable		8 0 0 0 00				8 0 0 0 00				8 0 0 0 00
12 J. Backlund, Capital		57 0 0 0 00				57 0 0 0 00				57 0 0 0 00
13 J. Backlund, Drawing	6 8 0 0 00				6 8 0 0 00				6 8 0 0 00	
14 Income Summary			(a) 42 1 6 0 00	(b) 44 3 0 0 00	42 1 6 0 00	44 3 0 0 00	42 1 6 0 00	44 3 0 0 00		
15 Sales		141 8 0 0 00				141 8 0 0 00		141 8 0 0 00		
16 Sales Returns and Allowances	1 3 1 0 00				1 3 1 0 00		1 3 1 0 00			
17 Purchases	81 3 0 0 00				81 3 0 0 00		81 3 0 0 00			
18 Purchases Returns and Allow.		2 9 0 0 00				2 9 0 0 00		2 9 0 0 00		
19 Purchases Discounts		1 5 1 0 00				1 5 1 0 00		1 5 1 0 00		
20 Freight-In	6 0 0 00				6 0 0 00		6 0 0 00			
21 Wages Expense	41 3 0 0 00		(f) 4 2 0 00		41 7 2 0 00		41 7 2 0 00			
22 Supplies Expense			(c) 8 6 0 00		8 6 0 00		8 6 0 00			
23 Telephone Expense	8 0 0 00				8 0 0 00		8 0 0 00			
24 Deprec. Expense—Equipment			(e) 9 0 0 00		9 0 0 00		9 0 0 00			
25 Insurance Expense			(d) 7 5 0 00		7 5 0 00		7 5 0 00			
26 Utilities Expense	1 3 0 0 00				1 3 0 0 00		1 3 0 0 00			
27 Advertising Expense	4 0 0 00				4 0 0 00		4 0 0 00			
28 Miscellaneous Expense	2 0 0 00				2 0 0 00		2 0 0 00			
29 Interest Expense	1 0 8 0 00				1 0 8 0 00		1 0 8 0 00			
30	259 2 1 0 00	259 2 1 0 00	89 3 9 0 00	89 3 9 0 00	304 8 3 0 00	304 8 3 0 00	173 3 8 0 00	190 5 1 0 00	131 4 5 0 00	114 3 2 0 00
31 Net Income							17 1 3 0 00			17 1 3 0 00
32							190 5 1 0 00	190 5 1 0 00	131 4 5 0 00	131 4 5 0 00

4 **PROBLEM 15B3 FINANCIAL STATEMENT RATIOS**   Use the work sheet and financial statements prepared in Problem 15B2. All sales are credit sales. The Accounts Receivable balance on January 1 was $38,200.

Prepare the following financial ratios:
a.   Working capital
b.   Current ratio
c.   Quick ratio
d.   Return on owner's equity
e.   Accounts receivable turnover and the average number of days required to collect receivables
f.   Inventory turnover and the average number of days required to sell inventory

MASTERY PROBLEM

Dominique Fouque owns and operates Dominique's Doll House. She has a small shop in which she sells new and antique dolls. She is particularly well known for her collection of antique Ken and Barbie dolls. A completed work sheet for 19-3 is shown on the next page. Fouque made no additional investments during the year and the long-term note payable is due in 19-9. No portion of the long-term note is due within the next year. Credit sales for 19-3 were $35,300 and receivables on January 1 were $2,500.

1.   Prepare a multiple-step income statement.
2.   Prepare a statement of owner's equity.
3.   Prepare a balance sheet.
4.   Compute the following measures of performance and financial condition for 19-3:
    a.   Current ratio
    b.   Quick ratio
    c.   Working capital
    d.   Return on owner's equity
    e.   Accounts receivable turnover and average number of days required to collect receivables
    f.   Inventory turnover and the average number of days required to sell inventory
5.   Prepare adjusting entries and indicate which should be reversed and why.
6.   Prepare closing entries.
7.   Prepare reversing entries for the adjustments where appropriate.

Mastery Problem (cont.)

Dominique's Doll House
Work Sheet
For Year Ended December 31, 19-3

	ACCOUNT TITLE	TRIAL BALANCE DEBIT	TRIAL BALANCE CREDIT	ADJUSTMENTS DEBIT	ADJUSTMENTS CREDIT	ADJUSTED TRIAL BALANCE DEBIT	ADJUSTED TRIAL BALANCE CREDIT	INCOME STATEMENT DEBIT	INCOME STATEMENT CREDIT	BALANCE SHEET DEBIT	BALANCE SHEET CREDIT	
1	Cash	5 2 0 0 00				5 2 0 0 00				5 2 0 0 00		1
2	Accounts Receivable	3 2 0 0 00				3 2 0 0 00				3 2 0 0 00		2
3	Merchandise Inventory	22 3 0 0 00		(b) 24 6 0 0 00	(a) 22 3 0 0 00	24 6 0 0 00				24 6 0 0 00		3
4	Office Supplies	8 0 0 00			(c) 6 0 0 00	2 0 0 00				2 0 0 00		4
5	Prepaid Insurance	1 2 0 0 00			(d) 4 0 0 00	8 0 0 00				8 0 0 00		5
6	Store Equipment	85 0 0 0 00				85 0 0 0 00				85 0 0 0 00		6
7	Accum. Deprec.—Store Equip.		15 0 0 0 00		(e) 5 0 0 0 00		20 0 0 0 00				20 0 0 0 00	7
8	Accounts Payable		5 5 0 0 00				5 5 0 0 00				5 5 0 0 00	8
9	Notes Payable		6 0 0 0 00				6 0 0 0 00				6 0 0 0 00	9
10	Wages Payable				(g) 2 0 0 00		2 0 0 00				2 0 0 00	10
11	Sales Tax Payable		8 5 0 00				8 5 0 00				8 5 0 00	11
12	Unearned Rent Revenue		1 0 0 0 00	(f) 7 0 0 00			3 0 0 00				3 0 0 00	12
13	Long-Term Note Payable		10 0 0 0 00				10 0 0 0 00				10 0 0 0 00	13
14	Dominique Fouque, Capital		75 8 0 0 00				75 8 0 0 00				75 8 0 0 00	14
15	Dominique Fouque, Drawing	21 0 0 0 00				21 0 0 0 00				21 0 0 0 00		15
16	Income Summary			(a) 22 3 0 0 00	(b) 24 6 0 0 00	22 3 0 0 00	24 6 0 0 00	22 3 0 0 00	24 6 0 0 00			16
17	Sales		130 5 0 0 00				130 5 0 0 00		130 5 0 0 00			17
18	Sales Returns and Allowances	9 0 0 00				9 0 0 00		9 0 0 00				18
19	Rent Revenue		25 0 0 0 00		(f) 7 0 0 00		25 7 0 0 00		25 7 0 0 00			19
20	Purchases	72 0 0 0 00				72 0 0 0 00		72 0 0 0 00				20
21	Purchases Discounts		7 5 0 00				7 5 0 00		7 5 0 00			21
22	Freight-In	1 2 0 0 00				1 2 0 0 00		1 2 0 0 00				22
23	Rent Expense	6 0 0 0 00				6 0 0 0 00		6 0 0 0 00				23
24	Wages Expense	42 0 0 0 00		(g) 2 0 0 00		42 2 0 0 00		42 2 0 0 00				24
25	Office Supplies Expense			(c) 6 0 0 00		6 0 0 00		6 0 0 00				25
26	Telephone Expense	1 5 0 0 00				1 5 0 0 00		1 5 0 0 00				26
27	Deprec. Expense—Store Equip.			(e) 5 0 0 0 00		5 0 0 0 00		5 0 0 0 00				27
28	Utilities Expense	7 6 0 0 00				7 6 0 0 00		7 6 0 0 00				28
29	Insurance Expense			(d) 4 0 0 00		4 0 0 00		4 0 0 00				29
30	Interest Expense	5 0 0 00				5 0 0 00		5 0 0 00				30
31		270 4 0 0 00	270 4 0 0 00	53 8 0 0 00	53 8 0 0 00	300 2 0 0 00	300 2 0 0 00	160 2 0 0 00	181 5 5 0 00	140 0 0 0 00	118 6 5 0 00	31
32	Net Income							21 3 5 0 00			21 3 5 0 00	32
33								181 5 5 0 00	181 5 5 0 00	140 0 0 0 00	140 0 0 0 00	33
34												34

During the month of December, 19-7, TJ's Specialty Shop engaged in the following transactions:

Dec. 1 Sold merchandise on account to Anne Clark, $2,000 plus tax of $100. Sale no. 637.

2 Issued check no. 806 to Owen Enterprises in payment of December 1 balance of $1,600, less 2% discount.

3 Issued check no. 807 to Nathen Co. in payment of December 1 balance of $3,000, less 2% discount.

4 Purchased merchandise on account from Owen Enterprises $1,550. Invoice no. 763, dated December 4, terms 2/10, n/30.

4 Issued check no. 808 in payment of telephone expense for the month of November, $180.

6 Purchased merchandise on account from Evans Essentials, $2,350. Invoice no. 764, dated December 6, terms net 30.

8 Sold merchandise for cash, $4,840, plus tax of $242.

9 Received payment from Heather Waters in full settlement of account, $490.

9 Sold merchandise on account to Lucy Greene, $800 plus tax of $40. Sale no. 638.

10 Issued check no. 809 to West Wholesalers in payment of December 1 balance of $1,000.

11 Issued check no. 810 in payment of advertising expense for the month of December, $400.

12 Sold merchandise on account to Martha Boyle, $1,260 plus tax of $63. Sale no. 639.

12 Received payment from Anne Clark on account, $1,340.

13 Issued check no. 811 to Owen Enterprises in payment of December 4 purchase. Invoice no. 763, less 2% discount.

13 Martha Boyle returned merchandise for a credit, $740 plus sales tax of $37.

15 Issued check no. 812 in payment of wages (Wages Expense) for the two-week period ending December 14, $1,100.

15 Received payment from Lucy Greene on account, $1,960.

16 Sold merchandise on account to Kim Fields, $160 plus sales tax of $8. Sale no. 640.

17 Returned merchandise to Evans Essentials for credit, $150.

18 Issued check no. 813 to Evans Essentials in payment of December 1 balance of $1,250 less the credit received on December 17.

19 Sold merchandise on account to Lucy Greene, $620 plus tax of $31. Sale no. 641.

22 Received payment from John Dempsey on account, $1,560.

23 Issued check no. 814 for the purchase of supplies, $120.

24 Purchased merchandise from West Wholesalers on account, $1,200. Invoice no. 765, dated December 24, terms net 30.

Dec. 26 Purchased merchandise from Nathen Co. on account, $800. Invoice no. 766, dated December 26, terms 2/10, n/30.

27 Issued check no. 815 in payment of utilities expense for the month of November, $630.

27 Sold merchandise on account to John Dempsey, $2,020 plus tax of $101. Sale no. 642.

29 Received payment from Martha Boyle on account, $2,473.

29 Issued check no. 816 in payment of wages (Wages Expense) for the two-week period ending December 26, $1,100.

30 Issued check no. 817 to Meyers Trophy Shop for a cash purchase of merchandise, $200.

As of December 1, TJ's account balances were as follows:

Account	Account No.	Debit	Credit
Cash	111	$ 11,500	
Accounts Receivable	131	8,600	
Merchandise Inventory	141	21,800	
Supplies	151	1,035	
Prepaid Insurance	155	1,380	
Land	171	8,700	
Building	175	52,000	
Accum. Deprec.—Building	175.1		$ 9,200
Store Equipment	181	28,750	
Accum. Deprec.—Store Equip.	181.1		9,300
Accounts Payable	216		6,850
Wages Payable	219		
Sales Tax Payable	225		970
Mortgage Payable	231		12,525
Tom Jones, Capital	311		90,000
Tom Jones, Drawing	312	8,500	
Income Summary	313		
Sales	411		116,000
Sales Returns and Allowances	411.1	690	
Purchases	511	60,500	
Purchases Returns and Allow.	511.1		460
Purchases Discounts	511.2		575
Freight-In	512	175	
Advertising Expense	532	4,300	
Wages Expense	542	25,000	
Supplies Expense	543		
Telephone Expense	545	2,000	
Deprec. Expense—Building	547		
Deprec. Expense—Store Equip.	548		
Utilities Expense	555	6,900	
Insurance Expense	559		
Miscellaneous Expense	592	2,700	
Interest Expense	595	1,350	
		$245,880	$245,880

TJ also had the following subsidiary ledger balances as of December 1.

Accounts Receivable:

Customer	Accounts Receivable Balance
Martha Boyle 12 Jude Lane Hartford, CT 06117	$3,250
Anne Clark 52 Juniper Road Hartford, CT 06118	1,340
John Dempsey 700 Hobbes Dr. Avon, CT 06108	1,560
Kim Fields 5200 Hamilton Ave. Hartford, CT 06117	—
Lucy Greene 236 Bally Lane Simsbury, CT 06123	1,960
Heather Waters 447 Drury Lane West Hartford, CT 06107	490

Accounts Payable:

Vendor	Accounts Payable Balance
Evans Essentials 34 Harry Ave. East Hartford, CT 06234	$1,250
Nathen Co. 1009 Drake Rd. Farmington, CT 06082	3,000
Owen Enterprises 43 Lucky Lane Bristol, CT 06007	1,600
West Wholesalers 888 Anders Street Newington, CT 06789	1,000

At the end of the year, the following adjustments need to be made:

(a, b)   Merchandise inventory as of December 31, $19,700.
(c)   Unused supplies on hand, $525.
(d)   Unexpired insurance on December 31, $1,000.

(e) Depreciation expense on the building for the year, $800.

(f) Depreciation expense on the store equipment for the year, $450.

(g) Wages earned but not paid as of December 31, $330.

REQUIRED

1. If you are not using the working papers, open a general ledger and accounts receivable and accounts payable ledgers as of December 1. Enter the December 1 balance of each of the accounts, with a check mark in the Post. Ref. column.

2. Enter the transactions for the month of December in the proper journals. Post immediately to the Accounts Receivable and Accounts Payable ledgers.

3. Post from the journals to the general ledger. Post the journals in the following order: general, sales, purchases, cash receipts, and cash payments.

4. Prepare schedules of accounts receivable and accounts payable.

5. Prepare a year-end work sheet, income statement, statement of owner's equity, and balance sheet. The mortgage payable includes $600 that is due within one year.

6. Journalize and post adjusting entries.

7. Journalize and post closing entries. (Hint: Close all expense and revenue account balances listed in the Income Statement columns of the work sheet. Then close Income Summary and Tom Jones, Drawing to Tom Jones, Capital.)

8. Prepare a post-closing trial balance.

9. Journalize and post reversing entries for the adjustments where appropriate, as of January 2, 19-8.

PART

4

Specialized Accounting Procedures for Merchandising Businesses and Partnerships

16

Accounting for Accounts Receivable

Careful study of this chapter should enable you to:

LO1 Apply the allowance method of accounting for uncollectible accounts.

LO2 Estimate and write off uncollectible accounts using the percentage of sales method and the percentage of receivables method.

LO3 Apply the direct write-off method of accounting for uncollectible accounts.

When we make sales on account, we know that some customers will not pay their accounts. In fact, the easier our credit policies are, the more of such customers there are likely to be. How should we account for this expense? The matching principle says that expenses should be matched with the revenues they helped to produce. This implies that we should write off some accounts receivable in the current period so that the expenses are matched with the related sales. But, we don't know which accounts will prove uncollectible. How can we write them off before we know which ones they are? We could wait until we know which ones are uncollectible, but this seems to violate the matching principle. What should we do?

Businesses generally are willing to sell goods and services on account. A major reason for doing so is to increase sales. Most of us simply tend to buy more if we can "charge it" rather than pay cash. In fact, one way a business can increase sales is to have easy credit policies and sell on account to virtually anyone. Unfortunately, some businesses and individuals who "charge it" then are unwilling or unable to "pay for it." Thus, a cost to a business of selling goods and services on account is that some of the accounts receivable will be uncollectible. The more willing a business is to make sales on account, the more uncollectible accounts it is likely to have.

There are two methods of accounting for uncollectible accounts: (1) the allowance method, and (2) the direct write-off method. The purpose of this chapter is to learn how to use these methods.

ALLOWANCE METHOD

LO1 Apply the allowance method of accounting for uncollectible accounts.

The **allowance method** is a technique that attempts to recognize uncollectible accounts expense in the same period that the related credit sales are made. This method is consistent with the **matching principle**, which states that expenses should be matched with the revenues they helped to produce.

Under the accrual basis of accounting, the allowance method is generally required for financial reporting purposes. To use the allowance method, three steps are followed.

STEP 1   At the end of each accounting period, the amount of uncollectible accounts is estimated.

STEP 2   An adjusting entry is made to recognize the uncollectible accounts expense and reduce reported receivables for the amount of estimated uncollectible accounts. For example, if the estimated amount is $900, the entry is:

4			Uncollectible Accounts Expense		9 0 0 00		4
5			Allowance for Doubtful Accounts			9 0 0 00	5
6			Estimated uncollectible accounts				6

Note that the credit is not to Accounts Receivable. This is because at this time we do not know which specific customers will fail to pay. Instead, a contra-asset account, Allowance for Doubtful Accounts (also known as Allowance for Uncollectible Accounts or Allowance for Bad Debts) is credited. The balance of this account is deducted from Accounts Receivable on the balance sheet. The remaining amount is known as the **net receivables** or **net realizable value** of accounts receivable because it is the amount the firm expects to collect. Accounts receivable of $30,000 with an allowance of $900 would appear as follows:

Current assets:
Accounts receivable $30,000
Less allowance for doubtful accounts   900 $29,100

STEP 3   In a subsequent period, when a specific uncollectible account is identified, an entry is made to write off the account and reduce the balance in Allowance for Doubtful Accounts. For example, if the uncollectible account is $250, the entry is:

8		Allowance for Doubtful Accounts	2 5 0 00		8
9		Accounts Rec./Customer Name		2 5 0 00	9
10		Wrote off uncollectible account			10

ESTIMATING AND WRITING OFF UNCOLLECTIBLES

LO2 Estimate and write off uncollectible accounts using the percentage of sales method and the percentage of receivables method.

To use the allowance method, we need a way to estimate the amount of uncollectibles. Two basic methods are used: the percentage of sales method and the percentage of receivables method.

Percentage of Sales Method

The **percentage of sales method** is based on the relationship between the amount of credit sales and the amount of uncollectible accounts. Assume that during 19-1 and 19-2, Chris Co. had total credit sales of $200,000 and that $2,000 of those credit sales had become uncollectible. Based on this experience, Chris could estimate its uncollectible accounts at 1% of credit sales.

$$\frac{\text{Uncollectible Accounts}}{\text{Credit Sales}} = \frac{\$2,000}{\$200,000} = 1\%$$

If during 19-3 Chris had credit sales of $120,000, the estimate of uncollectible accounts would be made as follows:

Credit sales $120,000
Estimated percent uncollectible   × 1%
Estimated uncollectible accounts $ 1,200

Thus, the following adjusting entry would be made on December 31, 19-3:

4		Uncollectible Accounts Expense	1 2 0 0 00		4
5		Allowance for Doubtful Accounts		1 2 0 0 00	5
6					6

In T account form, Allowance for Doubtful Accounts would appear as follows:

Allowance for Doubtful Accounts

	19-3
	Dec. 31 1,200

Assume that during 19-4, uncollectible accounts totaling $1,100 were written off as follows:

8		Allowance for Doubtful Accounts	1 1 0 0 00		8
9		Accounts Rec./Customer Names		1 1 0 0 00	9
10		Wrote off uncollectible accounts			10
11					11

After posting this entry, Allowance for Doubtful Accounts would have a credit balance of $100.

Allowance for Doubtful Accounts

		19-3	
		Dec. 31 1,200	
19-4	1,100		
		19-4 Bal. 100	

Assume that during 19-4, Chris had credit sales of $130,000. Based on experience, Chris would still estimate its uncollectible accounts at 1% of credit sales. This would yield estimated uncollectible accounts of $1,300 ($130,000 × 1%), and the following adjusting entry would be made on December 31, 19-4.

4		Uncollectible Accounts Expense	1 3 0 0 00		4
5		Allowance for Doubtful Accounts		1 3 0 0 00	5
6					6

This would increase the Allowance for Doubtful Accounts balance to $1,400.

Allowance for Doubtful Accounts

		19-3	
		Dec. 31 1,200	
19-4	1,100		
		19-4 Bal. 100	
		Dec. 31 Adj. 1,300	
		Dec. 31 Bal. 1,400	

LEARNING KEY

Percentage of sales method: When making the adjusting entry, ignore any balance in Allowance for Doubtful Accounts.

This demonstrates an important feature of the percentage of sales method. Allowance for Doubtful Accounts may have a debit or credit balance prior to adjustment. This is a normal result of underestimating or overestimating uncollectible accounts. Under the percentage of sales method, any balance in Allowance for Doubtful Accounts prior to adjustment is generally ignored in making the current period's adjusting entry.

This is because the percentage of sales method focuses on the *current year's* credit sales. Any previous balance in the allowance account relates to credit sales and uncollectible accounts from *prior years*. In the above illustration, the balance was a credit of $100. This balance could have been a credit of $300 or a debit of $200, and it would not have mattered. The adjusting entry for uncollectible accounts would have been the same—$1,300.

There is one exception to ignoring the balance in Allowance for Doubtful Accounts in making the adjustment. When a large debit or credit balance accumulates in the allowance account, the percentage of credit sales used to estimate uncollectible accounts should be increased or decreased. This provides a better estimate based on recent experience.

Percentage of Receivables Method

The **percentage of receivables method** is based on the relationship between the amount of accounts receivable and the amount of uncollectible accounts. The simplest form of this method involves computing uncollectible accounts as a percentage of the Accounts Receivable balance. Assume that Craft Co. had an average Accounts Receivable balance at the end of the past two years of $110,000. If a total of $4,400 of these accounts had become uncollectible, Craft would estimate its uncollectible accounts percentage as follows:

$$\frac{\text{Uncollectible Accounts}}{\text{Average Accounts Receivable}} = \frac{\$4,400}{\$110,000} = 4\%$$

Assume that the Accounts Receivable balance at the end of the current year was $120,000. The estimate of uncollectible accounts would be made as follows:

Accounts receivable	$120,000
Estimated percent uncollectible	× 4%
Estimated uncollectible accounts	$ 4,800

The following adjusting entry would be made at year end:

4		Uncollectible Accounts Expense		4 8 0 0 00		4
5		Allowance for Doubtful Accounts			4 8 0 0 00	5
6						6

Although the above approach is simple, the estimate of uncollectible accounts is not very precise. Therefore, the percentage of receivables method usually is applied in a way that yields a better estimate. Instead of using the total accounts receivable in making the estimate, each customer balance is analyzed to determine how long it has been outstanding. The probability that a customer account will not be collected usually increases with the length of time the account has been outstanding. Because of the emphasis on the length of time the accounts have been outstanding, this process is called **aging the receivables**.

An aging schedule similar to the one shown in Figure 16-1 is often used to analyze the receivables and estimate the uncollectible amount. The following steps are used in preparing the aging schedule.

FIGURE 16-1   Aging Schedule

AGING SCHEDULE OF ACCOUNTS RECEIVABLE—December 31, 19-1

| CUSTOMER | TOTAL | NOT YET DUE | NUMBER OF DAYS PAST DUE | | | | | |
			1–30	31–60	61–90	91–180	181–365	OVER 365
W. Billiard	$ 300 00	$ 250 00	$ 50 00					
K. Campbell	95 00			$ 65 00		$ 30 00		
J. Farley	432 50	380 00			$ 52 50			
L. Gilbert	190 00	150 00		40 00				
E. Rome	395 00	317 00					$ 78 00	
B. Zimmerman	20 00					20 00		
Total	$100 500 00	$65 000 00	$18 000 00	$8 250 00	$6 310 00	$1 810 00	$ 780 00	$ 350 00
Estimated percent uncollectible			2 %	5 %	10 %	20 %	30 %	50 %	80 %
Total estimated uncollectible accounts	$ 5 500 00	$ 1 300 00	$ 900 00	$ 825 00	$1 262 00	$ 543 00	$ 390 00	$ 280 00
	($5,500	=	1,300	+	900	+	825	+	1,262	+	543	+	390	+	280)

STEP 1   Categorize each account receivable according to the length of time the amounts have been outstanding.

STEP 2   Multiply the amount of receivables in each category by an estimate of the percent that will be uncollectible. This percentage is based on past experience and increases as the number of days past due increases.

STEP 3   Total the estimates for each category to determine the amount that is not expected to be collected.

Based on the aging schedule in Figure 16-1, uncollectible accounts would be estimated as $5,500. Thus, the following adjusting entry would be made on December 31, 19-1:

4	Uncollectible Accounts Expense	5 4 0 0 00			4
5	Allowance for Doubtful Accounts		5 4 0 0 00		5
6	Estimated uncollectible accounts				6

In T account form, Allowance for Doubtful Accounts would appear as follows:

Allowance for Doubtful Accounts

	19-1
	Dec. 31 Adj. 5,500

Assume that during 19-2, uncollectible accounts totaling $5,200 were written off as follows:

8	Allowance for Doubtful Accounts	5 2 0 0 00			8
9	Accounts Rec./Customer Names		5 2 0 0 00		9
10	Wrote off uncollectible accounts				10
11					11

Allowance for Doubtful Accounts now would have a credit balance of $300.

Allowance for Doubtful Accounts

		19-1	
		Dec. 31 Adj. 5,500	
19-2	5,200		
		19-2 Bal. 300	

Assume that at the end of 19-2 another aging schedule, like the one in Figure 16-1, is prepared and that the estimated uncollectible amount is $5,700. To bring the credit balance in the allowance account to $5,700, an adjustment of $5,400 is needed.

Estimated uncollectible amount	$5,700
Current credit balance in account	−300
Adjustment needed	$5,400

Thus, the following adjusting entry would be made on December 31, 19-2.

4	Uncollectible Accounts Expense	5 4 0 0 00			4
5	Allowance for Doubtful Accounts		5 4 0 0 00		5
6					6

This would increase the Allowance for Doubtful Accounts balance to $5,700.

Allowance for Doubtful Accounts

		19-1	
		Dec. 31 Adj. 5,500	
19-2	5,200		
		19-2 Bal. 300	
		Dec. 31 Adj. 5,400	
		Dec. 31 Bal. 5,700	

LEARNING KEY Percentage of receivables method: Unlike the percentage of sales method, the balance in Allowance for Doubtful Accounts prior to adjustment must be considered when making the current period's adjusting entry.

This demonstrates an important feature of the percentage of receivables method. Allowance for Doubtful Accounts may have a debit or credit balance prior to adjustment. Under the percentage of receivables method, this balance must be considered in making the current period's adjusting entry.

This is because the percentage of receivables method focuses on the Accounts Receivable balance at the end of the year. That balance contains receivables from the current year and any remaining from prior years. The total Accounts Receivable balance consisting of current and prior year receivables is analyzed to determine the proper allowance account balance. The adjusting entry is then made to achieve that balance in the allowance account. In the above illustration, the balance before adjustment was a credit of $300. Therefore, the adjustment to bring the balance to $5,700 was $5,400 ($5,700 − $300). If the balance prior to adjustment had been a debit of $100, the necessary adjusting entry would have been $5,800.

Estimated uncollectible amount	$5,700
Current debit balance in account	+100
Adjustment needed	$5,800

Notice that the resulting credit balance in Allowance for Doubtful Accounts after adjustment would once again be $5,700.

Allowance for Doubtful Accounts

19-2 Bal.	100	19-2
		Dec. 31 Adj. 5,800
		Dec. 31 Bal. 5,700

Comparison of Methods

Let's summarize the differences between the percentage of sales and percentage of receivables methods of estimating uncollectibles. Figure 16-2 identifies the key features of the two methods.

Write Off of Uncollectible Accounts

Recall that to write off a $250 uncollectible account, the following entry is made.

FIGURE 16-2   Key Features of Allowance Methods

FEATURE	PERCENTAGE OF SALES	PERCENTAGE OF RECEIVABLES
1 Basis for estimate	Percentage of credit sales	Aging (percentage) of accounts receivable
2 Amount of year-end adjustment	Amount calculated in 1	Amount calculated in 1 Plus debit balance in allowance account before adjustment or Minus credit balance in allowance account before adjustment
3 Balance after adjustment	Amount calculated in 1 Plus credit balance in allowance account before adjustment or Minus debit balance in allowance account before adjustment	Amount calculated in 1

4		Allowance for Doubtful Accounts		2 5 0 00				4
5		Accounts Rec./Customer Name				2 5 0 00		5
6		Wrote off uncollectible account						6
7								7

This entry is the same under both the percentage of sales and the percentage of receivables methods.

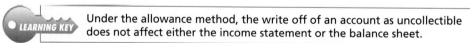

> **LEARNING KEY**   Under the allowance method, the write off of an account as uncollectible does not affect either the income statement or the balance sheet.

Note the effect of this entry on the income statement and balance sheet. No income statement accounts are used in the entry, so clearly there is no effect on the income statement. Not so obviously, the balance sheet is not affected either. Since Allowance for Doubtful Accounts is a contra-asset and Accounts Receivable is an asset, the effects offset each other. Let's look more closely at this perhaps surprising situation.

Effect of Entry on the Income Statement.   First, how can we write off an account as uncollectible and not affect the income statement? The answer lies in the adjusting entry we made at year end for the estimated uncollectibles. Assume the entry was for $900.

9		Uncollectible Accounts Expense	9 0 0 00			9
10		Allowance for Doubtful Accounts		9 0 0 00		10
11						11

The expense was already recognized with this adjusting entry. It would be double counting to recognize the expense again when the specific account is written off.

Effect of Entry on the Balance Sheet. Second, why is the balance sheet not affected? The best way to answer this question is with an example. Assume that on December 31, 19-1, the balance sheet showed the following information concerning Accounts Receivable:

Current assets:
Accounts receivable	$100,500	
Less allowance for doubtful accounts	5,500	$95,000

On January 15, 19-2, Bill McDonald's account for $500 is written off by making the following entry:

14	Jan. 15	Allowance for Doubtful Accounts	5 0 0 00			14
15		Accounts Rec./B. McDonald		5 0 0 00		15
16		Wrote off uncollectible account				16

If the balance sheet was prepared immediately after posting the above transaction, the following information would be reported for Accounts Receivable:

Current assets:
Accounts receivable	$100,000	
Less allowance for doubtful accounts	5,000	$95,000

Note that both Accounts Receivable and Allowance for Doubtful Accounts have been reduced by $500. Thus, the reported net receivables are not changed. The firm expected to collect $95,000 before writing off McDonald's account, and it still expects to collect $95,000 after writing off his account. Management knew that there would be uncollectible accounts. Now they know that McDonald is one of them.

Recovery of Accounts Previously Written Off

Occasionally an account that was written off is collected. For example, assume that a check for $500 was received on February 1 from Bill McDonald. Remember that his account was written off on January 15. This requires two entries: (1) reinstate the account, and (2) record the collection. To reinstate an account, the entry made to write off the account is simply reversed, as follows:

	19--															
5	Feb.	1	Accounts Receivable/B. McDonald			5	0	0	00							5
6			Allowance for Doubtful Accounts								5	0	0	00		6
7			Reinstated account receivable													7

To record the collection, the following entry is made:

9	Feb.	1	Cash			5	0	0	00							9
10			Accounts Receivable/B. McDonald								5	0	0	00		10
11			Collection on account													11

It might be simpler to debit Cash and credit Allowance for Doubtful Accounts. However, this shortcut should not be taken. Without the reinstatement, the subsidiary ledger will only report that McDonald's account was written off as uncollectible. With the reinstatement, the subsidiary ledger will reflect the fact that McDonald has paid his account. This information will be important to McDonald as well as the firm should he desire credit in the future.

DIRECT WRITE-OFF METHOD

LO3 Apply the direct write-off method of accounting for uncollectible accounts.

Under the **direct write-off method**, the uncollectible accounts expense is not recognized until it has been determined that an account is uncollectible. For example, assume that on August 15, John Lafollette's account for $500 is judged to be uncollectible. The following entry would be made:

	19--															
5	Aug.	15	Uncollectible Accounts Expense			5	0	0	00							5
6			Accounts Receivable/J. Lafollette								5	0	0	00		6
7			Wrote off uncollectible account													7

Advantage and Disadvantages of Direct Method

The direct write-off method has one advantage. It is very simple to apply. However, there are three disadvantages of using this method. First, efforts to collect the account often extend over many months. Thus, the revenue from the sale might be recognized in one period and the uncollectible account expense recognized in another. This violates the matching principle.

Second, the amount of uncollectible accounts expense recognized in a given period can be manipulated by management. This occurs because there is no general rule for deciding when an account becomes uncollectible. Thus, management can use its subjective judgment in deciding when to recognize uncollectible accounts expense.

Third, the amount of accounts receivable reported on the balance sheet does not represent the amount of cash actually expected to be collected. Thus, the assets are overstated by the amount of uncollectible accounts included in accounts receivable. For these reasons, the direct write-off method is generally not acceptable for financial reporting purposes. It is acceptable only if the amount of uncollectible accounts cannot be reasonably estimated or if the estimated amount is very small. This method is required, however, for income tax purposes.

Recovery of Accounts Previously Written Off

Occasionally, an account that was written off is collected. The proper entries for the recovery depend on the period in which the cash is collected.

Write-Off and Recovery in Same Accounting Period. Assume the write-off and recovery are made in the same accounting period. In this case, the first step is to reinstate the account by reversing the entry for the write-off. Then, the collection can be recorded in the usual manner, as shown below:

To write off account:

5	Aug.	15	Uncollectible Accounts Expense		5 0 0	00				5
6			Accounts Receivable/J. Lafollette					5 0 0	00	6
7			Wrote off uncollectible account							7

To reinstate account:

35	Dec.	20	Accounts Receivable/J. Lafollette		5 0 0	00				35
36			Uncollectible Accounts Expense					5 0 0	00	36
37			Reinstated account receivable							37

To record collection:

39	Dec.	20	Cash		5 0 0	00				39
40			Accounts Receivable/J. Lafollette					5 0 0	00	40
41			Collection on account							41

Write-Off and Recovery in Different Accounting Periods. Now assume that the write-off is made in one period and the recovery in the following accounting period. In this case, the first step is to reinstate the account by debiting Accounts Receivable and crediting Uncollectible Accounts Recovered. This account is credited instead of Uncollectible Accounts Expense because a credit to the expense account would understate uncollectible accounts expense for the current year. Uncollectible Accounts Recovered is reported on the income statement as other revenue. The entries for the write-off and recovery are as follows:

To write off account:

5	Aug.	15	Uncollectible Accounts Expense		5 0 0 00					5
6			Accounts Receivable/J. Lafollette				5 0 0 00			6
7			Wrote off uncollectible account							7

To reinstate account:

35	Jan.	20	Accounts Receivable/J. Lafollette		5 0 0 00					35
36			Uncollectible Accounts Recovered				5 0 0 00			36
37			Reinstated account receivable							37

To record collection:

39	Jan.	20	Cash		5 0 0 00					39
40			Accounts Receivable/J. Lafollette				5 0 0 00			40
41			Collection on account							41

KEY POINTS

1 To use the allowance method, apply three steps:

STEP 1   At the end of the period, estimate the uncollectible amount.

STEP 2   Make the following adjusting entry:

4			Uncollectible Accounts Expense		x x x xx					4
5			Allowance for Doubtful Accounts				x x x xx			5

STEP 3   When an uncollectible account is identified, make the following entry:

8			Allowance for Doubtful Accounts		x x x xx					8
9			Accounts Rec./Customer Name				x x x xx			9
10			Wrote off uncollectible account							10

2 The percentage of sales method is based on the relationship between the amount of credit sales and the amount of uncollectible accounts. Any balance in Allowance for Doubtful Accounts prior to adjustment is ignored in making the current period's adjusting entry.

The percentage of receivables method is based on the relationship between the amount of accounts receivable and the amount of uncollectible accounts. The estimate of uncollectibles is usually based on an aging of receivables. Any balance in Allowance for Doubtful Accounts prior to adjustment is considered in making the current period's adjusting entry.

Under the allowance method, the actual write off of an uncollectible account does not affect either the income statement or the balance sheet.

When an account is collected that has been written off, the account is reinstated and then the collection is recorded.

3   Under the direct write-off method, Uncollectible Accounts Expense is not recognized until an account is written off as uncollectible.

The entries for collection of an account previously written off depend on when the collection occurs. If the collection is in the same period as the write-off, the credit is to Uncollectible Accounts Expense. If the collection is in the following period, the credit is to Uncollectible Accounts Recovered.

KEY TERMS

aging the receivables 561   The process of estimating the uncollectible amount by analyzing account balances according to the length of time the accounts have been outstanding.

allowance method 557   A technique that attempts to recognize the uncollectible accounts expense in the same period that the related credit sales are made.

direct write-off method 566   A method in which the uncollectible accounts expense is not recognized until it has been determined that an account is uncollectible.

matching principle 557   A concept that requires expenses to be matched with the revenues they helped to produce.

net realizable value 557   The amount a firm expects to collect from its accounts receivable; calculated as Accounts Receivable less Allowance for Doubtful Accounts. Also called net receivables.

net receivables 557   See net realizable value.

percentage of receivables method 560   A method in which the current year's uncollectible accounts are estimated based on the relationship between the amount of accounts receivable and the amount of uncollectible accounts in prior years.

percentage of sales method 558   A method in which the current year's uncollectible accounts are estimated based on the relationship between the amount of credit sales and the amount of uncollectible accounts in prior years.

REVIEW QUESTIONS

1. What method of accounting for uncollectible accounts is generally required for financial reporting purposes?
2. Describe the steps to follow when using the allowance method to account for uncollectible accounts.
3. Explain how to compute net realizable value.
4. Describe the process followed when estimating uncollectible accounts under the percentage of sales method.

5. Describe the process followed when estimating uncollectible accounts under the percentage of receivables method based on aging the receivables.
6. How does the balance in Allowance for Doubtful Accounts before adjustment affect the amount of the year-end adjustment under the percentage of sales method? Under the percentage of receivables method?
7. Under the allowance method, what impact does the write off of a customer's account have on the financial statements?
8. Under the allowance method, what journal entries are made if an account is collected that was previously written off?
9. Describe the accounting procedures used under the direct write-off method to account for uncollectible accounts.
10. What are three disadvantages of using the direct write-off method?

MANAGING YOUR WRITING

The heads of the marketing and finance areas at your business are arguing about tight versus easy credit policies. One feels the policy should be tightened and the other feels it should be eased. The division manager is concerned about what approach to use and asks for your advice. Prepare a memo to the division manager stating arguments for and against tight and easy credit policies. The manager will use this information to help determine which policy to establish.

DEMONSTRATION PROBLEM

Budke and Budke, a landscaping service, uses the allowance method to record the following transactions related to accounts receivable. Adjusting and closing entries also completed during the current year ended December 31, 19--, are described below.

Mar.   6   Received 50% of the $12,000 balance owed by Columbia Gardens, a bankrupt business, and wrote off the remainder as uncollectible.

June 12   Reinstated the account of Ronald Stillman, which had been written off in the previous year, and received $2,250 cash in full settlement.

Sept. 19   Wrote off the $13,800 balance owed by Kelly Richeson, who has no assets.

Nov.   9   Reinstated the account of Jackie Kwas, which had been written off in the preceding year, and received $2,175 cash in full settlement.

Dec. 27   Wrote off the following accounts as uncollectible, in compound entry form: Blair & Smith, $10,480; Landscapes Unlimited, $8,570; Beekman Brothers, $22,500; B. J. McKay, $9,300.

Dec. 31   Based on an aging analysis of $1,460,000 of accounts receivable, it was estimated that $73,500 will be uncollectible. Made the adjusting entry.

31   Made the entry to close the appropriate account to Income Summary.

Selected accounts and beginning balances on January 1 of the current year are as follows:

131.1   Allowance for Doubtful Accounts $95,000 credit
313   Income Summary   —
554   Uncollectible Accounts Expense   —

REQUIRED
1. Open the three selected accounts.
2. Enter the transactions and the adjusting and closing entries described above in general journal form. After each entry, post to the three accounts named.
3. Determine the net realizable value as of December 31, 19--.

SOLUTION

1, 2.

GENERAL LEDGER

ACCOUNT: **Allowance for Doubtful Accounts**   ACCOUNT NO. **131.1**

DATE		ITEM	POST. REF.	DEBIT	CREDIT	BALANCE DEBIT	BALANCE CREDIT
19-- Jan.	1	Balance	✓				95 000 00
Mar.	6		J12	6 000 00			89 000 00
June	12		J13		2 250 00		91 250 00
Sept.	19		J13	13 800 00			77 450 00
Nov.	9		J13		2 175 00		79 625 00
Dec.	27		J13	50 850 00			28 775 00
	31		J13		44 725 00		73 500 00

ACCOUNT: **Income Summary**   ACCOUNT NO. **313**

DATE		ITEM	POST. REF.	DEBIT	CREDIT	BALANCE DEBIT	BALANCE CREDIT
19-- Dec.	31		J13	44 725 00		44 725 00	

ACCOUNT: **Uncollectible Accounts Expense**   ACCOUNT NO. **554**

DATE		ITEM	POST. REF.	DEBIT	CREDIT	BALANCE DEBIT	BALANCE CREDIT
19-- Dec.	31		J13	44 725 00		44 725 00	
	31		J13		44 725 00	—	

2.

			GENERAL JOURNAL				PAGE 12	
	DATE		DESCRIPTION	POST. REF.	DEBIT		CREDIT	
1	Mar. 19--	6	Cash		6 0 0 0 00			1
2			Accounts Rec./Columbia Gardens				6 0 0 0 00	2
3			Collection on account					3
4								4
5		6	Allowance for Doubtful Accounts	131.1	6 0 0 0 00			5
6			Accounts Rec./Columbia Gardens				6 0 0 0 00	6
7			Wrote off uncollectible account					7
8								8
9								9

			GENERAL JOURNAL				PAGE 13	
	DATE		DESCRIPTION	POST. REF.	DEBIT		CREDIT	
1	June 19--	12	Accounts Receivable/R. Stillman		2 2 5 0 00			1
2			Allowance for Doubtful Accounts	131.1			2 2 5 0 00	2
3			Reinstated account receivable					3
4								4
5		12	Cash		2 2 5 0 00			5
6			Accounts Receivable/R. Stillman				2 2 5 0 00	6
7			Collection on account					7
8								8
9	Sept.	19	Allowance for Doubtful Accounts	131.1	13 8 0 0 00			9
10			Accounts Receivable/K. Richeson				13 8 0 0 00	10
11			Wrote off uncollectible account					11
12								12
13	Nov.	9	Accounts Receivable/J. Kwas		2 1 7 5 00			13
14			Allowance for Doubtful Accounts	131.1			2 1 7 5 00	14
15			Reinstated account receivable					15
16								16
17		9	Cash		2 1 7 5 00			17
18			Accounts Receivable/J. Kwas				2 1 7 5 00	18
19			Collection on account					19
20								20
21	Dec.	27	Allowance for Doubtful Accounts	131.1	50 8 5 0 00			21
22			Accounts Rec./Blair & Smith				10 4 8 0 00	22
23			Accounts Rec./Landscapes Unl.				8 5 7 0 00	23
24			Accounts Rec./Beekman Bros.				22 5 0 0 00	24
25			Accounts Rec./B. J. McKay				9 3 0 0 00	25
26			Wrote off uncollectible accounts					26
27								27
28			Adjusting Entry					28
29		31	Uncollectible Accounts Expense	554	44 7 2 5 00			29
30			Allowance for Doubtful Accounts	131.1			44 7 2 5 00	30
31								31
32			Closing Entry					32
33		31	Income Summary	313	44 7 2 5 00			33
34			Uncollectible Accounts Expense	554			44 7 2 5 00	34
35								35

3.	Accounts receivable, December 31, 19--	$1,460,000
	Less allowance for doubtful accounts	73,500
	Net realizable value	$1,386,500

SERIES A EXERCISES

2 EXERCISE 16A1 UNCOLLECTIBLE ACCOUNTS EXPENSE—PERCENTAGE OF SALES   Ryan's Express has total credit sales for the year of $180,000 and estimates that 3% of its credit sales will be uncollectible. Record the end-of-period adjusting entry on December 31, in general journal form, to enter the estimate for uncollectible accounts expense. Assume the following independent conditions existed prior to the adjustment:

a.   Allowance for Doubtful Accounts has a credit balance of $925.
b.   Allowance for Doubtful Accounts has a debit balance of $385.

2 EXERCISE 16A2 UNCOLLECTIBLE ACCOUNTS EXPENSE—PERCENTAGE OF RECEIVABLES   Tammie's Toyota Sales and Service estimates the amount of uncollectible accounts using the percentage of receivables method. After aging the accounts, it is estimated that $4,250 will not be collected. Record the end-of-period adjusting entry on December 31, in general journal form, to enter the estimate for uncollectible accounts expense. Assume the following independent conditions existed prior to the adjustment:

a.   Allowance for Doubtful Accounts has a credit balance of $690.
b.   Allowance for Doubtful Accounts has a debit balance of $275.

2 EXERCISE 16A3 ENTRIES FOR UNCOLLECTIBLE ACCOUNTS—ALLOWANCE METHOD   Julia Alvarez, owner of Alvarez Rentals, uses the allowance method in accounting for uncollectible accounts. Record the following transactions in general journal form.

July   7 Wrote off $5,350 owed by Randy Dalzell, who has no assets.
Aug.   12 Wrote off $2,870 owed by Jason Flint, who declared bankruptcy.
Sept. 27 Reinstated the account of Randy Dalzell, which had been written off on July 7, and received $5,350 cash in full settlement.

2 EXERCISE 16A4 UNCOLLECTIBLE ACCOUNTS EXPENSE—PERCENTAGE OF SALES AND PERCENTAGE OF RECEIVABLES   At the end of the current year, the accounts receivable account of Glenn's Nursery Supplies has a debit balance of $390,000. Credit sales are $2,800,000. Record the end-of-period adjusting entry on December 31, in general journal form, to enter the estimate for uncollectible accounts expense. Assume the following independent conditions existed prior to the adjustment:

1. Allowance for Doubtful Accounts has a credit balance of $1,760.
   a. The percentage of sales method is used and uncollectible accounts expense is estimated to be 1% of credit sales.
   b. The percentage of receivables method is used and an analysis of the accounts produces an estimate of $30,330 in uncollectible accounts.
2. Allowance for Doubtful Accounts has a debit balance of $1,900.
   a. The percentage of sales method is used and uncollectible accounts expense is estimated to be 3/4 of 1% of credit sales.
   b. The percentage of receivables method is used and an analysis of the accounts produces an estimate of $29,890 in uncollectible accounts.

3 **EXERCISE 16A5 DIRECT WRITE-OFF METHOD** Rudy Wray, owner of Wray Pharmacy, uses the direct write-off method in accounting for uncollectible accounts. Record the following transactions in general journal form.

July 20 Wrote off $2,325 owed by Joe Balouka, who has no assets.
Oct. 15 Wrote off $1,675 owed by Alice Rose, who declared bankruptcy.

3 **EXERCISE 16A6 COLLECTION OF ACCOUNT WRITTEN OFF— DIRECT WRITE-OFF METHOD** Como's Music Store uses the direct write-off method in accounting for uncollectible accounts. Record the following transactions in general journal form.

19-7
May 8 Wrote off $1,745 owed by Vickie Lawrence, who has no assets.
July 15 Wrote off $1,300 owed by Dan Utter, who declared bankruptcy.
Sept. 2 Reinstated the account of Vickie Lawrence, which had been written off on May 8, and received $1,745 cash in full settlement.

19-8
May 15 Reinstated the account of Dan Utter, which had been written off the previous year, and received $1,300 cash in full settlement.

1 **EXERCISE 16A7 CALCULATION OF NET REALIZABLE VALUE** J. B. Bucks owns a department store that has a $45,000 balance in Accounts Receivable and a $3,000 credit balance in Allowance for Doubtful Accounts.

a. Determine the net realizable value of the accounts receivable.
b. Assume that an account receivable in the amount of $400 was written off using the allowance method. Determine the net realizable value of the accounts receivable after the write off.

SERIES A PROBLEMS

1/2 **PROBLEM 16A1 UNCOLLECTIBLE ACCOUNTS—ALLOWANCE METHOD** Emery Nurseries used the allowance method to record the following transactions, adjusting entries, and closing entries during the year ended December 31, 19--.

Feb. 9 Received 60% of the $5,000 balance owed by Patty's Petunias, a bankrupt business, and wrote off the remainder as uncollectible.

May 28 Reinstated the account of Danielle Bell, which had been written off in the preceding year, and received $2,400 cash in full settlement.

Aug. 16 Wrote off the $8,200 balance owed by Rich Bouie as uncollectible.

Oct. 5 Reinstated the account of Bonnie McCelland, which had been written off in the preceding year, and received $3,600 cash in full settlement.

Dec. 28 Wrote off the following accounts as uncollectible, in compound entry form: Bloudeck & Rhodes, $14,450; Creative Landscapers, $16,100; Ramona Randol, $12,750.

31 Based on an aging analysis of the $980,000 of accounts receivable, it was estimated that $58,700 will be uncollectible. Made the adjusting entry.

31 Made the entry to close the appropriate account to Income Summary.

Selected accounts and beginning balances on January 1 of the current year are as follows:

131.1	Allowance for Doubtful Accounts	$52,000 credit
313	Income Summary	—
554	Uncollectible Accounts Expense	—

REQUIRED
1. Open the three selected accounts.
2. Enter the transactions and the adjusting and closing entries described above in a general journal (page 6). After each entry, post to the three accounts named.
3. Determine the net realizable value as of December 31.

2 **PROBLEM 16A2 DOUBTFUL ACCOUNTS—PERCENTAGE OF SALES AND PERCENTAGE OF RECEIVABLES**   At the completion of the current fiscal year ending December 31, the balance of Accounts Receivable for Yang's Gift Shop was $30,000. Credit sales for the year were $355,200.

REQUIRED
Make the necessary adjusting entry in general journal form under each of the following assumptions. Show calculations for the amount of each adjustment and the resulting net realizable value.
1. Allowance for Doubtful Accounts has a credit balance of $330.
   a. The percentage of sales method is used and uncollectible accounts expense is estimated to be 2.0% of credit sales.
   b. The percentage of receivables method is used and an analysis of the accounts produces an estimate of $6,950 in uncollectible accounts.

   2. Allowance for Doubtful Accounts has a debit balance of $400.
   a. The percentage of sales method is used and uncollectible accounts expense is estimated to be 1.5% of credit sales.
   b. The percentage of receivables method is used and an analysis of the accounts produces an estimate of $5,685 in uncollectible accounts.

1/2 **PROBLEM 16A3 AGING ACCOUNTS RECEIVABLE**   An analysis of the accounts receivable of Johnson Company as of December 31, 19--, reveals the following.

Age Interval	Balance	Estimated Percent Uncollectible
Not yet due	$65,000	2%
1–30 days past due	4,500	5
31–60 days past due	3,550	10
61–90 days past due	1,650	25
91–180 days past due	1,200	35
181–365 days past due	650	55
Over 365 days past due	400	85
Total	$76,950	

REQUIRED
1. Prepare an aging schedule as of December 31, 19--, by adding the following column to the three columns shown above: Estimated Amount Uncollectible.
2. Assuming that Allowance for Doubtful Accounts had a credit balance of $620 before adjustment, record the end-of-period adjusting entry in general journal form to enter the estimate for the uncollectible accounts expense.

3 **PROBLEM 16A4 DIRECT WRITE-OFF METHOD**   Williams & Hendricks Distributors use the direct write-off method in accounting for uncollectible accounts.

19-5
Feb.   18 Sold merchandise on account to Merry Merchants, $17,500.
Mar.   22 Sold merchandise on account to Utter Unicorns, $14,300.
June   3 Received $10,000 from Merry Merchants and wrote off the remainder owed on the sale of February 18 as uncollectible.
Sept.   9 Received $8,000 from Utter Unicorns and wrote off the remainder owed on the sale of March 22 as uncollectible.
Nov.   13 Reinstated the account of Merry Merchants, which had been written off on June 3, and received $7,500 cash in full settlement.

19-6
Jan.   17 Reinstated the account of Utter Unicorns, which had been written off on September 9 of the previous year, and received $6,300 cash in full settlement.

REQUIRED
Record the above transactions in general journal form.

SERIES B EXERCISES

2   **EXERCISE 16B1 UNCOLLECTIBLE ACCOUNTS EXPENSE—PERCENTAGE OF SALES**   Nicole's Neckties has total credit sales for the year of $380,000 and estimates that 2% of its credit sales will be uncollectible. Record the end-of-period adjusting entry on December 31, in general journal form, to enter the estimate for uncollectible accounts expense. Assume the following independent conditions existed prior to the adjustment:

a.   Allowance for Doubtful Accounts has a credit balance of $430.
b.   Allowance for Doubtful Accounts has a debit balance of $295.

2   **EXERCISE 16B2 UNCOLLECTIBLE ACCOUNTS EXPENSE—PERCENTAGE OF RECEIVABLES**   Charlie's Chevy Sales and Service estimates the amount of uncollectible accounts using the percentage of receivables method. After aging the accounts, it is estimated that $3,935 will not be collected. Record the end-of-period adjusting entry on December 31, in general journal form, to enter the estimate for uncollectible accounts expense. Assume the following independent conditions existed prior to the adjustment:

a.   Allowance for Doubtful Accounts has a credit balance of $245.
b.   Allowance for Doubtful Accounts has a debit balance of $560.

2   **EXERCISE 16B3 UNCOLLECTIBLE ACCOUNTS—ALLOWANCE METHOD**   Raynette Ramos, owner of Ramos Rentals, uses the allowance method in accounting for uncollectible accounts. Record the following transactions in general journal form.

July   9   Wrote off $6,040 owed by Sue Sanchez, who has no assets.
Aug.   15   Wrote off $4,790 owed by Lonnie Jones, who declared bankruptcy.
Sept. 23   Reinstated the account of Sue Sanchez, which had been written
            off on July 9, and received $6,040 cash in full settlement.

2   **EXERCISE 16B4 UNCOLLECTIBLE ACCOUNTS EXPENSE—PERCENTAGE OF SALES AND PERCENTAGE OF RECEIVABLES**   At the end of the current year, the accounts receivable account of Parker's Nursery Supplies has a debit balance of $350,000. Credit sales are $2,300,000. Record the end-of-period adjusting entry on December 31, in general journal form, to enter the estimate for uncollectible accounts expense. Assume the following independent conditions existed prior to the adjustment:

1.   Allowance for Doubtful Accounts has a credit balance of $1,920.
  a.   The percentage of sales method is used and uncollectible accounts expense is estimated to be 1% of credit sales.
  b.   The percentage of receivables method is used and an analysis of the accounts produces an estimate of $24,560 in uncollectible accounts.

2. Allowance for Doubtful Accounts has a debit balance of $1,280.
   a. The percentage of sales method is used and uncollectible accounts expense is estimated to be ¾ of 1% of credit sales.
   b. The percentage of receivables method is used and an analysis of the accounts produces an estimate of $22,440 in uncollectible accounts.

3 **EXERCISE 16B5 DIRECT WRITE-OFF METHOD**   Brent Mussellman, owner of Brent's Barbells, uses the direct write-off method in accounting for uncollectible accounts. Record the following transactions in general journal form.

July   19 Wrote off $1,935 owed by Arnold Swartz, who has no assets.
Oct.   12 Wrote off $2,125 owed by Janice Strong, who declared bankruptcy

3 **EXERCISE 16B6 COLLECTION OF ACCOUNT WRITTEN OFF— DIRECT WRITE-OFF METHOD**   Madonna's Music Store uses the direct write-off method in accounting for uncollectible accounts. Record the following transactions in general journal form.

19-4
May   5 Wrote off $2,360 owed by Neal Dammond, who has no assets.
July   18 Wrote off $1,255 owed by Maxine Mouse, who declared bankruptcy.
Sept. 20 Reinstated the account of Neal Dammond, which had been written off on May 5, and received $2,360 cash in full settlement.

19-5
May   11 Reinstated the account of Maxine Mouse, which had been written off the previous year, and received $1,255 cash in full settlement.

1 **EXERCISE 16B7 CALCULATION OF NET REALIZABLE VALUE** Mary Martin owns a department store that has a $65,200 balance in Accounts Receivable and a $5,175 credit balance in Allowance for Doubtful Accounts.

   a. Determine the net realizable value of the accounts receivable.
   b. Assume that an account receivable in the amount of $900 was written off using the allowance method. Determine the net realizable value of the accounts receivable after the write off.

SERIES B PROBLEMS

1/2 **PROBLEM 16B1 ALLOWANCE METHOD**   Lewis Warehouse used the allowance method to record the following transactions, adjusting entries, and closing entries during the year ended December 31, 19--.

Feb.   7 Received 70% of the $8,000 balance owed by Luxury Sofas, a bankrupt business, and wrote off the remainder as uncollectible.
May   26 Reinstated the account of Sandy Johnson, which had been written off in the preceding year, and received $3,725 cash in full settlement.

continued

Aug. 15 Wrote off the $9,350 balance owed by Becky Goss as uncollectible.

Oct.   6 Reinstated the account of Doreen Woods, which had been written off in the preceding year, and received $4,320 cash in full settlement.

Dec. 29 Wrote off the following accounts as uncollectible, in compound entry form: Schmidt & Yeager, $13,945; Economy Homes, $15,830; Davis Industries, $11,865.

      31 Based on an aging analysis of the $1,175,000 of accounts receivable, it was estimated that $67,150 will be uncollectible. Made the adjusting entry.

      31 Made the entry to close the appropriate account to Income Summary.

Selected accounts and beginning balances on January 1 of the current year are as follows:

131.1	Allowance for Doubtful Accounts	$49,850 credit
313	Income Summary	—
554	Uncollectible Accounts Expense	—

REQUIRED
1. Open the three selected accounts.
2. Enter the transactions and the adjusting and closing entries described above in a general journal (page 6). After each entry, post to the three accounts named.
3. Determine the net realizable value as of December 31, 19--.

2   **PROBLEM 16B2 DOUBTFUL ACCOUNTS—PERCENTAGE OF SALES AND PERCENTAGE OF RECEIVABLES**   At the completion of the current fiscal year ending December 31, the balance of the accounts receivable account for Anderson's Greeting Cards was $180,000. Credit sales for the year were $1,950,000.

REQUIRED
Make the necessary adjusting entry in general journal form under each of the following assumptions. Show calculations for the amount of each adjustment and the resulting net realizable value.
1. Allowance for Doubtful Accounts has a credit balance of $2,600.
   a. The percentage of sales method is used and uncollectible accounts expense is estimated to be 1.5% of credit sales.
   b. The percentage of receivables method is used and an analysis of the accounts produces an estimate of $30,250 in uncollectible accounts.
2. Allowance for Doubtful Accounts has a debit balance of $1,900.
   a. The percentage of sales method is used and uncollectible accounts expense is estimated to be 1.0% of credit sales.
   b. The percentage of receivables method is used and an analysis of the accounts produces an estimate of $20,500 in uncollectible accounts.

1/2 **PROBLEM 16B3 AGING ACCOUNTS RECEIVABLE**   An analysis of the accounts receivable of Matsushita Company as of December 31, 19--, reveals the following.

Age Interval	Balance	Estimated Percent Uncollectible
Not yet due	$250,000	1.5%
1–30 days past due	17,000	4
31–60 days past due	12,800	9
61–90 days past due	8,200	20
91–180 days past due	4,600	30
181–365 days past due	4,200	45
Over 365 days past due	1,400	75
Total	$298,200	

REQUIRED

1. Prepare an aging schedule as of December 31, 19--, by adding the following column to the three columns shown above: Estimated Amount Uncollectible.
2. Assuming that Allowance for Doubtful Accounts had a credit balance of $1,750 before adjustment, record the end-of-period adjusting entry in general journal form to enter the estimate for the uncollectible accounts expense.

3 **PROBLEM 16B4 DIRECT WRITE-OFF METHOD**   Lee and Chen Distributors uses the direct write-off method in accounting for uncollectible accounts.

19-8
Feb.   16   Sold merchandise on account to Biggs and Daughters, $16,000.
Mar.   23   Sold merchandise on account to Lloyd Place, $12,800.
June   8   Received $12,000 from Biggs and Daughters and wrote off the remainder owed on the sale of February 16 as uncollectible.
Sept.   27   Received $7,000 from Lloyd Place and wrote off the remainder owed on the sale of March 23 as uncollectible.
Nov.   18   Reinstated the account of Biggs and Daughters, which had been written off on June 8, and received $4,000 cash in full settlement.

19-9
Jan.   11   Reinstated the account of Lloyd Place, which had been written off on September 27 of the previous year, and received $5,800 cash in full settlement.

REQUIRED
Record the above transactions in general journal form.

MASTERY PROBLEM

Sam and Robert are identical twins. They opened identical businesses and experienced identical transactions. However, they decided to estimate uncollectible accounts in different ways. Sam elected to use the percentage of sales method and Robert elected to use the percentage of receivables method. Listed below are the summary transactions and other relevant information for both businesses for 19--. Remember, both businesses experienced the same events: credit sales, collections of receivables, and write-offs. The only difference between the businesses is the method of estimating uncollectible accounts.

		Sam	**Robert**
a.	Balance of Cash, January 1, 19--	$300,000	$300,000
b.	Balance of Accounts Receivable, January 1	50,000	50,000
c.	Balance of Allowance for Doubtful Accounts, January 1	5,000	5,000
d.	Sales on account during 19--	550,000	550,000
e.	Collections on account during 19--	530,000	530,000
f.	Uncollectible accounts written off during 19--	4,500	4,500
g.	Collections made on accounts written off during 19--	500	500

REQUIRED
1. Enter items (a) through (c) in two sets of general ledger accounts: one for Sam and one for Robert.
2. Prepare entries in a general journal (page 4) for summary transactions (d) through (g) for Sam.
3. Post the entries to a general ledger for Sam, using the following accounts and numbers:

Cash	111
Accounts Receivable	131
Allowance for Doubtful Accounts	131.1
Sales	411
Uncollectible Accounts Expense	554

4. Sam estimates that 1% of all sales on account will be uncollectible. Calculate the estimated uncollectible accounts expense and make the appropriate adjusting entry in a general journal. Post the entry to the general ledger accounts on December 31, 19--.
5. Compute the net realizable value of Sam's accounts receivable on December 31, 19--.
6. Prepare entries in a general journal (page 4) for summary transactions (d) through (g) for Robert.
7. Post the entries to a general ledger for Robert, using the same accounts and numbers as were used for Sam.
8. Robert bases the estimate of uncollectible accounts on an aging schedule of accounts receivable. Using the following information, compute the estimated uncollectible amounts and make the appropriate adjusting entry in a general journal. Post the entry to the general ledger accounts on December 31, 19--.

Customers	Invoice Dates and Amounts for Unpaid Invoices					
Beets, D.	10/7	$2,300	11/15	$1,200	12/18	$8,500
Cook, L.	6/1	1,200	8/15	2,500		
Hylton, D.	9/23	4,300	10/22	2,500	12/23	2,800
Martin, D.	10/15	5,400	11/12	3,200	12/15	1,500
Stokes, D.	9/9	200	12/15	9,500		
Taylor, T.	11/20	400	12/10	1,400		
Thomas, O.	12/2	5,500				
Tower, R.	12/15	2,300				
Williams, G.	11/18	2,800	12/8	8,000		

All sales are billed n/30. The following aging chart is used to estimate the uncollectibles using the percentage of receivables method.

Age Interval	Estimated Percent Uncollectible
Not yet due	2%
1–30 days	5
31–60 days	10
61–90 days	25
91–120 days	50
Over 120 days	80

9. Calculate the net realizable value for Robert on December 31, 19--.

17

Accounting for Notes and Interest

You recently arranged to borrow $3,000 at the bank. The term was 12 months and the interest rate was set at 9%. At the closing meeting on the loan, the loan officer gave you a check for $2,730, explaining that "the interest of $270 had been deducted in advance." Is the bank trying to cheat you? What interest rate are you really paying to borrow the $2,730 (rather than the $3,000 you had wanted)?

In Chapter 16, we learned how to account for accounts receivable. Recall that an account receivable is an unwritten promise by a customer to pay for goods or services. In this chapter, we will learn how to account for a more formal, written type of receivable called a promissory note.

After completing our study of notes receivable, we will learn to account for notes payable. You will see that a note payable is similar to a note receivable. Both are promissory notes. We simply look at the note from two different points of view. A note receivable is someone's promise to pay you. A note payable is your promise to pay someone else.

THE PROMISSORY NOTE

LO1   Describe a promissory note.

A **promissory note** (usually called a note) is a written promise to pay a specific sum at a definite future date. The note must be signed by the person or business agreeing to make the payment, known as the **maker** of the note. The note must be payable to a specific person or business, known as the **payee**.

Notes are often used when credit is extended for 60 days or more, or when large amounts of money are involved. Figure 17-1 shows one form of promissory note. Paul DeBruke, the maker of the note, promises to pay a specific amount of money ($1,500) at a definite future time (90 days after June 9). Sarah Morney, the payee of the note, is to receive the specified amount of money. Notice that to DeBruke it is a note payable while to Morney it is a note receivable.

FIGURE 17-1   Promissory Note

$ 1,500.00	June 9 19 --
Ninety days *after date* I *promise to pay to*	
the order of Sarah Morney	Payee
One thousand five hundred and 00/100 *Dollars*	
Payable at Brentwood Bank	
With interest at 9% per annum from date	
No. 6 *Due* Sept. 7, 19-- *Paul DeBruke*	Maker

Notes may be interest-bearing or non-interest bearing. An **interest-bearing note** is one with an explicit interest rate stated on the face of the note. The note in Figure 17-1 is a 9% interest-bearing note. A **non-interest bearing note** is one on which no rate of interest is specified, although the note does include an interest component. Notes signed when borrowing from a bank often are of this type. This type of transaction is illustrated later in the chapter.

CALCULATING INTEREST AND DETERMINING DUE DATE

LO2 Calculate interest on and determine the due date of promissory notes.

To calculate interest on notes, three factors are used:

1. Principal of the note
2. Rate of interest
3. Term of the note

The **principal of the note** is the face amount of the note that the maker promises to pay at maturity. The principal is the base on which the interest is calculated. The principal of the note in Figure 17-1 is $1,500.

The **rate of interest** usually is expressed as a percentage, such as 8% or 10%. Ordinarily an annual rate is used, but in some cases a monthly rate is quoted, such as 1.5% a month. A rate of 1.5% a month is equivalent to a rate of 18% a year payable monthly (1.5% x 12 = 18%). The rate of interest on the note in Figure 17-1 is 9% per year.

The **term of the note** is the months or days from the date of issue to the date of maturity. The term of the note is used to calculate **time**, which is the term of the note stated as a fraction of a year. When the term of the note is specified in months, time is calculated on the basis of months. For example, a three-month note issued on June 1 is payable on September 1, and time is calculated as follows:

Time

3 months ÷ 12 months = 1/4 year

When the term of a note is specified in days or when the due date is specified in a note, time is computed using the exact number of days from the date of the note to the date of its maturity. In making this computation, the maturity date is counted, but the date of issue is not. For example, for a $1,000, 9% note dated March 1, with a due date of June 1, time is computed as follows:

LEARNING KEY ▸ To compute the time of a note, count the maturity date; do *not* count the date of issue.

Days in March	31	
Less: Date of note, March 1	1	
Days remaining in March		30
Add: Days in April		30
Days in May		31
Maturity date, June 1		1
Total time in days		92

Time = 92/360

Notice the use of 360 in the denominator in the above calculation. In computing interest, it is common to use 360 days as a year. Most banks and business firms follow this practice, although some banks and all federal government agencies use 365 days as the base in computing daily interest.

The due date of the note in Figure 17-1 is September 7. The term of the note is 90 days, calculated as follows:

Days in June	30	
Less: Date of note, June 9	9	
Days remaining in June		21
Add: Days in July		31
Days in August		31
Days in September (up to and including maturity date)		7
Total time in days		90

Calculating Interest

The principal, interest rate, and time of the note are used in the following formula to calculate interest:

Interest = Principal x Rate x Time

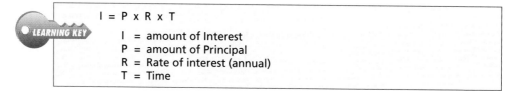

I = P x R x T

I = amount of Interest
P = amount of Principal
R = Rate of interest (annual)
T = Time

For the $1,000, 9% note described on page 584, interest is calculated as follows:

$$I = P \times R \times T$$
$$= \$1,000 \times 9\% \times 92/360$$
$$= \$23$$

For a $2,000, 8% note due in 3 months, interest is calculated as follows:

$$I = P \times R \times T$$
$$= \$2,000 \times 8\% \times 3/12$$
$$= \$40$$

For the note in Figure 17-1, interest is calculated as follows:

$$I = P \times R \times T$$
$$= \$1,500 \times 9\% \times 90/360$$
$$= \$33.75$$

The principal of the note plus interest equals the **maturity value** of the note. For example, the maturity value of the $1,000 note on page 586 is $1,023. Similarly, the maturity value of the $2,000 note is $2,040. Figure 17-2 uses a time line to illustrate the gradual accumulation of interest on the $1,000 note to its $1,023 maturity value.

FIGURE 17-2   Accumulation of Interest Time Line

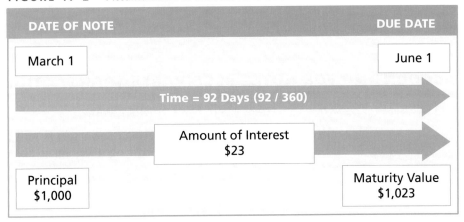

Determining the Due Date

As explained above, the period of time between the date of issue and the maturity date of a note may be stated in either months or days. If the term of the note is stated in months, then the due date is determined by counting the number of months from the date the note was issued. The note is due on the date in the month of maturity that corresponds with the date the note was issued. For example, a three-month note dated August 10 would be due November 10. If there is no date in the month of maturity corresponding to the issue date, the due date is the last day of the month. For example, a three-month note dated January 31 would be due April 30.

If the term of the note is stated in days, the due date is the specified number of days after the issue date. To determine the due date, apply the following three steps:

STEP 1   Subtract the date on which the note was issued from the number of days in the month of issuance.

STEP 2   Add to the result of STEP 1 the number of days in as many months as possible without exceeding the time of the note.

STEP 3   Subtract the result of STEP 2 from the time of the note. The result is the date of the month the note is due.

To calculate the due date of the note in Figure 17-1, a 90-day note dated June 9, apply the three steps as follows:

STEP 1   Days in June   30
          Less: Date of note, June   9
          Result of STEP 1   21

STEP 2   Result of STEP 1   21
          Add: Days in July   31
                Days in August   31
          Result of STEP 2   83

STEP 3   Time of note   90 days
          Less: Result of STEP 2   83
                Due date: September   7

ACCOUNTING FOR NOTES RECEIVABLE TRANSACTIONS

LO3 Account for notes receivable transactions and accrued interest.

Businesses other than banks and savings and loans generally encounter six types of transactions involving notes receivable:

1. Note received from a customer to obtain an extension of time for payment of an account
2. Note collected at maturity
3. Note renewed at maturity
4. Note discounted before maturity
5. Note dishonored
6. Collection of dishonored note

Note Received from a Customer to Extend Time for Payment

When a customer's account is due, the customer may issue a note for all or part of the amount. A business may be willing to accept the note for two reasons. First, the note is a formal, written promise to pay. This note can be converted to cash at a bank if necessary. Second, the note is likely to bear interest.

Assume that Michael Putter owes Linesch Hardware Co. $2,000 on account. To settle the account, Putter gives Linesch a 90-day, 10% note dated June 8. This transaction is entered by Linesch as follows:

15	June	8	Notes Receivable	2 0 0 0 00		15
16			Accounts Receivable/M. Putter		2 0 0 0 00	16
17			Received note to settle account			17

If instead, Putter gives a check for $250 and a note for $1,750 to settle the account, Linesch makes the following entry:

15	June	8	Cash		2 5 0 00			15
16			Notes Receivable		1 7 5 0 00			16
17			Accounts Receivable/M. Putter			2 0 0 0 00	17
18			Received cash and note to				18
19			settle account				19

Note Collected at Maturity

When a note receivable matures, it may be collected:

1. By the payee,
2. By the bank named in the note (in Figure 17-1, Brentwood Bank), or
3. By a bank where it was left for collection.

Assume that on September 6, Putter pays Linesch the $2,000 principal plus $50 interest on the note described above. Linesch makes the following entry:

31	Sept.	6	Cash		2 0 5 0 00			31
32			Notes Receivable			2 0 0 0 00	32
33			Interest Revenue			5 0 00	33
34			Received payment of note with				34
35			interest				35

When a bank makes the collection, it notifies the payee that the net amount has been added to the payee's account. The bank uses a **credit advice** like the one shown in Figure 17-3 for this purpose.

FIGURE 17-3   Credit Advice

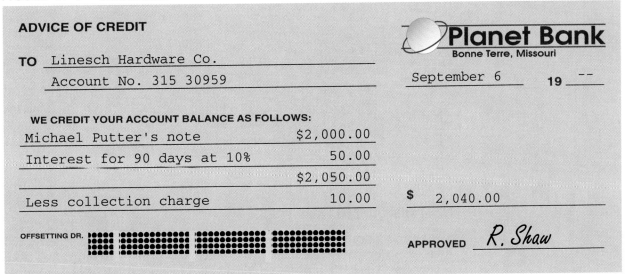

Assume that Linesch left Putter's 90-day, 10% note for $2,000 at Planet Bank for collection. On September 6, the bank notifies Linesch that the note plus $50 interest have been collected. The bank fee for collecting the note was $10. Linesch enters this transaction as follows:

38	Sept. 6	Cash		2 0 4 0 00				38
39		Collection Expense		1 0 00				39
40		Notes Receivable				2 0 0 0 00		40
41		Interest Revenue				5 0 00		41
42		Received payment of note with						42
43		interest, less collection fee						43

Note Renewed at Maturity

If the maker of a note is unable to pay the amount due at maturity, the payee may allow the maker to renew all or part of the note. Assume that at maturity of the $2,000 note, Putter pays only the $50 interest and gives a new 60-day, 10% note. Linesch enters this transaction as follows:

31	Sept. 6	Cash		5 0 00				31
32		Notes Receivable (new note)		2 0 0 0 00				32
33		Notes Receivable (old note)				2 0 0 0 00		33
34		Interest Revenue				5 0 00		34
35		Received new note plus						35
36		interest on old note						36

If Putter pays $50 interest plus $500 on the principal and gives a new 90-day, 11% note for $1,500, Linesch makes the following entry:

38	Sept. 6	Cash		5 5 0 00				38
39		Notes Receivable (new note)		1 5 0 0 00				39
40		Notes Receivable (old note)				2 0 0 0 00		40
41		Interest Revenue				5 0 00		41
42		Received new note plus partial						42
43		payment and interest on old						43
44		note						44

Note Discounted

If a business needs cash before the due date of a note, it can endorse the note and transfer it to a bank. This process is called **discounting a note receivable**. The bank charges an interest fee called a **bank discount** for the time between the date of discounting and the due date of the note. The difference between the maturity value of the note and the bank discount is called the **proceeds**. This is the amount of cash received by the business discounting the note.

Maturity Value – Discount = Proceeds

 LEARNING KEY | To calculate the discount amount, use the maturity value of the note, not the principal amount.

Assume that the $2,000, 10%, 90-day note receivable from Putter dated June 8 is discounted by Linesch at the bank on July 8 at a rate of 12%. To calculate the discount and proceeds, apply the following four steps:

STEP 1   Compute the maturity value of the note.

Principal + Interest = **Maturity Value**
  $2,000   + $50   = $2,050

STEP 2   Compute the number of days in the discount period—from the discount date to the due date.

Discount date	July 8	
Days in July		31
Less: Discount date	July	8
Remaining days in July		23
Add: Days in August		31
Due date	September	6
Days in **discount period**		60

STEP 3   Compute the discount amount.

Maturity Value* × Discount Rate × Discount Period = **Discount Amount**
      $2,050   ×   12%   ×   60/360   = $41

*Note that in calculating the discount amount, the *maturity value* of the note is used, not the principal.

STEP 4   Compute the proceeds.

Maturity Value – Discount Amount = **Proceeds**
      $2,050   – $41   = $2,009

Figure 17-4 shows a time line illustration of this transaction.
The excess of the $2,009 proceeds over the $2,000 face value of the note represents interest revenue of $9. Linesch enters this transaction as follows:

26	July	8	Cash		2 0 0 9 00			26
27			Notes Receivable			2 0 0 0 00		27
28			Interest Revenue				9 00	28
29			Discounted note receivable					29

FIGURE 17-4 Discounted Note Receivable Time Line

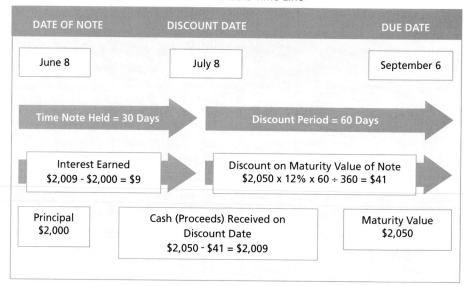

If the proceeds from discounting a note are less than the face value of the note, the difference represents interest expense. For example, if the proceeds from discounting Putter's $2,000 note were only $1,992, Linesch would make the following entry:

33	July	8	Cash			1 9 9 2	00						33
34			Interest Expense			8	00						34
35			Notes Receivable						2 0 0 0	00			35
36			Discounted note receivable										36

When a note receivable is discounted, the business that endorses the note becomes potentially liable to the bank. If the maker of the note does not pay it at maturity, the business that discounted the note must pay the maturity value and any bank fees to the bank. This kind of potential liability that may become a real liability, depending on future events, is called a **contingent liability**. A contingent liability does not affect the accounting records. It is disclosed in the notes to the financial statements.

Note Dishonored

If the maker of a note does not pay or renew it at maturity, the note is said to be **dishonored**. The maker of the note is still liable to the payee for the principal amount plus interest. But, a dishonored note loses its legal status as a note receivable. Therefore, the payee transfers the amount due from Notes Receivable to Accounts Receivable. For example, if the $2,000, 10%, 90-day note from Putter is dishonored, Linesch makes the following entry:

16	19-- Sept.	6	Accounts Receivable/M. Putter		2 0 5 0	00							16
17			Notes Receivable					2 0 0 0	00				17
18			Interest Revenue							5 0	00		18
19			Note receivable dishonored										19

Notice that the $50 difference between the maturity value and principal of the note is credited to Interest Revenue. This is done even though the amount has not been collected. Recall that under accrual accounting, revenue is recognized when earned, regardless of when cash is received. The time period of the note has passed, so the interest has been earned.

If the claim against Putter turns out to be worthless, the $2,050 will be treated as an uncollectible account receivable. Chapter 16 showed how to account for this type of transaction.

If the dishonored note is one that was discounted at a bank, the endorser usually must pay the bank the principal, interest, and any bank fees. The endorser records the total amount paid to the bank as an account receivable from the maker of the note. Assume that the $2,000 note receivable discounted on July 8 for proceeds of $2,009 was dishonored by Putter at maturity. The bank bills Linesch for the $2,000 principal of the note, $50 interest, and a $10 bank fee, a total of $2,060. Linesch pays the bank and makes the following journal entry:

23	19-- Sept.	6	Accounts Receivable/M. Putter		2 0 6 0	00							23
24			Cash					2 0 6 0	00				24
25			Paid bank for dishonored note										25

Note that the $10 bank fee is included in the amount receivable from Putter. This is because the fee was incurred as a result of Putter's dishonoring of the note, and this is not Linesch's expense.

Collection of Dishonored Note

What if a note that has been dishonored eventually is collected? When this occurs, the payee records collection of the account receivable. In addition, interest usually is charged for the period from the due date of the original note to the final collection date. Interest is based on the maturity value of the note plus the bank fee, if any, incurred when the note was dishonored. Let's go back to Putter's $2,000 note that Linesch held until maturity when it was dishonored and transferred to Accounts Receivable on September 6. Assume that on October 16, Putter pays the original maturity value of the note ($2,050) plus interest for the period from September 6 to October 16. Interest would be computed as follows:

Original Maturity Value x Rate x   Time

$$\$2,050 \times 10\% \times 40*/360 = \$22.78$$

*Days in September	30
Less: Date of note, September 6	6
Days remaining in September	24
Add: Days in October	16
Total time in days	40

Linesch would make the following journal entry:

16	Oct. 19--	16	Cash			2	0	7	2	78				16
17			Accounts Receivable								2	0	5 0 00	17
18			Interest Revenue										2 2 78	18
19			Collected dishonored note with											19
20			interest											20

Notes Receivable Register

When a business receives many notes, it may keep a **notes receivable register**. This is a detailed auxiliary record of notes receivable. Figure 17-5 shows an abbreviated version of such a register. A more complete register might also include the number of each note and where the note is payable. The information contained in the register is obtained directly from the notes.

FIGURE 17-5   Notes Receivable Register (Left Side)

NOTES RECEIVABLE REGISTER

DATE RECEIVED		MAKER	TIME	DUE DATE		AMOUNT
19-- Apr.	4	L. Peters	60 day	June	3	4 0 0 00
	21	I. Slaw	60 day	June	20	6 0 0 00
May	2	S. Alpart	30 day	June	1	7 0 0 00
	19	L. Shein	90 day	Aug.	17	8 0 0 00
June	20	J. Slaw	60 day	Aug.	19	5 0 0 00

FIGURE 17-5   Notes Receivable Register (Right Side)

PAGE 1

INTEREST		DISCOUNTED		DATE COLLECTED		REMARKS
RATE	AMOUNT	BANK	DATE			
8%	5 33			June	3	
9%	9 00			June	20	Renewal for $500
9%	5 25			June	1	Sent for collection 5/30/--
9%	1 8 00					
9%	7 50					Renewal of 4/21/-- note

Accrued Interest Receivable

Under accrual accounting, revenue is recognized when it is earned. For notes receivable, interest literally is earned day by day. It would be impractical, however, to record the interest revenue each day. Instead, for notes that are received and due within a single accounting period, no entry is made for interest revenue until the note is due.

For notes that are received in one period and due in the following period, however, accrued interest must be recorded at the end of the period. **Accrued interest on notes receivable** is interest revenue that has been earned but not yet received. The amount of accrued interest can be computed from the notes themselves or from the notes receivable register. The notes receivable register in Figure 17-5 can be used as an example. On June 30, the end of this company's fiscal year, two notes are outstanding. Accrued interest on these notes is calculated as follows:

Principal	Date of Issue	Rate of Interest	Days From Issue Date to June 30	Accrued Interest June 30
$800.00	May 19	9%	42	$8.40
500.00	June 20	9%	10	1.25
Total accrued interest on notes receivable				$9.65

The following adjusting entry is made on June 30 for the accrued interest:

16	19-- June	30	Accrued Interest Receivable			9 65		16
17			Interest Revenue				9 65	17
18								18

Accrued Interest Receivable is reported as a current asset on the balance sheet. Interest Revenue is reported as other revenue on the income statement.

ACCOUNTING FOR NOTES PAYABLE TRANSACTIONS

LO4 Account for notes payable transactions and accrued interest.

Businesses generally encounter four types of transactions involving notes payable:

1. Note issued to a supplier to obtain an extension of time for payment of an account
2. Note issued as security for cash loan
3. Note paid at maturity
4. Note renewed at maturity

Note Issued to a Supplier to Extend Time for Payment

When a firm's account with a supplier is due, the supplier may be willing to accept a note for all or part of the amount due. Assume that Linesch Hardware Co. owes Bella & Co. $700 on June 11. If Linesch issues Bella a 90-day, 10% note for $700, Linesch makes the following entry:

26	June 11	Accounts Payable		7 0 0 00		26
27		Notes Payable			7 0 0 00	27
28		Issued note to settle account				28

If instead, Linesch gives Bella a check for $200 and a 90-day, 10% note for $500, the entry by Linesch is:

32	June 11	Accounts Payable		7 0 0 00		32
33		Cash			2 0 0 00	33
34		Notes Payable			5 0 0 00	34
35		Made partial payment and				35
36		issued note to settle account				36

Note Issued as Security for Cash Loan

Businesses sometimes have brief periods during which receipts from customers are not adequate to finance operations. During such periods, businesses commonly borrow money from banks on short-term notes. Assume that on June 16, Linesch borrows $6,000 from the Planet Bank on a 60-day, 10.5% note. This transaction is entered as follows:

38	June 16	Cash		6 0 0 0 00		38
39		Notes Payable			6 0 0 0 00	39
40		Issued note for bank loan				40

 **LEARNING KEY**   To calculate the discount amount, use the maturity value of the note.

When making a loan, banks often deduct interest in advance, using a procedure known as **discounting**. The nature of this transaction and the procedures for handling it are similar to those used for discounting notes receivable (see pages 590–592). To illustrate, suppose that Linesch borrowed $6,000 on a 60-day, non-interest bearing note which the bank discounted at 10.5%. The bank calculates the **bank discount** at 10.5% and deducts this amount from the $6,000 principal of the note. The amount of the discount and the proceeds to Linesch are calculated using the following three steps:

STEP 1 Compute the maturity value of the note.

Principal + Interest = **Maturity Value**
  $6,000 +   0   = $6,000

STEP 2 Compute the discount amount.

Maturity Value* × Discount Rate × Discount Period = **Discount Amount**
    $6,000   ×   10.5%   ×   60/360   = $105

*Note that in calculating the discount amount, the *maturity value* of the note is used.

STEP 3 Compute the proceeds.

Maturity Value − Discount Amount = **Proceeds**
   $6,000   − $105   = $5,895

Figure 17-6 shows a time-line illustration of this transaction.

FIGURE 17-6   Time-Line for Discounted Note Payable

Linesch records receipt of the $5,895 proceeds ($6,000 − $105) from the loan as follows:

14	June 16	Cash		5 8 9 5 00				14
15		Discount on Notes Payable		1 0 5 00				15
16		Notes Payable				6 0 0 0 00		16
17		Issued note for bank loan						17

The $105 debit to Discount on Notes Payable is an offset to the $6,000 note payable. Linesch's liability at this time is only $5,895, which is the net amount, or **proceeds**, received from the bank. Discount on Notes Payable is a contra-liability account. As shown in Figure 17-7 it is reported as a deduction from Notes Payable on the balance sheet.

FIGURE 17-7   Notes Payable and Related Discount on the Balance Sheet

Current liabilities:		
Notes payable	$6 0 0 0 00	
Less: Discount on notes payable	1 0 5 00	$5 8 9 5 00

Stated Versus Effective Interest Rate.   The stated rate of interest was 10.5% on both the "interest-bearing" and "discounted" notes. Notice, however, that the real interest rates on the two notes are not the same. With the interest-bearing note, Linesch obtained $6,000 for 60 days at a cost of $105—exactly 10.5%.

$$\frac{\$105}{\$6,000} = \frac{1.75\%}{\text{for 60 days}} \times \frac{360 \text{ days}}{60 \text{ days}} = 10.5\% \text{ for 360 days}$$

With the discounted note, Linesch paid $105 for the use of only $5,895 for 60 days—a rate of nearly 10.7%. This rate is known as the **effective rate** of interest.

$$\frac{\$105}{\$5,895} = \frac{1.781\%}{\text{for 60 days}} \times \frac{360 \text{ days}}{60 \text{ days}} = 10.686\% \text{ for 360 days}$$

Note Paid at Maturity

The proper entry to make when a note is paid at maturity depends on whether the note is interest bearing or non-interest bearing. For an interest-bearing note, the same entry is made for payment to a supplier or to a bank. For example, let's reconsider Linesch's $6,000, 60-day, 10.5% note due August 15. When the note is paid on August 15, Linesch will make the following entry:

	19--				
21	Aug.	15	Notes Payable	6 0 0 0 00		21
22			Interest Expense	1 0 5 00		22
23			Cash		6 1 0 5 00	23
24			Paid note with interest at			24
25			maturity			25

For a non-interest bearing note from a bank, the entry to record the payment of the note is different. This is because Discount on Notes Payable was debited when the money was borrowed. For example, recall Linesch's $6,000, 60-day, non-interest bearing note discounted by the bank at 10.5%. When the money was borrowed, the following entry was made:

	19--				
14	June	16	Cash	5 8 9 5 00		14
15			Discount on Notes Payable	1 0 5 00		15
16			Notes Payable		6 0 0 0 00	16
17			Issued note for bank loan			17

The $105 discount gradually becomes interest expense. This expense is recognized when the $6,000 principal amount of the note is repaid on August 15, the due date. Linesch will enter the payment of the note at maturity as follows:

22	Aug. 15	Notes Payable	6 0 0 0 00			22
23		Interest Expense	1 0 5 00			23
24		Cash		6 0 0 0 00	24
25		Discount on Notes Payable		1 0 5 00	25
26		Paid note at maturity			26

Note Renewed at Maturity

The payee of a note may allow the maker to renew all or part of the note at maturity. For example, let's reconsider the $6,000 interest-bearing note that Linesch issued to Planet Bank on June 16. Assume that on August 15 Linesch pays $105 interest and $1,000 on the principal of this note and gives a new 60-day, 10.5% note for $5,000. Linesch enters this transaction as follows:

27	Aug. 15	Notes Payable (old note)	6 0 0 0 00			27
28		Interest Expense	1 0 5 00			28
29		Cash		1 1 0 5 00	29
30		Notes Payable (new note)		5 0 0 0 00	30
31		Paid interest and part of			31
32		principal on old note and			32
33		issued new note			33

Notes Payable Register

When a business issues many notes, it may keep a **notes payable register**. This is a detailed auxiliary record of notes payable. An abbreviated version of one is shown in Figure 17-8. A more complete register might also include the number of each note and where the note is payable. The information contained in the register is obtained directly from the notes.

FIGURE 17-8   Notes Payable Register

NOTES PAYABLE REGISTER

DATE ISSUED	PAYEE	TIME	DUE DATE	AMOUNT	INTEREST RATE	INTEREST AMOUNT	DATE PAID	REMARKS
Apr. 14	L. Knoop	60 days	June 13	2 0 0 0 00	9%	3 0 00	June 13	Settled 2/14/-- invoice
May 13	Apex Bank	90 days	Aug. 11	8 0 0 0 00	10%	2 0 0 00		
June 2	S. Bront	30 days	July 2	1 5 0 0 00	11%	1 3 75		Settled 4/2/-- invoice

Accrued Interest Payable

As with notes receivable, it also is necessary to record accrued interest on notes payable at the end of the period. For notes payable issued in one period and due in the following period, accrued interest payable must be recorded. **Accrued interest on notes payable** is interest expense that has been incurred but not paid. The amount of accrued interest can be computed from the notes themselves or from the notes payable register.

 The adjusting entry for accrued interest on an interest-bearing note payable is different from the adjusting entry for accrued interest on a non-interest bearing note from a bank.

The proper entry for accrued interest on notes payable depends on whether the note is interest bearing or non-interest bearing. Assume that a $900, 60-day, 10% note was issued on May 31. On June 30, this company's fiscal year end, an adjusting entry for accrued interest of $7.50 ($900 × 10% × 30/360) is recorded as follows:

19	19-- June	30	Interest Expense			7 50			19
20			Accrued Interest Payable				7 50		20
21									21

Assume instead that the $900, 60-day note was non-interest bearing and discounted at the bank at 10%. When the money was borrowed, the following entry was made:

23	19-- May	31	Cash			8 8 5 00			23
24			Discount on Notes Payable*			1 5 00			24
25			Notes Payable				9 0 0 00		25
26			Issued note for bank loan						26
27			*$900 x 10% x 60/360 = $15						27

On June 30, part of the discount must be transferred from Discount on Notes Payable to Interest Expense. The note was issued on May 31, so 30 days of the 60-day life of the note has passed. Thus, half of the balance in Discount on Notes Payable should be recognized as interest expense. The following adjusting entry is made on June 30:

29	19-- June	30	Interest Expense			7 50			29
30			Discount on Notes Payable				7 50		30
31									31

Interest Expense is reported as other expense on the income statement. Accrued Interest Payable is reported as a current liability on the balance sheet. As previously illustrated in Figure 17-7 (page 598), Discount on Notes Payable is reported as a contra-liability to Notes Payable on the balance sheet.

KEY POINTS

1 A promissory note is a written promise to pay a specific sum at a future date. Notes are used when credit is extended for periods of 60 days or more, or when large amounts of money are involved. To the maker of a note, the note is a note payable. To the payee of a note, the note is a note receivable.

2 The following formula is used to calculate interest on notes receivable and payable:

$$I \;=\; P \;\times\; R \;\times\; T$$
$$\text{Interest} = \text{Principal} \times \text{Rate} \times \text{Time}$$

3 Businesses generally encounter six types of transactions involving notes receivable:

1. Note received from a customer to extend time for payment
2. Note collected at maturity
3. Note renewed at maturity
4. Note discounted before maturity
5. Note dishonored
6. Collection of dishonored note

When a note receivable is discounted at a bank, four steps are applied to calculate the discount and proceeds:

STEP 1   Compute the maturity value of the note.
STEP 2   Compute the number of days in the discount period.
STEP 3   Compute the discount amount.
STEP 4   Compute the proceeds.

If a note receivable that was discounted at a bank is dishonored, the endorser of the note is liable to the bank for the maturity value of the note and any bank fees.
    Notes that are received in one period and due in the following period require an adjustment for accrued interest at the end of the period.

4 Businesses generally encounter four types of transactions involving notes payable:

1. Note issued to a supplier to extend time for payment
2. Note issued as security for cash loan
3. Note paid at maturity
4. Note renewed at maturity

When money is borrowed at a bank on a non-interest bearing note that is discounted by the bank, three steps are used to calculate the discount and proceeds:

STEP 1   Compute the maturity value of the note.

STEP 2   Compute the discount amount.

STEP 3   Compute the proceeds.

Notes payable that are issued in one period and due in the following period require an adjustment for accrued interest at the end of the period. The proper entry depends on whether or not the note is interest-bearing.

KEY TERMS

accrued interest on notes payable 600   Interest expense that has been incurred but not yet paid.

accrued interest on notes receivable 595   Interest revenue that has been earned but not yet received.

bank discount (note payable) 596   The amount that the bank deducts from the principal of a note.

bank discount (note receivable) 590   An interest fee that the bank charges for the time between the date of discounting and the due date of the note.

contingent liability 592   A potential liability that may become a real liability, depending on future events. In the case of a note discounted at a bank, the business that discounted the note must pay the maturity value and any bank fees if the maker of the note does not pay it at maturity.

credit advice 589   A notification to the payee that the bank has collected interest on a note and added the amount to the payee's account.

discounting (note payable) 596   The procedure, which banks often use, of deducting interest in advance when making a loan.

discounting a note receivable 590   Transferring a note receivable to a bank for cash before the due date of the note.

dishonored 592   If the maker of a note does not pay or renew it at maturity, the note is said to be dishonored.

effective rate 598   The interest amount paid divided by the proceeds received on a discounted note. This amount will differ from the stated rate on a discounted note.

interest-bearing note 585   A note with an explicit interest rate stated on the face of the note.

maker 584   The person or business agreeing to make the payment on a note.

maturity value 587   The principal of the note plus interest equals the maturity value of the note.

non-interest bearing note 585   A note on which no rate of interest is specified, although the note does include an interest component.

notes payable register 599   A detailed auxiliary record of notes payable.

notes receivable register 594   A detailed auxiliary record of notes receivable.

payee 584 The specific person or business to whom the note is payable.

principal of the note 585 The face amount of the note that the maker promises to pay at maturity. The principal is the base on which the interest is calculated.

proceeds (note payable) 597 The net amount received from the bank.

proceeds (note receivable) 591 The difference between the maturity value of the note and the bank discount. This is the amount of cash received by the business discounting the note.

promissory note 584 A written promise to pay a specific sum at a definite future date.

rate of interest 585 The rate at which interest is charged, usually expressed as an annual percentage, but in some cases a monthly rate is quoted.

term of the note 585 The months or days from the date of issue to the date of maturity.

time 585 The term of the note stated as a fraction of a year.

REVIEW QUESTIONS

1. What is the formula for calculating interest on promissory notes?
2. In the formula for calculating interest, how is time computed?
3. What number of days is considered as a year by most banks and business firms in computing interest?
4. What six types of transactions involving notes receivable do businesses generally encounter?
5. If a note receivable is discounted at a bank, on what amount and for what time period does the bank compute the discount?
6. If a note receivable that was discounted at a bank is dishonored by its maker, what is the responsibility of the person or business discounting the note?
7. On which notes receivable and notes payable is it necessary to record accrued interest at the end of the period?
8. What four types of transactions involving notes payable do businesses generally encounter?
9. When a business borrows money from a bank on a non-interest bearing note, how are the bank discount and proceeds calculated?
10. What kind of account is Discount on Notes Payable and how is it reported on the balance sheet?
11. What is the appropriate entry for accrued interest on notes payable for an interest-bearing note? For a non-interest bearing note from a bank?
12. How are Accrued Interest Receivable and Accrued Interest Payable reported on the balance sheet?

MANAGING YOUR WRITING

You are purchasing a new car and plan to finance it through your employee credit union. The credit union has offered you two different promissory note plans, as follows:

Option 1: Three years at 9% interest, with interest payable annually.
Option 2: One year at 8% interest, renewable each year for up to three
more years at the then current interest rate. Interest is payable at
the end of each year.

Prepare a written report summarizing the advantages and disadvantages of
each of these options.

DEMONSTRATION PROBLEM

Barbar Brothers, partners in a wholesale hardware business, completed
the following transactions involving notes and interest during the first
half of 19--:

Jan. 11 Received a $900, 60-day, 10% note from Paul Heinsius in
payment of an account receivable.

18 Borrowed $10,000 from Landmark Bank issuing a 90-day,
11% note.

Feb. 6 Received an $875, 30-day, 9% note from Deborah Douglas in
payment of an account receivable.

21 Issued a $650, 60-day, 11% note to Swanson & Johnson, a
supplier, in payment of an account payable.

Mar. 1 Received a $1,000, 90-day, 10% note from Steve Roberts, a
customer, in payment of an account receivable.

9 Received a check for $881.56 from Deborah Douglas in pay-
ment of note due March 8, including interest.

12 Paul Heinsius dishonored his $900 note due March 12.

31 Discounted the $1,000 note from Steve Roberts at
Manchester Bank at a discount rate of 12%.

Apr. 11 Paul Heinsius paid the original maturity value of his note
due March 12, plus interest at 10% for the 30 days from
March 12 to April 11.

18 Paid Landmark Bank for $10,000 note due today, including
interest. (See January 18 transaction.)

22 Paid Swanson & Johnson $61.92 on the note due today
(interest of $11.92 plus $50 toward the principal), and issued
a new $600, 60-day, 11% note.

May 31 Steve Roberts dishonored his $1,000 note due at the
Manchester Bank yesterday. Paid Manchester Bank $1,000,
plus interest, plus a $10 bank fee, for the dishonored note.

June 20 Issued a $750, 90-day, 9% note to Greene Acres, a supplier,
in payment of an account payable.

REQUIRED

Record each transaction in a general journal.

SOLUTION

	DATE		DESCRIPTION	POST. REF.	DEBIT	CREDIT	
			GENERAL JOURNAL			PAGE 5	
1	Jan.¹⁹⁻	11	Notes Receivable		9 0 0 00		1
2			Accounts Receivable/P. Heinsius			9 0 0 00	2
3			60-day, 10% note				3
4							4
5		18	Cash		10 0 0 0 00		5
6			Notes Payable			10 0 0 0 00	6
7			90-day, 11% note—Landmark				7
8			Bank				8
9							9
10	Feb.	6	Notes Receivable		8 7 5 00		10
11			Accounts Receivable/D. Douglas			8 7 5 00	11
12			30-day, 9% note				12
13							13
14		21	Accounts Payable/Swanson & Johnson		6 5 0 00		14
15			Notes Payable			6 5 0 00	15
16			60-day, 11% note				16
17							17
18	Mar.	1	Notes Receivable		1 0 0 0 00		18
19			Accounts Receivable/S. Roberts			1 0 0 0 00	19
20			90-day, 10% note				20
21							21
22		9	Cash		8 8 1 56		22
23			Notes Receivable			8 7 5 00	23
24			Interest Revenue			6 56	24
25			Principal and interest—				25
26			D. Douglas note				26
27							27
28		12	Accounts Receivable/P. Heinsius		9 1 5 00		28
29			Notes Receivable			9 0 0 00	29
30			Interest Revenue			1 5 00	30
31			Note dishonored				31
32							32
33							33
34							34
35							35
36							36
37							37
38							38
39							39
40							40

GENERAL JOURNAL   PAGE **6**

	DATE		DESCRIPTION	DEBIT	CREDIT	
1	Mar.	31	Cash	1 0 0 4 50		1
2			Notes Receivable		1 0 0 0 00	2
3			Interest Revenue		4 50	3
4			Discounted Steve Roberts' note			4
5			at Manchester Bank			5
6						6
7			Principal $1,000.00			7
8			Interest to maturity 25.00			8
9			Maturity value $1,025.00			9
10			Less: Discount			10
11			($1,025 x 12% x 60/360) 20.50			11
12			Cash Proceeds $1,004.50			12
13						13
14	Apr.	11	Cash	9 2 2 63		14
15			Accounts Receivable/P. Heinsius		9 1 5 00	15
16			Interest Revenue		7 63	16
17			Collection of dishonored note			17
18						18
19		18	Notes Payable	10 0 0 0 00		19
20			Interest Expense	2 7 5 00		20
21			Cash		10 2 7 5 00	21
22			Paid Landmark Bank note due today			22
23						23
24		22	Notes Payable (old note)	6 5 0 00		24
25			Interest Expense	1 1 92		25
26			Cash		6 1 92	26
27			Notes Payable (new note)		6 0 0 00	27
28			Partial payment and issuance of			28
29			new note to Swanson & Johnson			29
30						30
31	May	31	Accounts Receivable/S. Roberts	1 0 3 5 00		31
32			Cash		1 0 3 5 00	32
33			Paid Manchester Bank for			33
34			dishonored note			34
35						35
36			Principal $1,000.00			36
37			Interest 25.00			37
38			Bank fee 10.00			38
39			$1,035.00			39
40						40
41	June	20	Accounts Payable/Greene Acres	7 5 0 00		41
42			Notes Payable		7 5 0 00	42
43			90-day, 9% note			43

2 **EXERCISE 17A1 TERM OF A NOTE**   Calculate total time in days for the following notes. (Assume there are 28 days in February.)

Date of Note	Due Date	Time in Days
May 4	July 17	_____
August 17	October 1	_____
July 5	September 5	_____
December 11	February 5	_____
March 24	May 16	_____
January 6	March 18	_____

2 **EXERCISE 17A2 CALCULATING INTEREST**   Using 360 days as the denominator, calculate interest for the following notes using the formula $I = P \times R \times T$.

Principal	Rate	Time	Interest
$5,000	6.00%	30 days	_____
1,000	7.50	60	_____
4,500	8.00	120	_____
950	6.80	95	_____
1,250	7.25	102	_____
2,900	7.00	90	_____

2 **EXERCISE 17A3 DETERMINING DUE DATE**   Determine the due date for the following notes. (Assume there are 28 days in February.)

Date of Note	Term of Note	Due Date
August 12	90 days	_____
September 1	60	_____
January 3	120	_____
March 18	88	_____
June 11	200	_____
May 17	38	_____

3 **EXERCISE 17A4 JOURNAL ENTRIES (NOTE RENEWED, THEN COLLECTED)**   Prepare general journal entries for the following transactions.

Jan. 15 Received a 30-day, 9% note in payment for accounts receivable balance of $20,000.

Feb. 15 Received $150 (interest) on the old (January 15) note; the old note is renewed for 30 days at 11%.

Mar. 17 Received principal and interest on the new (February 15) note.
    19 Received a 60-day, 9% note in payment for accounts receivable balance of $10,000.

May   6 Received $120 (interest) plus $1,000 principal on the old (March 19) note; the old note is renewed for 60 days (from May 6) at 9%.

July 5 Received principal and interest on the new (May 6) note.

3 **EXERCISE 17A5 JOURNAL ENTRIES (NOTE DISCOUNTED, NOTE DISHONORED)** Prepare general journal entries for the following transactions.

Apr. 6 Received 120-day, 11% note in payment for accounts receivable balance of $3,000.
26 Discounted the note at a rate of 12%.
May 3 Received a 30-day, 10% note in payment for accounts receivable balance of $900.
June 2 The $900, 30-day, 10% note is dishonored.
5 The dishonored note is paid, plus interest at 10% on the maturity value.

3 **EXERCISE 17A6 JOURNAL ENTRIES (ACCRUED INTEREST RECEIVABLE)** At the end of the year the following interest is earned, but not yet received. Record the adjusting entry in a general journal.

Interest on $4,000, 90-day, 12% note (for 15 days)	$20.00
Interest on $7,000, 60-day, 11% note (for 18 days)	38.50
	$58.50

4 **EXERCISE 17A7 JOURNAL ENTRIES (NOTE ISSUED, RENEWED)** Prepare general journal entries for the following transactions.

May 1 Purchased $5,000 worth of equipment from a supplier on account.
June 1 Gave a $5,000, 30-day, 10% note in payment of the account payable.
July 1 Paid $500 cash plus interest to the supplier, extending the note for 30 days from July 1.
31 Paid the note in full.

4 **EXERCISE 17A8 JOURNAL ENTRIES (NOTE DISCOUNTED)** Prepare general journal entries for the following transactions.

July 15 Borrowed $5,000 cash from the bank, giving a 60-day, non-interest bearing note. The note is discounted 12% by the bank.
Sept. 13 Paid the $5,000 note, recognizing the discount as interest expense.

4 **EXERCISE 17A9 JOURNAL ENTRIES (ACCRUED INTEREST PAYABLE)** At the end of the year, the following interest is payable, but not yet paid. Record the adjusting entry in the general journal.

Interest on $5,000, 60-day, 9% note (for 12 days)	$15.00
Interest on $2,500, 30-day, 12% note (for 9 days)	7.50
	$22.50

SERIES A   PROBLEMS

2/3   **PROBLEM 17A1 NOTES RECEIVABLE ENTRIES**   J. K. Pratt Co. had the following transactions:

19-1
July   1 Sold merchandise on account to J. Akita, $750.
July   20 J. Akita gave a $750, 30-day, 10% note to extend time for payment on merchandise purchased on account.
Aug.   21 J. Akita paid note issued July 20 plus interest.
       25 Sold merchandise on account to L. Beene, $1,100.
Sept.   5 L. Beene paid $100 and gave a $1,000, 30-day, 12% note to extend time for payment.
Oct.   5 L. Beene paid note issued September 5, plus interest.
       10 Sold merchandise to R. Harris for $750: $50 plus a $700, 30-day, 11% note.
Nov.   9 R. Harris paid $200 plus interest on note issued October 10, and extended the note ($500) for 30 days.
Dec.   9 R. Harris paid note extended on November 9, plus interest.
       10 Sold merchandise on account to B. Kraus, $1,500.
       15 B. Kraus paid $150 on merchandise purchased on account, and gave a $1,350, 30-day, 12% note to extend time for payment.
19-2
Jan.   14 B. Kraus' note of December 15 is dishonored.
Feb.   13 Collected B. Kraus' dishonored note, plus interest at 12% on the maturity value.

REQUIRED
Record the transactions in a general journal.

PROBLEM 17A2 NOTES RECEIVABLE DISCOUNTING   Movado
2/3   Suppliers had the following transactions:

Mar.   1 Sold merchandise on account to R. Sticca, $5,000.
       20 R. Sticca gave a $5,000, 90-day, 12% note to extend time for payment.
       30 R. Sticca's note is discounted at Commerce Bank at a discount rate of 15%.
Apr.   1 Sold merchandise on account to K. Jones, $3,600.
       20 K. Jones paid $600 and gave a $3,000, 60-day, 10% note to extend time for payment.
May   5 K. Jones' note is discounted at Commerce Bank at a discount rate of 12%.
June   19 K. Jones' note is dishonored. The bank bills Movado for the maturity value of the note plus a $40 bank fee.
July   31 K. Jones' dishonored note is collected; Jones pays Movado the maturity value of the note, the $40 bank fee, and interest at 10% on the maturity value.
Aug.   1 Sold merchandise on account to R. Brown, $5,600.
       12 R. Brown paid $400 and gave a $5,200, 30-day, 12% note to extend time for payment.

continued

Sept. 11 R. Brown paid $400, plus interest, and gave a new $4,800, 60-day, 14% note to extend time for payment.

    26 R. Brown's note is discounted at Commerce Bank at a discount rate of 16%.

Nov. 10 R. Brown's note is dishonored. The bank bills Movado for the maturity value of the note plus a $40 bank fee.

Dec. 15 R. Brown's dishonored note is collected. Brown pays Movado the maturity value of the note, the $40 bank fee, and interest at 14% on the maturity value.

REQUIRED

Record the above transactions in a general journal.

3 **PROBLEM 17A3 ACCRUED INTEREST RECEIVABLE**   The following is a list of outstanding notes receivable as of December 31, 19--.

Maker	Date of Note	Principal	Interest	Term	No. of Days
K. Savelin	12/15/--	$1,000	10%	60 days	16
R. Hillier	12/3/--	5,000	12	90	28
B. Miller	11/30/--	2,800	8	90	31
R. Hansen	11/18/--	7,500	9	120	43

REQUIRED

1. Compute the accrued interest at the end of the year.
2. Prepare the adjusting entry in the general journal.

4 **PROBLEM 17A4 NOTES PAYABLE**   Milo Radio Shop had the following notes payable transactions:

Apr. 1 Borrowed $5,000 from the Builder's Bank, signing a 90-day, 8% note.

    5 Gave a $2,000, 60-day, 10% note to Breaker Parts Co. in full payment of an account payable.

    10 Paid $500 cash and gave a $1,500, 30-day, 12% note to M. K. Reynolds in payment of an account payable.

May 10 Paid $500 cash, plus interest, and issued a new $1,000, 30-day, 14% note to M. K. Reynolds.

    20 Borrowed $3,500 for 60 days from the Builder's Bank on a non-interest bearing note. The discount rate is 12%.

June 4 Paid $500 cash, plus interest, to Breaker Parts Co. (see April 5) and gave a new $1,500, 30-day, 12% note to extend time for payment.

    9 Paid the principal and interest due on the $1,000 note to M. K. Reynolds. (See May 10.)

    30 Paid the principal and interest due on the $5,000 note to the Builder's Bank. (See April 1.)

July 4 Paid the principal and interest due on the $1,500 note to Breaker Parts Co. (See June 4.)

    19 Paid the $3,500 non-interest bearing note to Builder's Bank. (See May 20.)

REQUIRED

Record the above transactions in a general journal.

4 **PROBLEM 17A5 ACCRUED INTEREST PAYABLE** The following is a list of outstanding notes payable as of December 31, 19--:

Maker	Date of Note	Principal	Interest	Term	No. of Days
B. Jones	12/1/--	$1,000	11%	90 days	30
M. Adkins	11/25/--	2,500	9	80	36
T. Plant	12/14/--	3,800	12	120	17
W. Brand	11/19/--	1,900	10	180	42

REQUIRED

1. Compute the accrued interest at the end of the year.
2. Prepare the adjusting entry in the general journal.

SERIES B EXERCISES

2 **EXERCISE 17B1 TERM OF A NOTE** Calculate total time in days for the following notes. (Assume there are 28 days in February.)

Date of Note	Due Date	Time in Days
August 17	October 10	_____
January 12	March 10	_____
July 15	September 13	_____
December 3	February 1	_____
April 11	July 6	_____
October 6	December 18	_____

2 **EXERCISE 17B2 CALCULATING INTEREST** Using 360 days as the denominator, calculate interest for the following notes using the formula $I = P \times R \times T$.

Principal	Rate	Time	Interest
$4,000	7.00%	60 days	_____
3,000	9.50	30	_____
7,500	8.00	150	_____
850	7.90	99	_____
2,250	7.55	122	_____
1,900	8.80	82	_____

2 **EXERCISE 17B3 DETERMINING DUE DATE** Determine the due date for the following notes. (Assume there are 28 days in February).

Date of Note	Term of Note	Due Date
July 11	45 days	_____
December 23	90	_____
April 18	120	_____
October 3	77	_____
January 1	180	_____
August 13	65	_____

3 **EXERCISE 17B4 JOURNAL ENTRIES (NOTE RENEWED, THEN COLLECTED)**   Prepare general journal entries for the following transactions.

May   22   Received a 30-day, 9% note in payment for accounts receivable balance of $22,000.00.

June   21   Received $165.00 cash (interest) on the old (May 22) note; the old note is renewed for 30 days at 10%.

July   21   Received principal and interest on the new (June 21) note.

        28   Received a 45-day, 7% note in payment for accounts receivable balance of $11,600.00.

Sept. 11   Received $101.50 cash (interest) plus $1,600.00 principal on the old (July 28) note; the old note is renewed for 60 days (from September 11) at 9%.

Nov.   10   Received principal and interest on the new (September 11) note.

3 **EXERCISE 17B5 JOURNAL ENTRIES (NOTE DISCOUNTED, NOTE DISHONORED)**   Prepare general journal entries for the following transactions.

Aug.   4   Received a 120-day, 12% note in payment for accounts receivable balance of $4,000.

       14   Discounted the note at a rate of 14%.

Sept. 6   Received a 30-day, 11% note in payment for accounts receivable balance of $1,200.

Oct.   5   The $1,200, 30-day, 11% note is dishonored.

Nov.   4   The dishonored note is paid, plus interest at 11% on the maturity value.

3 **EXERCISE 17B6 JOURNAL ENTRIES (ACCRUED INTEREST RECEIVABLE)**   At the end of the year the following interest is earned, but not yet received. Record the adjusting entry in a general journal.

Interest on $6,000, 60-day, 11% note (for 24 days) $44.00
Interest on $9,000, 90-day, 12% note (for 12 days)   36.00
                                                       $80.00

4 **EXERCISE 17B7 JOURNAL ENTRIES (NOTE ISSUED, RENEWED)**   Prepare general journal entries for the following transactions.

June   15   Purchased $6,000 worth of equipment from a supplier on account.

July   15   Gave a $6,000, 30-day, 12% note in payment of the account payable.

Aug.   14   Paid $600 cash plus interest to the supplier, extending the note for 30 days from August 14.

Sept. 13   Paid the note in full.

4 **EXERCISE 17B8 JOURNAL ENTRIES (NOTE DISCOUNTED)**   Prepare general journal entries for the following transactions.

Sept. 15 Borrowed $7,000 cash from the bank, giving a 60-day, non-interest bearing note. The note is discounted 12% by the bank.

Nov. 14 Paid the $7,000 note, recognizing the discount as interest expense.

4 **EXERCISE 17B9 JOURNAL ENTRIES (ACCRUED INTEREST PAYABLE)** At the end of the year, the following interest is payable, but not yet paid. Record the adjusting entry in the general journal.

Interest on $8,000, 90-day, 8% note (for 18 days)	$32.00
Interest on $4,500, 60-day, 10% note (for 7 days)	8.75
	$40.75

SERIES B PROBLEMS

2/3 **PROBLEM 17B1 NOTES RECEIVABLE ENTRIES** M. L. DiMaurizio had the following notes receivable transactions:

19-3

June 1 Sold merchandise on account to K. Lance, $2,400.

   20 K. Lance gave a $2,400, 30-day, 10% note to extend time for payment.

July 20 K. Lance paid the note plus interest.

   25 Sold merchandise on account to R. Boone, $5,600.

Aug. 4 R. Boone paid $600 and gave a $5,000, 30-day, 12% note to extend time for payment.

Sept. 3 R. Boone paid the note plus interest.

   10 Sold merchandise to T. Akins for $3,000: $400 plus a $2,600, 30-day, 11% note.

Oct. 10 T. Akins paid $600, plus interest, and extended the note ($2,000) for 30 days.

Nov. 9 T. Akins paid the note, plus interest.

   10 Sold merchandise on account to J. Brown, $5,000.

   25 J. Brown paid $1,000 and gave a $4,000, 30-day, 12% note to extend time for payment.

Dec. 25 J. Brown's note is dishonored.

19-4

Jan. 13 J. Brown's dishonored note is collected, plus interest at 12% on the maturity value.

REQUIRED

Record the transactions in a general journal.

2/3 **PROBLEM 17B2 NOTES RECEIVABLE DISCOUNTING** Madison Graphics had the following notes receivable transactions:

May 1 Sold merchandise on account to L. Carney, $5,600.

   20 L. Carney gave a $5,600, 90-day, 12% note to extend time for payment.

continued

May 30 L. Carney's note is discounted at Commercial Bank at a discount rate of 15%.

June 1 Sold merchandise on account to P. Arnst, $2,800.

20 P. Arnst paid $400 and gave a $2,400, 60-day, 10% note to extend time for payment.

July 5 P. Arnst's note is discounted at Commercial Bank at a discount rate of 12%.

Aug. 19 P. Arnst's note is dishonored. The bank bills Madison Graphics for the maturity value of the note plus a $30 bank fee.

31 P. Arnst's dishonored note is collected. Arnst pays Madison the maturity value of the note, the $30 bank fee, and interest at 10% on the maturity value.

Sept. 1 Sold merchandise on account to B. Faust, $6,400.

12 B. Faust paid $400 and gave a $6,000, 30-day, 12% note to extend time for payment.

Oct. 12 B. Faust paid $400, plus interest, and gave a new $5,600, 60-day, 14% note to extend time for payment.

26 B. Faust's note is discounted at Commercial Bank at a discount rate of 14%.

Nov. 11 B. Faust's note is dishonored. The bank bills Madison Graphics for the maturity value of the note plus a $30 bank fee.

Dec. 15 B. Faust's dishonored note is collected. Faust pays Madison the maturity value of the note, the $30 bank fee, and interest at 14% on the maturity value.

REQUIRED

Record the above transactions in a general journal.

3 **PROBLEM 17B3 ACCRUED INTEREST RECEIVABLE** The following is a list of outstanding notes receivable as of December 31, 19--.

Maker	Date of Note	Principal	Interest	Term	No. of Days
P. Harrison	12/17/--	$1,200	11.0%	60 days	14
T. Rieber	12/3/--	4,000	12.0	90	28
K. Burke	12/1/--	2,200	9.0	90	30
A. Rogers	11/28/--	4,500	8.5	120	33

REQUIRED

1. Compute the accrued interest at the end of the year.
2. Prepare the adjusting entry in the general journal.

4 **PROBLEM 17B4 NOTES PAYABLE** Mary's Travel Agency has the following notes payable transactions:

Apr. 1 Borrowed $4,000 from Finance Bank, signing a 90-day, 8% note.

5 Gave a $3,000, 60-day, 10% note to Krenshaw Airline in full payment of an account payable.

10 Paid $400 and issued a $1,600, 30-day, 12% note to Andrew Adams in payment of an account payable.

continued

May 10 Paid $400, plus interest, and gave a new $1,200, 30-day, 14% note to Andrew Adams.

　　20 Borrowed $4,500 for 60 days from Finance Bank on a non-interest bearing note. The discount rate is 14%.

June 4 Paid $500, plus interest, to Krenshaw Airline (see April 5) and gave a new $2,500, 30-day, 12% note to extend time for payment.

　　9 Paid the principal and interest due on the $1,200 note to Andrew Adams. (See May 10.)

　　30 Paid the principal and interest due on the $4,000 note to Finance Bank. (See April 1.)

July 4 Paid the principal and interest due on the $2,500 note to Krenshaw Airline. (See June 4.)

　　19 Paid the $4,500 non-interest bearing note to Finance Bank. (See May 20.)

REQUIRED

Record the above transactions in a general journal.

4 **PROBLEM 17B5 ACCRUED INTEREST PAYABLE**   The following is a list of outstanding notes payable as of December 31, 19--:

Payee	Date of Note	Principal	Interest	Term	No. of Days
X. Rayal	12/1/--	$1,200	11%	90 days	30
G. Richards	11/28/--	2,300	8	80	33
A. Gray	12/16/--	3,400	12	120	15
O. Hankins	11/13/--	2,900	10	180	48

REQUIRED

1. Compute the accrued interest at the end of the year.
2. Prepare the adjusting entry in the general journal.

MASTERY PROBLEM

Eddie Edwards and Phil Bell own and operate The Second Hand Equipment Shop. The following transactions involving notes and interest were completed during the last three months of 19--.

Oct. 1 Issued $6,800, 60 day, 10% note to Mac Farm Equipment in payment of an account payable.

　　15 Received a $2,000, 60-day, 12% note from R. Chambers in payment of an account receivable.

Nov. 1 Discounted the note received from R. Chambers on October 15 at Merchants National Bank. The discount rate is 14%.

　　1 Borrowed $5,000 from First National Bank on a three-month, non-interest bearing note that was discounted at 10%.

　　20 Received a $4,000, 90-day, 9% note from L. Revsine in payment of an account receivable.

　　30 Issued a check to Mac Farm Equipment in payment of the note issued on October 1, including interest.

continued

Dec.   10   Issued a $3,000, 90-day, 9% note to Remak Tractors to extend the time for payment of an account payable.

16   Received notification from Merchants National Bank that R. Chambers has dishonored his note. A check is issued to cover the note plus a $20 bank fee that must be paid to the bank.

REQUIRED

1.   Prepare general journal entries for the above transactions.
2.   Prepare necessary adjusting entries for the notes outstanding on December 31.

18

Accounting for Merchandise Inventory

As you walk through a grocery store, have you ever wondered what the store paid for each item? It would be nice to know which items were really "good buys" and which were "over priced." What happens when management pays different amounts for identical units on the shelf? The selling price is the same. Otherwise, we could have customers fighting over the item marked with the lower price. If the units, such as cans of beans, look identical, how does the store "know" which unit was sold: the one with the higher, or lower, purchase price? Does it matter?

One of the major reasons for keeping accounting records is to determine the net income (or net loss) of a business. For a merchandising firm, the cost of merchandise available for sale during the accounting period must be divided between the cost of goods (merchandise) sold and the ending merchandise inventory. (Recall that the terms "goods" and "merchandise" mean the same thing and are used interchangeably.) End-of-period adjustments for merchandise inventory were illustrated in earlier chapters. In those illustrations, the costs assigned to the cost of goods sold and ending inventory were provided. In this chapter, you will learn how to determine the dollar amounts assigned to the cost of goods sold and ending merchandise inventory.

THE IMPACT OF MERCHANDISE INVENTORY ON FINANCIAL STATEMENTS

LO1 Explain the impact of merchandise inventory on the financial statements.

A firm's ending inventory must be reported accurately. An error in the reported inventory will cause errors on the income statement, statement of owner's equity, and balance sheet. In addition, since this year's ending inventory becomes next year's beginning inventory, financial statements for the following year will also contain errors.

Figure 18-1 illustrates the impact of an error in the *ending inventory.* The first pair of columns presents partial financial statements when the ending inventory is correct. For this illustration, sales, cost of goods sold and operating expenses are assumed to be the same for 19-1 and 19-2. Thus, the same net income of $30,000 and beginning and ending merchandise inventories of $20,000 are reported for both years.

The second pair of columns in Figure 18-1 illustrates the effects of understating the ending inventory. Understating the ending inventory for 19-1 by $5 causes the cost of goods sold to be overstated by $5 and net income to be understated by $5. Since net income is reported on the statement of owner's equity, Erv Bultman's capital on December 31 is understated by $5. The understated capital also appears in the owner's equity section of the balance sheet. The understated ending inventory is reported in the current assets section of the balance sheet.

Even if the ending inventory for 19-2 is accurately reported, we still have a problem with the income statement. Since the ending inventory for 19-1 was understated, the beginning inventory for 19-2 is understated also ($15 instead of $20). This error causes cost of goods sold to be understated by $5 and net income to be overstated by $5.

At this point, we can see that this inventory error "washes out" over the two-year period. The understated net income for 19-1 is offset by overstated net income in 19-2. Thus, Bultman's capital account as of December 31, 19-2, is reported accurately on the statement of owner's equity and balance sheet at $160. Assuming no future inventory errors, the financial statements for 19-3 and thereafter will be correct.

 LEARNING KEY If the ending inventory for 19-1 is understated, net income for 19-1 is understated and net income for 19-2 is overstated.

FIGURE 18-1   Effect of Inventory Errors on Net Income

	ENDING INVENTORY FOR 19-1 IS CORRECT		ENDING INVENTORY FOR 19-1 IS UNDERSTATED		ENDING INVENTORY FOR 19-2 IS OVERSTATED	
	19-1	19-2	19-1	19-2	19-1	19-2
Income Statement						
Sales	80	80	80	80	80	80
Cost of goods sold:						
Beginning merchandise inventory	20	20	20	15	20	25
Add: Purchases (net)	40	40	40	40	40	40
Cost of goods available for sale	60	60	60	55	60	65
Less: Ending merchandise inventory	(20)	(20)	(15)	(20)	(25)	(20)
Cost of goods sold	(40)	(40)	(45)	(35)	(35)	(45)
Gross profit	40	40	35	45	45	35
Operating expenses	(10)	(10)	(10)	(10)	(10)	(10)
Net Income	30	30	25	35	35	25
Statement of Owner's Equity						
Erv Bultman, capital, January 1	100	130	100	125	100	135
Net income	30	30	25	35	35	25
Erv Bultman, capital, December 31	130	160	125	160	135	160
Balance Sheet (Partial)						
Current assets:						
Merchandise inventory	20	20	15	20	25	20
Owner's equity:						
Erv Bultman, capital	130	160	125	160	135	160

The third pair of columns in Figure 18-1 illustrates the effects of overstating the ending inventory for 19-1. This causes net income to be overstated in 19-1 and understated in 19-2. As discussed above, these errors "wash out" by the end of 19-2. Thus, Bultman's capital account is correct in the 19-2 financial statements.

 LEARNING KEY   If the ending inventory for 19-1 is overstated, net income for 19-1 is overstated and net income for 19-2 is understated.

TYPES OF INVENTORY SYSTEMS: PERIODIC AND PERPETUAL

LO2 Describe the two principal systems of accounting for inventory—the periodic system and the perpetual system.

The two principal systems of accounting for inventory are the periodic and the perpetual systems. The previous chapters discussed the **periodic inventory system** without identifying it by name. Under this system, the balance in the merchandise inventory account is merely a record of the most recent count of the physical inventory. The purchases account is debited for the cost of all goods purchased. The sales account is credited for the selling prices of all goods sold. Under this system, the current merchandise inventory and the cost of goods sold are not determined until the end of the accounting period, when a physical inventory is taken. At that time, the following formula is applied to calculate cost of goods sold.

> **LEARNING KEY**   Under the periodic inventory system, the ending inventory and cost of goods sold are determined at the end of the accounting period, when a physical inventory is taken.

Beginning Inventory (last year's ending physical count)
\+   Net Purchases (account balance at end of this year)

=   Cost of Goods Available for Sale
−   Ending Inventory (this year's ending physical count)

=   Cost of Goods Sold (for this year)

Recall that adjusting entries are needed at the end of the fiscal year to update the merchandise inventory account. These entries are illustrated as Transaction 6 for the periodic method in Figure 18-2.

Under the **perpetual inventory system**, the merchandise inventory account is debited for the cost of all goods purchased, including freight charges, and credited for the cost of all goods sold. In addition, this account is debited when customers return merchandise and is credited when returns

FIGURE 18-2   Entries for Periodic and Perpetual Inventory Systems

TRANSACTION	PERIODIC SYSTEM		PERPETUAL SYSTEM	

1. Purchased merchandise on account, $100.	Purchases
	    Accounts Payable
		100
		100
			Merchandise Inventory
			    Accounts Payable
				100
				100

2. Paid freight charge, $30.	Freight-In
	    Cash
		30
		30
			Merchandise Inventory
			    Cash
				30
				30

3. Sold merchandise on account, $80. The cost of the merchandise sold was $50.	Accounts Receivable
	    Sales
		80
		80
			Accounts Receivable
			    Sales
			
			Cost of Goods Sold
			    Merchandise Inventory
				80
				80
				
				50
				50

4. Merchandise costing $10 was returned to the supplier.	Accounts Payable
	    Purchases Ret. & Allow.
		10
		10
			Accounts Payable
			    Merchandise Inventory
				10
				10

5. Customers returned merchandise sold for $20. The cost of the merchandise was $15.	Sales Ret. and Allow.
	    Accounts Receivable
		20
		20
			Sales Ret. and Allow.
			    Accounts Receivable
			
			Merchandise Inventory
			    Cost of Goods Sold
				20
				20
				
				15
				15

6. Adjusting entries made at the end of the accounting period.	Income Summary
	    Merchandise Inventory
	
	Merchandise Inventory
	    Income Summary
		xx
		xx
		
		xx
		xx
			Not necessary if physical inventory agrees with amount reported in merchandise inventory account.	

and allowances are granted by suppliers. Thus, the balance of the account represents the cost of goods on hand at all times. When goods are sold, the cost of goods sold account is debited for the same amount that the merchandise inventory account is credited. No year-end adjusting entry is necessary as long as the physical inventory agrees with the amount reported in the merchandise inventory account. Figure 18-2 compares entries made under the periodic and perpetual inventory systems.

> **LEARNING KEY** Under the perpetual inventory system, cost of goods sold and the amount of merchandise inventory on hand are continually updated as merchandise is bought and sold.

ASSIGNING COST TO INVENTORY AND COST OF GOODS SOLD

LO3 Compute the costs allocated to the ending inventory and cost of goods sold using different inventory methods.

To determine the cost of goods sold and ending inventory, it is important to understand:

1. the purpose of a physical inventory,
2. the specific calculations used under the periodic and perpetual systems, and
3. the role of the lower-of-cost-or-market rule.

Taking a Physical Inventory

Under the periodic system, the goods on hand at the end of the period are counted to allocate merchandise costs between sold and unsold goods. This process is called taking a **physical inventory**. A physical inventory is also important under the perpetual system. It verifies that the amount of merchandise actually held agrees with what is reported in the accounting records.

Taking a physical inventory can be a sizable task. Frequently, it is done after regular business hours. Some firms even cease operations for a few days to take inventory. The ideal time to count the goods is when the quantity on hand is at its lowest level. A fiscal year that starts and ends at the time the stock of goods is normally at its lowest level is known as a **natural business year**. Such a year is used by many businesses for accounting purposes.

Various procedures are followed in taking an inventory to be sure that no items are missed and that no items are included more than once. Frequently, persons taking inventory work in pairs: one counts the items and the other records the information. Usually this information is entered on a special form called an **inventory sheet**, like the one illustrated in Figure 18-3. The inventory sheet has columns for recording the description of each item, the quantity on hand, the cost per unit, and the extension.

Only goods that are the property of the firm should be included in a physical inventory. Two special situations that require care to determine

FIGURE 18-3   Inventory Sheet

INVENTORY Aug. 31 **19** -- **Page** 1					
Sheet No. 1				Costed by C.M.H.	
Called by L.M.M.	Department A			Extended by C.M.H.	
Entered by K.N.	Location Storeroom			Examined by C.J.C.	

Description	Quantity	Unit	Unit Cost	Extensions	
Table lamp	20	ea.	62.80	1,256.00	
Wall rack	18	ea.	19.70	354.60	
Bookcase	7	ea.	88.10	616.70	
End table	13	ea.	53.20	691.60	

Desk	6	ea.	158.30	949.80	
Total					6,465.10

ownership are (1) goods acquired and later sold on **consignment** and (2) goods **in transit**. Goods held on consignment remain the property of the shipper (**consignor**). They should not be included in the inventory of the company holding the goods (**consignee**).

To determine whether goods in transit at year end should be included in inventory, we must know the FOB (free on board) terms. If goods are shipped FOB shipping point, the buyer pays for shipping and the goods belong to the buyer as soon as they are shipped. If goods are shipped FOB destination, the seller pays for shipping and the goods belong to the seller until they are received by the buyer.

> **LEARNING KEY**   Under FOB shipping point, the goods belong to the buyer as soon as they are shipped. Under FOB destination, the goods belong to the seller until they are received by the buyer.

After calculating the quantities of goods owned at the end of the period, the proper cost must be assigned to the inventory. In addition to the purchase price, we include delivery costs (freight-in), insurance, and, occasionally, storage fees. Therefore, cost means all necessary and reasonable costs incurred to get the goods to the buyer's place of business.

If all purchases of the same item were made at the same price per unit, computing the cost of the ending inventory would be simple. We would multiply the number of units by the cost per unit. In a world of changing prices, however, identical items are purchased at different times and at different costs per unit. Of the goods available for sale, how do we decide which units were sold and which units remain on the shelf? As shown in

Figure 18-4, this decision affects the income statement and balance sheet. The four inventory methods listed below have become generally accepted for answering this question.

1. specific identification
2. first-in, first-out (FIFO)
3. weighted-average
4. last-in, first out (LIFO)

These methods may be applied under the periodic or perpetual inventory systems.

FIGURE 18-4   Allocation of Goods Available for Sale to Cost of Goods Sold and Ending Inventory

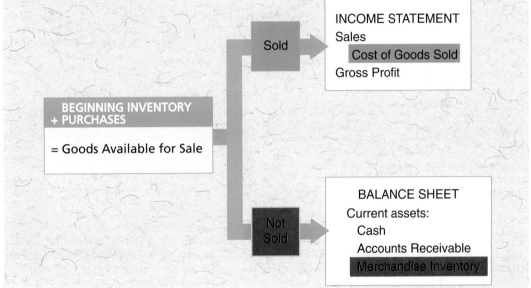

The Periodic Inventory System

Specific Identification Method. When each unit of inventory can be specifically identified, the **specific identification method** can be used. To use this method, inventory items must be physically different from each other, or they must have serial numbers. Examples include cars, motorcycles, furniture, appliances, and fine jewelry. When a unit is sold, its cost is determined from the supplier's invoice. This method is practical only for businesses in which sales volume is relatively low and inventory unit value is relatively high. Otherwise, record keeping becomes expensive and time consuming.

 The specific identification method requires that each inventory item have a distinguishing feature or marking to assure proper identification.

To illustrate how specific identification costing works, assume the following data for an inventory of one specific model of children's bicycles:

Children's Bicycles (Model ZX007)

	Units	Unit Price	Total Cost
On hand at start of period	40	$62	$ 2,480
Purchased during period:			
1st purchase	60	65	3,900
2nd purchase	80	67	5,360
3rd purchase	70	68	4,760
Number of units available for sale	250		$16,500
On hand at end of period	50		
Number of units sold during period	200		

Of the 200 units sold during the period, the bicycle serial numbers show that 30 were from the beginning inventory, 50 were from the first purchase, 60 were from the second purchase, and 60 were from the last purchase. The cost of goods sold and the cost of inventory at the end of the period are determined as shown in Figure 18-5.

FIGURE 18-5   Specific Identification Inventory Method

	COST OF GOODS SOLD			COST OF ENDING INVENTORY		
	Units	Unit Price	Total	Units	Unit Price	Total
Beginning inventory	30	$62	$ 1,860	10	$62	$ 620
First purchase	50	65	3,250	10	65	650
Second purchase	60	67	4,020	20	67	1,340
Third purchase	60	68	4,080	10	68	680
Total	200		$13,210	50		$3,290
Alternative calculation given goods available for sale and cost of goods sold or ending inventory.	Cost of goods available for sale Less: Cost of ending inventory Cost of goods sold		$16,500 (3,290) $13,210	Cost of goods available for sale Less: Cost of goods sold Cost of ending inventory		$16,500 (13,210) $ 3,290

 LEARNING KEY   FIFO means First-In, First-Out.

First-In, First-Out (FIFO) Method. Another widely used method of allocating merchandise cost is called the **first-in, first-out, or FIFO, method.** This costing method assumes that the first goods purchased were the first goods sold. Therefore, the latest goods purchased remain in inventory.

Whenever possible, a business will attempt to sell the older goods first. This is particularly true of businesses that sell perishable items or merchandise that may become obsolete. Grocery stores, fresh fruit stands, and computer software businesses are good examples. These businesses must rotate their stock forward. They pull the oldest bread, milk, fruit, and vegetables to the front of the shelves and try to sell all copies of the current software before a new version arrives. FIFO costing is, therefore, widely used because it often follows the actual movement of goods. It assumes that the oldest units have been sold and the newest or freshest units are in the ending inventory.

Applying FIFO to the bicycle inventory data, the cost of goods sold and the cost of inventory at the end of the period are determined as shown in Figure 18-6.

FIGURE 18-6   FIFO Inventory Method

	COST OF GOODS SOLD			COST OF ENDING INVENTORY		
	Units	Unit Price	Total	Units	Unit Price	Total
Beginning inventory	40	$62	$ 2,480		$62	$ 0
First purchase	60	65	3,900		65	0
Second purchase	80	67	5,360		67	0
Third purchase	20	68	1,360	50	68	3,400
Total	200		$13,100	50		$3,400
Alternative calculation given goods available for sale and cost of goods sold or ending inventory.	Cost of goods available for sale		$16,500	Cost of goods available for sale		$16,500
	Less: Cost of ending inventory		(3,400)	Less: Cost of goods sold		(13,100)
	Cost of goods sold		$13,100	Cost of ending inventory		$ 3,400

Note that the 50 items on hand at the end of the period are considered to be those most recently purchased.

FIFO costing is widely used because firms have used this method for a long time. Accountants are reluctant to change a long-followed method of accounting when such a change would affect the comparability of their income calculations over a period of years. **Consistency** based on comparability is an important accounting principle.

 The consistency principle of accounting suggests that a business should use the same accounting techniques from year to year.

Weighted-Average Method. Another method of allocating merchandise cost is called the **weighted-average method,** or **average cost method.** This costing method is based on the average cost of identical units.

Consider the bicycle inventory data again. The average cost of identical units is determined by dividing the total cost of units available for sale ($16,500) by the total number of units available for sale (250).

$$\frac{\$16,500 \text{ (cost of units available for sale)}}{250 \text{ (units available for sale)}} = \$66 \text{ weighted-average cost per unit}$$

The cost of goods sold and the cost of the end-of-period inventory are calculated as follows:

Cost of goods sold	200 units @ $66 =	$13,200
Cost of ending inventory	50 units @ $66 =	3,300
Total	250 units	$16,500

There is a logical appeal to the weighted-average method of allocating cost between goods sold and goods on hand. In this example, one-fifth (50) of the total units available (250) were unsold. The weighted-average method assigns one-fifth ($3,300) of the total cost ($16,500) to these goods.

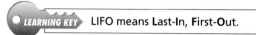 **LEARNING KEY** LIFO means Last-In, First-Out.

Last-In, First-Out (LIFO) Method. A fourth method of allocating merchandise cost is called the **last-in, first-out, or LIFO, method.** It assumes that the sales in the period were made from the most recently purchased goods. Therefore, the earliest goods purchased remain in inventory.

This physical flow is associated with businesses selling products that are not perishable or likely to become obsolete, and may be difficult to handle. Imagine a large barrel of nails at a lumber yard. Customers take nails from the top of the barrel. When the supply gets low, new nails are simply piled on top of the old ones. There is no need to rotate the nails from the bottom to the top of the barrel.

Applying LIFO to the bicycle inventory data, the cost of goods sold and the cost of inventory at the end of the period are determined as shown in Figure 18-7.

FIGURE 18-7   LIFO Inventory Method

	COST OF GOODS SOLD			COST OF ENDING INVENTORY		
	Units	Unit Price	Total	Units	Unit Price	Total
Beginning inventory	0	$62	$ 0	40	$62	$2,480
First purchase	50	65	3,250	10	65	650
Second purchase	80	67	5,360		67	0
Third purchase	70	68	4,760		68	0
Total	200		$13,370	50		$3,130
Alternative calculation given goods available for sale and cost of goods sold or ending inventory.	Cost of goods available for sale		$16,500	Cost of goods available for sale		$16,500
	Less: Cost of ending inventory		(3,130)	Less: Cost of goods sold		(13,370)
	Cost of goods sold		$13,370	Cost of ending inventory		$ 3,130

Note that the 50 units on hand at the end of the period are considered to be the 40 units in the beginning inventory plus 10 of the units from the first purchase.

The LIFO method has been justified on the grounds that the physical movement of goods in some businesses is actually last-in, first-out. This is rarely the case, but the method has become popular for other reasons. One persuasive argument for the use of the LIFO method is that it matches the most current cost of items purchased against the current sales revenue. When the most current costs of purchases are subtracted from sales revenue, the impact of changing prices on the resulting gross profit figure is minimized. In the opinion of many accountants, this is proper and desirable.

Another major reason for the popularity of the LIFO method is its effect on income taxes. When prices are rising, net income calculated under the LIFO method is less than net income calculated under either the FIFO or the weighted-average method. Since the net income amount under LIFO is less, the related income tax will be less. The reverse would be true if prices were falling. However, periods of falling prices over the past two centuries have been few and very brief.

Opponents of the LIFO method contend that its use causes old, out-of-date inventory costs to be shown on the balance sheet. The theoretical and practical merits of FIFO versus LIFO are the subject of much professional debate.

Physical Flows and Cost Flows. Of the four inventory costing methods described, only the specific identification costing method will necessarily reflect cost flows that match physical flows of goods. Each of the other three methods—FIFO, weighted-average, and LIFO—is based on assumed cost flows. The assumed cost flows *are not required to reflect the actual physical movement of goods* within the company. Any one of the three assumed cost flow methods can be used under any set of physical flow conditions. For example, a fresh fruit stand with an actual FIFO flow of inventory may use LIFO for accounting purposes. Similarly, a supplier of building materials that sells nails, lumber, and sand off the top of the pile may use FIFO even though the physical flow of goods is LIFO.

 LEARNING KEY   The inventory method used does not have to match the physical flow of goods.

Comparison of Methods. To compare the results of the four inventory methods, let's assume that the 200 bicycle units in our example were sold for $18,000. Figure 18-8 contrasts the ending inventory, cost of goods sold, and gross profit under each of the four methods.

FIGURE 18-8   Comparison of Inventory Methods

	SPECIFIC IDENTIFICATION		FIFO		WEIGHTED-AVERAGE		LIFO	
Sales		$18,000		$18,000		$18,000		$18,000
Cost of goods sold:								
Beginning inventory	$ 2,480		$ 2,480		$ 2,480		$ 2,480	
Purchases	14,020		14,020		14,020		14,020	
Goods available for sale	$16,500		$16,500		$16,500		$16,500	
Less ending inventory	3,290		3,400		3,300		3,130	
Cost of goods sold		$13,210		$13,100		$13,200		$13,370
Gross profit		$ 4,790		$ 4,900		$ 4,800		$ 4,630

Note that in all cases the total cost of goods available for sale ($16,500) is the same. It is the allocation between goods sold and goods on hand at the end of the period that differs. For example, under FIFO, $13,100 is assigned to cost of goods sold and $3,400 to ending inventory. Under conditions of rising prices, the gross profit is lowest if LIFO is used. This is because the most recent, and therefore the highest, purchase costs are matched against sales revenue.

In periods of rising prices, LIFO produces the lowest net income and FIFO produces the highest net income.

The Perpetual Inventory System

Under the perpetual inventory system, a continuous record is maintained for the quantities and costs of goods on hand at all times. The general ledger account for Merchandise Inventory under such a system is somewhat like the account for Cash. It provides a chronological record of each addition (purchase) and subtraction (sale). The balance of the account at any time shows the cost of goods that should be on hand.

A controlling account and subsidiary ledger are maintained for inventory in much the same way as for accounts receivable and accounts payable.

When perpetual inventory records are kept, the merchandise inventory account in the general ledger is usually a controlling account. A subsidiary ledger is maintained with an account for each type of merchandise. These accounts are often recorded on cards or in computer files. As shown in Figure 18-9, the accounts are designed to handle additions and subtractions and determine the new balance after each change. Goods sold usually are assigned cost on either a FIFO, weighted-average, or LIFO basis. Procedures for applying the FIFO method in a perpetual inventory system are similar to those illustrated for a periodic system. The first merchandise purchased is treated as the first merchandise sold. The illustration in Figure 18-9 is based on the FIFO method. The specific techniques used to apply the weighted-average and LIFO methods in a perpetual system are more complicated. They are illustrated in more advanced texts.

A physical inventory is still important under the perpetual inventory method. It is used to verify the accuracy of the inventory records.

Perpetual inventories do not eliminate the need for taking periodic physical inventories. The perpetual records must be compared with the physical inventory to discover and correct any errors or losses of merchandise from theft or breakage. If a difference is found between the physical count and the amount in the perpetual inventory records, the records must be corrected by an adjusting entry. Normally an account called **Inventory Short and Over** is used. For example, if the book balance is $3,840 and the physical count shows $3,710 worth of merchandise, the $130 shortage would be entered as follows:

FIGURE 18-9   Perpetual Inventory Record: FIFO Method

				CHILDREN'S BICYCLES							
	PURCHASES			**COST OF GOODS SOLD**				**INVENTORY**			
DATE	QUAN-TITY	COST PER UNIT	TOTAL	QUAN-TITY	COST PER UNIT	TOTAL	CUM. TOTAL	QUAN-TITY	COST PER UNIT	SUB-TOTAL	TOTAL
1/1/--								40	62	2,480	2,480
2/15/--				30	62	1,860	1,860	10	62	620	620
3/1/--	60	65	3,900					10 60	62 65	620 3,900	4,520
4/1/--				10 30	62 65	620 1,950	4,430	30	65	1,950	1,950
5/15/--	80	67	5,360					30 80	65 67	1,950 5,360	7,310
6/30/--				30 60	65 67	1,950 4,020	10,400	20	67	1,340	1,340
8/28/--	70	68	4,760					20 70	67 68	1,340 4,760	6,100
10/30/--				20 20	67 68	1,340 1,360	13,100	50	68	3,400	3,400

4		Inventory Short and Over		1 3 0 00			4
5		Merchandise Inventory			1 3 0 00		5
6		To adjust inventory per					6
7		physical count					7

Similarly, if the book balance is $3,840 and the physical count shows $3,900 worth of merchandise, this $60 overage would be entered as follows:

4		Merchandise Inventory		6 0 00			4
5		Inventory Short and Over			6 0 00		5
6		To adjust inventory per					6
7		physical count					7

If Inventory Short and Over has a debit balance, the account is listed with other expenses on the income statement. If it has a credit balance, the account is listed with other revenues on the income statement.

 LEARNING KEY   Inventory Short and Over is reported as other expense or other revenue on the income statement.

A business that sells a wide selection of low-cost goods may not find it practical to keep a perpetual inventory. In contrast, a business that sells a few high-cost items (cars, fine jewelry, stereo equipment) can maintain such a record without incurring excessive processing costs. The increasing use of computers and optical scanning devices at the point-of-sale has enabled more businesses to switch from using the periodic to using the perpetual inventory method.

Lower-of-Cost-or-Market Method of Inventory Valuation

It is a well-established tradition in accounting that gains should not be recognized unless a sale has occurred. If the value of an asset increases while it is being held, no formal entry of the gain is made on the books. On the other hand, if an asset's value declines while it is being held, it is generally considered proper to recognize a loss. This is in keeping with the accounting practice of **conservatism,** which states that when in doubt, the lower asset value and net income measure should be used. Thus, we should never anticipate gains, but we should always anticipate and account for losses.

> The accounting practice of conservatism states that when in doubt, the lower asset value and net income measure should be used. Thus, when in doubt, we should not record gains, but we should record losses.

As applied to inventory, conservatism means that if the value of inventory declines while it is being held, the loss should be recognized in the period of the decline. The purpose of the **lower-of-cost-or-market method** is to recognize such losses on the income statement and to report the lower inventory valuation on the balance sheet.

In applying the lower-of-cost-or-market method, **"cost"** means the dollar amount calculated using one of the four inventory costing methods. **"Market"** means the cost to replace. It is the price in the market in which goods are purchased by the business—not the price in the market in which they are normally sold by the business. The lower-of-cost-or-market method assumes that a decline in the purchase (replacement) price of inventory is accompanied by a decline in the selling price. In this sense, a decline in the purchase (replacement) price signals a decline in the value of the inventory.

> Under lower-of-cost-or-market, market represents the cost to replace the inventory item, not the selling price.

To illustrate the lower-of-cost-or-market method, assume the following end-of-period inventory data for three items:

Item	Recorded Purchase Cost	End-of-Period Market Value	Lower-of-Cost or-Market
1	$ 8,000	$ 7,000	$ 7,000
2	9,000	10,000	9,000
3	7,000	6,500	6,500
	$24,000	$23,500	$22,500

The illustration shows two ways to calculate the lower-of-cost-or-market. First, the lower-of-cost-or-market method can be applied to the total inventory. This involves comparing the $24,000 total cost with the $23,500 *total end-of-period market value*. Under the second approach, the method is applied to each item in inventory. This involves comparing the $24,000 total cost with the $22,500 lower-of-cost-or-market value determined by comparing cost with market value for *each item*. Either approach is acceptable, but the one chosen should be applied consistently across periods.

The difference between the cost and market value is considered a loss due to holding inventory. Normally it is charged to an account such as Loss on Write-Down of Inventory. For example, based on application of the method to the total inventory in the above illustration, a $500 loss ($24,000 – $23,500) is recognized as follows:

14		Loss on Write-Down of Inventory			5 0 0 00				14
15		Merchandise Inventory				5 0 0 00			15
16		To recognize loss in value of							16
17		inventory held							17

The loss due to write-down of inventory should be reported on the income statement as an expense. Although not a preferred treatment, some firms include it in cost of goods sold if the amounts are small.

ESTIMATING ENDING INVENTORY AND COST OF GOODS SOLD

LO4 Estimate the ending inventory and cost of goods sold by using the gross profit and retail inventory methods.

Many firms prepare monthly or quarterly financial statements. To do this, the firm must determine the inventory at the end of the month or quarter and the cost of goods sold for the period. This is not a problem for businesses using the perpetual inventory method. Although these amounts need to be verified by a physical inventory at the end of the year, the unverified amounts are generally reliable estimates and can be used for these "interim" statements.

Businesses using the periodic inventory method must use other methods to estimate the ending inventory and cost of goods sold. Two generally accepted methods are the gross profit method and the retail inventory method.

Gross Profit Method of Estimating Inventory

Under the **gross profit method,** the firm's normal gross profit (Net Sales – Cost of Goods Sold) is used to estimate the cost of goods sold and ending inventory. To illustrate the gross profit method, assume the following data with respect to Groomer Company:

Inventory, start of period	$ 80,000
Net purchases, first month	$ 70,000
Net sales, first month	$110,000
Normal gross profit as a percentage of sales	40%

The estimated cost of goods sold for the month and the estimated merchandise inventory at the end of the month would be determined as shown in Figure 18-10.

FIGURE 18-10   Steps for the Gross Profit Method

Step 1	Compute the cost of goods available for sale.	Cost of goods available for sale: Inventory, start of period $ 80,000 Net purchases, first month 70,000 Cost of goods available for sale $150,000
Step 2	Estimate cost of goods sold by deducting the normal gross profit from net sales.	Estimated cost of goods sold: Net sales $110,000 Normal gross profit ($110,000 x 40%) 44,000 Estimated cost of goods sold 66,000
Step 3	Estimate the ending inventory by deducting cost of goods sold from the cost of goods available for sale.	Estimated end-of-month inventory $ 84,000

This calculation is appropriate only if the firm's normal gross profit on sales has been relatively stable over time. This type of calculation also can be used to test the reasonableness of the amount of an inventory that was computed on the basis of a physical count. A large difference between the two amounts might indicate a mistake in the count or the costing of the items, or a marked change in the gross profit rate. The gross profit procedure also can be used to estimate the cost of an inventory that was destroyed by fire or other casualty.

Retail Method of Estimating Inventory

Many retail businesses, such as department and clothing stores, use a variation of the gross profit method to calculate cost of goods sold and ending inventory. The procedure used, called the **retail method** of inventory, requires keeping records of both the cost and selling (retail) prices of all goods purchased. This information can be used to estimate cost of goods sold and ending inventory, as shown in Figure 18-11.

KEY POINTS

1 The cost of merchandise available for sale during the accounting period must be divided between the cost of goods sold and the ending merchandise inventory. Cost of goods sold is reported on the income statement and used to determine the gross profit for the period. The ending merchandise inventory is reported as a current asset on the balance sheet. Figure 18-12

FIGURE 18-11   Steps in the Retail Inventory Method

			COST	RETAIL
Step 1	Compute the goods available for sale at cost and retail.	Inventory, start of period	$ 60,000	$ 85,000
		Net purchases during period	126,000	163,000
		Goods available for sale	$186,000	$248,000
Step 2	Compute the ending inventory at **retail** by subtracting sales at retail from goods available for sale at retail.	Less: Net sales for period		180,000
		Inventory, end of period, at retail		$ 68,000
Step 3	Compute the cost-to-retail ratio by dividing the **cost** of goods available for sale by the **retail** value of the goods available for sale.	Ratio of cost-to-retail prices of goods available for sale ($186,000 ÷ $248,000)		75%
Step 4	Estimate the cost of the ending inventory by multiplying the ending inventory at retail (Step 2) by the cost-to-retail ratio.	Inventory, end of period, at estimated cost (75% of $68,000)	(51,000)	
Step 5	Estimate cost of goods sold by a. multiplying sales at retail by the cost-to-retail ratio, or b. subtracting the estimated ending inventory from the cost of goods available for sale.	Estimated cost of goods sold (or, Sales of $180,000 x 75% = $135,000)	$135,000	

FIGURE 18-12   Allocation of Goods Available for Sale to Cost of Goods Sold and Ending Inventory

illustrates the allocation of cost of goods available for sale into cost of goods sold and ending inventory.

2 There are two systems of accounting for merchandise.

Periodic Inventory System

1. The purchases account is debited for the cost of all goods purchased.
2. The sales account is credited for the selling prices of all goods sold.
3. At the end of the accounting period, a physical inventory is taken and the following formula is applied to calculate cost of goods sold.

> Beginning inventory (last year's ending physical count)
> + Net Purchases (account balance at end of this year)
> = Cost of Goods Available for Sale
> − Ending Inventory (this year's ending physical count)
> = Cost of Goods Sold (for this year)

Perpetual Inventory System

1. The merchandise inventory account is debited for all purchases.
2. The cost of goods sold account is debited and the merchandise inventory account is credited for all sales.
3. Thus, the merchandise inventory account provides a running balance of the goods on hand.

3 One of four inventory methods is generally used to determine the costs assigned to the goods sold and ending inventory:

- Specific Identification
- FIFO: First-In, First-Out
- LIFO: Last-In, First-Out
- Weighted-Average

4 Firms using the periodic inventory method often need to estimate their inventory. Two methods are used for this purpose.

- Gross Profit Method
- Retail Inventory Method

KEY TERMS

average cost method 625   A method of allocating merchandise cost that is based on the average cost of identical units. See weighted-average method.

conservatism 630   The accounting practice of conservatism states that we should never anticipate gains, but always anticipate and account for losses. As applied to inventory, conservatism means that if the value of inventory declines while it is being held, the loss should be recognized in the period of the decline.

consignee 622   The company holding the merchandise to be sold.

consignment 622 Goods that are held by one business but owned by another business.

consignor 622 The owner of the merchandise that is held by another business.

consistency principle 625 This principle states that a business should use the same accounting methods from period to period. This improves the comparability of the financial statements over time.

cost 630 In applying the lower-of-cost-or-market method, cost means the dollar amount calculated using one of the four inventory costing methods.

first-in, first-out (FIFO) method 624 A method of allocating merchandise cost which assumes that the first goods purchased were the first goods sold and, therefore, that the latest goods purchased remain in inventory.

gross profit method 631 A method of estimating inventory in which the firm's normal gross profit percentage is used to estimate the cost of goods sold and ending inventory.

in transit 622 Goods that are in the process of being shipped between the seller and the buyer.

inventory sheet 621 A form used for recording inventory items. It has columns for recording the description of each item, the quantity on hand, the cost per unit, and the extension.

Inventory Short and Over 628 An account used to adjust the perpetual inventory records when a difference exists between the physical count and the amount in the perpetual inventory records.

last-in, first-out (LIFO) method 626 A method of allocating merchandise cost which assumes that the sales in the period were made from the most recently purchased goods. Therefore, the earliest goods purchased remain in inventory.

lower-of-cost-or-market method 630 An inventory valuation method under which inventory is valued at the lower of cost or market value (replacement cost).

market 630 In applying the lower-of-cost-or-market method, market means the cost to replace. It is the prevailing price in the market in which goods are purchased—not the prevailing price in the market in which they are normally sold.

natural business year 621 A fiscal year that starts and ends at the time the stock of goods is normally at its lowest level.

periodic inventory system 619 Under this system, the ending inventory and cost of goods sold are determined at the end of the accounting period, when a physical inventory is taken.

perpetual inventory system 620 Under this system, cost of goods sold and the amount of merchandise inventory on hand are updated when merchandise is bought and sold.

physical inventory 621 Counting the goods on hand at the end of the period to allocate merchandise costs between sold and unsold goods.

retail method 632 A variation of the gross profit method that is used by many retail businesses, such as department and clothing stores, to calculate the cost of goods sold and ending inventory.

specific identification method 623   A method of allocating merchandise cost in which each unit of inventory is specifically identified.

weighted-average method 625   A method of allocating merchandise cost based on the average cost of identical units. The average cost of identical units is determined by dividing the total cost of units available for sale by the total number of units available for sale.

REVIEW QUESTIONS

1. What financial statements are affected by an error in the ending inventory?
2. What is the main difference between the periodic system of accounting for inventory and the perpetual system of accounting for inventory?
3. Is a physical inventory necessary under the periodic method? Why or why not?
4. Is a physical inventory necessary under the perpetual method? Why or why not?
5. In a period of rising prices, which inventory method will result in:
    a. the highest cost of goods sold?
    b. the lowest cost of goods sold?
    c. the highest ending inventory?
    d. the lowest ending inventory?
    e. the highest gross profit?
    f. the lowest gross profit?
6. What two factors are taken into account by the weighted-average method of merchandise cost allocation?
7. Which inventory method always follows the actual physical flow of merchandise?
8. When lower-of-cost-or-market is assigned to the items that comprise the ending merchandise inventory, what does "cost" mean? What does "market" mean?
9. List the three steps followed under the gross profit method of estimating inventory.
10. List the five steps followed under the retail method of estimating inventory.

MANAGING YOUR WRITING

Does your local grocery store have optical scanning devices at the checkout stands? Most major grocery chains have installed them and they certainly reduce the time required to check out. What benefits do they provide to the business? Next time you go to the grocery store, take a few minutes to chat with the manager. Ask the manager to describe the benefits of the scanning devices over the old machines that required the clerk to key-in each purchase. Pay particular attention to the linkage between the scanning devices and the inventory systems. Be sure to ask whether the grocery store is on a periodic or perpetual system.

After your visit, write a memo to your instructor describing the benefits of the scanning devices and how they are linked with the inventory system.

DEMONSTRATION PROBLEM

The Fialka Company's beginning inventory and purchases during the fiscal year ended October 31, 19-2, were as follows.

	Units	Unit Price	Total Cost
November 1, 19-1, beginning inventory	500	$25.00	$ 12,500
November 12, 19-1, 1st purchase	600	26.25	15,750
December 28, 19-1, 2nd purchase	400	27.50	11,000
March 29, 19-2, 3rd purchase	1,000	28.00	28,000
May 31, 19-2, 4th purchase	750	28.50	21,375
July 29, 19-2, 5th purchase	350	29.00	10,150
August 30, 19-2, 6th purchase	675	30.00	20,250
October 21, 19-2, 7th purchase	225	31.00	6,975
	4,500		$126,000

There are 1,600 units of inventory on hand on October 31, 19-2.

REQUIRED

1. Calculate the total amount to be assigned to cost of goods sold for 19-2 and ending inventory on October 31, 19-2, under each of the following methods:
   a.   FIFO.
   b.   LIFO.
   c.   Weighted-average cost (round calculations to two decimal places).
2. Assume that the market price per unit (cost to replace) of Fialka's inventory on October 31, 19-2, was $29. Calculate the total amount to be assigned to the ending inventory on October 31, 19-2, under each of the following methods:
   a.   FIFO lower-of-cost-or-market.
   b.   Weighted-average lower-of-cost-or-market.
3. Now let's assume that a fire destroyed Fialka's store and all inventory on October 31, just prior to taking a physical inventory. Thus, Fialka must estimate the ending inventory and cost of goods sold. During the fiscal year ended October 31, 19-2, net sales of $134,000 were made. The normal gross profit rate is 40%. Use the gross profit method to estimate the cost of goods sold for the fiscal year ended October 31, 19-2, and the inventory on October 31, 19-2.

SOLUTION

1,a.

FIFO INVENTORY METHOD							
DATE		**COST OF GOODS SOLD**			**COST OF ENDING INVENTORY**		
19-1/-2		Units	Unit Price	Total	Units	Unit Price	Total
Nov. 1	Beg. Inv.	500	$25.00	$12,500		$25.00	$ 0
Nov. 12	1st purchase	600	26.25	15,750		26.25	0
Dec. 28	2nd purchase	400	27.50	11,000		27.50	0
Mar. 29	3rd purchase	1,000	28.00	28,000		28.00	0
May 31	4th purchase	400	28.50	11,400	350	28.50	9,975
July 29	5th purchase		29.00	0	350	29.00	10,150
Aug. 30	6th purchase		30.00	0	675	30.00	20,250
Oct. 21	7th purchase		31.00	0	225	31.00	6,975
	Total	2,900		$78,650	1,600		$47,350

Alternative calculation given goods available for sale and cost of goods sold or ending inventory.	Cost of goods available for sale	$126,000	Cost of goods available for sale	$126,000
	Less: Cost of ending inventory	(47,350)	Less: Cost of goods sold	(78,650)
	Cost of goods sold	$ 78,650	Cost of ending inventory	$ 47,350

1,b.

LIFO INVENTORY METHOD							
DATE		**COST OF GOODS SOLD**			**COST OF ENDING INVENTORY**		
19-1/-2		Units	Unit Price	Total	Units	Unit Price	Total
Nov. 1	Beg. Inv.		$25.00	$ 0	500	$25.00	$12,500
Nov. 12	1st purchase		26.25	0	600	26.25	15,750
Dec. 28	2nd purchase		27.50	0	400	27.50	11,000
Mar. 29	3rd purchase	900	28.00	25,200	100	28.00	2,800
May 31	4th purchase	750	28.50	21,375		28.50	0
July 29	5th purchase	350	29.00	10,150		29.00	0
Aug. 30	6th purchase	675	30.00	20,250		30.00	0
Oct. 21	7th purchase	225	31.00	6,975		31.00	0
	Total	2,900		$83,950	1,600		$42,050

Alternative calculation given goods available for sale and cost of goods sold or ending inventory.	Cost of goods available for sale	$126,000	Cost of goods available for sale	$126,000
	Less: Cost of ending inventory	(42,050)	Less: Cost of goods sold	(83,950)
	Cost of goods sold	$ 83,950	Cost of ending inventory	$ 42,050

1,c. Weighted-average method:

Average cost per unit: $126,000 ÷ 4,500 units = $28.
Inventory, October 31, 19-2:

1,600 units @ $28 =	$44,800

Cost of Goods Sold for 19-2:

2,900 units @ $28 =	$81,200

2,a. FIFO lower-of-cost-or-market:

FIFO cost	$47,350
Market 1,600 @ $29	$46,400
Choose market	$46,400

2,b. Weighted-average lower-of-cost-or-market:

Weighted-average cost	$44,800
Market 1,600 @ $29	$46,400
Choose weighted-average cost	$44,800

3. Estimated inventory on October 31, 19-2:

Inventory, November 1, 19-1		$ 12,500	
Net purchases, November 1, 19-1 through October 31, 19-2		113,500	
Cost of goods available for sale			$126,000
Estimated cost of goods sold:			
Net sales		$134,000	
Normal gross profit ($134,000 × 40%)		53,600	
Estimated cost of goods sold			80,400
Estimated inventory on October 31, 19-2			$ 45,600

SERIES A   EXERCISES

1

EXERCISE 18A1 INVENTORY ERRORS   Assume that in year 1, the ending merchandise inventory is overstated by $50,000. If this is the only error in years 1 and 2, indicate which items will be understated, overstated, or correctly stated for years 1 and 2.

	Year 1	Year 2
Ending merchandise inventory	————	————
Beginning merchandise inventory	————	————
Cost of goods sold	————	————
Gross profit	————	————
Net income	————	————
Ending owner's capital	————	————

2

EXERCISE 18A2 JOURNAL ENTRIES—PERIODIC INVENTORY
Bill Diamond owns a business called Diamond Distributors. The following

transactions took place during January of the current year. Journalize the transactions in a general journal using the periodic inventory method.

Jan. 5 Purchased merchandise on account from Prestigious Jewelers, $3,700.
      8 Paid freight charge on merchandise purchased, $200.
     12 Sold merchandise on account to Diamonds Unlimited, $4,900.
     15 Received a credit memo from Prestigious Jewelers for merchandise returned, $600.
     22 Issued a credit memo to Diamonds Unlimited for merchandise returned, $800.

2 EXERCISE 18A3 JOURNAL ENTRIES—PERPETUAL INVENTORY

Sandy Johnson owns a small variety store. The following transactions took place during March of the current year. Journalize the transactions in a general journal using the perpetual inventory method.

Mar. 3 Purchased merchandise on account from City Galleria, $2,700.
      7 Paid freight charge on merchandise purchased, $175.
     13 Sold merchandise on account to Amber Specialties, $3,000. The cost of the merchandise was $1,800.
     18 Received a credit memo from City Galleria for merchandise returned, $500.
     22 Issued a credit memo to Amber Specialties for merchandise returned, $400. The cost of the merchandise was $240.

3 EXERCISE 18A4 ENDING INVENTORY COSTS

Sandy Chen owns a small specialty store, named Chen's Chattel, whose year end is June 30. Determine the total amount that should be included in Chen's Chattel's year-end inventory. A physical inventory taken on June 30 reveals the following:

Cost of merchandise on the showroom floor and in warehouse	$37,800
Goods held on consignment (Consignor is National Manufacturer)	6,400
Goods that Chen's Chattel, as the consignor, has for sale at the location of the Grand Avenue Vista	4,600
Sales invoices indicate that merchandise was shipped on June 29, terms FOB shipping point, delivered at buyer's receiving dock on July 3	3,800
Sales invoices indicate that merchandise was shipped on June 25, terms FOB destination, delivered at buyer's receiving dock on July 5	3,100

3 EXERCISE 18A5 JOURNAL ENTRY—INVENTORY SHORT AND OVER

Tiger Industries uses the perpetual inventory method in accounting for inventory. Prepare the necessary adjusting entry for each of the following independent cases, using the account Inventory Short and Over. How would Inventory Short and Over be reported on the income statement for each independent case?

continued

Case 1:

Physical count as of April 30	$48,300
Perpetual inventory records as of April 30	46,800

Case 2:

Physical count as of April 30	$43,600
Perpetual inventory records as of April 30	45,200

3 **EXERCISE 18A6 LOWER-OF-COST-OR-MARKET**   Stalberg Company's beginning inventory and purchases during the fiscal year ended December 31, 19--, were as follows:

		Units	Unit Price	Total Cost
Jan. 1	Beginning inventory	10	$20	$200
Mar. 5	First purchase	10	22	220
Sept. 9	Second purchase	10	25	250
Dec. 8	Third purchase	10	30	300
		40		$970

There are 10 units of inventory on hand on December 31.

1. Calculate the total amount to be assigned to the ending inventory under each of the following methods:
   a. FIFO
   b. Weighted-average (round calculations to two decimal places)
2. Assume that the market price per unit (cost to replace) of Stalberg's inventory on December 31, 19--, was $26. Calculate the total amount to be assigned to the ending inventory on December 31 under each of the following methods:
   a. FIFO lower-of-cost-or-market
   b. Weighted-average lower-of-cost-or-market

SERIES A PROBLEMS

3 **PROBLEM 18A1 SPECIFIC IDENTIFICATION, FIFO, LIFO, AND WEIGHTED-AVERAGE**   The Hamilton Company's beginning inventory and purchases during the fiscal year ended September 30, 19-2, were as follows:

	Units	Unit Price	Total Cost
October 1, 19-1, beginning inventory	300	$20.00	$ 6,000
October 18, first purchase	500	21.50	10,750
November 25, second purchase	400	22.00	8,800
January 12, 19-2, third purchase	800	23.00	18,400
March 17, fourth purchase	900	23.50	21,150
June 2, fifth purchase	600	24.00	14,400
August 21, sixth purchase	500	25.00	12,500
September 27, seventh purchase	400	25.75	10,300
	4,400		$102,300

continued

There are 1,000 units of inventory on hand on September 30, 19-2. Of these 1,000 units:

100 are from the October 18, 19-1, first purchase
300 are from the January 12, 19-2, third purchase
100 are from the March 17, fourth purchase
200 are from the June 2, fifth purchase
100 are from the August 21, sixth purchase
200 are from the September 27, seventh purchase

REQUIRED
Calculate the total amount to be assigned to cost of goods sold for 19-2 and ending inventory on September 30, 19-2, under each of the following methods:
a.   FIFO
b.   LIFO
c.   Weighted-average (round calculations to two decimal places)
d.   Specific identification

3   **PROBLEM 18A2 COST ALLOCATION AND LOWER-OF-COST-OR-MARKET**   The Douglas Company's beginning inventory and purchases during the fiscal year ended December 31, 19--, were as follows:

	Units	**Unit Price**	**Total Cost**
January 1, 19--, beginning inventory	1,100	$ 8.00	$ 8,800
March 5, first purchase	900	9.00	8,100
April 16, second purchase	400	9.50	3,800
June 3, third purchase	700	10.25	7,175
August 18, fourth purchase	600	11.00	6,600
September 13, fifth purchase	800	12.00	9,600
November 14, sixth purchase	400	14.00	5,600
December 3, seventh purchase	500	14.05	7,025
	5,400		$56,700

There are 1,000 units of inventory on hand on December 31.

REQUIRED
1. Calculate the total amount to be assigned to the ending inventory and cost of goods sold on December 31 under each of the following methods:
   a. FIFO
   b. LIFO
   c. Weighted-average (round calculations to two decimal places).
2. Assume that the market price per unit (cost to replace) of Douglas' inventory on December 31 was $13. Calculate the total amount to be assigned to the ending inventory on December 31 under each of the following methods:
   a. FIFO lower-of-cost-or-market
   b. Weighted-average lower-of-cost-or-market

4 **PROBLEM 18A3 GROSS PROFIT METHOD**   A fire completely destroyed all the inventory of Glisan Lumber Yard on August 5, 19--. Fortunately, the books were not destroyed in the fire. The following information is taken from the books of Glisan Lumber Yard for the time period, January 1 through August 5:

Beginning inventory, January 1, 19--	$100,000
Net purchases, January 1 through August 5	420,000
Net sales, January 1 through August 5	732,000
Normal gross profit as a percentage of sales	40%

REQUIRED

Estimate the amount of merchandise inventory destroyed in the fire on August 5 using the gross profit method.

4 **PROBLEM 18A4 RETAIL INVENTORY METHOD**   The following information is taken from the books of Raynette's Pharmacy for the last quarter of their fiscal year ending on March 31, 19--.

	Cost	Retail
Inventory, start of period, January 1, 19--	$ 32,000	$ 52,000
Net purchases during the period	176,000	268,000
Net sales for the period		260,000

REQUIRED

1. Estimate the ending inventory as of March 31 using the retail inventory method.
2. Estimate the cost of goods sold for the time period, January 1 through March 31 using the retail inventory method.

SERIES B EXERCISES

1 **EXERCISE 18B1 INVENTORY ERRORS**   Assume that in year 1, the ending merchandise inventory is understated by $40,000. If this is the only error in years 1 and 2, indicate which items will be understated, overstated, or correctly stated for years 1 and 2.

	Year 1	Year 2
Ending merchandise inventory		
Beginning merchandise inventory		
Cost of goods sold		
Gross profit		
Net income		
Ending owner's capital		

2 **EXERCISE 18B2 JOURNAL ENTRIES—PERIODIC INVENTORY** Amy Douglas owns a business called Douglas Distributors. The following transactions took place during January of the current year. Journalize the transactions in a general journal using the periodic inventory method.

Jan.   5 Purchased merchandise on account from Elite Warehouse, $4,100.
       8 Paid freight charge on merchandise purchased, $300.
     12 Sold merchandise on account to Memories Unlimited, $5,200.
     15 Received a credit memo from Elite Warehouse for merchandise returned, $700.
     22 Issued a credit memo to Memories Unlimited for merchandise returned, $400.

2   **EXERCISE 18B3 JOURNAL ENTRIES—PERPETUAL INVENTORY**
Doreen Woods owns a small variety store. The following transactions took place during March of the current year. Journalize the transactions in a general journal using the perpetual inventory method.

Mar.   3 Purchased merchandise on account from Corner Galleria, $3,500.
      7 Paid freight charge on merchandise purchased, $200.
     13 Sold merchandise on account to Sonya Specialties, $4,250. The cost of the merchandise was $2,550.
     18 Received a credit memo from Corner Galleria for merchandise returned, $900.
     22 Issued a credit memo to Sonya Specialties for merchandise returned, $500. The cost of the merchandise was $300.

3   **EXERCISE 18B4 ENDING INVENTORY COSTS**   Danny Steele owns a small specialty store, named Steele's Storeroom, whose year end is June 30. Determine the total amount that should be included in Steele's Storeroom's year-end inventory. A physical inventory taken on June 30 reveals the following:

Cost of merchandise on the showroom floor and in warehouse	$42,600
Goods held on consignment (consignor is Quality Manufacturer)	7,600
Goods that Steele's Storeroom, as the consignor, has for sale at the location of the Midtown Galleria	8,300
Sales invoices indicate that merchandise was shipped on June 28, terms FOB shipping point, delivered at buyer's receiving dock on July 6	4,350
Sales invoices indicate that merchandise was shipped on June 26, terms FOB destination, delivered at buyer's receiving dock on July 1	2,800

3   **EXERCISE 18B5 JOURNAL ENTRY—INVENTORY SHORT AND OVER**   Hanson Industries uses the perpetual inventory method in accounting for their inventory. Prepare the necessary adjusting entry for each independent case, using the account Inventory Short and Over. How would Inventory Short and Over be reported on the income statement for each independent case?

continued

Case 1:

| Physical count as of April 30 | $44,150 |
| Perpetual inventory records as of April 30 | 47,300 |

Case 2:

| Physical count as of April 30 | $38,400 |
| Perpetual inventory records as of April 30 | 36,200 |

3   **EXERCISE 18B6 LOWER-OF-COST-OR-MARKET**   Bouie Company's beginning inventory and purchases during the fiscal year ended December 31, 19--, were as follows:

		Units	Unit Price	Total Cost
Jan. 1	Beginning inventory	20	$30	$ 600
Mar. 5	First purchase	22	34	748
Sept. 9	Second purchase	24	35	840
Dec. 8	Third purchase	22	40	880
		88		$3,068

There are 20 units of inventory on hand on December 31.

1. Calculate the total amount to be assigned to the ending inventory under each of the following methods:
   a.   FIFO
   b.   Weighted-average (round calculations to two decimal places)
2. Assume that the market price per unit (cost to replace) of Bouie's inventory on December 31, 19--, was $39. Calculate the total amount to be assigned to the ending inventory on December 31 under each of the following methods:
   a.   FIFO lower-of-cost-or-market
   b.   Weighted-average lower-of-cost-or-market

SERIES B   PROBLEMS

3   **PROBLEM 18B1 SPECIFIC IDENTIFICATION, FIFO, LIFO, AND WEIGHTED-AVERAGE**   The Boyce Company's beginning inventory and purchases during the fiscal year ended September 30, 19-2, were as follows:

	Units	Unit Price	Total Cost
October 1, 19-1, beginning inventory	400	$15.00	$ 6,000
October 18, first purchase	300	16.50	4,950
November 25, second purchase	600	17.00	10,200
January 12, 19-2, third purchase	700	17.25	12,075
March 17, fourth purchase	800	18.00	14,400
June 2, fifth purchase	400	19.00	7,600
August 21, sixth purchase	300	21.00	6,300
September 27, seventh purchase	500	21.75	10,875
	4,000		$72,400

continued

There are 900 units of inventory on hand on September 30, 19-2. Of these 900 units:

50 are from the October 18, 19-1, first purchase
300 are from the January 12, 19-2, third purchase
100 are from the March 17, fourth purchase
200 are from the June 2, fifth purchase
50 are from the August 21, sixth purchase
200 are from the September 27, seventh purchase

REQUIRED

Calculate the total amount to be assigned to cost of goods sold for 19-2 and ending inventory on September 30, 19-2, under each of the following methods:

a.   FIFO
b.   LIFO
c.   Weighted-average (round calculations to two decimal places)
d.   Specific identification

3   **PROBLEM 18B2 COST ALLOCATION AND LOWER-OF-COST-OR-MARKET**   The Hall Company's beginning inventory and purchases during the fiscal year ended December 31, 19--, were as follows:

	Units	Unit Price	Total Cost
January 1, beginning inventory	800	$11.00	$ 8,800
March 5, first purchase	600	12.00	7,200
April 16, second purchase	500	12.50	6,250
June 3, third purchase	700	14.00	9,800
August 18, fourth purchase	800	15.00	12,000
September 13, fifth purchase	900	17.00	15,300
November 14, sixth purchase	400	18.00	7,200
December 3, seventh purchase	500	20.30	10,150
	5,200		$76,700

There are 1,100 units of inventory on hand on December 31.

REQUIRED

1. Calculate the total amount to be assigned to the ending inventory and cost of goods sold on December 31 under each of the following methods:
a.   FIFO
b.   LIFO
c.   Weighted-average (round calculations to two decimal places)
2. Assume that the market price per unit (cost to replace) of Hall's inventory on December 31 was $16. Calculate the total amount to be assigned to the ending inventory on December 31 under each of the following methods:
a.   FIFO lower-of-cost-or-market
b.   Weighted-average lower-of-cost-or-market

4 **PROBLEM 18B3 GROSS PROFIT METHOD**   A flood completely destroyed all the inventory of Bayside Waterworks Company on July 1, 19--. Fortunately, the books were not destroyed in the flood. The following information is taken from the books of Bayside Waterworks for the time period January 1 through July 1, 19--:

Beginning inventory, January 1, 19--	$ 60,000
Net purchases, January 1 through July 1	$380,000
Net sales, January 1 through July 1	$650,000
Normal gross profit as a percentage of sales	45%

REQUIRED

Estimate the amount of merchandise inventory destroyed in the flood on July 1 using the gross profit method.

4 **PROBLEM 18B4 RETAIL INVENTORY METHOD**   The following information is taken from the books of Beverly's Basket Corner for the last quarter of their fiscal year ending on March 31, 19--.

	Cost	**Retail**
Inventory, start of period, January 1, 19--	$ 50,000	$ 80,000
Net purchases during the period	220,000	352,000
Net sales for the period		310,000

REQUIRED

1. Estimate the ending inventory as of March 31 using the retail inventory method.
2. Estimate the cost of goods sold for the time period January 1 through March 31 using the retail inventory method.

MASTERY PROBLEM

The Tiller Company's beginning inventory and purchases during the fiscal year ended December 31, 19-2, were as follows:

	Units	**Unit Price**	**Total Cost**
January 1, 19-2, beginning inventory	1,500	$10.00	$15,000
January 12, first purchase	500	11.50	5,750
February 28, second purchase	600	14.50	8,700
June 29, third purchase	1,200	15.00	18,000
August 31, fourth purchase	800	16.50	13,200
October 29, fifth purchase	300	18.00	5,400
November 30, sixth purchase	700	18.50	12,950
December 21, seventh purchase	400	20.00	8,000
	6,000		$87,000

There are 1,200 units of inventory on hand on December 31, 19-2.

continued

REQUIRED

1. Calculate the total amount to be assigned to the cost of goods sold for 19-2 and ending inventory on December 31 under each of the following methods:
   a.   FIFO
   b.   LIFO
   c.   Weighted-average (round calculations to two decimal places)
2. Assume that the market price per unit (cost to replace) of Tiller's inventory on December 31 was $18. Calculate the total amount to be assigned to the ending inventory on December 31 under each of the following methods:
   a.   FIFO
   b.   Weighted-average lower-of-cost-or-market
3. In addition to taking a physical inventory on December 31, Tiller decides to estimate the ending inventory and cost of goods sold. During the fiscal year ended December 31, 19-2, net sales of $100,000 were made at a normal gross profit rate of 35%. Use the gross profit method to estimate the cost of goods sold for the fiscal year ended December 31 and the inventory on December 31.

19

Accounting for Long-Term Assets

Betty's Flower Bowl just opened for business this year. Betty believes that the business needs two delivery vans, but she can afford only one at this time. The expected useful life of the van is four years, but it will be used especially heavily during the first year or two until Betty can purchase a second van. Betty knows about straight-line depreciation, but does not believe that this method would be the appropriate way to depreciate this initial van. Are there other depreciation methods that could be used?

Assets that are expected to provide benefits for a number of accounting periods are called **long-term assets.** Long-term assets that are **tangible** (have physical substance), and that are used in the operations of the business, are called **property, plant, and equipment; plant assets;** or **fixed assets.** Examples include land, buildings, furniture, and equipment. Assets whose physical substance consists of natural resources that are consumed in the operation of the business are often called **wasting assets.** Examples include mines (coal, salt, and gold), stands of timber, and oil and gas wells. Long-term assets that have no physical substance are called **intangible assets.** Common examples include patents, copyrights, and trademarks.

All long-term assets except land gradually wear out or are used up as time passes. As an asset's useful life expires, a portion of the asset's cost is recognized as an expense. A different term is used to describe this expense for the different types of long-term assets. For plant assets, the expense is called **depreciation;** for natural resources, it is called **depletion**; and for intangible assets, it is called **amortization.** In this chapter, proper accounting for property, plant, and equipment; natural resources; and intangible assets is described and illustrated.

 LEARNING KEY Since land does not wear out, no depreciation is recognized.

ACQUISITION COST OF PROPERTY, PLANT, AND EQUIPMENT

LO1 Determine the cost of property, plant, and equipment.

The cost of a long-term asset includes all amounts spent to acquire the asset and prepare it for its intended use. Purchases of long-term assets are entered by debiting the proper asset account and crediting either cash or the proper liability account.

Often, businesses must borrow money to buy major long-term assets. Are the interest costs on such loans part of the cost of the long-term assets? Absolutely not. The method of financing the purchase of an asset has no effect on the measurement of the asset's cost. We always use the **cash equivalent price,** which is the amount of cash that could have been paid for the asset on the date of purchase.

Land

All costs incurred to purchase land and prepare it for its intended use are debited to the land account. These costs include legal and real estate fees as well as the cost of removing old buildings and grading the land to prepare it for its intended use. Special tax assessments for streets, sewers, or parks also are debited to the land account, because they are viewed as permanent.

Land Improvements

Costs related to the land that are not permanent in nature are normally debited to the land improvements account. Common examples include the costs of planting trees and shrubs, installing fences, and paving parking areas. Items debited to the land improvements account are depreciated over their expected useful lives.

Buildings

The cost of buildings that are purchased includes the purchase price, realtor and legal fees, and related taxes. If the purchase price includes land, the cost of the land and building must be determined and accounted for separately. If the building is constructed, costs include all normal construction costs for material and labor and architectural and engineering fees. In addition, insurance premiums and interest on construction loans *while the building is being constructed* are considered part of the cost of the asset.

Equipment

The cost of equipment includes the purchase price, transportation charges, insurance while in transit, installation costs, and any other costs that are incurred up to the point of placing the asset in service.

DEPRECIATION

LO 2 Explain the nature and purpose of depreciation.

The purpose of depreciation is to match a plant asset's cost with the revenues it helps to produce. As discussed in earlier chapters, the following is a typical adjusting entry made at the end of each accounting period.

	19—						
5	Dec.	31	Depr. Expense—Delivery Equip.	547	1 0 0 00		5
6			Accum. Depr.—Delivery Equip.	185.1		1 0 0 00	6

 LEARNING KEY Depreciation matches a plant asset's cost with the revenues it helps to produce.

Recall that Depreciation Expense is reported on the income statement and Accumulated Depreciation is reported on the balance sheet as a contra-asset. It is deducted from the asset account to report the book value, or undepreciated cost, of the asset.

Keep in mind that depreciation is a process of *cost allocation*, not a process of valuation. Many factors cause the market values of plant assets to change over time. The recognition of depreciation is not intended to approximate market values on the balance sheet. The net amounts reported on the balance sheet (book values) are merely the portions of the original costs that have not yet been allocated to expense.

Market Value = Amount Asset Can Be Sold For

Book Value = Cost − Accumulated Depreciation

The recognition of depreciation is not intended to represent market values on the balance sheet.

The two major types of depreciation are physical and functional. **Physical depreciation** is the loss of usefulness because of deterioration from age and wear. **Functional depreciation** is the loss of usefulness because of inadequacy or obsolescence. As a business grows, some of its plant assets may become inadequate to handle the increased workload. As new manufacturing methods are developed, assets may become obsolete.

DEPRECIATION METHODS

LO3 Compute depreciation using the straight-line, declining-balance, sum-of-the-years'-digits, and units-of-production methods.

Before we discuss the methods of calculating depreciation, there are several terms to be defined.

Cost	The sum of all amounts spent to acquire an asset and prepare it for its intended use.
Useful Life	The amount of service expected to be obtained from an asset. It can be expressed in years, hours of operation, units of production, or miles driven. There is no way of knowing exactly how long an asset will last or exactly what its output will be. Therefore, estimates must be made based on past experience and information from trade associations and engineers. Uncertainty surrounds all depreciation calculations.

Recall the concepts of physical and functional depreciation. The useful life is based on an estimate of the period of time that an asset *will be useful* to the business, not necessarily the actual life of the asset.

Salvage Value	The estimated **scrap**, or market value for the asset on its expected disposal date. This amount can be difficult to predict. Often, a zero salvage value is used if the asset is expected to have little or no value at the end of its useful life.
Depreciable Cost (Base)	The original cost less salvage (or scrap) value.

Depreciable Cost = Original Cost − Salvage Value

Book Value	The undepreciated cost of the asset.

Book Value = Cost − Accumulated Depreciation

There are several different ways of calculating the amount of depreciation for each period. The most commonly used methods for financial reporting purposes are the following:

1. Straight-line method
2. Declining-balance method
3. Sum-of-the-years'-digits method
4. Units-of-production method

Straight-Line Method

Under the **straight-line method**, the depreciable cost of an asset is allocated equally over the years of the asset's useful life. To illustrate, assume that a new asset cost $10,000, has an expected life of four years, and has a $1,000 estimated salvage value. Using the straight-line method, the amount of depreciation allocated to each year would be $2,250, computed as follows:

Original Cost – Salvage Value = Depreciable Cost

$10,000   – $1,000   = $9,000

$$\frac{\text{Depreciable Cost}}{\text{Estimated Useful Life}} = \frac{\$9,000}{4 \text{ years}} = \$2,250 \text{ annual depreciation}$$

The annual *rate* of depreciation is 25% (100% ÷ 4 years) of the depreciable cost.

 LEARNING KEY Under the straight-line method, the same amount of depreciation is recorded each period.

A month is usually the shortest period that is used in depreciation accounting. An asset purchased on or before the fifteenth of the month is considered to have been owned for the full month. An asset purchased after the fifteenth of the month is considered to have been acquired the first of the next month.

 LEARNING KEY An asset purchased on or before the fifteenth of the month is considered to have been owned for the full month. An asset purchased after the fifteenth of the month is considered to have been acquired the first of the next month.

With the straight-line method, the book value of the asset decreases uniformly period by period. As shown in Figure 19-1, the book value over several periods is a downward-sloping, perfectly straight line. That is how the method got its name.

Declining-Balance Method

Many plant assets require repairs and replacement of parts to keep them in service. Such expenses usually increase as the assets get older. Some accountants believe that depreciation expense, therefore, should be higher in the early years to offset the higher repair and maintenance expenses of

FIGURE 19-1   Comparison of Depreciation Methods

Straight-Line Method

Year	Depr. Exp.	Accum. Depr.	Book Value
			10,000
1	2,250	2,250	7,750
2	2,250	4,500	5,500
3	2,250	6,750	3,250
4	2,250	9,000	1,000

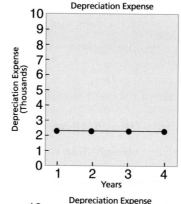
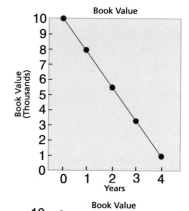

Double-Declining-Balance Method

Year	Depr. Exp.	Accum. Depr.	Book Value
			10,000
1	5,000	5,000	5,000
2	2,500	7,500	2,500
3	1,250	8,750	1,250
4	250	9,000	1,000

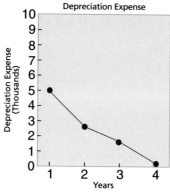
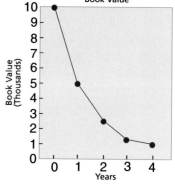

Sum-of-the-Years'-Digits Method

Year	Depr. Exp.	Accum. Depr.	Book Value
			10,000
1	3,600	3,600	6,400
2	2,700	6,300	3,700
3	1,800	8,100	1,900
4	900	9,000	1,000

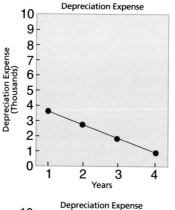
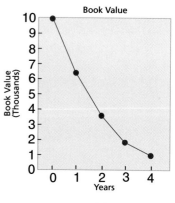

Units-of-Production Method

Year	Depr. Exp.	Accum. Depr.	Book Value
			10,000
1	2,400	2,400	7,600
2	4,000	6,400	3,600
3	2,000	8,400	1,600
4	600	9,000	1,000

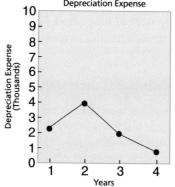
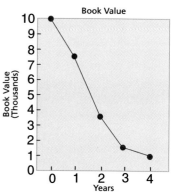

the later years. Others suggest that assets contribute more to the business when they are comparatively new. For these reasons, it may be desirable to calculate depreciation in a way that will give larger write-offs in the early years of the asset's life. Depreciation methods that provide for a higher depreciation charge in the first year of an asset's life and gradually decreasing charges in subsequent years are called **accelerated depreciation methods.**

One popular accelerated method is the **declining-balance method.** Under this method, the book value is multiplied by a fixed rate. This results in successively smaller depreciation charges as the book value declines year by year. The most common rate used is double the straight-line rate. For this reason, this technique is sometimes referred to as the **double-declining-balance method.**

> "Double" means double the straight-line rate. "Declining balance" means that we should multiply the rate by the declining beginning book value balance.

To illustrate, let's use the same asset as for the straight-line method. The asset cost $10,000, has an expected life of four years, and has a $1,000 estimated salvage value. Using the double-declining-balance method, the depreciation rate to be applied to the book value of the asset each year is 50%, computed as follows:

Straight-line rate = 25% (100% ÷ 4 years)
Double-declining-balance rate = 50% (2 × 25%)

The annual depreciation and the book value at the end of each year are as follows:

Year	Book Value Beginning of Year	Rate	Annual Depreciation	Accumulated Depreciation End of Year	Book Value End of Year
1	$10,000	50%	$5,000	$5,000	$5,000
2	5,000	50	2,500	7,500	2,500
3	2,500	50	1,250	8,750	1,250
4	1,250	—	250	9,000	1,000

The salvage value is not considered in determining the annual depreciation. However, the asset's book value should not be allowed to fall below its estimated salvage value. Thus, the amount of depreciation actually recorded in the final year (year 4) is limited to $250 ($1,250 − $1,000).

> Do not subtract the salvage value from the original cost before multiplying by the declining-balance rate.

As shown in Figure 19-1, with the declining-balance method, the book value declines rapidly in the early years and more slowly in the later years of an asset's life.

If the asset was acquired at some time other than the beginning of the year, a change would be necessary in the computation of depreciation for the year. For example, if the asset was acquired on April 1, the depreciation for year 1 would be calculated as follows:

Year 1: $10,000.00 x 50% = $5,000.00 x 9/12 = $3,750.00

Depreciation for years 2 through 4 would then be calculated by applying the 50% depreciation rate to the book value of the asset at the beginning of each year, as follows:

Year 2: $6,250.00 x 50% = *$3,125.00*
Year 3: $3,125.00 x 50% = *$1,562.50*
Year 4: $1,562.50 – $1,000.00 (salvage value) = *$562.50*

Depreciation in year 4 is limited to $562.50 because the asset should not be depreciated below its estimated salvage value. If the asset continued to be used in year 5, no depreciation would be recorded.

 LEARNING KEY   An asset should not be depreciated below its estimated salvage value.

Sum-of-the-Years'-Digits Method

With the **sum-of-the-years'-digits method,** the depreciation each year is determined by multiplying the depreciable cost by a schedule of fractions. The numerator in any year is the number of years of remaining life for the asset, measured from the beginning of the year. The denominator for all fractions is determined by listing the digits that represent the years of the estimated life of the asset and adding these digits. For example, suppose that the estimated life of an asset is four years. The sum of the digits (4 + 3 + 2 + 1) equals 10 (the denominator). The following formula can also be used to determine the denominator:

Calculating the Sum-of-the-Years'-Digits

$$S = N \times \frac{(N + 1)}{2}$$

S = sum of the digits
N = number of years of estimated life

If the life of the asset is four years:

$$S = 4 \times \frac{(4 + 1)}{2} = 4 \times (2.5) = 10$$

The denominator equals 10. Therefore, the fractions used for an asset with a four-year life would be 4/10, 3/10, 2/10, and 1/10. Applying these fractions to the asset in our illustration, the results are as follows:

Year	Depreciable Cost	Rate	Annual Depreciation	Accumulated Depreciation End of Year	Book Value End of Year
1	$9,000	4/10	$3,600	$3,600	$6,400
2	9,000	3/10	2,700	6,300	3,700
3	9,000	2/10	1,800	8,100	1,900
4	9,000	1/10	900	9,000	1,000

As shown in Figure 19-1, the pattern of decline in the book value using the sum-of-the-years'-digits method is accelerated. However, the write-off is not as rapid as it is with the double-declining-balance method.

If the asset is acquired at some time other than the beginning of the year, a modification is necessary in the calculation. For example, if the asset is acquired on April 1, the depreciation for years 1 through 3 is calculated as follows:

Year 1: $9,000 x 4/10 = $3,600 x 9/12 = *$2,700*

Year 2: $9,000 x 4/10 = $3,600 x 3/12 = $ 900
        9,000 x 3/10 = 2,700 x 9/12 = 2,025

                                        $2,925

Year 3: $9,000 x 3/10 = $2,700 x 3/12 = $ 675
        9,000 x 2/10 = 1,800 x 9/12 = 1,350

                                        $2,025

Depreciation for years 4 and 5 is calculated in a similar manner.

Units-of-Production Method

With the **units-of-production method,** depreciation is based on the extent to which the asset was used during the year. This method can be used for certain types of machinery, equipment, and vehicles. It is most appropriate for assets that receive varying amounts of use over time. For example, assume that a company purchases a new car at a cost of $10,000 and expects that it can be sold for $1,000 after 90,000 miles of service. The calculation of depreciation for the first year when the car was driven 24,000 miles is shown below.

Depreciable cost = $10,000 Original Cost − $1,000 Salvage Value = $9,000

$$\text{Depreciation per mile} = \frac{\$9,000 \text{ Depreciable Cost}}{90,000 \text{ Total Miles}} = \$.10$$

First-year depreciation = 24,000 miles x $.10/mile = $2,400

As shown in Figure 19-1, the depreciation expense and book value for each year do not follow a particular pattern. They are a function of the miles driven each year (24,000; 40,000; 20,000; and 6,000 in this illustration).

Depreciation for Federal Income Tax Purposes

A business is allowed to deduct depreciation expenses in calculating taxable income. Allowable depreciation methods for tax purposes vary depending on when the asset was acquired. For plant assets acquired before 1981, any of the four methods described in the previous sections is permitted. For plant assets acquired between 1981 and 1986, either the straight-line method or the **Accelerated Cost Recovery System (ACRS)** must be used. ACRS classifies all business plant assets into four different useful life categories. Most business assets fall into one of three categories: 3-year, 5-year, or 18-year property. For plant assets acquired after 1986, either the straight-line method or the **Modified Accelerated Cost Recovery System (MACRS)** must be used. MACRS identifies eight categories of useful life for plant assets. Most business assets other than real estate fall into one of two categories: 5-year or 7-year property. ACRS and MACRS define depreciation rates for various categories. For example, the rates for 5-year property are shown below. In using these rates, salvage value is ignored. Note that depreciation for a 5-year asset must be spread over 6 years. This is because ACRS and MACRS assumes one-half year's depreciation in year 1 and one-half year's depreciation in year 6.

Depreciation Rates for Five-Year Assets
ACRS and MACRS Depreciation

Year	ACRS	MACRS
1	15%	20.0%
2	22	32.0
3	21	19.2
4	21	11.5
5	21	11.5
6		5.8
	100%	100.0%

REPAIRS, MAINTENANCE, ADDITIONS, AND IMPROVEMENTS TO PLANT AND EQUIPMENT

LO4 Account for repairs, maintenance, additions, and improvements to plant and equipment.

Plant and equipment require normal repairs and maintenance for proper operating efficiency and quality. Replacement of minor parts, lubrication, and cleaning are typical examples of normal repairs and maintenance. These expenditures are debited to Repairs Expense, as shown below.

5		Repairs Expense			x x x xx		5
6		Cash or Supplies Inventory				x x x xx	6
7		Made repairs					7

Additions or improvements to plant and equipment are accounted for in two ways. All additions and some improvements increase the usefulness of the buildings or equipment and will provide benefits in future periods. For example, the addition of a wing to a building and improvements like the installation of partitions, shelving, sprinkler systems, or air conditioning systems, enhance the quality and efficiency of the building. These expenditures are debited to the building account and credited to either the cash or proper liability account, as shown below.

9		Building or Equipment			x x x xx		9
10		Cash or Proper Liability				x x x xx	10
11		Made addition					11

Since these improvements will benefit future periods, depreciation will be recognized in future periods.

Some improvements extend the useful life of the asset, but do not increase its usefulness or efficiency. For example, a business may replace the engine in a truck. This extends the life of the truck, but it does not improve the truck's usefulness or efficiency. This expenditure is debited to Accumulated Depreciation and credited to either the cash or proper liability account, as shown below.

14	Accum. Depr.—Building or Equip.		x x x xx		14
15	Cash or Proper Liability			x x x xx	15
16	Made improvement				16

Accumulated Depreciation is debited because the depreciation taken on the original engine has been recaptured by replacing it with a new one. The debit to Accumulated Depreciation increases the book value of the asset. Since the new engine will benefit future periods, additional depreciation will be taken in future periods.

Notice that the book value of the asset is increased regardless of whether we debit the asset account or the accumulated depreciation account. This increase in book value leads to an increase in the amount of depreciation recognized in future periods. To illustrate, assume that a business owns the following two computers that were purchased on January 1, 19-1.

	Computer A	**Computer B**
Cost	$6,500	$6,500
Salvage Value	500	500
Depreciable Base	6,000	6,000
Estimated Life	3 years	3 years
Depreciation Method	Straight-Line	Straight-Line
Depreciation Expense 19-1	$2,000	$2,000

At the beginning of 19-2, a disk drive is replaced on computer A and a new tape drive backup unit is added to computer B. Let's assume that the disk drive and tape backup units cost $400 each. The entries for the improvement to computer A, which extends its life but does not increase its usefulness, and the addition to computer B are shown in T account form below.

Computer A	
6,500	

Computer B	
19-2 Jan. 1 6,500	
400	
Bal. 6,900	

Accum. Deprec.—Computer A	
	19-1 Dec. 31 2,000
19-2 Jan. 1 400	
	Bal. 1,600

Accum. Deprec.—Computer B	
	19-1 Dec. 31 2,000

Note that after recording the expenditures on January 1, 19-2, computers A and B both have book values of $4,900, as shown below.

	Computer A	Computer B
Asset Account Balance	$6,500	$6,900
Accumulated Depreciation	(1,600)	(2,000)
Book Value	$4,900	$4,900

To compute depreciation expense for 19-2:

1. Compute the new depreciable base by deducting the salvage value from the book value of the computers following the expenditures.
2. Divide the new depreciable base by the remaining useful life, two years.

	Computer A	Computer B
Book Value	$4,900	$4,900
Salvage Value	(500)	(500)
New Depreciable Cost	$4,400	$4,400
Remaining Useful Life	2 years	2 years
Depreciation Expense	$2,200	$2,200

Thus, Depreciation Expense is $2,200 for each computer in 19-2 and 19-3.

DISPOSAL OF PLANT ASSETS

LO5 Account for the disposition of property, plant, and equipment.

A plant asset can be disposed of in several ways:

1. It may be discarded or retired.
2. It may be sold.
3. It may be exchanged or traded in for another asset.

Regardless of the method of disposal, any gain or loss that occurred on the disposal must be determined. This is done by comparing the market and book values of the asset on the date of disposal. To determine the book value on the date of disposal, an adjusting entry must be made to record depreciation from the end of the previous period to the disposal date.

Determining Gains and Losses on Disposal of Assets

Gain = Market Value greater than Book Value

Loss = Market Value less than Book Value

Gains are similar to revenue and increase net income. Losses are similar to expenses and reduce net income. They are reported on the income statement under Other Revenues and Other Expenses.

Discarding or Retiring Plant Assets

A plant asset may be discarded or retired at any time. If its book value on the disposal date is zero, no gain or loss will be realized. If greater than zero, the book value of the discarded asset will represent a loss.

To illustrate, assume that a printer with a cost of $800 and accumulated depreciation of $800 is discarded. Because the printer is fully depreciated, its book value is zero and no gain or loss results from this transaction. The removal of the asset and related accumulated depreciation is recorded as follows:

5		Accum. Deprec.—Office Equipment	8 0 0 00		5
6		Office Equipment		8 0 0 00	6
7		Discarded printer			7

However, if at the time the printer is discarded, the accumulated depreciation is $720, the book value is $80 and a loss results. In this case, the discard of the asset and recognition of the loss are recorded as follows:

9		Accum. Deprec.—Office Equipment	7 2 0 00		9
10		Loss on Discarded Office Equipment	8 0 00		10
11		Office Equipment		8 0 0 00	11
12		Discarded printer			12

Selling Plant Assets

Now, let's assume that this same printer is sold for $80 at the time its book value is $80. This transaction is entered as follows:

5		Cash	8 0 00		5
6		Accum. Deprec.—Office Equipment	7 2 0 00		6
7		Office Equipment		8 0 0 00	7
8		Sold printer			8

No gain or loss results from this transaction because the printer's selling price, or market value, is equal to its book value.

If the printer is sold for $120 at the time its book value is $80, there would be a gain of $40. In this case, the journal entry is as follows:

5		Cash	1 2 0 00		5
6		Accum. Deprec.—Office Equip.	7 2 0 00		6
7		Office Equipment		8 0 0 00	7
8		Gain on Sale of Printer		4 0 00	8
9		Sold printer			9

If, instead, the printer is sold for $50, there is a loss of $30. This transaction is recorded as follows:

5		Cash			5 0 00				5
6		Accum. Deprec.—Office Equip.			7 2 0 00				6
7		Loss on Sale of Printer			3 0 00				7
8		Office Equipment					8 0 0 00		8
9		Sold printer							9
10									10

> Gains and losses are always computed by comparing the market and book values of the asset being sold or exchanged.

Exchange or Trade-In of Plant Assets

If one asset is traded in on the purchase of another similar asset, a **trade-in allowance** may be granted. This trade-in allowance may be greater than, less than, or equal to the book value of the asset traded in.

If you have ever traded in a car for a newer model, you know that trade-in allowances frequently are not equal to the fair market value. Therefore, the fair market value of the asset traded in must be determined to calculate the gain or loss on the exchange. For simplicity, we will assume in our illustrations that the trade-in allowance is equal to the market value of the old asset being traded.

To illustrate accounting for the exchange of similar assets, let's assume that an old delivery truck is traded for a new one. Relevant information for this transaction is provided below.

Old Delivery Truck		**New Delivery Truck**	
Cost	$8,000	Market Value	$30,000
Accumulated Depreciation	6,900	Trade-in Allowance	1,000
Book Value	$1,100	Cash Required	$29,000

Gain or Loss on Exchange	
$ 1,100	Book Value
(1,000)	Market Value (Trade-In Allowance)
$ 100	Loss

If the new truck has a fair market value of $30,000 and the **trade-in value** of the old truck is $1,000, then $29,000 is due in cash ($30,000 – $1,000). As discussed earlier, the gain or loss on the exchange is determined by comparing the market value of the old asset ($1,000) with its book value ($1,100). In this case, there is a $100 loss. The transaction is entered as follows:

5		Delivery Equipment (new truck)	30 0 0 0 00			5
6		Accum. Deprec.—Delivery Equip.	6 9 0 0 00			6
7		Loss on Exchange of Delivery Equip.	1 0 0 00			7
8		Delivery Equipment (old truck)		8 0 0 0 00		8
9		Cash		29 0 0 0 00		9
10		Purchased a new truck				10

The above entry has the following effects on the accounting records:

1. The original cost ($8,000) and accumulated depreciation ($6,900) for the old truck are removed from the books.
2. Cash is credited to show the amount paid ($29,000).
3. The new delivery equipment is entered on the books at its market value ($30,000).
4. The loss on the exchange is recognized ($100).

Now let's assume the same event, except that the market value and trade-in allowance for the old truck is $1,500. As shown below, this means that only $28,500 in cash is required and there is a $400 gain on the exchange ($1,500 – $1,100 = $400).

Old Delivery Truck		**New Delivery Truck**	
Cost	$8,000	Market Value	$30,000
Accumulated Depreciation	6,900	Trade-in Allowance	1,500
Book Value	$1,100	Cash Required	$28,500

Gain or Loss on Exchange	
$ 1,500	Market Value (Trade-In Allowance)
(1,100)	Book Value
$ 400	Gain

Because of the practice of conservatism, we are not allowed to recognize this gain for financial reporting purposes. **Conservatism** states that *when in doubt* we should *choose the reporting technique that is least likely to overstate assets or net income.* Since an old delivery truck was replaced with a new delivery truck, the company intends to continue earning revenues by making deliveries. Thus, the earnings process of the delivery service has not been completed. This raises doubt about the amount of earnings to recognize at this time. As noted in Chapter 18, conservatism states that we should never anticipate gains. Thus, no gain should be recognized when recording this transaction. The proper entry is shown below:

5		Delivery Equipment (new truck)	29 6 0 0 00			5
6		Accum. Deprec.—Delivery Equip.	6 9 0 0 00			6
7		Delivery Equipment (old truck)		8 0 0 0 00		7
8		Cash		28 5 0 0 00		8
9		Purchased a new truck				9

The entry shown on page 663 has the following effects on the accounting records:

1. The original cost ($8,000) and accumulated depreciation ($6,900) for the old truck are removed from the books.
2. Cash is credited to show the amount paid ($28,500).
3. The new delivery equipment is entered on the books at its market value less the amount of the gain ($30,000 – $400). This must be done to avoid the recognition of the gain.

For tax purposes, neither gains nor losses are recognized on the exchange of similar assets ("like-kind" exchanges).

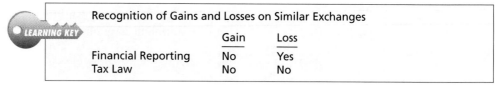

Recognition of Gains and Losses on Similar Exchanges		
	Gain	Loss
Financial Reporting	No	Yes
Tax Law	No	No

Property, Plant, and Equipment Records

If a business has many depreciable assets, a summary general ledger account will be kept for each major class of assets. For example, separate accounts might be kept for buildings, equipment, and furniture. Each summary account has a related accumulated depreciation account. These summary accounts are supported by subsidiary records in the form of cards or computer files. A typical property, plant, and equipment record is shown in Figure 19-2.

Fully Depreciated Plant Assets

A plant asset is fully depreciated when the book value is equal to the salvage value. When an asset is fully depreciated, no further depreciation should be entered. Since the rate of depreciation is based on its *estimated* useful life, an asset may still be used after it is fully depreciated. In this case, the cost of the asset and the accumulated depreciation are left in the accounts. When the asset eventually is disposed of, the cost and accumulated depreciation should be removed from the accounts, as illustrated in previous sections.

NATURAL RESOURCES

LO6 Explain the nature, purpose, and accounting for depletion.

The consumption or exhaustion of *natural resources* is called *depletion*. The purpose of depletion is to allocate the cost of these assets to the periods in which they are consumed. Computing *cost depletion* is similar to computing depreciation using the units-of-production method. The cost of the property, less the estimated salvage or residual value, is divided by the estimated

FIGURE 19-2   Property, Plant, and Equipment Record

PROPERTY, PLANT, AND EQUIPMENT RECORD

Description   Computer

Age when acquired   New

Estimated life   5 years

Account   Office Equipment

Estimated salvage value $400

Rate of annual depreciation based on cost less salvage value   20%

COST			DEPRECIATION RECORD			
Date Purchased	Description	Amount	Year	Rate	Amount	Total To Date
19-4 Jan. 9	ABC DE/3 MODEL 50	3,000 00	19-4	20%	520 00	520 00
	Serial No. 8403637		19-5	20%	520 00	1,040 00
	American Micro		19-6	20%	260 00	1,300 00
	Less estimated salvage value	400 00	19			
	Depreciable cost	2,600 00	19			
			19			
			19			
			19			
			19			

SOLD, EXCHANGED, OR DISCARDED					19	
Date	Explanation	Amount Realized	Book Value on Disposal Date	Gain (Loss)	19	
19-4 July 1	Sold	1,750 00	1,700 00	50 00	19	
					19	
					19	
					19	

number of units that the property contains. The result is the depletion expense per unit. This amount times the number of units removed and sold during the period is the depletion expense for the period.

 LEARNING KEY   The consumption or exhaustion of natural resources is called depletion.

To illustrate, assume a coal mine is acquired at a cost of $1,000,000. No salvage value is expected. The estimated recoverable amount of coal in the mine is 1,000,000 tons. During the current year, 180,000 tons of coal are mined and sold. The computation of the amount of depletion expense is as follows.

$$\frac{\$1,000,000}{1,000,000 \text{ tons}} = \$1 \text{ per ton}$$

180,000 tons x $1 per ton = $180,000 depletion expense

An adjusting entry is made at the end of the accounting period to recognize the depletion expense. For the coal mine, this entry is as follows:

11		Depletion Expense—Coal Mine	180 0 0 0 00		11
12		Accum. Depletion—Coal Mine		180 0 0 0 00	12
13		Depletion based on 180,000			13
14		tons of coal @ $1 a ton			14

The difference between the cost of the mine and the amount of the accumulated depletion is the undepleted cost of the property:

Cost of coal mine	$1,000,000
Less: Accumulated depletion	180,000
Undepleted cost of mine	$ 820,000

Depletion Expense is reported as an operating expense on the income statement. Accumulated Depletion is reported on the balance sheet as a deduction from the related asset account, with the difference identified as undepleted cost of the asset. As was explained for depreciation, this undepleted cost of the wasting asset simply represents the cost not yet charged to operations. It is not intended to reflect the market value of the asset.

INTANGIBLE ASSETS

LO7 Explain the nature of and account for intangible assets.

In an accounting sense, the term "intangible" has come to have a very restricted meaning. Intangible assets refers to a limited group of valuable legal or economic rights that a firm may acquire. All items classified as intangibles are considered to be long-term assets. Major examples of intangibles include patents, copyrights, and trademarks.

Patents

A **patent** is a grant by the federal government to an inventor giving the exclusive right to produce, use, and sell an invention for a period of seventeen years. A firm may purchase a patent from a prior patent owner or may develop its own and acquire an original patent from the government. If purchased, the amount paid represents the cost of the patent.

If a company carries on regular research and development activities to develop its own patents, the costs of such activities are treated as current expenses. If the government grants a patent on an invention the company develops, the cost of this patent includes only the fees paid to the government and to patent attorneys for their services. This amount is debited to an asset account and amortized over the patent's useful life.

Since the life of a patent is specifically limited, any cost assigned to it is allocated over no more than the number of years that the patent right will exist. The greatest number of years would be seventeen if the firm had acquired the patent at the time of its original issuance. If the expected useful or economic life of a patent is less than its legal life, the cost should be allocated over the shorter period.

With the straight-line method, the amortization each year is determined by dividing the cost of the patent by its expected life. Let's assume that a patent with thirteen years to run is purchased at a cost of $12,000, and that the buyer expects the useful life of the patent to be only ten years. In that event, $1,200 ($12,000 ÷ 10 years) would be amortized as expense for each of the ten years. The adjusting entry for the amortization at the end of each year is as follows:

6		Adjusting Entry				6
7		Patent Amortization	1 2 0 0 00			7
8		Patents		1 2 0 0 00		8

Patent amortization is usually treated as an operating expense. Since patents are assets, their unamortized cost is reported on the balance sheet as an intangible long-term asset.

Copyrights

A **copyright** is similar in many respects to a patent. It consists of a federal grant of the exclusive right to the reproduction and sale of a literary, artistic, or musical composition. A copyright is granted for life plus 50 years after the death of the holder. The cost of obtaining the initial copyright on a composition is nominal. It is treated as an ordinary expense. However, if an existing copyright is purchased, the cost may be large enough and the expected future value sufficient to warrant charging the cost to an asset account entitled Copyrights.

It is a rare case in which a copyright would have an economic life as long as its legal life. In most cases the cost of a copyright is written off in a very few years. The write-off can be on a straight-line basis or in the proportion of the actual sales of the copyrighted item during the period to the total expected sales of the item. The amount of the write-off for each period is debited to Copyright Amortization (or Copyright Expense) and credited to Copyrights. Copyright amortization is treated as an operating expense. Any unamortized portion of the cost of copyrights is reported on the balance sheet as an intangible long-term asset.

Trademarks

The practice of using a **trademark** or registered trade name to identify a firm's merchandise is widespread. Such designations can be legally protected by registering them with the United States Patent Office. As long as the trademark or trade name is continuously used, the trademark is legally enforceable.

Research and development costs incurred to develop a trademark are expensed as incurred. However, costs incurred to register a trademark are debited to an asset account and amortized over the trademark's useful life. These costs include attorney and registration fees.

If a trademark is acquired by purchase, its cost is debited to an asset account entitled Trademarks. The future value of a trademark or a trade name is highly uncertain. Conservatism suggests that any cost incurred in purchasing a trademark should be written off within a few years.

The amount written off each period is debited to Trademark Amortization and credited to Trademarks. The amount written off is reported as an operating expense in the income statement. Any unamortized portion of the cost of trademarks or trade names is reported on the balance sheet as an intangible long-term asset.

KEY POINTS

1 The cost to acquire an asset includes the purchase price and all costs incurred to prepare the asset for its intended use.

2 The purpose of depreciation is to match a plant asset's cost with the revenues it helps to produce.

3 Depreciation methods for financial reporting purposes:

Straight-Line Method

$$\text{Annual Depreciation} = \frac{(\text{Cost} - \text{Salvage Value})}{\text{Estimated Useful Life}}$$

Declining-Balance Method

$$\text{Annual Depreciation} = \text{Depreciation Rate} \times \text{Book Value at Beginning of Year}$$

Sum-of-the-Years'-Digits Method

$$\text{Annual Depreciation} = (\text{Cost} - \text{Salvage Value}) \times \frac{\text{Remaining Useful Life}}{\text{Sum-of-the-Years'-Digits}}$$

Units-of-Production Method

$$\text{Depreciation per Unit} = \frac{(\text{Cost} - \text{Salvage Value})}{\text{Estimated Useful Life in Units}}$$

$$\text{Annual Depreciation} = \text{Depreciation per Unit} \times \text{Number of Units Produced this Year}$$

4 Entry for additions and improvements that increase the usefulness of equipment:

Building or Equipment	xxx	
Cash or Proper Liability		xxx

Entry for improvements that extend the life of the asset, but do not improve usefulness or efficiency:

Accumulated Depreciation—Building or Equipment xxx
    Cash or Proper Liability account xxx

To compute straight-line depreciation expense for the year following an addition or improvement:

1. Compute the new depreciable base by deducting the salvage value from the book value of the asset following the expenditures for the addition or improvement.

2. Divide the new depreciable base by the remaining useful life.

5 Disposal of Assets

When an asset is discarded:

1. Remove cost and accumulated depreciation from accounting records.

2. If book value is greater than zero, recognize loss.

When an asset is sold:

1. Remove cost and accumulated depreciation from accounting records.

2. Debit cash for amount received.

3. Recognize gain or loss (Market Value – Book Value of asset sold).

When an asset is traded in for another similar asset:

1. Remove cost and accumulated depreciation for asset traded in from accounting records.

2. Credit cash for amount paid.

3. Treatment of gain or loss (Market Value – Book Value of asset traded in):
    a. Always recognize losses.
    b. Do not recognize gains on the exchange of similar assets.

4. Valuation of new asset:
    a. When exchanged at a loss,
        Cost = Market Value of new asset.
    b. When similar assets are exchanged at a gain,
        Cost = Market Value of new asset – Gain.

6 The consumption or exhaustion of natural resources is called depletion. The purpose of accounting for depletion is to allocate the cost of these assets to the periods in which they are consumed.

7 The term intangible assets is used to refer to a limited group of valuable legal or economic rights (patent, copyright, and trademark) that a firm may acquire. Since the life of an intangible asset is limited, any cost assigned to it is allocated over no more than the number of years that the asset will exist.

KEY TERMS

Accelerated Cost Recovery System (ACRS) 657 A method of depreciation used for federal income tax purposes for plant assets acquired between 1981 and 1986.

accelerated depreciation methods 655   Depreciation methods that provide for a higher depreciation charge in the first year of an asset's life and gradually decreasing charges in subsequent years.

amortization 650   The portion of an intangible asset's cost that is recognized as expense.

book value 652   The undepreciated cost of the asset (Cost – Accumulated Depreciation).

cash equivalent price 650   The amount of cash that could have been paid for the asset on the date of purchase.

conservatism 663   The practice stating that when in doubt, choose the reporting technique that is least likely to overstate assets or net income.

copyright 667   Similar to a patent, a copyright consists of a federal grant of the exclusive right to the reproduction and sale of a literary, artistic, or musical composition.

cost 652   The sum of all amounts spent to acquire an asset and prepare it for its intended use.

declining-balance method 655   An accelerated depreciation method in which the book value is multiplied by a fixed rate. A common rate is double the straight-line rate (the double-declining-balance method).

depletion 650   The consumption or exhaustion of natural resources.

depreciable cost 652   The original cost less salvage (or scrap) value.

depreciation 650   The portion of a plant asset's cost that is recognized as expense.

double-declining-balance method 655   An accelerated depreciation method in which the book value is multiplied by double the straight-line rate.

fixed assets 650   See property, plant, and equipment.

functional depreciation 652   The loss of usefulness from inadequacy or obsolescence.

intangible assets 650   Long-term assets that have no physical substance (patents, copyrights, and trademarks).

long-term assets 650   Assets that are expected to provide benefits for a number of accounting periods.

Modified Accelerated Cost Recovery System (MACRS) 657   A method of depreciation used for federal income tax purposes for plant assets acquired after 1986.

patent 666   A grant by the federal government to an inventor giving the exclusive right to produce, use, and sell an invention for a period of seventeen years.

physical depreciation 652   The loss of usefulness because of deterioration from age and wear.

plant assets 650   See property, plant, and equipment.

property, plant, and equipment 650   Long-term tangible assets that are used in the operations of the business. Also called plant assets or fixed assets.

salvage value 652   The estimated market value of an asset on its expected disposal date.

scrap value 652   See salvage value.

straight-line method 653   A depreciation method in which the depreciable cost of an asset is allocated equally over the years of the asset's useful life.

sum-of-the-years'-digits method 656   A depreciation method in which the annual depreciation is determined by multiplying the depreciable cost by a schedule of fractions.

tangible assets 650   Long-term assets that have physical substance.

trade-in allowance 662   If one asset is traded in on the purchase of another similar asset, an allowance may be granted.

trade-in value 662   See trade-in allowance.

trademark 667   A registered trade name or symbol that identifies a firm's merchandise.

units-of-production method 657   A depreciation method in which depreciation is based on the extent to which the asset was used during the year.

useful life 652   The amount of service expected to be obtained from an asset.

wasting assets 650   Assets whose physical substance consists of natural resources that are consumed in the operation of the business.

REVIEW QUESTIONS

1. What costs should be included when measuring the total cost to acquire a long-term asset?
2. How should additions or improvements representing an increase in the usefulness of plant assets be entered?
3. How should the cost of such activities as planting trees and shrubs be entered?
4. What are the two major causes of depreciation?
5. What is meant by the "depreciable cost" of a plant asset?
6. What are the four most commonly used methods of calculating depreciation for financial reporting purposes? How do they differ in their application?
7. Which depreciation method provides the fastest write-off of an asset?
8. Explain how the depreciation method selected affects the balance sheet and income statement.
9. For assets acquired after 1986, what depreciation methods are allowed for federal income tax purposes?
10. Explain what is meant by additions and identify the two types of improvements.
11. What are the three major ways of disposing of a plant asset?
12. For what time interval should depreciation be entered on the date of an asset's disposal?
13. When a plant asset is sold, what must be known about the asset in order to determine the proper amount of gain or loss on the sale?
14. What details about a particular asset are provided by a property, plant, and equipment record?
15. What is the purpose of depletion?
16. Which depreciation method is similar to the method used to compute depletion expense?

17. Over what period of time should the cost of a patent be allocated if its economic life is expected to be less than its legal life?

18. How should the unamortized portion of the cost of a copyright be reported on the balance sheet?

19. How does conservatism suggest that the cost of a trademark or trade name be accounted for subsequent to acquisition?

MANAGING YOUR WRITING

A friend owns and operates her own business and is concerned about completing her tax return. She owns several assets and uses straight-line depreciation for business purposes. She intended to use straight-line depreciation for tax purposes also, but recently heard about another method called MACRS. She has asked for your advice on which method to use on her tax return. Write a brief memo recommending a depreciation method and explaining why you believe it should be used.

DEMONSTRATION PROBLEM

The Stillman Company purchased a new machine at the start of their current year at a cost of $37,500. The machine is expected to serve for five years and to have a salvage value of $3,000. Ronald L. Stillman, the Chief Executive Officer, has asked for information as to the effects of alternative depreciation methods.

REQUIRED

1. Calculate the annual depreciation expense for each of the five years of expected life of the machine, the accumulated depreciation at the end of each year, and the book value at the end of each year using the:
   a. Straight-line method
   b. Double-declining-balance method
   c. Sum-of-the-years'-digits method

2. Assume that in year 2 and year 4 of the five-year life of this machine, revenues are $45,000 and costs and expenses other than depreciation are $25,000. Calculate the net income for year 2 and year 4 using the same three depreciation methods used in Requirement 1.

3. Assume that Stillman chose the double-declining-balance method of depreciation for this machine. Then, in the first week of year 5, the machine was exchanged (traded in) for similar equipment costing $45,000. The market value and trade-in allowance on the old machine was $4,000 and cash was paid for the balance. Prepare the necessary journal entry to record this exchange.

SOLUTION

1.

	Year	Annual Depreciation Expense	Accumulated Depreciation End of Year	Book Value End of Year
a.	1	$ 6,900	$ 6,900	$30,600
	2	6,900	13,800	23,700
	3	6,900	20,700	16,800
	4	6,900	27,600	9,900
	5	6,900	34,500	3,000
b.	1	$15,000	$15,000	$22,500
	2	9,000	24,000	13,500
	3	5,400	29,400	8,100
	4	3,240	32,640	4,860
	5	1,860*	34,500	3,000
c.	1	$11,500	$11,500	$26,000
	2	9,200	20,700	16,800
	3	6,900	27,600	9,900
	4	4,600	32,200	5,300
	5	2,300	34,500	3,000

*The machine is not depreciated below its estimated salvage value of $3,000.

2.

Year 2	(a) Straight-Line Method	(b) Double-Declining-Balance Method	(c) Sum-of-the-Years'-Digits Method
Revenue	$45,000	$45,000	$45,000
Costs and expenses other than depreciation	25,000	25,000	25,000
Depreciation	6,900	9,000	9,200
Net income	$13,100	$11,000	$10,800
Year 4			
Revenue	$45,000	$45,000	$45,000
Costs and expenses other than depreciation	25,000	25,000	25,000
Depreciation	6,900	3,240	4,600
Net income	$13,100	$16,760	$15,400

3.

5		Equipment (new machine)	45 0 0 0 00				5
6		Accum. Deprec.—Equipment	32 6 4 0 00				6
7		Loss on Exchange of Equipment	8 6 0 00				7
8		Equipment (old machine)		37 5 0 0 00			8
9		Cash		41 0 0 0 00			9
10		Purchased a new machine					10

Old Equipment		New Equipment	
Cost of old equipment	$37,500	Market Value	$45,000
Accumulated Depreciation	32,640	Trade-in Allowance	4,000
Book Value	$ 4,860	Cash required	$41,000
Book Value	$4,860		
Trade-in (Market Value)	(4,000)		
Loss	$ 860		

SERIES A EXERCISES

1 **EXERCISE 19A1 COST OF PROPERTY, PLANT, AND EQUIPMENT**
Consider the following list of expenditures and indicate whether each
would be debited to Land, Building, or Equipment as part of the cost to
purchase these assets. Place a check mark in the appropriate column.

	Yes	No
Land		
Real estate fees		
Cost to remove old buildings		
Cost to pave parking areas		
Tax assessment for streets		
Building		
Cost of land on which the building is located		
Legal fees related to purchase		
Taxes related to purchase		
Realtor fees		
Equipment		
Transportation charges		
Insurance while in transit		
Installation costs		
Interest on loan to buy equipment		

3 **EXERCISE 19A2 STRAIGHT-LINE, DECLINING-BALANCE, AND
SUM-OF-THE-YEARS'-DIGITS METHODS** A light truck is purchased on January 1 at a cost of $27,000. It is expected to serve for eight
years and have a salvage value of $3,000. Calculate the depreciation
expense for the first and third years of the truck's life using the:

1. Straight-line method
2. Double-declining-balance method (round to two decimal places)
3. Sum-of-the-years'-digits method (round to two decimal places)

3 **EXERCISE 19A3 UNITS-OF-PRODUCTION METHOD** The truck
purchased in Exercise 19A2 is expected to be used for 96,000 miles over its
eight-year useful life. Using the units-of-production method, calculate the

depreciation expense for the first and third years of use if the truck is driven 20,000 miles in year 1 and 18,000 miles in year 3.

4   **EXERCISE 19A4 JOURNAL ENTRIES: REPAIRS, MAINTENANCE, ADDITIONS, AND IMPROVEMENTS**   Prepare the entries for the following transactions for Stepanski's Food Mart in a general journal.

1. Replaced the checkout computer in checkout stand A for $2,000 cash. The computer is part of the checkout stand.
2. Added a laser scanner to checkout stand B for $3,000 cash to decrease checkout time.
3. Cleaned scanner window on checkout stand A for $20 cash (normal maintenance).

5   **EXERCISE 19A5 JOURNAL ENTRIES: DISPOSITION OF PLANT ASSETS**   Prepare the entries for the following transactions using a general journal.

1. Discarding an asset.
   a. On January 4, shelving units, which had cost $6,400 and had accumulated depreciation of $5,900, were discarded.
   b. On June 15, a hand cart, which had cost $1,500 and had accumulated depreciation of $1,350, was sold for $150.
   c. On October 1, a copy machine, which had cost $7,200 and had accumulated depreciation of $6,800, was sold for $450.
2. Exchange or trade-in of assets.
   a. On December 31, a drill press, which had cost $60,000 and had accumulated depreciation of $48,000, was traded in for a new drill press with a fair market value of $75,000. The old drill press and $65,000 in cash were given for the new drill press.
   b. On December 31, the old drill press in (a) above and $60,000 in cash were given for the new drill press.

6   **EXERCISE 19A6 DEPLETION**   Prepare the following entries using a general journal.

1. A silver mine was acquired at a cost of $1,500,000 and estimated to contain 6,000,000 tons of ore. During the year, 100,000 tons were mined and sold. Prepare the journal entry for the year's depletion expense.
2. A coal mine was acquired at a cost of $3,000,000 and estimated to contain 750,000 tons of ore. During the year, 125,000 tons were mined and sold. Prepare the journal entry for the year's depletion expense.

SERIES A PROBLEMS

3   **PROBLEM 19A1 STRAIGHT-LINE, DECLINING-BALANCE, AND SUM-OF-THE-YEARS'-DIGITS METHODS**   A machine is purchased January 1 at a cost of $59,000. It is expected to serve for eight years and have a salvage value of $3,000.

continued

REQUIRED

Prepare a schedule showing depreciation for each year and the book value at the end of each year using the:
a. Straight-line method
b. Double-declining-balance method (round to two decimal places)
c. Sum-of-the-years'-digits method (round to two decimal places)

3 PROBLEM 19A2 UNITS-OF-PRODUCTION METHOD A machine is purchased January 1 at a cost of $59,000. It is expected to produce 130,000 units and have a salvage value of $3,000 at the end of its useful life.

Units produced are as follows:

Year 1 10,000
Year 2 8,000
Year 3 12,000
Year 4 16,000
Year 5 11,000

REQUIRED

Prepare a schedule showing depreciation for each year and the undepreciated cost at the end of each year using the units-of-production method.

3 PROBLEM 19A3 CALCULATING AND JOURNALIZING DEPRECIATION Equipment records for Johnson Machine Co. for the year are given below. Johnson Machine uses the straight-line method of depreciation. In the case of assets acquired before the fifteenth day of the month, depreciation should be computed for the entire month. In the case of assets acquired after the fifteenth day of the month, no depreciation should be considered for the month in which the asset was acquired.

Asset	Purchase Price	Useful Life	Salvage Value	Date Purchased
Truck #1	$20,000	8 years	$4,000	January 1
Truck #2	24,000	8	4,000	April 10
Tractor #1	18,000	5	3,000	May 1
Tractor #2	14,000	6	2,000	June 18
Fork Lift	40,000	10	4,000	September 1

REQUIRED

1. Calculate the depreciation expense for Johnson Machine as of December 31, 19--.
2. Prepare the entry for depreciation expense using a general journal.

4 PROBLEM 19A4 IMPACT OF IMPROVEMENTS ON THE CALCULATION OF DEPRECIATION On January 1, 19-1, two flight simulators were purchased by a space camp for $68,000 each with a salvage value of $4,000 each and estimated useful lives of eight years. On January 1, 19-2, the jacks supporting simulator A were replaced for $3,000 cash and an updated computer for more advanced students was installed in simulator B for $10,000 cash.

REQUIRED
1. Using the straight-line method, prepare general journal entries for depreciation on December 31, 19-1, for simulators A and B.
2. Enter the transactions for January 19-2 in a general journal.
3. Assuming no other additions or improvements, calculate the depreciation expense for each simulator for 19-2 through 19-8.

5 **PROBLEM 19A5 DISPOSITION OF ASSETS: JOURNALIZING**
Mitchell Parts Co. had the following plant asset transactions during the year.

1. Assets discarded or sold:
Jan. 1 Motor #12, which had cost $2,800 and had accumulated depreciation of $2,800, was discarded.
    8 Motor #8, which had cost $4,400 and had accumulated depreciation of $4,000, was sold for $200.
   14 Motor #16, which had cost $5,600 and had accumulated depreciation of $5,400, was sold for $450.

2. Assets exchanged or traded-in:
Feb. 1 Motor #6, which had cost $6,000 and had accumulated depreciation of $4,800, was traded in for a new motor (#22) with a fair market value of $7,000. The old motor and $5,600 in cash were given for the new motor.
    9 Motor #9, which had cost $5,500 and had accumulated depreciation of $5,000, was traded in for a new motor (#23) with a fair market value of $6,500. The old motor and $6,200 in cash were given for the new motor.

REQUIRED
Prepare general journal entries for the above transactions.

6 **PROBLEM 19A6 DEPLETION: CALCULATING AND JOUR-NALIZING** Mineral Works Co. acquired a salt mine at a cost of $1,700,000. The estimated number of units available for production from the mine is 3,400,000 tons.

a. During the first year, 200,000 tons are mined and sold.
b. During the second year, 600,000 tons are mined and sold.

REQUIRED
1. Calculate the amount of depletion expense for both years.
2. Prepare general journal entries for depletion expense.

7 **PROBLEM 19A7 INTANGIBLE LONG-TERM ASSETS** Track Town Co. had the following transactions involving intangible assets.

Jan. 1 Purchased a patent for leather soles for $10,000 and estimated its useful life to be 10 years.

continued

Apr. 1 Purchased a copyright for a design for $15,000 with a life left on the copyright of 25 years. The estimated remaining (economic) life of the copyright is 5 years.

July 1 Purchased a trademark at a cost of $50,000. The estimated economic life of the trademark is 25 years. However, conservatism suggests it should be written off in 5 years.

REQUIRED

1. Using the straight-line method, calculate the amortization of the patent, copyright, and trademark.

2. Prepare general journal entries to record the end-of-year amortizations.

SERIES B EXERCISES

1 **EXERCISE 19B1 COST OF PROPERTY, PLANT, AND EQUIPMENT**
The Lam Company purchased the following long-term assets. Determine the purchase cost of each asset.

a. Ten computers:

Purchase price	$60,000
Transportation costs	500
Insurance during transportation	100
Installation	800
Interest on loan to purchase computers	3,000

b. Three acres of land:

Purchase price	$30,000
Grading of land in preparation to build	10,000
Planting of trees around border	5,000
Fence on southern border	3,000
Tax assessment for sewer	1,000
Legal fees related to purchase	900

c. Five-thousand square foot building:

Purchase price	$102,000
Real estate fees	5,000
Land on which building is located	10,000
Legal fees related to purchase	600
Taxes related to purchase	800

3 **EXERCISE 19B2 STRAIGHT-LINE, DECLINING-BALANCE, AND SUM-OF-THE-YEARS'-DIGITS METHODS** A light truck is purchased on January 1 at a cost of $19,000. It is expected to serve for five years and have a salvage value of $1,000. Calculate the depreciation expense for the first and third years of the truck's life using the:

1. Straight-line method
2. Double-declining-balance method
3. Sum-of-the-years'-digits method

3 **EXERCISE 19B3 UNITS-OF-PRODUCTION METHOD**   The truck purchased in Exercise 19B2 is expected to be used for 100,000 miles over its five-year useful life. Using the units-of-production method, calculate the depreciation expense for the first and third years of use if the truck is driven 18,000 miles in year 1 and 22,000 miles in year 3.

4 **EXERCISE 19B4 JOURNAL ENTRIES: REPAIRS, MAINTE-NANCE, ADDITIONS, AND IMPROVEMENTS**   Enter the following transactions for Larry's Lawn Service in a general journal.

1. Added a second mower deck to tractor A for $550 cash to decrease mowing time.
2. Replaced the engine in mower D for $200 cash.
3. Lubricated engine of tractor A for $25 cash (normal maintenance).

5 **EXERCISE 19B5 JOURNAL ENTRIES: DISPOSITION OF PLANT ASSETS**   Prepare the entries for the following transactions using a general journal.

1. Discarding an asset.
    a. On January 4, shelving units, which had cost $7,200 and had accumulated depreciation of $6,900, were discarded.
    b. On June 15, a hand cart, which had cost $2,500 and had accumulated depreciation of $2,250, was sold for $250.
    c. On October 1, a copy machine, which had cost $5,200 and had accumulated depreciation of $4,800, was sold for $500.

2. Exchange or trade-in of assets.
    a. On December 31, a drill press, which had cost $50,000 and had accumulated depreciation of $37,500, was traded in for a new drill press with a fair market value of $55,000. The old drill press and $40,000 in cash were given for the new drill press.
    b. On December 31, the old drill press in (a) above and $45,000 in cash were given for the new drill press.

6 **EXERCISE 19B6 DEPLETION**   Prepare the following entries using a general journal.

1. A silver mine was acquired at a cost of $1,750,000 and estimated to contain 2,500,000 tons of ore. During the year, 110,000 tons were mined and sold. Prepare the journal entry for the year's depletion expense.
2. A coal mine was acquired at a cost of $2,000,000 and estimated to contain 500,000 tons of ore. During the year, 75,000 tons were mined and sold. Prepare the journal entry for the year's depletion expense.

SERIES B   PROBLEMS

3 **PROBLEM 19B1 STRAIGHT-LINE, DECLINING-BALANCE, AND SUM-OF-THE-YEARS'-DIGITS METHODS**   A machine is purchased

January 1 at a cost of $77,000. It is expected to serve for eight years and have a salvage value of $5,000.

REQUIRED

Prepare a schedule showing depreciation for each year and the undepreciated cost at the end of each year using the:
a. Straight-line method
b. Double-declining-balance method (round to two decimal places)
c. Sum-of-the-years'-digits method (round to two decimal places)

3 **PROBLEM 19B2 UNITS-OF-PRODUCTION METHOD**   A machine is purchased January 1 at a cost of $58,000. It is expected to produce 110,000 units and have a salvage value of $3,000 at the end of its useful life.

Units produced are as follows:

Year 1	18,000
Year 2	16,000
Year 3	20,000
Year 4	16,000
Year 5	12,000

REQUIRED

Prepare a schedule showing depreciation for each year and the undepreciated cost at the end of each year using the units-of-production method.

3 **PROBLEM 19B3 CALCULATING AND JOURNALIZING DEPRECIATION**   Equipment records for Byerly Construction Co. for the year are given below. Byerly Construction uses the straight-line method of depreciation. In the case of assets acquired before the fifteenth day of the month, depreciation should be computed for the entire month. In the case of assets acquired after the fifteenth day of the month, no depreciation should be considered for the month in which the asset was acquired.

Asset	Purchase Price	Useful Life	Salvage Value	Date Purchased
Truck #1	$22,000	7 years	$1,000	January 17
Truck #2	24,000	5	4,000	March 23
Molding #1	18,000	5	3,000	May 14
Molding #2	24,000	6	6,000	July 1
Fork Lift	35,000	8	3,000	September 19

REQUIRED

1. Calculate the depreciation expense for Byerly Construction as of December 31, 19--.
2. Prepare the entry for depreciation expense using a general journal.

4 **PROBLEM 19B4 IMPACT OF IMPROVEMENTS ON THE CALCULATION OF DEPRECIATION**   On January 1, 19-1, Dan's Demolition purchased two jackhammers for $2,500 each with a salvage value of $100 each and estimated useful lives of four years. On January 1, 19-2, a stronger blade to improve performance was installed in jackhammer A for $800 cash and the compressor was replaced in jackhammer B for $200 cash.

REQUIRED
1. Using the straight-line method, prepare general journal entries for depreciation on December 31, 19-1, for jackhammers A and B.
2. Enter the transactions for January 19-2 in a general journal.
3. Assuming no other additions or improvements, calculate the depreciation expense for each jackhammer for 19-2 through 19-4.

5 **PROBLEM 19B5 DISPOSITION OF ASSETS: JOURNALIZING**
Mayer Delivery Co. had the following plant asset transactions during the year.

1. Assets discarded or sold:
Jan.   1 Van #11, which had cost $8,800 and had accumulated depreciation of $8,800, was discarded.
        8 Van #7, which had cost $9,400 and had accumulated depreciation of $9,000, was sold for $200.
       14 Van #13, which had cost $7,600 and had accumulated depreciation of $7,400, was sold for $250.

2. Assets exchanged or traded-in:
Feb.   1 Van #8, which had cost $11,000 and had accumulated depreciation of $8,800, was traded in for a new van (#20) with a fair market value of $13,000. The old van and $10,500 in cash were given for the new van.
        9 Van #3, which had cost $7,500 and had accumulated depreciation of $7,000, was traded in for a new van (#21) with a fair market value of $9,500. The old van and $9,200 in cash were given for the new van.

REQUIRED
Prepare general journal entries for the above transactions.

6 **PROBLEM 19B6 DEPLETION: CALCULATING AND JOUR-NALIZING**   Mining Works Co. acquired a copper mine at a cost of $1,200,000. The estimated number of units available for production from the mine is 3,000,000 tons.

a. During the first year, 400,000 tons are mined and sold.
b. During the second year, 700,000 tons are mined and sold.

REQUIRED
1. Calculate the amount of depletion expense for both years.
2. Prepare general journal entries for depletion expense.

7 **PROBLEM 19B7 INTANGIBLE LONG-TERM ASSETS**   B. J. Bakery had the following transactions involving intangible assets.

Jan.   1 Purchased a patent for a new pastry for $10,000 and estimated its useful life to be 10 years.

Apr.   1 Purchased a copyright for a cookie cutter design for $5,000 with a life left on the copyright of 15 years. Estimated that the future remaining (economic) life of the copyright is 5 years.

July   1 Purchased a trademark at a cost of $40,000. The estimated economic life on the trademark is 20 years. However, conservatism suggests it should be written off in 5 years.

REQUIRED

1. Using the straight-line method, calculate the amortization of the patent, copyright, and trademark.
2. Prepare journal entries to record the end-of-year amortizations using a general journal.

MASTERY PROBLEM

On April 1, 19-3, Kwik Kopy Printing purchased a copy machine for $50,000. The estimated life of the machine is five years and it has an estimated salvage value of $5,000. The machine was used until July 1, 19-6.

REQUIRED

1. Assume that Kwik Kopy uses straight-line depreciation and prepare the following entries.
    a. Adjusting entries for depreciation on December 31 of 19-3 through 19-5.
    b. Adjusting entry for depreciation on June 30, 19-6, just prior to trading in the asset.
    c. On July 1, 19-6, the copy machine was traded in for a new copy machine. The market value of the new machine is $38,000. Kwik Kopy must trade in the old copy machine and pay $22,000 for the new machine.
2. Assume that Kwik Kopy uses sum-of-the-years'-digits depreciation and prepare the following entries.
    a. Adjusting entries for depreciation on December 31 of 19-3 through 19-5.
    b. Adjusting entry for depreciation on June 30, 19-6, just prior to trading in the asset.
    c. On July 1, 19-6, the copy machine was traded in for a new copy machine. The market value of the new machine is $38,000. Kwik Kopy must trade in the old copy machine and pay $22,000 for the new machine.

20

Accounting for Partnerships

A professional associate has asked you to consider going into business together as partners. You have heard about partnerships, but you do not know the advantages and disadvantages of this form of ownership structure. Do you need to make a substantial cash investment? How will the profits be distributed? Would you have a regular salary to live on? Should any of these issues be placed in writing?

When two or more individuals engage in an enterprise as co-owners, the organization is known as a **partnership.** This form of organization is common to practically all types of enterprises. However, it is more popular among personal service enterprises than among merchandising businesses. For example, the partnership form of organization is quite common in the legal and public accounting professions. In this chapter, the important features and accounting procedures for partnerships will be discussed and illustrated.

PARTNERSHIP FORMATION

LO1 Explain how a partnership is formed and account for the formation.

The Uniform Partnership Act states that "a partnership is an association of two or more persons who carry on, as co-owners, a business for profit." Partnerships are formed for many reasons. Primarily, however, they are formed on the belief that individuals with complimentary resources and abilities can operate more profitably together than as individuals.

The Partnership Agreement

A written agreement containing the various provisions for operating a partnership is known as a **partnership agreement.** There is no standard form of partnership agreement, but the following provisions are essential.

1. Date of agreement
2. Names of the partners
3. Kind of business to be conducted
4. Length of time the partnership is to run
5. Name and location of the business
6. Investment of each partner
7. Basis on which profits or losses are to be shared by the partners
8. Limitation of partners' rights and activities
9. Salary allowances to partners
10. Division of assets upon dissolution of the partnership
11. Signatures of the partners

Figure 20-1 is an example of a partnership agreement.

Forming a partnership may lead to a great working relationship where partners can pool their assets, talents, and enthusiasm for the business. However, it is important to have a clear understanding of the key elements of the partnership: expectations for each partner, payments to partners in various forms, sharing of profits and losses, and dissolution of the partnership. The best way to ensure a clear understanding is to put everything in writing.

Characteristics of Partnerships

The characteristics of a partnership are different from those of the sole proprietorships we have accounted for in previous chapters. Some of the more important of these characteristics are listed on page 686.

FIGURE 20-1   Partnership Agreement

PARTNERSHIP AGREEMENT

THIS CONTRACT, made and entered into on the first day of July, 19--, by and between Robert Mitchell of Indianapolis, Indiana, and Jessica Jenkins of the same city and state.

WITNESSETH: That the said parties have this day formed a partnership for the purpose of engaging in and conducting a wholesale and retail business in the city of Indianapolis under the following stipulations which are a part of this contract:

FIRST: The said partnership is to continue for a term of twenty-five years from July 1, 19--.

SECOND: The business is to be conducted under the firm name of Mitchell & Jenkins, at 2200 East Washington Street, Indianapolis, Indiana.

THIRD: The investments are as follows: Robert Mitchell, cash, $350,000; Jessica Jenkins, cash, $200,000. These invested assets are partnership property.

FOURTH: Each partner is to devote his/her entire time and attention to the business and to engage in no other business enterprise without the written consent of the other partner.

FIFTH: During the operation of this partnership, neither partner is to become surety or bonding agent for anyone without the written consent of the other partner.

SIXTH: Robert Mitchell is to receive a salary allowance of $36,000 a year, payable $1,500 in cash on the fifteenth day and last business day of each month. Jessica Jenkins is to receive a salary allowance of $48,000 a year, payable $2,000 in cash on the fifteenth day and last business day of each month. At the end of each annual fiscal period, the net income or the net loss shown by the income statement, after the salaries of the two partners have been allowed is to be shared as follows: Robert Mitchell, 60 percent; Jessica Jenkins, 40 percent.

SEVENTH: Neither partner is to withdraw assets in excess of his/her salary, any part of the assets invested, or assets in anticipation of net income to be earned, without the written consent of the other partner.

EIGHTH: In the case of the death or the legal disability of either partner, the other partner is to continue the operations of the business until the close of the annual fiscal period on the following June 30. At that time the continuing partner is to be given an option to buy the interest of the deceased or incapacitated partner at not more than 10 percent above the value of the deceased or incapacitated partner's proprietary interest as shown by the balance of his/her capital account after the books are closed on June 30. It is agreed that this purchase price is to be paid one half in cash and the balance in four equal installments payable quarterly.

NINTH: At the conclusion of this contract, unless it is mutually agreed to continue the operation of the business under a new contact, the assets of the partnership, after the liabilities are paid, are to be divided in proportion to the net credit of each partner's capital account on that date.

IN WITNESS WHEREOF, the parties aforesaid have hereunto set their hands and affixed their seals on the day and year above written.

Robert Mitchell _____ (Seal)
Robert Mitchell

Jessica Jenkins _____ (Seal)
Jessica Jenkins

Co-Ownership of Assets. All assets held by a partnership are co-owned by all partners. If one partner contributes an asset to the business, the asset is jointly owned by all partners.

Mutual Agency. Any partner can bind the other partners to a contract if he or she is acting within the general scope of the business. Thus, if Mitchell signs a contract to purchase merchandise for the business, Jenkins is bound by that contract. On the other hand, if Mitchell contracts to buy a personal automobile, this is not part of normal business operations, and Jenkins would not be bound by it.

Limited Life. A partnership has a limited life. It may be dissolved as the result of any change in the ownership. These include the death, bankruptcy, incapacity, withdrawal of a partner, addition of a new partner, or expiration of the time specified in the partnership agreement.

Unlimited Liability. Each partner is personally liable for all debts incurred by the partnership. If the partnership cannot pay a bill, creditors will expect payment from the personal assets of the partners.

Federal Income Taxes. Partnerships are not subject to federal income taxes. However, individual partners must report and pay taxes on their share of partnership earnings as required on their individual federal income tax returns.

Advantages and Disadvantages

In comparison with the sole proprietorship, the partnership form of business offers certain advantages.

1. The ability and the experience of the partners are combined in one enterprise.
2. More capital may be raised because the resources of the partners are combined.
3. Credit may be improved because each general partner is personally liable for partnership debts.

There also are some disadvantages of the partnership form of organization.

1. As explained in the previous section, each partner is personally liable for all of the debts of the business. Under the laws of some states, certain partners may limit their liability. At least one partner, however, must be a general partner who has unlimited liability.
2. The interest of a partner in the partnership cannot be transferred without the consent of the other partners.
3. Termination of the partnership agreement, bankruptcy of the firm, or death of one of the partners dissolves the partnership.

Accounting for Initial Investments

Accounting for a partnership is basically the same as accounting for a sole proprietorship. The main difference is that separate capital and drawing accounts are maintained for each partner. Care should be used when preparing the opening entry and entering any transactions that affect the respective interests of the partners.

Cash Investments.   A partnership may be formed by the investment of cash by the partners. In opening the books for a partnership, a separate journal entry is made for each partner's investment. The opening entries for Mitchell & Jenkins based on the partnership agreement shown in Figure 20-1 are as follows:

5		Cash	350 0 0 0 00		5
6		Robert Mitchell, Capital		350 0 0 0 00	6
7		R. Mitchell invested $350,000			7
8		in cash			8
9					9
10		Cash	200 0 0 0 00		10
11		Jessica Jenkins, Capital		200 0 0 0 00	11
12		J. Jenkins invested $200,000			12
13		in cash			13

Investment of Cash and Other Assets.   A partnership may also be formed by the investment of cash and other assets by the partners. Certain liabilities also may be assumed by the partnership. Each partner's capital account should be credited for the difference between the market value of the assets invested and liabilities assumed.

Instead of investing $200,000 in cash, assume that Jenkins invested:

1 inventory valued at $47,500 on which $10,500 was owed,
2 office equipment valued at $40,000,
3 delivery equipment valued at $92,000, on which $19,000 was owed on a note, and
4 $50,000 in cash.

The following opening entry would be made.

5		Cash	4	50 0 0 0 00		5
6		Inventory	1	47 5 0 0 00		6
7		Office Equipment	2	40 0 0 0 00		7
8		Delivery Equipment	3	92 0 0 0 00		8
9		Accounts Payable			1 10 5 0 0 00	9
10		Notes Payable			3 19 0 0 0 00	10
11		Jessica Jenkins, Capital			200 0 0 0 00	11
12		J. Jenkins' investment in				12
13		partnership				13

Partnerships Formed from Existing Businesses.   Two or more sole proprietors may combine their businesses to form a partnership. Their respective balance sheets serve as the basis for the opening entries for the investments of such partners. For example, assume that on April 1, Don Morning and Larry Knight form a partnership under the firm name of Morning & Knight Sports. The balance sheets shown in Figure 20-2 are made a part of the partnership agreement. They agree to invest their assets and that the partnership will assume the liabilities shown in their respective balance sheets. Each partner's investment is measured by the difference between the assets invested and the liabilities assumed. The profits and losses are to be shared on a 50-50 basis. In case of dissolution, the assets are to be distributed between the partners in the ratio of their capital interests at the time of dissolution.

 LEARNING KEY Each partner's investment is measured by the difference between the assets invested and the liabilities assumed.

FIGURE 20-2 Balance Sheets for Morning Sports and Knight Athletics Prior to the Formation of the Partnership

Morning Sports
Balance Sheet
March 31, 19--

Assets				Liabilities		
Cash			$ 6 3 4 4 00	Accounts payable	$10 0 8 2 00	
Accounts receivable	$5 5 2 4 00			Notes payable	3 6 0 0 00	
Less allowance for doubtful				Total liabilities		$13 6 8 2 00
accounts	4 3 0 00	5 0 9 4 00				
Merchandise inventory		24 5 7 4 00				
Store equipment	$3 8 4 0 00			Owner's Equity		
Less accumulated				Don Morning, capital		25 1 7 0 00
depreciation	1 0 0 0 00	2 8 4 0 00		Total liabilities and		
Total assets		$38 8 5 2 00		owner's equity		$38 8 5 2 00

Knight Athletics
Balance Sheet
March 31, 19--

Assets				Liabilities		
Cash			$ 3 5 4 4 00	Accounts payable	$13 2 3 8 00	
Accounts receivable	$5 2 8 0 00			Notes payable	6 0 0 0 00	
Less allowance for doubtful				Total liabilities		$19 2 3 8 00
accounts	7 2 0 00	4 5 6 0 00				
Merchandise inventory		29 6 9 2 00				
Supplies		2 8 6 00				
Office equipment	$4 3 2 0 00					
Less accumulated						
depreciation	1 1 0 0 00	3 2 2 0 00				
Store equipment	$4 8 0 0 00			Owner's Equity		
Less accumulated				Larry Knight, capital		25 6 6 4 00
depreciation	1 2 0 0 00	3 6 0 0 00		Total liabilities and		
Total assets		$44 9 0 2 00		owner's equity		$44 9 0 2 00

> **LEARNING KEY** When two sole proprietors decide to combine their businesses, assets should be recorded at their fair market values as of the date of formation of the partnership.

When two sole proprietors decide to combine their businesses, assets should be recorded at their fair market values as of the date of formation of the partnership. For Morning and Knight, any accounts receivable known to be uncollectible as of March 31, 19--, should be written off. None was considered uncollectible in this case. The balance in Accounts Receivable is debited and the amount of the Allowance for Doubtful Accounts is credited in the books of the partnership. In this way, the accounts receivable are entered at their approximate fair market value.

Both Morning and Knight had been using the first-in, first-out (FIFO) method of inventory costing. Recall that under FIFO, the most recently purchased inventory is considered to be on hand. Thus, the values shown for merchandise inventories on their respective balance sheets are close to their fair market value as of March 31, 19--. If Morning or Knight had been using some other inventory costing method, the merchandise inventory amounts might have required restatement to reflect fair market value.

The fair market value of Morning's store equipment as of March 31, 19--, is $3,600. This amount should be entered on the books of the new partnership, rather than the book value of $2,840 shown on Morning's balance sheet in Figure 20-2. In like manner, the fair market values of Knight's office equipment and store equipment as of March 31, 19--, are $3,850 and $4,200, respectively. These amounts should be entered on the books of the new partnership, rather than the respective book values of $3,220 and $3,600 shown on Knight's balance sheet. Once again, the difference between assets invested and liabilities assumed is credited to each partner's capital account. The opening entries for Morning & Knight Sports are shown on the next page.

PARTNER COMPENSATION AND THE ALLOCATION OF NET INCOME

LO2 Explain how partners are compensated and account for the allocation of net income.

> **LEARNING KEY** The basis on which profits and losses are shared is a matter of agreement between the partners, and not necessarily the same as their investment ratio.

The basis on which profits and losses are shared is a matter of agreement between the partners, and not necessarily the same as their investment ratio. Factors other than the assets invested may enter into a profit-and-loss sharing agreement. For example, one partner may contribute most of the assets but render no services, while the other partner may contribute less in assets but devote full time to the partnership.

In the absence of any agreement between the partners, profits and losses must be shared equally regardless of the ratio of the partners' invest-

	DATE		DESCRIPTION	POST. REF.	DEBIT	CREDIT	
1	Apr.	1	Cash		6 3 4 4 00		1
2			Accounts Receivable		5 5 2 4 00		2
3			Merchandise Inventory		24 5 7 4 00		3
4			Store Equipment		3 6 0 0 00		4
5			Allowance for Doubtful Accounts			4 3 0 00	5
6			Accounts Payable			10 0 8 2 00	6
7			Notes Payable			3 6 0 0 00	7
8			Don Morning, Capital			25 9 3 0 00	8
9			D. Morning's investment in				9
10			partnership				10
11							11
12		1	Cash		3 5 4 4 00		12
13			Accounts Receivable		5 2 8 0 00		13
14			Merchandise Inventory		29 6 9 2 00		14
15			Supplies		2 8 6 00		15
16			Office Equipment		3 8 5 0 00		16
17			Store Equipment		4 2 0 0 00		17
18			Allowance for Doubtful Accounts			7 2 0 00	18
19			Accounts Payable			13 2 3 8 00	19
20			Notes Payable			6 0 0 0 00	20
21			Larry Knight, Capital			26 8 9 4 00	21
22			L. Knight's investment in				22
23			partnership				23

GENERAL JOURNAL — PAGE 1

ments. If the partnership agreement specifies how profits are to be shared but does not specify how losses are to be shared, the losses must be shared on the same basis as profits.

Profits and Losses Shared Equally

If the Mitchell and Jenkins partnership agreement shown in Figure 20-1 did not specify how the partners would be compensated, the profits and losses would be shared equally. If net income for the year was $190,800, the allocation would be reported on the income statement as shown in Figure 20-3.

Maintaining a record of each partner's share of net income and the amount of drawing each year requires a minor change in the way closing entries are made. Recall that four closing entries are made for sole proprietorships at the end of the accounting period. For a partnership, separate capital and drawing accounts are maintained for each partner. Thus, entries three and four must be changed as shown in Figure 20-4.

FIGURE 20-3   Allocation of Profit and Loss (Equal Division)

Mitchell and Jenkins
Income Statement (Partial)
For Year Ended December 31, 19--

	R. MITCHELL	J. JENKINS	TOTAL
Net income			$190 8 0 0 00
Allocation of net income	$95 4 0 0 00	$95 4 0 0 00	$190 8 0 0 00

FIGURE 20-4   Closing Entries

CLOSING ENTRIES—SOLE PROPRIETOR	CLOSING ENTRIES—PARTNERSHIP
1. Close all revenues to Income Summary.	1. Close all revenues to Income Summary.
2. Close all expenses to Income Summary.	2. Close all expenses to Income Summary.
3. Close Income Summary to the owner's capital account.	3. Close Income Summary by allocating each partner's share of net income or loss to the individual capital accounts.
4. Close Drawing to the owner's capital account.	4. Close each partner's drawing account to the individual capital accounts.

Based on the net income allocation shown above, the third closing entry is:

5		Income Summary	190 8 0 0 00		5
6		R. Mitchell, Capital		95 4 0 0 00	6
7		J. Jenkins, Capital		95 4 0 0 00	7

If Mitchell and Jenkins withdrew $36,000 and $48,000, respectively, the fourth closing entry would be:

9		R. Mitchell, Capital	36 0 0 0 00		9
10		R. Mitchell, Drawing		36 0 0 0 00	10
11					11
12		J. Jenkins, Capital	48 0 0 0 00		12
13		J. Jenkins, Drawing		48 0 0 0 00	13

The four closing entries for a partnership are summarized in T account form in Figure 20-5.

FIGURE 20-5   Closing Process for a Partnership

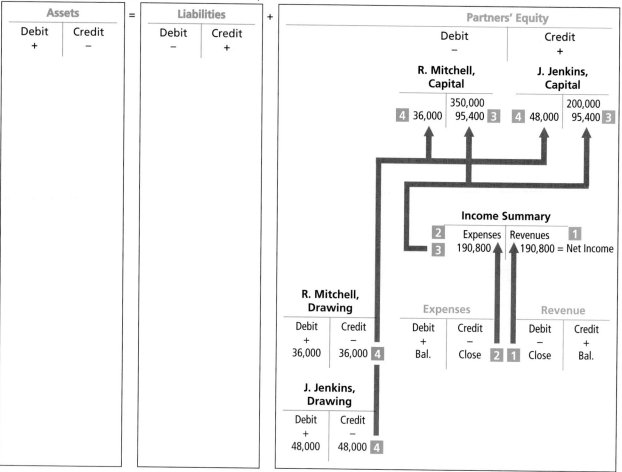

Allocation of Profits and Losses with Salary Allowances

The partnership agreement in Figure 20-1 specifies that after providing for salary allowances of $36,000 for Mitchell and $48,000 for Jenkins, the remaining net income or loss is divided on a 60-40 basis. Since the partners are not employees, many argue that payments made to the partners should not be reported as expenses. Instead, salary payments (or allowances) are debited to the partners' drawing accounts. Under these conditions, the allocation of net income would be reported on the income statement as shown in Figure 20-6.

If net income is greater than the salary allowances, the remaining income is allocated according to the ratio specified in the partnership agreement.

Net income	$190,800
Less: Total allowances	84,000
Remaining income	$106,800

60% of $106,800 = $64,080
40% of $106,800 = $42,720

FIGURE 20-6   Allocation of Profit and Loss on Income Statement (60–40 Basis)

Mitchell and Jenkins
Income Statement (Partial)
For Year Ended December 31, 19--

	R. MITCHELL	J. JENKINS	TOTAL
Net income			$190 8 0 0 00
Allocation of net income:			
Salary allowance	$ 36 0 0 0 00	$ 48 0 0 0 00	$ 84 0 0 0 00
Remaining income	64 0 8 0 00	42 2 7 0 00	106 8 0 0 00
Allocation of net income	$100 0 8 0 00	$ 90 7 2 0 00	$190 8 0 0 00

Based on the net income allocation shown above, the closing entry is:

5	Dec. 31	Income Summary	190 8 0 0 00		5
6		R. Mitchell, Capital		100 0 8 0 00	6
7		J. Jenkins, Capital		90 7 2 0 00	7

Assuming that Mitchell and Jenkins withdrew their salaries as described in the partnership agreement, the balances in the drawing accounts at year end would be $36,000 and $48,000, respectively. The drawing accounts would be closed to the partners' capital accounts at year end as follows:

9	Dec. 31	R. Mitchell, Capital	36 0 0 0 00		9
10		R. Mitchell, Drawing		36 0 0 0 00	10
11					11
12		J. Jenkins, Capital	48 0 0 0 00		12
13		J. Jenkins, Drawing		48 0 0 0 00	13

If the salary allowances are greater than net income, the excess is allocated to the partners according to the ratio specified in the partnership agreement. If net income for Mitchell and Jenkins is $44,000, the allocation is made as shown in Figure 20-7. Based on the preceding net income allocations in Figure 20-7, the closing entries are:

5	Dec. 31	Income Summary	44 0 0 0 00		5
6		R. Mitchell, Capital		12 0 0 0 00	6
7		J. Jenkins, Capital		32 0 0 0 00	7
8					8
9		R. Mitchell, Capital	36 0 0 0 00		9
10		R. Mitchell, Drawing		36 0 0 0 00	10
11					11
12		J. Jenkins, Capital	48 0 0 0 00		12
13		J. Jenkins, Drawing		48 0 0 0 00	13

FIGURE 20-7   Allocation of Profit and Loss on Income Statement when Salary Allowances are Greater than Net Income

Salary allowances	$84,000
Less net income	44,000
Excess of salary allowances over net income	$40,000

60% of $40,000 = $24,000
40% of $40,000 = $16,000

Mitchell and Jenkins
Income Statement (Partial)
For Year Ended December 31, 19--

	R. MITCHELL	J. JENKINS	TOTAL
Net income			$44 0 0 0 00
Allocation of net income:			
Salary allowance	$ 36 0 0 0 00	$ 48 0 0 0 00	$ 84 0 0 0 00
Excess of salary allowance over net income	24 0 0 0 00	16 0 0 0 00	40 0 0 0 00
Allocation of net income	$12 0 0 0 00	$ 32 0 0 0 00	$44 0 0 0 00

Allocation of Profits and Losses with Salary and Interest Allowances

Partners may agree that the best method of allocating profits and losses is to base salaries on the services rendered by each partner as well as to provide interest on capital investments. The remainder is then shared equally, or according to a predefined ratio. Assume that B. K. Kelly and S. B. Arthur form a partnership on January 1 of the current year. Kelly will devote full time to operating the business, invests $50,000, and will draw a salary of $35,000 per year. Arthur will devote about 10 hours per week, invests $150,000, and will draw a salary of $10,000 per year. The partners will be allowed interest of 10% on capital balances on January 1 of each year and the balance of earnings will be divided equally. Net income of $80,000 in the first year of operation would be allocated as reported in Figure 20-8.

Interest allowance:	Kelly	$50,000 x 10% =	$ 5,000
	Arthur	$150,000 x 10% =	$15,000
Net income		$80,000	
Less: Total allowances		65,000	
Remaining income		$15,000	

Based on the net income allocation shown in Figure 20-8, the closing entry is:

	19--								
5	Dec.	31	Income Summary			80 0 0 0 00			5
6			B. K. Kelly, Capital				47 5 0 0 00		6
7			S. B. Arthur, Capital				32 5 0 0 00		7

FIGURE 20-8   Allocation of Profit and Loss on Income Statement (Interest and Salary Allowances)

Kelly and Arthur
Income Statement (Partial)
For Year Ended December 31, 19--

	B. K. KELLY	S. B. ARTHUR	TOTAL
Net income			$80 0 0 0 00
Allocation of net income:			
Salary allowance	$35 0 0 0 00	$10 0 0 0 00	$45 0 0 0 00
Interest allowance	5 0 0 0 00	15 0 0 0 00	20 0 0 0 00
Remaining income	7 5 0 0 00	7 5 0 0 00	15 0 0 0 00
	$47 5 0 0 00	$32 5 0 0 00	$80 0 0 0 00

If Kelly and Arthur incurred a net loss of $20,000 in year 1, the allocation would be made as shown in Figure 20-9.

FIGURE 20-9   Allocation of Net Loss on Income Statement

Kelly and Arthur
Income Statement (Partial)
For Year Ended December 31, 19--

	B. K. KELLY	S. B. ARTHUR	TOTAL
Net loss			$(20 0 0 0 00)
Allocation of net income:			
Salary allowance	$35 0 0 0 00	$ 10 0 0 0 00	$ 45 0 0 0 00
Interest allowance	5 0 0 0 00	15 0 0 0 00	20 0 0 0 00
Excess of allowances over income allocated equally	(42 5 0 0 00)	(42 5 0 0 00)	(85 0 0 0 00)
	$ (2 5 0 0 00)	$(17 5 0 0 00)	$(20 0 0 0 00)

Net loss	$20,000
Plus: Total allowances	65,000
Excess of allowances over income	$85,000

$85,000 ÷ 2 = $42,500 allocated to each partner

The following closing entry would be made to allocate the loss of $20,000.

5	Dec. 31	B. K. Kelly, Capital	2 5 0 0 00			5
6		S. B. Arthur, Capital	17 5 0 0 00			6
7		Income Summary		20 0 0 0 00		7

STATEMENTS FOR PARTNERSHIPS

LO3 Prepare financial statements reporting the allocation of net income and partnership equity.

> The allocation of net income and its impact on the partners' capital balances should be disclosed in the financial statements.

The allocation of net income and its impact on the partners' capital balances should be disclosed in the financial statements. All three financial statements are affected: the income statement, statement of owners' (partners') equity, and balance sheet. As illustrated in the preceding section, the allocation is often reported in the lower portion of the income statement. In addition, the statement of partners' equity reflects the equity of each partner and summarizes the allocation of net income for the year.

Recall that the capital balances for Kelly and Arthur on January 1, 19--, were $50,000 and $150,000, respectively. Let's assume that Arthur invested an additional $10,000, net income was $80,000, and the partners withdrew only the salary portion of their compensation ($35,000 and $10,000, respectively) during the first year of operation. As shown in Figure 20-10, the statement of partners' equity reports this information and the income allocations reported on the income statement.

FIGURE 20-10   Statement of Partners' Equity

Kelly and Arthur
Statement of Partners' Equity
For Year Ended December 31, 19--

	B. K. KELLY	S. B. ARTHUR	TOTAL
Capital, January 1, 19--	$50 0 0 0 00	$150 0 0 0 00	$200 0 0 0 00
Additional investments during the year		10 0 0 0 00	10 0 0 0 00
	$50 0 0 0 00	$160 0 0 0 00	$210 0 0 0 00
Net income for the year	47 5 0 0 00	32 5 0 0 00	80 0 0 0 00
	$97 5 0 0 00	$192 5 0 0 00	$290 0 0 0 00
Withdrawals (salaries during the year)	35 0 0 0 00	10 0 0 0 00	45 0 0 0 00
Capital, December 31, 19--	$62 5 0 0 00	$182 5 0 0 00	$245 0 0 0 00

> Interest allowances for year 2 would be computed as follows:
>
> Kelly $ 62,500 x 10% = $ 6,250
> Arthur $182,500 x 10% = $18,250
>
> The additional investment is reported in the same manner as for a sole proprietorship.

Finally, the partners' equity section of the balance sheet reports the equity of each partner, as illustrated on the next page:

Partners' Equity								
B. K. Kelly, capital	$ 62	5	0	0	00			
S. B. Arthur, capital	182	5	0	0	00			
Total partners' equity						$245	0 0 0	00

DISSOLUTION OF A PARTNERSHIP

LO4 Describe the actions that result in the dissolution of a partnership and account for the dissolution.

One of the primary characteristics of the partnership form of organization is its limited life. Any change in the members of the partnership results in **dissolution.** Dissolution of a partnership may occur because of the addition of a new partner, the death or withdrawal of one of the partners, or bankruptcy.

 LEARNING KEY   Any change in the members of the partnership results in dissolution.

Dissolution of the partnership does not necessarily imply that business operations will halt. It simply means that the partnership is dissolved. The business may continue with a new group of partners, or a different form of ownership.

Admitting a New Partner

A new partner may be admitted by agreement among the existing partners. When this happens, the old partnership is dissolved and a new one is created. A new partner may buy into the business in three ways: (1) by purchasing an interest directly from existing partners, (2) by making a cash investment in the business, or (3) by contributing assets from an existing business.

Assume that Morning and Knight admit Sunny Noon as a new partner as of July 1, 19--, when Morning and Knight have capital interests of $30,000 and $20,000, respectively. Noon pays $12,000 to Morning for one-third of his interest and $12,000 to Knight for one-half of his interest. These cash payments go to the partners directly, not to the business. Thus, the following entry is made by the partnership.

1	July 1	Don Morning, Capital	10 0 0 0 00*			1
2		Larry Knight, Capital	10 0 0 0 00**			2
3		Sunny Noon, Capital		20 0 0 0 00		3
4		S. Noon admitted to partnership				4
5		*$30,000 x 1/3 = $10,000				5
6		**$20,000 x 1/2 = $10,000				6

The extra $2,000 ($12,000 – $10,000) paid to both Morning and Knight represents profit to the partners and has no effect on the *partnership's* financial statements.

Now, assume instead that Noon invested $25,000 cash in the new partnership. In this case, the following entry would be made to admit Noon.

	19--					
1	July 1	Cash		25 0 0 0 00		1
2		Sunny Noon, Capital			25 0 0 0 00	2
3		S. Noon admitted to				3
4		partnership				4
5						5

Finally, let's assume that Noon had been operating her own business, which was then taken over by the new partnership. In this case the balance sheet for Sunny Noon's Golf, shown in Figure 20-11, would serve as a basis for preparing the opening entry. The assets listed in the balance sheet are taken over, the liabilities are assumed, and Noon's capital account is credited for the difference.

FIGURE 20-11   Balance Sheet for Sunny Noon's Golf

Sunny Noon's Golf
Balance Sheet
June 30, 19--

Assets			Liabilities		
Cash		$ 5 0 0 0 00	Accounts payable	$7 5 5 0 00	
Accounts receivable	$14 2 9 0 00		Notes payable	9 0 4 8 00	
Less allowance for doubtful			Total liabilities		$16 5 9 8 00
accounts	1 0 7 8 00	13 2 1 2 00			
Merchandise inventory		27 2 9 0 00	Owner's Equity		
			Sunny Noon, capital		28 9 0 4 00
			Total liabilities and		
Total assets		$45 5 0 2 00	owner's equity		$45 5 0 2 00

Noon has no knowledge of any uncollectible accounts receivable as of June 30, 19--, and has been using the FIFO method of inventory costing. Thus, the amounts reported on the balance sheet are reasonable approximations of market values. The entry to admit Noon as a partner, therefore, is as follows:

	19--					
1	July 1	Cash		5 0 0 0 00		1
2		Accounts Receivable		14 2 9 0 00		2
3		Merchandise Inventory		27 2 9 0 00		3
4		Allowance for Doubtful Accounts			1 0 7 8 00	4
5		Accounts Payable			7 5 5 0 00	5
6		Notes Payable			9 0 4 8 00	6
7		Sunny Noon, Capital			28 9 0 4 00	7
8		S. Noon admitted to				8
9		partnership				9
10						10

Withdrawal of Partner

By agreement, a partner may retire and be permitted to withdraw assets equal to, less than, or greater than the amount of his or her interest in the partnership. The book value of a partner's interest is shown by the credit balance of the partner's capital account. The balance is computed after all profits or losses have been allocated in accordance with the partnership agreement and the books closed. If a retiring partner withdraws cash or other assets equal to the credit balance of his or her capital account, the transaction will have no effect on the capital of the remaining partners.

To illustrate, assume that several years after the formation of Morning, Noon, and Knight Sports, Sunny Noon decided to retire. The partners agreed to the withdrawal of cash equal to the amount of Noon's equity in the assets of the partnership. After bringing all accounts up to date, assume that the partners' capital accounts had credit balances as follows:

Don Morning	$55,000
Sunny Noon	40,000
Larry Knight	45,000

If Noon withdraws $40,000 in cash, the entry on the books of the partnership is as follows:

2		Sunny Noon, Capital	40 0 0 0 00		2
3		Cash		40 0 0 0 00	3
4		S. Noon retired, withdrawing			4
5		$40,000 in equity settlement			5

Note that this transaction decreases cash and decreases the total capital of the partnership, but it does not affect the equity of the remaining partners. Morning still has an equity of $55,000 and Knight an equity of $45,000 in the partnership assets.

If a retiring partner agrees to withdraw less than the amount in his or her capital account, the transaction will increase the capital accounts of the remaining partners. For example, if Noon withdraws only $30,000 in settlement of the interest, the entry in the books of the partnership is as follows:

2		Sunny Noon, Capital	40 0 0 0 00		2
3		Cash		30 0 0 0 00	3
4		Don Morning, Capital		5 5 0 0 00	4
5		Larry Knight, Capital		4 5 0 0 00	5
6		S. Noon retired, withdrawing			6
7		$30,000 in equity settlement			7

The difference between Noon's equity in the assets of the partnership and the amount of cash withdrawn is $10,000 ($40,000 − $30,000). This difference is divided between the remaining partners on the basis stated in the partnership agreement. In this case it is divided according to the ratio of their capital interests after allocating net income and closing their drawing accounts. On this basis, Morning's capital account is credited for $5,500 and Knight's is credited for $4,500. The calculations are shown below.

Remaining Equity in Partnership

Morning	$ 55,000
Knight	45,000
Total	$100,000

Allocation to Morning: ($55,000 ÷ $100,000) × $10,000 = $5,500
Allocation to Knight: ($45,000 ÷ $100,000) × $10,000 = $4,500

If a retiring partner withdraws more than the amount in his or her capital account, the transaction will decrease the capital accounts of the remaining partners. Thus, if Morning and Knight allow Noon to withdraw $45,000 in settlement of Noon's interest, the entry in the books of the partnership is as follows:

2		Sunny Noon, Capital	40 0 0 0 00			2
3		Don Morning, Capital	2 7 5 0 00			3
4		Larry Knight, Capital	2 2 5 0 00			4
5		Cash		45 0 0 0 00		5
6		S. Noon retired, withdrawing				6
7		$45,000 in equity settlement				7

The excess of the amount of cash withdrawn over Noon's equity in the partnership ($5,000) is divided between the remaining partners on the basis stated in the partnership agreement. Thus, Morning, Capital is debited for $2,750 ($55/100$ of $5,000), while Knight, Capital is debited for $2,250 ($45/100$ of $5,000).

When a partner retires from the business, the partner's interest may be purchased by one or more of the remaining partners or by an outside party. If the retiring partner's interest is sold to one of the remaining partners, the retiring partner's equity is merely transferred to the other partner. For example, assume that Noon's equity is sold to Morning. The entry for the transaction on the books of the partnership is as follows:

2		Sunny Noon, Capital	40 0 0 0 00		2
3		Don Morning, Capital		40 0 0 0 00	3
4		D. Morning purchased S. Noon's			4
5		interest in the partnership			5

The amount paid to Noon by Morning is a personal transaction and is not entered on the books of the partnership. Any gain or loss resulting from the transaction is a personal gain or loss of the withdrawing partner and not of the firm. Thus, whatever amount is involved, the credit in Noon's account is transferred to Morning's account.

Death of a Partner

The death of a partner dissolves the partnership. On the date of death, the accounts are closed and the net income for the year to date is allocated to the partners' capital accounts. Most agreements call for an audit and revaluation of the assets at this time. The balance of the deceased partner's capital account is then transferred to a liability account with the deceased's estate. The surviving partners may continue the business or liquidate. If the former action is chosen, the procedures for settling with the estate are the same as those described earlier for the withdrawal of a partner. Liquidation procedures are described in the following section.

LIQUIDATION OF A PARTNERSHIP

LO5 Describe how a partnership is liquidated and prepare associated entries and a statement of partnership liquidation.

Liquidation of a partnership generally means that the assets are sold, liabilities are paid, and the remaining cash or other assets are distributed to the partners. When normal operations are discontinued, adjusting and closing entries are made. Thus, only the assets, liabilities, and partners' equity accounts remain open. As the assets are sold, the cash realized is applied first to the claims of creditors. Once all liabilities are paid, the remaining cash is distributed to the partners according to their ownership interests as indicated by their capital accounts.

> Liquidation of a partnership generally means that the assets are sold, liabilities are paid, and the remaining cash or other assets are distributed to the partners.

To illustrate, assume that after several years of operations the partnership of Morning, Noon, and Knight Sports is to be liquidated. After making closing entries on May 31, 19--, the accounts listed below remain open. For simplicity, "Other Assets" and "Liabilities" are used as account titles. In actual practice several asset, contra-asset, and liability accounts would be involved.

Account Title	Account Balance	
	Debit	**Credit**
Cash	$ 10,000	
Inventory	120,000	
Other Assets	220,000	
Liabilities		$ 80,000
Don Morning, Capital		95,000
Larry Knight, Capital		120,000
Sunny Noon, Capital		55,000

Using these account balances, accounting for the liquidation of the partnership is illustrated on the next page. For convenience, let's assume that all assets are sold in one transaction on June 1, 19--, and all liabilities are paid at once on June 15, 19--. On June 18, cash settlements are made with the partners who share equally in all profits and losses.

Gain on Sale of Assets

Assume that the noncash assets are sold for $370,000. Since these assets have a book value of $340,000, a gain of $30,000 on the sale is recognized. The gain is allocated to the partners' capital accounts according to the profit-and-loss sharing ratio. In this case, the gain is shared equally. Next, the liabilities are paid and the remaining cash distributed to the partners according to their capital account balances. A statement of partnership liquidation summarizing these transactions is provided in Figure 20-12.

FIGURE 20-12 Statement of Partnership Liquidation

Morning, Noon, and Knight Sports
Statement of Partnership Liquidation
For Period June 1–18, 19--

	CASH	INVENTORY	OTHER ASSETS	LIABILITIES	CAPITAL D. MORNING	CAPITAL L. KNIGHT	CAPITAL S. NOON
Balance before sale of assets	$ 10 0 0 0 00	$120 0 0 0 00	$220 0 0 0 00	$80 0 0 0 00	$ 95 0 0 0 00	$120 0 0 0 00	$55 0 0 0 00
Sale of noncash assets and allocation of gain	370 0 0 0 00	(120 0 0 0 00)	(220 0 0 0 00)		10 0 0 0 00	10 0 0 0 00	10 0 0 0 00
Balance after sale	$380 0 0 0 00	0	0	$80 0 0 0 00	$105 0 0 0 00	$130 0 0 0 00	$65 0 0 0 00
Payment of liabilities	(80 0 0 0 00)			(80 0 0 0 00)			
Balance after payment of liabilities	$300 0 0 0 00	0	0	0	$105 0 0 0 00	$130 0 0 0 00	$65 0 0 0 00
Distribution of cash to partners	(300 0 0 0 00)				(105 0 0 0 00)	(130 0 0 0 00)	(65 0 0 0 00)
Final balance	0	0	0	0	0	0	0

The entries for these transactions are illustrated below.

1	June 1	Cash	370 0 0 0 00		1
2		Inventory		120 0 0 0 00	2
3		Other Assets		220 0 0 0 00	3
4		Gain on Sale of Assets		30 0 0 0 00	4
5		Sale of assets			5
6					6
7	1	Gain on Sale of Assets	30 0 0 0 00		7
8		Don Morning, Capital		10 0 0 0 00	8
9		Larry Knight, Capital		10 0 0 0 00	9
10		Sunny Noon, Capital		10 0 0 0 00	10
11		Allocation of gain			11
12					12
13	15	Liabilities	80 0 0 0 00		13
14		Cash		80 0 0 0 00	14
15		Payment of liabilities			15
16					16

17	18 Don Morning, Capital	105 0 0 0 00					17
18	Larry Knight, Capital	130 0 0 0 00					18
19	Sunny Noon, Capital	65 0 0 0 00					19
20	Cash			300 0 0 0 00			20
21	Distribution of cash to partners						21

Loss on Sale of Assets

Using the same information for Morning, Noon, and Knight as illustrated above and on page 702, assume that the noncash assets are sold for $295,000, resulting in a loss of $45,000. A statement of partnership liquidation reflecting the equal allocation of the loss on the sale of assets, payment of the liabilities, and distribution of the cash to the partners is illustrated in Figure 20-13.

FIGURE 20-13 Statement of Partnership Liquidation

Morning, Noon, and Knight Sports
Statement of Partnership Liquidation
For Period June 1–18, 19--

	CASH	INVENTORY	OTHER ASSETS	LIABILITIES	CAPITAL D. MORNING	L. KNIGHT	S. NOON
Balance before sale of assets	$ 10 0 0 0 00	$120 0 0 0 00	$220 0 0 0 00	$80 0 0 0 00	$95 0 0 0 00	$120 0 0 0 00	$55 0 0 0 00
Sale of noncash assets and allocation of loss	295 0 0 0 00	(120 0 0 0 00)	(220 0 0 0 00)		(15 0 0 0 00)	(15 0 0 0 00)	(15 0 0 0 00)
Balance after sale	$305 0 0 0 00	0	0	$80 0 0 0 00	$80 0 0 0 00	$105 0 0 0 00	$40 0 0 0 00
Payment of liabilities	(80 0 0 0 00)			(80 0 0 0 00)			
Balance after payment of liabilities	$225 0 0 0 00	0	0	0	$80 0 0 0 00	$105 0 0 0 00	$40 0 0 0 00
Distribution of cash to partners	(225 0 0 0 00)				(80 0 0 0 00)	(105 0 0 0 00)	(40 0 0 0 00)
Final balance	0	0	0	0	0	0	0

The entries for these transactions are as follows:

1	June 19-- 1 Cash	295 0 0 0 00			1
2	Loss on Sale of Assets	45 0 0 0 00			2
3	Inventory		120 0 0 0 00		3
4	Other Assets		220 0 0 0 00		4
5	Sale of assets				5
6					6
7	1 Don Morning, Capital	15 0 0 0 00			7
8	Larry Knight, Capital	15 0 0 0 00			8
9	Sunny Noon, Capital	15 0 0 0 00			9
10	Loss on Sale of Assets		45 0 0 0 00		10
11	Allocation of loss				11

13		15	Liabilities		80	0	0	0	00							13
14			Cash							80	0	0	0	00		14
15			Payment of liabilities													15
16																16
17		18	Don Morning, Capital		80	0	0	0	00							17
18			Larry Knight, Capital		105	0	0	0	00							18
19			Sunny Noon, Capital		40	0	0	0	00							19
20			Cash							225	0	0	0	00		20
21			Distribution of cash to partners													21
22																22
23																23
24																24

KEY POINTS

1 The main points of a partnership agreement are:

1. Date of agreement.
2. Names of the partners.
3. Kind of business to be conducted.
4. Length of time the partnership is to run.
5. Name and location of the business.
6. Investment of each partner.
7. Basis on which profits or losses are to be shared by the partners.
8. Limitation of partners' rights and activities.
9. Salary allowances to partners.
10. Division of assets upon dissolution of the partnership.
11. Signatures of the partners.

2 Partner compensation may be based on salary and interest allowances as well as an allocation of remaining profits as stated in the partnership agreement.

3 Partnership financial statements report the allocation of net income and partnership equity (see statements on next page).

4 Any change in the members of the partnership results in the dissolution of the partnership.

5 The steps in the liquidation process are:

1. Assets are sold.
2. Gains or losses are allocated to the partners.
3. Liabilities are paid.
4. Remaining cash and other assets are distributed to the partners.

Kelly and Arthur
Income Statement (Partial)
For Year Ended December 31, 19--

	B. K. KELLY	S. B. ARTHUR	TOTAL
Net income			$80 0 0 0 00
Allocation of net income:			
Salary allowance	$35 0 0 0 00	$10 0 0 0 00	$45 0 0 0 00
Interest allowance	5 0 0 0 00	15 0 0 0 00	20 0 0 0 00
Remaining income	7 5 0 0 00	7 5 0 0 00	15 0 0 0 00
	$47 5 0 0 00	$32 5 0 0 00	$80 0 0 0 00

Kelly and Arthur
Statement of Partners' Equity
For Year Ended December 31, 19--

	B. K. KELLY	S. B. ARTHUR	TOTAL
Capital, January 1, 19--	$50 0 0 0 00	$150 0 0 0 00	$200 0 0 0 00
Additional investments during the year		10 0 0 0 00	10 0 0 0 00
	$50 0 0 0 00	$160 0 0 0 00	$210 0 0 0 00
Net income for the year	47 5 0 0 00	32 5 0 0 00	80 0 0 0 00
	$97 5 0 0 00	$192 5 0 0 00	$290 0 0 0 00
Withdrawals (salaries during the year)	35 0 0 0 00	10 0 0 0 00	45 0 0 0 00
Capital, December 31, 19--	$62 5 0 0 00	$182 5 0 0 00	$245 0 0 0 00

Kelly and Arthur
Balance Sheet (Partial)
December 31, 19--

Partners' Equity		
B. K. Kelly, capital	$ 62 5 0 0 00	
S. B. Arthur, capital	182 5 0 0 00	
Total partners' equity		$245 0 0 0 00

KEY TERMS

dissolution 697   Dissolving of the partnership resulting from any change in the members of the partnership.

liquidation 701   The process of selling the assets, paying the liabilities, and distributing the remaining cash or other assets to the partners.

partnership 684   The form of organization in which two or more individuals engage in an enterprise as co-owners.

partnership agreement 684   A written agreement containing the various provisions for operating a partnership.

REVIEW QUESTIONS

1. Identify eleven essential provisions of a partnership agreement.
2. Identify three advantages of a partnership as compared with a sole proprietorship.
3. Identify three disadvantages of a partnership form of business organization.
4. When two sole proprietors decide to combine their businesses, at what values should the noncash assets be taken over by the partnership?
5. In the absence of any agreement between the partners, how must profits and losses be shared? If the partnership agreement specifies how profits are to be shared, but there is no agreement as to how losses are to be shared, what must be true with respect to losses?
6. What factors generally are considered in determining the allocation of profits and losses?
7. Identify three ways in which a partnership may be dissolved.
8. When a new partner who has been the sole owner of a business is admitted to a partnership by having the partnership take over the old business, what usually serves as the basis for preparing the opening entry?
9. Describe the four accounting entries for the liquidation of a partnership.

MANAGING YOUR WRITING

A friend, Joan Mellencamp, has mentioned that she is thinking about forming a partnership with a small group of colleagues. She is interested in learning about the advantages and disadvantages of the partnership form of ownership. In addition, she has asked for your advice on the kinds of issues that should be agreed upon in advance of the formation of the partnership. Write a memo to your friend explaining the advantages and disadvantages of a partnership and offer your advice on the issues that should be settled in advance.

DEMONSTRATION PROBLEM

Mascha Schuurmans, Jolijn Brouwer, and Mirjam van Tuil are partners in Holland Law. They share profits and losses in a 50-30-20 ratio. The partnership agreement calls for annual salaries of $40,000, $35,000, and $30,000, respectively, and interest of 12% on their January 1 capital balances.* Any remaining net income (or net loss) is to be divided in accordance with the ratios used for sharing profits and losses.

The partners' capital balances as of January 1, 19-1, were Schuurmans, $120,000; Brouwer, $75,000; and van Tuil, $50,000. No additional investments were made during the year. The net income of the partnership for the year 19-1 was $160,000. Partners' withdrawals for the year were Schuurmans, $50,000; Brouwer, $40,000; and van Tuil, $35,000.

On March 4, 19-2, the partners decide to liquidate their law firm. On that date, the firm has a cash balance of $46,000, noncash assets of $274,000, and liabilities of $40,000. No additional investments or withdrawals were made in 19-2. Between March 5 and March 31, the noncash assets are sold for $290,000, the gain is divided according to the profit and loss sharing ratio, and the liabilities are paid. The remaining cash is then distributed to the partners.

*Salaries and interest are not recognized as expenses in the determination of net income.

REQUIRED

1. Prepare the lower portion of the income statement of Holland Law for the year ended December 31, 19-1, showing the division of the partnership net income for the year.
2. Prepare the general journal entry to close Income Summary to the partners' capital accounts as of December 31, 19-1.
3. Prepare a statement of partners' equity for Holland Law for the year ended December 31, 19-1.
4. Prepare a statement of partnership liquidation for Holland Law for the period March 5 through March 31, 19-2.
5. Prepare the general journal entries as of March 31, 19-2, for:
   a. The sale of the noncash assets of the partnership
   b. The division of any loss or gain on realization
   c. The payment of partnership liabilities
   d. The distribution of remaining cash to the partners

SOLUTION

2.

4					4
5	19-1 Dec. 31	Income Summary	160 0 0 0 00		5
6		Mascha Schuurmans, Capital		67 2 0 0 00	6
7		Jolijn Brouwer, Capital		51 6 8 0 00	7
8		Mirjam van Tuil, Capital		41 1 2 0 00	8
9					9
10					10
11					11

1.

Holland Law
Income Statement (Partial)
For Year Ended December 31, 19-1

	M. SCHUURMANS	J. BROUWER	M. VAN TUIL	TOTAL
Net income				$160 0 0 0 00
Allocation of net income:				
Salary allowance	$40 0 0 0 00	$35 0 0 0 00	$30 0 0 0 00	$105 0 0 0 00
Interest allowance	14 4 0 0 00	9 0 0 0 00	6 0 0 0 00	29 4 0 0 00
Remaining income	12 8 0 0 00	7 6 8 0 00	5 1 2 0 00	25 6 0 0 00
	$67 2 0 0 00	$51 6 8 0 00	$41 1 2 0 00	$160 0 0 0 00

3.

Holland Law
Statement of Partners' Equity
For Year Ended December 31, 19-1

	M. SCHUURMANS	J. BROUWER	M. VAN TUIL	TOTAL
Capital, January 1, 19-1	$120 0 0 0 00	$ 75 0 0 0 00	$50 0 0 0 00	$245 0 0 0 00
Net income for the year	67 2 0 0 00	51 6 8 0 00	41 1 2 0 00	160 0 0 0 00
	$187 2 0 0 00	$126 6 8 0 00	$91 1 2 0 00	$405 0 0 0 00
Withdrawals	50 0 0 0 00	40 0 0 0 00	35 0 0 0 00	125 0 0 0 00
Capital, December 31, 19-1	$137 2 0 0 00	$ 86 6 8 0 00	$56 1 2 0 00	$280 0 0 0 00

4.

Holland Law
Statement of Partnership Liquidation
For Period March 5–31, 19-2

	CASH	NONCASH ASSETS	LIABILITIES	CAPITAL M. SCHUURMANS	J. BROUWER	M. VAN TUIL
Balance before sale of assets	$ 46 0 0 0 00	$274 0 0 0 00	$40 0 0 0 00	$137 2 0 0 00	$86 6 8 0 00	$56 1 2 0 00
Sale of noncash assets and allocation of gain	290 0 0 0 00	(274 0 0 0 00)	0	8 0 0 0 00	4 8 0 0 00	3 2 0 0 00
Balance after sale	$336 0 0 0 00	0	$40 0 0 0 00	$145 2 0 0 00	$91 4 8 0 00	$59 3 2 0 00
Payment of liabilities	(40 0 0 0 00)	0	(40 0 0 0 00)	0	0	0
Balance after payment of liabilities	$296 0 0 0 00	0	0	$145 2 0 0 00	$91 4 8 0 00	$59 3 2 0 00
Distribution of cash to partners	(296 0 0 0 00)	0	0	(145 2 0 0 00)	(91 4 8 0 00)	(59 3 2 0 00)
Final balance	0	0	0	0	0	0

5.

GENERAL JOURNAL PAGE 1

	DATE		DESCRIPTION	POST. REF.	DEBIT	CREDIT	
1	Mar. 19-2	31	Cash		290 0 0 0 00		1
2			Noncash Assets			274 0 0 0 00	2
3			Gain on Sale of Assets			16 0 0 0 00	3
4			Sale of assets				4
5							5
6							6
7		31	Gain on Sale of Assets		16 0 0 0 00		7
8			Mascha Schuurmans, Capital			8 0 0 0 00	8
9			Jolijn Brouwer, Capital			4 8 0 0 00	9
10			Mirjam van Tuil, Capital			3 2 0 0 00	10
11			Division of gain				11
12							12
13		31	Liabilities		40 0 0 0 00		13
14			Cash			40 0 0 0 00	14
15			Payment of liabilities				15
16							16
17		31	Mascha Schuurmans, Capital		145 2 0 0 00		17
18			Jolijn Brouwer, Capital		91 4 8 0 00		18
19			Mirjam van Tuil, Capital		59 3 2 0 00		19
20			Cash			296 0 0 0 00	20
21			Distribution of cash to partners				21
22							22

(a. rows 1–4, b. rows 7–11, c. rows 13–15, d. rows 17–21)

SERIES A EXERCISES

1 **EXERCISE 20A1 PARTNERSHIP OPENING ENTRIES**   Lisa Morris and Joyce Laski agreed on September 1 to go into business as partners. According to the agreement, Morris is to contribute $45,000 cash and Laski is to contribute $65,000 cash. Provide a separate journal entry for the investment of each partner.

2 **EXERCISE 20A2 ENTRIES FOR ALLOCATION OF NET INCOME**
Karen Rhea and Wayne Sellevaeg decided to form a partnership on July 1, 19–4. Rhea invested $100,000 and Sellevaeg invested $50,000. On June 30, 19–5, the end of the fiscal year, a net income of $90,000 was earned. Determine the amount of net income that Rhea and Sellevaeg would receive under each of the following independent assumptions:

1. There is no agreement concerning the distribution of net income.
2. Each partner is to receive 10% interest on their original investment. The remaining net income is to be divided equally.

continued

3. Rhea and Sellevaeg are to receive a salary allowance of $30,000 and $40,000, respectively. The remaining net income is to be divided equally.
4. Each partner is to receive 10% interest on their original investment. Rhea and Sellevaeg are to receive a salary allowance of $30,000 and $40,000, respectively. The remaining net income is to be divided as follows: Rhea 40% and Sellevaeg 60%.

3   **EXERCISE 20A3 PARTIAL FINANCIAL STATEMENTS**   Karen Cooper and Alex Orme formed a partnership on May 1, 19-1. Cooper contributed $80,000 and Orme contributed $50,000. During the year, Cooper contributed an additional $20,000. The partnership agreement states that Cooper is to receive $30,000 and Orme is to receive $60,000 as a salary allowance. Any remaining net income is to be divided as follows: Cooper 20% and Orme 80%. For the fiscal year ending April 30, 19-2, the partnership earned $140,000 in net income. The partners withdrew only the salary portion of their compensation during the first year of operation.

1. Prepare the lower portion of the income statement showing the allocation of net income between Cooper and Orme for the fiscal year ended April 30, 19-2.
2. Prepare a statement of partners' equity showing each individual partner's equity for the fiscal year ended April 30, 19-2.

4   **EXERCISE 20A4 ADMITTING NEW PARTNERS**   Jeff Bowman and Kristi Emery, who have ending capital balances of $100,000 and $60,000, respectively, agree to admit two new partners to their business on August 18, 19--. Dan Bridges will buy one-fifth of Bowman's equity interest for $30,000 and one-fourth of Emery's equity interest for $20,000. Anna Terrell will invest $50,000 in the business for which she is to receive a $50,000 equity interest.

1. Prepare general journal entries showing the transactions admitting Bridges and Terrell to the partnership.
2. Calculate the ending capital balances of all four partners after the transactions.

5   **EXERCISE 20A5 ENTRIES: PARTNERSHIP LIQUIDATION**   On liquidation of the partnership of J. Hui and K. Cline, as of November 1, 19--, inventory with a book value of $180,000 is sold for $230,000. Given that Hui and Cline share profits and losses equally, prepare the entries for the sale and the allocation of gain.

SERIES A   PROBLEMS

1   **PROBLEM 20A1 PARTNERSHIP OPENING ENTRIES**   On July 1, 19--, Susan Woodworth and Barbara Holly combined their two businesses to form a partnership under the firm name of Woodworth and Holly. The balance sheets of the two sole proprietorships are shown on the next page.

Woodworth's Antiques
Balance Sheet
June 30, 19--

Assets				Liabilities		
Cash		$ 7 1 0 0 00		Accounts payable	$8 4 0 0 00	
Accounts receivable	$4 5 0 0 00			Notes payable	2 5 0 0 00	
Less allowance for doubtful				Total liabilities		$10 9 0 0 00
accounts	6 2 0 00	3 8 8 0 00				
Merchandise inventory		21 4 3 0 00				
Store equipment	$8 2 0 0 00			Owner's Equity		
Less accumulated				Susan Woodworth, capital		28 4 1 0 00
depreciation	1 3 0 0 00	6 9 0 0 00		Total liabilities and		
Total assets		$39 3 1 0 00		owner's equity		$39 3 1 0 00

Holly's Unfinished Furniture
Balance Sheet
June 30, 19--

Assets				Liabilities		
Cash		$ 4 5 2 0 00		Accounts payable	$6 3 0 0 00	
Accounts receivable	$3 2 7 5 00			Notes payable	8 0 0 0 00	
Less allowance for doubtful				Total liabilities		$14 3 0 0 00
accounts	4 7 5 00	2 8 0 0 00				
Merchandise inventory		28 1 9 0 00				
Supplies		9 6 0 00				
Office equipment	$7 4 0 0 00					
Less accumulated						
depreciation	1 8 0 0 00	5 6 0 0 00				
Store equipment	$7 7 0 0 00			Owner's Equity		
Less accumulated				Barbara Holly, capital		33 9 7 0 00
depreciation	1 5 0 0 00	6 2 0 0 00		Total liabilities and		
Total assets		$48 2 7 0 00		owner's equity		$48 2 7 0 00

The balance sheets reflect fair market values except for the following:
a. The fair market value of Woodworth's store equipment is $7,500.
b. The fair market value of Holly's office equipment and store equipment are $6,100 and $6,800, respectively.

REQUIRED
Prepare the opening entry for the formation of Woodworth and Holly partnership as of July 1, 19--, using fair market values. The difference between assets invested and liabilities assumed should be credited to each partner's capital account. Neither partner has knowledge of any uncollectible accounts receivable.

3   **PROBLEM 20A2 PREPARING PARTIAL FINANCIAL STATE-MENTS AND CLOSING ENTRIES**   The partnership of Hiller and Roundtree, CPAs, showed revenues of $195,000 and expenses of $52,000 on their end-of-year work sheet. Their capital balances as of January 1, 19--, were $52,000 for B. Hiller and $48,000 for O. Roundtree. No additional investments were made during the year. As stated in their partnership agreement, after withdrawing salary allowances of $60,000 for Hiller and $40,000 for Roundtree, the partners each withdrew 5% interest on their January 1 capital balances. No additional withdrawals were made. Any remaining net income is to be divided on a 45–55 basis.

REQUIRED

1. Prepare the lower portion of the income statement of the partnership for the year ended December 31, 19--, showing the division of the partnership net income for the year.
2. Prepare a statement of partners' equity for the year ended December 31, 19--, and the partners' equity section of the balance sheet on that date.
3. Prepare closing entries for the partnership as of December 31, 19--. (For simplicity, use the account titles "Revenues" for all revenues and "Expenses" for all expenses.)

4   **PROBLEM 20A3 ENTRIES FOR DISSOLUTION OF PARTNER-SHIP**   The Kelly and Kelly Wrecking Company, a partnership, operates a general demolition business. Ownership of the company is divided among the partners, Mike Kelly, Kim Kelly, Larry Dennis, and Jim Wheeles. Profits and losses are shared equally. The books are kept on a calendar year basis.

On September 15, after the business had been in operation for several years, Dennis died. Mrs. Dennis wished to sell her husband's interest in the partnership for $25,000. After the books were closed, the partners' capital accounts had credit balances as follows:

Mike Kelly	$50,000
Kim Kelly	25,000
Larry Dennis	35,000
Jim Wheeles	25,000

REQUIRED

1. Prepare the general journal entry required to enter the check issued to Mrs. Dennis in payment of her deceased husband's interest in the partnership. According to the partnership agreement, the difference between the amount paid to Mrs. Dennis and the book value of Larry Dennis' capital account is allocated to the remaining partners based on their ending capital account balances.
2. Instead of the foregoing, assume that Mrs. Dennis is paid $50,000 for the book value of Larry Dennis' capital account. Prepare the necessary journal entry.

continued

3. Instead of the foregoing, assume that Jim Wheeles (with the consent of the remaining partners) purchased Dennis' interest for $40,000 and gave Mrs. Dennis a personal check for that amount. Prepare the general journal entry for the partnership only.

5 **PROBLEM 20A4 STATEMENT OF PARTNERSHIP LIQUIDATION WITH GAIN**   After several years of operations, the partnership of Baldwin, Cowan, and Stewart is to be liquidated. After making closing entries on June 30, 19--, the following accounts remain open:

	Account Balance	
Account Title	**Debit**	**Credit**
Cash	$ 5,000	
Inventory	55,000	
Other assets	180,000	
Liabilities		$40,000
R. J. Baldwin, capital		50,000
N. R. Cowan, capital		90,000
K. M. Stewart, capital		60,000

The noncash assets are sold for $250,000. Profits and losses are shared equally.

REQUIRED

1. Prepare a statement of partnership liquidation for the period July 1–20, 19--, showing the following:
    a. The sale of the noncash assets on July 1
    b. The allocation of any gain or loss to the partners on July 1
    c. The payment of the liabilities on July 15
    d. The distribution of cash to the partners on July 20
2. Journalize these four transactions in a general journal

5 **PROBLEM 20A5 STATEMENT OF PARTNERSHIP LIQUIDATION WITH LOSS**   After several years of operations, the partnership of Nelson, Pope, and Williams is to be liquidated. After making closing entries on March 31, 19--, the following accounts remain open:

	Account Balance	
Account Title	**Debit**	**Credit**
Cash	$ 15,000	
Inventory	40,000	
Other assets	220,000	
Liabilities		$ 75,000
C. W. Nelson, capital		40,000
J. R. Pope, capital		60,000
M. L. Williams, capital		100,000

The noncash assets are sold for $230,000. Profits and losses are shared equally.

continued

REQUIRED

1. Prepare a statement of partnership liquidation for the period April 1–15, 19--, showing the following:
   a. The sale of the noncash assets on April 1
   b. The allocation of any gain or loss to the partners on April 1
   c. The payment of the liabilities on April 12
   d. The distribution of cash to the partners on April 15
2. Journalize these four transactions in a general journal

SERIES B EXERCISES

1   **EXERCISE 20B1 PARTNERSHIP OPENING ENTRIES**   Sharon Usher and Leann Gomez agreed on September 1 to go into business as partners. According to the agreement, Usher is to contribute $30,000 cash and Gomez is to contribute $50,000 cash. Provide a separate journal entry for the investment of each partner.

2   **EXERCISE 20B2 ENTRIES FOR ALLOCATION OF NET INCOME**   John Clark and David Haase decided to form a partnership on July 1, 19–6. Clark invested $60,000 and Haase invested $40,000. On June 30, 19–7, the end of the fiscal year, a net income of $80,000 was earned. Determine the amount of net income that Clark and Haase would receive under each of the following independent assumptions:

1. There is no agreement concerning the distribution of net income.
2. Each partner is to receive 10% interest on their original investment. The remaining net income is to be divided equally.
3. Clark and Haase are to receive a salary allowance of $25,000 and $30,000, respectively. The remaining net income is to be divided equally.
4. Each partner is to receive 10% interest on their original investment. Clark and Haase are to receive a salary allowance of $25,000 and $30,000, respectively. The remaining net income is to be divided as follows: Clark 30% and Haase 70%.

3   **EXERCISE 20B3 PARTIAL FINANCIAL STATEMENTS**   Randy Nolan and Jill Brenton formed a partnership on May 1, 19-1. Nolan contributed $50,000 and Brenton contributed $25,000. During the year Nolan contributed an additional $10,000. The partnership agreement states that Nolan is to receive $15,000 and Brenton is to receive $50,000 as a salary allowance. Any remaining net income is to be divided as follows: Nolan 40% and Brenton 60%. For the fiscal year ending April 30, 19-2, the partnership earned $110,000 in net income. The partners withdrew only the salary portion of their compensation during the first year of operation.

1. Prepare the lower portion of the income statement showing the allocation of net income between Nolan and Brenton for the fiscal year ended April 30, 19-2.
2. Prepare a statement of partners' equity, showing each individual partner's equity for the fiscal year ended April 30, 19-2.

4 **EXERCISE 20B4 ADMITTING NEW PARTNERS**   Maria Rhodes and Craig Blair, who have ending capital balances of $90,000 and $40,000, respectively, agree to admit two new partners to their business on September 1, 19--. Lori Kinder will buy one-third of Rhodes' equity interest for $40,000 and one-fifth of Blair's equity interest for $12,000. Todd Gilbert will invest $30,000 in the business for which he is to receive a $30,000 equity interest.

1. Prepare general journal entries showing the above transactions admitting Kinder and Gilbert to the partnership.
2. Calculate the ending capital balances of all four partners after the above transactions.

5 **EXERCISE 20B5 ENTRIES: PARTNERSHIP LIQUIDATION**   On liquidation of the partnership of L. Straw and M. Maury, as of February 9, 19--, assets with a book value of $156,000 are sold for $140,000. Given that the profit-and-loss ratio is 60% for Straw and 40% for Maury, prepare the entries for the sale and the allocation of loss.

SERIES B   PROBLEMS

1 **PROBLEM 20B1 PARTNERSHIP OPENING ENTRIES**   On July 1, 19--, Lisa Bush and Wally Dodge combined their two businesses to form a partnership under the firm name of Bush and Dodge. The balance sheets of the two sole proprietorships are shown below and on the next page.

Bush's Grooming & Pet Supplies
Balance Sheet
June 30, 19--

Assets				Liabilities			
Cash		$ 4 6 0 0 00		Accounts payable	$7 6 9 0 00		
Accounts receivable	$4 2 0 0 00			Notes payable	3 6 0 0 00		
Less allowance for doubtful				Total liabilities			$11 2 9 0 00
accounts	4 8 0 00	3 7 2 0 00					
Merchandise inventory		28 5 8 0 00					
Store equipment	$9 2 6 0 00			Owner's Equity			
Less accumulated				Lisa Bush, capital			32 4 7 0 00
depreciation	2 4 0 0 00	6 8 6 0 00		Total liabilities and			
Total assets		$43 7 6 0 00		owner's equity			$43 7 6 0 00

Wally's Pet World
Balance Sheet
June 30, 19--

Assets					Liabilities			
Cash			$3 3 5 0 00		Accounts payable	$5 5 0 0 00		
Accounts receivable	$4 1 5 0 00				Notes payable	6 0 0 0 00		
Less allowance for doubtful					Total liabilities			$11 5 0 0 00
accounts	2 5 0 00		3 9 0 0 00					
Merchandise inventory			27 2 4 0 00					
Supplies			8 4 5 00					
Office equipment	$8 8 3 0 00							
Less accumulated								
depreciation	3 4 0 0 00		5 4 3 0 00					
Store equipment	$9 1 7 5 00				Owner's Equity			
Less accumulated					Wally Dodge, capital			34 1 9 0 00
depreciation	4 2 5 0 00		4 9 2 5 00		Total liabilities and			
Total assets			$45 6 9 0 00		owner's equity			$45 6 9 0 00

The balance sheets reflect fair market values except for the following:

a. The fair market value of Bush's store equipment is $7,350.

b. The fair market values of Dodge's office equipment and store equipment are $5,875 and $6,100, respectively.

REQUIRED

Prepare the opening entry for the formation of Bush and Dodge partnership as of July 1, 19--, using fair market values. The difference between assets invested and liabilities assumed should be credited to each partner's capital account. Neither partner has knowledge of any uncollectible accounts receivable.

3 **PROBLEM 20B2 PREPARING PARTIAL FINANCIAL STATE-MENTS AND CLOSING ENTRIES** The partnership of Rummel and Kang, Stonecutters, showed revenues of $133,000 and expenses of $41,000 on their end-of-year work sheet. Their capital balances as of January 1, 19--, were $41,000 for C. Rummel and $25,000 for V. Kang. No additional investments were made during the year. As stated in their partnership agreement, after withdrawing salary allowances of $43,000 for Rummel and $34,000 for Kang, the partners each withdrew 10% interest on their January 1 capital balances. No additional withdrawals were made. Any remaining net income is to be divided on a 60–40 basis.

REQUIRED

1. Prepare the lower portion of the income statement of the partnership for the year ended December 31, 19--, showing the division of the partnership net income for the year.

2. Prepare a statement of partners' equity for the year ended December 31, 19--, and the partners' equity section of the balance sheet on that date.

continued

3. Prepare closing entries for the partnership as of December 31, 19--. (For simplicity use the account titles "Revenues" for all revenues and "Expenses" for all expenses.)

4

PROBLEM 20B3 ENTRIES FOR DISSOLUTION OF PARTNERSHIP

The Cummings and Stickel Construction Company, a partnership, is operating a general contracting business. Ownership of the company is divided among the partners, Katie Cummings, Julie Stickel, Roy Hewson, and Patricia Weber. Profits and losses are shared equally. The books are kept on the calendar year basis.

On August 10, after the business had been in operation for several years, Patricia Weber died. Mr. Weber wished to sell his wife's interest for $30,000. After the books were closed, the partners' capital accounts had credit balances as follows:

Katie Cummings	$90,000
Julie Stickel	60,000
Roy Hewson	50,000
Patricia Weber	40,000

REQUIRED

1. Prepare the general journal entry required to enter the check issued to Mr. Weber in payment of his deceased wife's interest in the partnership. According to the partnership agreement, the difference between the amount paid to Mr. Weber and the book value of Patricia Weber's capital account is allocated to the remaining partners based on their ending capital account balances.
2. Instead of the foregoing, assume that Mr. Weber is paid $60,000 for the book value of Patricia Weber's capital account. Prepare the necessary journal entry.
3. Instead of the foregoing, assume that Julie Stickel (with the consent of the remaining partners) purchased Weber's interest for $70,000 and gave Mr. Weber a personal check for that amount. Prepare the general journal entry for the partnership only.

5

PROBLEM 20B4 STATEMENT OF PARTNERSHIP LIQUIDATION WITH GAIN

After several years of operations, the partnership of Leonard, Mitchell, and Swanson is to be liquidated. After making closing entries on June 30, 19--, the following accounts remain open:

	Account Balance	
Account Title	**Debit**	**Credit**
Cash	$ 4,000	
Inventory	40,000	
Other assets	150,000	
Liabilities		$44,000
B. J. Leonard, capital		60,000
W. T. Mitchell, capital		15,000
J. C. Swanson, capital		75,000

continued

The noncash assets are sold for $211,000. Profits and losses are shared equally.

REQUIRED

1. Prepare a statement of partnership liquidation for the period July 1–20, 19--, showing the following:
   - a. The sale of the noncash assets on July 1
   - b. The allocation of any gain or loss to the partners on July 1
   - c. The payment of the liabilities on July 15
   - d. The distribution of cash to the partners on July 20
2. Journalize these four transactions in a general journal

5 **PROBLEM 20B5 STATEMENT OF PARTNERSHIP LIQUIDATION WITH LOSS** After several years of operations, the partnership of Delco, Smith, and Walker is to be liquidated. After making closing entries on March 31, 19--, the following accounts remain open:

Account Title	Account Balance	
	Debit	Credit
Cash	$ 7,000	
Inventory	25,000	
Other assets	185,000	
Liabilities		$17,000
D. W. Delco, capital		30,000
C. S. Smith, capital		90,000
T. R. Walker, capital		80,000

The noncash assets are sold for $165,000. Profits and losses are shared equally.

REQUIRED

1. Prepare a statement of partnership liquidation for the period April 1–15, 19--, showing the following:
   - a. The sale of the noncash assets on April 1
   - b. The allocation of any gain or loss to the partners on April 1
   - c. The payment of the liabilities on April 12
   - d. The distribution of cash to the partners on April 15
2. Journalize these four transactions in a general journal

MASTERY PROBLEM

Jim Bond, a plumber, has been working for Fleming's Plumbing Supplies for several years. Based on his hard work and the fact that he recently married Ivan Fleming's daughter, Jim has been invited to enter into a partnership with Fleming. The new partnership will be called Fleming and Bond's Plumbing Supplies. The terms of the partnership are provided on the next page.

a. Fleming will invest the assets of Fleming's Plumbing Supplies and the partnership will assume all liabilities. The market values of the office and store equipment are estimated to be $18,000 and $8,000, respectively. All other values reported on the balance sheet below are reasonable approximations of market values. Neither partner has knowledge of any uncollectible accounts receivable.

Fleming's Plumbing Supplies
Balance Sheet
December 31, 19-1

Assets				Liabilities		
Cash		$ 13 5 4 4 00		Accounts payable	$18 0 8 2 00	
Accounts receivable	$15 2 8 0 00			Notes payable	36 0 0 0 00	
Less allowance for doubtful				Total liabilities		$ 54 0 8 2 00
accounts	1 7 2 0 00	13 5 6 0 00				
Merchandise inventory		89 6 9 2 00				
Supplies		1 2 8 6 00				
Office equipment	$14 3 2 0 00					
Less accumulated						
depreciation	1 1 0 0 00	13 2 2 0 00				
Store equipment	$8 8 0 0 00			Owner's Equity		
Less accumulated				Ivan Fleming, capital		83 8 2 0 00
depreciation	2 2 0 0 00	6 6 0 0 00		Total liabilities and		
Total assets		$137 9 0 2 00		owner's equity		$137 9 0 2 00

b. Bond will invest $50,000 cash.
c. Fleming will draw a salary allowance of $50,000 per year and Bond will receive $30,000.
d. Each partner will receive 10% interest on the January 1 balance of his capital account.
e. Profits or losses remaining after allocating salaries and interest will be distributed as follows: Fleming 60% and Bond 40%.

REQUIRED
1. Prepare the entries on January 1, 19-2, for the formation of the partnership.
2. Net income for the partnership for 19-2 was $150,000. Prepare the lower portion of the income statement reporting the allocation of the profits to each partner.
3. In December, 19-4, Fleming's daughter, Penny, graduated from business college and asked to join the business as a partner. She has $30,000 to invest and it is agreed that Penny will be given a capital interest of $30,000. Profits and losses will be shared as follows: I. Fleming 50%; J. Bond 30%; P. Fleming 20%. Prepare the entry for Penny's investment on January 1, 19-5.

continued

4. After several years of operations it is decided to liquidate the partnership. After making closing entries on July 31, 19-9, the following accounts remain open.

Cash	$ 20,000	
Inventory	150,000	
Office Equipment	30,000	
Accum. Depreciation—Office Equipment		$18,000
Store Equipment	22,000	
Accum. Depreciation—Store Equipment		15,000
Notes Payable		20,000
Ivan Fleming, Capital		80,000
Jim Bond, Capital		50,000
Penny Fleming, Capital		39,000

a. On August 1, 19-9, the inventory is sold for $130,000.
b. On August 3, the office equipment is sold for $10,000.
c. On August 5, the store equipment is sold for $12,000.
d. On August 10, the Notes Payable are paid.
e. On August 15, the remaining cash is distributed to the partners according to the balances in their capital accounts.

Prepare a statement of partnership liquidation and related journal entries for the period August 1–15, 19-9.

INDEX

Page references in bold indicate defined terms.

A

finding errors, 134
  fig., 134
income statement columns, 133

preparing for a merchandising firm, 470
steps in preparing, 132A–132H, 216
ten-column, 132